Joseph Rodriguez Ed.D, CCFT

Joseph Rodriguez Ed.D, CCFT

The
Columbia University College
of Physicians and Surgeons

COMPLETE
HOME GUIDE TO
MENTAL HEALTH

◆ ◆ ◆

Editors

FREDERIC I. KASS, M.D.

JOHN M. OLDHAM, M.D.

HERBERT PARDES, M.D.

Editorial Director

LOIS B. MORRIS

Managing Editor: Ellen Watson

· T H E ·

Columbia University College of Physicians and Surgeons

COMPLETE HOME GUIDE TO MENTAL HEALTH

◆ ◆ ◆ ◆ ◆

A G. S. Sharpe Communications, Inc. Publication

HENRY HOLT AND COMPANY · NEW YORK

Library of Congress Cataloging-in-Publication Data
The Columbia University College of Physicians and Surgeons complete home guide to
mental health / editors, Frederic I. Kass, John M. Oldham, Herbert Pardes, Lois B. Morris.
p.   cm.
Includes index.
1. Mental illness.   2. Psychiatry—Popular works.   3. Family—Mental health.
I. Kass, Frederic I.   II. Oldham, John M.   III. Pardes, Herbert.
IV. Columbia University. College of Physicians and Surgeons.
[DNLM: 1. Mental Disorders—popular works.   WN 75 C726]
RC460.C59   1992   616.89—dc20   92-1534
DNLM/DLC for Library of Congress   CIP

ISBN 0-8050-0724-5

Henry Holt books are available at special discounts for bulk purchases for
sales promotions, premiums, fund-raising, or educational use. Special editions
or book excerpts can also be created to specification.
For details contact: Special Sales Director, Henry Holt and Company, Inc.,
115 West 18th Street, New York, New York 10011.

First Edition—1992

Book design by Victoria Hartman

Printed in the United States of America
Recognizing the importance of preserving the written word,
Henry Holt and Company, Inc., by policy, prints all of its
first editions on acid-free paper. ∞

1   3   5   7   9   10   8   6   4   2

Contents

Foreword:
How to Use This Book

Frederic I. Kass, M.D., John M. Oldham, M.D., Herbert Pardes, M.D., and Lois B. Morris

The publication of *The Columbia University College of Physicians and Surgeons Complete Home Guide to Mental Health* represents the culmination of a unique, six-year effort by the Columbia Department of Psychiatry to make a single point: that mental suffering and disability can be understood and treated. The contributors to this volume are among the country's most distinguished mental health researchers and practitioners. All have pooled their knowledge to create the most authoritative guide ever published for individuals and families to the state-of-the-art treatments for all common forms of mental suffering—from short-lived but problematic to severe and disabling, from infancy to oldest age.

The book is designed to be comprehensive, interesting, informative, practical, and above all useful: We intend it to be a book readers consult frequently to understand their own or a family member's troubling symptoms as well as to comprehend the diagnosis and treatment provided by a mental health professional. For those who are curious, we offer the latest scientific understandings and discoveries about mental illness. For everyone, we offer *what to do about it*, including practical advice for oneself and for family members. Throughout we provide sources for additional information and for mutual support.

Although, as explained in chapter 3, the various mental health professions sometimes view mental symptoms differently, here we present the diagnoses and treatments as formulated by American psychiatry today. The functions of mental health professionals overlap in many areas (such as in the practice of psychotherapy), but only psychiatrists are medical doctors. Only they are permitted by law to provide medical workups, rule out medical illness that may cause mental symptoms, and offer physical treatments, including medication, in addition to psychotherapy.

The book is divided into four broad sections. Most readers will probably wish to consult individual chapters that deal with the symptoms, disorders, or issues that concern them at a specific time. However, we urge everyone first to read the six chapters that comprise part 1, "Mental Illness Assessment and Treatment." Beginning with "What Is Mental Illness?" and ending with "Is Treatment Effective?" these chapters present the background and viewpoint necessary to understand the definitions, treating professionals, diagnostic terminology, and treatment methods that are referred to in all succeeding chapters.

Part 2 deals with the causes, range, and treatments of the most common mental difficulties and disorders that afflict adults today: anxiety, depression, alcohol and substance abuse, eating disorders, sexual disorders, sleep difficulties, personality disorders, schizophrenia, and the dementias and other physical causes of mental suffering.

Part 3 covers the symptoms and disorders of mental disturbance and developmental difficulty from infancy through adolescence. Because diagnosis and treatment of children differ in important ways from those of adults, be sure to read the introduction to part 3 before consulting individual chapters. The chapters in this section emphasize not only signs of difficulty among children but also frameworks for understanding what is normal behavior and development during the first decades of life. In addition to discussing common problems and disorders in preschool children, school-age children, and adolescents, the section includes a chapter on the common and uncommon stresses and traumas of childhood, including birth of a sibling, severe medical illness in childhood, divorce in the family, death of a loved one, and child abuse.

Part 4, called "Special Issues and Problems," presents a wide range of topics, many of them of interest to particular populations: women, men, older people, and AIDS victims (sufferers and their loved ones). Here too we include mental health challenges for everyone, including stress and stress management, emotional crises, and coping with medical illness and dying. Chapters on suicide and violence are included here as well. Finally, part 4 includes chapters on the legal and ethical issues involved with mental health treatment (including, for example, commitment procedures, protecting your rights, and what to do if a person believes he or she is receiving inadequate care), national mental health concerns (including the woeful state of mental health insurance coverage), and a concluding chapter on research findings and their implications for the future.

Organizations that help sufferers of mental illness and their families are listed in chapter 31.

A glossary of psychiatric terms follows part 4.

A note about case histories: In many chapters we have used actual case histories to illustrate the mental disorders and their successful treatments. Because confidentiality is essential to mental health treatment, the identities and life circumstances of the individual patients have been disguised and the names are pseudonymous.

Throughout this book, we have labored to remove the mystery from mental illness. The state of knowledge today is vast, and much is to be gained from recognizing the symptoms of mental illness for what they are, having compassion for those who suffer, and reaching out for help or to help.

About the Editors

MEDICAL EDITORS

FREDERIC I. KASS, M.D., is Professor of Clinical Psychiatry and Associate Chairman of the Department of Psychiatry at the Columbia University College of Physicians and Surgeons. As Clinical Director of Psychiatry for Presbyterian Hospitals, he has directed the psychiatric service and implemented a variety of programs for indigent patients. As Chair of the American Psychiatric Association's Task Force on the Homeless Mentally Ill, he has published recommendations for a national initiative on effective treatment for homeless patients. Dr. Kass is Co-Chair of the Psychotherapy Division of the Columbia Psychoanalytic Center for Training and Research, and he also maintains a private practice.

JOHN M. OLDHAM, M.D., is Professor of Clinical Psychiatry and Associate Chairman of the Department of Psychiatry at the Columbia University College of Physicians and Surgeons. He is Director of the New York State Psychiatric Institute, the renowned research facility on the Columbia-Presbyterian Medical Center campus that is affiliated with the State of New York and with the Columbia University College of Physicians and Surgeons. Dr. Oldham serves also as the Chief Medical Officer for the New York State Office of Mental Health. Maintaining a private practice, he is a Training and Supervising Analyst at the Columbia Psychoanalytic Center for Training and Research.

HERBERT PARDES, M.D., is Vice President for Health Sciences, Dean of the Faculty of Medicine, Professor and Chairman of the Department of Psychiatry at the Columbia University College of Physicians and Surgeons. From 1978 to 1984, Dr. Pardes served as Director of the National Institute of Mental Health (NIMH). A past president of the American Psychiatric Association, Dr. Pardes has led the way in developing alliances with citizen mental health groups. He serves as President of the Scientific Board of the National Alliance for Research on Schizophrenia and Depression (NARSAD), the Chairman of the Research Council of the American Psychiatric Association, a Charter Associate member of the National Depressive and Manic Depressive Association, and advisor to the National Alliance for the Mentally Ill (NAMI) and the Mental Health Association.

EDITORIAL DIRECTOR

LOIS B. MORRIS is an editor and writer specializing in health and behavior. A journalist whose work appears frequently in magazines, she has written five books on mental health topics, including, most recently, *The Personality Self-Portrait*, with John M. Oldham, M.D.

List of Contributors

JOHN BARSA, M.D.
Assistant Clinical Professor of Psychiatry
Director of Geriatrics for the Department of Psychiatry

JUDITH BECKER, Ph.D.
Former member of the Department of Psychiatry, Columbia
University College of Physicians and Surgeons, now
Professor of Psychiatry and Psychology, University of
Arizona Health Sciences Center

HECTOR R. BIRD, M.D.
Professor of Clinical Psychiatry
Deputy Director of Child and Adolescent Psychiatry, New
York State Psychiatric Institute
Supervising Psychoanalyst, William Alanson White Institute

EVE CALIGOR, M.D.
Assistant Clinical Professor of Psychiatry
Assistant Attending Psychiatrist, Psychiatric Consultant
for the Anesthesia Pain Service, Presbyterian Hospital
Faculty, Columbia Psychoanalytic Center for
Training and Research

FRANCINE COURNOS, M.D.
Associate Clinical Professor of Psychiatry
Director, Washington Heights Community Service, New
York State Psychiatric Institute

SUSAN DEAKINS, M.D.
Assistant Clinical Professor of Psychiatry
Senior Supervisor, Biosocial Treatment Research Division,
New York State Psychiatric Institute

DAVANGERE P. DEVANAND, M.D.
Assistant Professor of Clinical Psychiatry
Assistant Director, Memory Disorders Clinic, and Director,
ECT Service, New York State Psychiatric Institute

JEAN ENDICOTT, Ph.D.
Professor of Clinical Psychology in Psychiatry
Chief, Department of Research Assessment and Training,
New York State Psychiatric Institute

ROBERT E. FEINSTEIN, M.D.
Assistant Clinical Professor of Psychiatry
Director of Behavioral Medicine, St. Joseph's Hospital,
Stamford, Connecticut
Faculty, Columbia Psychoanalytic Center
for Training and Research

KENNETH A. FRANK, Ph.D.
Associate Clinical Professor of Medical Psychology
in Psychiatry
Senior staff member, Behavioral Medicine Program,
Columbia-Presbyterian Medical Center

ALEXANDER H. GLASSMAN, M.D.
Professor of Clinical Psychiatry
Chief, Clinical Psychopharmacology, New York State
Psychiatric Institute

ROBERT ALAN GLICK, M.D.
Clinical Professor of Psychiatry
Training and Supervising Analyst, Admitting Analyst,
Columbia Psychoanalytic Center for Training and Research

JACK M. GORMAN, M.D.
Professor of Clinical Psychiatry
Chief, Department of Psychobiology, New York State
Psychiatric Institute
Attending Psychiatrist, Presbyterian Hospital

ARTHUR H. GREEN, M.D.
Clinical Professor of Psychiatry
Attending Psychiatrist; Medical Director, Family Center
and Therapeutic Nursery, Presbyterian Hospital
Collaborating Analyst, Columbia Psychoanalytic Center
for Training and Research

BARRY J. GURLAND, M.D.
John E. Borne Professor of Clinical Psychiatry
Director, Columbia University Center for Geriatrics
and Gerontology
Chief, Geriatrics Research, New York State Office
of Mental Health

FREDERIC I. KASS, M.D.
Professor of Clinical Psychiatry
Associate Chairman of the Department of Psychiatry
Clinical Director of Psychiatry and
Attending Psychiatrist, Presbyterian Hospital
Co-Chair, Psychotherapy Division, Columbia
Psychoanalytic Center for Training and Research

NEIL KAVEY, M.D.
Associate Clinical Professor of Psychiatry
Associate Attending Psychiatrist; Director, Sleep Disorders
Center, Columbia-Presbyterian Medical Center

ROBERT M. KERTZNER, M.D.
Assistant Professor of Clinical Psychiatry
Training Director, Behavioral Sciences Research in HIV
Infection, HIV Center, New York State Psychiatric Institute

CLARICE J. KESTENBAUM, M.D.
Clinical Professor of Psychiatry
Director of Training, Division of Child and
Adolescent Psychiatry

RACHEL G. KLEIN, Ph.D.
Professor of Clinical Psychology in Psychiatry
Director, Psychological Services, New York State
Psychiatric Institute and Presbyterian Hospital

DONALD S. KORNFELD, M.D.
Associate Dean, Faculty of Medicine
Professor of Clinical Psychiatry
Attending Psychiatrist; Chief, Consultation-Liaison
Psychiatry and Behavioral Medicine, Presbyterian
Hospital

THOMAS KRANJAC, M.D.
Associate Clinical Professor of Psychiatry
Clinical Director of Psychiatry, Associate Attending
Psychiatrist, Presbyterian Hospital
Attending Psychiatrist, New York State Psychiatric Institute
Collaborating Analyst, Columbia Psychoanalytic Center
for Training and Research

ELLIOT M. KRANZLER, M.D.
Assistant Professor of Clinical Psychiatry

FREDERICK M. LANE, M.D.
Clinical Professor of Psychiatry
Associate Director for Student Affairs and Training and
Supervising Analyst, Columbia Psychoanalytic Center
for Training and Research

MICHAEL R. LIEBOWITZ, M.D.
Professor of Clinical Psychiatry
Director, Anxiety Disorders Clinic, New York State
Psychiatric Institute

ROGER A. MacKINNON, M.D.
Professor of Clinical Psychiatry
Attending Psychiatrist, Presbyterian Hospital
and New York State Psychiatric Institute
Director and Supervising and Training Analyst,
Columbia Psychoanalytic Center for Training
and Research

RICHARD MAYEUX, M.D., M.S.E.
Gertrude H. Sergievsky Professor of Neurology
and Psychiatry
Director, Memory Disorder Center, New York State
Psychiatric Institute

SUKDEB MUKHERJEE, M.D.
Former member of the Department of Psychiatry, Columbia
University College of Physicians and Surgeons, now
Professor of Psychiatry, Medical College of Georgia

PHILIP R. MUSKIN, M.D.
Associate Professor of Clinical Psychiatry
Associate Chief, Consultation-Liaison Psychiatry,
Presbyterian Hospital
Collaborating Analyst, Columbia Psychoanalytic Center
for Training and Research

EDWARD V. NUNES, M.D.
Assistant Professor of Clinical Psychiatry
Research Psychiatrist, Depression Evaluation Service,
New York State Psychiatric Institute

JOHN M. OLDHAM, M.D.
Professor of Clinical Psychiatry
Associate Chairman of the Department of Psychiatry
Director, New York State Psychiatric Institute
Chief Medical Officer, New York State Office
of Mental Health
Training and Supervising Analyst, Columbia
Psychoanalytic Center for Training and Research
Attending Psychiatrist, Presbyterian Hospital

LEWIS A. OPLER, M.D., Ph.D.
Clinical Professor of Psychiatry
Director of Psychiatric Research, Presbyterian Hospital
Special Adjunct Research Professor, Department of
Psychology, Long Island University
Research Associate, Hispanic Research Center,
Fordham University

HERBERT PARDES, M.D.
Vice President for Health Sciences and Dean
of the Faculty of Medicine
Professor and Chairman of the Department
of Psychiatry

ETHEL SPECTOR PERSON, M.D.
Professor of Clinical Psychiatry
Training and Supervising Analyst, Columbia
Psychoanalytic Center for Training and Research

JOHN PETRILA, J.D., LL.M.
Former Deputy Commissioner and Counsel, New York State
Office of Mental Health, now Chairman, Department of
Law of Mental Health, Florida Mental Health Institute,
University of South Florida
Assistant Adjunct Professor, Stetson Law School

TIA POWELL, M.D.
Assistant in Clinical Psychiatry
Chairman, Consultation Subcommittee, Medical Ethics
Advisory Committee, Presbyterian Hospital

FREDERICK M. QUITKIN, M.D., D.M.Sc.
Professor of Clinical Psychiatry
Attending Psychiatrist, Presbyterian Hospital
and Long Island Jewish Hospital

JUDITH GODWIN RABKIN, Ph.D., M.P.H.
Professor of Clinical Psychology in Psychiatry
Research Scientist, New York State Psychiatric Institute

RONALD O. RIEDER, M.D.
Professor of Clinical Psychiatry
Director of Postgraduate Education, Department
of Psychiatry
Attending Psychiatrist, Presbyterian Hospital

STEVEN P. ROOSE, M.D.
Associate Professor, Clinical Psychiatry
Director, Research Depression Unit, New York State
Psychiatric Institute

BORIS RUBINSTEIN, M.D., M.P.H.
Assistant Clinical Professor, Psychiatry and Pediatrics
Director, Pediatric Psychiatry Consultation-Liaison
Service, Presbyterian Hospital

L. MARK RUSSAKOFF, M.D.
Associate Professor of Clinical Psychiatry
Deputy Director, New York State Psychiatric Institute

HAROLD A. SACKEIM, Ph.D.
Professor of Clinical Psychology in Psychiatry
Chief, Department of Biological Psychiatry, New York State
Psychiatric Institute
Adjunct Professor of Psychology, New York University

DAVID SHAFFER, M.D., F.R.C.P., F.R.C. Pysch.
Irving Phillips Professor of Child Psychiatry
Director, Division of Child and Adolescent Psychiatry

MICHAEL SHEEHY, M.D.
Associate Clinical Professor of Psychiatry
President and Medical Director of Silver Hill Hospital,
New Canaan, Connecticut

JONATHAN M. SILVER, M.D.
Associate Professor of Clinical Psychiatry
Director of Neuropsychiatry, Presbyterian Hospital
Chief of Psychiatry, Allen Pavilion

ANDREW E. SKODOL, M.D.
Associate Professor of Clinical Psychiatry
Director, Unit for Personality Studies, New York State
Psychiatric Institute
Associate Attending Psychiatrist, Presbyterian Hospital

HENRY I. SPITZ, M.D., F.A.P.A.
Clinical Professor of Psychiatry
Director, Training Programs in Group Psychotherapy
and Marital Therapy, Department of Psychiatry
Attending Psychiatrist, Presbyterian Hospital

ROBERT L. SPITZER, M.D.
Professor of Psychiatry
Chief, Biometrics Research, New York State
Psychiatric Institute

ELLEN STEVENSON, M.D.
Assistant Clinical Professor of Psychiatry
Director, Emergency and Community Services,
Presbyterian Hospital

PAUL D. TRAUTMAN, M.D.
Former member of the Department of Psychiatry, Columbia
University College of Physicians and Surgeons, now
Assistant Professor of Psychiatry, Assistant Professor of
Psychiatry in Pediatrics, and Director of the Division of
Pediatric Mental Health, New York Hospital/Cornell
Medical Center

B. TIMOTHY WALSH, M.D.
Professor of Clinical Psychiatry
Research Psychiatrist and Director, Eating Disorders Unit,
New York State Psychiatric Institute

GAIL A. WASSERMAN, Ph.D.
Associate Clinical Professor of Medical Psychology
in Psychiatry
Associate Professional Psychologist, Division of Child and
Adolescent Psychiatry
Research Scientist, New York State Psychiatric Institute
Director, Lowenstein Center

JANE ALLEN WATERS, M.S.
Assistant Clinical Professor of Psychiatric Social Work
in Psychiatry
Director of Social Work, New York State
Psychiatric Institute

DIANE WATTENMAKER, M.Ed., R.N., C.S., C.N.A.A.
Former member of the Department of Psychiatry, Columbia
University College of Physicians and Surgeons, now
Clinical Practice Director and Instructor, Psychiatric
Nursing, Norwalk Hospital, Norwalk, Connecticut

JAMIE WHYTE, M.D.
Fellow and Research Scientist, Sleep Disorders Center,
Columbia-Presbyterian Medical Center

JANET B. W. WILLIAMS, D.S.W.
Professor of Clinical Psychiatric Social Work in Psychiatry
and Neurology
Research Scientist and Deputy Chief, Biometrics Research,
New York State Psychiatric Institute

STUART YUDOFSKY, M.D.
Former member of the Department of Psychiatry, Columbia
University College of Physicians and Surgeons, now D. C.
Irene Ellwood Professor and Chairman, Department
of Psychiatry and Behavioral Sciences, Baylor College of
Medicine; Chief, Psychiatric Services, The Methodist
Hospital, Houston, Texas

Acknowledgments

We have been privileged to work with numerous dedicated and talented people in the creation of *The Columbia University College of Physicians and Surgeons Complete Home Guide to Mental Health.* Although it would be impossible to mention by name all who have offered advice, support, and direct contributions, we wish to cite those whose efforts have truly made it possible for us to bring this volume to fruition.

First, we would like to acknowledge the support and assistance of the entire faculty of the Department of Psychiatry. Special mention goes to Thomas Kranjac, M.D., and Francine Cournos, M.D., for their editorial comments and advice, and to David Kahn, M.D., Ellen Stevenson, M.D., and Nancy Petersmeyer, M.D., for their review of our earliest efforts. We appreciate the diligence of Helen (Sam) McGowan, Brenda Miles, Mary Sefring, and Eileen Asarnow. Special thanks, too, to Steven Papp, for his continuing faith in our efforts.

A superb team of skilled medical writers, researchers, and editors has labored long and hard to get it right. They include Marian Cohn, Lynn Dumas, Alicia Fortinberry, Robert Garrett and Ursula Wald-meyer, Mae Rudolph, Ellen Watson, and Ann West. Densie Webb, Rhoda Donkin, and Caroline Tapley also participated early on.

We have also worked with leading medical artists, to whom we offer grateful thanks: Vaune Hatch and Kristin Kuzamaki in Robert Demarest's department at the College of Physicians and Surgeons Center for Biomedical Communications.

For their guidance, professionalism, and indeed, their patience, we gratefully acknowledge the staff at Henry Holt. At the untimely death of Don Hutter, William Strachan stepped in and steered us to completion. Channah Taub provided invaluable insight, and Alison Juram kept us on our toes with patient determination. Thanks, too, to Rebecca Holland for guiding the complex production of such a large work, and to Victoria Hartman for her ability to make it work visually.

Finally, we thank Eugene Borkan, M.D., and Layton Borkan, M.S.W., for their suggestions; our agent, Barbara Lowenstein, a driving force from the very beginning; and Genell Subak-Sharpe, who conceived this book and set it in motion.

one

· · ·

MENTAL ILLNESS ASSESSMENT AND TREATMENT

1

What Is Mental Illness?

Michael Sheehy, M.D., and Francine Cournos, M.D.

People vary greatly in their abilities to cope with life's conflicts and stresses. Likewise, the nature and severity of life's difficulties vary from person to person. Someone able to adapt to the demands and carry out the basic tasks of life is generally considered mentally healthy. But when problems interfere with a person's ability to function day to day at home or at work, or with one's emotional experience or efforts to achieve personal goals, some degree of mental illness may be present.

Mental illness is common and amenable to treatment. Yet few health concerns are so cloaked in ignorance, secrecy, and fear. The fact is, most of those who suffer even the most debilitating symptoms of mental illness can be helped in a variety of ways, their suffering (and that of their families) alleviated, their lives made more comfortable and more productive.

In this chapter we show that mental illness consists of identifiable conditions with predictable patterns of symptoms. We explain that states of mental suffering and debility range along a spectrum of severity and consequence to the individual and to others, and we provide information on recognizing when to seek help on behalf of oneself or another. Finally, we discuss what experts now believe are the causes of mental illness.

IT'S COMMON, IT'S COSTLY . . . AND IT'S TREATABLE

No one is immune to mental suffering, and few families are without a member who battles with depression, anxiety, a drug problem, an emotional crisis, a behavior problem, a sexual dysfunction, insomnia, schizophrenia, dementia, or any of the numerous varieties of disorders or symptoms of disorder that have afflicted human beings throughout time.

Billions of dollars are spent on mental health care yearly in the United States, and billions more disappear in lost productivity. The personal, social, and economic burden of mental illness is comparable to that for cancer, heart disease, and other major physical illnesses. One analysis puts the total cost to the nation at nearly $300 billion a year.

As with any illness, by seeking treatment early in the course of the disease, the most severe consequences are often avoided. Without timely professional care, few mental problems are short-lived; many become severely disabling. For instance, someone with severe depression can usually expect, without treatment, that the condition will persist for some time or, if it ebbs, that it will eventually recur; suicide is often a direct consequence of untreated depression. Without help, a retarded person will neither develop to his or her full potential nor even approach a productive or independent life. Without treatment, a person whose personality disorder leads to difficulty getting or keeping a job will most likely face that problem indefinitely. Anxiety and panic can plague people throughout life, leading to immense personal suffering and poor job performance.

Unfortunately, victims of mental illness often believe "That's the way I am" rather than "I'm suffering from a treatable condition."

Following are some of the facts about the common occurrence of mental illness and the possibilities for successful treatment.

- One-third of all Americans will suffer a serious mental problem at some point in life. Twenty-seven million adults suffer from mental illness within any six-month period. Although an overall 80 percent of them can be helped, only 20 percent ever seek the help that is available.
- Among children, 12 million suffer from a mental disorder in any six-month period, and 4 million are debilitated by mental disorders. More than 40 percent of mentally troubled children are not brought for help.
- More than 15 percent of Americans will suffer an anxiety disorder at some time. Of these, 22 million suffer from panic disorders or phobias. More than 75 percent do not seek treatment, although current therapies are successful in 70 to 90 percent of cases.
- Severe depression strikes more than 11 million Americans yearly. Twenty-five percent of all women and 10 percent of men will have a serious bout of depression at least once in their lives. Current therapies relieve this suffering in 80 to 90 percent of cases, usually within weeks. Seventy percent of depressed people do not get help.
- Schizophrenia afflicts more than 2 million Americans in any year, 40 percent of whom never receive treatment. Medications can provide relief for the acute, devastating symptoms in eight out of ten cases.
- An estimated 30 percent of all older Americans who are diagnosed with some form of dementia are actually suffering from depression, which, if treated, would go away.
- Alcohol and substance abuse disorders take 100,000 American lives every year.
- Suicide is the second leading cause of death among teenagers in the United States. The suicide rate is highest among the elderly.
- Estimates suggest that one out of four people seeking medical help for a physical problem actually have an undetected mental illness.

CATEGORIES OF MENTAL ILLNESS

Like physical illnesses, mental disorders fall into several categories of severity and impairment, from mildly troublesome to life threatening.

The Medical Model of Mental Illness

Psychiatry is the branch of medicine that studies and treats mental disorder. As a medical discipline, psychiatry approaches suffering and disease by identifying patterns of symptoms that can be grouped together and labeled as specific illnesses or conditions. The field has made vast strides in identifying the various types and subtypes of mental disorder, determining diagnostic criteria (see those for panic disorder, for example, below), understanding their natural course, and developing treatments for them. Although the feelings, thoughts, behaviors, and physical problems that are symptomatic of mental disorders are confusing or frightening to society or to the troubled person, they are not mysterious to mental health professionals and can be understood in a logical framework.

As a result of the identification of specific types of mental disorders, vague descriptive phrases such as "being neurotic," "having a nervous breakdown," "going crazy," or even "getting senile" have been replaced by specific diagnostic categories that result in particular types of suffering and dysfunction, such as major depression, panic disorder, bulimia, social phobia, adjustment disorders, dementia, and schizophrenia, among many others. As with physical illnesses, a person can suffer from more than one mental disorder at the same time; for example, someone with a personality disorder can also receive a diagnosis of a sexual disorder, a sleep disorder, a mood disorder, and so on.

Each diagnosis, as will be explained in detail in appropriate chapters throughout this book, has identifiable symptoms and a generally predictable course. Once a clinician decides on the diagnosis (discussed at length in chapter 2), he or she chooses the appropriate treatment or combination of treatments that research, training, and experience indicate are likely to be effective for that individual with that condition.

DIAGNOSTIC CRITERIA FOR PANIC DISORDER

Psychiatric disorders consist of specific sets of symptoms that occur together. For example, the American Psychiatric Association, in the third revised edition of its *Diagnostic and Statistical Manual of Mental Disorders* (1987), has established the diagnostic criteria for panic disorder as follows. (See chapter 7 for a full discussion of this debilitating disorder.)

A. At some time during the disturbance, one or more panic attacks (discrete periods of intense fear or discomfort) have occurred that were (1) unexpected (i.e., did not occur immediately before or on exposure to a situation that almost always causes anxiety, and (2) not triggered by situations in which the person was the focus of others' attention.

B. Either four attacks, as defined in criterion A, have occurred within a four-week period, or one or more attacks have been followed by a period of at least a month of persistent fear of having another attack.

C. At least four of the following symptoms developed during at least one of the attacks:
   (1) shortness of breath (dyspnea) or smothering sensations
   (2) dizziness, unsteady feelings, or faintness
   (3) palpitations or accelerated heart rate (tachycardia)
   (4) trembling or shaking
   (5) choking
   (6) nausea or abdominal distress
   (7) depersonalization or derealization
   (8) numbness or tingling sensations (paresthesias)
   (9) flushes (hot flashes) or chills
   (10) chest pain or discomfort
   (11) fear of dying
   (12) fear of going crazy or of doing something uncontrolled

Note: Attacks involving four or more symptoms are panic attacks; attacks involving fewer than four symptoms are limited symptom attacks.

D. During at least some of the attacks, at least four of the C symptoms [listed above] developed suddenly and increased in intensity within ten minutes of the beginning of the first C symptom [listed above] noticed in the attack.

E. It cannot be established that an organic factor initiated and maintained the disturbance, e.g., amphetamine or caffeine intoxication, hyperthyroidism.

Source: American Psychiatric Association: *Diagnostic and Statistical Manual of Mental Disorders*, 3rd ed. revised (Washington, D.C.; APA 1987).

Mental Illness, Emotional Problems, and Problems of Living

Throughout all the medical disciplines, the point at which "illness" begins is frequently unclear and often depends on the aggregation of many persistent symptoms rather than the appearance of just one. Having a slightly abnormal blood test or X ray is often not enough to diagnose physical illness, but it could be a warning sign that problems may be occurring. Similarly, having a depressed mood for a week or having difficulty coping with the death of a loved one does not in itself warrant a diagnosis of major depression. Likewise, an adolescent may react to his parents' divorce by behaving aggressively but not necessarily earn a diagnosis of conduct disorder. And his father may react to his divorce by throwing himself into a bad relationship—a so-called problem of living or emotional reaction that may represent how he deals with stress but for which "mental illness" would not be an appropriate label. (See "Evaluating the Symptoms," on page 8.)

Throughout most of the remaining chapters of this book we tend to avoid the term "mental illness." We do this largely to avoid confusion over what type or degree of difficulty we are referring to. When we refer to the diagnosable syndromes of mental illness, we prefer to call them psychiatric or mental disorders. When we deal with problems of living or psychological reaction patterns that do not warrant psychiatric diagnoses but that nonetheless can be troublesome, we call them emotional problems or difficulties.

About Labels and Stigma

By whatever term, however, a person who contemplates receiving a psychiatric diagnosis and entering treatment may have many anxieties, including fears of being stigmatized, of "going crazy," or of being asked to give up a valued part of him- or herself that is perceived as creative or unconventional. Yet a psychiatric diagnosis also provides the person with a tool to understand what is wrong, to recognize that others have suffered similar symptoms, and to know that professionals can recognize and treat the syndrome. An ever-increasing number of people understand that mental illness is no more shameful than heart disease or injuries suffered in an accident. Most of what people fear about treatment for themselves or for family members is unfounded, because the goal of treatment is to reduce unwanted symptoms and free people of problems that interfere with developing their full potential.

HOW MENTAL ILLNESS AFFECTS LIFE

Mental disorders and difficulties reveal themselves in varying degrees of distress and dysfunction in three key domains of human functioning: (1) the way people experience and express their feelings; (2) how they think, reason, and learn; and (3) the way they behave. Mental disorders also influence physical experiences and sensations. (Likewise, physical disorders affect mental processes and experiences.)

The Key Symptom Areas

There are four major symptom areas: emotions, thoughts, behavior, and physical functioning and sensation.

Emotions

In response to common events of life, everyone feels unhappy, nervous, confused, frightened, or, conversely, overjoyed from time to time. An episode of "stage fright" preceding a speech is altogether nor-

mal, as is intense sadness over the loss of a loved one, a sense of disorientation when change occurs, or fear when facing obvious danger. So too do most people react with ecstasy or extreme happiness to extraordinary events, such as the birth of a child or a stroke of good fortune. In mental disorders, however, these extremes of feelings tend to be profound, pervasive, and/or inappropriate. The absence of appropriate feelings can also signal mental problems.

For a person with major depression (chapter 8), a low mood, emotional pain, frequent crying, and hopelessness dominate his or her feelings most or all of the day; some depressed people do not react at all to normally pleasurable experiences. Someone who experiences panic attacks (chapter 7) whenever leaving the security of home may eventually be overwhelmed by terror even upon walking to the mailbox. In the midst of a manic episode, a person with bipolar disorder (chapter 8) may grow euphoric over his or her "amazing" powers, or become irritable or angry over the smallest frustration. For someone experiencing a psychotic episode (chapter 14), irrational excitement or fear may mount to intolerable intensity.

Thoughts

Adults usually think along logical lines, even when thoughts seem to skip arbitrarily from subject to subject. In psychotic disorders, such trains of thought are seriously interrupted, and thoughts may surface at random, not discernibly connected to each other. In manic episodes, thoughts may race. In organic mental disorders such as dementia (chapter 15), thinking processes gradually degenerate.

Thought content too is usually affected in mental disorders. Mood disorders affect the way one interprets events, either overly negatively or unrealistically positively. Narcissistic personality disorder (chapter 13) is commonly marked by unrealistic convictions about the self, as with a person who is sure he or she will get a promotion despite a lack of experience or other qualifications. Someone with schizophrenia (chapter 14) in the midst of an acute episode usually will not know the difference between what is going on in his or her mind and in real life; delusions, such as the belief that one is the focus of a government investigation, or that one's actions have a disproportionate effect on some distant person or event, are common. Impaired judgment also can be a sign of mental disorder, as with a person who repeatedly loses at gambling and goes into debt but continues to believe that his or her luck will turn.

Failure to learn or develop mature thinking patterns are also significant. For example, children who are mentally retarded (chapter 17) lack such capacity to a varying degree, usually for neurological reasons.

Behavior

Society and culture establish norms of acceptable behavior. (See the box on page 8.) Within this range of social acceptability, every individual has his or her own unique repertoire of behaviors. Many unusual behavior patterns merely reflect individual personalities, eccentricities, or habits. But in certain mental disorders, behavior is extreme and debilitating, causing severe personal and social impairment. Aberrant behavior might include sexual perversions (called paraphilias; chapter 11); repetitive, useless gestures or activities (such as the hand-wringing or pacing common in some forms of depression, chapter 8, or the rocking seen frequently in autism, which is discussed in chapter 17); compulsions such as repeated hand-washing that mark obsessive-compulsive disorder (chapter 7). It can also show up in patterns of speech (that is, uninterruptible rapid speech or speaking in rhymes without apparent purpose, or slowed, tortured speech). The regular choice of clothing inappropriate to the season (wearing shorts in a blizzard) might also be a notable sign of mental problems. Inability to control spending, sexual activity, drug-taking, or other risky behaviors are still other manifestations of obvious difficulty.

In children, mental and emotional problems usually reveal themselves through behavior at home or in school, such as hyperactivity, aggressiveness, reluctance to leave home, poor attention span in school, lack of friendships, or drug use (chapters 17–20).

However, troubled behavior need not be so obvious. Often subtly self-defeating behavior patterns at work, at home, or in social situations are symptomatic of mental or emotional difficulty—as with the person who never can seem to get along with the boss, the man or woman who becomes overly subservient in relationships, or the person who always procrastinates and misses important deadlines. Indeed, the repertoire of possible troubled behavior is enormous.

Physical Functioning and Sensation

Mental life affects physical functioning in a host of ways. Indeed, unaware that they have a mental difficulty, many people go to their family doctors for help because they feel inexplicably tired; because they have problems with sleep, sexual functioning, or appetite; because they're subject to disturbing aches and pains; because they have heart palpitations; because they have odd physical sensations (such as being plagued by a smell that no one else seems aware of); or even because without any obvious physical cause they become unable to see or to walk. These and other symptoms might signal the presence of physical illness, but they could also be an expression of a psychiatric problem, such as depression, anxiety, eating disorders (chapter 10), or schizophrenia. Sometimes the physical symptoms are a reflection of an organic component of a mental disorder (in anxiety, for example, the body often exhibits a physical stress reaction, including shortness of breath; depression is believed to affect brain centers that control energy and appetite as well as mood; in schizophrenia, presumably malfunctioning brain chemicals produce sensations of hearing voices or perceiving odors that don't exist). In some cases, a troubled person diverts attention to existing physical maladies instead of recognizing the emotional pain he or she is experiencing.

Evaluating the Symptoms

Human beings differ in their feelings, thoughts, and behaviors. From time to time, normal people can be subject to some of the same experiences and behaviors (such as bad moods, sudden anxiety, feelings of being not quite real, or excessive anger) that can be symptomatic of mental illness. To establish the presence of mental disorder, the symptoms and symptom patterns must be evaluated as to the impairment they cause, their degree of intensity and distress, their persistence, and their duration.

Degree of Impairment or Distress

A person whose everyday life is in large measure unaffected by a mental difficulty, who continues relating well to family and friends, who carries on appropriately at work, and who feels reasonably satisfied will likely not be diagnosed as mentally ill. By contrast, someone no longer able to converse with family members or hold down a job, due to the constant distraction of hallucinations or peculiar, unrealistic thoughts, is an example of a person who is most likely mentally ill. One individual may get along quite well despite experiencing constant anxiety when traveling on an airplane, while another person might be so terrified that he or she refuses to fly and turns down career opportunities that might involve having to travel. This latter person experiences more severe consequences from his or her mental problem.

Persistence

Mental illness does not generally appear and disappear from day to day or week to week. Rarely occurring without warning signs, most mental illnesses have distinct histories of symptoms, usually becoming more and more noticeable and bothersome and worsening over time. An occasional feeling that "life is too confusing to handle" or "the boss is spying on me" does not always point to illness. But if such thoughts become persistent—arising with regularity or lasting even in a new situation and after making efforts to dismiss them—then a mental illness may well be present.

Duration

Without treatment, mental illness virtually always lasts for an extended period. Completely normal and natural sorrow over the death of a loved one may endure for weeks or months. But when such a mental state lasts for an unusually long period of time, with little or no change in the intense sense of loss, a vague line may have been crossed into the realm of mental disorder. Unless its duration is unusually long, however, and accompanied by life impairment, psychiatrists are loathe to call a completely understandable emotional reaction to the tragic events of life a mental illness. Indeed, some people will recover from a traumatic event quickly, while others will take much longer. But at some point, the expected signs of recovery should become apparent. If they do not, professional treatment may be needed.

MENTAL ILLNESS, CULTURE, AND SOCIETY

Within every culture and society, there are certain acceptable norms of behavior, attitude, and even personality. Those who demonstrate feelings, thoughts, and behaviors that are substantially outside these norms are likely to be viewed as mentally ill within that society.

Karl A. Menninger, the American psychiatrist who co-founded the Menninger Clinic and Foundation in Topeka, Kansas, was prominent among the many psychiatrists particularly interested in the link between society and mental well-being. He called mental health "the adjustment of human beings to the world and to each other with a maximum of effectiveness and happiness."

Cross-cultural psychiatrists, who study and treat mental disorders in varying cultural contexts and populations, have learned that for immigrants, attempts or expectations to "fit in" with the social standards of the newly adopted country are a common source of mental distress. Also, mental symptoms themselves may be expressed differently in various cultures. For example, newcomers from Latin America often reveal their depression through largely physical maladies and complaints, whereas depressed mood and feelings of guilt are generally more prominent among Americans of northern European background. Thus, mental health professionals who treat mental illness must always be alert to culture and social context. Nevertheless, although the expression of illness may vary, the major psychiatric disorders produce symptoms of distress and disability in all human beings, regardless of where they come from.

DEGREES OF SEVERITY OF MENTAL PROBLEMS: SOME EXAMPLES

As mentioned, there is no clear dividing line between the psychiatric disorders and milder problems that cause some of the same symptoms but less distress or life impairment. In adults as well as children, it is often useful to recognize mental problems along a spectrum of severity, as the following cases illustrate. Milder problems, although less disabling, can be troublesome to the individual, who may alter his or her lifestyle in ways that others might not even notice. These problems are often amenable to assistance by mental health professionals and sometimes respond to brief treatment. For the problems at the more severe end of the spectrum, impairment is greater and professional evaluation and treatment become more urgent.

Anxiety

Louis R., 29, a factory worker in a nonunion shop who earned a modest wage, had a mild problem with anxiety. Although he was content with his family life, enjoyed being with friends, and took particular joy in watching his children grow up, he was too nervous and shy to request a well-deserved raise. He wanted to send his children to college eventually and worried more each month about how he would ever be able to afford it. Although Mr. R. was a relatively well-adjusted person, his inability to assert himself was potentially harmful to his family, and his tendency to worry could eventually affect his health. At the urging of his wife, he finally discussed his problem with his pastor, who recommended that he sign up for an assertiveness training workshop sponsored by his church. Mr. R.'s wife urged him to go, because, she admitted, she would be happier with him if he would speak out more at home too. Mr. R. said he'd think about it. He did agree, however, to go with his wife for pastoral counseling.

Nickie B., who was once merely shy, in recent years had grown increasingly withdrawn from social contact. She even dropped out of her favorite Tuesday evening get-togethers with her old friends from college and became afraid to leave the house. Her symptoms are those of agoraphobia, and she requires treatment to regain any semblance of a fulfilling life. She spoke to a psychiatrist on the telephone but was afraid to go out to his office. She finally agreed to attend treatment accompanied by her elderly mother; after two months she was able to take the bus by herself. In the third month of treatment, Ms. B. agreed to join a therapy group consisting of others with her condition. Outside of therapy, they often accompany each other to go shopping or to go to the movies.

Depression

Immediately after her six-year marriage broke up, Joanne A. became sad and tearful, lost her appetite, had trouble sleeping, and was certain she would never feel good about anything again. Her reaction was understandable, and she was able to continue functioning fairly well at work and be emotionally available to her child. Common sense told her that she would probably begin to feel better after she got used to her changed circumstances, but that time seemed so far off that she decided to talk to the psychologist her company's employee assistance program provided. She found the sessions supportive and helpful, and she feels she is beginning to understand some of the issues over which her marriage broke up.

Howard L. slid into deep despair without apparent provocation. A prominent business executive, Mr. L. seemed to have all the good things of life, including wealth, a healthy body, an adoring family, and a wide range of interests. But shortly after he turned 50, he gradually lost interest in his work, no longer wanted to go out with friends or family, and preferred to retreat alone to their country cabin, where he would drink bourbon and brood. He could not eat or sleep or find pleasure, even from his wife or children. He felt that events had moved beyond his control and that there was little chance he would ever again take full charge of his life. Mr. L. began to find himself glancing frequently at the hunting rifles that he kept at the cabin, wondering whether his finances were in sufficient order that the family could get by if he died. His wife went out to the cabin one day without telling him and found Mr. L. looking over his will. She became so alarmed that she called their family doctor, who arranged for Mr. L. to have an emergency consultation with a psychiatrist nearby. Mr. L. agreed to brief hospitalization. Following treatment, his severe depression has completely resolved.

Childhood Conduct Problems

Tricia T. was seven when her brother was born. She began to have temper tantrums at home and to be truculent and difficult with her teachers at school. Always an active child, she now began hitting other children over small provocations, and they began to avoid her. When her brother was six months old, she pushed him roughly and he hit his head on the side of the crib. He was not hurt seriously, but Tricia's mother lost her temper and hit her daughter. Mr. T. came in the room and began to scream at his wife for hitting Tricia. That night Mrs. T. insisted that her husband sleep on the couch. The next week she consulted the school psychologist about Tricia. The psychologist recommended family therapy. In the course of six month's treatment, the family, including Tricia, was able to regain its equilibrium.

At 12, Max S. was becoming even more difficult than he had always been. He took his brother's pet goldfish out of the water and watched it struggle for life, and was caught trying to set fire to the family cat. At school he was a bully and respected no one's personal property. Although smart, he was stubborn in class and cursed at teachers. The school contacted his mother repeatedly about his behavior, but she invariably failed to show up at meetings with the teacher or the principal. Finally, when Max attempted to rape a six-year-old girl, the police took him into custody. Eventually, with the intervention of the family court, he was placed in a residential treatment program in the community, where his mother, a single woman with three other children, also comes for counseling. Mrs. S. has also joined a support group of parents with children with similar problems.

Personality Style, Personality Disorder, and Schizophrenia

All his life, Jordan C. was "different." In high school he would wear only black and carried a small flute with him, which he called his "magic flute." He would play it when he was under stress, even during a test. He had few close friends but was not lonely. He excelled in science and music and did extremely well in college. Working his way through graduate school, he was fired from office temporary jobs because of his strange habits, including his flute-playing. At present, he's finishing his dissertation for his doctorate in physics. He continues to play the flute, but now he is more likely to play it at home, alone in his lab, or sometimes in a small musical group with other graduate students. Mostly he is a loner and has lately taken up writing poetry with metaphysical themes. In a rare personal confidence, he once told his advisor that he wished he were more like everybody else. But Mr. C. seems unaffected by his eccentricities most of the time, is well adjusted and certainly productive, and is no less happy than many of his fellow students. In all he is an interesting, unusual person, who functions well.

Patricia W. kept to herself too, but her existence was neither happy nor useful. Although intellectually gifted, she quit college because she couldn't concentrate and because she found it increasingly difficult to relate to the other students. Now she has a job as a word processor, and when she gets home retreats immediately to her room. She has told her mother that she believes her dead brother shares the room with her. She became angry when her mother wanted her to go for help; she refused. Her mother went to see a psychiatrist herself, to talk about her daughter and how to deal with her. She is hoping that Ms. W., who has a probable schizotypal personality disorder, will go with her soon.

During his second year at college, Timothy G. began to talk to himself, or so his roommate at first believed. In fact Mr. G. was responding to voices that he had begun to hear. Within the course of several months, he stopped bathing and changing his clothes. One night his roommate awoke to find Mr. G. hovering over him screaming and cursing. He ran out of the room, woke up a dorm counselor, and Mr. G. was taken to the university hospital. He was soon diagnosed as having schizophrenia. He was forced to take a leave of absence from school, but with medication and family counseling, there is every hope that he may resume his studies.

Suspiciousness in the Elderly

Mary K., 79, moved into her oldest daughter's house after Mrs. K.'s husband died. She tended to keep to herself and did not participate in family conversation. After a few months, her children could hardly fail to notice that she was becoming convinced that they were whispering about her and planning to move her into a nursing home. The more she accused them of this plan, the more they actually began to consider it, since they thought she was getting "senile." They mentioned their concerns to their mother's physician. He reevaluated her physical condition and discovered that her hearing had worsened drastically. Because she couldn't hear them any longer when they spoke to each other in her presence, Mrs. K. withdrew and jumped to the conclusion that her family was planning to "put her away." A new hearing aid cleared up the problem.

Sam M., a bachelor, had always had a tendency to be suspicious of other people's motives. When he was 68, however, it became apparent that his problem had become more serious. He began to "overhear" people talking about him. Then he began to accuse his neighbor of spying on him and of training his dog to defecate in Sam's vegetable garden. The neighbor called the police when Sam threatened him with a shovel. Mr. M. was taken for a psychiatric evaluation and diagnosed with a late-onset paranoid disorder (chapter 23). When he was finally convinced to take antipsychotic medication, his condition improved greatly.

WHEN TO SEEK HELP

The exact point at which help should be sought for a mental or emotional problem—for yourself or someone you care about—is often a personal decision, based on the intensity and duration of symptoms and the degree of discomfort experienced. (See also the box on page 13.) Some situations, however, require *immediate* professional care, some even requiring emergency hospitalization, to prevent injury and save lives.

Recognizing Mental Health Emergencies

Suicidal Behavior
Suicidal actions always require emergency attention. Don't waste time trying to distinguish suicidal "gestures," such as relatively minor wrist-cutting, from more lethal actions such as deep wrist-cutting or dangerous overdoses of drugs. Seek help immediately by getting the person to an emergency room, calling the local suicide or crisis hot-line, or even phoning your local police. Suicidal statements are more difficult to assess. The person who says "I wish I were dead" may be expressing frustration, but if that same person has been depressed, has a drug or alcohol problem or a known psychiatric illness such as schizophrenia, seek help right away as you would for a suicidal action. (For more advice, consult chapter 26.)

Physical Danger
An emotionally unstable person bearing a weapon poses an imminent threat, as does someone demonstrating particularly aggressive or violent behavior. Physical danger is also present with someone whose mental illness has resulted in plans or impulses to commit violence, even if nothing has happened yet. Anyone who represents a physical danger to him- or herself or someone else because of mental illness should receive *immediate* care from a professional and might even require police intervention and/or hospitalization. If the threat is imminent, remove yourself from the premises and call the police or other appropriate emergency service. (See also chapter 27.)

When an Evaluation Is Appropriate

Mental health specialists generally agree that a professional evaluation should be considered when certain kinds of thoughts, feelings, or actions occur. While indicating that help may be needed, these events usually do not require emergency care. Among them:

On Your Own Behalf

- *An emotional or mental difficulty makes you change some important aspect of your life.* Examples: (1) You no longer go out with friends because your mind keeps returning to a problem you just can't seem to resolve. (2) You find yourself withdrawing from family or friends because you're feeling inexplicably angry at them. (3) You're taking sick days at work because when you get there you can't seem to concentrate. (4) You have decided not to continue school because you can't take the social pressure or the competition. (5) You've stopped driving your car because sometimes you get terribly panicky.

- *You feel generally displeased with yourself.* Examples: (1) You hate yourself because you think you are fat or ugly. (2) You feel you should be doing better than you are in various aspects of your life but for some reason you're not. (3) You feel lonely and isolated and you don't know why you can't seem to connect to others. (4) You feel continuously guilty or bad about some of your thoughts, feelings, or actions toward others. (5) You can't assert your feelings or desires. (6) You wish you weren't so nervous all the time.

- *You feel generally displeased with life or with others.* Examples: (1) People you meet always seem to have things better than you do. (2) The activities you have always enjoyed enormously no longer seem fun. (3) Life seems to have no purpose or point to it, and you don't see much hope that it ever will. (4) You feel out of touch with those around you or with life in general. (5) People are always blaming you for things that you believe are their fault. (6) You believe that your life is too stressful and you are losing your ability to cope. (7) You feel your habits or actions are out of control. (8) You are angry at your doctor, who keeps telling you that your physical symptoms have no organic basis.

- *You are unhappy about your relationships.* Examples: (1) You always seem to get into relationships with people who harm or take advantage of you. (2) You can't seem to grow really close to or become intimate with others. (3) You and your partner cannot establish a satisfying relationship, sexually or otherwise. (4) You are never happy for long in a relationship. (5) You worry so much all the time or are so moody that nobody seems to want to put up with you.

- *You have a hunch that your drinking or drug use is getting out of control.* Examples: (1) You've been drinking early in the morning. (2) You drove a car while you were high on drugs. (3) You've been asking your family doctor for more and more sleeping pills or tranquilizers. (4) People in your life are telling you that you have a drinking or drug problem, and you find yourself reacting angrily at them.

- *You've heard, seen, or felt something that other people tell you is impossible.* Examples: (1) When no one is around you sometimes hear voices giving you advice. (2) You occasionally see visions of a dead relative. (3) You smell bad odors that other people say aren't there. (4) You feel peculiar sensations on or beneath your skin, as if insects were crawling on you.

- *You firmly believe something, but when other people tell you it's false, you can't let your idea go or you get into arguments about it.* Examples: (1) You believe an actor or actress is sending you personal messages through the dialogue in a movie, even though the two of you have never met. (2) You're convinced that someone is poisoning your food, even though your family doctor tells you there is nothing physically wrong with you. (3) You're positive your spouse is having an affair, despite reports to the contrary from a private investigator.

On Someone Else's Behalf

Certain types of behavior might cause you to become concerned for someone who is close to you. Where feasible, it is best for the troubled person to initiate treatment personally. It can be difficult, however, to convince a reluctant individual to seek mental health assistance (see chapter 2). You may wish to arrange for a consultation in which you discuss the problem with a professional yourself and clarify whether you have grounds for your concerns. In any case, if the demeanor or behavior of someone close to you causes you concern, always talk to him or her about it first. For people who are troubled, support, attention from others, and the chance to air their worries can provide great comfort and relief. In the case of children or relatives whom you believe are mentally incompetent (see chapter 30), you may wish to arrange for the evaluation personally.

Following are examples of behaviors in others that may alert you to their need for help.

- *The person reacts to events in disproportionate ways.* Examples: (1) Your spouse or child repeatedly loses his or her temper over trivial events. (2) Your child's bitterness over an "unfair" grade seems to increase rather than ebb as the weeks pass. (3) Your relative believes that your concern for him or her means "You're out to get me."

- *The person has had a major mood or behavior change.* Examples: (1) Your spouse has lost interest in talking about the day's events and prefers just to sit alone every evening. (2) Your father hasn't recovered from the death of your mother three years ago and seems to be getting even sadder day by day. (3) Your normally happy-go-lucky daughter has not smiled in weeks and has begun to do poorly in school after having performed well in the past. (4) A family member has become extremely forgetful and confused. (5) Since the birth of your child, your wife has been weeping all the time and claiming she's not a good mother. (6) Your teenage son, a longtime fan of rock music, has started giving away all his favorite recordings. (7) An always-neat relative has begun to go to work grossly unkempt. (8) You've begun to notice that every time your spouse is about to leave the house, he or she must return to the kitchen repeatedly to check that the stove is turned off. (9) A family member suddenly has become fearful of situations that he or she tolerated in the past. (10) Your apparently healthy relative has been visiting one doctor after another searching for the physician who will *finally* diagnose and treat some mysterious illness. (11) Your child, spouse, or relative has periods in which he or she seems *too* happy over nothing, overly optimistic, and excessively energetic, with strangely little need for sleep. (12) The person has begun acting in extremely risky ways while denying that his or her behavior is dangerous.

- *The person has begun to express bizarre or inexplicable thoughts or beliefs.* Examples: (1) Your spouse refuses to eat dinner because "it's been poisoned." (2) Your oldest friend doesn't want to see you any more because "they'll use *you* to get to *me*." (3) Your relative starts talking about having a peculiar "special mission" in life. (4) Your child has begun seriously to believe that he or she was born on another planet and is not human.

THE VALUE AND LIMITS OF SELF-DIAGNOSIS

Usually, if a person perceives that he or she has a mental or emotional problem, some kind of problem does exist. However, the affected person often does not have an accurate view of his or her own diagnosis or the severity of the situation. For example, a person undergoing a life crisis (chapter 25) may be managing as well as can be expected under the circumstances and yet still worry about being unable to cope or about "going crazy." Sometimes a few sessions with a skilled professional are all that is necessary to put things in perspective.

On the other hand, certain illnesses—for example mania, schizophrenia, and narcissistic personality disorder—can interfere with a person's ability to see that something is seriously wrong. Such a person may act unreasonably with other people or do things that could cause injury, and yet feel that his or her own behavior is justified and that any negative results are someone else's fault.

One purpose of a professional opinion is to obtain an objective perspective on a problem. Don't hesitate to seek professional care, or encourage others to do so, if you find yourself wondering if you or someone you are close to has a mental problem.

. . . AND SELF-HELP

Helping oneself or a close friend or relative cope with a mental problem can prove invaluable in times of need, but it should never be considered in lieu of professional evaluation. Sometimes the best self-help is the act of seeking professional assistance. As you will see throughout this book, many chapters provide tips on helping oneself and others and list names and often addresses of mutual-support groups. Chapter 31 (page 435) also lists citizen organizations that provide help of many kinds to those who suffer from mental disorders and their families. Avail yourself of the knowledge and support of these groups and organizations, many of which can provide names of skilled professionals to consult—but consider them adjuncts to treatment of a diagnosed disorder or, in some cases, ways to deal with a problem that hasn't gotten out of hand. If your efforts to help yourself or another person fail to resolve the difficulty, get professional help. Citizen advocacy and support groups often can help individuals and families negotiate the mental health system. Successful mental health treatment will provide you or the other person with new ways of coping and taking care of oneself in the future.

THE SEARCH FOR CAUSES

Everyone encounters psychic pain and problems coping with life to some degree. Why one person is able to "roll with the punches" while another must contend with more serious mental health problems is the subject of much research and speculation. Experts believe that there are two broad categories of causative factors. One is the biology of the human body, including the brain itself; the other is the psychological development of each individual in the context of family, culture, and life experience. These mind-body aspects of human functioning no longer are believed to be separate and distinct from one another.

Psychological processes—including mood, learning, and behavior—depend on a functioning physical organism. All or many mental illnesses thus probably have a biological aspect or underpinning, such as an under- or oversupply of vital neurotransmitters (see "Nerve-signal Transmission and Brain Metabolism," below). Subtle differences in brain chemistry, many of them probably inherited, may make some people vulnerable to illnesses such as depression, alcoholism, or schizophrenia.

Psychological processes can have great influence on the body, such as to produce changes in the functioning of the immune system via neurotransmitters that communicate throughout the brain and nervous system. Many people become vulnerable to physical illness through repeated "Type-A" stress (chapter 24).

Even though alterations in brain chemistry might well affect all those who suffer mental symptoms, psychiatry distinguishes between psychological illness and organic mental illness. Organic mental illnesses (chapter 15) are those in which a disease or injury directly damages brain tissue and in so doing produces alterations in thinking, feeling, or behaving. Such diseases include, for example, stroke, or Alzheimer's disease and other dementias, which cause deterioration of brain tissue and can make someone violent, confused, forgetful, and uncooperative. Other organic causes of mental symptoms include many hormonal abnormalities (such as thyroid disease), drug overdoses, and high fever, for example, which can interfere with how the brain functions, at least temporarily. As direct physical causes of such diseases as schizophrenia are discovered, perhaps they too will be classified as organic.

Together body and mind, plus life itself, create vulnerabilities to mental illness. For example, someone with a family history of depression may have no serious difficulty until a severe stress (perhaps a divorce) triggers the biological susceptibility. It is known that severe deprivation in infancy and early childhood can be a cause (although not the most common one) of mental retardation (chapter 17), which is a primarily neurological condition. Although many genetically influenced people who develop schizophrenia in late adolescence have been well nurtured and provided for by their families, in other victims the vulnerability to illness must be triggered by a stressful life experience or background. Also, although many people may have a genetic susceptibility to alcoholism, they would never develop the disease if they did not try alcohol.

Following is a brief discussion of the factors that are believed to cause mental illness, alone or in combination with other risk factors. How they contribute to the specific mental disorders that we discuss in this book is dealt with in the individual chapters. Chapter 32 includes an extensive discussion of research into the causes of mental illness.

Organic Factors

Nerve-signal Transmission and Brain Metabolism
As our understanding of brain mechanisms grows, researchers have been focusing on how the brain transmits nerve signals. They have identified numerous natural compounds, called neurotransmitters, that carry messages between nerve cells. Abnormal amounts of some chemicals, whether too high or too low, are associated with depression, schizophrenia, and suicidal and homicidal behavior. (See the box on page 15.) In addition, new testing techniques demonstrate that some people with mental illness have different patterns of metabolism in their brains.

Brain Structure
The brains of individuals with severe mental illness sometimes have overall physical attributes that differ from the brains of most other people, although as yet there is no firm correlation between these structural differences and any specific mental abnormalities. It is also known that the brain cells of some mentally disabled people have fewer connections between one another than those in other individuals' brains, dif-

ferences believed to be tied to intellectual development. As mentioned earlier, significant physical illness within the brain—for example, tumors or strokes—can also affect structure and functioning and produce symptoms of mental disorder.

Introduced Substances

Many drugs, prescription medicines, and over-the-counter medications can alter the functioning of the brain and influence mental processes. Caffeine and nicotine, for example, act as stimulants. Alcohol has an enormous influence on behavior and personality over the short and long term. Cocaine can lead to psychosis. In children, lead poisoning can lead to mental retardation and learning disabilities. Numerous prescribed drugs, including some of those that lower blood pressure, cause depression.

Heredity

Biological susceptibility to mental illness can be inherited. Various mood disorders, anxiety disorders, schizophrenia, and some forms of alcoholism are among the disorders that researchers believe have a strong genetic component. Genes probably do not confer an absolute certainty that the disorder will be passed on; rather, numerous psychological and environmental influences interact with an inherited vulnerability to various mental illnesses.

MESSAGES FROM THE BRAIN

Even a tiny portion of the brain—as much as might fit in a teaspoon—is more complex than the most powerful computer built to date. A typical brain might contain 100 billion neurons. Each neuron (see figure 1.1) has dozens of "tails," called dendrites, that accept messages from other neurons. Each also has a long axon, stretching through the brain to other neurons before branching into numerous tips, which sends messages. In all, the brain might contain more than 1,000,000,000,000,000 (1 quadrillion) links between cells, all of them together producing human thought and feelings.

Among the most important communication channels within the brain are those located at the tips of one cell's axons and another cell's dendrites. There, a tiny space—called a synaptic cleft, or synapse—keeps the cells slightly separated. A message being passed from one cell to another travels along the axon as an electrical signal. This stimulates the axon tip to release molecules of chemicals called neurotransmitters. In less than $1/10,000$ of a second, the chemicals reach the receptors of the nearby dendrite, which converts the message back into an electrical signal within the receiving cell.

There are dozens of distinctly different neurotransmitters, many remaining to be discovered (see chapter 32). Each one, it is believed, transmits a particular kind of signal. Some deal with emotions, such as sadness or elation. Other neurotransmitters appear responsible for thoughts and sensations, such as passing along signals caused by seeing colors, hearing a bell ring, or feeling heat from a match.

Some axons are able to release a wide variety of the chemicals but, depending on the electrical signal, might produce them only one at a time. Others are capable of doling out only a few different neurotransmitters, and they do so sparingly. At the same time, dendrites will accept varying numbers of chemicals and in limited amounts. Neurotransmitters sometimes remain "afloat" in the synaptic cleft until they are reabsorbed by the cell that emitted them, broken down by enzymes, or finally accepted by the receiving cell.

Substantial research in recent years has focused on the precise roles played by different neurotransmitters and receptors, and the effects seen when these chemical messengers remain in the synaptic cleft. When certain chemicals remain, they can block other important signals from being transmitted. When other neurotransmitters are reabsorbed too quickly, the signal they tried to convey is transmitted inadequately, like a telephone call where every other word is blocked by static.

Numerous modern drugs used in psychiatry act directly on the ever-changing chemical mix of neurotransmitters. Some affect neurotransmitters necessary to help an individual maintain concentration. Some inhibit the activity of enzymes that ordinarily would break down specific neurotransmitters. Others "fill up" receptors with inactive chemicals, so brain cells cannot accept messages that might be harmful mentally or emotionally. (See chapter 5 for more about how psychiatric drugs function and chapter 32 for more on neurotransmitter research.)

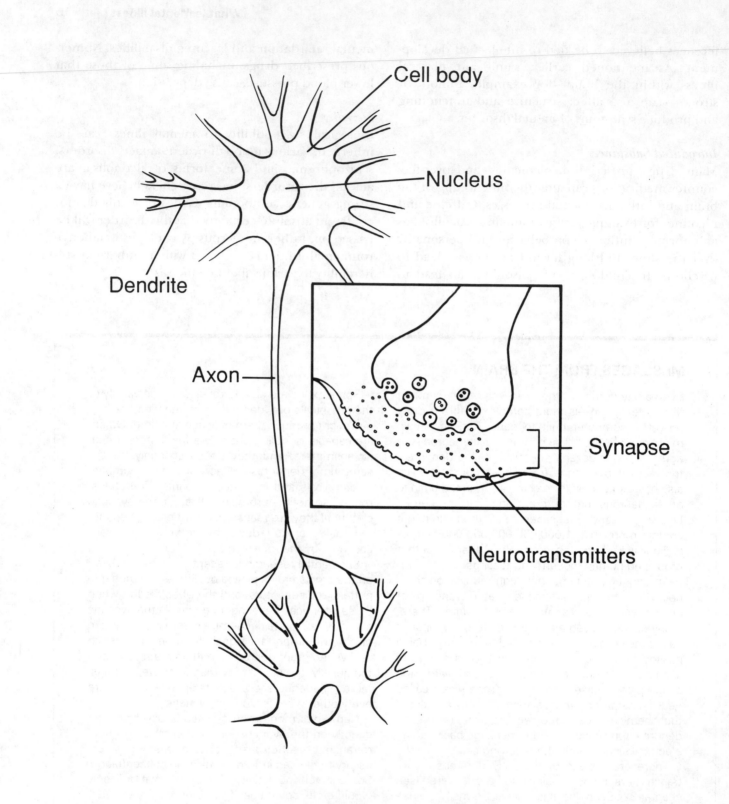

NEURONS: THE CELLS OF THE BRAIN

Figure 1.1: The typical brain contains 100 billion neurons. A neuron is composed of a cell body with a nucleus, dendrites ("tails" that receive messages from other neurons), and axons (long branches that send messages to other neurons). Between dendrites and axons is a tiny space called the synapse (see box); message-bearing chemicals called neurotransmitters are released from axons and picked up by dendrites.

Psychological Factors

As discussed at length in chapter 4, the many schools of thought in psychotherapy seek to account for what the human mind is, how it develops, and how and why it sometimes functions improperly. When considered all together, they explain in large measure many of the underlying mental processes that result in what we call "mental illness."

Psychoanalysts, for example, believe that events, feelings, fantasies, expectations, and other memories stored in the unconscious mind can create conflicts that produce symptoms of illness. Derived from psychoanalysis, psychodynamic therapies seek to unearth and resolve the conflicts that produce mental illness symptoms. Clinical and research specialists from many theoretical backgrounds have studied the importance of experiences during childhood and have noted the repetitions throughout later, adult relationships of early life patterns established with parents and siblings.

Experts from the behavioral and learning schools of psychology and psychotherapy theorize that behavior is learned through a series of positive and negative reinforcements—rewards and punishments—that occur throughout life. Mental illness can be viewed as the end result of a series of "bad habits" that can be overcome in treatment by relearning. (Such habits are often quite complex, such as the way a person customarily responds emotionally to a certain kind of situation, or someone's typical train of thought when presented with an intellectual challenge.) The relatively new discipline of cognitive therapy holds that a person's thoughts can produce maladaptive feelings and behaviors; clinicians work with patients to help them recognize and change these thinking patterns.

2

Going for Help: How Diagnoses Are Made and Appropriate Treatments Determined

L. Mark Russakoff, M.D., Steven Roose, M.D.,
Roger MacKinnon, M.D., Robert Spitzer, M.D.,
and Janet B. W. Williams, D.S.W.

A person seeking mental health assistance can begin the process in several ways. A prearranged appointment with a psychiatrist, a visit to a hospital clinic or emergency room, a meeting with a school psychologist, or a call to a crisis hotline, for example, can initiate a consultation and evaluation process that will lead to a diagnosis and a recommended type of treatment. In chapter 3 we discuss the various types of practitioners, their training, their scope of practice, and how to find and evaluate a therapist. This chapter covers what to expect during the evaluation process and how the practitioner makes a diagnosis and establishes a treatment plan.

The format and content of a mental health examination are flexible. The steps and tests involved vary depending on the nature or seriousness of the individual's problem and the type of professional consulted. Someone who wants help for a marital problem, for example, may well require a different type of assessment from someone with symptoms of confusion or depression or a problem with drugs.

This chapter discusses the many possible steps that could be taken in a complete diagnostic workup by a mental health professional. As discussed in the following chapter, a psychiatrist is a medical doctor who has specialized training in mental disorders. Nonmedical mental health practitioners refer patients to psychiatrists for evaluation when medication or hospital admission may be necessary, and when medical factors cause or complicate the problem. All the medical procedures and evaluations that are mentioned throughout this chapter must be performed by or under the auspices of a psychiatrist or other medical doctor.

THE PSYCHIATRIC INTERVIEW: TYPES OF QUESTIONS

In addition to very specific questions about your symptoms, mental health professionals might ask a number of the following questions during a first meeting.

- What brings you here to see me?
- Describe your childhood and adolescence.
- Provide information on your adult life—occupation, education, and marital history.
- Who are the people who are or have been important in your life? Describe your relationship with them.
- Tell me about your sex life and feelings about sexuality.

- What is your religious background and your family's attitude toward religion?
- Describe recent emotional experiences that have upset you and your reactions to them.
- How do others react to you? To your problem?
- Do you have a history of emotional problems?
- Is there any history of emotional problems in your family?
- What kinds of situations frustrate you? How do you become involved in them?
- How have your symptoms interfered with your life?
- Describe a typical day.
- What are your strengths? Your weaknesses?

THE EVALUATION PROCESS

Assembling all the information needed to make a diagnosis of a mental disorder or emotional problem is a difficult process that requires observation and interviews. Often the clinician makes an initial, tentative diagnosis, then refines it as testing and/or treatment response reveals additional information. Relief is provided as soon as possible for a person seeking help for acute painful symptoms. Once the clinician establishes the diagnosis, the formal treatment plan is set into motion.

As in all medical specialties, establishing a diagnosis is essential to the process of determining appropriate treatment. To make a diagnosis, clinicians organize data they gather in examinations, interviews, and testing. It is a complex procedure, because different disorders share common symptoms (inability to sleep can be a symptom of a sleep disorder or of depression, for example). Therefore pinpointing the precise diagnosis is all the more important.

Typically, on a first visit a clinician takes a history (a review of an individual's past life as well as a discussion of the current emotional problem) and performs a mental status examination (an evaluation of an individual's current mental state). If he or she considers it to be necessary, the practitioner sometimes schedules one or more psychological tests. A physical examination and laboratory tests also may be recommended to rule out organic illness or to assess how physical factors contribute to the mental problem. (All these steps are discussed at length below.)

Generally speaking, the first one or two meetings with a mental health professional focus on determining a diagnosis and formulating a direction for treatment.

Length of Time and Setting

The average interview lasts 45 to 50 minutes; it is usually conducted in a clinic or private office, with few or no interruptions. Many practitioners take some notes during an interview, but will stop if the patient finds it distracting. Those who use a tape recorder ask the patient for permission to tape. Notes are important to help the clinician review a patient's case and because he or she has a legal and professional responsibility to maintain adequate records of a patient's diagnosis and treatment.

CONFIDENTIALITY

Some people fear that their problem will be revealed to others. Be assured that the clinician will respect your confidentiality. (Certain exceptions to confidentiality are discussed at length in chapter 30.) If you and your psychiatrist agree that it is important to inform your relatives about your illness, he or she will do so without disclosing confidential information. Even if the clinician discusses aspects of your problem with other physicians or mental health practitioners, your name will not be revealed unless you have specifically given your consent.

The only time a mental health practitioner deliberately breaches the code of confidentiality is if he or she believes your life is in danger (that is, if it appears likely that you will commit suicide) or that you might harm another individual. In these cases, the therapist is legally, morally, and professionally obligated to disclose this information.

Interviews with Family and Friends

In order to assess a problem fully, it is sometimes helpful for the clinician to talk to family members and friends, particularly if the problem centers around family matters or is part of a family crisis. Usually, however, a family interview is not part of an initial consultation—although in an emergency situation or in the case of psychosis, close relatives often can provide information that is useful in determining a diagnosis. In family therapy, however, the initial consultation may include interviews with the entire family.

Sometimes an individual goes for help not because he or she feels the need for help but because someone else—a parent or a spouse—insists that seeing a mental health professional is necessary. In these cases, the clinician explores with the individual why others feel help is needed and determines if in fact a treatable problem exists. In some instances, psychiatric help may not be needed, and conveying this information to relatives can be very reassuring.

The History

Seeing a mental health specialist is in many ways similar to seeing any medical doctor. He or she will want to know the nature of mental and physical symptoms, the approximate date they began, the context in which they developed, and the person's lifetime mental and medical history.

The psychiatric history lays the foundation for the diagnosis. It begins with a discussion of the current problem and why the individual, the family, or a physician decided a consultation with a mental health professional would be helpful. The discussion includes questions about when the problem started, its symptoms and their severity, and any factors that may have caused it or may be related. The clinician usually asks questions to help organize the discussion.

Beyond the immediate problem, the therapist is interested in developing a therapeutic alliance with the patient (see chapter 6 for more information). To help develop this rapport, he or she may begin by asking basic details of a person's life, including such things as marital status, occupation, and educational background. As the interview progresses, the therapist begins to probe for more personal information, asking questions, for example, about current lifestyle, feelings about self and others, and different ways of coping with problems and stress.

Questions about previous episodes of emotional disorders yield important information. The practitioner needs to know the extent of incapacity, the type of and response to any previous treatment received, and whether or not the person was hospitalized. Also of importance is any family history of mental or medical illness.

Mental health professionals usually ask questions about past life in order to uncover how and to what extent past events affect current emotional problems. Major events—such as the death of a loved one or long-term separation from a parent in childhood, for example—can have a profound effect many years later. Information about key figures from current and past life, the roles that various people have played in the person's upbringing, and feelings about these individuals are explored, as are qualitative aspects of these relationships—their length, the depth of communication, and so forth.

From all this information, the mental health professional attempts to clarify the problem and to gain insights into an individual's personality and mental health problems and determine whether or not any physical conditions may be involved.

No one method or list of questions is used to obtain a history. (See the box on page 19.) Psychiatrists and other mental health professionals use different approaches for different problems or personality styles, but the goal is always the same: to understand and diagnose the mental or emotional problem and to plan a treatment.

SOME GUIDELINES FOR A FIRST VISIT

When referred to a psychiatrist or other mental health professional, it is natural to wonder and perhaps worry about what will happen during the evaluation. Often part of the concern stems from the very nature of a psychiatric consultation. Many people feel uncomfortable about revealing personal information to a stranger (even though that stranger is a doctor or other professional), while others are embarrassed to admit that they are unable to handle their problems on their own. Some people worry that their symptoms mean that they are "crazy" or that the therapist will somehow judge them negatively because of their problem.

These are all normal feelings. It should be remembered, however, that professionals who deal with mental health problems have a broad understanding of the many different kinds of human behavior. The mental health practitioner is there to help, to listen, and to direct a course of therapy.

To help the clinician and to get the most out of treatment, as a patient you should:

1. Be honest. Unless you are truthful and open, it will be difficult for your therapist to understand the problem correctly.
2. Express your thoughts and feelings freely.

3. Have confidence in the practitioner's professional abilities. Realize that he or she has treated many patients with similar problems and is an expert in human behavior.
4. Don't keep secrets from your therapist, and don't be concerned with the impression you are making. You will not lose the therapist's respect or concern, no matter how difficult or troubling your problem is.
5. As you tell the mental health professional of your problem, you may feel powerful emotions, such as intense anger or sadness, but do not be embarrassed to talk about your emotions or to let your therapist know how you are feeling.
6. Prepare a written or mental list of questions. Feel free to ask the practitioner what his or her opinion of your problem is and about the type of treatment he or she is thinking of recommending—as well as the risks, complications, benefits, and costs of treatment.
7. Don't feel ashamed or embarrassed if you find it difficult to talk. Often discussing emotionally charged information arouses intense anxiety. Even the most articulate person may find him- or herself unable to talk clearly or concisely.

The Mental Status Examination

The mental status examination provides information about a patient's current mental functioning; in this it is rather like a routine physical examination. Through this assessment process, the clinician gains information about the patient's emotional state and cognitive (his or her ability to think and reason) functioning. Results help determine whether psychological, medical, or neurological tests are necessary.

Aspects of functioning that a clinician looks for in the mental status examination include:

Appearance. Sometimes external factors, such as dress and grooming, can provide diagnostic hints to a patient's state of mind; some physical conditions (such as Graves' disease, a thyroid disorder) have distinctive physical characteristics.

Behavior/motor activity. Typical behaviors often mark specific disorders. For example, suspiciousness could indicate paranoia; apprehensiveness, an anxiety condition. Motor behaviors, such as tremors, could be signals of an underlying physical condition.

Speaking manner. Rapid and pressured speech, for example, could indicate bipolar disorder, while a flat monotone could indicate depression. Speech abnormalities might mean that the patient has brain damage.

Affect. This term refers to the type of emotion a person displays externally. Therapists assess the intensity as well as the duration of an affective state, such as the sadness that often accompanies depression. Often affect that is inconsistent with a given situation or that shifts rapidly is evidence of a psychiatric disorder.

Thought processes. The way a patient structures thoughts and reaches conclusions is important to the evaluation process. Does the patient actually answer the questions asked? Is he or she logical and able to describe clearly events and their relationship to problems?

Thought content. This term refers to specific, often unusual, concerns that a person may have, such as delusions (beliefs that are objectively incorrect and out of keeping with the person's background) and obsessions (ideas, recognized at least initially by the person as irrational, that intrude into his or her mind).

Intellectual function. Many psychiatric and physical conditions affect the ability to calculate, think abstractly, and use words correctly. Patients who have had strokes often have significant problems in this area, for example.

Memory. The focus is on both short-term and long-term memory. In many organic conditions (physical illnesses that influence brain functioning), short-term memory is particularly impaired.

Orientation. Whether a patient knows such facts as the date, the time, or who is the president are clues to cognitive functioning.

Insight. This term refers to the extent of an individual's self-understanding. Some people understand that they are suffering from an emotional disorder while others completely deny that a problem exists; still others know but blame it on other people or uncontrollable events.

Physical Examination

Frequently a comprehensive psychiatric evaluation includes a medical history and a physical examination to see if an organic condition is causing or contributing to the mental disorder. Although psychiatrists are trained to evaluate their patients medically, most usually do not conduct extensive physical examinations themselves; instead they refer patients to appropriate specialists, as do other mental health professionals.

Many psychiatric disorders are accompanied by physical complaints. For example, panic disorder is often marked by respiratory and cardiovascular symptoms; depression with appetite and sleep changes and gastrointestinal disturbances. Conversely, many physical conditions (ranging from thyroid disorders to brain tumors and including such illnesses as Parkinson's disease and Huntington's chorea) can cause psychiatric symptoms. (See chapter 28 for a fuller discussion of the relationship of physical illness to psychiatric problems.)

DIAGNOSTIC TESTS

No physical or psychological test exists that by itself can establish the diagnosis of any of the major mental disorders. However, diagnostic procedures and laboratory tests often can supplement data obtained from the psychiatric history and mental status examination, if the practitioner decides they are necessary. The choice of tests ordered depends on the diagnostic clues revealed during a patient's history and mental status examination as well as on the therapist's best judgment of what is needed.

Medical Tests

In order to make sure that a psychiatric symptom is not being caused by an organic disorder, physicians sometimes order laboratory studies. Some of these include the following.

Biochemical evaluations. Electrolyte (sodium, potassium, chloride, bicarbonate) abnormalities can cause a wide range of neuropsychiatric complications. For example, low levels of potassium (commonly associated with bulimia) can cause weakness and fatigue. Serum magnesium levels are often decreased in alcoholism. Biochemical testing also can include kidney and liver function tests, which are useful in determining if psychotropic drugs are having adverse effects.

Endocrine tests. Endocrine (hormonal) disturbances can cause a broad range of psychiatric symptoms, including those associated with depression, anxiety and panic attacks, dementia, delirium, and psychosis. Endocrine studies include screening tests for thyroid conditions and adrenal disease; pancreatic function also is frequently checked because diabetes and hypoglycemia can cause many symptoms that mimic psychiatric problems. Tests for specific endocrine problems might also be given—for example, a man suffering from impotence might be tested in order to measure the level of his serum testosterone.

Neuroendocrine tests. A number of diagnostic tests are being developed by researchers studying links between the endocrine and nervous systems. For years, the dexamethasone suppression test (DST), which provides information on the secretions of the adrenal hormone cortisol, has been of particular interest to psychiatrist researchers. Some researchers believe an abnormal DST reading can help confirm the diagnosis of major depression in some people, although this finding is far from being conclusively proven. Several other neuroendocrine tests show promise, but none is likely to be of value to the routine diagnosis and treatment of mental disorders in the foreseeable future.

Hematology tests. A complete blood count (CBC) is part of a routine hospital screen and is useful psychiatrically in a number of ways. Drug use, for example, can affect certain blood factors. Blood tests can also test for vitamin deficiencies that produce psychiatric symptoms. Vitamin B-12 deficiency, for example, has been connected to marked personality changes and symptoms of psychosis, paranoia, fatigue, and dementia.

Immunologic tests. Viruses and infectious agents cause a wide spectrum of psychiatric symptoms. Among the most common are syphilis, viral hepatitis, and tuberculosis. Lyme disease can cause fatigue, headache, and dementia-like symptoms. Epstein-Barr virus and cytomegalovirus infections can cause changes in mental functioning, motor behavior, and personality. HIV (human immunodeficiency virus) is responsible for a dementia condition that can appear before other symptoms of acquired immune deficiency syndrome (AIDS) are apparent.

Toxicology studies. Prescription, over-the-counter, and "street" drugs often cause psychiatric symptoms. Similarly environmental toxins that are breathed or ingested (such as lead, mercury, manganese, arsenic, aluminum, insecticides, industrial chemicals used to make inks, glue, paints, and solvents) also can cause behavioral abnormalities.

Neuropsychiatric Tests

Because of the close relationship and similarity of symptoms between organic brain dysfunction and psychiatric disorders, a new science called neuropsychiatry has evolved. This discipline uses a battery of neurological tests and diagnostic equipment to test for cognitive function and organic conditions that might be causing psychiatric symptoms.

New imaging technology has been developed that can provide detailed information on brain abnormalities associated with subtle behavioral and emotional changes long before more obvious symptoms are evident. In research settings, imaging studies are yielding information on schizophrenia, depression, and other mental disorders that are believed to have a strong biologic basis.

Neuropsychiatric testing can include the following.

Electroencephalogram (EEG). The EEG measures electrical activity from the brain. It is a noninvasive, relatively simple test in which electrodes are attached to the scalp; these record brain waves on a polygraph, and the pattern is then evaluated. EEGs are particularly useful in diagnosing seizure disorders.

Polysomnography (sleep EEG). Brain activity is recorded during sleep, in order to diagnose sleep disorders or monitor disorders that are characterized by abnormal sleep patterns, such as depression.

Computed tomography scan (CT or CAT scan). The first modern brain imaging technique in wide use, the CT scan is used to assess organic brain conditions. In research settings, it is being used to study a wide variety of psychiatric conditions that are accompanied by abnormalities in the brain structure, including schizophrenia, alcoholism, and anorexia

IMAGING STUDIES

Figure 2.1: Because physical disorders such as brain tumors can cause mental symptoms, a psychiatrist may suggest a variety of tests, including brain imaging studies, to rule out organic causes of mental illness. The two most common imaging studies are computed tomography (CT) scans and magnetic resonance imaging (MRI).

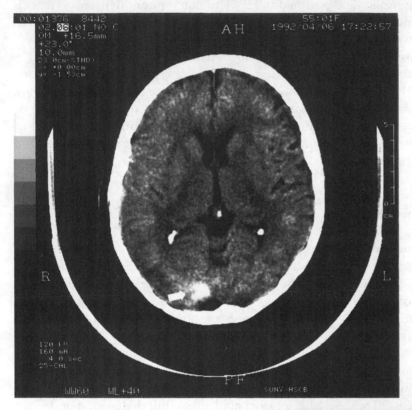

Left: CT scans reveal structural abnormalities within the brain. In this scan, a brain tumor in the right brain hemisphere (arrow) is revealed.

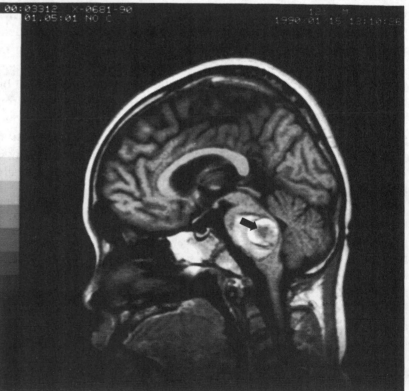

Right: MRI scan showing a large tumor in the brain stem (arrow). In addition to tumors, MRI can identify problems that cannot be seen on CT scans, such as small lesions caused by stroke.

nervosa. An X-ray beam scans the brain from different directions, producing images. In a contrast CT scan, a dye is injected into the patient in order to enhance the image.

Magnetic resonance imaging (MRI). Brain images are produced by alterations in a magnetic field. MRI can identify structural changes that cannot be seen on a CT scan, such as small lesions involved in stroke or multiple sclerosis. It is the best imaging device currently available to identify brain tumors. MRI technology has identified a number of abnormalities that appear to be associated with mental disorders such as schizophrenia, although the meaning of these abnormalities and their diagnostic implications are still unclear. Because MRI is a relatively new technology, researchers are still evaluating how best to use it in psychiatry.

Positron emission tomography (PET). PET technology uses radioactive compounds to image metabolic processes and provides a three-dimensional view of brain function, rather than structure. It allows researchers to study neurotransmitters and other brain chemicals that help the brain to communicate. Because the technology is new, its uses are still being studied and developed; a major application of PET is expected to be the identification of chemical abnormalities associated with specific psychiatric disorders.

Single photon emission computerized tomography (SPECT). Like PET, SPECT creates detailed, three-dimensional images of brain function, using machinery that is less complicated and expensive. SPECT, a new technology whose uses are still being developed, promises to be very useful in diagnosing stroke, because it provides a measure of cerebral blood flow. SPECT also may be used one day to differentiate Alzheimer's disease from other disorders such as depression.

Psychological Testing and Rating Scales

Psychological tests and symptom rating scales are used in the assessment of mental disorders. These tests can help determine an individual's personality, coping resources, and degree of emotional difficulties as well as cognitive functioning. Hundreds of tests have been developed; some check for general personality styles while others test for specific behavioral or cognitive dysfunctions.

As with medical tests, psychological tests alone cannot determine a diagnosis, but they can reveal important information about many aspects of a per-

son: self-image and self-esteem, motivation, values, patterns of relationships, and mood, among others. They can sometimes help predict what type of therapy may be most useful or what the focus of treatment should be. Tests conducted for an initial evaluation also are useful as a baseline for comparison to tests taken as treatment progresses.

Before a test is administered (often by a psychologist specializing in testing), the evaluating clinician advises a patient on the purpose of the test and the kind of information it provides. Because testing can take several hours (and several hours more for a qualified professional to assess the results), tests are not given during the initial interview but are scheduled separately, if necessary.

There are several categories of tests: IQ tests, neuropsychological test batteries, objective and projective psychological tests, and psychological rating scales.

IQ Tests

The most common IQ tests are the Wechsler Adult Intelligence Scale-Revised (WAIS-R) and the Wechsler Intelligence Scale for Children-Revised (WISC-R). These were developed in the 1940s and are revised periodically. They consist of 11 scales, some of which measure verbal abilities while others measure performance. IQ tests can aid in identifying cognitive problems. They are useful in evaluating a psychiatric disorder because often people suffering from emotional disorders have scores that deviate from what are considered to be normal standards. IQ testing can also be helpful in evaluating developmental disabilities in children and adolescents.

Neuropsychological Test Batteries

Several batteries of neuropsychological tests are currently in use. The Halstead-Reitan battery, for example, surveys a wide variety of brain functions. Likewise, the Luria battery has been used to assess individuals with presumed organic mental impairments. These tests can delineate specific areas in the brain that have been affected by illness such as strokes or tumors.

Objective Psychological Tests

Objective psychological tests usually consist of lists that have true/false or agree/disagree answers. A number of these tests have been in use for decades. More recently, a broad range of tests have been developed to assess specific disorders or aspects of personality and to better focus on therapeutic interventions. Because the answers are standardized, many of these tests are tabulated and scored by computers, providing reliable data that is useful for both treatment and research purposes.

One of the most common is the Minnesota Multiphasic Personality Inventory (MMPI). This test, recently revised, is designed to test for maladjustment. It generates scores on a variety of different scales that help practitioners in the diagnostic assessment process. It can help target specific areas of concern, such as suicidal thoughts and psychosis.

Projective Psychological Tests

In projective tests, an individual is asked to make up stories or to tell what he or she sees in ambiguous pictures. The theory underlying these tests is that the responses will reveal fundamental aspects of the way a person thinks, feels, or experiences the world. There is no "right" answer to these tests.

Two of the most common projective tests are:

The Rorschach test. A person is shown ten symmetrical "inkblot" shapes and instructed to describe what they look like. A psychologist then interprets the results, with particular emphasis on how a person thinks and organizes information.

The thematic apperception test (TAT). This test consists of a series of pictures that portray different ambiguous situations. The test-taker is asked to make up a story for each picture that includes what each character in the picture is thinking and feeling. TAT provides insights on motivation and behavior.

Rating Scales

Dozens of rating scales have been developed to allow researchers and trained observers, relatives, or even the individual him- or herself to rate symptoms and behaviors along a continuum of intensity. One example of a rating scale is the Hamilton Rating Scale for Depression (HRSD), shown on page 114, which helps a clinician evaluate the degree of depression an individual is experiencing.

THE "DSM"

The American Psychiatric Association has standardized the criteria for the diagnoses of all mental disorders. It has published these in the *Diagnostic and Statistical Manual of Mental Disorders,* or DSM, which is revised and updated periodically to reflect research and clinical findings; the fourth edition (or DSM-IV) is scheduled for publication in 1994.

Although the manual presents the official psychiatric diagnostic system, its influence has spread to the other mental health professions as well, for several reasons. By using these standardized diagnostic criteria, which are relatively free of the influence of different theoretical systems, research teams can build a more reliable body of information. Second, clinicians of different professions and/or theoretical approaches can communicate more easily using one diagnostic "language." Finally, insurance companies have adopted the DSM diagnostic system, and all claims for mental health care must include a current DSM diagnosis.

How Mental Health Professionals Use the DSM System

Although not all psychiatrists or other practitioners endorse its guidelines, the manual nonetheless demonstrates a contemporary scheme for organizing the biological, psychological, and psychosocial information gleaned during the evaluation process, all of which lead to the treatment selection decision.

The manual summarizes and clearly describes every official diagnosis used in psychiatry (there are over 100) and lists the symptoms of each disorder. It organizes this information into categories of information called "axes" that evaluate a patient in different ways. A clinician can develop a fairly complete picture of a psychiatric problem by using the axes to evaluate symptoms, conditions, and factors that may be contributing to the problem. Many patients have more than one diagnosis. There are five axes.

Axis I describes the diagnostic criteria for the major syndromes, such as schizophrenia and the mood disorders.

Axis II lists personality disorders and developmental disorders.

Axis III lists the various physical conditions, such as heart disease or diabetes, that may be relevant to diagnosis or treatment.

Axis IV quantifies the severity of psychosocial stressors—family crises, occupational setbacks, financial difficulties, legal problems—and alerts the prac-

Table 2.1   DSM-III-R CLASSIFICATIONS

Here are some of the diagnoses established by the third revised edition of the American Psychiatric Association's *Diagnostic and Statistical Manual.* Many of these disorders are discussed at length in the chapters throughout this book.

AXIS I

Disorders of Childhood

Attention-deficit hyperactivity disorder
Conduct disorder
Oppositional defiant disorder
Separation anxiety disorder
Overanxious disorder
Pica
Gender identity disorder of
    childhood
Gender identity disorder of adolescence or adulthood
Elective mutism
Identity disorder
Stereotypy/habit disorder

Adult Disorders

Organic mental disorders
Primary degenerative dementia
    of the Alzheimer type
Multi-infarct dementia
Delirium
Dementia
Organic mood disorder

Substance abuse disorders
Alcohol (dependence/abuse)
Amphetamine or similarly acting substance (dependence/abuse)
Cannabis (dependence/abuse)
Cocaine (dependence/abuse)
Hallucinogen (dependence/abuse)
Inhalant (dependence/abuse)
Nicotine (dependence)
Opioid (dependence/abuse)
Phencyclidine (PCP) or similarly acting
    substance (dependence/abuse)
Polysubstance dependence

Psychotic disorders
Schizophrenia
Brief reactive psychosis

Mood disorders
Bipolar disorder
    mixed
    manic
    depressed
Major depression
    single episode
    recurrent
Dysthymia

Anxiety disorders
Panic disorder
Agoraphobia
Social phobia
Simple phobia
Obsessive-compulsive disorder
Post-traumatic stress disorder
Generalized anxiety disorder

Somatoform disorders
Somatoform pain disorder
Undifferentiated somatoform
    disorder

Sexual disorders
Paraphilias
    Exhibitionism
    Fetishism
    Frotteurism
    Pedophilia
    Sexual masochism and sadism
    Transvestic fetishism
    Voyeurism

Sexual dysfunctions
Hypoactive sexual desire disorder
Sexual aversion disorder
Female sexual arousal disorder
Male erectile disorder
Inhibited orgasm
Premature ejaculation
Dyspareunia
Vaginismus

Sleep disorders
Primary insomnia
Primary hypersomnia
Sleep-wake schedule disorder
Dream anxiety (nightmare) disorder
Sleep terror disorder
Sleepwalking disorder

Eating disorders
Anorexia nervosa
Bulimia nervosa

Adjustment disorder
With anxious mood
With depressed mood
With disturbance of conduct

AXIS II

Developmental disorders
Mild mental retardation
Moderate mental retardation
Severe mental retardation
Profound mental retardation
Autistic disorder

Personality disorders
Paranoid
Schizoid
Schizotypal
Antisocial
Borderline
Histrionic
Narcissistic
Avoidant
Dependent
Obsessive compulsive
Passive-aggressive

Source: American Psychiatric Association: *Diagnostic and Statistical Manual of Mental Disorders,* 3rd ed. revised (Washington, D.C.; APA, 1987).

titioner to any personal factors that might be relevant to diagnosis. Comparing Axis IV with Axis I provides information on the relationship between these stressors and an individual's mental difficulties. For example, an acute episode of depression could be related to a stressor such as recent loss of employment.

Axis V is a global assessment of the overall level of functioning and psychological health. Assessments are recorded for current functioning as well as functioning over the past year. Such evaluations help generally determine the need for treatment and also can aid in predicting what level of functioning might be expected after treatment.

USING THE DSM TO DIAGNOSE: THE CASE OF JOHN Q.

John Q., a 32-year-old paralegal who worked for a busy New York law firm, was referred to a psychiatrist by his physician, whom Mr. Q. had consulted because he had trouble sleeping and felt constantly fatigued. Mr. Q., an only child whose mother had died when he was 18, was unmarried.

During his first visit with the psychiatrist, Mr. Q. revealed that his father had died four months earlier, after a prolonged illness that had consumed much of Mr. Q.'s free time. Mr. Q. had taken care of all of the details of his father's illness—including the ultimate decision not to put him on a respirator, which had been emotionally wrenching.

A "workaholic," Mr. Q. returned to his job the day after the funeral. Since then things had not gone well at work. Mr. Q. described his intense anger about being criticized for failure to turn in a complicated project on time. He talked about how his problems were unique, that no one in his office was capable of understanding them, and the complexity of the decisions he was called on to make. He also complained bitterly about his supervisor's failure to recognize the extraordinary contribution Mr. Q. was making to the law firm. He bragged that he understood the law better than many of the lawyers in his office. When asked why he had not become a lawyer, he responded that he had had to spend so much time caring for his father that he was unable to attend to his career or even to pursue a relationship with a woman.

In order to evaluate Mr. Q. fully, the psychiatrist had to determine the answers to a number of questions. Did Mr. Q. show any symptoms of a psychiatric disorder? What factors in Mr. Q.'s family and business life were contributing to his feelings of stress? Was therapy necessary? If so, what type would be most likely to be effective?

After reviewing his notes from the consultation, Mr. Q.'s clinician diagnosed him as having an adjustment disorder with depressed mood, combined with a possible narcissistic personality disorder. This is the picture he drew of Mr. Q., using the DSM.

Axis I. Mr. Q.'s symptoms of insomnia, tiredness, and feelings of guilt, coupled with his difficulties at work, suggested symptoms of an adjustment disorder (see chapter 24) with a mood component, because they appeared to be a reaction to the death of his father, but not sufficiently severe to qualify as a mood disorder.

Axis II. His feelings that his work was unique, his rage at being criticized, and his preoccupation with fantasies of brilliance all pointed toward a narcissistic personality disorder (see chapter 13).

Axis III. Mr. Q. did not have any physical disorders that would account for his symptoms of insomnia and fatigue. The referring physician had performed a thorough physical before referring Mr. Q. to the psychiatrist; all of the tests were negative.

Axis IV. Mr. Q.'s father's death had placed severe stress on him. On the DSM's scale of stressors, categorized from 1 (none) to 6 (catastrophic), it rated a number 5 (extreme). The stress Mr. Q. was experiencing at work fell at about 4 (moderate to severe).

Axis V. This category rates functioning from 0–90. Mr. Q.'s psychiatrist felt that Mr. Q.'s functioning fell somewhere between fair and poor, at about 35.

Given this clinical picture, the psychiatrist recommended that Mr. Q. join a therapy group. He felt that this type of therapy would help both deal with his grief and rage over the death of his father and understand the effects of his personality disorder on his relationships at work and in his social life.

THE CHOICE OF TREATMENT

Finally, once the diagnosis has been established, the clinician must determine both the setting and the type of treatment that is most appropriate for that patient.

The Treatment Setting

Mental health treatment is provided in three broad settings: inpatient (hospital), outpatient (clinic or practitioner's office), or day hospital.

Inpatient Treatment

The hospital is often the most appropriate setting in emergencies. An emergency exists when the clinician has little time in which to act because of safety concerns—because the patient is acutely ill medically, perhaps experiencing severe malnutrition due to depression or anorexia nervosa; is experiencing serious toxic reactions from drugs or medications; or is in danger of causing harm to him- or herself or to others.

Even in nonemergencies, however, the severity of the illness generally determines whether the patient needs to be hospitalized. For example, some severely depressed people, although not in immediate life-threatening danger, may nonetheless deteriorate if not treated promptly. They may require the skilled nursing care that only an inpatient hospital setting can provide. As another example, a person suffering from bulimia whose binge-eating and vomiting is out of control may require hospitalization for direct intervention in the behavior. At times, however, a patient may need to be hospitalized simply because the diagnostic workup is so complex that the hospital is the most efficient place to coordinate the evaluation.

The hospital may also be the appropriate setting for an individual who is severely disoriented or unable to provide routine self-care; for drug detoxification; for electroconvulsive treatment; and for stabilization of medications.

Intensive inpatient treatment is often the best and fastest way to stabilize an individual, and it can help him or her feel most secure in a time of extreme difficulty. Unfortunately, however, hospitalization can be more stigmatizing and embarrassing to some people than outpatient treatment—a factor that the mental health practitioner will also weigh. (See the discussion of stigma in chapter 31.)

In most states, only psychiatrists can admit patients to hospitals (although other mental health professionals can provide psychological treatment once they are there). However, most nonmedical mental health professionals work with psychiatric consultants, who will admit an individual to the hospital and provide the necessary care.

Day Hospitals and Other Structured Living Programs

Day programs are intermediate between full hospitalization and outpatient treatment. Individuals spend the day in special structured programs in hospitals or other treatment facilities, returning home for the night. Such programs are suitable for a wide range of individuals with varying levels of disability. Day hospitals also may be suitable for patients with less serious disorders who need the structure and support of a formal program. In some cases, people who are acutely ill, such as those with schizophrenia, can be helped in this setting, as can those who have just been discharged from a hospital.

Outpatient Treatment

Provided in the clinician's office (which may be in or outside a hospital), outpatient treatment is appropriate when there is no immediate safety concern and the individual functions adequately.

Which Treatment to Choose?

Broadly, mental health treatments consist of two categories: somatic (drugs and electroconvulsive treatment) and psychosocial (the psychotherapies). For some diagnoses, certain types of treatments have proved particularly effective. Generally, the more severe, acute conditions are treated with medications (the choice of drug depending on the specific diagnosis), usually in combination with some form of psychotherapy. Other conditions are treated with a form of psychotherapy alone. However, as discussed in chapter 6, differing approaches can often provide significant benefit to the same patient.

Thus, the treatment that the therapist recommends to the patient commonly depends not only on the diagnosis but on the clinician's particular training, the resources available in the community, the patient's preferences, and other "patient variables," including his or her finances (see the next section).

Research suggests that practitioners are most likely to recommend those treatments with which they are most comfortable and skilled. The assignment of a patient to one treatment or another, particularly with the psychotherapies, may be more an issue of personal comfort—for both the clinician and the patient—than a scientific one.

(The specific treatments are described at length in chapter 4 and chapter 5; the range of approaches for each disorder are discussed in the individual chapters dealing with disorders throughout the book.)

"Patient Variables" Influencing the Treatment Decision

In addition to a person's diagnosis, numerous other factors are involved in the decision to provide a particular course of treatment. Following are some of these factors.

- *Motivation.* Does the person want treatment, or has he or she come for a consultation only because of pressure from relatives? Does he or she acknowledge that a problem exists?
- *Compliance.* Will this person appear for regular visits over a long period of time? Is he or she likely to follow "doctor's orders" for the use of medications?
- *Treatment goals.* Does the person desire only symptom relief and a quick return to functioning, or does he or she wish to work longer, toward some deeper change?
- *The patient's personality.* Is the person too shy to participate in group therapy? Is the person more interested in learning new habits or in taking medication than in delving deeply into his or her psyche?
- *Capacity for insight.* Is this person psychologically minded, interested in self-exploration? If not, noninsight-oriented treatments may be preferable.
- *Social support.* Does the individual have the support of family or friends? If so, outpatient treatment may be possible in some more serious cases that might usually require inpatient treatment.
- *Finances.* An individual without adequate financial resources or insurance coverage may not be able to take advantage of longer-term treatments. Sometimes inpatient treatment is preferable because hospital stays are covered while outpatient visits are not.

EVALUATING THE DIAGNOSIS AND TREATMENT RECOMMENDATIONS

As has been stressed throughout this chapter, psychiatric diagnosis rests on a comprehensive assessment of a range of a person's activities, often supplemented by tests. Using the DSM, a diagnosis is made and a treatment plan formulated. Because many treatment modalities are available to mental health practitioners, two patients with identical diagnoses may have different treatment plans, both of which are correct.

When seeking help for a mental or emotional problem, patients and their families should always ask what the diagnosis is; what are the treatment alternatives; what are the risks, complications, benefits, and costs of them all; and why the practitioner has recommended a particular treatment plan.

For lists of specific questions to consider, see the box on page 42 in chapter 3 and those in chapter 6.

WEIGHING THE FACTORS ASSOCIATED WITH THE CHOICE OF TREATMENT PLAN: THE CASE OF MRS. L.

Mrs. L., 54, has been persistently depressed for three months. She has no energy, can't sleep, has no desire to eat, and has occasional thoughts of killing herself (especially in the morning). She feels that she's a bad wife and mother and that even if she lives, the best part of her life is over. At the insistence of her husband and the recommendation of her internist, who has conducted a thorough physical evaluation and found no organic cause to her depression, she has come to see Dr. A., a psychiatrist, at his office.

Dr. A. determines that Mrs. L. is not in immediate danger of suicide. Many depressed people become medically ill from poor self-care (suffering from dehydration, for example), but Mrs. L. is able, with her family's help, to take care of herself. Because she is not immediately suicidal and can take care of her basic needs, Dr. A. decides that hospitalization is not required. Even though she is having some thoughts of killing herself, he decides that he can treat her on an outpatient basis because she seems willing to participate actively in getting better, they seem to be establishing a good rapport, and she has strong support from her family to sustain the treatment endeavor.

Dr. A.'s initial diagnostic impression is that Mrs. L. is suffering an episode of major depression. He now needs to confirm the diagnosis and decide on specific treatment interventions. He continues taking Mrs. L.'s history, and decides to speak to her husband to confirm his own impression of the signs and symptoms of her illness. Reviewing her history before finally determining the best course of treatment, Dr. A. finds possible evidence of two or three prior similar, although less severe, episodes; finds no conditions that might complicate treatment (such as a prior history of substance abuse); and observes the specific pattern of symptoms that she experiences, such as that she is sleeping more and eating much less than usual.

Because Mrs. L. has prominent and enduring symptoms of disturbed sleep, appetite, and energy—symptoms often labeled "neurovegetative"—Dr. A. considers prescribing antidepressant medication as the initial treatment intervention. Dr. A. has a number of other treatment options that have all been proven effective in this condition, including medication plus cognitive psychotherapy, and cognitive or other types of psychotherapy alone. In considering psychotherapy alone, Dr. A. would have to determine whether Mrs. L. could benefit from it; for example, would she be able to and interested in examining her feelings and behavior? Would she do the "homework" necessary to successful cognitive therapy? Dr. A. decides to leave the psychotherapy decision for later and to proceed with medication, which is likely to provide the quickest response and be least costly to his patient.

As always when he prescribes medication, Dr. A. provides supportive psychotherapy, helping Mrs. L. to understand the psychological impact of having an illness, to cope with her symptoms until the medication takes effect, and to follow the medication regimen.

Within four weeks, the antidepressant medication has begun to work. Mrs. L. is eating and sleeping again, and her mood has begun to lift. Although she will continue the medication for at least several months after the remission of symptoms, Dr. A. has decided it's time to consider whether more intensive psychotherapy would be helpful. He has focused his reevaluation on whether Mrs. L. has a personality disorder and whether this episode of depression has had severe consequences on her life. He has determined that Mrs. L., who has relied on her husband, elderly mother, and older children to help her make most of her decisions, possibly suffers from dependent personality disorder. Although her husband and family have been helpful to her in her illness, this depressive episode seemed to have strained the marriage. Mrs. L. recently revealed to Dr. A. that she has worried for a long time that her husband would leave her.

Personality disorders are generally responsive to psychotherapy. The question Dr. A. now needs to determine is: which type of psychotherapy? In general, individual psychodynamic psychotherapy is appropriate for people who are aware of internal emotional distress and who conceptualize their problems as reflecting problems within themselves (see chapter 4 for the full range of approaches, however). Group psychotherapy is often prescribed for those who experience the bulk of their problems in their relationships with others and who, in particular, have great difficulty in seeing how their behavior affects others. Those individuals who experience most of their problems at home, or who can't leave home when that would be the appropriate course in life, are often best treated in a family therapy situation.

(Continued)

Probably, thinks Dr. A., Mrs. L. would be a good candidate for any of these approaches. He discusses them all with her, adding that he is not skilled in family therapy but could refer her to a colleague if she and her family agreed to seek that type of help. Mrs. L. has become quite attached to her psychiatrist, however, and wants to stay in treatment with him. Dr. A. therefore recommends that Mrs. L. come to see him twice a week for more intensive individual therapy. He also suggests that once a month she and her husband come together for marital therapy, but Mr. L. is reluctant, so Dr. A. and Mrs. L. decide to reconsider that option in the future.

3

Mental Health Professionals and Treatment Facilities

Ronald O. Rieder, M.D., Rachel G. Klein, Ph.D.,
Jane Allen Waters, M.S.,
and Diane Wattenmaker, M.Ed., R.N. C.S., C.N.A.A.

The decision to seek mental health care for oneself or on behalf of a family member can be difficult to make. Then comes the quandary of whom to consult, which type of therapy or treatment to choose, and—if not consulting an individual in private practice—at what type of facility. The purpose of this chapter is to acquaint readers with the range of *trained* professionals and facilities that offer mental health care services to the public.

Mental health professionals can train in any one of several fields, most commonly psychiatry, psychology, social work, and nursing. Although offering overlapping services, each discipline has a somewhat different approach and its members offer varying treatments, consistent with their respective backgrounds.

It is common for practitioners from different disciplines to collaborate with each other, either in a consulting role or as part of a multidisciplinary treatment team. This is because, traditionally or legally, certain kinds of services are provided by specific practitioners only. For example, by law, in most states only physicians may prescribe medications or admit a patient to a hospital; in general, it is the role of psychologists to administer psychological testing.

In order to assess options and to make the most informed choice, it is important to know the training required of each group of mental health professionals and the types of services they provide. Be aware that in most states, anyone can call him- or herself a psychotherapist, counselor, and the like, without any training whatsoever; the terms "psychotherapist," "psychoanalyst," and "counselor" do not in themselves define the extent of training or other qualifications that a practitioner may have. Although the laws vary, in most states these terms are not defined legally nor are there licensing requirements for them per se. Various professional bodies, however, such as the American Psychoanalytic Association, have extensive requirements and procedures for certification. To ensure that the mental health professional has specific training and professional experience, prospective patients should verify that the practitioner they consult has been certified within his or her respective discipline by an authoritative organization.

For information on the specific therapies or somatic (bodily) treatments that a qualified mental health professional may recommend or offer, see chapters 4 and 5 as well as the chapters specific to the various disorders. The box at the end of this chapter discusses how to obtain names of qualified mental health professionals and how to choose among them.

THE PRACTITIONERS

Psychiatrists

Psychiatrists are physicians who specialize in the treatment of mental disorders. There are some 41,000 psychiatrists practicing in the United States. They are medical doctors (M.D.'s) or doctors of osteopathy (D.O.'s). Physicians must be licensed by the state in which they practice.

To specialize in psychiatry, a physician must complete four years of medical school followed by one year of internship and three years of training in a psychiatric residency. During their residency, psychiatrists receive instruction in clinical medical care and neurology as well as in inpatient and outpatient treatment, psychiatric emergency treatment, and child and adolescent psychiatry. They are exposed to and gain experience in treating the full range of psychiatric disorders, with intensive, case-by-case instruction from experienced psychiatrists.

Upon graduation from a residency program, a psychiatrist may seek specialty certification in psychiatry from the American Board of Psychiatry and Neurology (ABPN). Those psychiatrists who successfully complete its written and oral examinations are designated as "board certified." Though not required by law for the practice of psychiatry, as is medical licensure, most psychiatrists, especially in recent years, seek such board certification. While the vast majority of psychiatrists today opt to take the board exams, there are many well-trained psychiatrists who have not.

Psychiatrists may practice either general psychiatry or elect to specialize in such areas as child psychiatry, geriatric psychiatry, substance abuse treatment, or psychoanalysis. Formal subspecialty certification requirements and procedures have been established in child psychiatry and in psychoanalysis. The ABPN also has recently established "added qualifications" certifications for geriatric and addiction psychiatry.

Because of their medical training, psychiatrists can diagnose and evaluate the extent to which organic illness plays a role in a psychiatric condition. They can ensure that appropriate medical care is given, consulting with other medical specialists as needed and coordinating whatever combination of psychological and medical treatment is necessary. Psychiatrists also have a unique role in prescribing medications, either as primary therapists or in collaboration with mental health professionals from other disciplines. This is an important consideration for those seeking treatment for mental disorders that can be treated with medications, such as depression, bipolar disorder, schizophrenia, panic and anxiety disorders, eating disorders, and obsessive-compulsive disorder. Generally speaking, the more serious the problem, the more likely a person is to require the services of a psychiatrist, because medications are often part of the treatment in such cases.

All psychiatrists receive training in psychotherapy (a number of techniques based on communication between the patient and the professional; see chapter 4), and most practice it as well as prescribe medications. Psychiatrists whose primary clinical and research focus is the therapeutic use of medications are known as psychopharmacologists. If a mental disorder is not responding to standard drug treatment, evaluation by a psychopharmacologist can be very helpful. The practitioner can recommend a consultation, or the psychiatric department of a major medical center (most psychopharmacologists are connected with such centers) can provide a recommendation.

Psychiatrists tend to charge more for their services than nonmedical mental health professionals.

The American Psychiatric Association (APA) (1400 K Street, NW, Washington, D.C. 20005, tel. 202 682–6000) is the professional organization to which most psychiatrists belong. The APA should be able to answer questions about a particular psychiatrist's credentials. It publishes a biographical directory of members that is available through public libraries.

Another source for locating a selection of qualified psychiatrists in each city and state is the directory published annually by the American Board of Medical Specialties (ABMS) (One American Plaza, Evanston, Illinois 60201) in collaboration with the American Board of Psychiatry and Neurology. Its *Directory of Certified Psychiatrists* contains biographical data and a geographic cross-reference that lists the names of certified psychiatrists by city and state.

Clinical Psychologists

Psychologists who treat patients have earned a Ph.D. (doctorate) in clinical psychology or a Psy.D. (doctor of psychology). In addition to several years of course work in such subjects as general psychology, personality theory, psychodynamics, and therapeutic techniques, their graduate training also involves intensive clinical work, including one year in full-time clinical training and one year of supervised part-time clinical practice. Clinical psychologists must pass licensing exams in all 50 states.

Clinical psychologists focus on the individual's personality and behavior to understand his or her emotional problems. They provide a wide variety of psychotherapeutic services and testing. Some specialize in areas such as child guidance, marital counseling, or vocational rehabilitation. Often psychologists work in collaboration with a psychiatrist: They provide psychological testing, personality assessment, and psychotherapeutic care, while the psychiatrist prescribes medications and directs any medical care that might be necessary.

The American Psychological Association (750 First Street, NE, Washington, D.C. 20002–4242, tel. 202 336–5500) is the professional organization to which a majority of the estimated 65,000 psychologists in the United States belong. Some clinical psychologists receive diplomas for excellence from the American Board of Professional Psychology, which is the only board that tests for competency in psychotherapy. Psychologists are eligible to take its exams only after five years of postdoctoral experience. The association publishes a directory of its members, available in some libraries.

Another way to check a psychologist's credentials is by calling the National Register of Health Service Providers in Psychology (1730 Rhode Island Avenue, NW, Suite 1200, Washington, D.C. 20036, tel. 202 833–2377). The register lists psychologists who are licensed or certified in each state. To be included, a psychologist must have a Ph.D. in psychology and at least two years of supervised experience. Listing in the register does not guarantee experience in psychotherapy, however, because an individual psychologist may have chosen to focus his or her skills in the areas of school counseling or research.

Social Workers

Social workers who have expertise in the treatment of patients with emotional and psychiatric problems are called clinical or psychiatric social workers, of which there are over 200,000 practicing in the United States. They provide psychotherapy for the full range of mental and emotional difficulties and, like clinical psychologists, often work in collaboration with psychiatrists. In smaller communities, social workers are often the only qualified mental health professionals available.

Most social workers whom individuals consult in clinical settings have a master's degree in social work (M.S.W., M.S.S.W., or M.S., depending on the type of degree a particular school grants its graduates). Training programs usually include two years of classroom instruction and a minimum of 900 hours of supervised clinical practice.

A doctorate in social work (D.S.W.) or a Ph.D. degree does not in itself necessarily mean that the individual is a more qualified therapist than a social worker with a master's degree, because many doctoral programs are geared more toward training in research, teaching, or administrative work rather than specific development of expertise in clinical social work.

All fifty states have procedures for licensing, certifying, or registering clinical social workers, although regulations, criteria, and professional titles vary from state to state.

Two professional social work organizations have developed criteria for formal credentials in clinical social work and monitor credentialing: the National Association of Social Workers, Inc. (NASW) and the American Board of Examiners in Clinical Social Work. Their respective nationwide listings of social work practitioners can be obtained by writing to: The NASW Register of Clinical Social Workers, 750 First Street, NE, Suite 700, Washington, D.C. 20002 (tel. 202 408-8600 or 800 638-8799); and the American Board of Examiners in Clinical Social Work, 8484 Georgia Avenue, Suite 800, Silver Spring, MD 20910 (tel. 301 587-8783). Neither registry lists all clinical social workers; both are simply listings of the social workers who applied and who met all of the credentialing criteria each agency has developed for its listing.

Psychiatric Nurses

After completing their general nursing training, psychiatric nurses receive additional, specialized training in mental health care through formal course work and/or hospital experience. Psychiatric clinical nurse specialists continue their education to the master's level and receive supervised training in individual, group, and family psychotherapy. Their education is grounded in the medical and social sciences, and they are knowledgeable about physical conditions that relate to mental disorders and the action and side effects of psychoactive medication. Increasingly, psychiatric clinical nurse specialists are turning to the private practice of psychotherapy, especially in states that have legislated insurance reimbursement for nurse providers.

In psychiatric hospitals, psychiatric nurses function in several roles simultaneously. They educate patients about their conditions and provide therapy. They interact with and observe the patients all hours of the day, documenting their behavior and sharing these observations with patients' psychiatrists and other members of the treatment team. In addition, they are responsible for maintaining a healthy social and psychological atmosphere during the patient's hospital stay.

Psychiatric clinical nurse specialists are certified by the American Nurses' Association. They generally take the qualifying exam after at least two years of postgraduate practice and 100 hours of postgraduate supervision. The American Nurses' Association (600 Maryland Avenue, SW, Suite 100, Washington, D.C. 20024-2571) can supply a list of certified clinical nurse specialists.

Mental Health Counselors

Many providers of mental health care refer to themselves as counselors. While some states regulate the use of the term "counselor," in most states anyone can legally use this term, even without training. Therefore, the credentials of a therapist who calls him- or herself a counselor should be checked thoroughly. "Counselor" also can refer to school counselor, career counselor, and unemployment counselor, to name a few.

A new professional degree at the master's level in mental health counseling has developed in the past 20 years. This degree is granted after a two-year graduate program in counseling that includes courses and supervised clinical work. Graduates are certified by the National Academy of Certified Clinical Mental Health Counselors, and their professional organization is the American Mental Health Counselors Association (AMHCA) (5999 Stevenson Avenue, Alexandria, VA 22304, tel. 703 823-9800). Individuals with this degree receive the designation of "Certified Clinical Mental Health Counselor" if they have 3,000 hours of postgraduate supervised practice and pass a national qualifying exam. They are licensed to practice in 26 states. About 1,200 AMHCA members have met these requirements. They tend to call themselves counselors rather than psychotherapists, even though they are qualified to provide psychotherapy.

Many members of the clergy are qualified to provide individual, group, or family therapy. To be certified, a pastoral counselor must complete three years of study at a seminary (earning a degree in divinity studies) as well as complete a master's- or doctoral-level theology program that includes clinical training in crisis intervention. The professional organization that certifies these individuals is the American Association of Pastoral Counselors (9504A Lee Highway, Fairfax, VA 22031 tel. 703 385–6967). Certification is not required by law for the practice of pastoral counseling.

PRACTITIONERS IN CERTAIN SPECIALTY AREAS

Marriage and Family Therapists

Because the terms "marriage counselor" and "marital therapist" have no legal standing in most states, a qualified marriage therapist is likely to identify him- or herself by primary professional qualifications first; for example, as a psychologist who specializes in marital therapy rather than simply as a marriage counselor.

Some psychiatrists, psychologists, social workers, and nurse clinical specialists obtain special expertise in the practice of family therapy from a family therapy training institute. As discussed in chapter 4, family therapy may involve all members of the family going through therapy together or selected family members working together with the therapist. Sixteen states regulate, license, or certify family therapists, although there is no national certification program. The American Association of Marriage and Family Therapists examines the credentials of marriage and family therapists, but membership in this national organization is not required by law to practice in this area. This organization also accredits specialized training programs in marital and family therapy. The American Family Therapy Association (2020 Pennsylvania Avenue, NW, Suite 273, Washington, D.C. 20006 (tel. 202 994-2776) is a society for clinicians, researchers, and educators with advanced expertise in the field.

Sex Therapists

There is no standardized educational program for a psychiatrist, other physician, psychologist, social worker, or nurse who seeks specialized training as a sex therapist. Some of the major medical centers

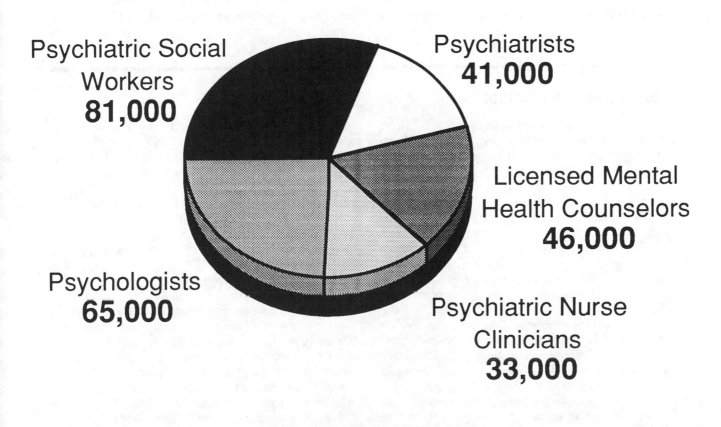

Psychiatric Social Workers
81,000

Psychiatrists
41,000

Licensed Mental Health Counselors
46,000

Psychologists
65,000

Psychiatric Nurse Clinicians
33,000

MENTAL HEALTH PROFESSIONALS

Figure 3.1: **Approximate numbers of certified mental health professionals practicing in the United States.**

around the country offer such programs, but the orientation and curriculum vary from program to program. Because there are, unfortunately, unqualified and unethical persons who are presenting themselves as "sex therapists" and because the practice of sex therapy is at this time largely unregulated by state governmental agencies, it is very important to find a competent professional when seeking help for a sexual dysfunction or other problems related to sexuality. (See chapter 11.)

Part of the initial evaluation of a sexual dysfunction should be performed by a physician, and it should include a physical exam and a careful medical history to rule out any underlying physical or medication problem. A gynecologist, urologist, or family physician may be able to make these determinations or provide a referral to a specialized medical clinic where a team of experts, including physicians with special expertise in this area, can evaluate the complaint.

The examination also includes a thorough evaluation of the individual's sexual history, interpersonal relationships, and any possible psychological problems or psychiatric disorders. Information from an ongoing sexual partner may be important, because many problems in sexual functioning are problems between two people. These aspects of the evaluation may be done by a physician or another mental health professional, or someone with specialized training in sexual problems who is working with a team of professionals.

Prospective patients should inquire whether this general approach is taken before making an appointment. At all times, a prospective patient should be cautious in consulting with individuals or clinics whose sole "background" and "training" is in sex therapy and who operate independent of supervision or affiliation with competent physicians and other health professionals.

One national professional organization to which many qualified sex therapists belong is the American Association of Sex Educators, Counselors and Therapists (435 N. Michigan Avenue, Suite 1717, Chicago, IL 60611–4067, tel. 312 644-0828). This organization provides the most rigorous certification for sex counselors and sex therapists who are psychiatrists, psychologists, nurses, social workers, or marriage and family therapists and who have had a sufficient degree

FINDING HELP FOR A CHILD

If your child is experiencing problems that might be helped by a mental health professional (see chapters 16 through 20 for a discussion of disorders and common problems by age group), it is best to find a practitioner who is specially trained to treat children.

There are several ways to locate such an expert. One good way is by asking your child's pediatrician or your own primary physician for a recommendation. Your child's teacher, school guidance counselor, or school nurse may also know of practitioners who have been able to help other children, as may the parents of other children who have had similar problems. The American Psychiatric Association and American Psychological Association can provide the names of practitioners in your area who have been certified as having expertise in treating children. If your child has a severe problem or one that is not responding to treatment, call an academic medical center to find out if it has a program or is conducting research in the area of your child's problem, or if personnel there can refer you to another center involved in such studies.

Part of the assessment of a child includes an evaluation of the family as well as input from the school and other sources that may provide insight into the child's problem. A practitioner who works with children must probe into a family's history to understand the interactions that may be causing the problem. Parents should not feel offended by prying questions.

The treatment decided on to some extent involves the entire family—within limits. As with adults, what goes on in a session with a child is subject to the rules of confidentiality (see chapter 30); however, most child practitioners make every effort to keep the family informed on the issues, without revealing a child's confidences.

Ask the practitioner about credentials and whether he or she is certified by the American Psychiatric Association (or, for nonpsychiatrists, by their professional accrediting association) to treat children.

of sex therapy courses, clinical experience, and supervised training. Not all qualified sex therapists, however, seek certification by this organization.

Substance Abuse Counselors

In addition to mental health practitioners with various professional degrees who specialize in substance abuse treatment, individuals from many backgrounds receive specialized training to counsel patients suffering from drug and alcohol abuse. Many states regulate the certification process for drug and alcoholism counselors. The letters "C.A.C." after someone's name means "Certified Addiction Counselor." The exact mix of educational training and numbers of hours of supervised treatment experience in drug and alcohol counseling varies from state to state. Usually an individual is certified for either drug or alcohol counseling but not necessarily for both.

A number of national associations for substance abuse counselors are attempting to develop uniform state-to-state criteria. One such organization is the National Association of Alcohol and Drug Counselors (Suite 300, 3717 Columbia Pike, Arlington, VA 22204, tel. 703 920-4644). Their criteria mandate two years' clinical experience working with addicted patients, 180 hours of course work in the area, and 220 hours of supervised training. In addition, candidates for certification must make case presentations of their work to three certified counselors who must then approve it. If candidates are seeking certification for both drug and alcoholism counseling, these certification criteria increase to three years' clinical experience covering both fields, 270 hours of course work, and 300 hours of supervision in the area, in addition to the case presentations.

MENTAL HEALTH TREATMENT FACILITIES

Most people who seek mental health care are treated in outpatient clinics or a practitioner's private office. Some individuals with psychiatric disorders require hospitalization to stabilize their symptoms. Patients with schizophrenia (discussed in chapter 14), severe depression (chapter 8), and eating disorders (chapter 10), for example, sometimes require hospitalization for diagnostic purposes, to get "back on track," or to treat symptoms that cannot be controlled on an outpatient basis.

There are a number of different types of facilities—some publicly funded, others run by for-profit corporations—offering a variety of care plans. If a mental health professional believes that a patient needs hospitalization, he or she will recommend a facility based on a variety of factors, including the needs of the patient, the availability of local services, and a patient's ability to pay, among others.

Following is a brief review of the types of treatment facilities.

Hospital Facilities

Hospital care is offered in public and private settings and in community clinics.

Major Medical Centers

Generally located in or near large cities, major medical centers combine hospital care with research facilities; many are connected to medical schools, in which case they are called academic medical centers. These centers generally have separate psychiatric departments that conduct a variety of research projects in addition to providing inpatient and outpatient clinical care for the widest range of mental health problems. Some centers offer diagnostic and treatment options that are innovative or still under study for patients whose psychiatric illness is not responding to standard treatment. Medical centers can also be a superb source of referral or information.

Private Psychiatric Hospitals

No two private psychiatric hospitals are alike; there is a wide variation in the type of care and services they offer. Most are small, containing fewer than 150 beds, with good staff-to-patient ratios. They usually offer a wide variety of types of treatment, tailored to fit the individual needs of each patient. In general, private hospitals specialize in short-term care (less than six months), although a few do offer the option of long-term stays.

Private hospitals often offer greater privacy and nicer surroundings than public hospitals, and they usually provide a greater range of recreational and rehabilitative activities.

Some private facilities specialize in treating specific disorders (such as substance abuse, personality or eating disorders, or phobias) or types of patients (such as adolescents or older individuals).

When a private psychiatric facility is being considered, prospective patients should ask whether or not it has been accredited by the Joint Commission of Accreditation of Hospitals—one way of assuring that the facility meets basic standards of care. Fees and charges should also be discussed, and the patient's insurance company should be contacted to find out how much, if any, will be covered.

Community Hospitals

Local hospitals sometimes have separate psychiatric units for inpatient care, but many community hospitals place patients with psychiatric problems in the general hospital wards. Community hospitals vary a great deal in regard to the treatment programs offered; prospective patients should ask the treating mental health professional if the local hospital provides the best option for treatment. Many community hospitals do not have full-time psychiatric staff; instead psychiatrists under contract to the hospital offer treatment.

Public Facilities

Every state and major metropolitan area has facilities for mental health care for those who cannot afford other alternatives. Like private facilities, publicly funded treatment facilities offer treatment and rehabilitation. They also offer long-term custodial care for severely ill patients who are unable to care for themselves or who have been committed because they are dangerous to themselves or others.

Many public facilities are affected by funding problems and staffing problems; often the staff-to-patient ratio in public facilities is not as good as in private facilities. Nor are the amenities as varied.

Veterans Administration (VA) Hospitals are government-funded hospitals that offer medical care, including psychiatric services, to veterans. As is true of public facilities generally, the population of VA psychiatric wards is poorer (many patients taking advantage of the care offered in VA hospitals have exhausted their insurance), and patients are more seriously ill than in private facilities. Patients

have short stays and readmissions are frequent. Many of those seeking psychiatric treatment at VA hospitals or at other public facilities also have a problem with substance abuse.

Freestanding Clinics

Many communities have freestanding mental health or psychotherapy clinics. Sometimes these are run by a group of mental health professionals who have banded together to form an independent practice. Others are run under the aegis of a hospital or state or local health agency; they often receive government grants and base their fees on ability to pay. Still others are run in conjunction with specialized training institutes, such as analytic institutes.

Psychiatric Emergency Care

Hospital emergency rooms vary widely in their ability to provide psychiatric care. Larger hospitals in urban areas frequently have physicians trained in psychiatry on their emergency services staff. Small community hospitals may rely on psychiatric social workers or nurse clinical specialists. Persons who are or who have a family member under treatment for a disorder that might require emergency hospitalization (such as schizophrenia, an eating disorder, severe depression, or substance abuse), should ask the attending mental health worker what local facilities are best equipped to handle psychiatric emergencies.

Partial Care

Some hospitals and freestanding clinics offer partial care (frequently called day hospitalization, although some partial care programs also offer evening or weekend care alternatives). These programs are for patients who require more intensive care than offered in outpatient clinics but who do not need round-the-clock supervision or nursing care.

Most partial hospitalization programs offer at least eight hours of care a week. They usually provide a full range of therapy options, including individual, group, and family counseling. Generally speaking, partial care programs provide supervision during the day or evening as well as recreational or rehabilitative training activities. The emphasis is usually on intensive short-term therapy.

Nonhospital Residential Care

Halfway houses are "in-between" living arrangements for individuals with mental illness. There are many different kinds of halfway houses offering varying levels of supervision. *Nonmedical residential support facilities,* for example, provide overnight care and supervised living; *residential treatment facilities* provide overnight care and intensive treatment. Often residential treatment facilities house only individuals with the same disorder, such as substance abuse or schizophrenia.

Halfway houses have many different names: adult foster homes, board and care homes, personal care homes, and group homes, to name a few. Some halfway houses have medical staff that spend time on the premises daily; others have only a manager who may or may not have some training in working with a population with mental illness. Some halfway houses are meant to be a place where a patient who does not need hospitalization but is not ready to function on his or her own can stay while treatment proceeds; eventually independence is achieved. Other halfway houses, however (especially for individuals with chronic mental illness, such as schizophrenia) provide long-term housing on a permanent basis.

Cooperative apartments are different from halfway houses in that they are independent apartments that do not have a live-in manager. Instead, they are sponsored by a community agency that provides supportive mental health services as necessary.

How to Find a Mental Health Treatment Facility

The best way to find a treatment facility is to ask for a recommendation from the treating mental health professional. He or she probably is familiar with treatment alternatives in the community as well as facilities that specialize in specific disorders. Or the practitioner can be asked to recommend a psychiatric social worker who has had experience in placing individuals with problems similar to the patient's. For long-term residential care, the state department of health (or whatever similarly named state agency oversees mental health care) can be asked for a list of licensed facilities.

The following manuals list different types of facilities. Libraries often carry these manuals, or the publisher can be contacted directly.

- *The Psychiatric Hospital Directory,* published by the National Association of Private Psychiatric Hospitals, Suite 1000, 1319 F Street NW, Washington, D.C. 20004, tel. 202 393–6700.
- *The American Hospital Association Guide to the Health Care Field,* published by the American Hospital Association, 840 North Lake Shore Drive, Chicago, IL 60611, tel. 312 280–6000. (To order the guide, call 800 242–2626.)
- *Mental Health Directory* (Publication No. [ADM] 90-1707) published by the U.S. Department of Health and Human Services, Institute of Mental Health. Available through the Superintendent of Documents, Government Printing Office, Washington, D.C. 20402, tel. 202 783–3238.

Finally, support or advocacy groups for mental illness victims or their families, including those listed in chapter 31, page 435, as well as those mentioned in individual chapters throughout this book (such as the Association for Retarded Citizens, page 245), are often among the best sources of information on mental health professionals and treatment facilities in specific communities.

FINDING AND EVALUATING A THERAPIST

Numerous sources exist to locate mental health professionals and evaluate their credentials. Asking key questions can simplify the process.

Getting a Professional Evaluation

Ideally, mental health treatment begins with a thorough evaluation and diagnosis of the difficulty, which may require a medical examination to rule out physical causes of mental symptoms. The evaluation, diagnosis, and treatment-choice process are described at length in chapter 2.

To obtain a referral for professional evaluation and diagnosis, prospective patients should ask a personal physician (internist, pediatrician, gynecologist, or the like), friends who have sought treatment themselves, or mental health professionals they know personally. If personal contacts are not available, the psychiatry

CHOOSING THE RIGHT MENTAL HEALTH PROFESSIONAL FOR YOU

Once you have been referred to a therapist, or you have obtained two or three names on your own, you must evaluate for yourself whether you have reached an individual who will be able to provide help for your particular problem. You should find a therapist with whom you feel reasonably comfortable and are able to speak freely. Success in therapy depends a great deal on the rapport that develops between you and your therapist. Keep in mind, however, that a good therapist will ask you to speak about relevant matters that trouble you and will challenge your ideas on certain issues, making you feel anxious, even defensive at times. This may be uncomfortable, but it is necessary for effective therapy to occur. Therefore, it is important that you feel that the prospective therapist possesses sufficient qualities of warmth, understanding, and professionalism.

Although the professional qualifications listed earlier in the chapter are very important, a trusting relationship between you and your therapist is crucial if you are to keep working together effectively. If you feel that you still need more information about the therapist's qualifications in order to have that trust, the first visit is the time to ask.

Don't be afraid to ask questions about the therapist's training, goals for you in therapy, approach to using or recommending medications, intention to involve other members of the family, and anything else about which you are concerned. In addition, any strong preference you may have about age,

religion, sexual orientation, marriage status, personal philosophy, smoker versus nonsmoker, and the like should be brought out and explored at this initial meeting. Although the therapist may not wish to divulge personal information, a discussion of these issues may lead you to think through why you consider them important and help you and the therapist decide whether to continue working together.

Following is a checklist of questions to ask yourself after the first session.

- Did you feel at ease with the therapist?
- Was the therapist able to help you to discuss your problem and your reasons for deciding to seek treatment?
- Did he or she seem competent and responsive to your problem?
- Did you discuss possible therapeutic goals, and do you agree with them?
- Were you able to ask questions, and were they answered adequately?
- Are you able to arrange for appointments at times that are convenient for you? Is the fee structure acceptable?

If you are not satisfied with the answers to these questions, seek an additional consultation with someone else on your list.

For another set of questions to ask yourself during the course of your treatment, see chapter 6.

---

department at a well-respected hospital nearby should be called and asked for the names of staff members who can provide a consultation and evaluation.

Once the evaluation is complete, expect an explanation of the nature of the problem and a discussion of the advantages and disadvantages of different types of treatment. The evaluator should recommend the particular type of treatment that is indicated and provide the names of well-qualified local practitioners. The evaluator may offer his or her own services as well.

Finding a Mental Health Professional

Another way to find a therapist for oneself or for a member of one's family is to contact the following organizations or people.

Professional organizations and credentialing bodies. As mentioned earlier, these national organizations often can provide a list or directory of qualified local practitioners. State or local branches of these organizations may be more likely to suggest names of specific therapists.

Psychoanalytic and other psychotherapy training institutes. For those seeking psychoanalytic treatment (see chapter 4), institutes offering postgraduate psychoanalytic training provide referrals for treatment with member analysts who have completed their training or who are currently in training. Other types of psychotherapy training institutes also exist. As always, it pays to check the background and credentials of any individual who is recommended.

Friends and acquaintances. Asking friends who have received mental health care about their therapists can be helpful, although a friend's therapist may not be able to provide the appropriate treatment. Friends' therapists may also be willing to provide names of other qualified individuals in the community.

The Yellow Pages. Listings in the telephone book can do no more than provide names and, sometimes, degrees and areas of specialization. The telephone company does not screen qualifications before listing someone in the telephone book. Any information given there should be double checked with the appropriate organizations.

4

Common Approaches to Psychotherapy

Robert Alan Glick, M.D., and Henry I. Spitz, M.D., F.A.P.A.

Psychotherapy is a category of psychological treatments for mental and emotional distress that relies specifically on verbal and nonverbal communication between the therapist and the person who seeks help—the so-called talking cure.

Almost all individuals who receive mental health care are treated with some form of psychotherapy, often in conjunction with drugs or other somatic (bodily) treatments. The process of psychotherapy itself involves no invasive bodily treatments. Whereas drugs and other somatic treatments alter the functioning of the brain directly, psychotherapy intervenes in the processes of mind—the patterns of feeling, thinking, perceiving, adapting, coping, behaving, and relating that develop over time.

The modern approach to psychotherapy began in late-19th-century Vienna when Sigmund Freud began treating patients with his newly discovered techniques of psychoanalysis. In the century since, it has flowered into as many as 400 types of treatment, practiced by a wide range of mental health professionals. (See chapter 3.) Although the proliferation of approaches is a distinctly contemporary development, psychotherapy in some form probably has existed as long as human beings have lived in civilized groups. The practice presumably began when a person with problems sought out the expert-healer for advice and counsel.

In recent decades, the understanding and effectiveness of the psychotherapeutic process have become scientific. As discussed at length in chapter 6, psychological treatments of emotional disturbances derive their beneficial or curative influence from complex processes of communication between suffering patient and healing psychotherapist. These processes usually include forms of emotional release

as well as emotional learning based on new information and ways of understanding oneself and one's environment. They take place within a confidential relationship with the therapist, who provides expert knowledge, support and acceptance, hope, safety, and a model for someone with whom to identify.

Effective psychotherapy can make profound changes in people's lives. All psychotherapies provide opportunities to view oneself and deal with life in new ways. Even people suffering from the most crippling inhibitions, self-defeating behavior patterns, and anxieties have been cured of their disorders and aided in making their lives more satisfying and successful.

The use of psychotherapy in the treatment of specific mental disorders and emotional difficulties is detailed in the appropriate individual chapters throughout this book. Chapter 6 provides further discussion on how psychotherapy works and how to evaluate a treatment, as well as some case histories that illustrate different types of psychotherapy.

Goals of Psychotherapy

In its broadest definition, psychotherapy has three main goals. First and foremost, it seeks to alleviate psychological pain. This pain is usually in the form of distressing feelings or emotions, including anxiety and depression, and/or in the form of symptoms, such as phobias, obsessions, compulsions, inhibitions, panic attacks, psychologically based physical problems, sexual problems, and mental "blocks" that prevent accomplishment, emotional comfort, or happiness in many areas.

A second, more ambitious goal includes the modification of distressing behavior patterns and problematic personality traits. These difficulties manifest themselves in the two major areas of life: love and work. Relationship difficulties, self-esteem problems, deep-seated insecurities, self-hatred, and self-defeating behaviors are among the targets of the various psychotherapeutic approaches.

Most ambitiously, psychotherapy seeks to increase self-awareness and self-knowledge, insight that can lead to improvement in judgment, emotional flexibility, maturation, and successful adaptation to the demands of life.

Indications for Treatment

Modern scientific psychotherapy has been shown to be helpful to people suffering from a wide spectrum of psychological conditions. Indeed, some form of psychotherapy now exists for almost every type of mental disorder in children and adults, sometimes constituting the sole form of treatment and other times in conjunction with a somatic (bodily) approach. Yet psychotherapy can also benefit relatively normal people, suffering from no psychiatric disorder, for whom deepened self-knowledge affords enhanced capacity for emotional growth and satisfaction.

Forms of Psychotherapy

Psychotherapy is conducted with individuals, groups of patients, couples, or families. It lasts a limited, predetermined amount of time, or it continues over a longer term, until the therapist and patient consider that the goals have been met.

Within each of these settings or formats, the most common psychotherapeutic approaches offered by trained mental health professionals fall within the following four broad categories: supportive, psychodynamic (psychoanalytic), behavioral, and cognitive. A fifth category, the experiential, humanistic, or "alternative," includes a variety of approaches, some of them popularly rather than scientifically conceived, that may aim to help healthy individuals achieve personal growth or achieve their potential rather than to solve specific mental health problems. Finally, the burgeoning number of self-help and peer support groups form a fast-growing, extremely popular category of therapies.

The different psychotherapeutic approaches determine the kind of information the therapist seeks from the patient and how the therapist attempts to influence that individual to bring about the desired change. For example, in supportive psychotherapy, the therapist may be interested mainly in allowing the individual to vent his or her feelings, focusing mostly on current life problems and coping mechanisms. In behavior therapy, the practitioner will be interested in the specific problematic behaviors or habits and will provide, in effect, a "training program" to alter them. In psychodynamic approaches, the therapist may seek to understand and impart to the patient the determinants of his or her emotional problems that lay buried in the unconscious mind, and in the impact of past emotions and relationships on present experiences.

Ideally, in a thorough evaluation, as described in chapter 2, the mental health professional matches the patient and his or her difficulties and current life circumstances to a particular form of treatment.

Often, however, the type of treatment recommended to a patient depends on the skills of the therapist consulted or on the options available in the community. Fortunately, as discussed in chapter 6, when practiced by competent professionals, all types of psychotherapy tend to yield positive results. Also, although some psychotherapists concentrate on specific techniques only, a great number of mental health professionals bring a variety of techniques from many forms of psychotherapy to bear on the patient's difficulties and individual needs.

In the rest of this chapter, the most widely used and best-studied psychotherapies are discussed in the context of individual and group formats.

Individual Psychotherapies

Individual psychotherapy is the most common treatment format and is indicated in the widest variety of psychiatric and psychological problems. It focuses on the specific individual, his or her problems, coping mechanisms, defenses (see the box on page 48), and troublesome behaviors. Individual psychotherapies range along a spectrum from the most supportive, advice-giving, and directive treatments to the most explorative or "uncovering" approaches, the most intensive of which is psychoanalysis.

SUPPORTIVE PSYCHOTHERAPY

In all forms of psychotherapy (as in all healing), the relationship with the therapist is extremely important to the outcome of the treatment. In supportive psychotherapy, this relationship, and the active emotional assistance that the therapist provides, is central. The goals of this type of treatment are to provide psychological support and reduce distressing psychological symptoms, and to help the individual to regain his or her emotional balance, find solutions to immediate problems, and function as well as or better than before. As the most widely provided form of individual psychotherapy, it is often used in conjunction with pharmacological or other somatic treatment and with hospitalization.

Supportive psychotherapy differs from other forms of psychotherapy in that it does not aim to produce major change or to provide substantial insight into underlying psychological conflicts that may have contributed to the current difficulty, although some patients may nonetheless achieve some such understanding. Clinicians who treat individuals with supportive therapy are generally versed in psychodynamic (psychoanalytic) techniques, however, and some patients, once their immediate problems have resolved, may proceed to more "searching" forms of therapy.

Indications for Treatment

Supportive psychotherapy is particularly useful as a short-term "situationally focused" treatment for people who are relatively healthy psychologically but who are experiencing emotional difficulties and find they cannot cope under the stress. (See "Crisis Intervention" on page 47.) In this regard, it can be very helpful for people who are suffering the emotional effects of medical illness. (See chapter 28.) It is also commonly used to treat people who are having mental and emotional symptoms who are not psychologically minded or introspective—in other words, they are not interested in or able to explore their feelings, behaviors, or relationships.

Long-term supportive psychotherapy is appropriate for people suffering from severe and chronic psychiatric illness and personality disorders who cannot sustain the emotional rigors of intensive psychodynamic forms of treatment. Such individuals require the emotional support and "how-to" direction for daily living that this form of treatment provides.

How It Works

Supportive therapy is a directive form of therapy, in which the therapist actively engages the patient and guides the treatment. Therapists provide empathy, understanding, and reassurance, encourage release of painful emotions, give advice, bolster the patient's ability to function in the present, and strengthen (rather than question or analyze, as in psychodynamic therapies) his or her defense mechanisms.

Defense mechanisms (see the box on page 48) are ways in which a person processes inner emotional experiences, usually without conscious awareness. Often defense mechanisms shield people from being overwhelmed by emotional pain. For example, many people who receive frightening medical diagnoses, such as cancer or heart disease, protect themselves from their terror of dying by denying that they are sick or by avoiding appropriate treatment. Supportive therapists can help bolster the positive or adaptive elements of a patient's denial that allow him or her to retain hope ("I can lick this thing"), while encouraging the patient to accept treatment ("If I go ahead with the chemotherapy, I'll have an even better chance to get better"). When defense mechanisms fail to keep the pain at bay, supportive therapists can help restore their usefulness. People who suffer a major personal blow such as a divorce or job loss, for example, often feel like failures and withdraw in despair. The therapist can help them release and redirect their overpowering anger, rage, or resentment, bolster their self-esteem, and encourage a return to more adaptive ways of coping with reality.

For people who have difficulty distinguishing between fact and fantasy, supportive therapists can enhance their appreciation of reality and help them behave more appropriately and productively. Thus, for example, a therapist can help a woman tell the difference between the voices in her head and those she hears around her on the street; help a man to recognize whether people are talking about him or about the next election; or teach someone who is very withdrawn to look into the face of the waitress when trying to order lunch.

Techniques of cognitive or behavior psychotherapy (see pages 51–55) can also be used in a supportive capacity, such as teaching social skills to a highly withdrawn individual or methods of relaxation to someone suffering from anxiety.

Crisis Intervention

A form of brief, intense supportive psychotherapy for individuals in acute crises, who are currently in severe emotional turmoil, crisis intervention helps people in a wide variety of circumstances. Unexpected and intense stress, such as a death in the family, job loss, or an accident, can precipitate overwhelming anxiety and depression or leave someone with the incapacitating sense that he or she is out of control. In allowing the patient to express the intense painful feelings and receive support and some insight, the therapist bolsters the patient's coping capacities and helps restore his or her mental equilibrium.

Frequently, other forms of psychotherapy are very useful and important as a follow-up to crisis intervention in order to understand the reasons for the crisis and prevent a recurrence. Crisis intervention usually requires one to three weeks of treatment with sessions two to four times per week.

See also chapter 25.

PSYCHODYNAMIC PSYCHOTHERAPIES

Also known as insight-oriented, psychoanalytic, or explorative treatments, psychodynamic psychotherapies derive from psychoanalysis. All psychodynamic psychotherapies have in common the assumption that a person's feelings and behavior are influenced by past experience as well as present circumstances. Through their varying techniques, psychodynamic psychotherapies attempt to help individuals achieve insight into their emotional life, including the influence of the past on the present, in order to resolve current difficulties and produce change in personality and behavior.

The various psychodynamic psychotherapies share certain assumptions and principles, including:

The dynamic unconscious. A large part of mental life exists outside awareness but nonetheless continually influences and motivates current experience. Many behaviors (including, for example, a slip of the tongue), symptoms (anxiety, depression, and so on), dreams, and fantasies provide clues to the workings of the unconscious mind.

The importance of early experience and development. From birth, each stage of life affects the next one and has lasting impact on emotions and behavior.

Because they set the stage for later experiences, early life experiences are particularly important.

Intrapsychic conflict. From earliest childhood and throughout life, needs and wishes often conflict with one another and with societal and parental prohibitions (such as a two-year-old's wish to kill a newborn in order to remain the only child, or an adult's excessive fear of rejection as punishment for "bad" or unacceptable feelings). Because these conflicts are too painful or frightening to tolerate, they are kept from awareness through various defense mechanisms (see the box below), and sometimes turned into the symptoms that bring the individual for help (such as headaches, phobias, anxiety). These wishes and fears profoundly influence current mental life. Indeed, most of what people do is determined by the interplay of current experience with dynamic unconscious efforts to resolve competing wishes and fears.

All psychodynamic psychotherapies in one way or another attempt to uncover unconscious conflicts and reveal how they are underlying or influencing current experiences.

Psychoanalysis

Psychoanalysis is the most intensive form of psychodynamic treatment. It is also the most demanding on the patient's emotions, time, and, usually, his or her financial resources. For these reasons it is the least common form of psychodynamic treatment. However, because it is the "grandfather" of all the therapies in this category, it bears scrutiny first.

Sigmund Freud, a Viennese neurologist, began the practice of psychoanalysis late in the 19th century. Subsequent generations of psychoanalysts have developed its theories and techniques considerably since Freud's time. Today psychoanalysis has evolved as a rigorous intellectual, psychotherapeutic, and research discipline.

DEFENSE MECHANISMS

From childhood, each individual employs a variety of psychological mechanisms for processing emotional experience, gaining pleasure, and keeping anxiety and painful conflicts out of awareness. Beginning with Sigmund Freud, psychodynamic theorists have identified a long list of these unconscious defenses, sometimes classifying them as *immature* and *mature* defenses. Immature defenses result in behaviors that distort a person's experience of life, whereas mature defenses help him or her to cope successfully.

Immature Defenses

- *Projection* is attributing one's own feelings or motives to another person. For example, people who avoid dating because "all they want from me is sex" may not be able to acknowledge their own sexual desires.
- *Denial* is the refusal to acknowledge painful reality. For example, some people insist on seeing themselves as victims because they cannot face the consequences of their own actions; some middle-age married men have affairs with young women in order to deny that they are aging.
- *Displacement* is inappropriately transferring feelings from one person to another. For example, a woman who has a fight with her ex-husband might displace the anger onto the children, or a boss might take out his marital difficulties on his employees.
- *Avoidance* means avoiding life situations, tasks, challenges, or involvements, such as by not taking a driver's test for fear of losing control of the car.

Mature Defenses

- *Altruism* is deriving vicarious pleasure and gratification from helping others.
- *Humor* buffers the experience of pain through laughter and amusement.
- *Sublimation* redirects unacceptable impulses, such as sexual or aggressive drives, into acceptable activities, such as creative pursuits or sports.
- *Suppression* means postponing or delaying response to unpleasantness, such as by trying to "look at the bright side" or by deciding to wait until an appropriate time to react ("I'll sleep on it"). Suppression operates on a conscious level.
- *Identification* is appropriately taking on the attitudes, goals, ideals, and ambitions of valued others.

There are numerous theoretical approaches to psychoanalysis, such as Freudian, Jungian, Kleinian, object relations, self psychological, and others. They vary in the importance they give to certain unconscious motives and conflicts and the role of early experiences. Jungian analysis, for example (based on the work of Carl Jung, a contemporary and at one time a follower of Sigmund Freud), draws on notions of universal myths and symbols and a collective, universal unconscious that is beyond an individual's unconscious.

Although in common parlance the terms "psychotherapist" and "psychoanalyst" are sometimes used interchangeably, in fact to become a psychoanalyst, a clinician must receive specialized advanced training following receipt of a professional degree and undergo a personal psychoanalysis in a training institute.

The goals of psychoanalysis are the most global and ambitious of all the psychotherapies: Rather than to target and solve specific, current problems, it attempts to understand personality and produce major character and behavior change. In order to do this, it relies on specific techniques, to be discussed, to enable the patient to recover childhood experiences and fantasies and to bring into consciousness the conflicts that influence current feelings and behavior.

Most often, psychoanalysis is a long, slow process of progressive insight, leading to greater self-knowledge, maturation, and emotional growth. It has been likened to peeling an onion layer by layer until the unconscious determinants of current behavior and feelings—infantile wishes and fears—slowly come into focus. Once uncovered, the conflicts eventually can be tolerated, understood, accepted, and resolved. As a result, behavior and feelings change and the individual achieves a new maturity. Very often people emerge from analysis with a greater appreciation and richer view of themselves and others in their lives.

Treatment requires sessions three to five times a week for an average of three to five years.

Indications for Treatment

Psychoanalysis is a nondirective form of therapy, in which the analyst explores with the patient the way his or her mind works. Because psychoanalysts do not give advice or problem-solving direction, this treatment is not recommended for people in crisis, who require a more active approach. However, psychoanalysis is sometimes used in conjunction with medication for certain conditions (such as severe mood disorders) in which the medication stabilizes the person and allows him or her to continue the analytic treatment process.

Psychoanalysis requires at least average intelligence, a degree of psychological-mindedness, ability to tolerate frustration and painful feelings, and some ability to form a relationship. Therefore it is not appropriate for overtly psychotic, highly impulsive, addicted, or severely depressed people, although psychoanalysis may later help some such individuals understand and change patterns of behavior and emotional experience that contributed to the acute difficulties.

Chronic difficulties and frustrations in relationships, severe inhibitions, and persistent problems at work or other pursuits, as well as symptoms such as anxiety and moderate depression all can be indications for psychoanalysis. Many people with mild to moderate difficulties in life probably can benefit from psychoanalysis.

How It Works

Although theories of psychoanalysis have advanced considerably since Freud's day, techniques remain much as he discovered them.

Therapeutic neutrality. The therapeutic posture of the analyst is one of neutrality, anonymity, and abstinence; that is, the analyst, although always empathic, generally does not take sides or become involved in the patient's choices or goals. Neither does the analyst reveal much about his or her views, feelings, or personal life, because the analyst's focus is always on how the patient's mind works.

The patient lies on a couch, facing away from the analyst. This position promotes deepening introspective experience and awareness as well as free association.

Free association. The fundamental rule of the analytic situation is for the patient to attempt to say, without editing, everything that comes to mind during the treatment—all thoughts, feelings, wishes, fantasies, and experiences, no matter how unpleasant, embarrassing, frightening, trivial, or unrelated. Although the analyst may seem passive and inactive, he or she actively listens and is interested in the patient's dreams and fantasies as well as his or her current feelings, thoughts, and actions. By free associating, the patient begins to reveal clues to the hidden meanings and unconscious determinants of his or her emotional life.

Interpretation. The analyst asks questions, encourages the patient to be more specific about his or her behavior and feelings, and sometimes confronts the patient about inconsistencies or patterns (for example, "Every time you talk about you and me, you get more intellectual"). Most important, at appropriate times the analyst provides interpretations of the patient's feelings and behavior. The most important therapeutic "tool" in psychoanalysis, interpretations are the analyst's method of expressing what he or she perceives about the unconscious elements underlying the patient's experiences. The interpretation of dreams and the way they link past and present experience is a common feature of psychoanalytic interpretation.

Interpretation is also used to help the patient understand the defenses he or she uses in *resistance* to the treatment. It is not uncommon, for example, for patients to forget an appointment or to find they have "nothing to say" prior to the analyst's departure for vacation. This forgetting may serve to protect a patient from experiencing anger, sadness, or rage over the analyst's "abandonment" of him or her. Interpreting resistance helps increase the patient's tolerance of unacceptable feelings and thoughts and provides a growing insight into the inner workings of his or her mind.

Transference reaction. Transference is a common process in all areas of life, through which a person unconsciously repeats childlike patterns of relating that developed in reference to important people in the past, such as parents or siblings. In the transference, a person displaces onto a present-day individual the same feelings and attitudes that were associated with early-life figures. Thus, for example, people often relate—unconsciously—to spouses, teachers, or employers as if they were their parents, and as if they were making the same demands of them their parents did or threatening them with punishment. Understanding transference helps people recognize how they distort their perceptions of others.

As the psychoanalytic treatment progresses, the patient gradually develops an intensely powerful transference reaction to the analyst. This reaction becomes the major crucible of the therapeutic process—the lens through which the unconscious conflicts and dynamics of the patient's emotional life are recognized, interpreted, revised, and changed. The patient increasingly relates to the analyst (who remains neutral in reality) as if he or she were an important early figure and reexperiences the conflicting wishes, fantasies, sorrows, frustration, shame, guilt, anger, fear, joy, and pain that he or she felt in relation to key figures in infancy and childhood.

Through the exploration of the transference—how the patient relates to the analyst and what he or she believes the analyst is feeling and thinking—the patient reveals the roots of disturbed psychological functioning hidden in "the child within."

Working through. In the analysis, the patient comes to experience the transference in a kind of "split screen," simultaneously experiencing and observing how these early conflicts influence past and present life. As the individual repeatedly brings up the buried hopes and pains and unrealistic wishes of childhood, he or she becomes slowly able to accept rather than to defend against them. Most important, in this process of working through, which forms the major work of the analysis, the patient begins to change the behaviors and reactions that were based on these unconscious, anachronistic notions. For example, a patient gradually may come to see that her inhibitions and intense self-criticism have been based on the need to see others as judgmental parents whose love and acceptance she relentlessly seeks. As this recognition deepens, she can at last move beyond her childhood needs and test new behaviors.

Psychoanalytic (or Psychoanalytically Oriented) Psychotherapy

A modification of psychoanalytic technique, psychoanalytic psychotherapy is a much more widely used form of treatment. It holds to the same psychodynamic principles of uncovering unconscious conflict, but its goals are less ambitious and the process is less intense. The focus of this form of psychotherapy is more on helping patients achieve the necessary insights that will allow them to work out major life problems. Usually the therapist is more active than in psychoanalysis.

Psychoanalytic therapy is practiced by therapists who are psychoanalysts as well as by those who have not received specialized analytic training.

Patient and therapist meet one to three times a week for, usually, two to five years.

Indications for Treatment

The indications are the same as for psychoanalysis, except that psychoanalytic psychotherapy is appropriate for a wider range of patients, including those who require more active support and intervention from the therapist and who have more difficulty tolerating the frustrations that are necessary to the psychoanalytic process. Like psychoanalysis, it works best with patients who are interested in the workings of their minds and are motivated to find solutions.

How It Works

The patient and therapist sit face to face, although some psychoanalytic psychotherapists also have patients lie on the couch. As in psychoanalysis, the patient is encouraged to say everything that is on his or her mind. Although the nature of the patient's relationship to the therapist is important, psychoanalytic psychotherapy usually does not focus on the establishment and interpretation of an intense, regressive or childlike transference (page 50). The therapist is more likely to use techniques of clarification of specific behaviors and attitudes, confrontation (pointing out discrepancies between what a patient says and what he or she does, for example), suggestion, and other techniques that actively influence the course of the treatment.

Brief Dynamic Psychotherapy

In brief dynamic psychotherapy (also called brief or time-limited psychotherapy), therapist and patient explicitly agree that treatment will end after a specific number of sessions or on a scheduled date, usually 12 to 20 sessions over three to six months. Therapist and patient direct their attention to a particular, well-defined problem (for example, a student's reluctance to write his or her doctoral dissertation). Through the exploration of this one issue or problem, certain underlying conflicts are resolved (such as the student's fear of growing up and leaving home).

Indications for Treatment

Brief dynamic psychotherapy requires that the individual be relatively healthy psychologically, highly motivated to solve the problem, and able to become involved quickly with the therapist. Like the other forms of dynamic therapy, it is not recommended for people with severe depression, disorders marked by impulsiveness, addictive behaviors, or an inability to form relationships.

It is appropriate, however, to help someone handle a specific, identifiable problem. This positive resolution often has a "ripple effect" on the person's life. Being able to resolve a pressing or nagging problem (such as persistent reluctance to look for a better job) increases a person's self-esteem, which can lead to more effective functioning in other areas of life. It is also appropriate as a "trial" of the psychotherapeutic process, which can be pursued in greater intensity for other, deeper issues.

How It Works

Early on, the therapist identifies the unconscious conflict that seems to explain the patient's current problem. Throughout the treatment he or she actively keeps the central conflict at the forefront, using clarification, confrontation, and interpretation. The transference also is important for what it reveals about this same conflict. For example, a man comes for help because he is failing at his job. The therapist determines that he has an excessive fear of authority. In their sessions, the man behaves in a very placating way toward the therapist. The therapist interprets the man's behavior as a way of avoiding the central conflict—his fear of authority.

BEHAVIOR THERAPY

Known also as behavior modification and behavioral therapy, behavior therapy is a form of psychotherapy aimed at changing specific thoughts, feelings, and actions. It is based on the assumption that abnormal behavior results from faulty or inadequate learned responses.

Behavior therapy employs various techniques, to be discussed, to reduce or eliminate unwanted, problematic, painful, or stressful behaviors and to foster, reinforce, or introduce new, more rewarding behaviors. The therapy emphasizes the connection between problematic behaviors and stimuli in the environment that trigger them. Attention focuses on the current behavior and not on deeper emotional processes or underlying psychological conflicts.

Success in behavior therapy is often quick and tangible—such as finally, after 20 years, stopping smoking or binge-eating. In addition to the immediate benefits of changing a problematic behavior, the patient feels renewed confidence and hence self-esteem and mastery: "If I can do this, I can do anything!"

Behavior therapy is often a short-term treatment structured around a prescribed number of sessions.

Background and Some Basic Principles

Whereas psychodynamic psychotherapies derived from the theories and practices of Sigmund Freud, behavior therapy grew out of the work of experimental psychologists, such as the Russian physiologist Ivan Pavlov and American psychologists John B. Watson and B. F. Skinner. Like psychodynamic psychotherapies, it has grown considerably in theory and technique since its earlier days. Unlike these therapies, it focuses on the individual's actions and their triggers rather than on the meanings of and reasons for them.

Classical and Operant Conditioning

Many of the techniques used today in behavior therapy derive from the discoveries of classical and operant conditioning. Pavlov demonstrated the principles of classical conditioning when he trained a dog to salivate at the sound of a bell. Pavlov's experiments demonstrated fundamental ways in which behavior is learned and how it can be changed.

In human terms, a person who is afraid of having a life-threatening accident may develop a reluctance or fear of going to work and may thus give up a vital activity. This learned, maladaptive behavior can be *deconditioned*, however. For example, through training in the use of relaxation techniques, the person who grows anxious on the street eventually can learn to associate muscular relaxation and calm with getting to work.

Operant conditioning is the process whereby behavior is *reinforced* by its consequences. For example, one can train a dog to sit by feeding it or praising it afterward, in other words providing rewards or positive reinforcement.

Behaviors can be *extinguished*, however, using operant conditioning techniques. For example, for a child who neglects homework, threats to reduce television time or offers to reward him or her with a favorite video can sometimes serve to alter the undesired behavior.

Indications for Treatment

Behavior therapy is used in a wide range of disorders, especially for symptoms that interfere drastically with the quality of life, such as stuttering or repetitive, compulsive behaviors such as hand-washing. As detailed in the appropriate chapters throughout this book, behavior therapy techniques are considered quite useful alone or in combination with other therapies in the treatment of anxiety disorders, in particular the phobias and obsessive-compulsive disorder; depression and other mood disorders; eating disorders; sexual disorders; sleep disorders; schizophrenia; childhood conduct disorders, attention-deficit hyperactivity disorder, and learning disabilities; autism and other developmental disorders; and speech impediments.

In addition, it has important applications in stress management and treatment of medical conditions such as hypertension, headache, asthma, certain gastrointestinal disorders including irritable bowel syndrome, and chronic pain. Indeed, many of the methods of stress reduction, including biofeedback and relaxation training (chapter 24), are behavior therapy interventions.

How It Works

Because behavior therapy is highly specific and focused, it depends on, first, a careful assessment of the behaviors to be targeted. The therapist identifies the problematic behavior (such as a phobia) and aspects of the patient's life that arouse it (such as getting in a car).

Following are some common techniques of behavior therapy. (See also techniques of cognitive therapy later in this chapter. These techniques are often combined with behavioral treatments in cognitive/behavior therapy.

Relaxation Training

To learn to relax muscles and reduce tension, patients are taken through a series of exercises, instructed to breathe deeply and to tense and relax major muscles in a particular order, perhaps beginning with the toes and moving toward the head. The process usually lasts up to 30 minutes and is used as the basis of other therapeutic techniques, such as desensitization.

Desensitization

Following relaxation exercises, patients gradually are exposed to anxiety-generating situations. A therapist using this approach will instruct a patient to confront in small steps the fearful object, person, or situation, or to imagine such a confrontation. For example, a person who is afraid of elevators might be accompanied to an elevator and encouraged to go quickly in and out the door, then to stay inside with the door closed before pressing the "open" button, then to ride up one floor, and so on, until he or she has grown comfortable riding elevators. Through these repeated exposures, the person eventually becomes desensitized to the fear.

Flooding

Akin to getting back on a horse after being thrown, flooding, a less commonly used technique, exposes patients to the full force of their anxieties all at once, rather than little by little, until, within the controlled treatment situation, they learn to overcome their fears. The exercise can be in the imagination or a real-life confrontation. The person with the elevator fear, for instance, might be escorted up and down on one for hours, or asked in therapy to imagine the worst possible accident that could happen to someone when the elevator doors close. When the technique is an exercise in imagination only, it is often called *implosion*.

Self-control, Self-monitoring, and Self-reinforcement

A variety of "self-management" techniques are used not only to extinguish overt behaviors but to alter thought processes. Patients observe and evaluate their own behaviors, especially those targeted for change. They also initiate rewards and punishments. Such a self-reinforcing reward might be congratulating oneself verbally for performing a previously avoided task— "Hey, I'm really great!" says the person with writer's block who finally gets a paragraph down on paper.

Self-control and self-reinforcement techniques are used widely in altering habits such as overeating. In these cases, patients might be instructed to keep a written account of what they eat, when, and what they were feeling (self-monitoring), and to reward themselves in some way for sticking to the diet.

Behavioral Rehearsal, Assertiveness Training, Social Skills Training

Behavioral rehearsal addresses social problems and is used most often for assertiveness training. People who are handicapped by shyness, for instance, practice what to say in social situations. Often, using techniques of *role reversal*, the patient plays the role of a significant person in his or her life and the therapist takes on the patient's role.

Assertiveness training in particular guides people through the difficulties of asking for help, saying no, expressing feelings and opinions, and showing affection. Patients are instructed in how to handle themselves as the therapist models specific situations.

Social skills training can help people with schizophrenia and developmental disabilities learn how to behave in basic interactions with others in daily life. It is also useful in drug abuse treatment to teach people how to socialize without being intoxicated.

Modeling

Modeling involves imitating the behavior of another person in order to improve social skills or overcome fears. Also called vicarious learning, it is used frequently with children and adolescents. For example, a child who is afraid to speak in front of others will watch another child get up in front of a group and talk, then imitate the same behavior.

Token Economies

Used primarily with chronically mentally ill patients in hospital settings, techniques that use tokens promote improved behavior through a specified system of rewards. Good behavior "buys" patients "reinforcers" such as extra dessert, more television time, a private room. Tokens (plastic chips, stars, and the like) are dispensed by staff or volunteers who act as "bankers" for patients working toward achieving their goals.

COGNITIVE THERAPY

A relatively new form of psychotherapy, cognitive therapy is a short-term treatment that, like behavior therapy, targets specific symptoms. Unlike behavior therapy, however, it focuses on a person's thoughts and thought processes rather than his or her behaviors. Variants of the cognitive therapy approach include rational emotive therapy and cognitive-behavior therapy.

Cognitive therapy was developed in the 1960s by psychiatrist Aaron Beck originally to treat depression. (Another, newer short-term therapy specifically for depression, interpersonal therapy, is discussed in chapter 8.) Cognitive therapy derives in part from theories of information processing. According to cognitive theorists, the way people think about themselves and the world—their views, attitudes, and assumptions—determines what they do and how they feel. Thus, for example, a man who believes himself incapable of finding a better job will not look for one, or do well in interviews, and will feel discouraged and depressed. Negative thinking, in other words, leads to negative experiences. Cognitive therapists intervene in this thinking process (most of which is outside the individual's awareness) to help patients identify and change their fundamental assumptions and, therefore, the behaviors that derive from them. In the course of usually less than 20 sessions, with follow-up, refresher, and "booster" sessions, many patients develop effective techniques to think less negatively, test their beliefs, and alter their behaviors.

Indications for Treatment

Cognitive therapy was originally devised to treat nonpsychotic depression. Increasingly it is also being used in stress management and to treat anxiety, panic, phobias, substance abuse, marital conflict, and personality disorders. The treatment may be particularly useful to help people cope with situational crises.

How It Works

Cognitive therapists actively work with patients to identify their distortions in thinking (see the box below) that lead to disordered emotional states and self-defeating behaviors. They structure sessions, give advice, and propose methods to test new ways of thinking and experiencing. Homework is an important part of the process. Homework assignments at first involve learning to monitor thinking styles and recognize logical errors that lead to bad feelings. During sessions therapist and patient, using the patient's experiences, discuss how the distorted thinking patterns and assumptions lead directly to self-defeating behaviors and emotional symptoms.

As the therapy proceeds, the therapist and patient devise ways for the individual to test false assumptions as well as newer, more reasonable ones. For example, Mr. N., who is a perfectionist ("If I don't do my work perfectly, my boss won't like me") was asked to *not*

COMMON ERRORS IN THINKING

Aaron Beck and other cognitive theorists have identified a number of logical errors in thinking that are common among people who are depressed or suffering other emotional problems. Some of these—to which many people are prone on occasion—include:

- *Arbitrary inference.* Drawing a conclusion without the facts to support it. For example, recently married friends to whom Ms. R. gave a gift have not written to thank her. She thinks: "They hate my taste."
- *Selective abstraction.* Taking a fact out of context while ignoring the rest of the evidence. For example, although eventually the groom's parents tell Ms. R. how much their son and his wife like her gift and have in fact featured it prominently on their mantelpiece, she still thinks the absence of a thank-you note "tells the real story."
- *Overgeneralization.* Drawing a sweeping conclusion based on one incident. For example, Mr. M. asks a woman for a date. She turns him down. He thinks, "No woman I like will ever go out with me."

- *Magnification* and *minimization.* Overestimating the negative and underestimating or dismissing the positive. For example, Mrs. C., who is depressed, calls her granddaughter and asks her to visit. Her granddaughter says she is going out of town that week but will visit when she returns. Even though the young woman calls her during the business trip, Mrs. C. feels unwanted by her only granddaughter.
- *Personalization.* Relating external events to oneself without substantiating evidence. For example, Mr. B. loses a customer. He thinks, "It's all my fault," without considering that the customer may be having business reversals or other possible explanations.
- *Dichotomous thinking.* Explaining situations in all-or-nothing, black-and-white terms. For example, Ms. A. submits a magazine article for publication. When the editor asks her to rewrite parts of it, she thinks, "I'm a bad writer," instead of recognizing that revision is part of the process.

revise a report before submitting it to his boss. Because Mr. N. did not take the additional time to read and reread the report and make continual changes, for once he was able to submit it on time. Although the report contained a few minor spelling errors, Mr. N.'s boss was delighted that he met his deadline.

HYPNOTHERAPY

A technique utilizing hypnosis, hypnotherapy can be used in most types of psychotherapy. Hypnosis, or trance, is an altered state of consciousness that allows heightened communication between mind and body. It is a condition of relaxed, focused concentration similar to the state of mind a person achieves when lost in a good book, when extraneous details—such as the first ring of the telephone—move temporarily outside awareness. Considered by some to be the oldest modern form of psychotherapy, practiced for more than two centuries, it is the first technique Sigmund Freud used to gain access to the unconscious mind.

Today, therapists provide hypnotherapy for a wide variety of purposes: to relieve pain and other physical symptoms; to control habits such as smoking and overeating; to treat anxiety, panic, phobias, and post-traumatic stress disorders; to restore memory; to uncover unconscious conflicts; to foster free association (page 49); and to resolve emotional difficulties and creative blocks.

Most people are capable of being hypnotized, although some people enter a deeper state of trance than do others. Those who are most hypnotizable often are capable of reliving childhood experiences as if they were occurring in the present. Many methods exist to test hypnotizability, including the "eye roll." The individual tries to roll his or her eyes up inside the head. The more white showing beneath the iris, the more hypnotizable the person usually turns out to be, for reasons that remain unclear.

Therapists induce trance in many ways, usually involving concentration and deep relaxation techniques, such as focusing on relaxing the whole body one muscle group at a time. Once hypnotized, a person is relaxed and aware, capable of remembering the trance experience, and capable of coming out of it at any time. People do not act against their better judgment while in trance or get lost in that state of mind. At worst, they fall asleep.

Not all therapists are trained in hypnotherapy. To find out whether a clinician uses hypnosis in his or her therapy practice, ask.

OTHER THERAPIES

Hundreds of types of therapy fall into the large category of "other" psychotherapies. Often called "experiential" therapies, some aim at liberating emotions, expanding consciousness, and facilitating self-realization. Others emphasize emotional awareness and may provide massage and other body work as part of the treatment. Still others promote emotional control and/or spiritual awareness and use techniques of meditation. Many experiential therapies are associated with the New Age or human potential movement.

Although it is difficult to generalize, many of these therapies are most useful for enhancing day-to-day adjustment and personal fulfillment for individuals who are mentally healthy rather than for those who are suffering from severe, disabling symptoms.

A brief description of one more widely known therapy in this "other" category follows; see also the subsequent discussion of group therapies.

Client-centered Psychotherapy

Founded by psychologist Carl Rogers, client-centered psychotherapy grew out of the humanistic-existential movement of the 1940s and 1950s. Its aims are self-actualization (fulfilling one's potential) and growth of the whole person rather than diagnosis and treatment of specific disorders. Client-centered therapy rejects the medical model of illness for symptoms of mental suffering.

Client-centered therapists believe that each human being is born with the capacity and the drive for self-actualization. The nondirective therapy relies not so much on specific techniques as on the empathic relationship between the client and the totally accepting and attentive therapist. The therapist behaves as a real person during sessions, demonstrating here-and-now feelings. Principally through this therapeutic relationship, the client becomes able to experience feelings fully. The client's own inherent self-actualizing tendency helps return control over behavior and movement in life to him or her through this process.

Group Psychotherapies

Group therapy is an increasingly popular form of treatment, available in a wide variety of mental health-care settings. A therapist leads group treatments and utilizes the interactions of group members to bring about relief of symptoms, improvement in relationships, and personality change. (Groups are often leaderless in self-help or supportive formats, as discussed below.) Most forms of group treatment aim at helping members with individual problems. In family and marital therapies, however, the goal is also or entirely to improve the functioning of the group as a whole.

Group therapy offers numerous advantages. Because a number of people can be treated simultaneously, at a lower price than individual psychotherapy, it is often the most efficient and economical way to provide help. In self-help formats, the experience is often free of charge. Also, within the therapy group, individuals end up demonstrating their difficulties with others rather than just talking about them, which can often make it easier to work out those problems. Finally, therapy groups provide a sense of community, an understanding that there are others with the same or similar problems, models for overcoming difficulties, and sources of practical problem-solving information.

Some Basics of Group Therapy

Many types of psychotherapy exist in group formats. The style of the leader or leaders as well as the goals of the group work depend on which type of therapy is offered. For example, in behavior therapy groups, the leader is active and structures the sessions so that group members focus on particular behaviors that require change. In psychodynamic groups, the leader may tend more to watch, listen, question, and interpret rather than to direct the sessions.

In professionally led groups, members are selected carefully by the specially trained therapist. Most groups are heterogeneous, that is, composed of people who are different with respect to sex, age, race, socioeconomic status, religion, vocation, personality factors, and, often, the nature of their problem. These variations provide the basis for interactions and for discussion and understanding of differences.

A number of groups are homogeneous, however, consisting of members who are selected for their common characteristics or shared disorders. For example, some groups consist entirely of adolescents, medically ill patients, substance abusers, married couples, sex offenders, people with phobias, those suffering from eating disorders, and so on. Most self-help groups consist of people who share a common problem.

Some groups exist with the same members for the length of the treatment. Others introduce new members throughout the course of the therapy. Five to nine members is average. Sessions usually meet once a week and last one and a half hours.

Like individual therapies, group approaches can be short or long term. Generally, time-limited groups, which also tend to have fixed membership, work toward the achievement of attainable goals. Usually these groups have a large educational component, such as learning social skills, or are geared toward symptom removal, as in supportive, cognitive, or behavioral formats. Longer-term groups with changing membership aim toward increased self-awareness, personality change, and improvement in interpersonal relationships.

Indications for Group Therapy Treatment

Group therapy, like individual therapy, in one form or another is useful for the widest range of mental and emotional disorders and life situations. Often it is pro-

GROUP THERAPY: ADDITIONAL APPROACHES

Numerous types of group therapy are practiced in addition to those that apply the supportive, psychodynamic, behavioral, or cognitive principles and techniques that have been discussed. Following are some additional approaches.

- *Confrontational groups.* These groups utilize peer pressure to help members change behaviors that they are not necessarily eager to give up, such as drug use or gambling. In confronting people with long-standing, rigid attitudes and behaviors, the group experience can be highly emotional. Synanon, Daytop, and encounter groups use confrontational approaches.
- *Repressive/inspirational groups.* Alcoholics Anonymous, derivative "Twelve-Step" approaches (see chapter 9) such as Overeaters Anonymous, and religious support groups are among the examples of group experiences that are designed mainly to elevate group morale and create a positive group climate in which to promote change. Testimonials, group discussions, standardized literature, and meditation and relaxation experiences provide support and encouragement and create powerful group identification, which is the most potent therapeutic technique of such approaches.
- *Time-extended groups.* These are intensive experiences, lasting for many hours or sometimes days, that aim to break down psychological defenses and to accelerate group interactions. Exemplified by marathon groups, these groups tend to place a high value on self-disclosure and psychological intimacy. How group members behave in the present is usually more important than past experiences.
- *Psychodrama.* Developed by psychiatrist J. L. Moreno, psychodrama uses theatrical techniques to promote insight, self-awareness, and individual growth. Psychodramas include a subject (the patient), director (the therapist), therapeutic aides (called auxiliary egos), and an audience. The players act out various conflicts and relationship problems in group members' lives.
- *Transactional analysis groups.* The "TA" approach, originated by psychiatrist Eric Berne, focuses on the here and now. Group interactions help uncover members' inner conflicts, which often have to do with the "parent," "child," and "adult" that each individual unconsciously keeps hidden within him- or herself. According to Berne, understanding which role a person is playing out at any given time can explain why he or she is feeling or behaving in a particular way. They also help explain the "games," or relationship patterns, that people establish with one another and that are revealed within the group therapy.
- *Gestalt therapy groups.* A holistic approach developed by psychologist Fritz Perls, gestalt groups concern themselves with the emotional and sensory awareness of members in the present. They commonly employ exercises, role playing, and other specific techniques to enable group members to become aware of how they feel rather than how they think and to promote individual growth and development of potential personal resources.
- *Structured group experiences.* These include various group therapies that are primarily supportive, educational, and nonstressful in nature, such as medication groups, discussion/education groups, quiet activity groups (music and poetry therapy), and physical activity groups (dance therapy). Therapeutic community meetings (such as in group homes for substance abusers or in psychiatric hospitals) also fall into this category.
- *Special population groups.* All members in these groups share the same diagnosis or symptoms for which they seek psychotherapy—for example, patients with cancer or phobias or those who have difficulty coming to terms with their sexual identity. They rely on group support and identification, role modeling, and universality of experience to facilitate open discussion and sharing of mutual problems.

vided along with individual therapy, where it becomes particularly useful for people who have difficulties in their relationships. Group therapy is believed to be a particularly useful form of treatment for people with interpersonal problems who need to recognize the impact of these problems on other people.

THE CASE OF MS. B.

Ms. B. was a 35-year-old single woman who consulted a psychiatrist because of her difficulty establishing a long-term relationship with a man. She had always wanted to get married and raise a family, but she had had a series of unsuccessful liaisons and was puzzled and distressed about her inability to be successful in love. She also mentioned that at work she felt isolated from others and sometimes had arguments with her fellow employees and supervisors, whom she felt took advantage of her.

Ms. B. came from a family in which she was the younger of two sisters. Her older sister was favored by both parents, and Ms. B. described herself as a "second-class citizen" in the family. Although she was attractive, intelligent, and articulate, she lacked self-confidence and viewed herself as inadequate or deficient.

Because many of her issues centered around interpersonal themes—within her family, with men, at work—the psychiatrist decided to place her in a psychodynamically oriented psychotherapy group. The psychiatrist hoped that not only could she gain more experience in relationships within the group, but also that her interactions with group members would reveal the extent to which her beliefs about herself contributed to her problems in relationships.

The group chosen for Ms. B. consisted of eight people, four men and four women, ranging in age from 25 to 45. All members were experiencing career concerns, relationships problems, and symptoms of anxiety or depression that intruded into the conduct of their everyday lives. The group met once weekly for one and a half hours over the course of many months.

Ms. B. experienced great apprehension about her entry into the group, fearing that she would be poorly received and relegated to its periphery—the same feelings that she had had about her family. To her surprise, she found that almost all members could identify with her concerns about rejection and that they too were initially fearful of joining the group.

Once integrated into the group, Ms. B. was able to share her concerns about specific problems areas in her current life. She learned a great deal through listening to problems that other people had as well. In addition, she began to feel that she was able to help others, which boosted her self-esteem.

As usually happens in psychodynamic psychotherapy groups, Ms. B. began to understand how her experiences with the psychiatrist and members of the therapy group "replayed" the interactions she originally experienced in her family. For example, she often expressed annoyance or frank outrage at what she felt was the psychiatrist's "preference" for other group members, particularly one woman who was slightly older than she was, who provoked her age-old feelings of rivalry with her sister.

The group therapy process also gave her insights into the genesis of many of her difficulties with other people. Her low self-esteem combined with her envious feelings toward others made it difficult for her to get close to people; she often acted as if she had a chip on her shoulder, so people frequently steered clear of her. With men, her desperate need to be loved and accepted had the reverse effect: It scared them away. But with those men who wanted to get to know her anyway, she was the one who pulled away. Through the group therapy process she began to discover that she was afraid that a man who got too close to her would see through to her "real" self.

As she began to replace antiquated fears and misconceptions that were interfering with her relationships, she began to make great progress with people in her personal and professional life. By the time she had been in group therapy for a year and a half, Ms. B. was involved with a man she cared for very much and they had begun to talk about marriage.

FAMILY THERAPY

Most approaches to psychotherapy, including those provided in a group setting, view a person's problems and the solutions to them as emanating in some way from within him- or herself. Family therapy takes a different perspective: that the individual's difficulties or those of the family as a whole arise and are maintained within the shared context in which they live. Deemphasizing individual psychopathology and avoiding diagnostic labels, family therapy works with the entire family system—its structure, communication, and styles of interaction—to produce change.

Family therapy refers to any treatment that deals with the family group, including the marital (or cohabiting) couple, children and grandparents, extended families, and stepfamilies and nonrelated individuals who constitute "blended" families. Within the rapidly growing field of family therapy, there are many practical and theoretical approaches. The prevailing orientations are psychodynamic, behavioral, and systems-derived schools; this last, which approaches the family as an interdependent unit rather than as a collection of individuals, is currently the most influential.

Indications for Treatment

Marital problems and difficulties among generations (parents and children, stepfamilies, grandparents) are the major indications for treatment. Often, however, one family member comes for treatment because he or she is having symptoms of emotional distress or is behaving problematically. The therapist suggests family therapy because the individual's problems reflect a disturbance in the whole family, or because the family, perhaps unwittingly, undermines the person's treatment.

Eating disorders, substance abuse, school phobias, and problems related to leaving home are among the typical family situations for which a systems-oriented family therapy perspective frequently is employed. Family therapy is also becoming increasingly important in the treatment of schizophrenia, and it also can be very helpful to families in which one member suffers from a devastating medical illness. In all such cases, family therapy helps to strengthen the organization of the family so it can better withstand the disruptive effects of one member's illness on family functioning.

How It Works

Family therapists are interested in how the entire family functions. During the evaluation process, family therapists prefer to see all members of the immediate family, including young children, and perhaps also important members of the extended family and "blended" family, although not everyone is necessarily involved in the treatment process at all times. Some family therapists prepare a genogram, a chart of family relationships and emotional history over three or more generations.

Family therapists look at the nature of the limits that parents set for their children, the kind of boundaries they draw between the generations, and the point during the life cycle of the family when symptoms of dysfunction emerge. Additional concerns include:

- *Patterns of alliances* (parents vs. children, parents and one child vs. the other child; children vs. stepparent).
- *Emotional triangles* (parents and child; for example, when the parents are having marital difficulties, the child may develop problems that focus their attention on him or her and end up keeping them together).
- *Power hierarchy* (who makes the decisions, whose opinions count and whose do not).
- *Verbal and nonverbal communication styles* (who puts whom down and who interrupts whom; conflicting messages; intimidating gestures).
- *Scapegoating* (who gets blamed or is seen as the one with "problems").
- *Emotional interactions* (are some family members routinely hostile to one another, and does this style reflect fear of intimacy?; do the family's unwritten rules prevent expression of emotions?; does the father, perhaps, project onto his son his own sense of not being "man enough"?).
- *Self-differentiation* (do the children have a sense that they are individual and different from other family members?; often family members who lack self-differentiation become vulnerable to the emotional pressures of other members and end up having overt symptoms that require help).
- *Family roles* (what are the role expectations of the father, the mother, the girl, the boy, the grandparents; who is the "sick" one, the "strong" one?).

The therapist or therapists (often family therapists work in male-female teams, to provide a role model of both sexes) work with each member of the family as parts of the whole. Although they may support efforts of individual family members to behave differently or to become more independent, they generally do not take sides. Indeed, family therapists form a working alliance with each member of the

THE GENOGRAM: YOUR FAMILY'S EMOTIONAL TREE

Figure 4.1: A genogram is an outline of a family tree, annotated with information about your family. Psychotherapists use it to illustrate family dynamics between generations.

In addition to diagramming the significant people within a family network, a genogram usually contains a description of the personality characteristics and mental and physical illnesses of each person in the family.

CONSTRUCTING YOUR FAMILY GENOGRAM

1. **Make a simple diagram of your family tree. Use a circle for each woman and a square for each man. Draw your position and that of your spouse, as indicated here, and then your children.**

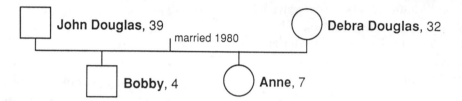

2. **Then branch out. Add parents, grandparents, and grandchildren.**

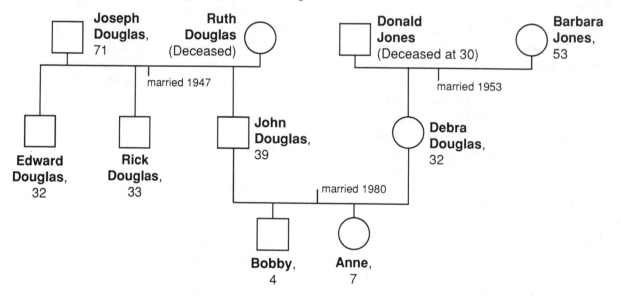

family, which helps to promote an atmosphere in which change can take place. Change in one family member, even if it is positive, often upsets the entire family's equilibrium, and the therapist needs to work with all members to help them recognize the forces that underlie the integrity of the system.

Usually family therapy is practical, problem-focused, and short term. The therapist helps guide the family toward solutions to their problems, which may involve the need to: set limits for children; establish firmer boundaries between the roles each generation plays; understand and accept individual differences; learn new ways to communicate, interact, and express feelings; alter destructive alliances; or (as in family

therapy for schizophrenia) learn about the illness and how to live with it as a family. Interventions tend to be behaviorally oriented, using specific homework assignments and exercises to build trust, empathy, and differentiation among family members.

Family therapy treatment is sometimes offered in conjunction with individual forms of treatment.

Marital (Couples) Therapy

Many practitioners of family therapy also work separately with couples, and some specialize in helping couples. The couple is the cornerstone of the family. When their coalition is strong, they usually can col-

3. Now add personality characteristics as well as any significant illnesses (emotional or physical).

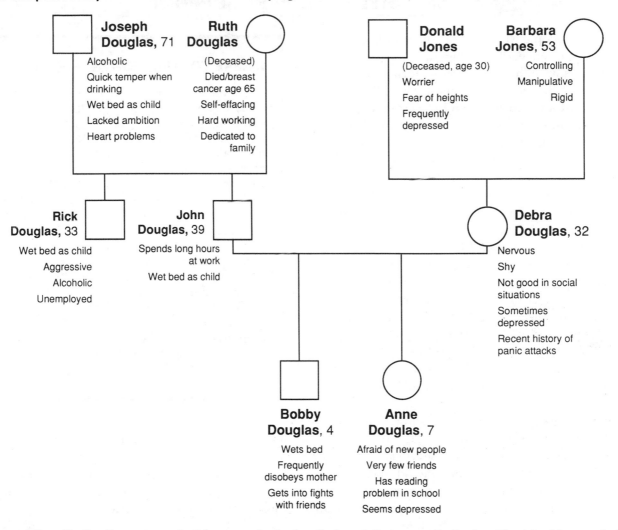

Joseph Douglas, 71
Alcoholic
Quick temper when drinking
Wet bed as child
Lacked ambition
Heart problems

Ruth Douglas
(Deceased)
Died/breast cancer age 65
Self-effacing
Hard working
Dedicated to family

Donald Jones
(Deceased, age 30)
Worrier
Fear of heights
Frequently depressed

Barbara Jones, 53
Controlling
Manipulative
Rigid

Rick Douglas, 33
Wet bed as child
Aggressive
Alcoholic
Unemployed

John Douglas, 39
Spends long hours at work
Wet bed as child

Debra Douglas, 32
Nervous
Shy
Not good in social situations
Sometimes depressed
Recent history of panic attacks

Bobby Douglas, 4
Wets bed
Frequently disobeys mother
Gets into fights with friends

Anne Douglas, 7
Afraid of new people
Very few friends
Has reading problem in school
Seems depressed

4. Now analyze the family system. In this example the family found that enuresis (bedwetting) had been a trait shared by three generations. Seven-year-old Anne's fearfulness and depression can be seen in relation to her mother's and grandfather's emotional histories.

laborate well with each other, with their children, or with others in their social system. Marital therapists often work with any committed couple, married or living together, heterosexual or homosexual.

Often the nature of the distress dictates the choice between marital or family therapy approaches. For sexual problems, issues related to separation and the prospect of divorce, and spouse abuse, marital therapy is usually the treatment that is recommended initially. Any couple unable to resolve conflicts can be helped by this form of therapy. Marital therapy also may be recommended for patients who are in individual therapy who have unstable marriages.

As with family therapy generally, there are many approaches to marital therapy, but the focus is usually on problem-solving approaches that emphasize improving communication patterns and trust. In the course of treatment, couples may explore their expectations of one another, learn to recognize the tactics they have been using in unsuccessful attempts to resolve conflict, and are helped to see each other as separate and individual people with different needs and perhaps emotional styles. In psychodynamic marital therapy, there also may be emphasis on how conflicts or styles of relating within families of origin influence each person's difficulties now.

SELF-HELP AND PEER SUPPORT

Groups of people who share a common need, stressful life experience, illness, disability, or concern currently constitute the most popular form of therapy in the United States. An estimated 15 million Americans attend some form of self-help group each week. Offering mutual support, assistance, spiritual direction, habit control, substance abuse recovery, and/or personal growth to those who choose to attend, self-help groups generally are either leaderless, run by laypersons without mental health training, or, sometimes, directed by a mental health professional who has suffered from the same problem.

Self-help groups can offer numerous advantages to those who attend. Because every member shares a common experience, these groups ideally can provide a sense of community, social support, and identification that can greatly benefit an individual's well-being, motivation, and mastery over difficulty. Also, they offer those who attend the chance to help others, which can enhance one's own healing. Importantly, they offer the opportunity to share practical advice and coping resources.

Many individuals who do not require formal mental health treatment attend self-help groups. When professional interventions are necessary, however, support groups can often provide additional benefits. In substance abuse treatment particularly, peer support groups often constitute an important

WHERE TO TURN FOR SELF-HELP

A self-help or support group exists for virtually every ailment, condition, life stress, or predicament that you might have—including living with somebody who has a predicament. Suggestions for locating some of them are provided in various chapters of this book. In addition, in chapter 31 we provide a list of mental health advocacy groups, which also may help mental illness sufferers and their families locate self-help mutual-aid resources.

For information about the enormous number of support groups for virtually any interest, write the National Self-Help Clearinghouse (33 West 42nd Street, New York, NY 10036).

The quality of self-help groups varies widely. See if you like what a particular group has to offer, and if you have anything to offer it. But don't seek out a self-help group in lieu of professional evaluation and care.

adjunct to the formal treatment process, and indeed attendance at one of the various so-called Twelve-Step groups based on principles of Alcoholics Anonymous (chapter 9, page 130) is now mandatory in most substance abuse programs.

5

The Use of Drugs and Other Somatic Treatments

Lewis A. Opler, M.D., Ph.D.

Treatment of the body—somatic treatment—is the mainstay of medical practice. As physicians, psychiatrists always have used available somatic treatments—drugs in particular—to relieve the suffering and distress of their patients. Today psychiatrists have at their disposal increasing numbers of drugs that, when administered in precise dosages for specified periods of time, can profoundly modify mental states, behavior, and feelings of people afflicted with serious mental and emotional illnesses.

Until the 1950s, however, when a chance discovery revolutionized the somatic treatments used within psychiatry, no drugs were known that could target specifically the symptoms or syndromes that psychiatrists were called upon to treat—including anxiety, depression, and psychosis. Drug treatment consisted mostly of the use of nonspecific medications, especially sedatives, which quiet an agitated or upset individual but provide no further benefit. Even for chronic psychotic conditions, psychotherapy remained the focus of treatment in the United States. For patients who found it difficult or impossible rationally to engage in such therapy, little could be done. As the second half of the twentieth century began, many of those who showed bizarre or dangerous behavior were confined in locked wards where their basic physical needs could be met and where they could be protected from themselves and from others.

The Breakthrough

In the early 1950s the French surgeon and physiologist Henri Laborit began to use the drug chlorpromazine as a sedative to be given to patients prior to surgery. French psychiatrists Jean Delay and Paul Deniker decided to try chlorpromazine to sedate their chronically psychotic inpatients. To the doctors' astonishment, chlorpromazine caused a remarkable amelioration of hallucinations and delusions in patients who had been plagued by them for years. In some patients these symptoms virtually vanished, while in others they lessened to the point that previously "unreachable" men and women could be engaged in therapeutic programs and even discharged from the hospital.

Soon Delay and Deniker's finding was replicated around the world. Chlorpromazine (marketed in the United States as Thorazine) spurred the development not only of other antipsychotics but also of other classes of psychopharmacological agents, or *psychotropics*. By the end of the 1950s, highly specific agents targeting psychosis or depression were available worldwide, altering forever and for the better our treatment approaches and our understanding of the major mental disorders.

At about the same time these powerful new drugs were becoming available, other nondrug somatic treatment modes were being developed and refined as additions to the therapeutic repertoire. A few failed the test of time, eventually proving too dangerous for widespread use or providing scant benefit; others have newly been developed and added to the treatment repertoire. Electroconvulsive therapy (ECT), phototherapy, and biofeedback, discussed toward the end of this chapter, have been demonstrated to be highly effective and are in widespread use today.

HOW SOMATIC TREATMENTS WORK

As with chlorpromazine, the discovery of many other effective psychotropics resulted more from chance observation than from rationally designed searches for new agents. Little was known about the biochemistry of mental disorders in the 1950s when these drugs were introduced. Subsequently, rigorous study in basic science laboratories to determine how these new drugs worked began to unravel the biochemical components of the major mental disorders. For example, the discovery that chlorpromazine and the other antipsychotic drugs all block the action of the neurotransmitter (chemical messenger) dopamine has led to the hypothesis that schizophrenia, the most devastating of the psychotic disorders, results at least in part from an overactivity of this same substance. Similarly, discovering that antidepressant drugs influence the monoamine neurotransmitters norepinephrine and serotonin makes it reasonable to implicate these neurotransmitter systems in the genesis of at least some major depressive disorders. (For a definition and discussion of neurotransmitters, see chapter 1, page 15.) Research into what electroshock therapy does to the biochemistry and

physiology of the brain no doubt will lead to further understanding of the mechanisms of depression and of psychosis.

Even without a full understanding of how the somatic treatments function, they nevertheless are used extensively today to ameliorate symptoms in most of the major psychiatric disorders. Psychotropic drugs play the largest role, though they are not the only form of treatment, nor are they always appropriate. Thus, for the best treatment of anxiety disorders, affective (mood) disorders, and psychotic disorders, it is essential to consult with a psychiatrist knowledgeable and skilled in the practice of *both* psychotherapy and pharmacotherapy, as drug treatment is often called.

Do Drugs "Cure" Mental Illness?

Antibiotics are prescribed to "cure" infections by helping to destroy the organisms that have invaded the body. Surgeons sometimes "cure" cancer by removing it with a scalpel. Much of the time, however, medical interventions *manage symptoms*, helping the person to be more able to function normally—without necessarily curing the underlying disease. For example, insulin is essential in managing diabetes, but it does not cure the underlying disease. Similarly, antihypertensives manage and even correct high blood pressure, but they do not alter the disorder that causes the blood pressure to be so high.

Numerous drugs used in psychiatry regularly produce results that may look like cures, in that a person's symptoms fade, signs of the illness disappear, and normal life resumes. Yet psychiatrists seldom say their patients are "cured." In large part this is because so much remains to be learned about why mental illness occurs in the first place, how drugs function to combat certain symptoms, and the conditions under which a mental illness may reappear.

A patient whose chronic depression dissipates with the help of drugs may continue to need drug treatment, along with psychotherapy when it is required. In a like manner, severe psychotic symptoms—hallucinations, delusions, and thought disorders in particular—often ebb with the help of antipsychotic drugs but, unfortunately, may recur when drugs are discontinued.

Modern psychiatry is finding that for anxiety disorders, affective (mood) disorders, and psychotic disorders, the best results are achieved by combining psychotherapy with drug treatments, although we still have much to learn about the nature of these interactions.

To best understand how drugs are used in psychiatric treatment, in addition to reading about each drug type in the next sections, the following chapters should be consulted: chapter 2 for how clinicians make treatment decisions, the chapters on the individual disorders, and chapter 6, concerning the effectiveness of treatment. In the discussion that follows, the generic or chemical name of a drug is given first, followed in parentheses by the trade name by which it is commonly sold.

ANTIANXIETY DRUGS (TRANQUILIZERS) AND SEDATIVE–HYPNOTICS (SLEEPING PILLS)

Technically termed anxiolytics and often called minor tranquilizers or antianxiety drugs, tranquilizers and sedative-hypnotics are used mainly for the short-term treatment of anxiety, tension, and fear. They are especially helpful when the anxiety is due to a clearly defined circumstance—impending surgery, an upcoming trip, or a situation expected to be traumatic.

In the sedative-hypnotic category are numerous anxiolytics that cause sleepiness among other major effects, as well as medications prescribed primarily for their sleep-inducing properties and used to treat such disorders as insomnia—sleeping pills, in other words.

The Benzodiazepines

Throughout history, many substances have been used for their calming effects. Alcohol is one of the oldest anxiolytics, and several herbs brewed into tea have been used similarly. In the nineteenth century, bromides were introduced as antianxiety agents, followed by barbiturates. The toxic or addictive side effects of most of the drugs led to the quest for safer chemicals. Today most drugs used to treat anxiety and related problems belong to the single chemical group known as benzodiazepines. Chlordiazepoxide (Librium) was the first benzodiazepine introduced, in 1960. Since then numerous additional benzodiazepines have been developed, among them diazepam (Valium) and, more recently, alprazolam (Xanax). While benzodiazepines are less dangerous than their predecessors, they too are not without substantial risk (see "Risks and Interactions" on page 66).

Despite their known dangers, benzodiazepines are widely prescribed. In an international survey of the United States and nine Western European countries, 10 to 17 percent of adults in each country reported using an antianxiety drug during the preceding year. The figure for the United States was about 15 percent.

How They Work

Benzodiazepines appear to enhance the actions of the neurotransmitter gamma-aminobutyric acid (GABA), which reduces nerve impulse transmissions and slows down certain brain activity. In the 1980s researchers discovered that some brain cells have receptors into which benzodiazepine molecules fit as neatly as a hand in a glove, leading to the supposition that these man-made drugs in some way emulate as-yet undiscovered chemicals made by the body that have a naturally tranquilizing effect. (For more on this topic see chapters 7 and 32.)

While all the major benzodiazepines are similar in their antianxiety, sedative, and/or sleep-inducing effects, they vary in the rate at which they remain active in the body. All benzodiazepines take effect fairly rapidly, usually within an hour or two. *Short-acting* benzodiazepines, whose effects last for only a few hours, usually are prescribed when the anxiety-producing event is likely to end soon afterward or when a physician wishes to keep a close watch on dosage levels (particularly in the elderly, who metabolize the drugs very slowly). For a continuing effect, they must be taken several times throughout the day. *Long-acting* benzodiazepines, which can be taken in a single daily dose, are prescribed when the need for the drug is expected to continue for a lengthy period. Regardless of length of activity, however, it takes about two days for all the effects of any benzodiazepine to disappear after the medication is discontinued.

Side Effects

The most prominent benzodiazepine side effects are sleepiness, drowsiness, and reduced coordination and alertness. These reactions usually become less of a problem after the first few weeks of treatment. Some people report that judgment and memory are affected when they begin taking these drugs or when they take the drugs occasionally, as for intermittent insomnia. Other symptoms, such as blurred vision, slurred speech, tremor, skin rash, excessive weight gain, hypotension (low blood pressure), and "sun-downing" (a disorientation that occurs among the elderly; see chapter 23) may develop. It is important to discuss with a physician what types of activities should be avoided while taking these drugs.

Euphoria (an exaggerated sense of well-being) is *not* a common side effect of benzodiazepines. There is some evidence, however, that children of alcoholics may react with euphoria and should be monitored very closely to prevent abuse.

Risks and Interactions

Benzodiazepines can produce physical dependency (addiction) if taken at a higher level or more frequently than the recommended dosage. Even at the dosages required for a therapeutic effect, some people will become addicted to these drugs. Sudden termination of antianxiety drugs after prolonged use is not recommended. Serious withdrawal symptoms—similar to the syndrome experienced by alcoholics who stop drinking—may develop following abrupt drug discontinuation, and sometimes even when the drug is tapered off under a doctor's guidance. For many people, abrupt withdrawal also produces a "rebound"

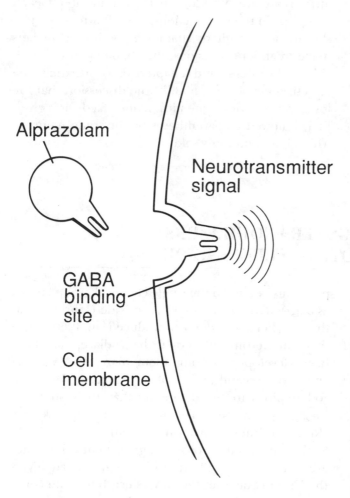

Alprazolam

Neurotransmitter signal

GABA binding site

Cell membrane

HOW PSYCHOACTIVE DRUGS WORK

Figure 5.1: A drug molecule—in this case from the benzodiazepine tranquilizer alprazolam (Xanax)—attaches to a receptor on the surface of a cell in the brain. After binding to the cell, the drug influences how the cell functions. Here it is transmitting a signal that enhances the calming effects of the GABA neurotransmitter—hence the drug's tranquilizing capabilities.

effect, during which symptoms for which the drugs were prescribed return more strongly than before. Although not definitively proven, there is some evidence that benzodiazepine use during the first trimester of pregnancy may lead to an increased incidence of cleft lip and cleft palate. Therefore, benzodiazepine use during early pregnancy is in general avoided.

Benzodiazepine overdose is a life-threatening emergency. People who take such an overdose become very drowsy or stuporous and fall into a deep sleep. In combination with alcohol or other drugs, an overdose can lead to death. Children and physically ailing people are at greater risk of a benzodiazepine overdose.

Alcohol and other central nervous system depressants increase the sedative effect of benzodiazepines. The combination can cause severe intoxication and even death. Therefore, when taking benzodiazepines, a person should not drink any alcohol or take other drugs (including tranquilizers, sleeping pills, barbiturates, narcotics, antihistamines, or anticonvulsants), unless specifically prescribed by a doctor. Benzodiazepines can be safely used with many other medications, however, if approved by the treating doctor. Patients always should tell a doctor or dentist who prescribes any drug that they are taking benzodiazepines. Likewise, they should tell the doctor who prescribes benzodiazepines that they are taking other drugs.

Other Drugs Used for Anxiety and Sleep Problems

One recently developed antianxiety drug, buspirone (BuSpar), carries a dramatically lower risk of dependency and addiction than the benzodiazepines, even though its antianxiety effects are very similar. Numerous other compounds without the major dangers of benzodiazepines are under investigation.

Beta-blocking drugs such as propranolol (Inderal), primarily used to treat high blood pressure, have shown some promise in lessening the symptoms of anxiety, especially those associated with performance anxiety. The use of these drugs in treating anxiety is currently under investigation.

Barbiturates—potent drugs including phenobarbital and secobarbital, among others—are still used in the short-term treatment of insomnia for people who cannot tolerate benzodiazepines, but they produce a high rate of mental confusion, are addictive, and carry greater overdose risks than benzodiazepines. Chloral hydrate, another choice for insomnia, often causes stomach disturbances.

Antidepressants have proved to be highly effective in the treatment of panic attacks.

COMMONLY PRESCRIBED TRANQUILIZERS AND SLEEPING PILLS

Benzodiazepines

Alprazolam (Xanax)	Lorazepam (Ativan)
Chlordiazepoxide (Librium)	Oxazepam (Serax)
Clonazepam (Klonopin)	Prazepam (Centrax)
Clorazepate (Tranxene)	Temazepam (Restoril)
Diazepam (Valium)	Triazolam (Halcion)
Flurazepam (Dalmane)	

Other Agents

Buspirone (BuSpar)	Hydroxyzine (Atarax, Vistaril)
Chlormezanone (Trancopal)	Meprobamate (Equanil, Miltown)

ANTIDEPRESSANTS

The most widely known antidepressants, available since the late 1950s, fall into two major classes—tricyclic antidepressants (TCAs) and monoamine oxidase inhibitors (MAOIs). In recent years additional agents—the so-called second-generation antidepressants—have been introduced, including serotonin reuptake inhibitors such as fluoxetine (Prozac), which are chemically unrelated to other available antidepressant agents.

In addition to the treatment of depression, antidepressants are often prescribed for anxiety disorders and eating disorders.

How They Work

TCAs, MAOIs, and the second-generation antidepressants by somewhat different mechanisms increase the amount or concentration of *monoamines*, which are neurotransmitters that are vital to mood regulation. The TCAs and the MAOIs influence the monoamines norepinephrine and serotonin, while the second-generation antidepressant fluoxetine, for example, affects primarily serotonin.

Treatment is similar regardless of the type of drug selected. Antidepressants are given most often in gradually increasing doses until a distinct therapeutic effect is achieved. (Treatment sometimes fails because insufficient doses were prescribed or because the drug was prescribed for too little time; see chapter 6.) For some people, antidepressants may take effect within a few days. For most people, the depression will begin to lift within weeks. If the depression continues after six weeks of treatment, generally the physician will switch to a different drug.

After the drug achieves its antidepressant effect, treatment continues for at least six months. Many individuals continue on the medication for a year or more to prevent relapse. Even though antidepressants are *not* addictive, it is important to taper off them slowly, in order to prevent a rapid return of symptoms.

Antidepressant Side Effects

Although the antidepressant effects of these drugs may be slow to appear, their side effects usually appear more rapidly—which may have some benefits. Because of a drug's initially sedating side effects, for example, the depressed person with insomnia may finally be able to sleep through the night. Likewise, the person who has had no appetite may begin to feel hungry again.

On the other hand, side effects may be an additional burden for a person already suffering from depression severe enough to warrant medication. Most of the side effects lessen or disappear alto-

BASIC RULES FOR DRUG USE

When taking psychotropic drugs, remember that:

- Only a medical doctor can determine which psychotropic drugs, if any, may help in a specific situation.
- Only a medical doctor can safely substitute drugs or change dosages.
- Take drugs exactly as prescribed. There are specific reasons why some drugs have to be taken before meals, others at bedtime, and so on.
- Always mention to your doctor any effects you experience while taking a drug. Only the physician can properly evaluate their importance, suggest ways to counteract them, change dosages, or prescribe another drug.
- Never abruptly stop taking psychotropic drugs that you have been taking regularly, even if you feel better. Consult your doctor about whether the time is right to stop taking the medication and how you can safely taper off the medication, if that is appropriate.
- If you have any questions about a drug, talk to your doctor. If you are not satisfied with the answers, get another opinion.

- Don't use more than one drug at a time unless your doctor is aware of it and has approved the combination. Remember, alcohol is a drug too; avoid drinking when taking psychotropic drugs. Tell your doctor if you smoke, since nicotine can alter metabolism of some drugs.
- Always tell all doctors or dentists you consult exactly which medications you are taking, including all "over-the-counter" (nonprescription) medications. If they don't ask, volunteer the information.
- Store drugs in the containers in which they were supplied, with labels intact. Keep containers tightly closed and out of extreme heat, cold, and dampness.
- Always keep all drugs out of the reach of children. A locked drawer is a good place to store drugs safely if children are present; the bathroom medicine cabinet is not.
- If you think you are experiencing unusually serious drug side effects, an allergic reaction, or an overdose, go to a hospital emergency room immediately. Take the medicine bottle with you so hospital personnel can identify the drug quickly and administer the appropriate treatment.

gether as treatment continues, and when they are troublesome the doctor can manage them in many ways. He or she may choose to cut back on the dose until side effects become tolerable, increasing to an effective dose more slowly. In some cases the physician may instruct the patient to take the drug in one daily dose at night, so that by morning the intense sedating effect of certain antidepressants will have passed. With those antidepressants that produce insomnia, the doctor also may prescribe sleeping pills for the first week or two of therapy. Or the doctor may switch to another antidepressant with a different side effect profile.

In general, TCAs and MAOIs are associated with either more or more intense side effects than the second-generation antidepressants. Nonetheless, all have at least some side effects, especially early in treatment. To determine the side effects that have been known to occur with any drug that a doctor prescribes, ask the doctor or the pharmacist who fills the prescription. The most common side effects associated with antidepressants as a whole (which vary from drug to drug) are: dry mouth, blurred vision, poor memory, constipation, diarrhea, difficulty urinating or frequent need to urinate, nausea, daytime sedation, insomnia, weight changes, sensitivity to sunlight, changes in sexual response, altered sense of taste, and headaches.

Some people may experience low blood pressure, particularly when they stand up; this is termed "postural" or "orthostatic hypotension" and can be dangerous, particularly for elderly individuals. Avoiding sudden changes in posture and learning to flex leg and calf muscles before standing up may help. If the problem persists, the doctor may decide to change to a different drug or—if the drug is otherwise helping in eliminating the depression—add an additional medication to counteract the side effect.

Antidepressants may impair mental and physical abilities. Persons taking these drugs should avoid activities requiring alertness and good coordination, such as driving a car or operating machinery, especially in the initial weeks.

As with any medication, some people may develop an allergic reaction; if a rash develops, the treating doctor should be contacted immediately. In addition to possible allergic reaction, the following serious side effects, although they occur rarely, should be reported immediately: convulsions, hallucinations, balance problems, bleeding, fever, yellowing eyes or skin, and difficulty breathing.

All side effects should be discussed with the physician, especially those that are frightening or persistently troublesome. He or she will offer advice on how to manage the symptoms or provide reassurance that drug therapy is proceeding normally. Enough antidepressants currently are available that the vast majority of people with major depression will be able to find relief without being defeated by side effects.

Tricyclic Antidepressants (TCAs)

Imipramine, the first TCA, was being studied in the late 1950s as a possible antipsychotic agent but was found instead to have antidepressant properties. Since then more than a dozen other TCAs have been developed.

TCAs are often the first choice for the treatment of most types of depression. A number of studies and a wealth of clinical experience also have shown them to be highly effective in the treatment of panic attacks and of bulimia. Some new TCAs appear promising for the treatment of obsessive-compulsive disorder.

Although the different TCAs are considered to be about equally effective in the average case of depression, individual characteristics make one preferable over another in specific cases. For example, some cause drowsiness and may be selected for people suffering from insomnia. Others have stimulating effects, making them preferable for those who need to remain alert at work.

Risks and Interactions

TCAs generally are not prescribed for anyone who has heart disease or urinary problems, among other medical conditions. Usually a complete physical examination is recommended before beginning antidepressant therapy.

Although antidepressants have not been proven to cause birth defects, their use during pregnancy and nursing should be discussed with the treating doctor.

TCAs interact with several widely used drugs, especially alcohol and medications used to treat high blood pressure. People using TCAs who drink alcohol become intoxicated more quickly, and the TCA side effects are likely to be enhanced. Combining TCAs with antihypertensive medications can lead to an excessive drop in blood pressure. Many other medications, among them sedatives, thyroid drugs, oral contraceptives, and blood-thinning drugs, also interact with TCAs.

A TCA overdose can result in life-threatening heart failure or fibrillations. Persons who suspect they have taken an overdose or who are experiencing any serious side effects should go to a hospital emergency room immediately. The medicine bottle should be taken so hospital personnel can quickly identify the drug and provide appropriate treatment.

TCAs have been used to commit suicide. Because depressed patients have a high suicide rate, the doctor may choose to prescribe only a few days' supply at a time.

Monoamine Oxidase Inhibitors (MAOIs)

Iproniazid, the first MAOI marketed for the treatment of depression, was originally developed to treat tuberculosis. After its mood-elevating effect on tuberculous patients was noted, the drug swiftly emerged as a treatment for depression. Other MAOIs were soon developed. Although several were withdrawn from the market because of their toxicity, three MAOIs are available in the United States to treat depression: phenelzine (Nardil), tranylcypromine (Parnate), and isocarboxazid (Marplan).

Because of dangers associated with MAOIs when they were first introduced, psychiatrists used to prescribe them only for people who failed to respond to TCA treatment. Now that the major risk of MAOIs can be prevented (see "Risks and Interactions" below and tables 5.1 and 5.2 on pages 71 and 72), psychiatrists are much more willing to prescribe them in lieu of TCAs, especially for people suffering from so-called atypical depression (marked by "reverse" symptoms, such as increased rather than decreased appetite and increased need for sleep rather than insomnia; see chapter 12); as well as anxiety and phobias that do not respond to other treatment.

Risks and Interactions

MAOIs can interact with a number of foods and drugs to produce a *hypertensive crisis*—a sudden, potentially life-threatening rise in blood pressure. People using these drugs, and their families, should learn to recognize the early signs of hypertensive crisis: heart palpitations, chest pain, irregular heart rhythms, heavy sweating, nausea, dizziness, vomiting, and most notably, a severe pounding headache. If any of these symptoms appear, it is *essential*

to visit a hospital emergency room immediately, where the hypertensive crisis can be treated rapidly and effectively with intravenous phentolamine (Regitine).

This risk can be eliminated by avoiding the foods and drugs listed in table 5.1. All these substances contain *pressor agents,* which can cause blood pressure to rise. Foods containing *tyramine,* which is usually produced as foods (such as cheese) age, ferment, or decay, are particularly dangerous.

Obviously, MAOIs are appropriate only for those people who are willing and able to adhere to strict dietary restrictions.

MAOIs will increase the effects of alcohol, sedatives, antianxiety drugs, and pain medication, possibly past the margin of safety. Patients requiring surgery may need to discontinue MAOIs in order to avoid adverse reactions to drugs administered before, during, and after surgery.

Note that the effects of MAOIs persist days to weeks after the drugs are stopped. Thus, while a person may no longer be taking MAOIs, the drugs can still result in dangerous interactions. The dietary and drug restrictions should be observed for at least two weeks after MAOI therapy is completed.

COMMONLY PRESCRIBED ANTIDEPRESSANTS

Tricyclics (TCAs)

Amitriptyline (Elavil, Endep)	Imipramine (Tofranil)
Clomipramine (Anafranil)	Nortriptyline (Pamelor)
Desipramine (Norpramin, Pertofrane)	Protryptiline (Vivactil)
Doxepin (Adapin, Sinequan)	Trimipramine (Surmontil)

Monoamine Oxidase Inhibitors (MAOIs)

Isocarboxazid (Marplan)	Tranylcypromine (Parnate)
Phenelzine (Nardil)	

Second-Generation Antidepressants

Amoxapine (Asendin)	Paroxetine (Paxil)
Bupropion (Wellbutrin)	Sertraline (Zoloft)
Fluoxetine (Prozac)	Trazodone (Desyrel)
Maprotiline (Ludiomil)	

Table 5.1 DIETARY RESTRICTIONS FOR PATIENTS TAKING MAOIs

(Avoid 1 day before and 2 weeks after taking drugs)

Danger of Blood Pressure Rise
*Minimal Danger   **Moderate Danger   ***Very Dangerous

A. *Foods*

1. *** All cheese

   *** All foods containing cheese (for example, pizza, fondue, many Italian dishes, and salad dressings)

   SAFE Fresh cottage cheese, cream cheese, and yogurt are safe in moderate amounts

   ** Sour cream

2. ** All fermented or aged foods, especially aged meats or aged fish (for example, aged corned beef, salami, fermented sausage, pepperoni, summer sausage, pickled herring)

3. ** Liver (chicken, beef, or pork)

   ** Liverwurst

4. *** Broad bean *pods* (English bean pods, Chinese pea pods)

5. ** Meat extracts or yeast extracts (for example, Bovril or Marmite)

   SAFE Baked products raised with yeast (for example, bread) are safe

   SAFE Yeast is safe

6. ** Spoiled fruit (for example, spoiled bananas, pineapple, avocados, figs, raisins)

   SAFE Fresh fruits are safe

B. *Drinks*

1. ** Red wine, sherry, vermouth, cognac

2. ** Beer and ale

3. SAFE Other alcoholic drinks are permitted in *true moderation* (for example, gin, vodka, whiskey)

C. *Drugs*

1. *** Cold medications (for example, Dristan, Contac)

2. *** Nasal decongestants and sinus medicine

3. *** Asthma inhalants

   SAFE Pure steroid asthma inhalants (for example, Vanceril) are safe

4. ** Allergy and hay fever medication

   SAFE Pure antihistamines (chlorpheniramine, brompheniramine)

5. *** Demerol

   SAFE Other narcotics (for example, codeine)—use lower doses

6. *** Amphetamines

   ** Antiappetite (diet) medicine

7. ** a. Sympathomimetic amines—direct acting: for example, epinephrine, isoproterenol, methoxamine, levarterenol (norepinephrine)

   *** b. Indirect acting: amphetamines, methylphenidate, phenylpropanolamine, ephedrine, cyclopentamine, pseudoephedrine, tyramine

   *** c. Direct and indirect acting: metaraminol, phenylephrine

8. ** a. Local anesthetics with epinephrine

   SAFE b. Local anesthetics without epinephrine (for example, Carbacaine Hydrochloride)

9. ** Levodopa for parkinsonism

   ** Dopamine

10. Blood sugar Diabetics on insulin may have increased hypoglycemia requiring a decreased dose of insulin (otherwise safe)

11. Blood Pressure (decreased)

    Patients on hypotensive agents for high blood pressure may have more hypotension requiring a decrease in their use of hypotensive agent (otherwise safe)

The following foods have been rarely reported to cause hypertensive reactions with MAOIs. The evidence supporting these claims is weak and often based on a single isolated case. Warnings based on such evidence have been uncritically perpetuated especially in view of the large numbers of patients on MAOIs who ate these foods with no problem.

In practice, a blanket prohibition of these foods seems unjustified, unless they are clearly spoiled or decayed, and except for specific patients in whom they have already caused symptoms.

Danger of Blood Pressure Rise

*Anchovies	*Curry powder	*Sauerkraut
*Beet root (beets)	*Figs, raisins, dates	*Snails
*Caviar	*Junket	*Soy sauce
*Chocolate	*Licorice	*Worcestershire
*Coffee	*Mushrooms	sauce
*Colas	*Rhubarb	

Source: *The Psychiatric Times*, March 1987.

Table 5.2   INSTRUCTIONS FOR PATIENTS TAKING MAOIs

While taking this medication:

1. Avoid all the food and drugs mentioned on the list in Table 5.1. Be particularly careful to avoid those foods and drugs with two and three stars.
2. In general, all the foods you should avoid are decayed, fermented, or aged in some way. Avoid *any* spoiled food even if it is not on the list.
3. If you get a cold or flu, you may use aspirin or Tylenol. For a cough, glycerin cough drops or *plain* Robitussin may be used.
4. All laxatives or stool softeners for constipation may be used.
5. For infections, all antibiotics may be safely prescribed (for example, penicillin, tetracycline, erythromycin).
6. Avoid all other medications without first checking with your doctor. This includes any over-the-counter medicines bought without prescription (for example, cold tablets, nose drops, cough medicine, diet pills).
7. Eating one of the restricted foods may cause a sudden elevation of your blood pressure. When this occurs, you get an explosive headache, particularly in the back of your head and temples. Your head and face will feel flushed and full, your heart may pound and you may perspire heavily and feel nauseated.
8. If you need medical or dental care while on this medication, show these restrictions and instructions to the doctor. Have the doctor call the physician who prescribed the MAOIs if he or she has any questions or needs further clarification or information.
9. Side effects such as postural light-headedness, constipation, delay in urination, delay in ejaculation and orgasm, muscle twitching, sedation, fluid retention, insomnia, and excess sweating are quite common. Many of these side effects lessen considerably after the third week.
10. Light-headedness may occur following sudden changes in position. This can be avoided by getting up slowly. If tablets are taken with meals, this and the other side effects are lessened.
11. The medication is rarely effective in less than three weeks.
12. Care should be taken while operating any machinery or while driving, because some patients have episodes of sleepiness in the early phase of treatment.
13. Take the medication precisely as directed. Do not regulate the number of pills without first consulting your doctor.
14. In spite of the side effects and special dietary restrictions, your medication (an MAOI inhibitor) is safe and effective when taken as directed.
15. If any special problems arise, call your doctor.

Source: *The Psychiatric Times,* March 1987.

Even though there is no evidence that MAOIs cause birth defects, the use of these drugs during pregnancy and nursing should be discussed with the treating doctor.

MAOI overdose is marked by intensification of the common side effects and may also include increased anxiety, confusion, and a hypertensive crisis. MAOI overdose is a medical emergency and must be treated immediately. As with TCAs, MAOIs may be dispensed a few days' supply at a time for suicidal people.

Also as with TCAs, a physical examination may precede MAOI therapy.

Second-Generation Antidepressants

Until the 1980s TCAs and MAOIs were the only types of antidepressant drugs known. While clinical experience with these drugs is long and favorable, the search has continued for other, more effective types of antidepressants with fewer side effects. Included among newer formulations are the so-called *tetracyclics* (chemically related to the TCAs), such as maprotiline (Ludiomil), and various unrelated drugs, including trazodone (Desyrel) and bupropion (Wellbutrin). The most rapidly developing drugs in this group are the serotonin reuptake inhibitors, with fluoxetine (Prozac), sertraline (Zoloft), and paroxetine (Paxil) currently available and fluvoxamine presently in development. Trazodone, fluoxetine, sertraline, paroxetine, and fluvoxamine are believed to work primarily by affecting the serotonin system in the brain.

While none of these newer drugs necessarily is more effective than the TCAs or MAOIs, their emergence is important for two reasons. First, they may work for people who have failed to find relief with other antidepressants. Second, they have a different spectrum of side effects (see page 73). For example, fluoxetine (Prozac) has become widely used because it has a low incidence of unpleasant side effects for most people and because it often produces weight loss rather than weight gain. Many clinicians now prescribe one or another of these second-generation drugs as a first choice, switching to the older varieties if treatment fails. Clinicians with many years of experience with TCAs and MAOIs, however, may prefer to rely on the drugs whose effects they know well.

Side Effects, Risks, and Interactions

Second-generation antidepressants may be freer of unpleasant side effects than TCAs and MAOIs. They are notably freer of effects on the heart than are TCAs and risk of hypertensive crisis than are MAOIs. Some of the drugs, fluoxetine, sertraline, and paroxetine included, have fewer of the annoying so-called anticholinergic side effects—such as dry mouth, blurred vision, and constipation.

Still, no drug is free of side effects or risks. Depending on the particular drug, second-generation antidepressants may present an increased risk of seizures; affect sexual functioning; and cause agitation, insomnia, headaches, nausea, weight changes, and dizziness. Reports that fluoxetine (Prozac) substantially increases risks of suicide and homicide remain unproven. As with other antidepressants, most of the side effects diminish as the body adjusts to the medication. Other medications, such as beta-blockers for agitation and benzodiazepines for insomnia, can often help during the adjustment process. Precautions about use during pregnancy and nursing are the same as for other classes of antidepressants. Additional side effects and risks may become apparent as experience with these drugs increases.

These drugs, like other antidepressants, interact with sedatives and alcohol. Some types will interact with thyroid medication, blood thinners (anticoagulants), blood pressure medications, oral contraceptives, and anticonvulsants, among other medications.

ANTIPSYCHOTICS

Also known as *neuroleptics,* antipsychotics dramatically reduce agitation, paranoia, delusions, hallucinations, bizarre behavior, and thought disorder—the so-called positive psychotic symptoms—in a variety of psychotic disorders. They are often used in psychotic dementia and in the treatment of mania, with or without psychosis. Two neuroleptics, haloperidol (Haldol) and pimozide (Orap), are approved by the Food and Drug Administration (FDA) for use in the treatment of Tourette's syndrome, a neuropsychiatric disorder characterized by involuntary movements and vocalizations. Haloperidol is also approved as an antipsychotic. While antipsychotics are sometimes called major tranquilizers, they are not recommended for the treatment of anxiety.

With the exception of clozapine (Clozaril) and pimozide (Orap), these drugs are less effective for the "negative" psychotic symptoms, such as the blunted emotional response and emotional and social withdrawal characteristic of schizophrenia.

How They Work

Since it began the psychotropic drug revolution in the early 1950s, chlorpromazine (Thorazine) has been joined by more than 30 additional antipsychotics. While they differ in their chemical structures, have different rates of onset, and have varying degrees of potency, they all eventually trigger roughly the same therapeutic response. This is because they all work by blocking the neurotransmitter dopamine—a fact that suggests that many of the symptoms of psychosis may result from too much dopamine activity in the brain.

As with antidepressants, antipsychotics are prescribed in gradually increasing doses until a noticeable therapeutic effect is achieved. Psychiatrists tend to select a particular antipsychotic based on its side effect profile; they switch to a different drug if a patient shows unusual sensitivity to the first one selected.

In many chronic psychotic conditions, discontinuation of these drugs after prolonged use causes a return of symptoms. The requirement for long-term maintenance therapy increases the risks of some serious side effects associated with antipsychotic drugs.

Managing the Major Risks

Except for clozapine (which has its own risks, discussed on page 74), all the antipsychotics produce motor (movement) side effects, known as *extrapyramidal symptoms.*

Early Extrapyramidal Symptoms

Early extrapyramidal symptoms are treatable and appear within hours to days after the start of antipsychotic therapy. They take three major forms.

Acute dystonia. This is an infrequent but severe muscular reaction, characterized by uncoordinated, spasmodic, involuntary body movements, and painful muscle spasms of the extremities, face, and neck.

Akathisia. This is an involuntary motor restlessness and pacing, or inability to sit still, often accompanied by anxiety or agitation.

Parkinson's syndrome. This mimics Parkinson's disease, with its characteristic shuffling gait, tremors, rigidity, and masklike expression.

Early extrapyramidal symptoms usually can be controlled with antiparkinson medication, in particular drugs called "anticholinergics," which include benztropine (Cogentin), trihexiphenidyl (Artane), and amantadine (Symmetrel). If the akathisia fails to respond to these medications, beta-blocking drugs such as propranolol (Inderal) or a benzodiazepine anticonvulsant drug, clonazepam (Klonopin), may work well.

Tardive Dyskinesia

Tardive dyskinesia is a neurological syndrome characterized by involuntary rhythmic movements, especially of the lips, tongue, and jaw, such as unintended protrusion of the tongue, chewing movements, and puckering of the cheeks. Sometimes these movements are accompanied by involuntary movements of arms and legs. These symptoms are scarcely noticeable in some people, but grossly disfiguring in others.

Tardive dyskinesia can occur at any age, but the risk appears to increase with age. In elderly people, the severity is often greater as well, and the chance for spontaneous remission diminishes. Women and people on high-dose therapy seem to be at increased risk.

There is no known treatment for tardive dyskinesia, although lithium is being tested as a possible preventive (see page 75). Tardive dyskinesia is associated with all antipsychotic drugs currently in use except clozapine, regardless of potency level or chemical class. Once the symptoms of tardive dyskinesia occur, the psychiatrist will discontinue antipsychotic treatment, unless the drugs are absolutely vital to the patient. As a preventive measure, antipsychotic medications should always be used conservatively, at the lowest effective dosage levels or for the shortest time possible. To reduce the risk in people with chronic schizophrenia, whose ability to manage their lives often depends on maintenance therapy with antipsychotics, experts in psychopharmacology strongly recommend reducing dose levels, taking drug "holidays" (periods in which no drugs are taken), and other strategies to minimize drug exposure.

Neuroleptic Malignant Syndrome (NMS)

Neuroleptic malignant syndrome (NMS) is a rare but exceedingly dangerous side effect that produces profound muscle rigidity throughout the body, often causes severe kidney damage, and can result in death. When symptoms appear, all antipsychotic drugs must be withdrawn immediately and emergency medical care provided. Treatments for NMS include amantadine (Symmetrel), bromocriptine (Parlodel), and dantrolene (Dantrium).

Other Risks and Drug Interactions

Clozapine (Clozaril) causes a reversible lowering of one component of the white blood cells (the granulocytes) in a very small percentage of those persons treated for more than four weeks. Because of this risk, it can be prescribed only to patients who comply with mandatory weekly blood tests. Clozapine also carries a slight risk of seizures.

All neuroleptics, except possibly clozapine, cause a sustained increase in levels of a hormone called prolactin, leading to *neuroendocrine side effects* in some people. Symptoms include lactation (the production of breast milk not related to childbirth, technically called *galactorrhea*), breast tenderness and swelling, decreased sexual interest, menstrual abnormalities or even cessation, and possible weight gain. Fortunately, neuroendocrine side effects are at least partially treatable with amantadine (Symmetrel) and with bromocriptine (Parlodel).

Some data suggest the possibility of a slightly increased incidence of birth defects when the fetus is exposed to antipsychotics during the first trimester. Therefore, if clinically possible, these drugs should be reduced or discontinued during pregnancy. They should also be withheld if the mother plans to nurse her baby, as antipsychotics will enter breast milk and expose the fetus to unwanted side effects. However, stopping the medication may not be a better option when a return of symptoms will jeopardize the life of a developing fetus or a newborn. If the mother must take antipsychotics, she should not breast-feed her newborn.

Antipsychotics interact with a variety of other drugs, including alcohol, antihistamines, sedatives, sleeping medications, barbiturates, tranquilizers, and narcotics. Such combinations can increase the strength of both the antipsychotic and the other

---

**Commonly Prescribed
Antipsychotics**

Chlorpromazine (Thorazine)
Chlorprothixene (Taractan)
Clozapine (Clozaril)
Fluphenazine (Prolixin, Permitil)
Haloperidol (Haldol)
Loxapine (Loxitane)
Mesoridazine (Serentil)
Molindone (Moban)
Pimozide (Orap)
   (Note: While FDA-approved in this country only for the treatment of Tourette's disorder, pimozide has been shown to be an effective antipsychotic agent.)
Thioridazine (Mellaril)
Thiothixene (Navane)
Trifluoperazine (Stelazine)

---

drug unpredictably. Antipsychotics also block the effects of several medications prescribed for high blood pressure, while at the same time directly inducing low blood pressure, so that blood pressure should be checked periodically.

Overdoses of antipsychotics are rare and seldom fatal. Signs of an overdose are usually the intensification of the transitory side effects listed below or symptoms of depression.

Transitory Side Effects

Side effects that often diminish during treatment include drowsiness, dizziness, and faintness. People experiencing these symptoms should refrain from activities requiring alertness or good coordination and avoid sudden changes in posture. Other possible side effects include dry mouth, nasal congestion, nausea, urinary retention, constipation, menstrual changes, sexual dysfunction, and blurred vision. Antipsychotics can cause increased sensitivity to sunlight, including a tendency to burn more quickly than usual; prolonged exposure to the sun should be avoided and sunscreening agents and protective clothing should be used.

LITHIUM

Lithium, a naturally occurring salt, is the treatment of choice in the manic phase of bipolar (manic-depressive) disorder. It restores normal sleep patterns and eradicates characteristic symptoms such as rapid speech, hyperactive movements, elation, grandiose ideas, poor judgment, aggressiveness, and hostility. Between 7 and 8 out of every 10 manic people respond well to lithium.

Lithium is also used as a maintenance drug, preventing or reducing the severity of future attacks of acute mania as well as of depression, to which people with bipolar disorder are also subject. With sustained medical supervision, lithium is a safe maintenance medication.

For some people, lithium may be prescribed for the treatment of acute depressive episodes in bipolar illness, especially if other treatments have failed. Sometimes lithium is used to augment the action of standard antidepressants in the treatment of major depression.

Depending on results of current research, lithium may become an accepted treatment for cluster headaches and for episodic aggression, as well as in preventing tardive dyskinesia (see page 74) and in restoring white blood cell count in patients on anti-cancer drugs. Lithium also may have a better impact on immune function than the antidepressants, so it may have a role in the treatment of people with both depression and HIV infection.

How It Works

Lithium alters the movement of sodium in nerves and muscles, and affects the way certain chemicals in the body are metabolized. It is not known exactly how lithium affects the manic phase of bipolar illness, but it is often effective within 4 to 10 days. It has no significant mood-changing effect on healthy people.

Australian psychiatrist John Cade first observed its effectiveness against acute mania by chance in 1949. In Europe and Australia, lithium was quickly accepted as a valid treatment. However, it was not approved by the U.S. Food and Drug Administration for treatment of acute manic episodes until 1970, over 20 years after its discovery, and its use as a maintenance drug was not approved until 1974. In the United States it has become widely prescribed only in the past decade, and there is considerable evidence that it still may be underprescribed.

Some of the delay in accepting lithium resulted from its reputation as dangerous and potentially lethal. The misconception stemmed in part from early use of lithium as a sodium substitute for heart patients, which resulted in numerous cardiac deaths. Only later was it learned that the drug is particularly dangerous when used by people with low sodium levels.

Risks and Interactions

The therapeutic dosage of lithium is very close to the amount capable of causing severe adverse reactions, some of which can be life-threatening. A mild lithium overdose can lead to general weakness, blurred vision, drowsiness, diarrhea, vomiting, and tremors, while a serious overdose can result in seizures and coma. Prior to prescribing lithium, a patient's overall physical status—sodium levels as well as thyroid, heart, and in particular kidney functions—must be evaluated. To maintain proper lithium levels in blood and to prevent adverse effects, tests should continue throughout the drug's use, even if no side effects occur.

Because there is evidence that lithium can cause birth defects, in particular cardiac malformations, lithium therapy should stop during the first trimester of pregnancy. As lithium is excreted in breast milk, the new mother and her doctors should discuss the pros and cons of nursing or of going off the drug.

Concerns about lithium causing long-term kidney damage appear unwarranted, as long as the drug is held to appropriate levels. Overdosage may lead to irreversible kidney damage, however. People on long-term maintenance therapy are kept on the lowest effective dose.

Lithium interacts with a variety of drugs, both prescribed and over-the-counter. Such interactions can increase or decrease the effect of the drug significantly, so it is very important that no other drug be taken with lithium without the doctor's knowledge and approval. As the amount of salt and fluids in the diet will affect lithium levels, people taking the drug should keep salt intake relatively constant and drink plenty of water.

FDA APPROVED: WHAT DOES IT MEAN?

Before a manufacturer can make a drug commercially available, the U.S. Food and Drug Administration (FDA) must approve its release. Approval is a long procedure involving considerable documentation of the drug's risks and safety. In the final stages of the process, the FDA must approve the wording on the informational package insert that accompanies all containers of each drug. The insert lists all FDA-approved uses of the drug that the manufacturer may claim and for which the manufacturer can promote the drug.

However, physicians are never limited to prescribing a medication only for those conditions that the FDA has approved. On the contrary, *if clinical and scientific evidence demonstrates that the drug is useful in a particular condition,* even if this use is not labeled on the package or officially approved by the FDA, it is legally acceptable for doctors to prescribe the drug for their patients.

Many state-of-the-art treatments in psychiatry (and other fields of medicine) represent non-FDA-approved uses of otherwise approved drugs. Antidepressants for bulimia, beta-blockers for some forms of anxiety, anticonvulsants for bipolar disorder—all are acceptable treatments that doctors may use as long as they can demonstrate that the treatment is indicated in the specific clinical instance.

Common Side Effects

Side effects that may appear for a brief period soon after lithium therapy begins include feelings of being slightly tired, dazed, or sleepy, as well as slurred speech, muscle weakness, nausea, stomach cramps, weight gain, swelling of ankles and wrists, impotence or reduction in sexual ability, and skin irritation.

Because lithium sometimes impairs coordination and alertness, activities such as driving a car or operating machinery should be avoided until those side effects diminish.

If they occur at all, a few minor side effects tend to persist for the duration of the lithium treatment, among them excessive thirst, hand tremors, and increased urination.

People taking lithium as maintenance treatment for bipolar illness sometimes complain about being less creative. This feeling may result more from the leveling out of their mood swings than from an actual decrease in creativity.

All side effects, however minor they may seem, should be reported to the doctor.

ANTICONVULSANTS

A small number of drugs that help control the kinds of convulsions (seizures) common in epilepsy are proving promising for the treatment of aggression, violence, impulsiveness, and hostile behavior that do not respond to other treatments. Studies also show these drugs to be effective against bipolar disorder, especially when characterized by rapid mood swings, in people who do not respond to lithium.

How They Work

The most widely used anticonvulsant for treating bipolar disorder is carbamazepine (Tegretol). How it works is unknown. Another anticonvulsant drug with mood-stabilizing properties, valproate (Depakene or Depakote), appears to affect the action of the neurotransmitter gamma-aminobutyric acid (GABA).

Risks, Side Effects, and Interactions

On rare occasions, carbamazepine (Tegretol) causes bone marrow suppression compromising blood cell-production and making periodic blood tests necessary during treatment. Although usually quite safe when prescribed to a healthy adult, valproate (Depakene or Depakote) may cause severe and even fatal liver damage. To be on the safe side, valproate should not be used by anyone suffering from liver disease. An overdose can result in deep coma and excessive bleeding and requires immediate medical attention. Possible side effects of valproate that may diminish with treatment include nausea, vomiting, indigestion, diarrhea, abdominal cramps, appetite disturbances, sleepiness, weakness, and partial hair loss.

Valproate is excreted in breast milk and should be used by nursing women only if absolutely necessary.

Valproate interacts strongly with depressant drugs such as barbiturates and should not be used simultaneously with them except under close medical supervision. Alcohol and over-the-counter drugs such as decongestants and cough medicines should be avoided while using valproate.

PSYCHOSTIMULANTS

Psychostimulants are not widely used for treating psychiatric disorders. However, for childhood attention-deficit hyperactivity disorder (ADHD) (see chapter 17), they are the best treatment available.

For ADHD, the drugs of choice are dextroamphetamine (Dexedrine), methylphenidate (Ritalin), and pemoline (Cylert). While these compounds function as stimulants in most people, they permit children with ADHD to resume normal school work and concentrate for longer periods on a single subject.

Various amphetamines and methylphenidate are also sometimes prescribed for narcolepsy (see chapter 12) and on a short-term basis as an adjunct treatment for depression that has not responded adequately to standard treatment. (However, their use for depression has not received FDA approval; the physician prescribing psychostimulants for this purpose should thoroughly explain why the drug's use may be advantageous and how long the patient should expect to take it.)

Psychostimulants are no longer approved as appetite suppressants.

How They Work

These stimulating and arousing drugs increase the amount and activity of the *catecholamines* group of neurotransmitters, including norepinephrine. These drugs are potentially addictive, however. Therefore they should be used for brief periods only, then withdrawn slowly under a doctor's close supervision. Withdrawal symptoms can include psychotic episodes and a depressive "crash," with sudden sharp episodes of crying and feelings of worthlessness.

Risks, Side Effects, and Interactions

Methylphenidate (Ritalin) should not be used by people with glaucoma, psychotic symptoms, seizure disorders, or high blood pressure. Side

NUTRITIONAL THERAPY

Some researchers have suggested that nutritional supplements might be helpful as psychiatric somatic treatments. They claim that nutrients can affect brain activity significantly while keeping to a minimum the undesirable side effects that may result from drug treatment. Megavitamin therapy (also known as orthomolecular therapy) has been suggested by some as a treatment for acute schizophrenia.

Although some nutritional approaches may help some people with psychiatric symptoms, research has yet to demonstrate that nutritional therapies alone are effective or appropriate treatments for the major psychiatric disorders. Unless well-designed studies reveal their benefits, their use instead of standard psychiatric treatments must be considered highly questionable.

effects can include headache, blurred vision, nervousness, insomnia, skin rashes, nausea, eating disturbances, drowsiness, and changes in the heart beat. Long-term use can result in changes in a child's growth rate.

Amphetamines should not be used by anyone with high blood pressure, glaucoma, symptoms of psychosis, or a history of drug dependence. Side effects can include euphoria, dysphoria (bad mood), increased blood pressure, restlessness, dizziness, insomnia, headache, dry mouth, stomach upset, appetite disturbances, and weight loss.

These drugs interact with alcohol and many over-the-counter drugs. Discuss with the treating physician what other drugs should or should not be taken.

NON-DRUG SOMATIC THERAPIES

In conjunction with psychotherapy, the expanded use of drug treatment for mental illness today is seen as the most important development in psychiatry since the work of Sigmund Freud. But other non-drug therapies are also undergoing increased study and gaining widespread support, most notably electroconvulsive therapy, light therapy, and biofeedback.

Electroconvulsive Therapy (ECT)

To many psychiatrists, electroconvulsive therapy (ECT) is the treatment of choice for severely depressed psychotic and suicidal people because of its rapid onset of therapeutic action and its relative safety. For nonsuicidal people with major depressive or bipolar disorders, psychiatrists recommend ECT when antidepressant drugs have not worked, when their side effects cannot be tolerated, or when patients are taking so many medications that antidepressants are too risky—a common situation among the elderly. ECT has also been used successfully in the treatment of certain intractable cases of schizophrenia and is being studied for use in dementia.

How It Works

ECT involves exposing the brain to carefully controlled pulses of electric current that induce brief seizures. Why this helps in treating depression is unknown, but some researchers believe ECT alters monoamine function, as do the antidepressant medications.

Convulsive therapy, using drugs rather than electricity to induce seizures, was introduced in 1934 by Hungarian neuropsychiatrist Ladislas Meduna, who speculated that seizures (similar to those occurring in epilepsy) might alleviate mental disorders. His theory was based on the then-common (although erroneous) belief that epileptic seizures prevented the symptoms of schizophrenia. In 1937 two Italian psychiatrists started using electric shocks to induce seizures, and by 1939 what is today know as ECT—popularly called shock therapy—was in wide use in the United States.

In those days, ECT techniques were unrefined. Many medical complications (including even bone fractures resulting from severity of the convulsions, along with panic, heart problems, and profound memory loss) came to be associated with the treatment. Furthermore, ECT was abused terribly in some situations. Literature and films soon painted a grisly view of the frightening aspects of treatment.

In its modern form, with appropriate monitoring ECT is a remarkably safe and effective treatment. Still, its previous reputation continues to discourage people from accepting it when it is recommended.

Treatment takes place in a specially equipped room where a clinical team first administers an intravenous general anesthetic, then a muscle relaxant. Oxygen is administered, and the electric current is applied through electrodes. Someone undergoing ECT does not feel the electric current, and the only noticeable reaction is likely to be a curling of the toes or mild finger movements. The entire procedure, from preparation through recovery, usually takes 20 to 40 minutes.

At present the best placement of the electrodes is a matter of ongoing research. In unilateral treatment, both electrodes are placed 2 to 3 inches apart on the same side of the head. The side chosen is on the same side of the body as the dominant hand (that is, right side of the head in right-handed people). Those who prefer this strategy claim that it causes less short-term memory loss and confusion. In bilateral treatment, electrodes are placed opposite each other over both temples. Proponents of this traditional method see it as more effective. They claim that after about two weeks the patient's memory loss will be approximately the same as in unilateral treatment placement.

ECT therapy consists of a series of treatments, usually scheduled two or three times a week for a total of 6 to 12 treatments for depression, 25 to 30 treatments for schizophrenia. The number of treatments, however, depends on response to therapy.

Risks

Temporary memory loss is the risk most often associated with modern ECT. After a treatment, a person will wake up appearing a bit drowsy and confused for an hour or so. The treatment and events, or even days, immediately preceding it may not be remembered. Most memories return within a few weeks. Occasionally learning new information may be more difficult for a short time.

Another risk of ECT is to the heart, both from the actual seizures as well as from the drugs used in treatment—anesthesia, muscle relaxants, and barbiturates.

Side effects may also include headaches, slight skin burns at the electrode sites, mild muscle soreness, or nausea. A few people may experience minor speech problems, changes in language use, and coordination difficulties, but these generally improve gradually after the last treatment and are substantially gone after six months.

Phototherapy (Light Therapy)

Phototherapy is used to treat depression resulting from seasonal affective disorder (SAD), a disorder that recently has captured the attention of many researchers and clinicians. (See chapter 8.)

How It Works

A patient sits a short distance from a bank of special lights much brighter than normal indoor illumination. The exposure to intense light appears to work best either very early in the morning, when it is still dark outside, or in the evening. This suggests that light therapy may work by tricking a person's own biological clock into thinking the day is longer than it is. Thirty minutes of exposure to the newest and highest intensity 10,000-lux systems gives results similar to two or more hours of exposure to more standard 2,500- to 3,500-lux systems. The procedure is somewhat similar to visiting a tanning salon, except that the lights designed for phototherapy produce no sun tans.

People undergoing phototherapy often notice improvement in their seasonal depression after just two or three days of treatment.

Risks

Phototherapy has almost no notable side effects. Significant overexposure to the powerful lights can cause burns, and eyes can be damaged unless properly protected during treatment. While repeated exposure to strong sunlight over several years is known to increase the risk of excessive wrinkling and can produce some kinds of skin cancer, research into light therapy has not yet shown evidence of this danger.

Biofeedback

Biofeedback is a process whereby a person is trained to exert control over voluntary and, to a more limited extent, involuntary physiological responses. In addition to being used in the treatment of a variety of medical disorders, biofeedback has many mental health applications, particularly in the treatment of anxiety and stress disorders and problems that may be made worse by anxiety or stress, such as difficulty falling asleep. It is very useful in training individuals with chronic tension headaches to relax the muscles that produce the headaches.

How It Works

Biofeedback has it roots in theories of learning, psychophysiology, meditation, and cybernetics (the study of automatic control systems). Since ancient times, masters of yoga have been able to control certain physiological functions thought to be totally involuntary, such as heart rate and blood pressure. Such feats are achieved only after years of dedicated study and practice. These individuals are also able to achieve states of complete relaxation. Now many of these same skills may be learned far more quickly through the process of biofeedback training.

A person learning biofeedback techniques is hooked up to various types of equipment to monitor heart rate, blood pressure, skin temperature, muscle tension, or brain waves. Then he or she is instructed to begin to use various mental techniques to lower the heart rate or blood pressure, raise skin temperature, relax muscles, or even change some brain waves. The feedback devices emit a visual or audible signal to alert the individual that a physiological change is taking place—hence the name "biofeedback." By using conscious thought, through trial and error, the person learns how to control some of these processes, perhaps with only a few days of training. As control becomes more automatic, the person no longer needs the feedback provided by the equipment in order to, for example, achieve a relaxed state whenever he or she feels anxious. Following successful treatment, the person can relax at will.

Risks

No risks are associated with biofeedback, except possibly the risk of ineffectual training. To be certain that a practitioner has attained generally accepted levels of professional competence, only biofeedback therapists with credentials from the Biofeedback Certification Institute of America (BCIA) should be consulted.

6

Is Treatment Effective?

Frederic I. Kass, M.D., Jonathan M. Silver, M.D.,
Ellen Stevenson, M.D., and Francine Cournos, M.D.

The effectiveness of any particular treatment—does it help? does it harm? does it have any effect at all?—is a major concern in all areas of health care. In mental health care, the question of effectiveness is both very important and difficult to answer, in part because the evaluation of the psychotherapies has proved to be elusive in many ways. Demonstrating that the psychotherapies work and why has been difficult, because all psychotherapeutic treatments aim to change intangible and hard-to-measure personality characteristics, and assessment of improvement may be subjective.

Throughout this book the range of psychological and biological approaches that are most often used by psychiatrists and allied mental health professionals in the treatment of mental suffering are presented. In this chapter we approach the overriding question of whether these treatments achieve their goals, whether one form is better than another, how the effectiveness can be determined, and what are the major factors that determine the success of any type of treatment. It is important to emphasize at the outset that in all areas of medicine, including psychiatry, treatment may have untoward side effects, and no treatment works for all people under all circumstances. The objective, then, is to find the treatment or combination of treatments that have the highest likelihood of helping a particular person with the least risk of adverse side effects.

STANDARDS FOR MEASURING EFFECTIVENESS

When a troubled individual goes to a mental health professional for help, how does the therapist know what will work? And how does the patient know that what the therapist is recommending will be effective? Substantial research has been conducted to answer these important questions.

Drug Research

The efficacy of a drug is established through controlled scientific studies. Study formats vary according to the drug being tested. A *controlled study* may simply entail comparing a treated and an untreated group of volunteers. In a *double-blind placebo trial,* one group receives the test drug and the other gets a placebo (an inactive substance, such as a "sugar pill," that has no effect on the body); if the researchers want to compare the test drug with other medications or treatments, additional groups of volunteer subjects may be incorporated in the study. "Double-blind" means that neither the volunteer test subjects nor the researchers know who is getting what, which helps ensure against bias. In a *cross-over study,* the groups will be switched—for example, those getting a placebo in one phase of the study will be given the test drug in another. At the end of the study, the results for all groups and phases are analyzed according to objective statistical criteria.

The drug is considered effective if a significantly larger number of people improve after treatment with the active drug compared to treatment with the placebo drug, or if the drug being tested is as helpful as a "standard" drug known to be effective on the basis of prior studies.

THE PLACEBO RESPONSE

In controlled clinical drug trials, a significant percentage of the test subjects responds positively even to the placebo drug, although it has no active ingredients. In studies of antidepressants, for example, 30 to 40 percent of patients will improve simply from taking a "sugar pill" that they believe may be a pharmacological treatment of their condition.

This positive response does not indicate that these people are not "really" ill. Rather, it reminds us that there is more to the treatment than the chemical alone. Knowing that there is someone with whom one can share problems often alleviates even severe feelings of anxiety and demoralization. Even if a psychiatrist's primary involvement with the individual is to prescribe medication, he or she offers a healing relationship, listening with understanding and empathy. Further, symptoms can and do improve spontaneously, sometimes because the stressors that triggered the symptoms have resolved.

Psychotherapy Research

Controlled testing has demonstrated that the benefits of medications, including those used to treat depression, anxiety, schizophrenia, and other psychiatric conditions, are far greater than their risks. Studying psychotherapy scientifically, however, is a far more formidable task. Therapy takes place behind closed doors and is subject to the rules of confidentiality. (See chapter 30.) The agents of change (such as the skills of the therapist and the complex bond that develops between therapist and patient) are difficult to observe objectively. Outcome may also be subjective and difficult to measure.

Over the last few decades, as approaches to psychotherapy have multiplied, research on psychotherapy outcome has become more rigorous and sophisticated. In addition, the application of a statistical procedure called meta-analysis permits investigators to pool data from many independent studies on the outcome of treatment; this allows the study of patients in numbers far beyond what would be possible in small clinical trials. Some short-term psychotherapies have been designed specifically to be accessible to research. For example, Dr. Gerald Klerman devised interpersonal therapy for depression (see chapter 8) to be administered in a specific number of sessions by trained therapists using techniques set forth in a detailed manual. His research, as well as that of many other investigators involving short-term psychiatric interventions (which are easier to study than treatments that last for several years), has demonstrated that psychotherapy has considerable effectiveness.

particular psycho-

legal or ethical
er 30), or has no
y he or she is not
undergo or con-

issue is whether
apist for *you.* To
d to first assess
prefer a particular
efore you begin
not the profes-
re of his or her
numerous types
techniques and
ting to a patient
eatment offered.
therapies, the
y talk very little.
es in techniques
scuss your treat-
her the therapist

In addition, as the treatment proceeds, ask yourself the following questions:

- Does the therapist give you feedback? Do you think that he or she has some understanding of how you think and feel?
- Does the therapist help you confront the issues? For example, if you're the kind of person who avoids problems, does your therapist allow you to continue to avoid problems or does he or she encourage you address them?
- Does your therapist insist that only his or her approach can help you? If a mental health professional says that he or she never recommends drug treatment for any problem (or conversely, that only drugs will work), you should consider getting additional advice from a different mental health professional.
- Does the treatment help you legitimize the choices you make based on who you are, rather than on what other people think or social convention dictates? A good therapist will be focused on you and what is going to work for you.

CTIVENESS OF PSYCHOTHERAPY

(which analyze
area) have indi-
erapy is benefi-
on data from
monstrated that
mproved by the
y three quarters
hs of treatment.
apy of any kind
than 80 percent
had no treat-
ment. Studies that evaluated the patients months and even years after the end of treatment found that initial improvements were usually maintained.

Factors Determining Outcome

For many years, researchers have tried to elucidate the specific factors that contribute to psychotherapeutic success.

Dr. Jerome Frank, for example, postulates that all

patients who seek psychiatric help suffer from demoralization and that all effective treatments share common factors that help alleviate demoralization. Many researchers have determined that as a healer, the therapist offers concern, trust, and intimacy as well as an explanation for the patient's distressing feelings and behavior. Based on the therapist's conceptual scheme, he or she then prescribes a plan for improvement that requires the active participation of both the patient and the therapist. Finally, whatever form this plan takes, both therapist and patient have confidence in it. Other factors that influence treatment outcome include mastery, the therapist's qualities, and the therapeutic relationship.

Mastery

Despite differences in orientation, all successful therapies attempt to change the patient's view of him- or herself from a person who is overwhelmed by problems to one who can identify, tackle, and master them. Biofeedback and relaxation training provide a

---

Question: There are so many different forms of mental health treatment. How do I know that the type of treatment I'm receiving is the best one for me?

Answer: The first step in considering the type of treatment is knowing what the diagnosis is and/or the goals you want or can expect to achieve. For disorders that have a distinct complex of treatable symptoms—such as depression, bipolar disorder, or panic disorder, for example—the appropriate chapters in this book detail the various treatment approaches that research has shown to be effective.

However, if the reason you are seeking help is less specific—if, for example, you are having difficulties in your relationships or your career, or would like to change aspects of your personality—the issue of what is the best treatment has not been as well studied. In this instance, the fact that you have chosen to seek help and be in treatment is probably more important than the specific type or school of therapy chosen. Read chapter 4 for information about the major schools of psychotherapy and the types of difficulties for which they are indicated.

---

patient with direct control over bodily responses. Cognitive therapy teaches an individual to become aware of pathological ways of thinking and to develop new, adaptive ways of approaching problems. Psychoanalysis increases the individual's understanding of unconscious processes in order to provide the patient with control over them. Behavioral therapy prescribes well-defined tasks and goals that ultimately allow the patient to conquer his or her anxiety. Group therapy allows the patient to identify maladaptive ways of interacting and to try out new and more successful ways of relating to others.

In an interesting series of studies performed at Johns Hopkins University, patients who attributed their improvement to medication did not sustain improvement, while those who viewed improvement as resulting from their own efforts did. These findings suggest that the difference between an unsuccessful and a successful therapy can be like the difference between driving someone to a destination versus teaching him or her how to drive. A person given the tools to negotiate life's vicissitudes is more likely to sustain a lasting recovery. These studies also suggest that it is useful for patients to think of medication as a helpful adjunct to psychotherapy—a tool that facilitates change by conferring the ability to control symptoms.

The Therapist's Qualities

Each therapist, like each patient, is unique. The therapist's variation in technique and personality can have a significant impact on the way the patient relates to the therapist and on the outcome of therapy.

Studies by Dr. David E. Orlinsky and Dr. Kenneth I. Howard demonstrate that patients' perceptions of their psychotherapists are important in predicting successful treatment. Regardless of the type of therapy they were undergoing, patients interviewed in these studies agreed that certain attributes were

---

Table 6.1   "WHY MY THERAPY WORKED"

Dr. Lestor Luborsky of the University of Pennsylvania has found that patients who benefit most from therapy rate the following factors as most important to treatment outcome.

As rated on a scale of 1 to 4:
1 = little or no importance; 4 = very important

Gaining understanding of reasons behind my behavior and feelings	4
Positive relationship with therapist	3.8
Talking about feelings that were not easy to talk about	3.8
Getting a feeling of hope	3.8
Getting aware of and in touch with my feelings	3.8
Getting guidance	3.6
Relief from getting things off my chest	3.6
Talking about my feelings toward or relationship with my therapist	3.2
Earning my therapist's approval	2.8
Having my feelings stirred up	2.4
My therapist making clear what he or she thought I should do in order to improve	2.2

Adapted with permission from Lester Luborsky, Paul Crits-Christoph, Jim Mintz, and Arthur Auerbach, eds., *Who Will Benefit from Psychotherapy?* (New York: Basic Books, 1988), p. 69.

Question: How do I know the treatment is working?

Answer: The answer lies in the nature of your problem and the goals you have set for yourself in treatment. In a disorder such as depression, your therapist should be able to give you predictive guidelines on the type of progress you should expect and how long it should take to experience some improvement in your symptoms. If you do not see improvement within the suggested period of time, discuss the problem your therapist. A change in the direction of therapy or a consultation with another mental health professional may be warranted.

For therapy directed at personality change or a problematic area of life rather than a specific diagnosable mental disorder, there may be no clear guidelines as to whether the therapy is maximally effective or how long you should expect to continue. Determining direction or values in life is subjective. Changing character traits that you have lived with all your life is less scientific than overcoming symptoms of anxiety, for example. You may have to depend on your own evaluation of whether or not the treatment has enabled you to overcome the difficulties that troubled you or to act or feel differently. Do you feel that you are making progress? Do you feel that you are getting closer to resolving the issue(s) for which you are seeking help? Do not keep such questions to yourself. Ask your therapist for guidance on how to answer them.

Question: How do I know that continuing my psychotherapy will help me? How do I know when costs begin to outweigh benefits?

Answer: Depending on your treatment goals in therapy, it takes months to years before various types of difficulty can be resolved. As explained in chapter 4, resistance to change is normal. As in creative processes, breakthroughs often occur after periods of great frustration. Often a person has to work over a problem again and again before solutions are found and undertaken. Therefore, it's important not to get discouraged too early. Ask your therapist about your feelings of lack of progress. Find out what he or she thinks about continuing therapy and, based on your current progress, what further benefit you are likely to gain.

If therapy goes on for some time without any apparent progress, and if discussing this impasse with your therapist provides no answers, then it may be time to consider going for a consultation and/or changing therapists. You may also decide that additional progress in psychotherapy is unlikely at this point in your life.

essential. For example, they preferred a "human" therapist: one who was understanding, spoke simply and directly, and was not averse to giving advice. Satisfied patients described their therapists as "warm," "attentive," "interested," "understanding," and "respectful."

Both patients and therapists felt that a practitioner's ability to empathize was crucial. Empathy is the ability to sense the feelings and ideas of another person beyond a mere intellectual understanding, as when someone says, "That really struck a chord with me." It is not surprising that in a treatment that deals so deeply with human emotions, the therapist must understand his or her patient's experience in a profound way.

The following case history illustrates just how important the therapist's human qualities can be in facilitating positive treatment outcome.

The Case of Mr. B.

Mr. B. entered a behavioral therapy for incapacitating fear of flying. He attended his sessions and did his homework assignments faithfully. During each session his therapist reviewed his progress and gave him slightly more anxiety-provoking assignments to complete by the next session. After several months he was able to take a plane trip by himself, an accomplishment that both enhanced his self-esteem and benefited his career.

He was contacted much later, and asked to describe the elements of his treatment that were most important to him. Surprisingly, he did not mention any of the behavioral techniques used by his therapist. Rather, he claimed that the therapist's warmth and patience helped him to continue. Mr. B. felt that his therapist's understanding and tolerance of even his "craziest" fears gave him the strength to overcome his phobia.

The Therapeutic Relationship

Research has shown that the most powerful predictor of success in psychotherapy is the presence of a good relationship between the patient and the therapist in

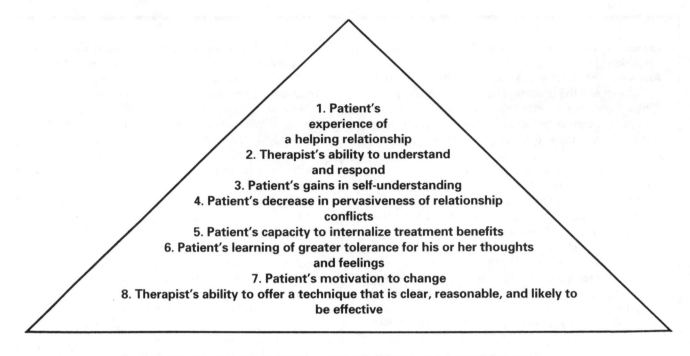

1. Patient's
experience of
a helping relationship
2. Therapist's ability to understand
and respond
3. Patient's gains in self-understanding
4. Patient's decrease in pervasiveness of relationship
conflicts
5. Patient's capacity to internalize treatment benefits
6. Patient's learning of greater tolerance for his or her thoughts
and feelings
7. Patient's motivation to change
8. Therapist's ability to offer a technique that is clear, reasonable, and likely to
be effective

WHY THERAPY WORKS —THE THERAPIST'S POINT OF VIEW

Figure 6.1: **Factors likely to contribute to the success of therapy. Adapted with permission from Lestor Luborsky, Paul Crits-Christoph, Jim Mintz, and Arthur Auerbach, eds.,** _Who Will Benefit from Psychotherapy?_ **(New York: Basic Books, 1988), p. 164.**

the early stage of psychotherapy. As with any relationship, some people "hit it off," while others do not. The patient and therapist who "click" are often similar in some respects. Psychotherapy researchers have found that similarities in social class, age, interests, and values foster a "therapeutic alliance." This term refers to the degree to which the patient is able to work with the therapist toward the achievement of therapeutic goals. Should the relationship be problematic initially, the therapy may or may not prove to be beneficial. If the therapy enables the patient to "work through" his or her early doubts or mistrust of the therapist, lasting change often ensues; this is particularly true when the initial mistrust is a function of the individual's negative early life experiences and emotional problems. However, psychiatrist Allen Frances of Duke University maintains that "a patient who finds that his experiences with a therapist are consistently unsatisfactory in the early sessions should consider seeing another therapist in hope of finding a better match."

In the initial sessions, the patient may see the therapist as an expert who has the burden of healing; as treatment progresses, however, success is characterized by both parties having the sense that they are working toward a common goal—as the following

case vignette of a woman in an extended psychotherapy illustrates.

The Case of Mrs. L.

A 45-year-old mother of three was referred to a psychiatrist by her internist, who could find no medical basis for her dizzy spells, palpitations, and worries about her health. She spent the initial sessions discussing her physical concerns. The therapist had noticed that she was always accompanied to his office by a woman friend. When he questioned her about it, Mrs. L. disclosed that she was afraid to be alone; she expressed a desire, however, to free herself from her fearfulness.

As the treatment proceeded, the woman revealed that she had been the adored "baby" in a large family ruled by the patriarch father, the central figure in her life as she was growing up. The family dubbed him "The Powerhouse" because of his feats of physical strength, which Mrs. L. delighted in recounting. She had felt safe and secure only in her father's presence. As soon as she had finished high school, she had married a man who served the same protective role. She began to view her therapist as her new protector, but whereas in the past she and the men in her life had placed a premium on her helplessness, the goals of treatment were independence and mastery. Patient and therapist discussed her unconscious wishes to remain "daddy's little girl" and the therapist's favorite patient.

Slowly, as she continued to discuss her wishes for a magic protector and developed insight into her need to give up her childhood role, Mrs. L. began to take buses by herself and experiment with other opportunities to be on her own. She felt encouraged by her therapist's pleasure in her independence. The successful treatment lasted two and a half years. Mrs. L.'s fearfulness and her physical symptoms and worries had long since diminished, and at this point she was ready, too, to give up her "powerhouse" therapist.

Question: My teenager is in treatment. She likes the therapist but won't tell me what goes on in her sessions. How can I be sure that her treatment is working?

Answer: The most obvious answer, of course, is whether or not your daughter has improved. If she hasn't improved, has she at least learned to cope better with her symptoms? Does she have more of an understanding of what the problem is? Does she feel comfortable calling the therapist if she feels that she needs help?

Question: I have tried to get information from my teenager's therapist, but he won't tell me anything.

Answer: Mental health professionals are bound by strict codes of confidentiality. A therapist cannot ethically divulge information to a patient's family. (See chapter 30.) However, a therapist must also balance both the patient's and the family's needs. Even if the therapist cannot answer all of a family's questions, he or she should still be accessible and provide whatever information can be shared without violating confidentiality.

Question: I don't think my husband's treatment is progressing the way it should. What can I do?

Answer: If the treatment isn't obviously harmful, there may be no way for a third party to intervene. Keep in mind that change often comes slowly and some conditions take longer to treat than others. Even though to you things seem not to be going well, your husband may have a very different perception than you of how well he is progressing.

Specialized Treatment Approaches

Although outcome is influenced by general factors such as the patient's expectation of improvement and a positive interaction between patient and therapist, research indicates that specific treatment techniques are indicated for certain problems and clinical syndromes. Careful assessment and diagnosis are, of course, very important in all types of mental health treatment, especially in identifying subgroups for whom specialized approaches are appropriate.

Behavioral techniques (see chapter 4), for example, have been found to be very effective in many of the anxiety disorders (detailed in chapter 7), in particular agoraphobia and obsessive-compulsive disorder and in the eating disorders (chapter 10). Specialized psychotherapeutic techniques involving support for the patient and education for the family are useful in treating schizophrenia, discussed at greater length later in this chapter (page 92). Group therapy can be an especially effective treatment when a person's primary difficulty is in interpersonal interactions and in developing social skills (chapter 4). Group experience allows a safe and controlled setting in which individuals can try out new ways of behaving in relationships. Gains made in the group setting can pave the way to more rewarding and intimate relationships outside the group.

Throughout this book, the chapters dealing with the various disorders indicate where particular approaches are appropriate.

When Psychotherapy Does Not Help

Despite the benefits experienced by the majority of patients undergoing psychotherapy, some patients do not improve and a smaller number may get worse.

During psychotherapy, a person may notice a return in the symptoms that brought him or her to therapy or the appearance of new symptoms. In addition, it is not uncommon for patients to feel significantly worse when they are working out their problems; indeed, a temporary setback can be a sign that progress is being made and that problems ultimately will be worked out. However, a negative trend over time—decreased self-esteem, increased anxiety and hostility, self-destructive behaviors, or suicidal thoughts in a person who had not previously been suicidal—can be a sign that treatment is not working and should be reevaluated by both patient and therapist. Under such circumstances, consultation with another clinician may be useful.

Stagnation in therapy may occur if patients intellectualize and do not implement life changes, and paradoxically use psychological insights to avoid the real problems. Patients may at times focus on psychotherapy as an end in itself. It is the job of the therapist to help patients overcome these blocks to progress, but sometimes therapists avoid the issue of how patients sabotage their own treatment, or why they are not making the gains they seek. For example, a patient may obtain gratification from the relationship with a therapist rather than be encouraged to take on the challenging task of making new acquaintances and friends. In some cases, therapists fail to set realistic goals with patients—that is, treatment may be approached as if it were timeless, with patient and therapist working toward vaguely defined goals that may not be obtainable. Or (as the case of Ms. R. demonstrates, below) the therapist may not feel the same sense of urgency as the patient.

Question: If I don't feel I'm making any progress, should I change therapists?

Answer: There is no easy answer to this question. Sometimes the best way to decide if you want to make a change is to go for a consultation with another therapist—someone whose role is explicitly to help you think through the problems you are having with the therapy you are currently undergoing. Important to consider is whether you would have the same problems with any therapist—because the problem is your outlook or your defense mechanisms. (See chapter 4, page 48.) You need to determine, on the other hand, whether you and the therapist are not a good match and whether you would do better with someone else.

As with treatment for medical problems, a second opinion can help confirm the benefit of the current therapy or suggest possible alternatives.

The Case of Ms. R.

A young investment banker, Ms. R. consulted a therapist after she had been offered a promotion that would necessitate her moving to another city, but was unable to make this important career decision. She felt paralyzed and extremely anxious.

In the initial sessions, the therapist asked Ms. R. to speak freely. Often Ms. R. felt lost and wondered what she should be speaking about. When the therapist would not respond to her direct questions, Ms. R. began to feel discouraged and misunderstood, and felt no closer to making a decision about her career.

Four weeks into treatment, her mother suffered a mild stroke. Ms. R. canceled her session and left a message on the therapist's telephone answering machine that made it clear that she was upset about her mother's health. When Ms. R. arrived for the next session, the therapist did not ask about her mother but rather sat silently and waited for Ms. R. to speak. Ms. R. left the session angry and confused. She called the therapist that evening and canceled all future sessions.

When asked at a later date why she had terminated treatment, Ms. R. explained that she had not liked her therapist much but felt that over time she might change her mind. She felt that she was given little guidance and structure from the start, considering the time pressure of her decision. Ms. R. remarked that when her therapist neglected to ask about her mother, "Even a stranger would have been warmer than that. I sensed no caring or understanding. I had no desire to tell her any of my problems again."

With the deadline for her job decision growing closer, Ms. R. sought a consultation with another therapist. She liked the second therapist right away and noted that she had a warm smile. Ms. R. immediately felt understood when her new therapist said, "We have a lot of work to do in a short period of time." This therapist also asked her to say what was on her mind, but often interjected comments and helped structure each session. Ms. R. felt that at the end of each session she had learned something new about herself. A month into therapy, she was much more relaxed and was able to see how the job promotion symbolized, for her, growing up and separating from her parents. Despite some continuing anxiety, she decided to accept the promotion and to move, feeling confident about her decision. After she settled in at her new job and location, she decided to reenter treatment to examine some issues raised in her successful brief therapy.

PSYCHOTHERAPY AND MEDICAL HEALTH

Several studies have now shown that patients who receive psychotherapy reduce their use of medical services. A meta-analytic study by Dr. Emily Mumford and colleagues found that psychotherapy results in a one-third decrease in medical care. The reductions were most noticeable in expensive hospital procedures. The evidence "argues for the inseparability of mind and body in health care, and . . . for the likelihood that mental health treatment may improve patients' ability to stay healthy enough to avoid hospital admission for physical illness," wrote Mumford and coworkers in their 1984 article in the *American Journal of Psychiatry.*

In a study of 86 women with metastatic breast cancer, Dr. David Spiegel found that supportive therapy, in a group setting, extended these women's survival time. The women in the control groups were randomly assigned to routine oncologic (cancer) care. The experimental group received, in addi-

tion, weekly supportive group psychotherapy. In these groups patients "discussed their fears about dying and ways of living the remainder of their lives as richly as possible, improving doctor-patient communication, strengthening family relationships, grieving losses within the group, [and] building a strong sense of mutual support," wrote Spiegel in a 1990 issue of *Psychosomatics.*

Spiegel and colleagues predicted correctly that the psychotherapy would improve the quality of life for these women. They never expected that the treatment would prolong life. Yet when Spiegel's group undertook a follow-up study of these women, they discovered that the women in the psychotherapy treatment group survived twice as long as those in the control group. This suggests that psychotherapy is an effective adjunct to the medical treatment of cancer and may be useful in other terminal illnesses. (See also chapter 28.)

THE EFFECTIVENESS OF PHARMACOLOGICAL TREATMENTS

For reasons noted earlier, drug-efficacy studies are easier to design, implement, and evaluate than those measuring the effectiveness of the various forms of psychotherapy. All the drugs currently approved by the Food and Drug Administration (FDA) for the treatment of psychiatric disorders have been found in clinical trials to have far greater benefits than risks for specific conditions. Nonetheless, even though a particular drug or a class of drugs has the potential to work, numerous physician, patient, and pharmacologic factors come into play in determining whether the treatment actually proves effective.

Factors Determining Outcome

Six factors affect the outcome of pharmacological treatments: diagnosis, dosage, drug choice, therapeutic trial, therapeutic alliance, and noncompliance.

Diagnosis

Psychiatric symptoms may appear to be unrelated, and each may be treated individually by a physician who fails to diagnose and treat the underlying disorder responsible for them all. Depression, for example, often includes feelings of sadness, appetite difficulties, problems sleeping, and nervousness. A 58-year-old accountant, who did not suspect that he was depressed, had been having great difficulty falling asleep for over a month. He had no appetite and tired easily during the day. He also felt sad and on edge. He went to his family doctor, who, after performing a physical examination that revealed no organic illness, prescribed a sleeping medication. Although his sleep improved somewhat, the man did not feel better. Eventually his physician referred him to a psychiatrist, who diagnosed depression and prescribed an antidepressant medication. All the man's symptoms resolved within four weeks.

In some cases, people go to different doctors for different complaints, gathering different prescriptions from each. Besides ineffective therapy for the primary disorder, multiple pharmacologic treatments can lead to dangerous side effects and drug interactions. (See chapter 5 for information on drug side effects.) Just as psychiatric symptoms can mimic medical disorders, medical conditions may cause symptoms that appear to be psychiatric in origin. (See chapters 23 and 28.) Sleep, energy, appetite, and mood disturbances are symptoms of depression, but also of thyroid disease and numerous other organic illnesses. Psychiatric medications are not effective treatments for underlying medical problems.

Question: How can I tell if the medication my psychiatrist has prescribed is the right one for my disorder? I have a friend who, like me, was diagnosed with depression, but she is taking a different medication.

Answer: Just as with cardiac medications, there is often more than one psychiatric drug that will effectively treat a given condition. The prescribing physician will decide on a specific drug based on your specific symptoms and physical history (you may have a condition, such as high blood pressure, for example, that would make one drug a better choice than another) and his or her clinical experience with various medications. Ask your doctor to explain the choice of medication and the advantages of the course of therapy he or she is recommending.

For a good general briefing on drugs, read chapter 5 in this book, as well as the specific chapters on the various disorders.

Dosage

Incorrect dosage (prescribing too much or too little of a medication) is one reason why drug treatment may fail. The brain is the intended site of action for psychoactive drugs, and if a drug does not get into the brain in sufficient concentrations, it will not work. Physicians unfamiliar with the correct use of psychoactive drugs may prescribe them in doses that are too low to achieve a full effect. People metabolize drugs differently, and thus even an experienced psychiatrist is not always able to predict how much medication will be needed to achieve an effect. Because of the obvious difficulty in monitoring how much drug is in the brain of any living person (doing so would involve sampling brain tissue), psychiatrists often measure the amount of drug in the blood as a reflection of the amount in the brain. Some drugs, such as several of the antidepressants, must be taken in sufficient doses to exceed a specific minimum blood level. Others must fall within a certain range, beyond which the drug may either lose its effectiveness or cause side effects. Continual monitoring of

dosage, to maintain effectiveness and control side effects, is important throughout drug treatment.

Choice of Drug

While drugs that receive FDA approval have been shown to be generally effective, not everyone responds to the same drug. In many cases, the psychiatrist must choose a specific drug from among several medications that are potentially equally effective. The choice is made easier if the patient has a history of responding to a particular drug. Sometimes diagnosing illness subtypes may help pinpoint the choice of drugs.

Often the choice depends on a particular drug's side effect profile. For example, there are well over two dozen antidepressant drugs, all of which are equivalent in potential effectiveness but which produce different side effects that can influence the course of the treatment. Some produce sedation, which can be very helpful for people who have insomnia but counterproductive for those who sleep too much when they are depressed. Still others have stimulating effects that may be inappropriate for individuals who are experiencing agitation.

Although psychiatrists have a wide range of drugs from which to choose in treating the major disorders, in most cases they begin treatment with a drug whose effects and appropriate use they have become most experienced.

Therapeutic Trial

Because of the immense suffering that people with emotional problems experience, the doctor, patient, and family want improvement to be immediate. Most of the drugs used in psychiatry take time to work, however, requiring an adequate "therapeutic trial" before effectiveness can be determined. Antidepressants often take two to three weeks before beginning to take effect, and antipsychotics can take up to six weeks before full response is noted. A trial of most psychiatric drugs requires three to six weeks at the full, therapeutic dosage. If the drug has no effect after six weeks, reassessment is needed.

Therapeutic Alliance

Even when treatment is primarily pharmacologic, the psychiatrist's concern and empathy and the patient's trust are essential. The two must see themselves as a team working toward the same goals, and the goals themselves need to be specified clearly. The more a patient understands about the reasons a medication is prescribed, how and when to take it, how it works, and what to expect in terms of the timing of response and side effects, the more effective the drug is likely to be. Similarly, during the course of treatment, the physician must be available to the patient to answer questions and monitor effects and side effects, to ensure that the treatment proceeds effectively. Once the medication produces beneficial results, the two need to determine how long treatment will be necessary. When symptoms have been absent for a specified time, and when both agree that the medication can be stopped, the clinician must assist the patient in tapering off the drug while carefully watching for a return of symptoms.

Noncompliance

Noncompliance—the patient failing to take the medication, or to take it the way the doctor prescribes—is the most common cause of apparent treatment failure. A person may neglect to take the medication or to follow doctor's orders for several reasons. Many people, although they are suffering immensely, have mixed feelings about taking medication; they feel it is a sign of "weakness" and that they "should" be able to get better by themselves. Sometimes, too, as with some people who are experiencing the manic phase of bipolar illness, a person may not wish to relinquish the symptoms and thus will not take the medication as prescribed. For others, medication side effects are initially unpleasant; for this reason they cut down the dosage or stop the medication without consulting the prescribing physician. Sometimes, too, when the pills need to be taken several times a day, people simply forget to take one or more of them and symptoms return or fail to resolve.

A good, open relationship between doctor and patient—in which the physician fully informs the patient of what to expect and the patient discusses reactions to the drug and to taking medication altogether—is key in assuring compliance. Side effects can usually be managed if the physician knows what the problem is.

A 34-year-old teacher began treatment for panic attacks. She was supposed to take an antidepressant medication three times a day, at mealtimes. She often forgot to take her lunchtime pill, however, because she had to supervise students in the lunchroom. Consequently, her condition was not improving as rapidly as the psychiatrist had predicted. When the doctor discovered that she was not always getting the full daily dosage, he suggested that she take all the medication at night. Her symptoms began to disappear one week later.

When Drug Treatment Fails

When a drug fails to be effective after a full therapeutic trial, the physician needs to reevaluate the diagnosis, change to another drug, or add a second medication in order to potentiate the effects of the first one. For example, adding lithium carbonate to a previously prescribed antidepressant can convert some depressed "nonresponders" into "responders."

Consulting with another doctor may also be appropriate. Nonpsychiatric physicians may be less skilled in psychiatric diagnosis and treatment, and referral to a psychiatrist would be in order if treatment fails. Although all psychiatrists can prescribe medication and most do, referral to a psychopharmacologist (a psychiatrist with special expertise in the use of medication) may be helpful for those individuals whose difficulties do not respond to the usual psychiatric treatments.

COMPARING AND COMBINING TREATMENTS

Psychiatric research and practice increasingly emphasize the integration of mind and body and the interactions between a person's biology and his or her environment. Thus, a drug or other somatic therapy (such as electroconvulsive therapy or biofeedback) is rarely the complete treatment. Even if the focus is primarily somatic, interacting with the prescribing psychiatrist and learning to cope with the illness and its consequences are important to the success of the treatment. In many if not most cases in which a psychiatrist prescribes medication, the patient also receives some type of psychotherapy.

Studies of combined treatments show that the different modalities work on separate aspects of the illness. According to a number of these studies, medication is particularly effective in ameliorating abnormalities of mood and thinking, while psychotherapy helps improve social functioning.

Most research in combining or comparing treatments has focused on depression. In general, these studies have found that psychotherapy is as effective as drugs in treating milder depressions. However, severely depressed patients benefit most from medication or a combination of medication and psychotherapy. The National Institute of Mental Health Treatment of Depression Collaborative Research Program (one of the most extensive comparative treatment trials ever conducted) compared drug treatment using imipramine (a commonly used antidepressant) with cognitive behavioral therapy, interpersonal therapy, and placebo. At the end of the 16-week trial, more than two-thirds of the treated patients were free of symptoms, although those who received imipramine recovered faster. Except for the most depressed group, who did best with imipramine, by the end of the trial all treatment groups benefited equally. In still another study, Dr. Ellen Frank found that for patients suffering from recurrent depression, those receiving long-term combined high-dose imipramine and interpersonal therapy continued the longest without a relapse, although either of the two treatments alone was helpful. (See chapter 8.)

Research has shown that the most effective treatment for schizophrenia is one that includes medication and supportive psychotherapy for the patient as well as education and psychotherapy for family members (see earlier in this chapter and chapter 14). In a representative study, investigators at the University of Southern California compared a group of patients with schizophrenia whose families received psychotherapy with a control group whose families did not. In the treatment group, families were educated about the nature, course, and treatment of schizophrenia; sessions were devoted to reducing family tensions and improving the family's problem-solving skills. The study found that patients whose families had received treatment had fewer exacerbations of their illness and a greater remission of their symptoms.

EVALUATING YOUR TREATMENT

Whatever the treatment, you as a patient should feel comfortable with your therapist. Together you should set and agree on appropriate goals. Within months, you should be functioning at least somewhat better and should at all times feel free to discuss doubts and ask questions of your therapist. An informed patient who participates fully in the therapy will be best able to use it as an aid to having a happier, more productive, less troubled life.

In chapter 3, page 42, we suggest a list of questions to ask following the initial visit with a mental health practitioner. Consider the following questions as treatment continues. (The question-and-answer boxes throughout this chapter may help you determine your own answers to some of them.)

- Are you comfortable discussing your problems with your therapist?
- Do you feel that your therapist understands and respects you and is interested in what you are saying?
- Does he or she answer your questions?
- Do you understand and agree with the goals of the treatment that you are receiving?
- Do you understand how the treatment works?

- Do you understand your role in the treatment process?
- Do you know how long the treatment you are receiving generally takes to achieve the results you and the therapist are working toward?
- If you are taking medication, did the psychiatrist tell you what side effects to expect and how to cope with them?
- Are you experiencing expected benefits from the treatment? Do you feel worse?
- If you are experiencing no benefits, have you followed through on the treatment plan, such as by taking the medication exactly as prescribed or doing possible homework exercises?
- If you are no better, have you asked the therapist why and what can be done about it?
- Do you like, respect, and trust the therapist and wish to continue?
- If you have achieved the benefits of the treatment you had gone for, have you discussed with your therapist when to leave treatment?

While definitive answers to all questions may not be possible, it is important to ask them and to evaluate the answers.

two

• • •

COMMON PROBLEMS
AND DISORDERS
AMONG ADULTS

7

Anxiety and Anxiety Disorders

Michael R. Liebowitz, M.D.

More people suffer from anxiety disorders than from any other form of psychiatric illness—13 million Americans are believed to suffer from them. Anxiety is also a common symptom of most other psychiatric disorders, from schizophrenia, to mood disorders, to sexual disorders.

Anxiety disorders are a group of clinically specific illnesses, each with its own characteristics, causes, and treatments. They include generalized anxiety disorder (GAD), panic disorder, phobias, obsessive-compulsive disorder (OCD), adjustment disorder with anxious mood, and post-traumatic stress disorder. (This last is covered in chapter 24.)

Despite their prevalence, anxiety disorders frequently are not recognized or treated for what they are. Because anxiety has many physical symptoms that can be severe, people suffering from anxiety disorders commonly think that they are physically ill and therefore seek medical diagnoses and treatments. While their physicians may recognize that there is nothing organically wrong with them, they may overlook the appropriate diagnosis and treatment.

Some people with anxiety disorders grow so used to their anxiety that they believe it is normal to be constantly nervous and on edge—that it's simply the way they are. Many sufferers turn to alcohol or drugs to alleviate their discomfort. As a result, alcohol-related problems are relatively common among people with anxiety disorders and may be the reason why they finally go for help.

Recent developments in pharmacologic and psychotherapeutic treatments have vastly improved the outlook for those who receive the correct diagnosis. In fact, over 80 percent of people with anxiety disorders can be helped with psychotherapy and/or medication. Those with milder forms of anxiety, phobias, and compulsions can even learn to tame their own responses.

STATES OF ANXIETY

On the one hand, anxiety is normal and human. On the other, it can be symptomatic of psychiatric disorder. Colloquially, the term "anxiety" is often used interchangeably with "stress" and "fear," with which it shares many characteristics. (See chapter 24.) All are states of physiological arousal in response to perceived danger.

Being fearful and dreading certain things or situations are not necessarily abnormal. Everyone has experienced the "nerves," clammy palms and dread associated with facing an audience, waiting for a family member who is out late in bad weather, or asking for a raise. Like stress and fear, mild anxiety can be a useful reaction, signaling the need to take action—perhaps to prepare for that speech or to warn the teenager not to stay out late when the roads are bad.

Many modern-day dangers are not so clear-cut or escapable, however. A persistent problem, such as a

---

ADAPTIVE OR MALADAPTIVE?

Evaluating Your Own Anxiety

While each of the anxiety disorders covered in this chapter has its own diagnostic criteria, it may be useful to evaluate your own anxiety or that of a family member in terms of whether it is adaptive or maladaptive. Does it encourage you to meet the challenges that face you—such as by studying for exams or practicing important new tasks? Or does it cause you such great discomfort that it interferes with pleasure and the ability to function in life?

Particular questions to consider are:

- How bad does the experience of anxiety make you feel? Do you worry that it will happen again?
- Does the experience that triggers the anxiety present some rational basis for concern? For example, a fear of sharks may be reasonable when swimming in ocean waters known to have sharks. It makes little sense when swimming in a lake or pool.
- To what length do you go to avoid experiencing anxiety, and how much does the avoidance interfere with your life? A fear of traveling on airplanes may cause no disruption for someone who does not travel much. But for the individual who wants to visit distant places or who needs to travel for career advancement, avoiding airplanes may severely limit happiness or success in life.

In many types of anxiety, such as with social anxiety, there is a continuum from normal to pathological levels. For example:

1. You may feel shy at social gatherings but will eventually overcome these feelings and have a good time.
2. You may feel uncomfortable throughout most social occasions, but you'll force yourself to go when necessary. You will be able to build a meaningful life in which "partying" plays little part.
3. You will experience such discomfort when having to endure a social gathering that you will begin to avoid socializing altogether—even though you wish you would be able to go and have a good time. You experience the quality of your life as diminished.
4. You are terrified of leaving the house and encountering other people, so you stay indoors. You are very unhappy but don't know what else to do.

In the third and fourth instances, the anxiety causes significant discomfort and robs you of a full and meaningful life. In such cases, you may want to seek professional help. Anxiety disorders clinics at major medical centers can be an excellent source of treatment.

bad relationship with the boss, may cause ongoing tension and anxiety. Experiencing a major life change, such as a divorce or change of residence, can bring on a period of tension and apprehension.

In anxiety-disordered states, people overreact to real or perceived dangers. The mental and physical symptoms of this overarousal are the result.

The Symptoms of Anxiety

Dread, apprehension, fear or terror, uncertainty, nervousness, impatience, irritability, difficulty concentrating, and feelings of unreality are among the common mental symptoms of anxiety. The list of possible physical symptoms is even longer. Many are cardiorespiratory, including pounding heart, difficulty breathing, faintness, dizziness, and chest pain. Other symptoms are gastrointestinal, such as stomach cramps, nausea, constipation, and diarrhea. Still other symptoms include trembling, chills, hot spells, clamminess or sweating, frequent urination, muscle aches, dry mouth, insomnia, and fatigue.

All these symptoms can range from mild to severe. In extreme anxiety states, some people think they're having heart attacks. When the anxiety becomes so severe that it significantly impairs a person's ability to function well and to enjoy life, it

ANXIETY SELF-MANAGEMENT

You can learn to calm your own mild anxiety. Chapter 24 provides practical techniques for relaxation, including controlled breathing, "Relax!" and exercise (pages 360–361).

You may find as well that you can tame your own fears by confronting them systematically rather than avoiding them. You can try techniques of desensitization on your own. Try to confront what you fear very gradually, one small stage at a time. For instance, if you are afraid of enclosed spaces, try standing in a semienclosed space such as a small room; leave the door open and stay there as long as you can. Repeat this step until the anxiety diminishes. Then try closing the door. After you can stand that stage, try entering a closet, first with the door open, then with the door closed. If the anxiety never seems to diminish no matter how assiduously you practice this exercise, you may want to go for professional help. Many people find, however, that by using methods such as these they can quiet many of the annoying discomforts they thought they would be stuck with forever.

begins to fall into one of the categories of psychiatric disorder.

THE PHYSIOLOGICAL AND PSYCHOLOGICAL BASES OF ANXIETY DISORDERS

Anxiety disorders provide an excellent example of the complex relationship between mind and body factors in mental illness.

The Biology of Anxiety

Some researchers believe that anxiety disorders are biological rather than psychological in origin. Whether or not this is true, biological components of anxiety disorders are strongly indicated. Early clues came from studies showing anxiety disorders tend to run in families. More recently, studies of fraternal and identical twins have shown that identical twins (who have identical genes) are more likely than fraternal (nonidentical) twins to suffer similarly from anxiety, even if the twins were separated at birth and raised by different families.

Although we still can't pinpoint the gene or genes responsible for anxiety disorders, or the exact nature of the biological abnormality that would predispose someone to suffer from them, there are many interesting leads.

According to one theory, abnormal anxiety is triggered by overactivity of norepinephrine, a neurotransmitter that stimulates certain brain functions. Norepinephrine is produced in an area of the brain called the locus ceruleus. If this area is stimulated electrically in animals, they experience fear and anxiety. Researchers believe that people with anxiety disorders have an abundance of norepinephrine or too many nerve cells utilizing norepinephrine, or that the nerve cells are hyperactive. In addition, the self-tranquilizing chemicals that the brain is believed to produce to balance norepinephrine (discussed

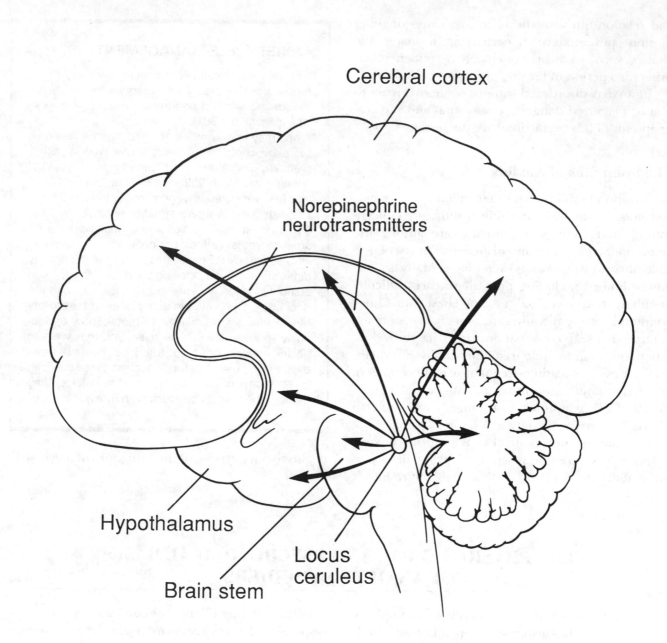

Cerebral cortex

Norepinephrine
neurotransmitters

Hypothalamus

Brain stem

Locus
ceruleus

HOW NOREPINEPHRINE TRANSMITTERS PLAY A ROLE IN ANXIETY

**Figure 7.1:** The norepinephrine neurotransmitter system arises in the locus ceruleus, a brain structure that is believed to play a role in fear and anxiety. In this diagram, norepinephrine arises from the locus ceruleus and exerts effects on almost every brain region, including the entire cerebral cortex (the thinking part of the brain), the hypothalamus (which plays a role in regulating emotions), and the brain stem (through which the brain communicates to the rest of the body, among other important functions).

below on page 100) are either too scarce or too weak to do the job.

Another possible culprit in anxiety disorders, particularly in panic attacks, is lactic acid, a chemical that occurs naturally in the body following vigorous exercise. Scientists became interested in this chemical after noting that some people suffer panic attacks after exercising strenuously. Researchers then tried giving people who had a history of panic attacks intravenous infusions of sodium lactate (a synthetic form of lactic acid) and found that the subjects experienced panic attacks. When the infusions ceased, so did the symptoms. Further evidence for the role of lactic acid or some related metabolic disturbance is that certain drugs—the monoamine oxidase inhibitors (MAOIs), tricyclics, and certain benzodiazepines (see chapter 5)—can prevent sodium lactate from causing panic attack symptoms in these patients.

Hyperventilation—rapid, shallow breathing that is caused by an imbalance of carbon dioxide levels in the blood—may also play a role. Hyperventilation is often a component of anxiety and panic attacks. Researchers have been able to stimulate panic attacks in most patients with these disorders by increasing the amount of carbon dioxide in their air supply. We are not sure of the exact role of hyperventilation and carbon dioxide in anxiety, but it may be that carbon dioxide stimulates the locus ceruleus, thus increasing the production or activity of norepinephrine.

The Psychology of Anxiety

There are many different psychological theories for anxiety and anxiety disorders, each with their own proponents and critics. They fall into two major categories: psychodynamic theories and learning or behavioral theories.

The psychodynamic view is basically that anxiety is generated by internal conflict. To some theorists, the anxiety serves as a signal that the ego is in danger from unconscious fantasies or desires. The psyche reacts to that signal by repressing this frightening material or by avoiding any object or event that is associated with those desires. Other psychodynamic theorists believe that the conflict is between people's idealized view of what they should be and the low self-esteem they actually feel, which prompts them to fear they will never succeed or be worthwhile people. This underlying conflict makes them vulnerable to many forms of anxiety. Still others hold that the conflict is between a person's own values and the forces of society that act against these convictions.

Learning theories are based on the idea that the causes of anxiety are to be found in the immediate environment and that experience conditions people to react with fear to certain events or objects. For instance, if a person had a heart attack once, even small palpitations might cause fear of a recurrence and a panic attack later.

Cognitive therapists have developed an interesting twist to learning theories. They believe that people are prone to anxiety when they perceive, however incorrectly, that their problem-solving abilities cannot meet the demands of a given situation. For example, Monica T., an excellent tennis player, often loses matches to players who are far less skilled than she is. Ms. T. underestimates her own abilities and overestimates her opponents'. These thoughts about herself undermine Ms. T.'s confidence and concentration and make her so anxious that she fumbles shot after shot.

Types of Anxiety Disorders

Anxiety disorders include: generalized anxiety disorder, adjustment disorder with anxious mood, panic attacks and panic disorder, phobias and phobic disorders, agoraphobia, and obsessive-compulsive disorder.

GENERALIZED ANXIETY DISORDER (GAD)

People suffering from generalized anxiety disorder (GAD) often say it is like having a chronic cloud of doom floating overhead. In GAD disorders, this *free-floating anxiety* ranges from mild tension and nervousness, to continuous feelings of dread, and it lasts at least six months. Often there is no precipitating factor or event, and sufferers may not remember when they first began to feel this anxious.

At various times, people suffering from GAD may experience other symptoms, such as a pounding heart, sweating, and a sinking feeling in the stomach. If left untreated, generalized anxiety can result in headaches, insomnia, and fatigue. These secondary symptoms, in fact, along with alcohol and drug abuse, are often what finally compel a person to seek treatment.

The Cases of Angela T. and Tom M.

Angela T., a 35-year-old account executive at a public relations firm, went to her physician complaining of chronic migraines and back pain. "I just never feel I'm well," she said. "I don't sleep well and I never go on vacations, because I'm always terrified that something will go wrong while I'm away." Ms. T. spoke rapidly, fidgeted with her purse, and kept glancing nervously at the door. When the phone rang she seemed startled.

A thorough physical showed no organic illness. Suggesting that she might be suffering from generalized anxiety, the physician referred her to a psychiatrist.

Because generalized anxiety is so chronic and pervasive, some people find that over time their memory, concentration, and ability to make decisions are affected. Tom M., a high school history teacher, worried about every assignment he gave his students and replayed in his mind each night how he had presented the material in class that day. He began to worry that the principal was getting ready to fire him, although in fact he received nothing but praise. If one of his students asked about a historical incident that Mr. M. had not mentioned in class, he took the question as a criticism and a sign of rejection. Mr. M. was constantly afraid his students were making fun of him behind his back and that he would not be able to control either the class or his own reactions.

As Mr. M.'s symptoms grew, he began to fear that he was going insane. He sought constant reassurance that his mental faculties were intact. Mr. M.'s anxiety finally eroded the administration's confidence in his abilities, and he eventually lost his job.

GAD and Depression

It is sometimes difficult to distinguish between pervasive anxiety and depression, because people who are depressed may also be anxious and agitated and may even have anxiety attacks. Moreover, people with anxiety disorders may become demoralized and depressed as their illness interferes with their ability to live a normal and happy life. There are, however, some major differences.

People with anxiety disorders generally do not suffer the same degree of lethargy as do those with depression. Anxious people are more apt to have trouble falling asleep, rather than waking up early, which is a hallmark of depression. Anxiety does not impair a person's ability to enjoy things or to be cheered up, as depression often does.

Possible Causes

No one knows for certain what causes generalized anxiety disorder. Most of the research on anxiety has focused on panic attacks and phobias, which are more intense and disabling, and which tend to drive people to seek treatment.

Researchers are currently studying possible links between GAD and malfunctioning of the brain's benzodiazepine-receptor system. Benzodiazepines—including diazepam (Valium), alprazolam (Xanax), and many other drugs—are a type of medication that have antianxiety or tranquilizing properties. (See chapter 5.) They work because their molecular shape allows them to fit precisely into specific brain receptors and to slow the too-rapid nerve transmissions that are believed to produce anxiety. Scientists theorize that the body produces a substance that fits into these brain receptors and has a naturally tranquilizing influence; GAD sufferers may have a defect that blocks this tranquilizing effect, causing a chronic state of anxiety.

Treatment

Clinicians use a variety of methods to treat GAD. At present no firm scientific data have established a clear advantage to any one treatment method.

Benzodiazepine drugs can be very effective for short-term relief of symptoms. Over the longer term, however, people can become physically dependent on them, which means clinicians must be careful to taper them off slowly when the drug is no longer necessary. There is some evidence that tricyclic antidepressants may also be effective in treating chronically anxious patients, but more studies are needed to confirm their efficacy for GAD sufferers.

Psychodynamic therapies are used when clinicians believe that unconscious conflicts contribute to GAD. Cognitive and behavioral forms of therapy, such as relaxation techniques, can help some people to manage or eliminate some or many of their symptoms.

Some individuals may require a combination of all three types of therapy—short-term medication to eliminate the more debilitating aspects of the anxiety disorder, behavioral approaches to change pervasive symptom patterns, and psychodynamic therapy to help resolve underlying conflicts.

ADJUSTMENT DISORDER WITH ANXIOUS MOOD

Adjustment disorder with anxious mood is in a category of short-term psychiatric illness. In this disorder, anxiety results from life changes such as divorce, job loss, or illness. While anxiety is quite normal in such situations, some people experience such debilitating anxiety that they cannot function normally. Usually mild tranquilizers and/or short-term counseling can help a person adjust to the situation and cope without feeling overwhelmed. (See page 362 in chapter 24 and chapter 25.)

PANIC ATTACKS AND PANIC DISORDER

Panic attacks are a far more acute and frightening form of anxiety than generalized anxiety. Attacks seem to come out of nowhere. For example, a man is engaged in routine activity, such as reading a book or attending a concert, when suddenly his heart begins to pound; he cannot catch his breath; he feels dizzy, light-headed, and faint; he is convinced he is about to die. Often people experiencing panic attacks are rushed to emergency rooms, where no physical problem can be discovered. They may go home, reassured, only to have the same thing happen a few days or weeks later.

The attacks usually last between 5 and 20 minutes, rarely as long as an hour. Other symptoms, mostly physical, are usually present as well: hyperventilation, chest pain or discomfort, choking or smothering sensations, hot and cold flashes, sweating, trembling, and nausea. The person may feel that nothing is real and have an overwhelming sense of impending doom and the desire to flee.

Although nothing seems to trigger these first attacks, often they are experienced during a time of transition or crisis: during a divorce or at the loss of a relationship, or when leaving home to go to college.

Course of the Disorder

Panic attacks most often start in young adulthood, usually when people are in their 20s. Also known as anxiety attacks, they are not uncommon; about 6 per-

cent of the population has had at least one attack some time in life. But if they become frequent (at least four in a four-week period) or when they cause a person to worry about recurrences and/or to avoid activities that are either necessary or very enjoyable, they constitute panic disorder.

People with a history of panic attacks often find themselves in a near-continuous state of *anticipatory anxiety* as their dread of the next attack grows greater. Anticipatory anxiety can be similar to, and may be misdiagnosed as, generalized anxiety. The anticipatory anxiety may grow to the point that the person is afraid of leaving home, driving a car, or doing any activity that has become associated with a panic attack. When avoidance becomes severe and disabling, the person is suffering from agoraphobia with panic attacks. (See page 104.) Most people with untreated panic disorder eventually develop some degree of agoraphobia. Because of the demoralizing limitations panic disorders can place on a person's life, 25 to 40 percent of sufferers will experience depression as well.

Panic Attacks and Separation Anxiety

We've already mentioned the apparent relationship between panic attacks and lactic acid and hyperventilation/carbon dioxide. (See pages 97 and 99.) Panic disorder may also be linked to acute separation anxiety experienced in childhood. In one study, for example, 20 to 50 percent of adults with panic disorder and agoraphobia recalled experiencing symptoms of severe anxiety whenever they had to be separated from their parents as youngsters, and many of them had resisted going to school.

Treatment

Many clinicians use medications to block the attacks. To date only one medication, the benzodiazepine Xanax, has been approved by the Food and Drug Administration specifically to treat panic disorder, although antidepressants can also be effective. However, while these drugs can prevent the attacks, they do not decrease the anticipatory anxiety a person may still feel. Clinicians therefore often prescribe benzodiazepine tranquilizers for a short time along with an antidepressant to reduce these symptoms. Once the panic attacks have ceased, the individual generally stays on the medication for at least six months.

Clinicians use psychotherapy in many ways to treat patients with panic disorder, either in conjunction with medication or alone, as the following cases demonstrate.

The Cases of Dean D. and Janet M.

Dean D., a 25-year-old house painter, gave up his job because he was afraid he would have a panic attack while on a ladder and seriously injure himself. Although antidepressants successfully prevented further attacks, Mr. D. remained terrified of returning to the work he loved to do. Supportive psychotherapy helped Mr. D. to understand his illness and become willing to try to overcome his fear. The therapist also used behavioral techniques to help Mr. D. rebuild his confidence. He gave Mr. D. specific tasks to help him gradually work up to his duties again. First, Mr. D. was simply to help out his co-workers by

mixing paints, setting up and holding ladders, and so on. Whenever Mr. D. felt symptoms of anxiety, such as a speeding heart, he was to say to himself "There go my anxiety symptoms again" rather than, as he had in the past, "I'm dying of a heart attack." Slowly, and with the support of both the therapist and his fellow house painters, Mr. D. eventually resumed his full duties.

Janet M., a 31-year-old homemaker with three young children, experienced severe panic attacks whenever her husband had to leave town on business. Even the suggestion that such a trip might be necessary triggered extreme anxiety, often accompanied by such symptoms as hyperventilation, dizziness, and faintness. Afraid that she might experience an attack in public, Mrs. M. became increasingly reluctant to leave the house. She hid her discomfort even from herself with such excuses as "It's a nuisance to pack all the kids into the car," or "I need to be by the phone in case someone is trying to contact me."

Finally, Mrs. M.'s husband persuaded her to seek professional help. In therapy, she remembered that when she was a child her parents seemed always to be fighting and threatening to divorce. Her insecurity at home had made her afraid to leave it, even to go to school, for unconsciously she feared that her parents would not be there when she returned.

Once both Mrs. M. and her husband began to understand the roots of her anxiety, they were able to work on it together with the therapist's direction. Her husband gave her ample warning of an impending trip. When she felt an attack coming on, she practiced relaxation techniques. Gradually these exercises (discussed in greater detail at the end of this chapter) became part of her morning routine, and with practice she became able to relax herself quickly and discreetly when she felt anxious in public. Gradually the attacks and the interim anxiety lessened and finally stopped altogether.

PHOBIAS AND PHOBIC DISORDERS

A phobia is a persistent and irrational fear of a specific object, activity, or situation that results in a compelling desire to avoid whatever is feared. Most people experience at least one phobia, perhaps a terror of spiders, of enclosed places (claustrophobia), or of public speaking. These situations arouse anxiety or even trigger severe panic, with

symptoms such as a racing heart, sweating, blushing, and the need to flee the experience at any cost.

When such intense fear forces a person who has no other major emotional problem to avoid common activities and to severely restrict his or her life, the problem is classed as a phobic disorder.

Phobias fall into two broad types: specific phobias (formally termed simple phobias) and social phobias. Agoraphobia (pages 104–105) is considered to be a separate category of anxiety disorder.

How Phobias Develop

Physiologically, anxiety is similar to the "fight-or-flight response," which prepares the body to react appropriately to external threat. (See chapter 24, page 353.) Many common fears that seem odd or out of place in the late 20th century—of heights, wide-open or enclosed spaces, or even of birds—may be "built-in" reactions to threats posed within the natural environment of our mammalian forbears.

In some cases, the fears may be a learned, or conditioned, response resulting from a childhood trauma, as is frequently the case with a fear of animals. Biological abnormalities or a genetic predisposition may prove to be factors in certain phobic people.

According to psychoanalysts, people associate certain objects or situations with repressed fears, thoughts, or desires. They control these threatening feelings by avoiding the object or situation. For example, a child who was punished for doing something he was ashamed of and placed in a dark room may thereafter associate that shame with a dark room. As a result, he or she may try to avoid dark rooms as a way of escaping the emotion.

Most experts agree that whatever the nature of the phobia, what people are trying to avoid is the feeling of being afraid and their response to the fear. For example, people who are phobic about appearing in public really are afraid of shaking, sweating, blushing, or otherwise making themselves look ridiculous.

The act of avoidance serves to reinforce the fear, however. Thus, a man who is afraid of snakes spots a garter snake on the golf course. He knows it's harmless, but his heart is racing, he goes into a sweat, and he's beginning to feel faint, so he hurries away. Away from the snake, his symptoms stop. He associates fleeing with relief. Because he always runs away from garter snakes—he's never encountered a truly dangerous snake—he never has the experience of facing and surviving the situation and by so doing losing his fear. Through association, phobic avoidance can generalize into phobic disorder, severely inhibiting enjoyment and opportunity in life. The golfer who is afraid of snakes prefers to avoid movies with snake scenes, he won't go to the zoo with his children, and now, even looking at grass makes him think of snakes.

He covers his small lawn with synthetic turf and finally gives up golf, losing his main source of pleasure and his primary opportunity for socializing with friends and business contacts.

Most phobias are chronic if not treated, although their influence may wax and wane.

Specific (Simple) Phobias

Fear of a specific place, thing, or situation without any apparent justification is called a specific phobia. Common examples of specific phobias are fear of snakes, mice, or dogs; fear of heights (acrophobia); fear of enclosed spaces (claustrophobia); excessive fear of blood or injury; fear of crowds; and fear of storms. Multiple specific phobias are common.

Incidence and Outlook

Specific phobias are quite widespread, although only a small percentage of sufferers seek treatment. Phobias of animals are usually acquired in early childhood and continue into adulthood if not addressed. Specific phobias of other things and situations can start any time, although at least one study has found that situational fears (for example, of darkness or thunderstorms) usually begin in early adulthood. Many specific phobias disappear spontaneously after running their course for a few months. After reading of a particularly gruesome murder in the subway, one woman was unable to ride subways for the rest of the summer, even though the murders had taken place late at night on a line she never took. By the time fall arrived, she had overcome her fear and was riding the subways again. Hers was a mild case; severe phobias, if left untreated for a year or more, seldom disappear spontaneously.

Treatment

Up to 75 percent of specific phobias are cured by desensitization, a process by which the person gradually is exposed to the object of his or her phobia. Once the person sees that he or she is not really harmed, the fear will usually diminish. The hard part is to get people to see that exposure is good for them, when all their impulses tell them to flee. There are many ways to get around this resistance. Sometimes simply imagining the experience, either with a therapist or on one's own, will decrease the fear. Relaxation and deep breathing techniques can help as well.

Groups of people with similar problems can help by encouraging members to confront their shared fears, by seeing how it is done, and even by going together into situations that frighten them, such as tunnels or crowded places. In addition to desensitization, some individuals may need psychotherapy and/or medications that block the anxiety.

Social Phobias

Most people are at least a little anxious before a social event, but the feeling usually passes as the occasion gets underway. Many people—31 percent of all adults and 40 percent of young adults—say they are shy people and that they are never completely comfortable outside their own circles. An estimated one in five people admits to strong social or performance fears, and some 2 to 3 percent of men and women suffer from full-blown social phobia.

People with social phobia are terrified of being embarrassed or humiliated in public. The phobia usually manifests itself as fear of performing in front of people, such as in public speaking; of socializing, as in talking to co-workers or asking someone out on a date; or of doing simple acts in public, such as eating in restaurants. Although equally severe, the symptoms of acute social phobia differ slightly from those of a panic attack. Social phobias may involve blushing or sweating, for instance, but not chest pain or pressure.

People with social phobia who go for treatment are likely to be male, single, and come from middle or upper socioeconomic brackets. Social phobias usually begin in adolescence and early adulthood. A person may begin fearing social situations after a humiliating social experience, but more commonly the problem grows slowly over time. If not treated, social phobia can remain with a person for life. Many people with this problem try to overcome their anxiety with alcohol or drugs, thus exacerbating their problems. The depression that results from both the drug use and the lifestyle is often the reason people with social phobia seek treatment.

Avoidant Personality Disorder

Some people suffer only in certain social situations and can function quite normally in all others. Oth-

ers, however, avoid all social situations. They may have what is called avoidant personality disorder (discussed in chapter 13, page 187). Out of fear they steer clear of all close relationships in all areas of life. Some researchers think avoidant personality disorder is just another term for severe social phobia.

Biological Clues

People who suffer from social phobia may inherit nervous systems that overreact to criticism and rejection. Scientists theorize that the mood response to social approval and disapproval may be regulated by one or more neurotransmitters, although which specific ones have yet to be identified. One clue may be that MAOIs, drugs that are used to treat depression because of their effect on the neurotransmitter dopamine (as well as norepinephrine and serotonin), also seem to reduce people's sensitivity to rejection.

Treatment

The MAOI antidepressant phenelzine (Nardil) seems to help a large majority of people with severe social phobia, including those suffering from a general fear of other people. Beta-blockers such as propranolol (Inderal) or atenolol (Tenormin) can help those suffering from stage fright.

Especially in cases where the phobia is the result of a traumatic experience, systematic desensitization may help. This involves gradual exposure to performance and social situations. A person with social phobia might first, for instance, practice having a nonbusiness conversation with a colleague and work his or her way up to asking a neighbor out on a date.

Very often, people who have long avoided socializing need to learn social skills. The therapist may demonstrate appropriate behavior, or the person may rehearse how he or she can act in a threatening situation. Role playing and assigned practice (usually in groups) help people learn how they are expected to behave socially and give them more self-confidence in social situations. Cognitive approaches strive to give people a more accurate sense of their self worth and of others' reactions to them.

AGORAPHOBIA

Agoraphobia (literally "fear of the marketplace") is one of the most common and chronically debilitat-

ing anxiety disorders, accounting for over half of all anxiety disorders treated. It is defined as a marked fear of leaving home, of being alone, or of being in public places from which escape might be difficult or help not easily accessible.

The underlying fear in all these situations is of losing control; people with agoraphobia say they worry about having a heart attack, fainting, embarrassing themselves in public, or even dying. They believe the only way to prevent disaster and/or humiliation is by avoiding any situation in which this might occur.

The most common situations to trigger an agoraphobic response are being in crowds, theaters, department stores, or tunnels; traveling a distance from home or on any public transportation; or waiting in line.

Agoraphobia usually begins with a series of panic attacks. The median age of onset is 28. If the first panic attack occurs in a supermarket, then all supermarkets may be the initial target of the phobia. The phobic response may then generalize to all markets, or even to all big stores, where exit may be difficult. Even when not in a phobic situation, the person may be worrying about where and when the next panic attack will occur.

In addition to (and perhaps because of) their panic attacks, multiple phobias, and chronic anxiety, people with agoraphobia frequently become demoralized and depressed. They become physically ill and tend to misuse alcohol and sedative drugs. If untreated, agoraphobia is chronic, although there may be times when it is better, times when it is worse.

Possible Causes

Theories about the causes of panic attacks, which play such a significant role in most cases of agoraphobia, have been discussed earlier. We do not know why panic attacks and phobias develop into agoraphobia in some people and not in others. Perhaps the panic disorder itself is simply more severe or chronic.

However, environment, gender, and genes all seem to play a part. Most people with agoraphobia are women who are married and unemployed, and therefore perhaps more susceptible to becoming housebound. Family studies point to genetic transmission of agoraphobia, both related to and independent of panic disorder.

Treatment

Because panic attacks and phobias are the precipitants for agoraphobia, the major means of preventing and treating agoraphobia is to block the panic attacks or cure the phobias by the methods discussed previously. Even after successful drug therapy, however, some patients need to be persuaded that they really can leave their home without experiencing a panic attack. Traditional psychotherapy usually is not helpful in treating agoraphobia, but behavioral and group approaches are.

The Case of Mary C.

Mary C., a college-educated librarian, experienced her first panic attack in her mid-30s, at a conference at which she was scheduled to speak. She then began to experience attacks during her commute to work and, over the next six months, gradually became more frightened and housebound. Although she consulted several psychologists for the problem, psychotherapy was not at all helpful.

Her illness continued to progress. Five years following the first attack, Mrs. C. was seriously disabled by agoraphobia. She hardly socialized with others and, unable to function well in daily life, was forced to leave her job. Her husband divorced her because of the illness. Finally she consulted a psychiatrist who specialized in panic disorders. He prescribed a course of imipramine to block the panic attacks that were responsible for the agoraphobia. In six weeks the panic attacks were blocked. Although not experiencing new attacks, Mrs. C. still needed help to get over her fear of leaving the house; she joined a therapy group. Gradually Mrs. C. started life again. She began to feel comfortable leaving the house, made new friends, and began to look for work. Within six months of starting drug therapy, her life was back to normal.

OBSESSIVE–COMPULSIVE DISORDER (OCD)

Short-lived, minor episodes of obsessive or compulsive behavior are fairly common. A person may check and recheck her purse, wash his or her hands frequently, or feel compelled to drive home from work at lunchtime to make sure the stove is turned off. In and of themselves, these behaviors are nothing to worry about.

For people with obsessive-compulsive disorder (OCD), however, such thoughts and behaviors become major preoccupations that take up most of their waking hours. Although the thoughts are against their will and better judgment, those with OCD are incapable of dismissing them.

The "obsession" in obsessive-compulsive disorder refers to the thought or mental image ("the stove might be on"), and the compulsion refers to the action that the person feels compelled to take (checking the stove repeatedly).

About half of the people with OCD are obsessed with dirt and contamination; they may wash their hands compulsively until they bleed and avoid any objects they feel are contaminated. Symptoms common to other OCD sufferers involve pathological counting and checking. They may check repeatedly to make sure they haven't run over someone with their car or left all the house lights on, but often the checking doesn't resolve the doubt.

Some people experience only the obsession, without compulsions; such a person might feel continuously invaded by sexual fantasies but not develop any ritual behavior to counteract them. Others slow down or repeat all movements so that it may take them hours to wash, dress, and eat breakfast. "Hoarders" are unable to throw anything away for fear they might need it someday.

OCD and Anxiety

OCD is classified as an anxiety disorder, and it often occurs in association with other anxiety disorders, such as phobias. OCD often resembles phobias. For example, people who are obsessed with dirt and contamination have been called germ phobics, and their avoidance may seem phobic. Attempting to resist the obsession or compulsion may flood the sufferer with anxiety, as with a phobia. However, while fleeing the object of avoidance always brings at least temporary relief to the phobic, giving in to the obsession or compulsion may not do so for the person with OCD. ("Did I *really* make sure the stove was off? Could I have been mistaken?") OCD also often is characterized by feelings of disgust toward the object or situation, which is not necessarily the case with phobias.

Course of the Disorder

Researchers now believe that OCD is much more common than previously thought. Some studies show it to be twice as prevalent as panic disorder or schizophre-

nia, for example. About 1 percent of Americans suffer from OCD at some time in their lives.

In adult OCD, there is an equal ratio of men to women. However, 75 percent of those whose OCD began when they were children are male. Twin studies suggest that some predisposition to obsessional behavior is inherited.

Most sufferers first experience OCD before they are 30. If untreated, about one-third of all people with OCD will have episodes on and off all their life. For over half, the disorder will progress steadily, causing increasing life impairment.

Possible Causes

OCD has long been of interest to psychoanalysts, who postulate that the compulsions are an unconscious attempt to control unacceptable sexual and aggressive impulses. Some see the disorder on a continuum with the obsessive-compulsive personality (chapter 13, page 188). Indeed, some of those people who later develop OCD show nervous or obsessional characteristics as children.

Most research now, however, focuses on theories relating to brain function and chemistry. The idea that OCD may be related to a dysfunction of the brain is backed by mounting instances of brain damage that produces OCD symptoms. One theory holds that OCD symptoms are due to the inability of the brain to inhibit activity among nerve fibers in the frontal cortex or basal ganglia, leading to lack of control over certain thoughts and actions. Surgery in this area of the brain eliminates symptoms in some individuals.

Serotonin, a neurotransmitter that mediates many thoughts and processes, including impulsivity, suicidality, and anxiety, seems also to play a role in OCD. Further research will show whether overproduction of this chemical contributes to the repetitive obsessions and ritualistic behavior of OCD patients.

Treatment

In spite of the fact that the symptoms of obsessive-compulsive patients seem loaded with unconscious meaning, psychoanalytic and other nondirective therapies have not proven very effective in treating the disorder. Active therapy that encourages patients to focus on the present and to take risks has helped patients live with and reduce their anxiety.

Behavioral therapy that involves having the person face his or her fears while avoiding the usual

---

FOR FURTHER HELP . . .

Contact the Anxiety Disorders Association of America, 6000 Executive Blvd., Rockville, MD; tel. 301 231-9350.

---

excessive response can be helpful. Those who dread dirt and contamination, for instance, would actually have to touch the things they are afraid of and refrain from washing, until they become convinced that nothing terrible will happen.

Two drugs that appear promising in treating OCD are the tricyclic antidepressant clomipramine (Anafranil) and fluoxetine (Prozac), which alters the level of serotonin. Although neither drug was developed specifically to treat obsessive-compulsive disorder, recent studies suggest that they are effective treatments.

8

Depression and Other Mood Disorders

Frederick M. Quitkin, M.D., D.M.Sc., and Jean Endicott, Ph.D.

Depression is one of the most common, most painful, and currently most treatable forms of mental suffering. Approximately 20 percent of the population will suffer an episode of depressive illness at least once in life; some estimates put the risk at 30 percent. Almost 7 percent of women and about 3 percent of men are diagnosed with depression each year. Depression afflicts every age group, from childhood through old age. For some people, the illness strikes once. For others, it is a chronic illness with frequent recurrences.

This miserable, persistent state of despair and despondency has been written about since early Egypt and Greece. In Shakespeare's time it was known as "the Elizabethan malady." The first popular book about it, *The Anatomy of Melancholy* by Robert Burton, was published in England in the seventeenth century.

Once thought to be the work of the devil, depression and bipolar disorder (manic-depression) are now known to be accompanied by disturbances in the brain's chemistry. Over the past 40 years, scientists have made rapid strides in identifying types of mood disorders, their patterns of occurrence, course, biochemistry, genetics, and possible causes. Treatments are effective in 80 to 90 percent of all cases.

WHAT IS A MOOD DISORDER?

Mood governs motivation, energy, emotional experience, and attitude toward life. Moods, even bad ones, are normal and necessary. Indeed, a person who did *not* react with a down mood to the loss of a job or a loved one, or with joy to winning the lottery, would not seem normal. The box on page 110 explains ways in which a normal mood differs from a clinical mood disorder. It may be useful to picture moods on a continuum from mild, transient, and appropriate to extreme, persistent, and inappropriate. At some point on this continuum, the mood difficulty enters the range of a clinical disorder, requiring and benefiting from treatment.

Mood disorders, also called *affective disorders,* represent disruptions of normal emotional regulation. The central feature is a persistent, recurrent low or high mood, sometimes both at different times. Many other symptoms can accompany a mood disorder, however, as explained on pages 111–113.

GOOD REASONS TO GET HELP

Eighty to 90 percent of people suffering from a mood disorder can be helped, most within a short time. That's the best reason to seek help. However, because an estimated two-thirds of those who are suffering do not go for help, or because their symptoms are not recognized for what they are (see page 113), depression continues to take a high toll.

- Fifteen percent of depressed people kill themselves. Among depressed young people, rates of suicide are on the rise, and death rates from suicide-related accidents are high. People who are in a manic state are also at increased risk to commit suicide.
- Among the elderly, depressed people have higher rates of chronic medical conditions, especially cardiovascular disease.
- According to a RAND Corporation study, people suffering from severe depression are as disabled as those with chronic physical illnesses; in fact, they spend more days in bed than those with hypertension, diabetes, angina, arthritis, back problems, lung problems, and gastrointestinal disease. In terms of lost work time alone, mood disorders cost the United States upward of $16 billion each year.
- Studies have begun to reveal some association between depression and lowered immunity in people of all ages, although whether or how depression makes people more vulnerable to disease is not yet understood.
- The toll of untreated depression on social and family life is incalculable. Depressed people withdraw from others. Depressed mothers and fathers have difficulty being parents and often cannot attend to their children's emotional needs.

The Unipolar (Depressive) and Bipolar (Manic-Depressive) Distinction

The two basic mood-disorder categories are *unipolar* and *bipolar.* In unipolar illness, mood is depressed. Bipolar disorders (manic-depressive illness) are marked by periods of manic, greatly elated moods or excited states as well as by periods of depression.

Unipolar depression (which we refer to as depression throughout this chapter) is far more common than bipolar illness.

When Is Severely Altered Mood *Not* a Mood Disorder?

Symptoms of depression and, less commonly, mania occur in a wide variety of mental and physical conditions. Depression, like anxiety (chapter 7), occurs in numerous psychiatric disorders, including many of the personality disorders, Alzheimer's disease and other dementias (which can also cause mania), drug-abuse disorders, eating disorders, anxiety disorders, and conditions of stress, among others. Mania can be caused by cocaine and other stimulant drugs. In addition, both mood states can be a side effect of some drugs used to treat mental disorders.

In medically ill individuals, altered mood can be a side effect of medication (such as antihypertensives) or a direct result of a medical condition (such as thyroid illness, multiple sclerosis, or various types of cancer). (It is also a common reaction to being ill; see chapter 28.)

In cases in which mood symptoms are *secondary* to another illness or condition, it is necessary to establish the correct diagnosis and treat the primary problem to remove or diminish the symptoms of depression.

IS IT THE BLUES, OR IS IT DEPRESSION?

From time to time, almost everybody experiences a blah or blue mood, particularly in response to the loss of something or someone valued, failure to achieve an important goal, or drastic change in one's own life or in the world. It is natural to retreat somewhat after a blow, to lick one's wounds, in order to recover the strength to face life with renewed hope. In addition, some people by nature are moodier than others, experiencing mild changes in feelings frequently.

Some ways to tell whether a mood is within, or inching toward, the disorder range include:

- *How bad is the mood and how long have you been feeling it? Can you bounce back?* Although having a mildly depressed mood does not in itself rule out having a mood disorder, most normal bad moods are fleeting. Severe, painful, agonizing moods that last for more than a month and that recur frequently suggest a problem, as do mild depressions that never seem to lift.
- *Do you feel like killing yourself?* Suicidal thoughts and wishes are signs that help is warranted. If you or someone you know is suicidal, do not delay in seeking help. (See also chapter 26.)
- *Do you have other symptoms as well?* Depressive disorders are accompanied by a host of problems, including appetite and sleep changes, loss of desire for sex, and inability to concentrate or make decisions. (See pages 111–113 for a complete list.)
- *Are you drinking or using drugs to try to alter a persistent bad feeling?* Commonplace, transient blues do not propel most people toward increased substance use.
- *To what extent does your mood interfere with your life?* Normal moods do not substantially reduce a person's capacity to carry out usual roles, enjoy at least some pleasures, or to seek the company of other people.
- *When you're having a bad mood, do you feel as if you're worthless, unlovable, or to blame for bad things that happen?* Depression rather than the blues is likely to take a toll on self-esteem.
- *Is the mood appropriate to what you have experienced recently in life?* It is fitting to feel depressed when you separate from a spouse or lose a job, or to experience grief when a loved one dies. Feeling like killing yourself is not. Even when the mood is appropriate to the life event, however, in time it should resolve and lift. Regardless of the circumstances, if your mood remains persistently down, consider the possibility that you have depressive illness.

IS IT A GOOD MOOD, OR IS IT MANIA?

- *When you are in a really good mood, do you make decisions that you regret later?* Although a mild form of mania called hypomania (page 120) can be hard to distinguish from an extremely good mood, in a hypomanic state many people have grandiose, unrealistic ideas about their abilities, relationships, and finances. The reality hits home when the mood changes and they have to deal with the consequences of what they did.
- *Do you pay for a good mood with a bad mood?* Ordinary good moods and periods of high productivity and energy do not generally "crash" into periods of unhappiness, irritability, insomnia, and exhaustion.

If you answer yes to one or more of these questions, seek a professional evaluation. Symptoms of depression or mania accompany many mental and physical conditions. Even if your symptoms do not warrant a diagnosis of a mood disorder, they can be distressing and disruptive.

DEPRESSION

Depression appears in many forms, with manifold and varying symptoms, and has several patterns of occurrence and recurrence. It disrupts life to different degrees for different people. Some individuals feel that they are carrying a cloud over their heads wherever they go, but they can still function. Others are so despondent that they can barely summon the will to live; they may stop eating and drinking, risking death from malnutrition and dehydration. Some suffer with lower back pain and fatigue. Some feel a pervasive annoyance and boredom. Some can't sleep; others sleep too much. Some become so used to their symptoms that they don't recognize that anything is wrong with them—they think that's just the way they are or life is.

Current psychiatric classification subdivides depression into two predominant types: major depression and a milder, chronic variant called dysthymia. Numerous subtypes exist, however, with different symptom pat-

terns and courses of illness; some of these are discussed below. Depression that is marked also by occasional or frequent episodes of mild or severe mania is discussed under bipolar disorders later in this chapter.

Signs, Symptoms, and Associated Features

Various types of depression show differing patterns of occurrence and/or intensity of signs and symptoms,

WHO GETS DEPRESSED?

Although no one is invulnerable to depression, statistically depression does play favorites. Here, for example, are some of the high-risk groups:

- *Women.* Women are twice as vulnerable to depression as men. Research has never produced an explanation for this phenomenon. Of course, only women can experience the types of depression related to their reproductive biology, such as premenstrual syndrome and postpartum depression, but to date biology alone has not been shown to account for the differences in overall rates. Some experts currently postulate that women's social and gender roles and socioeconomic status make them more vulnerable to low self-esteem and to depressive illness. (See below, page 124, and chapter 21.)
- *People from families with a history of mood disorders.* Research indicates that children with one depressed parent are two to three times more likely to suffer from depression by the time they reach age 18 than children of nondepressed parents. If both parents are depressed, the risk doubles. Rates of bipolar disorder are also high in many of these families. See page 124 for a discussion of the genetics of mood disorders.
- *Anyone in the 25–44 age range.* These are the ages in which rates of depression peak. Although depression can occur at any age, including infancy, for most people it begins in the late 20s and 30s. Recent research, however, suggests an increase in rates of depression among younger people, from late adolescence through the 20s. Many elderly people suffer from depression (see chapter 23), and their symptoms often go unrecognized, but statistically it is less common in older age.

Although rates among children are lower, depression can cause much suffering among younger age groups too, especially when adults fail to recognize the symptoms.

- *Married women who are not getting along with their husbands.* According to a study by the National Institute of Mental Health, nearly half of all such women are clinically depressed. Whether the depression caused the marital problems or vice versa remains unknown.
- *Anyone who has experienced a recent loss or misfortune.* In the past, clinicians regularly differentiated between *endogenous* depression, arising from within the individual with no apparent provocation and believed to be a biological form of illness, and *reactive* depression, occurring in response to a life event or stressor and believed to be psychological and thus not responsive to somatic treatment. Today, however, it is recognized that an unfortunate life event triggers treatment-responsive depression in many people, whether they are predisposed biologically or psychologically to the illness. (See "The Search for Causes of and Contributions to Mood Disorders," page 122.)
- *Individuals who suffer from borderline personality disorder.* Although depression occurs in a wide range of mental disorders (as discussed on page 109), borderline personality disorder is highly associated with depression and mood swings. Indeed, depression is so common in this disorder (which is discussed in chapter 13) that some experts speculate that the two share the same biological underpinnings.
- *People dependent on alcohol, cocaine, and other substances of abuse.* Problems with drugs are known to be predisposing factors in many people.

as will be discussed below. Among all forms, however, depression reveals an extraordinary number of signs and symptoms that pervade all areas of life.

Mood

Depressed, sad, despondent mood is the most pervasive, common feature of depression, although it may not always be apparent to the person who is suffering from it, or it may be masked by other symptoms. As with all the symptoms, the depressed mood can be mild to severe. At its mildest, it may appear as a persistent "blah," flat emotional state, as if a cloud has settled over the person's head. As it increases in intensity, the feeling state becomes more recognizably painful and the person is definitely, sometimes unremittingly, unhappy, gloomy, hopeless, and despairing. For some depressed people, being alive becomes sheer torture.

The mood is often at its worst in the morning, although some people experience a nighttime worsening of symptoms. Crying is common; however, some depressed people would feel relieved if they *could* cry. Other associated mood features in depression are anxiety, irritability, and impatience.

Loss of Pleasure, Interest, and Motivation

Loss of the ability to experience pleasure, interest, or satisfaction in usual activities, known as *anhedonia*, is another hallmark of depression. (In children, the loss of interest in toys and games may be the most telling sign; see chapter 18.) Losing their motivation to pursue their usual ambitions or interests, depressed people often feel instead a pervasive boredom or emptiness. Some depressed people are able to enjoy some activities and to free their minds from their depression at least for a little while, while others can't react at all to anything pleasurable.

Thinking and Self-Esteem

Gloomy, negative thinking is characteristic of depressed people, who see their lives and prospects as hopeless and without meaning, themselves as worthless and helpless to change things. Tasks at work and at home seem overwhelming or impossible to accomplish. Depressed people often do not believe a therapist who tells them they will get better. The hopelessness can lead to thoughts of or plans for suicide.

Guilt appears frequently in the thoughts of depressed people as well, who think that the depression is their fault and that they are being punished. Some become preoccupied with their "badness" or

with mistakes they have made throughout their lives. In extremely severe cases, psychotic delusions and hallucinations drive home this "I'm bad" message. In psychotic depression, a person might have the delusion that a relative is trying to murder him or her for some imagined sin. Another might hear voices urging suicide. Some people also become convinced that they are dying from an incurable illness.

In addition to thought content, the process of thinking can become impaired. Intellectual functioning slows. Depressed people frequently are indecisive and have trouble concentrating on anything other than their dark thoughts. Some experience disorientation and memory problems as well, which, in elderly people, frequently is confused with symptoms of dementia. (See chapter 15.)

Social Problems

Depressed people tend to withdraw socially and emotionally from other people and to believe that they are inadequate in their various roles. They have difficulty maintaining eye contact and communicating with others; their typically downcast, sorrowful faces often discourage social contact. They may have little patience with others and have difficulty controlling their anger and irritation. Depressed mothers play less with their children and respond slowly to their cries.

Physical Problems

Of all the symptoms of depression, the physical complaints that accompany it are often what propel people for help. These symptoms come in two general categories: the so-called vegetative symptoms and general somatic problems.

Vegetative. Vegetative (or neurovegetative) functions—including among others appetite, sleep, and energy regulation—are controlled by areas of the brain that are believed to be affected in many forms of depression. Vegetative symptoms of depression include:

- *Changes in sleep patterns* (insomnia, often featuring early-morning awakening and restlessness, or excessive need for sleep).
- *Appetite disturbances* (loss of appetite and interest in food, sometimes with weight loss, or excessive appetite, sometimes with weight gain).
- *Loss of interest in and desire for sex.*
- *Energy loss and fatigue* (these can be so profound that some people think they are suffering from a life-threatening illness).

- *Psychomotor agitation* (restlessness, fidgeting, inability to sit still) or *psychomotor retardation* (slowing of body movements and of thought, action, and speech; sometimes, a feeling of inordinate heaviness in the limbs).

Other somatic symptoms. Depressed people commonly are plagued by a host of troubling bodily symptoms in addition to the vegetative ones. Because the gastrointestinal system slows in depression, constipation, nausea, heartburn, and even dry mouth are extremely common. Headaches, backaches, chest pains, shortness of breath, skin eruptions, and aches and pains throughout the body also occur frequently.

The Challenge of Diagnosis

Depression is diagnosed by the appearance of typical symptoms, their pattern, and the individual's past history and family history, since depression occurs frequently in members of the same family. Clinicians need to rule out the wide variety of other conditions that can produce symptoms of depression. (See page 110). Some have patients fill out symptom checklists and inventories. (See "The Hamilton Rating Scale for Depression," pages 114–115.)

New Tests

In research settings, numerous biochemical, imaging, and sleep-laboratory tests have been developed to investigate a variety of biological correlates of depression. All of the tests that are in development work on the assumption that some types of depression usually are accompanied by abnormalities in brain and body functions and that these abnormalities can be detected through the measurements of chemicals in body fluids, or by measuring brain waves or other brain functions.

These tests are considered experimental and thus not used in routine clinical practice.

Avoiding Misdiagnosis

Misdiagnosis of depression is common. Because so many people who are depressed suffer from physical symptoms, they tend to consult their primary-care physicians. Although some two-thirds of depressed people see their family doctors first, a recent study found that in medical settings, only about 50 percent of cases are discovered; the number increases to 80 percent in mental health care settings.

The high rate of misdiagnosis results from several factors. For one, many people do not recognize that they are having emotional symptoms as well as physical ones; indeed physical symptoms can mask the mood symptoms. Because of the stigma attached to mental illness, or a cultural or personal reticence to share feelings, people may not mention their moods or personal feelings to their doctors, who may be reluctant to ask about them. Similarly, to protect patients and their families from this same stigma, physicians may hesitate to diagnose depression, which, like many mental conditions, is frequently not covered, or not sufficiently covered, by insurance. (See chapter 31.)

As in the anxiety disorders (chapter 7), the sheer number of physical manifestations of depression can lead to numerous costly tests and procedures to track down a medical diagnosis by physicians who are not alert to the possibility that the patient is depressed. People who are medically ill can be and often are depressed, however (as discussed on page 109). Even among this group, depression is believed to be underdiagnosed substantially.

Attempts are underway by the U.S. Public Health Service, the National Institute of Mental Health, and the American Medical Association, among others, to educate health care providers about the diagnosis and treatment of depression. These attempts are expected to correct the high rate of misdiagnosis.

Major Depression

Of the two principal types of depression, as defined by the current psychiatric diagnostic system, major depression represents the more severe form. Onset of the mental and physical symptoms (see pages 111–113) can be sudden or gradual (sometimes preceded by anxiety, phobias, and panic attacks), but they spell a definite change from the person's previous functioning and state of mind. In extreme cases, the depression is so intense and severe that a person risks death from malnutrition and dehydration or from suicide. The depression leaves most people feeling blue and in relatively constant psychic pain.

To establish a diagnosis, depressed mood or loss of pleasure and interest must be accompanied by at least a few of the following: changes in appetite and sleep, psychomotor agitation or retardation, fatigue, feelings of worthlessness or guilt, trouble thinking or concentrating, and thoughts of or plans for suicide.

Table 8.1 HAMILTON RATING SCALE FOR DEPRESSION

For each item select the "cue" which best characterizes the patient.

1. **Depressed mood** (Sadness, hopeless, helpless, worthless)
   - 0 Absent
   - 1 These feeling states indicated only on questioning
   - 2 These feeling states spontaneously reported verbally
   - 3 Communicates feeling states nonverbally—i.e., through facial expression, posture, voice, and tendency to weep
   - 4 Patient reports *virtually only* these feeling states in his spontaneous verbal and nonverbal communication

2. **Feelings of guilt**
   - 0 Absent
   - 1 Self-reproach, feels he has let people down
   - 2 Ideas of guilt or rumination over past errors or sinful deeds
   - 3 Present illness is a punishment. Delusions of guilt
   - 4 Hears accusatory or denunciatory voices and/or experiences threatening visual hallucinations

3. **Suicide**
   - 0 Absent
   - 1 Feels life is not worth living
   - 2 Wishes he were dead or any thoughts of possible death to self
   - 3 Suicide ideas or gesture
   - 4 Attempts at suicide (any serious attempt rates 4)

4. **Insomnia early**
   - 0 No difficulty falling asleep
   - 1 Complains of occasional difficulty falling asleep—i.e., more than 1/4 hour
   - 2 Complains of nightly difficulty falling asleep

5. **Insomnia middle**
   - 0 No difficulty
   - 1 Patient complains of being restless and disturbed during the night
   - 2 Waking during the night—any getting out of bed rates 2 (except for purpose of voiding)

6. **Insomnia late**
   - 0 No difficulty
   - 1 Waking in early hours of the morning but goes back to sleep
   - 2 Unable to fall asleep again if gets out of bed

7. **Work and activities**
   - 0 No difficulty
   - 1 Thoughts and feelings of incapacity, fatigue, or weakness related to activities, work, or hobbies
   - 2 Loss of interest in activity, hobbies, or work—either directly reported by patient, or indirect in listlessness, indecision, and vacillation (feels he has to push self to work or activities)
   - 3 Decrease in actual time spent in activities or decrease in productivity. In hospital, rate 3 if patient does not spend at least three hours a day in activities (hospital job or hobbies) exclusive of ward chores
   - 4 Stopped working because of present illness. In hospital, rate 4 if patient engages in no activities except ward chores, or if patient fails to perform ward chores unassisted

8. **Retardation** (Slowness of thought and speech; impaired ability to concentrate; decreased motor activity)
   - 0 Normal speech and thought
   - 1 Slight retardation at interview
   - 2 Obvious retardation at interview
   - 3 Interview difficult
   - 4 Complete stupor

9. **Agitation**
   - 0 None
   - 1 "Playing with" hands, hair, etc.
   - 2 Hand wringing, nail biting, hair pulling, biting of lips

10. **Anxiety psychic**
    - 0 No difficulty
    - 1 Subjective tension and irritability
    - 2 Worrying about minor matters
    - 3 Apprehensive attitude apparent in face or speech
    - 4 Fears expressed without questioning

11. **Anxiety somatic**
    - 0 Absent
    - 1 Mild
    - 2 Moderate
    - 3 Severe
    - 4 Incapacitating

    Physiological concomitants of anxiety, such as:
    Gastrointestinal—dry mouth, wind, indigestion, diarrhea, cramps, belching
    Cardiovascular—palpitations, headaches
    Respiratory—hyperventilation, sighing
    Urinary frequency
    Sweating

12. **Somatic symptoms gastrointestinal**
    - 0 None
    - 1 Loss of appetite but eating without staff encouragement. Heavy feelings in abdomen
    - 2 Difficulty eating without staff urging. Requests or requires laxatives or medication for bowels or medication for G.I. symptoms

13. Somatic symptoms general
0　None
1　Heaviness in limbs, back or head. Backaches, head-ache, muscle aches. Loss of energy and fatigability
2　Any clear-cut symptom rates 2

14. Genital symptoms
0　Absent　　*Symptoms such as:* Loss of libido,
1　Mild　　　menstrual disturbances
2　Severe

15. Hypochondriasis
0　Not present
1　Self-absorption (bodily)
2　Preoccupation with health
3　Frequent complaints, requests for help, etc.
4　Hypochondriacal delusions

16. Loss of weight
a. when rating by history
0　No weight loss
1　Probable weight loss associated with present illness
2　Definite (according to patient) weight loss

b. on weekly ratings by ward psychiatrist, when actual weight changes are measured
0　Less than 1 lb. weight loss in week
1　Greater than 1 lb. weight loss in week
2　Greater than 2 lb. weight loss in week

17. Insight
0　Acknowledges being depressed and ill
1　Acknowledges illness but attributes cause to bad food, climate, overwork, virus, need for rest, etc.
2　Denies being ill at all

18. Diurnal variation
A.M.　P.M.
0　　0　Absent　　*If symptoms are worse in the morn-*
1　　1　Mild　　　*ing or evening, note which it is*
2　　2　Severe　　*and rate severity of variation*

19. Depersonalization and derealization
0　Absent　　*Such as:* Feelings of unreality,
1　Mild　　　nihilistic ideas
2　Moderate
3　Severe
4　Incapacitating

20. Paranoid symptoms
0　None
1　Suspiciousness
2　Ideas of reference
3　Delusions of reference and persecution
4　Persecutory hallucinations

21. Obsessional and compulsive symptoms
0　Absent
1　Mild
2　Severe

22. Helplessness
0　Not present
1　Subjective feelings which are elicited only by inquiry
2　Patient volunteers his helpless feelings
3　Requires urging, guidance, and reassurance to accomplish ward chores or personal hygiene
4　Requires physical assistance for dress, grooming, eating, bedside tasks, or personal hygiene

23. Hopelessness
0　Not present
1　Intermittently doubts that "things will improve" but can be reassured
2　Consistently feels "hopeless" but accepts reassurances
3　Expresses feelings of discouragement, despair, pessimism about future, which cannot be dispelled
4　Spontaneously and inappropriately perseverates "I'll never get well" or its equivalent

24. Worthlessness (Ranges from mild loss of esteem, feelings of inferiority, self-depreciation to delusional notions of worthlessness)
0　Not present
1　Indicates feelings of worthlessness (loss of self-esteem) only on questioning
2　Spontaneously indicates feelings of worthlessness (loss of self-esteem)
3　Different from 2 by degree. Patient volunteers that he is "no good," "inferior," etc.
4　Delusional notions of worthlessness—i.e., "I am a heap of garbage" or its equivalent

Source: Reprinted with permission from M. Hamilton, "A Rating Scale for Depression," *Journal of Neurology and Neurosurgical Psychiatry* 23(1960):56–62.

Some people suffer a major depressive episode once in life, which eventually remits. However, at least half of these people experience a relapse within one to five years. The median number of episodes in a lifetime is four to six. Without treatment, episodes can last a few months to more than a year. Between episodes, most people are their "usual selves." In a minority of cases, however, major depression takes a chronic course, causing continual impairment. It can also coexist with dysthymia, the milder chronic form of depression (described below) in a phenomenon known as *double depression.*

Treatment options include a wide range of biological and psychosocial treatments, which are explained on pages 117–119.

Other Patterns

Major depression has a variety of subtypes, including, among others, atypical depression and seasonal affective disorder.

Atypical depression. Excessive sleep and appetite as well as worsening of symptoms in the evening are characteristic of the so-called atypical variety, which often also features a craving for carbohydrates. People with this illness pattern are more able to cheer up temporarily. Extreme sensitivity to rejection is another feature that some experts believe to be associated with this pattern of symptoms. Often, atypical depression responds to a particular class of antidepressant drugs, the MAOIs (see "Drugs," on page 117).

Seasonal affective disorder (SAD). Many people associate different moods with different seasons. Some, however, experience full-blown episodes of SAD, or winter depression, beginning in the fall and remitting completely in the spring. (Some people switch into a mildly manic phase in spring.) Like atypical depression, it is marked more by oversleeping, overeating, and carbohydrate craving. People who have SAD also tend to suffer from daytime drowsiness (putting them at risk for accidents at work). It is clearly associated with a decrease in the amount of daylight as the days grow shorter, because it remits spontaneously as the days lengthen. Probably it is related to functioning of the hormone melatonin, which in animals helps regulate hibernation (see "The Search for Causes of and Contributions to Mood Disorders," on page 122).

Treatment with bright lights, also known as phototherapy (explained in detail in chapter 5, on page 79) is extremely effective for SAD. Traveling toward the equator, where days are longer in winter, also works.

Little is known about an opposite seasonal pattern, far less common, in which depression occurs in summer and lifts in winter.

Dysthymia

Dysthymia (or dysthymic disorder), the second principal type of depression, is a chronic state of mild depression that lasts for years. It is believed to affect about 3 percent of the population at any time and thus is the most common form of depression. In dysthymia, the mood never seems to quit for more than a day or two, draining all pleasure from life. Every couple of years it may vanish for a month or two, but it almost always returns. Some people grow so used to being depressed that they think it's part and parcel of who they are rather than an illness that can be treated. Because symptoms are not as severe as in major depression, sufferers are better able to function in the short run. In the long run, however, because their symptoms are chronic, their relationships and work life suffer.

In addition to the mood, which is sad, blue, or down in the dumps, individuals with the disorder can suffer many of the same symptoms as in major depression (except the psychotic symptoms) but in a less intense or acutely life-disruptive way, especially: sleep and appetite changes, fatigue or reduced energy, low self-esteem, indecisiveness and trouble concentrating, and feelings of hopelessness. In double depression, however, major depression and dysthymia coexist, so that the chronic state periodically is interrupted by intense, more severe episodes. Some researchers believe that in some people, especially those who develop the disorder in adulthood, dysthymia results from an episode of major depression suffered years before from which they never fully recovered.

People who suffer from this chronic depressive disorder are at high risk for other mental difficulties as well, notably disorders of anxiety, eating, personality, and substance abuse.

Personality Factors

Although it can appear at any age, dysthymia often begins earlier than major depression, in childhood, adolescence, or early adult life. Because of its usually early occurrence and its chronic nature, dysthymia seems to become embedded in a person's personality and to appear like a personality trait; people who have it have been thought to have a "depressive personality" or "depressive neurosis." Low self-worth coupled with reliance on others for self-esteem, exaggerated disappointment reactions, feelings of helplessness, a tendency to blame others, and an angry, unhappy attitude often characterize people with this disorder. It is unclear, however, whether these personality factors predispose a person to dysthymia or whether they are a consequence of having it. In any case, the diagnosis of dysthymia is made from the pattern of mental and physical symptoms just described.

Treatment

In the past, clinicians treated dysthymia primarily with psychotherapy. Increasingly, however, medication is also being used.

The Treatment of Depression

Depression is among the most treatable of mental disorders. In some cases it can be completely cured, never to recur. In other cases episodes can be treated as soon as they occur and recurrences can be diminished substantially. As long as it is diagnosed accurately and specifically, depression can be approached with a variety of effective treatments singly or in combination.

When depression is severe and potentially life-threatening, treatment usually begins in a hospital, where the individual can be stabilized, cared for, and protected.

The three basic treatment modalities include drugs, some form of psychotherapy, and electroconvulsive therapy (ECT). Current psychiatric research suggests that for individual episodes of severe depression, somatic approaches (medication or ECT) combined with psychotherapy are the most effective form of treatment. For milder episodes, short-term depression therapies (including cognitive and interpersonal therapies; see page 118) and medication appear to be equally effective. For recurrent or chronic major depression and dysthymia, treatment with medication and/or psychotherapy may need to continue for years. (See also chapter 6.)

Drugs

Numerous antidepressant medications have been developed that begin to resolve an episode of depression in a matter of weeks. As explained in chapter 5, these drugs fall into three general categories: tricyclics, monoamine oxidase inhibitors (MAOIs), and "second-generation" antidepressants, this last includ-

ing the newest drugs for depression. As explained in chapter 5 and below on page 122, all of them probably correct an imbalance or deficit in various brain neurotransmitters, thus normalizing mood. They generally take a few weeks to work, although some symptoms (such as insomnia) can disappear almost immediately. Usually improvement is sudden rather than gradual. After remaining depressed for the first three to six weeks of drug treatment, the individual feels profoundly better from one day to the next.

Most antidepressants are prescribed in gradually increasing dosages until the appropriate blood level is reached (this differs from one individual to another) and side effects can be tolerated. Not everyone responds to every drug, and side effects differ. It is important to be treated by a physician who is knowledgeable about all these drugs and skilled in their use; although any medical doctor can prescribe them, psychiatrists are most experienced with them, and some psychiatrists, called psychopharmacologists, specialize in drug treatment.

Results should be seen within six weeks after the individual has reached the effective dosage. If not, or if the person experiences difficulties with side effects, the doctor will either switch to another type of drug or sometimes add a second drug to the regimen. (Many side effects of antidepressants, discussed in chapter 5, page 68, prove to be no more than a passing nuisance.) A common error in depression treatment is to switch from one drug or approach to another, without giving any one a fair, therapeutic trial. (See also chapter 6.) Lithium, which is generally used to control mania and stabilize bipolar disorder (discussed later in this chapter), sometimes "boosts" the effect of an antidepressant drug.

The clinician may also decide to prescribe other drugs to counteract uncomfortable side effects or to target particular symptoms. For example, when psychotic symptoms are present, antipsychotics (chapter 5, pages 73–75) may be added to the treatment.

Length of Treatment

Because relapse can occur if medication is discontinued prematurely, for single episodes of depression antidepressant treatment generally lasts at least six months. For chronic depression treatment can continue at the same or a lowered dosage indefinitely. For people with a history of frequently recurring depression, drug treatment may continue, with or without psychotherapy, over a period of years. Some experts treat recurrent depression with long-term lithium treatment. Otherwise, episodes may be treated individually.

FOR MORE ABOUT DEPRESSION . . .

Depression and its treatment are covered in numerous other chapters in this book. Note that the specific treatments mentioned here are discussed individually in great detail in chapters 4 and 5. In addition, important treatment issues relating to depression are covered in chapters 2 and 6. For treatments of those types of depression that are related to women's reproductive biology, including premenstrual syndrome (PMS) and postpartum depression, see chapter 21. Finally, for treatment approaches for depressed children and adolescents, see chapters 16 through 20; for depression in the elderly, see chapter 23.

Electroconvulsive Therapy (ECT)

In its modern form, ECT is an extremely safe, fast, painless, humane, and effective form of treatment. Especially for people who are agitated, psychotic, suicidal, or malnourished, or who have not responded to antidepressants or who cannot tolerate them, ECT can be the most beneficial, life-saving treatment available. ECT bears no resemblance to the "shock therapy" of the past. The use of this form of treatment is described in chapter 5, pages 78–79.

Psychotherapy

Most forms of psychotherapy that are discussed in chapter 4 can be brought to bear on the treatment of depression. However, for severe, acute episodes of major depression, supportive or short-term approaches in which the therapist actively engages and works with the patient generally are recommended over the less directive, exploratory forms of therapy, at least until severe symptoms resolve. Even when treatment is primarily biological, however, the individual generally receives supportive psychotherapy, to help understand and deal with the effects of the illness on his or her current life, to learn to cope with stressors, to help with medication issues, and for reassurance and encouragement.

Two forms of short-term psychotherapy—cognitive and interpersonal (IPT)—have been developed specifically to treat depression. Because they are much easier to study than the longer-term, less structured therapies, they have been the subject of much research, which has found them highly effective. The psychodynamic therapies are much more difficult to study (for reasons that are explained in chapter 6), and thus their effectiveness specifically for depression is not known. However, many practitioners consider psychodynamic therapies quite useful, especially after the severe symptoms lift; these forms of treatment can help identify and resolve other issues.

Cognitive Therapy

Discussed fully in chapter 6, cognitive therapy was developed as a short-term treatment specifically for depression, although it now has many other applications. It is based on the premise that a person's emotions and behaviors are determined by how he or she views the world. Depressed people are notoriously negative, focusing on the dark or discouraging side of every experience (the proverbial glass-is-half-empty phenomenon). Lasting three to six months, sometimes with added "refresher" and follow-up sessions, cognitive therapy is a highly structured form of treatment that tackles the depressed person's negative thoughts about him- or herself, other people, the world, and the future. Once they recognize and correct their errors in thinking (see the list in chapter 4, page 54), many depressed people begin very quickly to have hope and experience pleasure and to behave in ways that produce more positive results.

Interpersonal Therapy for Depression (IPT)

IPT is the newest short-term psychotherapy to focus solely on depression. It is based on the concept that symptoms of depression evolve from disturbances in relationships. In weekly therapy sessions over three to four months, patient and therapist work on solving relationship problems that are found to be specifically related to the current depression: grief over the death of a loved one; disputes and role conflicts; role transitions, often associated with divorce or life-stage changes (such as retirement or having the children leave home); or loneliness, isolation, and lack of social skills.

Behavior Therapy

Sometimes combined with cognitive therapy (and called cognitive behavioral therapy), behavior therapy teaches specific techniques—such as assertiveness and social skills training—that help people cope with and overcome depression. (See chapter 4).

Phototherapy (Light Therapy)
Page 116 and chapter 5, page 79, discuss phototherapy (light therapy) in more detail. In addition to the use of phototherapy in seasonal affective disorder, researchers are studying its effectiveness in other forms of depression, including premenstrual syndrome.

Family Therapy
Family therapy views an individual's depression as arising from within the family system. Certainly families have more than one member who suffers from it, and depression in a parent, for example, can be devastating for the whole family. Chapter 4, pages 58–61, provides more information on family therapy.

Feminist Therapy
Less a specific technique than a point of view or philosophy, a feminist perspective can be brought to bear on many types of therapy. Because depression affects so many more women than men, feminist therapy emphasizes how social and cultural views of women, their roles, and the power structure within relationships influence their vulnerability to depression. See chapter 21 for more about the influence of women's roles on their symptoms and disorders.

BIPOLAR DISORDERS (MANIC–DEPRESSIVE ILLNESS)

Some people who experience clinical depression also have periods of euphoria, elation, or excitement known as mania and thus suffer from one of the forms of bipolar illness. They go from the depths of despair to the top of the world, or vice versa. From not being able to get out of bed or to talk to anyone, they become loquacious and hyperactive, with unbelievable reserves of energy and no desire to sleep. In mania, their judgment can become as skewed in a positive direction as it is overnegative during depres-

sion. Many people during a euphoric, manic phase go on spending sprees or stints of sexual activity, or board jets and go traveling the world over. Yet their experience can also be very unpleasant in this overexcited stage (See "Symptoms of Mania," below.)

The depression of bipolar disorders is indistinguishable from the unipolar varieties. The atypical pattern of symptoms (page 120) is quite common. The pattern of mild or severe mania in addition to depression warrants the diagnosis of bipolar disorder. Many people experience a predominance of episodes of one mood over the other, with occasional shifts to the opposite state. Rare individuals experience elevated mood only.

The severe, acute form of the illness is known as bipolar disorder. Compared with major depression, it is quite rare, affecting about 1 percent of the population. The milder, chronic form is called cyclothymia.

Symptoms of Mania

Mania generally refers to a state of extreme euphoria, enthusiasm, overconfidence, elation, and excitement. Most people in such a state have an inflated, grandiose sense of themselves. They are exceedingly talkative or seem pressured to keep talking, their thoughts race from one thing to another, and they are often highly distractible. The inexhaustibility of manic people can be amazing. They throw themselves into work, social, school, or sexual activity with hyperactive energy, and they show little need for

---

WHO'S AT RISK FOR MANIC–DEPRESSIVE ILLNESS?

People who suffer from bipolar illness tend to come from the following groups:

- *Men and women.* Unlike depression only, bipolar illness plays no favorites among the sexes.
- *Younger people.* Bipolar illness often strikes earlier than depression alone, in the late teens or early 20s.
- *Mood-disordered families.* Upward of 60 percent of people with bipolar disorder have mood disorders in the family.
- *Individuals who experience mild mania (hypomania) when they take tricyclic antidepressant drugs.* Research and clinical experience suggest that this reaction can help identify who is at risk for bipolar illness.

sleep. Typical of manic states, however, is their loss of restraint and impaired judgment about the consequences of their actions. Many people invest huge sums in grandiose business schemes; go on buying sprees; engage in relentless, high-risk sexual activity and/or drug abuse; or give away their savings.

Mania can be extremely unpleasant, though. It is frequently associated with agitation, irritability, and rage, sometimes in the absence of other manic symptoms. Some people experience paranoia, delusions, and hallucinations, making the disorder difficult to distinguish from schizophrenia or paranoid disorders. As in depression, delusions and hallucinations are in character with the mood; for example, a person may feel singled out for attack because of his or her extraordinary gifts. People in manic states also can become suicidal.

Although they do not recognize that they are ill, people in the full-blown manic states cannot function at work or in their relationships and often need to be hospitalized.

Hypomania, however, is a less extreme state of exaggerated well-being. Usually in a hypomanic state a person feels on top of the world and can function, often rather well.

Bipolar Disorder

Bipolar disorder is the major, severe form of the illness, in which, over time, episodes of mania and of major depression both appear.

Usually the illness appears suddenly, although onset may be gradual. Episodes of mania, which can last from days to weeks or months, are generally briefer than episodes of depression. Without treatment, symptoms usually become more severe and unpleasant. Some people cycle directly from one mood to the other, while others experience normal moods between episodes. Some people go for years without a recurrence, while others suffer from increasingly frequent episodes. As in depression, a small percentage suffer impaired mood chronically.

Other Patterns

Some clinicians distinguish between bipolar I disorder and *bipolar II* disorder, in which major depression alternates with hypomania only. In the *rapid cycling* pattern, moods alternate as frequently as several times a day, or week to week. In the *mixed pattern*, symptoms of mania and depression occur simultaneously.

Cyclothymia

The milder variant of bipolar disorder, cyclothymia is a chronic disorder marked by periods of both hypomania and mild depression (indistinguishable from dysthymia), with one type of mood sometimes more common than the other. Individuals with this disorder are rarely free of symptoms for long. It generally begins gradually in late adolescence or early adult life, and a large minority of sufferers eventually develop the more severe disorder. Once thought to be rare, cyclothymia is now recognized more frequently, especially among people seeking outpatient mental health care.

While in a hypomanic phase, individuals with cyclothymia can be unusually creative and productive. Indeed, numerous studies have shown mood disorders, especially the bipolar disorders, to be overrepresented among people in the creative professions.

Treatment of the Bipolar Disorders

To treat acute episodes of mania and depression, to reduce the cycling, and to prevent relapses, doctors use primarily biological measures.

Acute Mania

Acute mania may require hospitalization to protect the individual or others from impulsiveness. Lithium is generally the drug of choice to stabilize the person. Lithium treatment requires frequent testing; see chapter 5, page 76. If the individual is experiencing psychotic symptoms, antipsychotics usually are provided. Anticonvulsant drugs such as carbamazepine (Tegretol; see chapter 5, page 77) may also be used, especially if lithium fails.

Electroconvulsive therapy (ECT) is effective for acute mania too, although it is never used in conjunction with lithium.

Acute Depression

Lithium can be a very effective treatment for the depression that occurs in bipolar disorder. Antidepressants may be prescribed in addition.

Maintenance

Lithium is usually prescribed for long-term maintenance treatment. Testing to monitor potential side effects and to be certain the person is taking the medication is important. Antidepressant medication may also continue.

COMPLIANCE WITH MEDICATION: HOW FAMILIES CAN HELP

Many individuals with bipolar disorder keep their illness under good control as long as they continue taking medication. If they stop, however, their symptoms recur. When a cycling pattern of starting and stopping medication develops, the results can be difficult, even devastating, for both the person suffering from the disorder and those who live with him or her. Symptoms of illness reappear when blood levels of medication drop, and unpleasant side effects return when the body readjusts to resuming the drug therapy.

There is usually no one single reason why people with bipolar disorder—or, for that matter, any mental or physical disorder—stop complying with their medication therapy. If the result of taking medication is to make the person feel well, he or she may begin to believe, falsely, that further medication use is unnecessary. In the manic stages of the illness, the person's judgment is likely to be affected adversely; he or she may not want to take a medication that would curtail the feelings of euphoria and special powers.

For some, using medication has important symbolic meaning: taking a drug is equated with being ill, not taking it with being well. However misdirected, for these individuals, not taking drugs becomes a statement of being in control of their health. There are also physical reasons why someone might decide to stop taking medications. Lithium, for example, can have significant, unpleasant side effects—it can slow reflexes or distort thinking, for example. (See chapter 5.)

What the Family Can Do to Help

- The single most effective course of action is to get professional help. A manic episode can be a psychiatric emergency requiring immediate hospitalization for the patient's own safety. Call the individual's doctor or clinic.
- Whenever a family member suffers from a chronic mental illness, it is important to maintain an ongoing relationship with a mental health professional and/or treatment center so that you have somewhere to turn for help. Find out if there is a medical center or clinic in your area with a *psychiatric outreach program.* Some of these programs have crisis teams that make home visits to try to resolve problems.
- If the person is reluctant to continue medication or to take it properly, arrange for a group counseling session—either with the prescribing physician or another mental health professional—to talk about the problems that are being caused for everyone by the person's refusal to continue drug therapy.
- Sometimes an evaluation by a mental health professional who is not involved in the patient's ongoing treatment can help to uncover whether a conflict between the patient and the prescribing physician is causing the refusal of medication. Keep in mind, however, that ultimately it is the prescribing physician and patient who must resolve all the psychological and physical issues and develop an acceptable medication regimen.
- Remember, *you* are not the one suffering the illness or side effects from medication. It is the person taking the drug who ultimately must come to terms with both and decide whether the benefits of taking medication outweigh any negative side effects. However, you should explain that while you understand, you will need to insist on professional intervention if he or she is dangerous to him- or herself or to others as a result of not taking medication for the illness.
- Don't lose hope or perspective. Because the person is not taking medication appropriately now does not mean that in the future he or she will not recognize that maintenance medication is necessary and improves life. Sometimes people with severe illnesses such as bipolar disorder begin to accept a lifelong medication regimen only after repeatedly experiencing that they cannot stay well without it.

Psychotherapy

Between episodes, most people with bipolar disorder return to their usual functioning. Individuals with cyclothymia are almost always in one mood state or the other. For both types of disorder, psychotherapy is indicated to help the person deal with the effects of the illness on his or her life, to work on coping with the stresses that can trigger episodes, or to help those individuals who have psychological difficulties when their moods are stable. Family therapy can help all family members learn about the illness and deal with it better as a family.

THE SEARCH FOR CAUSES OF AND CONTRIBUTIONS TO MOOD DISORDERS

The mood disorders have not one cause but many, falling into biological and psychosocial categories. Every year, new pieces of this complex puzzle are being discovered. How all the pieces fit together is not yet understood, however. For example, although numerous biochemical factors involved in depression continue to be discovered, it is not clear whether the depression causes the biochemical changes or whether these biological factors cause the mood and physical changes associated with depression. Currently bipolar disorder is believed to result from primarily biological causes. Increasing evidence supports the importance of biology in most depressive disorders too, although psychosocial and biological factors frequently interact to create a vulnerability. Following are some of the many factors that cause or contribute to mood disorders.

SELF-HELP FOR DEPRESSION

Depression makes you feel worthless, useless, and hopeless. What's the use of trying, you might ask, when nothing's going to get better anyway? There *are* things you can do to help yourself, in the midst of an episode of depression, if you are troubled by chronic depression, or if you are subject to the blues from time to time.

- *Take your depressed thoughts with a grain of salt.* Recognize that negativity, hopelessness, and self-blame are symptoms of depression and do not represent the way life is or you are. Say to yourself, "This is the *depression* talking."
- *Keep busy.* When your mind is not occupied, you tend to dwell on your depressed thoughts. You need activity and tasks to distract you.
- *Do what you can.* Don't expect to accomplish what you were capable of before you became depressed. But instead of punishing yourself for your "failures," be kind to yourself and congratulate yourself for doing what you can.

- *Fight your inclination to withdraw.* Try to be with others for at least brief periods. People who have been depressed usually are easier to be with and talk to.
- *Try exercise.* Although you may not feel like doing it, you'll find that mild to moderate exercise, from walking to aerobic exercise, will probably make you feel better. The effect might be temporary, but every little bit helps.
- *Recognize the signs.* If you are subject to depression, learn to recognize all the symptoms of an impending episode. Call your doctor *before* an episode becomes full blown.
- *Give it time.* Nobody snaps out of depression instantly. If you are receiving treatment, give it the opportunity to work. If you are fighting the blues, do what you can to help yourself, and accept that the mood will pass. But if it doesn't pass, or the moods keep coming back . . .
- *Seek help.* For additional sources of information and support, see the box on page 124.

Neurotransmitters and Other Biochemical Factors

The earliest antidepressants were discovered before scientists had the technology to understand why or how they worked. Now scientists know that antidepressants affect the functioning of the brain's neurotransmitter systems. Neurotransmitters are the chemicals that transmit electrochemical nerve signals from one cell to another and control feelings, thoughts, and behaviors. Imbalance, depletion, and excess of various neurotransmitters, particularly norepinephrine and serotonin, are implicated in the mood disorders; these substances are involved in mood regulation and also in hunger, sex, and other of the "vegetative" functions that are affected in depression. The antidepressants increase the supply of or the sensitivity to norepinephrine and serotonin.

HOW TO HELP SOMEONE WHO'S DEPRESSED

Being around a person who is depressed can be very difficult. The negativity, exhaustion, irritability, physical complaints, helplessness, loss of interest and ability to pursue usual activities—all this can take the pleasure out of your life too. Following are some ways you can help the other person and help yourself as well.

- *Encourage the individual to seek help.* Reassure the person who thinks that depression is a defect of his or her own character or own fault that depression is a treatable condition. But if the person continues not to seek help and your family life is disrupted, insist if you have to.
- *If the person is suicidal, get help for him or her yourself.* Be alert for direct and veiled threats or unusual behavior. Call the person's doctor yourself, if he or she is in treatment. For specific advice on recognizing suicidal behavior and dealing with people who are suicidal, see chapter 26.
- *Don't blame the person.* Although depressed people often seem to lack the will to get better, that is symptomatic of the depression. Blame the illness, not the person.
- *Provide as much help, support, and patience as you can.* Try to understand the experience of

being depressed. Don't expect the person to be able to "get a grip on it."

- *Try to counter some of the negativity without judging the person.* For example, when a depressed person says, "There's no use. I'll never be able to get another job"—say, "It's natural for you to feel that way when you are depressed. Let's wait and see how you feel when you get better."
- *Encourage the person to go out and do things with you or with others.* Distraction from depressed thoughts and brooding is very important. Even if the individual can't socialize for long, every little bit helps.
- *Don't kid yourself.* When someone you care about is depressed, you may feel a range of emotions, including sadness, anger, annoyance, and frustration. In order to be able to help the depressed person, understand and accept that you have these feelings and avoid acting inappropriately. But don't blame the depressed person for the way you feel.
- *Seek support.* Many organizations offer self-help, sharing, and advice for families too. See the box on page 124.

Hormones

A substantial number of people with major depression show changes in the production and regulation of several hormones, including cortisol, which is produced in the adrenal gland and secreted during stress. In seasonal affective disorder, for example, melatonin regulation appears to be affected. Melatonin is a hormone produced by the pineal gland in the brain. Its production is suppressed by bright light, which is the treatment for this type of depression.

The depression-related or depression-producing hormonal problems may have less to do with the glands that produce the hormones than with the complex feedback mechanisms between them and the brain.

Hormonal factors also play a role in depression related to women's reproductive biology. See chapter 21.

Sleep and the Biological Clock

As with many of the hormonal oddities found in depression, including those associated with seasonal reactions, other of the body's cycles seem to be out of phase. Sleep disturbances are present in most types of depression, for example, and the timing of the normal stages of sleep is altered in many depressed people. Most particularly, a majority of clinically depressed people reveal in sleep-laboratory tests that they enter dream sleep or REM (see chapter 12, page 171) much quicker than normal and have more REM stages earlier in sleep rather than toward morning, which is the usual pattern. In addition, they experience less of the deepest, most refreshing stage of sleep. Sleep disturbances and changes in cortisol functioning (see above) seem to be related to the same biological clock malfunction.

RESETTING THE BIOLOGICAL CLOCK BY MANIPULATING SLEEP

A sure but temporary relief from the worst depression symptoms is to stay up all night and not go to sleep, or to sleep the first half of the night only. Symptoms return following sleep, unfortunately. Going to sleep four to six hours earlier than usual is another sleep technique that seems to be able to reset the biological clock temporarily. The method can switch off a depressed episode for some people, although symptoms come back within a week or two—but by the time they do, the antidepressant medication may be beginning to achieve its effects.

ORGANIZATIONS THAT CAN HELP

Depression/Awareness, Recognition, and Treatment (D/ART) Program
Public Inquiries
National Institute of Mental Health
5600 Fishers Lane
Room 15C-05
Rockville, MD 20857

National Depressive and Manic Depressive Association
53 West Jackson Boulevard
Room 618
Chicago, IL 60604
tel. 312 939–2442

Genetic and Familial Factors

Evidence is strong that vulnerability to mood disorders is inherited. In studies of twins, if one identical twin has a mood disorder, the other twin also has it approximately 70 percent of the time. This rate holds true even for identical twins who are reared apart. Identical twins have exactly the same genes. Nonidentical twins, who share only about half of their genes, share the same type of mood disorder only 15 to 20 percent of the time. Researchers have also found that depression in adopted children is much more likely to correlate with mood disorders in their biological parents than in their adoptive parents.

Bipolar disorder shows a higher rate of genetic transmission than unipolar illness. Both depression and bipolar illness can be transmitted in the same family, however.

Psychosocial Factors

Stress, sex roles, early life experiences, poverty, and individual psychology are among the many psychosocial factors that may contribute to the development of mood disorders or provoke episodes.

Any severe or sustained stress, particularly that which is related to loss, may trigger depression or mania. Loss of a relationship or loved one and loss of employment are high on the list. Some people, perhaps by virtue of early life experiences, are particularly sensitive to issues of loss and are thus more vulnerable to depression.

There is some evidence that rates of depression are higher in lower socioeconomic groups, reflecting that poor social conditions and lack of opportunities might be contributing causes. Poverty, hopelessness, and victimization could bestow a vulnerability to depression among women. Culturally, personality traits that are known to be associated with depression, including passivity and dependency, are inculcated particularly among women. (See chapter 21.) When people have no control over their experiences, depression can result from a phenomenon known as *learned helplessness.*

9

Alcoholism and Other Substance Abuse

Edward V. Nunes, M.D., Susan Deakins, M.D., and Alexander H. Glassman, M.D.

Using psychoactive substances—chemicals that affect the brain and nervous system—to change mood, alter perception and thought, and induce pleasure or relaxation is common in our society. Indeed, drug use has been present in every culture throughout history. Today, drinking alcohol, self-medicating with prescription medicines, getting "high" on illegal drugs, and smoking tobacco products are all acceptable behaviors in varying degrees to at least some people.

Without exception, all substances that cause such sought-after effects also have the potential for dependency and addiction. (See the box on page 128 for a definition of these terms.) In addition, many are capable of causing serious, sometimes fatal consequences to the user's health. Most people who drink socially or "experiment" with drugs are able to stop if their use begins to threaten their jobs, their health, and their personal lives. However, a significant minority of people continue alcohol or drug use despite mounting health and social consequences. In other words, they become substance *abusers*.

Most health professionals today conceptualize substance abuse as a disease (page 128), with a clear set of signs, symptoms, and potentially successful treatments. It is a progressive disease; once substance use becomes substance abuse, the illness will worsen as long as the substance continues to be taken.

WHAT IS SUBSTANCE ABUSE, WHO IS AT RISK, AND WHY?

Substance abuse is defined broadly as regular, habitual use of any substance (including psychoactive drugs, alcohol, and tobacco) to the degree that it causes self-detrimental behavior. Not all drugs are equally harmful. Moreover, from a medical point of view, use of a drug does not in itself imply that the user has a "drug problem," although he or she may be risking social disapproval or, depending on the substance, legal consequences. Likewise, use of a socially approved substance, such as alcohol, does not imply that the use bears no risk.

As it progresses, substance abuse entails physical and mental suffering for the abuser and almost inevitably affects other people. It damages personal relationships, breaks up families, causes absenteeism or unemployment, and can have devastating effects on the abuser's children.

Table 9.1 ALCOHOL AND DRUG ABUSE STATISTICS

- An estimated 100 million Americans drink alcohol; of these, some 10 million suffer from alcoholism and another 7 million abuse alcohol.
- Fifteen to 18 percent of the population will have a dependency problem with alcohol or other drugs at some time during life.
- Annually, 2.58 gallons of pure alcohol are consumed per person. Spirits account for 0.85 gallon per person, wine for 0.39 gallon per person, and beer for 1.34 gallons per person. The amount of pure alcohol consumed is the equivalent of approximately 2.1 gallons of spirits, 3 gallons of wine, and 29.8 gallons of beer per person.
- Every year there are 25,000 alcohol-related auto fatalities; 1.4 million arrests occur for driving while intoxicated.
- Twenty million people use marijuana and 7.5 million people use sedative/hypnotics without a doctor's prescription.
- Close to 22.7 million people—or 11 percent of the population—have tried cocaine; almost 3 million have tried crack.
- Alcohol costs the nation $65.6 billion annually in lost productivity; drug use other than alcohol costs the nation $33.3 billion.

Source: National Clearinghouse for Alcohol and Drug Information.

A Spectrum of Abuse

The behavior of the young man who goes out with friends every Saturday night, gets drunk, and spends Sunday sleeping it off appears on the surface to be very different from that of the intravenous heroin addict who can't last more than a few hours without a "fix" and who steals or deals to pay for the habit. These types of habits seem different from that of the wife and mother who self-medicates with tranquilizers obtained from a friend when the pressures of job, home, and children become overwhelming. Different still, apparently, is the pattern of use of the artist who has to smoke marijuana in order to work but can take it or leave it at other times.

Nevertheless, all of these people have a substance abuse problem. They differ chiefly in the ways their habit developed, in their choice of substance, in their degree of physical dependence, and in the severity and potential consequences of their problem.

Susceptibility and Risk Factors

Many factors may determine whether a person becomes a substance abuser and which substance he or she chooses. These vary from person to person and from drug to drug. For example, genetic predisposition is far more significant in alcoholism than in marijuana smoking.

However, it is important to know that while there are many similarities among the various forms of

HOW TO KNOW IF YOU HAVE AN ALCOHOL OR DRUG PROBLEM

The following items are among those that psychiatrists and health-care professionals use to diagnose substance abuse disorders. Do any of these behaviors apply to you? If so, you probably have an alcohol or drug problem. (See "Signs of Nicotine Dependence," page 143.)

- You drink or use drugs when you don't really want to or in larger amounts than you intended; you have irresistible cravings or a compulsion to drink or take drugs.
- You keep trying to stop or cut down but you can't, at least not for long; you feel helpless to control your use.
- You always use drugs or alcohol to help you perform important activities, including working and socializing; you can't perform without first drinking or using a drug; you are bored unless you are "turned on."
- You spend a lot of time and energy getting the substance, taking it, or recovering from it. You become worried and upset when you are about to run out. Your life revolves around getting and using; it occupies more of your attention than anything else.
- You use deceit or dishonesty to obtain the substance; you hide it from others and lie about your use; you have numerous hiding places and often forget where they are.
- You indulge your habit at times when you have important responsibilities for which you should be "clean" or sober: for example, drinking or taking drugs before an important job interview, while taking care of children, or when you have to drive or operate dangerous machinery.
- You have to take more and more of the substance in order to get the effect you want.
- You have blackouts; that is, you can't remember things that happened to you even though you were conscious at the time. For example, you forget where you parked your car or can't even remember driving home.
- You have withdrawal symptoms: shakes, headaches, chills, thirst, and a strong craving for your substance. You use more of the substance just to counteract these symptoms.
- You continue using the substance even if it is endangering your health, threatening your job, and/or destroying your relationships with your family; you keep telling yourself and others, "I don't have a drug problem."

drug abuse, there are striking differences both in a person's susceptibility to various substances and in the health and behavioral consequences of the individual drugs.

For example, perhaps 90 percent of all Americans drink, but only an estimated 10–13 percent of them develop problems with alcohol. By comparison, some 15 percent of people who take heroin and at least 30 percent of people who smoke one cigarette become addicted to these substances. (There are no reliable figures for cocaine or crack.)

Once addicted, there are also differences. It is easier in general for people to give up *any* other substance than it is for them to quit smoking. The ultimate risks are also different. Cigarette smoking carries a vastly higher mortality rate than most other substances.

The following are factors known to influence the development of substance abuse.

Age. For example, young men are more likely than older ones to drink, smoke, and use illicit drugs. Older individuals are more likely to abuse sleeping pills.

Sex. Women, especially older women, are more likely to use tranquilizers, for example.

Heredity. Children of alcoholics are more likely to drink, even if they are raised by nondrinking families, than are children of nonalcoholics. Furthermore, alcoholism is common among the relatives of abusers of other substances, such as heroin and cocaine, suggesting a broad vulnerability to a variety of substances. Abusers of other drugs also may inherit chemical imbalances in their brains that various drugs can temporarily correct.

Religion and culture. For example, Orthodox Jews almost never become alcoholics, and alcoholism is far more common in France than in Norway.

Peer influence. Peers may pressure young people into substance use but may also encourage each other to stop.

Availability and expense. Cocaine addiction was far less prevalent before "crack" cocaine became available. Prior to that time cocaine was extremely expensive and difficult to obtain.

Personality, coping style, and mental health. People who suffer from chronic depression or anxiety are more likely to use mood-altering substances as a form of self-medication. People who are excitable by nature tend to seek sedative substances such as alcohol; those who are lethargic and sad go for mood-lifting drugs such as amphetamines or cocaine. People with poor self-esteem are vulnerable to substances that make them feel more confident (cocaine) or that help them escape their anguish (marijuana or heroin). People with poor self-control are less likely to stop use when earliest consequences develop.

The substance itself. A fair number of people can experiment with some substances and not become dependent—although almost everyone who smokes even a moderate number of cigarettes for any length of time becomes "hooked."

The Disease Model

Rather than blaming substance abuse on lack of moral character, laziness, or weakness of will, most health and mental health professionals, every major medical association, most government and religious institutions, and even the major health insurers have come to accept it as a disease. This view of substance abuse recognizes that for some substances, there is probably a genetic susceptibility to dependence; that once a susceptible person begins to use a substance, he or she loses the ability to control its use; and that all psychoactive substances cause changes in brain chemistry that perpetuate substance-seeking behavior and cripple the individual's capacity to change. The disease model emphasizes that people with dependency disorders are not "bad," they are sick. Therefore, they should not be scorned or punished for the use itself, but understood and helped.

In fact, placing social stigmas on abusers or indicting them for moral turpitude or lack of willpower can interfere with their seeking and adhering to effective treatment. Defining substance abuse as a disease helps promote recovery. Studies have shown that alcoholics, for instance, respond better to treatment and attain abstinence more readily if they understand the disease model and accept what it implies: They are not at fault for getting the disease but, as with any other illness, they are responsible for taking steps to get well from it.

Like diabetics who must understand that sugar is acceptable for other people but is something like a poison to them, and like people with allergies who know that other people can eat strawberries and chocolate but they cannot, substance abusers must learn to view mood-altering substances as something

---

SOME DEFINITIONS

■ *Addiction and Dependence*
Increasingly these two terms are used interchangeably to mean the inability to stop using a substance without suffering some degree of discomfort. Sometimes addiction is used also to denote the development of tolerance and physical dependence (see below) and the compulsive use of the substance (that is, the inability to control the behavior despite adverse circumstances).

Dependence is the more commonly used term among substance abuse specialists, with the following distinctions:

Psychological dependence is a condition in which the effects produced by a chemical substance are necessary for mental and physical performance and to maintain feelings of well-being. Psychological dependence is always present in substance abuse.

Physical dependence is a state that occurs when a chemical substance is taken on such a frequent and regular basis that it becomes physiologically necessary to the body; stopping drug use abruptly causes a physical withdrawal syndrome (explained on page 129). Not all drugs cause physical dependence.

■ *Tolerance*
Tolerance occurs when a chemical is taken repeatedly over a period of time to the point where the usual amounts produce less of an effect and increasingly larger amounts are required. Development of tolerance varies widely with the substance used and with the regularity of use. Increasing the use of a substance once tolerance develops also increases the mental and physical risks associated with drug use, including the risk of dependency/addiction.

they cannot have "just a little" of. For susceptible people, any psychoactive substance, not just the preferred drug of abuse, can destroy the ability to control intake and to manage their behavior and their lives.

How Drug Abuse Develops

The most basic property of substances that are abused is that they change the person's mood. In most cases, they create euphoria (a state of well-being or elation) or at least provide relief from emotional pain. Once this feeling is experienced, the substance user will seek repeatedly to recapture it.

The second essential property is that the habitual or regular use of these substances can lead to impaired functioning and damage work performance, social and family life, and physical health. (As mentioned earlier, and dealt with at greater length in the discussion of individual drugs later in this chapter, the extent of the damage depends on the type of substance and the extent of its use.)

Denial and Rationalization

The more trouble a substance causes a vulnerable individual, the more he or she tends to use it in order to escape from that trouble and to relieve the pain. Typically, substance abusers react to this vicious cycle with denial and rationalization. Denying a problem exists, they insist to themselves and everyone around them that their drinking or drug-taking is "perfectly normal" or "not out of hand." They describe themselves as "social drinkers" or say they use drugs only "recreationally." Many people continue denying or rationalizing their substance abuse even when they are facing the loss of everything they care about.

Withdrawal

Most substances that are abused produce a withdrawal syndrome. Deprived of the usual chemical, the substance abuser experiences symptoms that range from the unpleasant to the extremely dangerous. Many people continue to use drugs not for their positive effects but just to avoid the withdrawal symptoms. A substance abuser may decide to quit but will feel so uncomfortable he or she will have "just one" to ward off the symptoms.

Seeking professional help when withdrawal symptoms occur helps to make cessation of the habit easier. In addition, seeking help can prevent serious medical consequences that sometimes result from the drug being eliminated from the system. For substances that cause physical dependence (page 128), a period of detoxification is necessary. During this time, the abuser is monitored medically and, when appropriate, provided with medication to ease withdrawal symptoms. Such symptoms occur when the body's cells and systems react to the sudden lack of the substance on which they have come to rely in order to function. (See sections on specific substances for particulars).

Relapse

Nearly every substance abuse habit carries with it the possibility of relapse after recovery. The strength of the temptation to relapse varies with the chemical; cocaine users, for instance, can suffer powerful cravings just at the sight of any white powdery substance. The guidelines for avoiding relapse, however, are virtually the same for every substance of abuse. (See the box on page 131.)

TREATMENT APPROACHES

Recovery from substance abuse is not usually done on one's own. Because lack of willpower is not the cause of the disease, willpower alone may not be enough for a "cure." Without the help of others, a person may not be able to resist the temptation and may not develop attitudes and behaviors that promote abstinence. Many studies have demonstrated that the relapse rate is highest among people who try to give up a substance without any professional help or group support.

Many different kinds of treatment are available. These include short- or long-term inpatient treatment in a hospital or rehabilitation center, individual therapy or counseling, halfway houses, and support groups.

The choice of a treatment program requires consultation with a health-care professional who is trained in substance abuse diagnosis and treatment or who can refer people to the appropriate source.

To find a trained professional, a family doctor, school psychologist, employee assistance program, or religious counselor might be consulted; the nearest hospital or medical center also may provide referrals; or local or state substance abuse service agencies may also supply referrals.

Outpatient Treatment Programs

Outpatient treatment programs are operated within hospitals or free-standing clinics or facilities. They are staffed by substance abuse counselors (who are often recovered abusers themselves), social workers, or psychologists. The programs generally have a group format and include a strong emphasis on education. They usually recommend involvement in "Twelve-Step" (see below) or other support groups. Participation in such programs is commonly limited to 18 months to two years.

Day Programs

Day programs are a form of treatment plan in which the individual checks into a treatment facility during the day, but returns home at night. They are usually appropriate for more severe and chronic problems than outpatient programs. An alternative to inpatient treatment programs, day programs provide a complete range of treatment services without the costs associated with 24-hour care. Individual and group therapy are generally available to help the recovering abuser cope and to treat any coexisting mental health problems. Educational programs aimed at both the patient and the family are often a part of treatment. And usually there is an emphasis on helping the individual to accept or become comfortable with involvement in such self-help groups as Alcoholics Anonymous. Day programs also offer a recovering abuser companionship and support during the day.

Inpatient Programs

Inpatient programs are residential programs in hospitals or special facilities. (The Betty Ford Center is one of the best known today.) They offer a supportive atmosphere where the substance abuser can go through detoxification (a process that varies depending on the particular substance, as explained throughout this chapter) and rehabilitation.

Rehabilitation. Usually lasting 28 days, rehabilitation is an intensive program that is usually provided on an inpatient basis. The goal is to help substance abusers learn to understand their disease, accept their problem and its chronic nature, review what their abuse has done to others, and begin to restructure their lives in more positive terms. The substance abuser participates in educational and therapy groups and, in many programs, is required to attend "Twelve-Step" meetings. The last stage of rehabilitation involves family education.

Aftercare. Aftercare is considered a crucial part of the inpatient treatment structure. After the individual leaves the residential facility, he or she engages in a series of aftercare activities such as individual counseling, regular group therapy sessions, and support group meetings. Aftercare is considered extremely valuable in easing the recovering substance abuser through the difficult transition between the safety of the residential setting and the "real" world.

Therapy and Counseling

Often, use of various mood-altering substances accompanies other emotional problems for which a person seeks help. Therapy and counseling can help the person understand factors contributing to and caused by the substance use, uncover denial, and motivate the person to do something about it. When a substance abuse disorder exists, however, a treatment program (alone or in addition to therapy) is usually required to help the individual discontinue use. Therapy and counseling are also useful in helping the individual cope with the stresses encountered during recovery.

Twelve-Step Support Programs

Many people voluntarily join one of the "Twelve-Step" support groups such as Alcoholics Anonymous (AA), Narcotics Anonymous (NA), or Cocaine Anonymous (CA) and do well without additional treatment, especially those whose problem is not severe. The term "Twelve-Step" refers to the AA guidelines for recovery, based on the principle that recovery requires not only abstinence from chemicals but fundamental changes in attitude and behavior. The program incorporates many fundamental psychotherapeutic principles. These include honest self-appraisal and recognition of personal shortcomings and weaknesses; "confessing" or sharing this self-appraisal with a qualified person; "catharsis" or "spiritual housecleaning" by correcting or making amends for damage done to others; and the elimination of self-centeredness by recognizing one's interdependence with other people and by helping others. Most American rehabilitation centers today incorporate "Twelve-Step" involvement as a part of therapy.

The telephone directory lists local chapters of these organizations and Alcoholics Anonymous, which can provide further information. The "Treatment" sections of the individual substances throughout this chapter also provide further information.

Controlled Use

The medical literature contains many reports of attempts to allow alcoholics in particular, and some drug users as well, to avoid total abstinence and to use chemical substances in a regulated, limited way. Attempts at teaching people to control their use of chemicals have had occasional success, especially if the people in the studies were carefully selected to include only those who were highly motivated, had not reached a point where they had lost jobs and family, were still functioning within normal limits, and who underwent expert, intensive training. The general consensus, however, is that the number of people who succeed is small, the therapy and training required for success calls for highly qualified professionals with well-conceived programs, and that, finally, the risks of attempting controlled use vastly outweigh the likelihood of long-term success.

GUIDELINES FOR AVOIDING RELAPSE

Relapse is an ever-present danger in the early stages of recovery from any substance abuse habit. Although it diminishes with time, users may never be entirely safe. People have been known to relapse, apparently for no compelling reason, after years of abstinence. Therefore, to avoid a relapse, follow these guidelines.

- Avoid "people, places, and things." This means staying away from bars or places where drugs are used; avoiding the companionship of people whose chief recreation is drinking or taking drugs; ridding the house of drugs and alcohol, drug-taking apparatus, and even reminders of drinking or drug-using, such as New Year's Eve party favors. Some people find it necessary to avoid listening to certain kinds of music that they always associated with getting high.
- When you can't avoid an occasion where drink or drugs might be available, stay close to someone who is "straight."
- Call counselors or support group members when the temptation to drink or use drugs is strong.
- Regularly practice techniques learned in rehabilitation, counseling, Alcoholics Anonymous, Narcotics Anonymous, or Cocaine Anonymous.
- Recognize and deal with relapse triggers. Letting too many irritations pile up and not dealing with them is one such trigger. Getting hungry, angry, and overtired can also provoke relapse. Triggers can be unique to each individual; an important goal of treatment and relapse prevention is learning to recognize them.
- Good nutrition, exercise, and other healthy habits are powerful relapse-preventers.
- If a relapse occurs, instead of taking it as a sign of total failure or an excuse to "throw in the towel," consider it a learning experience, an opportunity to reflect on what led to the relapse, and make plans for avoiding the same circumstances in the future.

In addition, for some recovering substance abusers, certain psychiatric problems, such as depression, may emerge in recovery and place the individual at risk for relapse. In such cases, the recovering person should be examined and treated by a psychiatrist knowledgeable about substance abuse. It is important that depression or other psychopathology not become an excuse to avoid substance abuse treatment.

The Substances of Abuse and Their Treatment

The drugs of abuse discussed in this section include alcohol, heroin and other opiates, cocaine and other stimulants, sedative-hypnotics and tranquilizers, marijuana, PCP, hallucinogens, the so-called designer drugs, and nicotine and tobacco products.

ALCOHOL

Alcohol is a sedative-hypnotic drug belonging to a large class of chemicals including sleeping pills and minor tranquilizers. (See chapter 5, page 65.) It is a central nervous system depressant that initially stimulates the brain and produces a euphoric effect, before depressing inhibition, judgment, and basic body functions such as breathing and heart rate. Alcohol use can cause behavioral change, including moodiness and irritability, and exaggerate personality traits.

Experts differ as to whether all heavy drinkers should be considered alcoholics. Some people confine their heavy drinking to certain days of the week or certain occasions, and can go without alcohol for days or weeks in between. These are in the "questionable" category. But many people cannot control their compulsion to drink. These people are alcoholics.

Alcoholism is a chronic disease that can be fatal. In addition to serious medical consequences (see below), alcohol has been implicated in many automobile accidents, acts of violence, and suicide. The disease is not cured by abstaining from alcohol; no matter how long an alcoholic goes without a drink, the first drink often triggers compulsive drinking, sometimes worse than previously. The disease does not pursue a straight line; over time, the negative effects of continued drinking grow worse, and deterioration becomes more rapid.

Health Consequences

Alcohol damages the body in numerous ways. It can cause brain atrophy, which leads to impaired memory and mental functioning. (Some brain damage is reversible with abstinence, but much is not.) The substance may cause or aggravate hypertension, which increases the risk of a stroke, heart attack, or kidney failure. It can also cause cardiomyopathy, a type of heart muscle disease, which can lead to heart failure and death.

Liver disease is common among alcoholics. The liver detoxifies alcohol; in time, chronic alcohol use can cause liver inflammation (a type of chronic hepatitis) and cirrhosis. Early liver damage can be reversed with abstinence. Pancreatitis, an inflammation of the pancreas that results in serious digestive disorders and abdominal pain, is also common among long-term alcoholics. So too are numerous gastrointestinal complaints, including diarrhea and increased incidence of ulcers.

Other deleterious effects of alcohol include depression of bone marrow, characterized by lowered resistance to infection, and various muscle disorders. Extended alcohol use is associated with cancers of the mouth, pharynx, larynx, esophagus, lung, breast, pancreas, and liver. The substance can also interfere with the absorption and utilization of certain nutrients, leading to vitamin deficiency diseases that affect the nervous system.

Intake of alcohol by pregnant women can lead to birth defects and to severe learning and developmental abnormalities (*fetal alcohol syndrome*), low birth weight, and an increased risk of stillbirths and miscarriages.

Effects on Mental Health

Chronic heavy alcohol use can cause or precipitate various psychiatric syndromes, particularly depression and anxiety. The suicide rate among alcoholics is high. (See chapter 26.) In most cases, depression and anxiety vanish after one or two weeks of detoxification and abstinence. However, in a significant minority (as many as 10 to 20 percent of alcoholics), depression or anxiety may persist, signaling the need for psychiatric consultation regarding the possibility of antidepressant or other specific treatment.

Alcohol use regularly contributes to sexual dysfunctions in men and women. (See chapter 11.)

Alcohol withdrawal may be accompanied by psychosis, characterized by illusions, hallucinations, and paranoid delusions, all of which disappear with abstinence. In rare cases delusions persist beyond the withdrawal period and may become permanent.

Table 9.2 FACTS FOR CHILDREN OF ALCOHOLICS

- There is strong scientific evidence that alcoholism tends to run in families.
- Children of alcoholics are more at risk for alcoholism and other drug abuse than children of nonalcoholics.
  - Children of alcoholics are two to four times more likely than children of nonalcoholics to develop alcoholism.
  - Physiological and environmental factors appear to place children of alcoholics at greater risk of becoming alcoholic.
  - Children of alcoholics are at increased risk for other drug use, especially as they approach late adolescence.
- Alcoholism affects the entire family.
- A relationship between parental alcoholism and child abuse is indicated in a large proportion of child abuse cases.
- Children of alcoholics score lower on tests measuring verbal ability.
- Children raised in alcoholic families have different life experiences than children raised in nonalcoholic families.
- Children of alcoholics exhibit more symptoms of depression and anxiety than children of nonalcoholics.
  - Young children show symptoms of depression and anxiety, such as crying, bedwetting, not having friends, being afraid to go to school, or having nightmares.

- Older children may stay in their rooms for long periods of time and not relate to other children, claiming they have "no one to talk to."
- Teenagers may show depressive symptoms by being perfectionistic in their endeavors, hoarding, staying by themselves, and being excessively self-conscious. They may also begin to develop phobias.
- Children of alcoholics often have difficulties in school.
- Children of alcoholics have greater difficulty with abstraction and conceptual reasoning.
- There is *no* clear relationship between being a child of an alcoholic and having an attention-deficit disorder, hyperactivity, conduct disorder, or delinquency.
- If the active alcoholic is confronted with his or her problem, if family rituals or traditions (vacations, mealtimes, church attendance, and the like) are highly valued, and if there are consistent significant others in the life of the children, children can be protected from the problems associated with growing up in an alcoholic family.

Source: "Alcoholism Tends to Run in Families," U.S. Department of Health and Human Services, Office for Substance Abuse Prevention.

Predisposing Factors

A growing body of research indicates that hereditary and familial factors predispose some people to alcoholism. The more alcoholics an individual has in the immediate and extended family, the higher that person's risk of alcoholism; studies have shown that children of alcoholics have a higher rate of alcoholism than children of nonalcoholic parents, even if they are reared by adopted or foster parents who do not drink. Preliminary evidence indicates that there actually may be several different forms of genetically influenced disease that result in different forms of abuse: sporadic "binge" drinking as opposed to regular, daily drinking, for example.

Scientists suspect that this genetic susceptibility is due to a difference in the brain chemistry of alcoholics from that of nonalcoholics. While this difference does not make people drink, it may cause them to respond more quickly and more intensely to alcohol than other people. In addition, once they begin to drink, the alcohol seems to alter the brain chemistry further in a way that perpetuates the disease, making them unable to control drinking and to crave increasing amounts. While abstinence from alcohol does not change the basic defect in brain chemistry, it effectively prevents the alcoholism from becoming manifest.

Cultural and environmental factors also influence the risk of alcoholism. In cultures where heavy drinking to the point of intoxication is encouraged as a sign of manhood or sociability, the rate of alcoholism is higher than in cultures where heavy drinking is frowned upon, restricted to highly ritualized settings, or expressly forbidden.

Persons who have become addicted to alcohol are at higher risk of becoming cross-addicted to other substances than are those people with no alcohol-dependency problem.

Treatment

Most alcoholics are coerced into treatment by families, employers, physicians, or courts of law. The effectiveness of different kinds of treatment programs varies with the individual and the extent of his or her problems. Alcoholics and their families should consult a knowledgeable health-care professional to discuss the best course of treatment. Common settings include Alcoholics Anonymous (AA), outpatient and inpatient treatment, and day programs (all described earlier, pages 129–131).

Detoxification. Many alcoholics require detoxification when entering a treatment program. It often entails giving the person another sedative-hypnotic drug (to substitute for the alcohol), which is gradually tapered off over a period of about five to seven days. The objective is to lessen the withdrawal symp-

toms; the danger is substituting one dependency for another. The need for detoxification depends on a number of medical factors and requires careful examination and evaluation.

Antabuse. The most frequently used drug in the direct treatment of alcoholism is disulfiram, more commonly known by its brand name, Antabuse. It blocks the enzyme acetaldehyde dehydrogenase in the liver, which metabolizes alcohol. If a person drinks while taking or for several days after stopping Antabuse, acetaldehyde builds up in the blood, causing an extremely unpleasant, sometimes frightening reaction. Symptoms include flushing of the skin, heart palpitations, nausea, vomiting, headache, tightening in the chest, and increased blood pressure followed by decreased blood pressure. People taking Antabuse quickly learn that they cannot drink while on the drug, because even a small amount of alcohol can produce a reaction. While on Antabuse care also must be taken to avoid hidden alcohol, such as that found in cough syrups and other medications or used in cooking.

Antabuse is not considered the first line of treatment for alcoholism, although it may be helpful for some individuals who need help controlling their impulse to drink. It is generally prescribed on a short-term basis, and the patient taking it must be monitored carefully by the prescribing physician. Most patients tolerate it well, although side effects

WARNING SIGNS OF ALCOHOLISM

Because of confusing and conflicting information about alcoholism, many people do not realize that they are living with an alcoholic. Here are some clear indications (also see the box on page 127), which in many cases apply to abusers of other substances as well.

- In a situation where alcohol is available, the alcoholic keeps drinking as long as possible. At a party, for instance, the alcoholic is often the last to leave. Even before going to a party, the alcoholic may have one or several drinks "to get started."
- Drinking has clearly become highly important to the individual, but when a friend, spouse, or other family member raises the issue, the individual denies it and usually says something like: "I don't have the problem—if you can't handle it, it's your problem."

- The individual has difficulty remembering events that occurred while drinking, starts missing time from work, repeatedly comes home late after drinking, or exhibits some kind of personality change. Typically, the person will call to say he or she is having a drink with friends and will be home in one hour, then shows up four or five hours later.
- The person becomes less sociable and more isolated than before, doesn't want to go out in the evenings (especially to any kind of nonalcoholic activity such as a movie), spends time alone in his or her room, and when seen again, has obviously had something to drink.
- Changes in the family's finances without any other known cause can be a sign that the individual is spending far more money on drinking than before.

can include fatigue, liver toxicity, cardiac complications, and, in rare cases, psychosis.

Antabuse is effective chiefly among people who have a strong motivation to stop drinking. (Some experts believe that such people would probably succeed in quitting even without the medication.) Its chief drawback is that it is relatively easy to "plan" a relapse by stopping the Antabuse a few days before an expected party or other excuse to drink. For this reason, some outpatient programs require the individual to take the daily Antabuse in the presence of the therapist or clinic physician.

For More Information

Information on alcoholism may be obtained by contacting the central office of the National Council on Alcoholism (12 West 21 Street, New York City, NY 10010; tel. 212 206–6770) or (800) NCA–CALL. The National Council on Alcoholism has local affiliates in major cities throughout the United States. Local telephone numbers are provided in the Yellow Pages under "Alcoholism."

HEROIN AND OTHER OPIATES

Opiates, also known as narcotic analgesics, form a class of drugs that create a sense of pleasure and well-being and serve to kill pain. Opium, distilled from the opium poppy flower, is the original opiate drug and has been used medicinally for thousands of years, especially in Middle Eastern and Eastern cultures. Physiologically, these drugs bind various receptors on brain cells to create an exaggerated, pleasurable response in the individual. Common opiates include heroin, morphine, Demerol, and methadone. In addition, a number of commonly prescribed painkillers, such as codeine, Darvocet, and Percocet, contain opiates.

Drug Types

Heroin is the opiate most commonly sold on the street, and it is usually injected intravenously, although its powdered form can also be "snorted" up the nose. It depresses the central nervous system, regulates the perception of pain, and stimulates the mood-regulating centers of the brain, including the hypothalamus, to produce euphoria. Heroin has a unique effect that users call "the rush," which has been compared to sexual orgasm. The rush is followed by "the nod," a kind of easy drowsiness. The final result, however, is a severe withdrawal syndrome which can be so terrifying that users will do anything to get another shot of heroin in order to avoid it. This combination of effects makes heroin addiction among the hardest chemical abuse to beat.

Methadone is an addicting synthetic opiate developed as a treatment for heroin addiction. It provides a lifting of mood similar to that of heroin but is not so sedating (thus allowing the user to function more normally) and creates less severe withdrawal symptoms. (See "Treatment" on page 136.) It is taken by mouth and is dispensed by legal treatment programs as a substitute for other opiates, although it is sometimes sold on the street and abused.

Morphine, Demerol, and fentanyl are commonly used as powerful painkillers in medical and surgical settings. When used under medical supervision for the treatment of pain, they are safe and generally do not lead to addiction. Health-care workers are particularly vulnerable to abuse of these drugs because they have access to them and to needles and syringes.

Predisposing Factors

Heroin use in the United States has remained relatively stable over the past few decades and involves only a small part of the population, mostly in urban centers. Nonmedical use of other opiates is thought to be more common.

There is little evidence to suggest a genetic or biological predisposition to opiate dependence, but abnormal family factors—especially the absence of one parent or severely disturbed family relationships—are often part of the heroin user's background.

As with other substances of abuse, acceptance within the culture and environment and ease of substance availability contribute to increasing an individual's risk for opiate dependency.

The Withdrawal Syndrome

Opiate users are likely to experience tolerance and withdrawal. Withdrawal symptoms vary greatly in intensity depending on the type of opiate, extent of use, and the speed with which it is removed from the system. Common withdrawal symptoms resemble those of a bad case of the flu, and include anxiety, sweating, broken sleeping patterns, hot and cold flashes, nausea, vomiting, diarrhea, weight loss, and fever. Symptoms are most severe for the first 7 to 10 days, but minor disturbances of mood or sleep can continue for months. Although it may be extremely unpleasant, the opiate withdrawal syndrome is rarely, if ever, dangerous or life-threatening. Still, because these symptoms are so uncomfortable, the opiate user who tries to quit often returns to substance use in order to alleviate them.

Health Consequences

Overdose of opiates can be fatal. Short of that, most of the serious health consequences of opiate abuse result from intravenous (IV) injection, which is the most common means of administration, particularly with heroin. Impure diluting substances and repeated use of unsterilized needles makes opiate abusers extremely vulnerable to deadly infections and other health problems.

The acquired immune deficiency syndrome (AIDS) virus can be transmitted through direct blood contact, such as that which occurs during the sharing of needles. Indeed, sharing needles has resulted in a dramatic increase in AIDS among drug users in recent years. (See chapter 29.) In some areas, up to two-thirds of patients at drug treatment clinics are infected with the AIDS virus, and they pass it on to their sexual partners or to their offspring during pregnancy.

As many as 80 percent of IV drug users contract hepatitis within the first two years of unsterile needle use. Hepatitis often goes into permanent remission but can also lead to death due to liver failure. Chronic hepatitis also is closely linked with an increased risk of liver cancer.

Unclean needles also put opiate abusers at risk for endocarditis and tetanus. Endocarditis is a bacterial infection and inflammation of the inner lining of the heart muscle and heart valves. It can lead to heart failure and death. Tetanus is a bacterial infection that causes muscular rigidity and can be fatal.

IV drug users have an increased incidence of tuberculosis, pneumonia, and other respiratory infections as well.

Effects on Mental Health

Like alcoholics, drug abusers are considered to be at risk for suicide. Accidental overdose and severe intoxication leading to respiratory arrest are also common. (While opiates are actually less toxic than other drugs of abuse, such as alcohol and cocaine, it is often impossible for abusers to judge the strength of drugs bought off the street.)

Many opiate addicts are chronically depressed, although the depression usually clears after the drugs are cleansed from their systems. Individuals who remain depressed after detoxification should seek psychiatric treatment for depression. Treatment can also help a number of other problems associated with heroin/opiate abuse. For example, many abusers are co-addicted to alcohol. Panic disorder and other anxiety disorders (see chapter 7) are common, as is antisocial personality disorder. (See chapter 13, page 186.) For some abusers, antisocial personality disorder dates back to childhood; for others, antisocial behaviors such as lying and stealing have been learned in order to sustain the drug-using lifestyle.

Treatment

Opiate abusers can be treated in either outpatient or inpatient programs. (See page 130.)

Support groups. Narcotics Anonymous (NA) is a self-help support program for opiate abusers that is modeled after Alcoholics Anonymous. Narconon is the self-help group for family members of narcotics abusers and is analogous to Al-Anon (page 142).

Methadone maintenance. In addition to various types of treatment programs, opiate dependency is often treated pharmacologically with methadone in a program called methadone maintenance. In such programs, opiate users substitute methadone for their original opiate. A government-regulated narcotic analgesic, methadone is relatively safe in that those who take it develop a strong tolerance to the effects of numerous other opiates. This means that they get little or no "high" either from methadone or from illicit opiates. When successful, methadone maintenance enables the opiate abuser to escape the drug-seeking lifestyle and to resume a stable, productive role in society. Methadone also can be used to help users detoxify (withdraw from the abused substance). They are given methadone to replace the opiate drug; then the amount of methadone is reduced slowly. Although some addicts remain on methadone for long periods, the eventual goal is to wean them away from this drug as well as any others.

Naltrexone. Known as an opiate antagonist, naltrexone blocks the "high" and creates no euphoria on its own. It is an effective treatment for motivated patients but has not found wide acceptance with most patients, perhaps because of its lack of substitute effects. Other opiate antagonists and agonists (which stimulate the system), such as buprenorphine, are currently being investigated.

Clonidine. A drug used to treat high blood pressure, clonidine can also block many of the symptoms of opiate withdrawal. It is useful for detoxifying from opiate dependence to a drug-free state and for making the transition from opiates to naltrexone. Careful medical supervision is necessary.

Therapeutic communities. Opiate abusers may also take advantage of these in-residence programs where they can live for up to several years. Therapeutic communities usually offer an intensive program of group therapy, often focusing on the theme of roles and responsibilities of the individual as a member of the community. The goal of therapy is to rebuild character by changing personality and ultimately to return to a normal and productive life outside of the therapeutic community. Well-known examples of such communities are Phoenix House and Odyssey House in New York.

COCAINE AND OTHER STIMULANTS

Cocaine is extracted from the leaves of the coca plant, which grows at high altitudes primarily in the Andes Mountains of South America. For centuries prior to the European discovery of the New World, Andean Indians chewed the leaves of this plant for energy to work at such high altitudes, a custom that continues to this day. The effect of leaf-chewing is considerably less pronounced than the use of cocaine in other forms.

The 1985 National Household Survey on Drug Abuse from the National Institute on Drug Abuse (NIDA) reported that cocaine usage in the United States increased from 4.2 million persons in 1982 to 5.8 million persons in 1985. Since 1985 cocaine use overall has declined, but the prevalence of heavy users has continued to increase, a result of the spread of "crack."

Cocaine and substances such as amphetamines ("speed") are drugs that stimulate the central nervous system. (See also chapter 5.) Specifically, they increase the activity of the brain's catecholamine nerve transmitters (mainly dopamine and norepinephrine) in a variety of ways that result, in the short term, in an intense feeling of euphoria and well-being. Such drugs also increase energy and alertness. However, the euphoria is very brief, about 15 to 30 minutes for cocaine and up to a few hours for some forms of "speed," and is followed by a "crash" consisting of fatigue, irritability, nervousness, dysphoria ("the blues"), and depression. At this point there is a strong urge to take more cocaine or other stimulants to counteract the crash. But an acute tolerance develops so that over a period of hours, less and less "high" results from successive stimulant doses, until finally there is none. The user typically takes more and more of the drug in binges while getting less and less high but avoiding the crash.

Cocaine has been called the "champagne" of drugs. A powerful stimulant and anesthetic, it produces a "rush" like heroin, which is followed not by heroin drowsiness but by a pervasive sense of heightened awareness and concentration, pleasure, and omnipotence.

The stimulant high is often described in sexual terms, and some users say they take cocaine to heighten sexual experiences. However, chronic use of cocaine and other powerful stimulants usually depletes sexual energy, leading to loss of sexual desire and even to impotence.

Routes of Administration

Cocaine is generally taken in three ways: by sniffing (snorting) the diluted white powder up the nose, through intravenous injection, and through smoking a preparation known as freebase. "Crack," a powerful street version of cocaine, is a form of smokable freebase cocaine. Freebase cocaine or crack is quickly absorbed through the lungs. Thus, the user can get high blood levels of cocaine rapidly. However, as the effect also wears off more rapidly, the user must smoke crack at shorter and shorter intervals to remain high. Crack, therefore, is extremely addictive and dangerous.

Amphetamines are taken in pill form or intravenously, the latter being the more intense, addictive, and dangerous route. Stimulant abusers commonly "self-medicate" some of the side effects such as sleeplessness with sedating drugs such as alcohol, opiates, and tranquilizers, and thus often have multiple drug problems.

Symptoms and Effects of Abuse

Symptoms of stimulant abuse vary widely. Tolerance and withdrawal symptoms occur, but these are less prominent than the preoccupation and craving for the drug, which seems to stem from the extraordinary pleasure sensation it creates. Former values and responsibilities become less important in the face of the desire for the drug; family, job, and personal responsibilities and commitments also are neglected.

All stimulants have a toxic, ultimately unpleasant effect on the central nervous system; chronic use leads to lethargy, depression, dysphoria, paranoia, and even to a state of paranoid psychosis that can be difficult to distinguish from acute psychosis or schizophrenia.

Indeed, among the most ravaging effects of cocaine and other stimulant abuse is the change in behavior and personality of the user. Stimulant abusers may become grossly irresponsible, spend far more money than their income allows, and become violent and abusive. Abusers may also become suicidal.

Health Consequences

Cocaine and other stimulants, which are fatal in overdoses, can cause several serious medical complications. The drugs put tremendous strain on the heart and can cause dangerous irregularities of heartbeat (cardiac arrhythmia), heart attacks, and sudden death. They can also cause epileptic seizures. Other problems include high blood pressure, stroke, perforated nasal septum (from snorting cocaine through the nose), weight loss, and malnutrition.

Intravenous stimulant users are also at high risk for all the complications of IV drug use, detailed earlier.

Pregnant women who use cocaine can severely damage the developing fetus.

Treatment

As with other substance abuse problems, inpatient and outpatient counseling and rehabilitation are the foundation of treatment for stimulant abuse. Programs need to help abusers find a sense of confidence, self-esteem, and mastery through everyday activities, rather than through the effects of drugs.

Support. Cocaine Anonymous is a self-help treatment program for cocaine users modeled after Alcoholics Anonymous. Local chapters are listed in the telephone directory.

Help for depression. Recent research reveals that a significant proportion of cocaine abusers suffer from coexisting depression. If this is suspected, psychiatric consultation is advisable, as treatment of the coexisting disorder may be important to overall recovery.

Pharmacological approaches. Several promising medical treatments for cocaine and other stimulant abuse have been proposed and are currently being researched. These include tricyclic antidepressants, bromocriptine and other drugs that influence the brain, dopamine system, and medications acting on the serotonin system. Although the effectiveness of these treatments has not yet been proven, they might be considered if standard rehabilitation treatments have failed.

Drug-related psychosis is treated with antipsychotic medications, and symptoms of anxiety and agitation may require tranquilizers.

SEDATIVE–HYPNOTICS AND TRANQUILIZERS

Sedative-hypnotics and tranquilizers are drugs that depress the central nervous system, inducing relaxation, sleep, or reduced anxiety. This class of drugs, used medically in anesthesia and to control certain types of epileptic seizures, includes barbiturates and benzodiazepines, which are also commonly prescribed as sleeping pills and to control anxiety. (Ativan, Dalmane, Halcion, Klonopin, Librium, Restoril, Valium, and Xanax are the brand names of commonly prescribed benzodiazepines; see chapter 5.) Quaalude (methaqualone) has also been a popular sedative drug of abuse, but it is more difficult to obtain as it is no longer available by prescription in this country. When taken in conjunction with alcohol, these drugs exaggerate the intensity of alcohol's effects. Drug abusers often use sedatives and/or alcohol to counteract the unpleasant effects of stimulants. The combination of sedatives and alcohol, however, can be fatal.

Because sedative-hypnotics and tranquilizers are often prescribed by physicians for therapeutic use, it is difficult to ascertain the incidence of nonmedical use and substance abuse. The National Institute on Drug Abuse, however, reports decreased nonmedical use of sedatives among people 18 to 26 years old during the 1980s. Among adults 26 and older, however, significant increases have occurred in nonmedical use of tranquilizers in this period.

These medications apparently present a risk of abuse only to some individuals, though it is difficult to assess the predisposing factors. Recent thinking points to a family history of drug and alcohol dependence as a key risk factor. These substances are similar to alcohol, and thus alcoholics are also at high risk for dependence on this class of drugs. Because risk factors of dependence are difficult to assess, it is imperative that anyone taking these drugs be alert to any changes in sleep patterns, mood, physical health, or behavior. These or any other signs of dependency should be reported to a physician immediately.

Symptoms of Intoxication and Abuse

Intoxication from sedative-hypnotics and tranquilizers can result in immediate loss of coordination and slowed reflexes. These can be dangerous, especially if the user is operating machinery or driving a car. These substances also can result in overdose and death. Barbiturates, for instance, can depress the respiratory center and thus cause death. Valium and other benzodiazapines also depress the respiratory center, especially when combined with alcohol, and thus can lead to death. Chronic sedative-hypnotic abuse can lead to depression, increased anxiety, insomnia, personality changes, and impaired memory.

Withdrawal

The withdrawal syndrome from this class of drugs resembles withdrawal from alcohol. When substance intake is curtailed abruptly, a wide range of potentially life-threatening symptoms may develop. Such symptoms include general malaise, sweats, hypertension, shakes, tremors, anxiety, irritability, seizures, delirium, psychosis, and a general confusional state.

Treatment

Complete cessation of the drug use and detoxification are essential first steps in treatment. Detoxification should always take place under medical supervision. A gradual reduction in dosage is usually necessary; serious withdrawal symptoms such as epileptic seizures may occur if use is stopped abruptly or if tapering off is too rapid. Once detoxification is achieved, counseling and rehabilitation programs designed for alcoholism are generally appropriate. (See pages 134–135.)

MARIJUANA

Marijuana, commonly called pot, consists of dried leaves of the cannabis (hemp) plant and is usually smoked in cigarette form or in pipes. Cannabis smoking probably began in various Old World cultures thousands of years ago. Marijuana users report a variety of effects, including relaxation, stimulation, increased anxiety, paranoia, increased appetite, enhanced sexuality, and a heightened sense of intellectual acumen. Marijuana also has several medical uses, including the relief of nausea that accompanies chemotherapy and the treatment of glaucoma, although it is not legal in most states even for these purposes.

Hashish is a tarlike substance distilled from the leaves of the cannabis plant. It contains higher concentrations of the psychoactive cannabinoid alkaloids and is therefore more potent than marijuana.

Patterns of Use

Use of marijuana is widespread. According to the National Institute on Drug Abuse, nearly a third of Americans have tried marijuana at least once in their lives. Marijuana is considered by some researchers to be a "gateway drug"; that is, it opens the gate to abuse of harder drugs such as heroin or cocaine. This theory has incited much controversy; while it is true that most people who go on to become heroin abusers did use pot regularly at one time in their lives, the vast majority of marijuana users do not go on to use heroin. Nevertheless, exposure to the drug subculture via marijuana use probably does increase the access to drugs and, therefore, the risk of hard drug abuse to at least some people. The NIDA reports that current users of marijuana are more likely to be users of other drugs than persons not currently using the substance.

Health Effects

Marijuana smoke is very irritating to the lungs and upper respiratory systems and may place heavy users at greater risk for bronchitis, sinusitis, and pharyngitis. Conjunctivitis and increased heart rate are common. Marijuana interferes with attention span in many people, and reaction time is often impaired.

Symptoms of Dependence and Abuse

Many persons may smoke marijuana socially or "recreationally" and seem to suffer little or no impairment. However, symptoms of dependence, such as preoccupation with the drug or impaired work or social functioning, can develop. Chronic heavy marijuana use may be associated with certain deleterious effects in some people, including apathy and decreased motivation, impaired cognitive and intellectual ability, and memory deficits. Chronic heavy marijuana users sometimes describe a sense of "coming out of a fog" after becoming abstinent.

Treatment

Self-help support programs and group and individual psychotherapy are usually sufficient for the treatment of people who are dependent on marijuana. Individuals who are dependent on other drugs in addition to marijuana may require a treatment program. Those who are dependent on marijuana and cannot achieve well-being without it may deny the existence of the problem. Their rationalization that marijuana is a "safe, recreational drug" may be difficult to overcome.

PCP (PHENCYCLIDINE)

PCP, commonly known as "angel dust," was originally used in veterinary medicine as a general anesthetic. Use as an anesthetic in humans, however, resulted in postoperative psychotic reactions in a high proportion of patients. Consequently, its medical use for humans was discontinued.

PCP comes in powder, capsule, tablet, or liquid form but is most commonly smoked in a mixture with marijuana. It may create euphoria but can also cause a psychotic reaction, including agitation, paranoia, delusions, hallucinations, and violence. Acute PCP intoxication easily can be confused with the acute psychosis of paranoid schizophrenia or mania. Other symptoms characteristic of PCP intoxication include acute anxiety, emotional instability, grandiosity, and sensation of slowed time.

PCP intoxication also creates a variety of physical symptoms, including vertical or horizontal nystagmus (rapid movement of the eyeballs, as in dizziness), increased blood pressure and heart rate, numbness or diminished response to pain, impairment of muscular coordination, and slurred speech.

Treatment

PCP abuse more commonly occurs as an occasional binge or episode in the setting of other drug use, but a pattern of chronic, habitual abuse can develop. As with other drug dependencies, treatment requires a commitment to abstinence from PCP and to a program of counseling and rehabilitation.

HALLUCINOGENS

Hallucinogens are a diverse class of drugs that cause euphoric effects, including a sense of an altered, heightened, or "expanded" consciousness. Users may also have false sensory experiences, that is, illusions or hallucinations. The most well-known hallucinogens are LSD and mescaline, which are synthetic compounds; peyote, a cactus that contains mescaline; and psilocybin mushrooms, which contain a related hallucinogenic drug. Very small doses of such drugs can lead to dramatic psychological effects.

Hallucinogen use was common in certain subgroups as part of the "psychedelic revolution" of the 1960s, but hallucinogens have fallen out of favor in recent years. The NIDA reports that in 1985, usage had declined among all age groups, although hallucinogen abuse still occurs sporadically.

Adverse Effects

Ingestion of an hallucinogen can lead to sweating, palpitations, blurred vision, tremors, pupil dilation, and lack of coordination. Thoughts and behavior may become disorganized, and the user may hallucinate, become paranoid or agitated, and lose touch with reality. "Flashbacks," in which users experience a brief, repeated effect of the hallucinogen days or weeks following use, may occur.

Hallucinogens are not especially addictive, and chronic patterns of habitual use are relatively unusual but can occur.

Antipsychotic medications may be prescribed temporarily should treatment be necessary.

INHALANTS

A wide range of gases and vapors of organic solvents produce euphoric effects when inhaled. They are easily available in a variety of inexpensive household and commercial products and include: toluene, contained in paint products and glues (hence the term "glue-sniffing"); gasoline and other petroleum products; halogenated hydrocarbons, such as trichloroethane, contained in solvents and spot removers; nitrous oxide, a medically useful general anesthetic present in some commercial products; ether; and nitrites or "poppers," related to vasodilators used to treat cardiac angina and sometimes sold as "incense" in shops selling drug paraphernalia.

Inhalant use occurs primarily in younger adolescents and is mostly sporadic. However, regular and chronic use occasionally develops with all the hallmarks of abuse and dependence syndromes, including craving, impairment of functioning, and withdrawal symptoms upon cessation. Inhalants may serve as an entry level drug in that young abusers often switch to other drugs or alcohol as they get older. Adults exposed to fumes in the workplace may also develop signs of dependence.

Heavy solvent use may result in severe intoxication with agitation, confusion, violent behavior, and seizures. The withdrawal syndrome resembles alcohol or sedative withdrawal in that it may be medically dangerous; it can include seizures and severe confusion. Longstanding solvent abuse or exposure is physically harmful and can damage the brain, the kidneys, the bone marrow, the upper respiratory tract, and the lungs.

Detoxification for regular users should take place under medical supervision so that withdrawal effects may be detected and treated. After detoxification, counseling and rehabilitation programs designed for alcohol and other drugs are generally appropriate.

DESIGNER DRUGS

Relatively new on the scene are the so-called designer drugs, which are synthesized by amateur chemists. Because they have emerged so recently, little is known about them. They are, however, related in effects to both brain stimulants and hallucinogens. The most popular of these drugs is MDMA (3,4-methylenodioxymethamphetamine), also called "ecstasy." Like hallucinogens, designer drugs are thought to create states of heightened awareness.

A major danger of designer drugs is that, like "bathtub gin" in the days of Prohibition, they are not tested for purity or safety. Consequently, users don't know what they are getting when using these drugs. In one instance, for example, a designer drug destroyed the dopamine cells in the brain of a young

HELP FOR FAMILIES OF SUBSTANCE ABUSERS

Getting Help for the Abuser

If someone in your family uses alcohol or drugs to the point of abuse, the first step is to *engage the help of a professional who is skilled in treating substance abuse and addiction.* For a referral, ask your personal physician, contact the psychiatric department of the closest medical center, or call one of the agencies or groups listed at the end of this chapter.

Substance abuse is not a problem that is likely to go away on its own; professional help is needed. Despite promises to the contrary, most abusers will not seek help until they "bottom out," that is, they reach an emotional, spiritual, or physical crisis that convinces them that they must get help. Forcing a person into help usually does not work; he or she has to want to seek help. In fact, forcing the issue may merely exacerbate the problem.

Even if you cannot convince the abuser to seek help, you should contact a mental health professional and get help for yourself and any other family members who are affected adversely by the abuser's behavior. Recognizing that his or her family is seeking professional advice may help to motivate the substance abuser to seek treatment.

A "family intervention" meeting sometimes is effective in convincing an abuser that he or she should get help. During an intervention, family members and other concerned persons, such as friends and coworkers, gather together for a meeting with the abuser. Each person voices his or her concerns about the substance abuser and asks the individual to enter treatment. Substance abuse clinicians can help set up this type of confrontation.

There is little point in attempting to reason or argue with the person while he or she is intoxicated. You cannot communicate effectively or reason with a user who is under the influence. When the person is not "high," be persistent; you will probably need to broach the subject over and over again before making any headway.

If someone is in a drug- or alcohol-induced crisis, get help immediately. If the person has taken an overdose or is unconscious, call 911.

If the person is psychotic (that is, he or she has lost touch with reality), call the police and explain the situation; tell them that the person needs to be taken to an emergency room with a psychiatric unit.

If the person is violent, *get out of the house.* Once out of reach, call 911 and explain the problem to the police. Let them assess the situation. A person who is suicidal or violent can be held at a hospital, but only until the immediate crisis has passed. See chapters 26, 27, and 30 for additional information.

Getting Help for Yourself

Help is also available for the families of substance abusers through the "Twelve-Step" programs mentioned throughout this chapter. Among the best known are Al-Anon and Alateen for families of alcoholics. These programs have been broadened to encompass groups for the families of people who abuse other substances.

It is helpful to the substance abuser to have the support of family members who are knowledgeable and understanding about the disease, but the more significant reason for a family member to join such groups is to get help for him- or herself. No one in a family is untouched by a substance user's illness. People who are close to a substance abuser can become "codependent," to use the currently popular term; that is, the abuser's behavior causes them to fall into habits of behavior and feelings that can be as destructive to them as the abuser's illness is to him or her.

There are also support groups for children and adult children of alcoholics (Children of Alcoholics, CoA; Adult Children of Alcoholics, ACoA) and drug abusers, because numerous scientific studies have shown that the children of substance abusers suffer emotional damage as a result of growing up in a family that doesn't function in normal, healthy ways because of a substance abuse problem.

Consult your telephone directory for local chapters of these organizations or for Alcoholics Anonymous, which can provide further information. See also the "Treatment" sections of the individual substances throughout this chapter.

user, which resulted in her developing Parkinson's disease, a debilitating neurological ailment. Adverse psychological reactions resembling those of co-caine, PCP, or hallucinogens can also occur. Symptoms include paranoia, delusions, agitation, and hallucinations.

NICOTINE AND TOBACCO-SMOKING

Nicotine, the psychoactive substance found in tobacco, is probably the most addictive of all substances of abuse. It is one of the three major components of cigarette smoke, along with tar and carbon monoxide, but it is also present in cigar and pipe smoke. People take nicotine into their system by smoking, chewing, or snuffing tobacco, all of which can lead to nicotine dependence. (Nicotine also is available in gum or pill forms, which are frequently used by people who are trying to stop smoking; see below.)

Nicotine can act as both a stimulant and sedative. Strong evidence suggests that the stimulating effect of nicotine improves smokers' performance. For instance, cigarettes help people perform repetitive tasks because they make users more alert and keeps them from being bored. The stimulating effect of smoking also counteracts the sedative effects of alcohol, accounting in part for the tendency of many alcohol users also to smoke. On the other hand, the sedative effects of nicotine serve to diminish negative feeling states; that is, nicotine can temporarily calm anxiety, minimize rage, and assuage depression.

Patterns of Use

According to United States government statistics, approximately 52 million adults smoke tobacco; stated another way, 31.5 percent of adult men and nearly 26 percent of adult women smoke. In addition, about 2 million teenagers smoke today.

Proportionately fewer adults smoke cigarettes today than in the past few decades. But despite the overall decline in the percentage of smokers in every income level and age group, the rate has declined much more slowly for women than for men. The percentage of teenage smokers has declined from 29 percent to 20 percent over the past 10 years.

Predisposing Factors

Studies have shown that people who have suffered persistent periods of depression that have affected sleep, appetite, and everyday functioning are at greater risk for becoming nicotine-dependent than those without such a history. Also at high risk are heavy drinkers and people with attention-deficit disorder. (See chapter 18.)

Social acceptability of smoking also increases the risk of nicotine addiction. Individuals who belong to a culture that encourages or at least tolerates smoking will be more likely to smoke, and thus become nicotine-dependent, than those who live in a culture that discourages or forbids smoking. This fact has been dramatically demonstrated by the recent experience in the United States where legal and social pressures have resulted in a marked decrease in smoking compared to other nations where laws and attitudes remain unchanged.

Furthermore, research indicates that individuals with a history of depression are twice as likely to fail in their efforts to stop smoking than individuals with no past history. This may explain why women, who are almost twice as likely as men to suffer from depression, seem to have a harder time quitting than men.

Effects of Smoking on Health

Smoking causes or contributes to 30 percent of all cancers in the United States and is the leading cause of cancer deaths among Americans. Lung cancer is the most notable example. Up to 85 percent of all lung

---

SIGNS OF NICOTINE DEPENDENCE

- The need to smoke immediately upon waking in the morning.
- The inability to curtail or reduce smoking despite several attempts to stop. It is important to note that the more cigarettes an individual smokes, the more difficult it is to stop.
- Continuation of the smoking habit even though it is causing some symptoms (such as chronic cough or hoarseness) or is obviously affecting the health of close members of the family.
- Attempts to reduce or curtail smoking result in *withdrawal syndrome* or "nicotine fits." During withdrawal, the individual may experience a variety of symptoms that include headaches, irritability, lack of concentration, insomnia, tremors, increased appetite, drowsiness, and, most significantly, a craving for cigarettes. Often the individual returns to smoking to counteract these unpleasant symptoms.

cancer deaths are attributable to smoking. Lung cancer has long been the leading cause of cancer mortality among men, and it has surpassed breast cancer as the number-one cause of cancer in women. Other cancers strongly associated with smoking include those of the larynx, esophagus, mouth, and bladder.

Smoking causes 85 percent of all chronic pulmonary disease and is the major cause of emphysema.

Approximately 30 to 40 percent of all deaths from heart attacks are attributable to smoking. The 1983 Report of the Surgeon General states that "cigarette smoking should be considered the most important of the known modifiable risk factors for coronary heart disease in the United States." Smokers also have an increased risk of stroke.

Smoking increases the flow of gastric acids and is associated with an increased incidence of peptic ulcers. It also causes mouth sores, diminished taste, gum disease, and other nonmalignant mouth disorders.

Women who smoke during pregnancy have an increased risk of miscarriage, stillbirths, and low-birthweight babies. Crib death also is more common among babies born to women who smoke.

Osteoporosis (weakening of the bones) occurs at a higher rate among smokers. Smoking also is associated with earlier menopause.

Moreover, when combined with other cardiovascular or respiratory risk factors, smoking greatly compounds the effects of both. For example, a smoker who is exposed to asbestos has a much higher risk of asbestos-related lung cancer than a nonsmoker exposed to asbestos. Similarly, a person with high blood pressure or high blood cholesterol who also smokes has a much higher risk of a heart attack than a nonsmoking counterpart.

Effects of Passive Smoking

Passive or involuntary smoke is smoke to which non-smokers are exposed in an indoor environment. Common effects of passive smoke on healthy nonsmokers include eye irritation, headaches, nasal problems, and coughing. People with asthma or allergic disorders may suffer more severe effects when exposed to smoke.

The 1986 Report of the Surgeon General concludes that "involuntary smoking is a cause of disease, including lung cancer, in healthy nonsmokers." Studies have shown that nonsmokers who live with heavy smokers have a threefold increase in lung cancer deaths, compared to nonsmokers who live in a smoke-free household. Children of smokers have double the normal rate of hospitalization for respiratory ailments.

The Surgeon General's report also states that passive smoking negatively affects the health of children of smokers by increasing the frequency of respiratory infections and symptoms.

Quit–Smoking Programs

The importance of quitting smoking cannot be overstated. Doing so can reduce substantially the ill effects on health and the risk of early death. For instance, within five years of quitting, a smoker can reduce his or her risk of heart disease to the level of a nonsmoker. Ten years after stopping, the risk of lung cancer is almost back to that of a nonsmoker. It is easier for some people to quit smoking than it is for others; some are able to quit immediately and permanently the first time they try.

The rate of relapse by smokers who attempt to quit is high, as with opiates and alcohol. The vast majority of relapses occur within the first three months; people who remain abstinent for this long have a good chance of succeeding permanently, and those who don't smoke for a year have an excellent long-term chance. As with stopping other substance abuse, early relapse is attributable primarily to the unpleasant withdrawal symptoms experienced during this time; the user returns to smoking to alleviate such symptoms. And as with other substances, once a smoker quits, he or she can never "have just one." The addiction returns quickly and powerfully.

Although the largest number of people who stop smoking successfully simply decide to quit and do so on their own ("cold turkey"), others try repeatedly and are unable to give it up. For such people, several kinds of smoking cessation programs can be helpful.

The first programs to try are those that are most accessible, convenient, free, and not too time-consuming. The American Cancer Society and the American Lung Association sponsor such programs, as do most hospitals. These programs rely largely on behavior change along with encouragement and support. They do not use medications.

There are a number of other programs recommended for those who do not succeed with the simpler programs.

GETTING READY TO QUIT

Thoughtful preparation before quitting is an important factor in the smoker's ultimate success. The following advice may help those who are trying to stop on their own.

- *Plan ahead.* Try listing the reasons you want to quit. Besides the well-known health reasons, include your own personal motivations, such as "My mate says smoking makes my breath smell foul." Or, "I want to stop to improve my athletic performance."
- *Keep a diary* for several days of when and where you smoke. Recognizing patterns of time, place, emotional framework, and associated activities can help you discover and then avoid high-risk smoking situations once you quit. For example, discovering that your smoking increases in late afternoon when you are tired and hungry will allow you, perhaps, to substitute a snack (such as fruit or fruit juice) as a pick-me-up.
- *Set the date for quitting.* Do not choose a time when you will be under a great deal of stress. Vacation time may be a good choice. Whatever date you choose, however, stick to it.
- *Change brands of cigarettes.* While there is no "safe" cigarette, low tar and low nicotine cigarettes may reduce your pleasure in smoking and therefore make it easier to quit. Also, buy only one pack at a time. This will make smoking a little less convenient.
- *Involve other people.* Some smokers are hesitant to make known their intentions to quit for fear of public failure. But most people, even nonsmokers, know that quitting is difficult and have some idea about what you are going through; chances are they will be very supportive and encouraging. A good way to involve someone is to ask a friend to quit with you or to bet someone that you will be able to quit. You may also wish to designate a phone buddy whom you can call when you have a craving to smoke. Cravings pass—just keep talking.
- *Increase your exercise.* You cannot smoke while you exercise, so start an exercise regimen. Your body is going to need all the help you can give it to repair itself from the damages of smoking; build up your strength, drink plenty of fluids, and get lots of rest.
- *Breathe deeply.* You may not be used to taking deep breaths unless you are taking a deep drag on a cigarette. Practice taking deep, slow breaths. Some people find this technique useful during craving attacks.
- *Expect to succeed.* But do not be afraid of an initial failure or backsliding. Slipping back does not indicate inevitable failure again—in fact, your chances of being successful increase each time you attempt to quit.

Remember if you can't do it on your own, you can join a quit-smoking program. A lot of people can't do it on their own. Make it easier on yourself and get help.

Use of nicotine gum and the nicotine patch. This is the best proven of all the methods. Studies have shown that people who use nicotine gum (combined with counseling) have doubled the success rate of those who chewed a placebo (a nonnicotine "dummy" gum). Nicotine gum initially allows the smoker to maintain nicotine dependence while curtailing smoking. Counseling is highly important in this approach. Many people worry about the health effects of the gum; although it is a good idea to taper off the gum eventually, there is no evidence so far of long-term ill effects.

A nicotine patch, which is applied to the skin, releasing nicotine directly into the bloodstream and eliminating the inconvenience and many of the side effects of gum, has also become available to physicians for use in quit-smoking treatment.

Clonidine and behavior therapy. A new treatment being studied involves the use of clonidine to lessen the symptoms of withdrawal. (This drug, commonly used to reduce high blood pressure, blocks certain nervous system responses.) In a study at The Columbia University College of Physicians and Surgeons, when administered to heavy smokers who also underwent behavioral therapy, clonidine was helpful, especially for women with severe addictions. The nicotine patch generally is easier to use, however, so it should be tried first.

Smoking aversion. This program repeatedly forces a smoker to inhale smoke rapidly to the point of feeling sick. Over time the smoker begins to associate smoking with a strong negative feeling that will encourage quitting. This is an expensive and time-consuming program; typically, the smoker spends a minimum of an hour every day for a week, then reduces the daily sessions progressively over many weeks or even several months. It must be done under expert medical supervision after careful medical evaluation.

Others. Acupuncture, hypnosis, and commercial programs have not been scientifically evaluated as the preceding programs have. The commercial programs, in addition, can be very expensive.

Weight Gain

Many people worry that they will gain weight once they quit, and indeed many people do, but the average gain is only eight pounds. Most people are able to lose the weight once they have succeeded in quitting; it is difficult to do this while trying to quit.

Helpful Numbers

Self-help Groups

If your telephone book does not list local chapters of self-help groups, you can obtain information from the following sources:

Alcoholics Anonymous
National Service Office
15 E. 26 Street
New York, NY 10010
tel. 212 686–1100
The national office can provide referrals to local chapters of Alcoholics Anonymous anywhere in the country.

Narcotics Anonymous
National Office
P.O. Box 9999
Van Nuys, CA 91409
tel. 818 780–3951
Provides referrals to local chapters both nationally and internationally, as well as literature for addicts written by addicts.

Cocaine Anonymous
World Service Office, Inc.
374 Overland Avenue
Suite-G
Los Angeles, CA 90034
tel. 213 559–5833

For referral to local chapters, call:
800 347–8998

Referrals and Information

National Clearinghouse for Alcohol and Drug Information (NCADI)
P.O. Box 2345
Rockville, MD 20852
tel. 800 729–6686

Callers can receive free alcohol and other drug materials and services: booklets, fliers, and posters; data base searches; referral; information; 24-hour telephone access. NCADI is a service of the U.S. Office for Substance Abuse Prevention.

National Institute of Drug Abuse and Confidential Referral Service
tel. 800 662–HELP
This is a publicly funded free telephone service.

10

Eating Disorders

B. Timothy Walsh, M.D.

Dieting and worrying about body image are an American pastime. At any given moment, some 50 million Americans are on a weight-loss regimen. Although few of those who wish they were thinner suffer from a true psychiatric eating disorder, the numbers of individuals who have either of the two major forms of eating disorder—anorexia nervosa and bulimia—have risen dramatically in recent decades.

Obesity is sometimes considered a third eating disorder. Technically, it is not viewed as a true psychiatric problem unless attempts to lose weight become abnormally obsessive, or unless concern about body image becomes so severe that it interferes with normal functioning and good mental health. These emotional problems do frequently accompany obesity.

Anorexia nervosa (severe self-starvation) and bulimia (binge-eating and purging) have striking, sometimes life-threatening physical features that must be treated medically. Nonetheless, the roots of these disorders are emotional and psychological, and treatment approaches are primarily psychological. While investigators do not agree on the causes of these disorders, numerous factors that contribute to their development have been identified.

ANOREXIA NERVOSA

Anorexia nervosa is a serious disorder that is estimated to affect as many as one out of every 100 to 200 adolescent girls and young women and about one-tenth as many boys and young men. The first case of this disorder was described in the medical literature 300 years ago; Sir William Gull named the disorder anorexia nervosa in the 19th century. However, anorexia nervosa did not become widespread until the 1960s and 1970s.

How It Starts

The problem usually begins when a girl in early adolescence becomes unhappy about her appearance, decides she needs to lose a few pounds, and goes on a diet. Most often this desire to diet first occurs at around age 12 to 14, but sometimes it happens as early as age 9 or 10 or as late as the 20s. Boys' concern with their weight is often related to sports participation; they diet in order to "reach weight" for a particular sport.

Among young teenage girls especially, such dieting is common, usually lasts only briefly, and rarely affects either physical or mental health. Among a susceptible group of young women and men, however, the dieting begins to take on a psychological significance that turns it into something potentially dangerous. They become obsessed with thinness and terrified of regaining weight. Dieting and food concerns become the central focus of their lives, turning all their energies and attention away from the real issues of growth and maturity with which they should be dealing at this age. The dieting is accompanied by baffling and distressing physical and behavioral changes. One of the most significant problems in anorexia nervosa is that it tends to become chronic, especially if not recognized and treated early.

Physical Changes

In girls, once weight falls below a critical level, and sometimes even when weight loss is not substantial, menstruation stops or may be delayed if it hasn't already started. Because the body's rate of metabolism slows down to compensate for fewer calories and lost fat reserves, the body temperature drops and the girls and boys become highly sensitive to cold. Sometimes their lips and fingers may become blue. They may develop lanugo, a fine body hair normally seen in newborn infants, especially over the trunk and back. They may have trouble sleeping.

Constipation is common, as is delayed stomach emptying, which may cause prolonged bloating after normal meals and increase the common belief among people with anorexia that they are "eating too much." Various symptoms may result from vitamin and other nutritional deficiencies, including mild to moderate anemia.

All of the physical symptoms thus far described improve or disappear when normal weight is regained, although it may take months and occasionally years for menstruation to resume. But some of the medical consequences of anorexia nervosa are more severe and can be fatal. Various estimates of long-term mortality due to anorexia nervosa range from 5 to 18 percent; today the rate is probably at the lower end of that scale. (When anorexia nervosa first began increasing in this country, it was poorly understood and few therapists had knowledge or experience in treating it; since then both understanding and therapy have improved.)

Changes in body chemistry (especially potassium depletion) can produce weakness, lethargy, and disturbances of heart rhythm, which can lead to death from sudden cardiac arrest, particularly among those who also purge themselves with vomiting, laxatives, and diuretics or water pills.

Lack of calcium and other nutrients along with lowered estrogen levels causes reduced bone density and increases the risk of serious osteoporosis and fractures in later life.

Behavioral Changes

Changes in mood, attitude, and behavior are often quite dramatic and may become a cause for concern even before the weight loss becomes severe. These changes can create confusion in those who are trying to understand the causes and solutions to the problem of anorexia nervosa, because some of the changes are the result of underlying emotional problems while others are the direct effects of starvation.

Obsessive preoccupation with food is prominent. People with anorexia nervosa often collect diet books, cookbooks, and recipes; begin taking over the responsibility for preparing food for the family; and sometimes cook elaborate and fattening meals that they themselves won't touch but that they insist other family members eat "until their plates are clean." They develop food fetishes, such as eating nothing but lettuce and tomatoes for a week, or arranging tiny portions of food in a precise pattern on a plate, then eating it in a specific order. Many become vegetarians and are fanatic about nutrition; others eat nothing but crackers and diet soda. Many refuse to eat with other people, saying they "can't stand to see everybody making pigs of themselves." Others take pride in watching other people overeat while they gloat over their own heroic self-restraint. They often lie about their eating habits, such as telling parents that they had lunch in school and telling the teacher or school nurse that they ate at home.

Although the term "anorexia nervosa" literally means "nervous loss of appetite," the fact is that appetite does not disappear, and people with eating disorders are perpetually hungry and chronically struggling against the normal urge to eat. Their food-obsessive behavior is indistinguishable from the behavior of people who have been deprived of food by famine or imprisonment, who may develop strange eating rituals during starvation and become obsessed with food and eating, talking constantly and often dreaming about food and recipes. The physical, biochemical, and psychological effects of semi-starvation and unremitting hunger contribute a great deal to the abnormal behavior.

Ritual plays a large part in the behavior of some people with anorexia nervosa. For example, the bathroom scales may have to be in the exact right spot, or a light has to be turned on and off a certain number of times before leaving the room. There may be an obsessive preoccupation with household and personal cleanliness. These procedures are a confused attempt by the affected person to gain control of her or his life, for the feeling that life is out of control is one of many underlying causes of anorexia nervosa.

This effort to gain control often includes battles within the family. The sufferer expects "special treatment" from everyone. Her or his precarious physical health and bizarre behavior usually do attract the attention of other family members, who may cater to the ill person's needs and give in to demands in a mistaken attempt to comfort or help the sufferer, or out of fear that she or he might die of the disease or by suicide. These young women and men may manipulate other family members to such an extent that others' schedules, needs, concerns, and social life suffer as a result. Parents are susceptible to considerable pain and guilt, from their fear that they may have caused the disorder and from their inability to stop it. (See the box on page 151.)

Self-starvers themselves may become increasingly isolated from society. Girls who were friendly and outgoing may become hermitlike, spending much of their time alone, neglecting old friendships and failing to make new ones. Rarely are they sexually active. They may become increasingly more serious about life and lose their sense of humor. Because of the physical effects of excessive dieting, they may begin to have trouble concentrating, and school work may suffer. They may exercise relentlessly, either in private or by participating in competitive

athletics, especially running. People are often astonished at the stamina and energy that can be put into exercise by an almost skeletal girl who looks emaciated to the point of feebleness.

WARNING SIGNS OF ANOREXIA NERVOSA

- Significant weight loss.
- Cessation or delayed onset of menstruation.
- Disturbances of body image: complaining of being "fat" when obviously underweight.
- Persistent "fad" dieting with poor nutrition.
- Continued dieting after an announced weight goal has been reached.
- Excessive exercise.
- Moodiness, impatience, rudeness, secretiveness, social isolation.
- Depression, complaints of "emptiness," remarks about "not wanting to go on."
- Intense fear of gaining weight or becoming fat, even when underweight.

Causes

Many influences have been identified as contributing to the development of anorexia nervosa, and in individual cases it may be possible to identify which combination of these plays the most crucial role. But there is no single unified "explanation" for anorexia nervosa. It is fairly well agreed that this disorder occurs among young women with some unexplained susceptibility when they are subjected to certain personal, familial, or societal pressures. The susceptibility may come from low self-esteem, a genetic predisposition, a particular metabolic and biochemical makeup, or various other components not yet identified.

Anorexia nervosa most often begins with the onset of the physical (and emotional) changes of puberty. It may be triggered by a commonplace but psychologically difficult event, such as leaving home for school or camp, entering the more competitive and "popularity conscious" atmosphere of junior high or high school, the loss of a parent or close relative, divorce or threat of divorce. It may begin with critical remarks or teasing by friends or family about weight or about the noticeable physical changes of puberty.

Among the many factors that have been recognized in the development of anorexia nervosa are the following.

The challenge of adolescence. Some young women and men are poorly equipped to deal with emerging sexuality, dramatic bodily changes, the responsibilities of adulthood, separation from parents, and developing good relationships with peers—the normal and essential tasks of the teen years. Those who are susceptible to eating disorders appear to have difficulty with this transition. Because they are ineffective in dealing with it, they unconsciously attempt to avoid it by taking refuge in a quest for total control over weight. Their behavior looks like an effort to return to preadolescence; their general "ideal" body image is that of an 11-year-old boy.

Lack of self-esteem. People with anorexia nervosa seem to be seeking some way of making themselves "special" by being thinner than anyone else, in the mistaken belief that if society believes thin is beautiful, the thinner you are, the more beautiful (and therefore "better") you are.

A leading pioneer in eating disorders, Hilde Bruch, said that none of the many people with anorexia she treated had ever started out with the intent to become emaciated: "All they had wanted to achieve was to feel better about themselves. Since they had felt that 'being too fat' was the cause of their despair, they were determined to correct it. Whatever weight they reached in this struggle for self-respect and respect from others, it was 'not right' for giving them self-assurance, and so the downhill course continued," she wrote in *Eating Disorders* (1973).

Societal pressures and standards. One reason suggested for the great increase in anorexia nervosa in recent years has been the general obsession with looks—especially fitness and leanness. Other researchers theorize that the general lack of structure and discipline in today's society leaves the adolescent without strong direction, value systems, or a sense of competence during the struggle for identity that takes place in the teen years. Confusion over the nature of femininity and of women's roles in today's society also may influence the potential anorexic. (See chapter 21.)

Family dysfunction. People with eating disorders sometimes come from families that may appear to be well adjusted on the surface but in which there are serious problems—excessive closeness (or what therapists call "enmeshment"), coldness and lack of affection, inability to solve conflict or to communicate, and alcoholism, among others.

Treatment

A crucial obstacle to treatment is that self-starvers don't want it. They are pleased with the results of their dieting and with the rewards accompanying it, including a unique sense of identity and an unprecedented feeling of mastery over at least one part of their lives. They deny that they even have a problem; they think their thinness is a solution. Ideally, treatment should be sought as soon as early warning signs of anorexic behavior appear (see page 149), well before the weight loss has become dramatic or dangerous and before the psychological rewards of excess thinness have become too compelling. At this stage, the disorder may be managed with brief psychotherapy and encouragement.

The longer the disorder remains untreated, the harder it is to treat and the more likely it is to become chronic and long term, causing difficulties not only with food and weight but with general emotional adjustment well into later life.

The first consultation is frequently with the pediatrician or family doctor rather than a mental health professional, to confirm the diagnosis in a familiar setting. Parents would be well advised to discuss the issue with the physician before the visit, to express their concerns about the possibility of anorexia nervosa and describe the abnormal behavior. Otherwise, the problem may be dismissed as just another case of overeager teenage dieting.

Behavior problems may be a better early signal of a serious disorder than weight loss alone. The behavior changes most often occur before the weight loss becomes dramatic.

Efforts to get the person to regain weight must be part of the initial treatment, as it will be difficult for the person to deal with the emotional problems while still suffering the effects of starvation. In addition, treatment aims to shift the focus away from food, weight, and appearance and onto the emotional and personal problems underlying the disorder. The therapist and the individual with anorexia nervosa work together to find normal and effective ways of dealing with these issues. Thus, the main emphasis is on establishing new patterns of thinking and behaving.

Hospitalization is usually required when the weight loss has reached a danger level, about 25 percent or more below normal weight. In most cases, weight can be restored by a combination of psychotherapy and learning new eating behavior patterns. Weight gain alone will not solve the problem. The underlying issues must be dealt with; otherwise, quite often people with eating disorders comply with the hospital rules until they gain enough weight to be released and then immediately return to serious dieting and weight loss.

Outpatient treatment generally entails individual psychotherapy but may also involve the family, especially in the case of the younger patient. Many experts in the field believe that a family approach is necessary. In *The Golden Cage* (1978), Hilde Bruch warns, "If the family problems are not attended to . . . increasingly turbulent situations will develop. . . . It is important that the underlying patterns of interaction are recognized and that the family accept help in changing them."

Sometimes it is recommended that families also seek guidance and support from a parents' mutual-help group, which usually can be found through the same sources used for finding therapists (see page 154). Mutual-help or self-help groups for people with eating disorders are not recommended as the only form of treatment, although they may be a useful adjunct to therapy if the therapist advises it. While they can be very effective for people with bulimia and for chronic dieters in general, mutual-help groups of people with anorexia do not seem as effective. One

reason is that self-starvers are so anxious to be thinner than anyone else that if they join a group and see others who are thinner, they may redouble their efforts to lose weight.

SUGGESTIONS FOR THE FAMILY

- Don't feel guilty. Concentrate on what can be done *now*.
- Don't make food an issue. Don't nag or criticize.
- Give sympathy, not pity. Don't coddle. Provide more opportunities for independence and responsibility.
- Don't be intimidated or let your judgment be distorted by fear.
- Be open and honest. Make it clear you know what the problem is and want to help.
- Maintain family normalcy. Apply family rules to *everyone* equally.
- Discourage perfectionism. Admit your own mistakes; forgive the mistakes of others.
- Be patient. Take each day as it comes.
- Get help for yourselves as well as the person with the eating disorder, especially if either parent has an addictive disorder such as alcoholism.

BULIMIA

Bulimia means "hunger of an ox," and people with this disorder regularly go on food binges, often feeling that they will not be able to stop eating. Afterward most attempt to purge themselves of the food—and the calories—by vomiting, using laxatives or diuretics, or exercising to excess.

Despite their purging, such people do not usually become emaciated, and despite their ingestion of large quantities of food, most are of normal weight. (Contrary to accepted folklore among people who binge and purge, laxatives do not eliminate all or even a very large part of a meal; despite repeated purging such people still retain enough calories to avoid weight loss, which makes it even more difficult for their disease to be recognized.) People who binge-eat without purging (who are sometimes said to have binge-eating disorder), however, usually are substantially overweight.

Often bulimia is compared to alcoholism. Like the alcoholic, people who binge feel guilty and full of shame after every episode. Many swear to themselves "never to do it again," but they have no apparent control over their impulses, and willpower alone is ineffective.

How It Starts, and Why

Sometimes bulimia develops out of self-starvation, when hunger and deprivation become intolerable. Then the individual with anorexia swings to the opposite extreme, eating with unrestrained appetite but continuing to try to control weight by purging with laxatives or by vomiting. An estimated one-fourth of all those with bulimia have a history of anorexia nervosa. In some cases, people with bulimia could not control their weight by dieting; that is, they never could lose enough weight to be classified as having anorexia, although they may have tried.

Most often, a young woman who wants to lose weight but has made only halfhearted attempts to diet or no effort at all learns about purging from friends. Besides being an apparently "easy" way to lose weight, purging is socially acceptable, even approved, among certain groups, which in part accounts for the high prevalence of bulimia in colleges (an estimated 1 to 5 percent of all female college students) and among professional women in their 20s and 30s.

Bulimia generally begins later in adolescence than anorexia, although age at onset can range from early teens to mid-30s. As with anorexia, the great majority of sufferers are female, and the disorder begins in association with dieting.

There is no one cause for bulimia. Factors that produce the behavior are often similar to those producing self-starvation. In addition, some investigators mention feelings of inadequacy, conflicts over feelings of dependency, and a need to appear perfect. Numerous studies have shown a high association between bulimia and depression. Although some workers hypothesize that bulimia is a form of mood disorder, research has yet to establish this point. People with bulimia have been found to have impaired senses of hunger, taste, and fullness, but these may result from the bingeing and purging behavior rather than cause it.

Physical Changes

Bulimia has medical consequences that range from mild to potentially deadly, although they are relatively "benign" compared to the physical and medical effects of anorexia nervosa. The emotional toll may be just as high with bulimia, but there are fewer serious physical consequences and far lower mortality.

In contrast to anorexia nervosa, the damage is caused not by weight loss but by the purging behavior and the use of laxatives or emetics (substances that induce vomiting). Abnormal menstruation is fairly common but not universal, as among those with very low weight anorexia nervosa. Constant exposure of the teeth to stomach acid from vomiting causes serious dental erosion, and bulimia may be diagnosed for the first time by a dentist.

The parotid glands (the salivary glands below and in front of the ear; the ones that swell up in mumps) may become enlarged from vomiting. This may make the face look more rounded. Those who have combined anorexia nervosa and bulimia may take advantage of this fact. Because they look better nourished than they are, they can deny that they are losing too much weight.

Laxative abuse can cause serious problems, including laxative dependence. When a laxative abuser tries to stop taking laxatives, it can take as long as several months for bowel function to get back to normal.

Bulimia can also cause severe medical emergencies that require immediate hospitalization. Among the potential threats to life are abnormal heart rhythms caused by imbalances in body chemistry, rupture of the esophagus from vomiting, and rupture of the stomach from overloading during a binge. Serious or fatal damage to the muscles and the heart, for example, may result from overuse of ipecac, a nonprescription emetic often kept in the medicine cabinet to induce vomiting in a child who has eaten or drunk something dangerous.

WARNING SIGNS OF BULIMIA

- Binge eating.
- Hoarding food.
- Leaving the table immediately after meals to "go to the bathroom."
- Spending long periods of time in the bathroom.
- Secretive behavior; pretending not to know what happened to missing food.
- Denial that anything is wrong.
- Depression, anger, anxiety.

Behavioral Changes

People with bulimia resemble alcoholics in their concern about their supplies; they hoard food and frequently steal food or the money to buy it. Shoplifting is common. They can be quite tyrannical in their rules regarding their food supply, insisting it not be touched by others in the household.

Compared to people with anorexia nervosa, who cannot easily hide their illness and are actually proud of their self-control and their achievement of dramatic losses of weight, people with bulimia are usually highly secretive and often will do anything to keep family members from knowing what they are doing. They usually consider their bingeing and purging to be repulsive and self-destructive; some call it "my dirty little secret." The person who binges may continue to deny it even when directly confronted with evidence.

People who binge and purge may be frightened by their inability to manage their impulsive eating. They may also share many of the obsessive behavior patterns of the self-starver, but are less likely to be socially isolated and more likely to be sexually active. Also unlike the self-starver, the person who binges and purges is more likely to be addicted to drugs or alcohol and to have problems controlling impulsive behavior in general.

Self-mutilation and suicidal thoughts or suicide attempts occur in some cases.

Treatment

The most generally accepted approaches to treatment of bulimia focus specifically on the eating behavior rather than on the underlying emotional problems, which can be addressed in other types of therapy after the behavior has resolved. In behavior therapy, people with bulimia maintain a record of their eating behavior and are taught to monitor their emotional state before each eating binge. They learn to recognize the warning signs of an impending binge as well as situations that make them vulnerable to binges, such as stress, loneliness, boredom, or long stretches without food. They learn to develop alternative methods for dealing with these situations, such as exercise, work, or calling a support person. Working with a nutritionist to learn how to plan nutritious and satisfying meals is especially helpful.

People with bulimia often benefit as well from group therapy or group support activities such as Overeaters Anonymous. (See page 156.)

Recently a number of leading scientists in the eating disorders field have had considerable success in treating bulimia with certain antidepressant medications, regardless of whether the person also is suffering from depression.

OBESITY AND CHRONIC DIETING

It is a long-held popular belief that obese individuals (who are at least 20 percent above what is considered the highest normal weight for their age and sex) are emotionally disturbed and overeat for psychological reasons—to relieve anxiety or depression, for example. Today mental health professionals have serious doubts about this notion. The current view of obesity is that it can result from a complex of factors, including genetics, behavior patterns, physical and metabolic characteristics, and social influences. In any case, obesity is not considered a mental disorder. However, both obesity itself and repeated efforts to lose weight can have serious emotional consequences.

Scientific studies have demonstrated convincingly that most obese people have no more psychological disturbances than normal-weight people, except perhaps for their distress about their weight. Obese people tend to view themselves more negatively than nonobese people, which undoubtedly reflects the prevailing social bias in this country.

Thus, in treating the obese patient, the chief role of the mental health professional is to alleviate the demoralizing effects of social stigma. As more and more people recognize the fact that obesity is not a psychological problem and weight loss through willpower is not the cure, overweight people may be relieved of some guilt and embarrassment. Psychotherapy may also play a part in this and in helping the obese person to learn new patterns of living and eating, which are the focus of most weight-control programs.

Psychotherapy also may be helpful in treating the obsessive behavior of people who repeatedly diet, lose weight, regain it, and diet again; people who repeatedly diet without any success; and people who suffer both obesity and bulimia. Recent studies have shown that chronic dieting can have severe negative effects, including irritability, anxiety, and depression. Moreover, chronic dieting tends to cause subsequent weight gain. Crash diets and starvation diets, without supportive therapy, also can produce symptoms of mental illness. These symptoms can be relieved by a therapy that includes behavioral change and nutritional counseling for gradual weight loss without restrictive dieting, as well as by other forms of individual and group therapy. Many people also find Overeaters Anonymous helpful. (See page 156.)

It is important for chronic dieters to keep this distinction in mind: Their dieting is not caused *by* a mental or emotional problem but can be the cause *of* such problems.

THE CASE OF NANCY D.

Nancy D. was the only girl in a family of four children. Her father had a history of alcoholism, and during her childhood there were difficulties between the mother and father as well as between the boys and their parents. At age 14, Nancy weighed 128 pounds and had reached her adult height of 5 feet 6 inches. She felt "terribly fat" and began to diet, without lasting success. By age 17 she weighed 165 pounds. She began to diet more seriously for fear that she would be ridiculed, finally going down to 130 pounds. She felt "depressed, overwhelmed, and insignificant," she said. In school Nancy began to avoid taking difficult classes so that she would never get less than an A. When she got Bs she felt humiliated and would lie about her school and grade performance. She had great social anxiety in dealing with boys, which culminated in her transferring to a girls' school for the last year of high school.

In college Nancy started using laxatives, working up to 250 to 300 Ex-Lax pills at a time, 20 in a gulp; she also used diuretics (water pills). Sometimes she lost as much as 20 pounds in 24 hours, mostly water; she was so dehydrated she couldn't stand and could barely speak. She was admitted numerous times to the college infirmary.

"I would not eat for days, then I'd eat something and feel so guilty, and so hungry, I would eat-eat-eat," she said. Another girl told her about vomiting, and Nancy discovered she could eat large amounts of food, vomit, and not gain weight. "I lost nearly 50 pounds over a few months, and my weight dropped to 90 pounds. My hair started coming out in handfuls and my teeth were loose. But I never felt lovelier or more confident about my appearance—physically liberated, streamlined, close-to-the-bone."

While still in college, Nancy began trying to eat a more healthful diet, but she continued to vomit and to control caloric intake so her weight stayed at about 105 pounds. The vomiting usually took her two to three hours. Eventually she dropped out of college.

"Fat—I can't *stand* it," she said. "That feeling is stronger and more desperate than any horror at what I am doing to myself. If I gain a few pounds I hate to leave the house and let people see me."

When she was 23, she spent several weeks in a medical center where research on anorexia and bulimia was being done. In this unit she was prevented from bingeing or vomiting, which was an important step in breaking her habit patterns. At the same time, a therapist talked with her about using her strengths—which included her insight and her ability to organize her life—to combat the impulse to binge or purge. She was encouraged to take advantage of her personality traits and not to think of them as liabilities, which she had done previously. Nutritional counselors also planned out a healthful diet to help her avoid dieting too strictly or, on the other hand, feeling as if she were overeating. As a result she was able to give up her laxative and diuretic abuse. After leaving the research unit she continued with private therapy, and at 25 had returned to college, was completing her course work satisfactorily, had reached a normal weight, and was being counseled by a nutritionist. Although she occasionally binged and vomited, she described herself as "doing much better."

Source: R. L. Spitzer, M. Gibbon, and J. B. W. Williams, *Psychopathology: A Case Book* (New York: McGraw-Hill, 1983).

GETTING HELP

People seeking help with eating disorders and persistent weight or dieting problems should consult experts who specialize in treating them or who have considerable experience in this area. The American Anorexia/Bulimia Association, Inc. (418 East 76th Street, New York, NY 10021, tel. 212 734–1114) can provide referrals to practitioners, hospitals, and support groups in your area. Appropriate mental health professionals can also be found through high school or college guidance counselors or health services, or through local medical schools. Many major university-affiliated medical centers

PATTERNS OF THINKING, FEELING, AND ACTING IN EATING DISORDERS

Do you have an eating disorder or a problem with body image? Ask yourself the following questions about the way you think, feel, and act about your eating and your weight.

- Are you obsessed with a need to lose weight even though your friends and your physician tell you your weight is fine?
- Do you often feel that you cannot control yourself around food?
- Are you embarrassed by the way or the amount you eat?
- Do you prefer to eat alone?
- In determining how you feel about yourself, is your weight one of the *most* important factors?

- Do you try to compensate for overeating by doing inappropriate things, such as making yourself vomit or taking laxatives or diet pills?
- Do you feel that you will lose control of your eating if you do not eat the same foods day after day?
- Do you often eat so much that you feel ill?

The more "yes" answers you accumulate, the more your patterns resemble those of people with eating disorders. If you think you have a problem, you may wish to consult a specialist in eating disorders and related problems.

TO DIET OR NOT TO DIET

Researchers in psychiatry and psychology have determined that American women especially are dissatisfied with their bodies and most believe incorrectly that they are "fat." To determine whether a man or woman is within the normal weight range, obesity researchers often measure the individual's *body/mass index,* or BMI. This figure is a ratio of both weight and height.

To determine your BMI, consult the following chart or divide your weight in kilograms by your height in meters squared (1 kilogram = 2.20 pounds; 1 meter = 39.3 inches). BMIs in the 20 to 25 range are considered normal and healthy; 26 to 34 is overweight; below 20 and above 35 are considered unhealthy.

Many people who diet frequently will find that according to their BMIs, they are well within the normal range. Admittedly, the current cultural ideal for female beauty emphasizes extreme thinness, and thus many women will proceed with their weight-reduction plans anyway. Experts caution that, overweight or not, frequent and intense dieting increases one's risk for eating disorders. Recent research has shown that "yo-yo" dieting—taking weight off and putting it back on—also may lead to cardiovascular disease and diabetes.

Successful weight loss or weight maintenance involves not a drastic reduction of calories but a change in eating habits and lifestyle that includes balanced nutrition, increased exercise, and positive body image.

Here are some sample BMIs:

height	weight	BMI	height	weight	BMI
5'1"	100	18.9	5'8"	235	35.8
5'2"	118	21.6	5'9"	150	22.2
5'3"	110	19.5		170	25.2
	125	22.2		200	29.6
5'4"	125	21.5	5'10"	150	21.6
	140	24.1		175	25.2
	160	27.5		200	28.8
5'5"	120	20.0	5'11"	145	20.3
	145	24.1		175	24.5
	160	26.6		200	28.0
5'6"	140	22.6	6'	160	21.8
	150	24.3		200	27.2
	200	32.3		250	34.0
5'7"	120	18.8	6'1"	175	23.1
	150	23.5		190	25.1
	175	27.4		230	30.4
5'8"	140	21.3	6'2"	200	25.7
	155	23.6		300	38.6

have eating disorder and weight programs. The phone book cites listings for Overeaters Anonymous; or its headquarters can be reached at 213 542–8363.

Therapists may achieve good results regardless of whether they are psychiatrists, clinical psychologists, or clinical social workers; the critical factors are skill and experience in these specific disorders, flexibility, and empathy. In recent years a number of residential and outpatient centers specializing in eating disorders have been established. Family physicians or psychotherapists should be able to help locate and evaluate them. A physician should be involved in any treatment program to diagnose and deal with any associated medical problems, and to prescribe medications when needed.

11

Sexual Dysfunctions and Disorders

Judith Becker, Ph.D.

Sexuality plays a vital role in human life and experience. As the means of procreating, sexuality of course is essential to survival of the species. For each individual, our genetic sex, or gender—being male or female—becomes a fundamental part of who we are; it shapes our basic physical appearance, influences our physiology and our roles, and impacts on our emotional, social, and even economic life. And the ability—or inability—to function sexually can affect psychological and interpersonal well-being profoundly.

When a person is unable to function or respond sexually, behave in conformity with prevailing sexual norms, or accept his or her gender, much suffering can result.

"ABNORMAL" AND "NORMAL" SEXUALITY

Many conditions and situations can interfere with sexuality. This chapter explores the common sexual dysfunctions and disorders that lead to an abnormal experience of sexuality and discusses the various therapies available to treat them.

Types of Sexual Dysfunctions and Disorders

Specifically, the sexual dysfunctions and disorders fall into three categories.

Sexual dysfunctions.   These occur when the normal sexual cycle (see page 158) is blocked, causing an impaired ability to perform. An example would be a man who is unable to obtain an erection, or a woman who does not become aroused when her partner stimulates her.

Paraphilias. This term covers a wide range of sexual behaviors that do not conform to acceptable social mores. They would include, for example, an adult man who engages in sexual activity with children or a man who enjoys exposing his penis to strangers.

Gender identity disorders. These are disorders in the perception of being male or female—as in the case of a male who believes that he is a woman trapped in a man's body.

Sexual Expression and Practices

It is important to note that from a mental health perspective, there is no universally accepted "normal" way to express sexuality. Between two consenting adults, what is "normal" or "right" is what is comfortable, safe, and satisfying for both.

Sexual customs and preferences vary enormously from group to group and individual to individual. Acceptable practices are shaped by cultural attitudes, family or religious upbringing, social movements as well as individual preferences. What is considered normal sexual activity in one culture, or even one family, may be prohibited in another, and cultural norms change with the times and events.

At present, Western cultures demonstrate a wide variation of sexual expression and choice. One can remain sexually abstinent, wait until marriage or engage in premarital sex, have more than one partner or remain sexually faithful to a spouse, or be bisexual or homosexual. Depending on individual preferences, sexual practices may include genital intercourse, oral sex, and anal sex.

Some cultures and religious groups discourage sex when a woman is menstruating. In some circles it is acceptable for a woman to initiate sex, while in others women are expected to wait until approached.

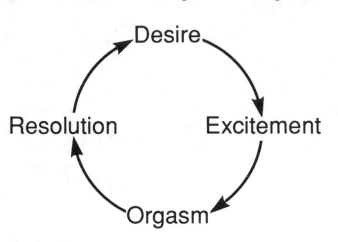

The Sexual Response Cycle

Desire → Excitement → Orgasm → Resolution →

Figure 11.1: The human sexual response cycle has four phases: desire, excitement, orgasm, and resolution. When a disruption in this cycle occurs, the person is said to have a sexual dysfunction.

Early in this century masturbation was considered to be an unhealthy practice. Today mental health professionals consider it a normal and healthy expression, although some groups may continue to discourage it. In a large number of societies, some individuals choose members of their own sex as sexual partners. Within our society, the mental health community in general does not consider consensual homosexuality to be a sexual disorder.

Conflicting attitudes toward sexual preferences and practices, however, can influence a person's ability to achieve a full sexual response and to accept his or her sexuality as normal. Also, the desire to express oneself sexually in socially deviant ways can lead to legal difficulties, social ostracism, and torment for oneself and others.

THE SEXUAL RESPONSE CYCLE

Human sexual functioning is the result of the complex interaction of the autonomic nervous system, which controls involuntary functions of the body; the vascular system, which conveys blood throughout the body; and the endocrine system, which controls the production and secretion of hormones. All act in concert with thoughts and emotions.

Sex researchers have found that the sexual response cycle consists of the following four phases.

Desire. Sexual arousal occurs in the presence of verbal, physical, or visual stimulation. Fantasies about sex can also generate arousal, causing a desire to engage in some type of sexual activity. (See the box on page 160.)

Excitement. This is the stage of sexual arousal and erotic pleasure. If adequate stimulation occurs, parasympathetic nerves trigger an increased flow of blood into the genital area. A man's penis becomes erect. A woman's vagina becomes engorged, her clitoris swells, and she begins to lubricate. Heart rate increases. If stimulation continues, the pleasurable tension heightens.

Orgasm. Sexual pleasure peaks in this phase. For men, semen is ejaculated from the penis in spurts. Orgasm in women consists of reflex rhythmic contractions of the muscles surrounding the vagina.

Resolution. The sexual organs return to a preexcitement state, with the heart and breathing rates slowing.

While women may be able to repeat the entire cycle almost immediately afterward, usually men are unable to achieve an erection for some time, ranging from minutes to hours. Called the refractory period, its duration changes with age. In a teenage boy, the refractory period may last only seconds. As a man approaches his late 30s, it lengthens to 30 minutes or more. By age 50, the average refractory period is eight to 24 hours.

Organic or psychological factors can interfere with this usual cycle of sexual response and activity. When a disruption occurs, the person is said to have a sexual dysfunction.

SEXOLOGY HISTORY: A BRIEF REVIEW

Mental health professionals have long recognized the importance of sexuality to the individual's well-being. During the late 19th and early 20th centuries, a number of sexologists (those who study the science of sexual behavior) made important contributions to the understanding of human sexuality. Richard von Krafft-Ebing, for example, investigated sexual deviance, which was thought to result from nervous system disorders. A German neurologist, he wrote a textbook on sexual disorders, *Psychopathia Sexualis,* published in 1886. Henry Havelock Ellis, who explored the range of sexual expression, wrote on topics such as female sexuality, masturbation, and homosexuality. The first volume of his *Studies in the Psychology of Sex* was banned as obscene in England when it was published in 1897.

Sigmund Freud, a Viennese physician and the founder of psychoanalysis, incorporated sexuality as a major theme in his theories. He believed that neuroses had their origin in childhood sexual conflicts. Freud was the first in modern times to emphasize the sexual drive as a dynamic inner force shaping personality and directing human behavior.

Prominent sexologists of the mid- and late 20th century include Alfred Kinsey and William H. Masters and Virginia E. Johnson. Kinsey, a biologist, is known for his surveys of sexual practices of American men and women, published in 1948 and 1953. Masters, a gynecologist, and Johnson, a psychologist, conducted laboratory studies of male and female sexual response. Their pioneering work, which they began to publish in the 1960s, laid the foundation for laboratory studies of sexuality in humans and for the sex therapies widely in use today.

SEXUAL DYSFUNCTIONS

A number of organic and psychological factors can interfere with the sexual response cycle, causing a wide range of problems, including loss of sexual desire or ability to become aroused, orgasm difficulties, painful sex, or aversion to sex.

While the exact number of people who experience these sexual dysfunctions during their lifetime is unknown, researchers do know that sexual dysfunctions occur quite frequently. In one survey, reported in the *New England Journal of Medicine* in 1978, 100 well-educated, happily married couples

were interviewed. Forty percent of the men reported ejaculating before they wanted to or having difficulty getting or maintaining an erection. Sixty-three percent of the women reported that they had difficulty in becoming aroused or experiencing orgasm. Half of the men surveyed and 77 percent of the women reported that at some time they lacked a desire for sex or had difficulty relaxing when they were sexual.

Organic and psychological factors each account for an approximately equal number of sexual dysfunctions. Some cases can be traced to a combination of both types of causes.

Organic Causes

Any illness involving the nervous, endocrine, or circulatory system can have an adverse effect on sexual functioning. Among the more common are multiple sclerosis, atherosclerosis (hardening of the arteries), thrombosis of the arteries or veins in the penis, diabetes, liver disease, hyperprolactinemia (excess secretions of the pituitary hormone prolactin), and dementia. Trauma to the lumbar or sacral spinal cord, a herniated disc, and prostate surgery can also damage penile nerves.

A multitude of prescription and nonprescription drugs affect sexual response, including antihistamines, diuretics, and medications widely used to control high blood pressure. Drugs prescribed for psychiatric disorders, including antidepressants and antipsychotics, may also interfere with the sexual response cycle in some people. Impotence and failure to achieve orgasm may be side effects of some antidepressants. For more about side effects of psychoactive drugs, see chapter 5.

Estrogen also can interfere with sexual functioning, as can the use of steroids. Legal and illicit "recreational" drugs—alcohol, cocaine, heroin, even tobacco and caffeine—are frequent causes of impaired sexual functioning.

SEXUAL FANTASIES

Fantasies are a normal and important part of sexuality. The fantasies may be fleeting images or extensive scenes involving different behaviors and different locations. They might involve the person's sexual partner, a potential partner, or a fantasy person. It is common for fantasy themes to change over time.

Some people may worry that their erotic fantasies are "wrong" or abnormal. But the mere fact that a person has a fantasy does not mean that he or she will act it out. In general, sexual fantasizing is normal and healthy—although there may be some cause for concern if an adult exclusively fantasizes about sex with children or about sex that is violent or coercive.

Psychiatric and Psychological Causes

The major mood disorders, including depression and bipolar illness (manic-depression), are very common psychiatric causes of sexual dysfunctions. People who are depressed, for example, commonly lose all desire for sex. Schizophrenia is also associated with sexual dysfunction. The personality disorders too often lead to difficulties in sexual functioning, as do the stress-related adjustment disorders.

Attitudes about what is "proper" sexual behavior and how one "should" behave sexually can strongly influence sexual response. For many people, ignorance or misconceptions about how their bodies respond leads to sexual dissatisfaction. For example, many women do not realize that without adequate stimulation to the clitoris, they may not achieve orgasm during sex. Sexual intercourse alone may not provide sufficient stimulation, which is why many women who do have orgasms perform the direct stimulation themselves or have partners who directly stimulate them. Men who are unaware that women require this clitoral stimulation may believe that they are not virile enough to bring their partners to orgasm through intercourse; this anxiety could lead to impotence.

Some common psychological causes of sexual problems include:

- depression
- unconscious guilt or anxiety about sex
- performance anxiety (worry over how well one is performing sexually and over meeting the partner's expectations)
- repressive inhibitions (those "don'ts" or "shouldn'ts" attributable to familial, cultural, or religious upbringing)
- sexual trauma (such as incest or rape, or embarrassing sexual failures)
- spectatoring (focusing on who is doing what to whom, rather than allowing oneself to experience the sexual act)
- problematic relationships (when one partner constantly berates or belittles the other, when one or both partners is angry, among other examples)
- intrapsychic conflicts (states of tension, usually unconscious, that arise when inner wishes, needs, or thoughts are in conflict with each other, as when a man who has unresolved sexual feelings about his mother loses sexual interest in his wife after she gives birth and—to him—becomes a mother figure)

One of the most frequent problems is the failure to communicate sexual needs. It is not uncommon for partners to know little about one another's sexual fantasies, preferences, dislikes, fears, and vulnerabilities. For example, a woman may expect that her partner should know what brings her to orgasm without communicating what she finds pleasurable. A man may be reluctant to discuss what he needs to provoke an erection. And all too often, partners fail to acknowledge to each other that a problem exists.

Finally, life changes, stress, fatigue, and ordinary ups and downs in moods can affect the sexual response cycle in anyone, temporarily. For example, mothers of infants may experience occasional periods of fatigue-related decrease in sexual desire. Following a divorce, a man might experience an increase or decrease in sexual functioning or desire because of lifestyle changes. In these cases, sexual functioning usually returns to normal when the situation stabilizes, energy returns to normal, or mood improves. If not, a sexual dysfunction may exist that requires treatment.

Male Erectile Disorder and Female Sexual Arousal Disorder

Male erectile disorder and female sexual arousal disorder are caused by failure of the sexual excitement phase of the sexual response cycle. Men may have difficulty achieving or maintaining an erection (impotence), or they may achieve only a partial erection. Women experience difficulty with vaginal lubrication.

Some people have a long history of erectile or arousal disorders, while others experience them suddenly, after a long period of successful sexual functioning. For example, a 50-year-old man had been married for 25 years and rarely experienced difficulty with erections. One year after the death of his wife he began dating; when he attempted to have intercourse with his partner, he could not get an erection. In another case, a 27-year-old woman found that in her current relationship she could not become sexually aroused even though she desired sex. In a previous relationship she almost always became excited during lovemaking. Further questioning revealed that this woman's partner did not touch her the way she liked to be stimulated.

Causes

When an erectile/arousal problem is present, the first step is to consult a physician and obtain a medical evaluation. As mentioned previously, a number of medications and illnesses may interfere with the sexual response cycle.

When a man has an erectile disorder, he may be referred to a urologist to assess whether the problem is related to organic factors or is psychologically caused. It is not unusual for the problem to be both organic and psychological in origin, as in the case of a man who could achieve only a partial erection. The problem began one year after he was diagnosed as having diabetes (a very common cause of impotence) and placed on insulin. His wife's complaints about the partial erection made him so anxious that he became unable to achieve any erection at all.

Organic tests for men include those that trace and measure the flow of penile blood, assess the condition of arteries and veins, and check for neurological impairment. Some men are referred for nocturnal penile tumescence (NPT) assessment. In these studies, a man will sleep for two or more nights in a laboratory equipped to monitor erection response during rapid-eye-movement (REM, or dream) sleep. (Portable test devices are also available for home use.) If he consistently fails to become erect during this sleep phase, when erections are the norm, an organic cause is suspected.

Unfortunately, the development of techniques to assess organic factors in female dysfunctions has lagged behind that of males, although a physical examination and hormonal studies may reveal an organic cause.

Treatments

Therapies that reduce anxiety have proven effective in the treatment of erectile/arousal disorders. Sensate focus exercises, discussed on page 164, are commonly prescribed. They encourage intimate contact and emotional warmth rather than focusing on the mechanics of intercourse. Both men and women are encouraged to involve their partner in treatment, particularly if the sexual problem is related to a problem in the relationship.

Many men have difficulties with erections because of performance anxiety. They may engage in spectatoring or be overly concerned about the size of their erections. Men with erectile disorders are particularly sensitive to their partners' comments and attitudes toward the lack of erection; often they feel inadequate or guilty. Therapy in these cases also focuses on helping partners accept other pleasurable aspects of sex, rather than insisting on intercourse only.

For those men who have an organically caused erectile disorder and who wish to have an erection sufficient for penetration, a penile prosthesis can be implanted. This surgery should be considered only after the man has had a psychological/psychiatric, sexual, and urologic evaluation.

In some cases, longer-term psychotherapy as well as behaviorally oriented sex therapy may be necessary if there are other psychological problems inhibiting the person from enjoying sex.

Orgasm Disorders

Orgasm disorders include inhibited female orgasm, premature ejaculation, and inhibited male orgasm.

Inhibited Female Orgasm

When a woman has never had an orgasm, or her orgasms are frequently delayed or difficult to achieve, inhibited female orgasm disorder (also called anorgasmia) may be the problem. It may be primary (the women has never had an orgasm), secondary (she used to have orgasms but now does not), or situational (she may with one partner but not with another, or she may with one form of stimulation but not another).

For a woman who has never had an orgasm, the most likely way for her to become orgasmic is through a program that trains her to explore and stimulate her own genitals (masturbation). Once able to experience orgasm by self-stimulation, she then can teach her partner the type of genital and nongenital stimulation she requires to have an orgasm.

Treatment of secondary and situational orgasm problems involves exploring the relationship. If a woman can achieve an orgasm through one means or with one partner, the logical conclusion is that it is a specific problem in her current relationship that blocks orgasm. Treatment of the couple is recommended and usually focuses on sensate focus exercises (page 164).

Premature Ejaculation

A man who regularly ejaculates too early, usually after a minimum of sexual stimulation, has premature ejaculation disorder. It is probably the most common sexual dysfunction among men. Treatment involves teaching a man to tolerate high levels of excitement without ejaculating and to reduce his anxiety about ejaculating prematurely.

The following experience of a man in his 30s is common: In his first sexual encounter after a long period of sexual abstinence, he ejaculated too rapidly.

The next time he had sex, worry that he would "come" too quickly interfered with his ability to control his level of excitement; again he ejaculated early. Because this pattern continued, he sought help from a sex therapist, who suggested two easily learned techniques for ejaculatory control. Using the *stop-start* technique, the man learned to become alert to impending ejaculation. He then signaled his partner to stop the stimulation. Once the feeling that he was about to ejaculate subsided, sexual activity resumed. He repeated the stop-start pattern as often as he needed. Using the *squeeze technique,* he taught his partner to squeeze the penis briefly and painlessly to stave off ejaculation until the moment was right.

As with most other sexual dysfunctions, sensate focus exercises (page 164) and concentrating on forms of lovemaking other than intercourse help reduce the anxiety and take the emphasis off of sexual performance.

Inhibited Male Orgasm

Also known as retarded ejaculation, inhibited male orgasm is the opposite of premature ejaculation. In this case, an erection is maintained for an excessive length of time prior to ejaculation, if ejaculation occurs at all. Treatment involves reducing anxiety, teaching sensate focus exercises, and making use of prescribed masturbation to teach control of ejaculation timing. For example, after a period of masturbating only, a man may be taught to enter his partner only when he recognizes he is about to ejaculate.

Hypoactive (Low) Sexual Desire Disorder

Low sexual desire is characterized by a pervasive or persistent loss of sexual desire. In general, people with this disorder report an absence of sexual fantasies and lack of desire or interest in having sex.

Some people report a lifelong history of a lack of desire for sex. Others develop this problem after years of good sexual appetite. Sometimes a person will develop this disorder after experiencing other sexual disorders, as in the case of a man who, after a long history of difficulty in achieving an erection with his wife, finally lost all interest in sex. Similarly, a woman who found intercourse to be painful subsequently lost her desire for sex.

Causes and Treatments

Hypoactive sexual desire disorder can be organic and requires a medical workup first. The problem may be hormonal in nature, and therapy with hormones may help. Other causes may be depression, intrapsychic conflicts (such as a fear of asserting oneself), or problems in the relationship.

The most effective treatments involve a combination of cognitive therapy, to explore the person's beliefs about sex; behavioral treatment, such as sensate focus exercises to facilitate sexual communications (page 164); and couple therapy, to address any problems in the relationship—for example, when sex is used to gain control, as in the case of a young married woman who felt like having sex only after her husband gave her presents.

Sexual Aversion Disorder

Sexual aversion disorder is a persistent or recurrent aversion to virtually all sexual activity with a partner, characterized by fear and avoidance of sex. Sexual trauma is a common cause. A 33-year-old woman, for example, had been raped by her stepfather when she was nine years old. The experience scarred her both physically and psychologically; as a consequence she avoided any sexual contact in her adulthood. Other possible causes include fear of intimacy and intrapsychic conflicts.

Sex therapy for this disorder focuses on reducing the individual's fear and avoidance of sex by exposing the patient, first in imagination and then in the privacy of his or her home and with the partner, to the actual sexual situations that generate the anxiety. Tricyclic antidepressant medications may also be helpful.

Sexual Pain

When a man or woman experiences recurrent genital pain during intercourse, the diagnosis is *dyspareunia*. The disorder is more common among women, who should have a medical workup to rule out organic causes of genital pain, including vaginitis, urinary tract infection, vaginal scarring, ligament injuries, endometriosis, and ovarian tumors. In the absence of organic cause, treatment involves addressing the patient's underlying anxieties about sex. Often the individual unconsciously fears being hurt, and discussing these fears can help alleviate the problem.

If a woman experiences involuntary muscle spasms of the outer third of the vagina that are sufficiently intense to prevent penetration, she is diagnosed as having *vaginismus*. Sexual trauma and the anxiety caused by it is the leading cause of this disorder. Treatment involves systematic desensitization, a process that involves inserting dilators of graduated sizes, tampons, or fingers to increase vaginal tolerance gradually until penile penetration can be achieved.

PARAPHILIAS

When a sexual fantasy or act involves a nonconsenting person or an inanimate object, and when that fantasy or act occurs regularly or dominates a person's sexual interest, a paraphilia may exist. Formerly, paraphilias were known as perversions. A diagnosis of paraphilia requires that the fantasies existed for at least six months and that the person either acted on the fantasies or suffered serious distress because of them.

Among the recognized paraphilias are:

Exhibitionism. Exhibitionists expose their genitals to an unsuspecting stranger. Some exhibitionists will masturbate while exposing themselves or progress to actually touching their victims.

Frotteurism. This is defined as touching and rubbing against a nonconsenting person. It generally occurs in crowded places such as subways, buses, or elevators.

Fetishism. This involves intense sexual stimulation by inanimate objects, often a woman's clothing (bras, panties, stocking, shoes, and so on), or by body parts such as the foot. It commonly leads to masturbation while fondling the selected object. Transvestic fetishism involves a fetish for clothing used in cross-dressing (dressing as a member of the opposite sex).

Sexual masochism. Individuals with this paraphilia are strongly attracted sexually to being beaten, bound, humiliated, or otherwise made to suffer. Sometimes they have a sex partner perform these acts on them, or they can hurt themselves by self-inflicted acts while masturbating. Masochism can be extremely dangerous; one form (hypoxyphilia) involves the near strangulation of the sufferer, either alone or with the help of a partner during a sexual event.

Sexual sadism. This is a powerful sexual attraction to inflicting suffering on someone else, either physically or psychologically. The sexual acts, which might include whipping, beating, or mutilation, can be extremely dangerous to the victim, whether he or

SENSATE FOCUS EXERCISES

Sensate focus exercises are used to treat a number of sexual dysfunctions. They consist of a series of sessions in which the individual engages initially in nongenital, undemanding (and hence nonthreatening) caressing with his or her partner. The emphasis is on providing "pleasuring"; as the exercises progress, the partners switch roles so that they both have an opportunity to pleasure one another. Gradually, over time, the focus becomes more genital.

Sensate Focus I

Each partner is required to be totally receptive for 15 to 20 minutes while the other partner explores, stimulates, and caresses all parts of the body except the genital area and breasts. All types of manual and oral stimulation may be used. The touching should encompass everything from light touch to stroking or rubbing, and can include using other parts of the body besides the hands, such as the lips or hair. Partners should take turns in initiating sensate focus exercises.

Sensate Focus II

The exercises are continued but now include the genital areas. Feedback from the partner is encouraged so that those aspects of stimulation found most pleasurable are integrated into the stimulation exercises. Orgasm and penetration are still prohibited, but in some instances oral-genital contact is encouraged.

Sensate Focus III

The exercises are continued. Penetration and continued activity to orgasm is now encouraged, depending on the specific sexual dysfunction.

The sensate focus exercises in the sequence outlined here are valuable for any couple that wishes to resume sex after a period of inactivity. They also help enhance sexual activity when it has become routine and unimaginative. Couples are not advised to proceed to the next exercise stage until the previous one has been mastered.

Source: These exercises have been adapted with permission from *The Columbia University College of Physicians and Surgeons Complete Home Medical Guide*, Donald F. Tapley, M.D., Robert J. Weiss, M.D., and Thomas Q. Morris, eds. (New York: Crown, 1985).

---

she willingly cooperates or is forced to do so. The severity of the acts tends to increase over time.

Pedophilia. Pedophiliacs have an intense sexual attraction to children, and in some cases prefer them as sexual partners. Some pedophiliacs are sexually attracted only to children who meet specific criteria, perhaps those with blond hair or of a certain age. Others may molest both male and female children without regard for specific physical characteristics. Unfortunately, pedophilia is a common occurrence in our society, although it should be noted that not all child molesters are pedophiles. (Some may have antisocial personality disorder, for example.)

Voyeurism. This is a strong sexual attraction to observing unsuspecting people who are getting undressed, are naked, or are engaged in sexual activity. (Voyeurs are sometimes called "peeping toms.") No contact with the victims is sought, but the act of watching leads to sexual arousal and, usually, masturbation either during or after the event.

Less common paraphilias include necrophilia (sexual attraction to or acts with corpses), zoophilia (animals), coprophilia (feces), klismaphilia (enemas), urophilia (urine), and telephone scatologia (obscene phone calls).

Sexual activities involving an adult and child (pedophilia) or an adult and a nonconsenting partner (exhibitionism, voyeurism, frotteurism) are inappropriate, illegal, and potentially harmful to the victim.

No one knows the true extent of paraphilias in society, because most known cases come from police reports or case studies from individual therapists. It is also unclear if the incidence of certain paraphilias is increasing. Pedophilia, for instance, appears to be on the rise—but this may be a case of increased reporting rather than increasing occurrence.

Causes

The overwhelming majority (about 90 percent) of those persons with paraphilias are men, and many

Partners concentrate on giving each other pleasure through stimulating but nongenital touch.

Exercise I

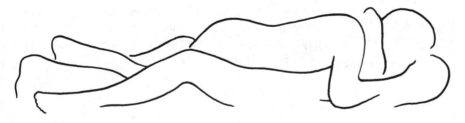

Exercise II

Touching extends to erogenous zones.

Exercise III

The exercises progress to sexual intercourse.

<u>**SENSATE FOCUS EXERCISES**</u>

<u>***Figure 11.2:***</u> **Sensate focus exercises are used to treat sexual dysfunctions such as impotence and lack of sexual desire. The exercises concentrate on achieving increasing levels of comfort with physical intimacy. Couples are advised to achieve mastery over each level of exercise before proceeding on to the next stage.**

have two or more paraphilias. Most of these men first develop the disorder in adolescence, before the age of 18, but are clearly identified as paraphiliacs only after being arrested for a sex-related crime.

It is not clear why someone develops a paraphilia. Some researchers believe a physiological factor is partly responsible, perhaps a defect in the brain. Others credit it to a chemical imbalance in the body, such as too much testosterone. Still others place part of the blame on early childhood fears of castration, to hostility toward women, or to anxiety caused by a parent who withheld love or was brutal.

One theory explains paraphilia as a learned response to early sexual arousal. When a young boy becomes aroused while wearing female clothing, for example, he might continue to associate crossdressing with sexual arousal well into adulthood.

Diagnosis and Treatment

To determine whether a person has a paraphilia, one must first distinguish paraphilias such as fetishism and transvestism from normal variations of sexual behavior. For example, a couple may on occasion augment their usual sexual activities

---

COUNSELING FOR A SEXUAL DYSFUNCTION

Sex therapy is a specific form of treatment for sexual disorders or problems, most of which are rooted in faulty learning or communication. It works best when both partners participate, although individuals can also benefit from it.

Sex therapy emphasizes the following:

- Confronting sexual myths (such as that couples usually have simultaneous orgasms).
- Providing sex education.
- Challenging inappropriate attitudes and beliefs (such as that self-stimulation is "wrong," dangerous, or immature).
- Recommending specific behavioral exercises.
- Fostering more effective communication.

If you or your partner think you have a sexual disorder and would like help for the problem, you should:

- Realize that sexual problems are relatively common occurrences.

- See a medical specialist to rule out an organic basis for the sexual problem. Schedule an appointment with your primary care physician and explain the nature of your problem.
- Ask for a referral to a urologist or gynecologist if your primary care physician does not have expertise in sexual disorders.

The specialist will take a sexual history and conduct other medical tests. If organic pathology has been ruled out, your physician will suggest you see a sex therapist. (Even people with organically based problems, however, can benefit from sex therapy.) Sex therapy can sometimes include brief psychotherapy.

Treatment for sexual difficulties also occurs within other settings, such as marital therapy or individual psychotherapy for associated problems such as depression or personality disorders.

FINDING A SEX THERAPIST

Your physician may give you the name or names of sex therapists, or you may want to select one on your own. The following recommendations are suggested for finding a qualified sex therapist.

- Contact your local university medical center and request the name of faculty members who specialize in treating sexual disorders. Many university medical centers have sexual behavior, sexual disorder, or human sexuality departments.
- States have licensing boards that govern who can provide mental health services. Contact psychological, psychiatric, or social work licensing

boards and request the name of individuals who specialize in treating sexual disorders.
- When you contact a therapist, inquire as to whether the person has expertise in treating the specific sexual problem you have. Ask the therapist what the course of therapy involves.
- No ethical therapy would involve the therapist having sex with you. If a therapist ever proposes this, contact the state licensing board under which he or she is licensed.

For more information on sex therapists, see chapter 3.

with activities such as consensual bondage or cross-dressing. It is only when these activities are the exclusive or preferred means of achieving sexual excitement and orgasm or when the sexual behavior is not consensual that the diagnosis of paraphilia is conclusive.

A diagnosis of paraphilia begins with a thorough evaluation of the subject's sexual history, including the frequency of any unusual behavior and the intensity of sexual fantasies. The therapist must rule out other possible causes of the paraphilia, for example, psychosis or dementia.

Assessment includes an evaluation of any faulty beliefs a person may have about his or her behavior. Many rapists, for instance, believe that women like to have sex forced upon them. Many pedophiles believe that sex with a child is permissible as long as they do not physically hurt the child. Exhibitionists believe that women stare at exposed genitals because they like what they see. Therapy is aimed at altering these patients' cognitive distortions and developing more appropriate behavior and social skills.

The treatment for a paraphilia can range from relatively benign to drastic. Some nations castrate paraphiliacs who repeatedly violate sexual-conduct laws. In theory, because levels of hormones released by the testicles are closely tied to sexual activity, castration reduces hormone levels and thus eliminates the activity. However, results of this method are mixed. Another treatment approach is to alter hormone levels with drugs that reduce sexual drive (chemical castration). Drug therapy is best used in conjunction with a psychotherapeutic intervention.

Behavior therapies have been found to be successful in the treatment of paraphilias, including techniques to decrease deviant arousal and increase nondeviant arousal. As part of this therapy, penile erection is measured to assess arousal levels. This involves presenting paraphiliac and nonparaphiliac stimuli (slides, videos, and audio tapes) to the individual while his erection response is monitored.

IF YOU SUSPECT THAT SOMEONE YOU KNOW HAS A PARAPHILIA

Because a number of the paraphilias are against the law and involve victims, it is important that people with paraphilias receive treatment for their sexually deviant behavior. You should know that:

- Paraphilias usually don't just go away. The person who has a paraphilia needs professional help in gaining control of the behavior.
- Most people who have paraphilias are not motivated to receive treatment. Motivation usually needs to be provided by others.

- Treatment is available and effective in the majority of cases.

To obtain help, contact the psychiatry or psychology department at the nearest university medical center and ask for the name or names of faculty who specialize in treating people with paraphilias. When you speak with the person to whom you have been referred, inquire about his or her experience in working with the specific problem and ask what the course of therapy will involve.

GENDER IDENTITY DISORDERS

A person's genetic sex, or gender, is determined at the moment of conception when the sperm unites with the ovum. From that point on, development as male or as female is influenced by a complex interaction of both prenatal and postnatal factors.

Gender identity is the person's perception of being male or female—a perception not always defined by

the person's biologic genitalia. *Gender role* is the behavior that identifies an individual as being male or female. Gender roles are strongly influenced by parental, peer, and societal spoken and unspoken messages about how boys and girls, or men and women, are supposed to behave. For more on gender roles, see chapters 21 and 22.

During the first two or three years of life, a child's environment is critical in establishing which sex the child thinks he or she is. For example, an infant raised as a boy will usually consider "himself" to be a boy (that is, his gender role), even if "he" is physically female. Occasionally a child is born with the genitals of both sexes (ambiguous genitals). Parents' belief that such a child is either male or female and the way they raise the child will influence the child's subsequent gender identity.

Theories abound to explain the many factors involved in the creation of gender identity. Hormone production during prenatal development is thought to play a strong role. It is widely believed that a host of other as-yet-unknown sensory, biochemical, and psychological factors come into play, only some involving the way parents interact with a child during early development. But no explanation is completely satisfactory. Mixing traditional boy or girl activities seems to have little effect on the future development of sexual identity. That is, very young boys may enjoy playing with dolls and young girls may enjoy mechanical toys.

Once firmly entrenched, a child's gender identity likely will remain throughout life. When a girl is raised as a boy, for instance, she usually will continue thinking of herself as a boy—even though "he" begins to develop obvious female physical characteristics. It is sometimes possible to resolve a gender identity problem by reinforcing behavior that links the child to the appropriate gender. In some cases, surgery can correct anatomic abnormalities.

Note that a person's gender identity is not the same as his or her *sexual orientation,* which defines his or her erotic attraction toward other people. Someone whose gender identity is female, for instance, might be sexually attracted to either males or females.

Gender Identity Disorder of Childhood

Gender identity disorder of childhood is a disorder of children who perceive themselves as being of the opposite sex. It is characterized by a repeated pattern of opposite gender role behavior accompanied by a disturbance in the child's perception of being a boy or girl. The origins of this rare disorder are unclear.

It has been hypothesized that parents' indifference to, or encouragement of, opposite-sex behavior may contribute to the cause, as when a parent who wanted a female child but had a male child dresses the boy in feminine clothes and tells him how pretty he is.

Treatment of these children focuses on helping them feel comfortable with their genetic sex and helping them avoid peer ostracism or humiliation. Behavior therapy has been helpful in modifying specific cross-gender conduct. Psychodynamic therapy has been utilized to address any maladaptive family or individual conflicts that contribute to the problem. For more about gender identity disorder of childhood, see chapters 17 and 22.

Transsexualism

The gender identity disorder known as transsexualism (also called *gender dysphoria syndrome*) attracts much press coverage but is actually quite unusual, with only about 30,000 verified cases recorded worldwide.

In transsexualism, an individual's gender identity is at variance with his or her anatomical sex. In these cases, a boy or man strongly believes that he is really a girl or woman, and vice versa. Most transsexuals have a personal history of sexual confusion, often including episodes of cross-dressing and other opposite-sex activities. For a diagnosis to be made, there must be strong evidence that the situation has been continuous for a long period (usually since childhood) and that it is almost certain to continue.

These cases usually come to light when the individual requests sexual reassignment, most often seeking surgery to change the sexual organs. A physician must be alert to the possibility that a recent emotional problem led to the sexual identity crisis and that this crisis might resolve without surgery.

Psychotherapy is widely urged for those seeking sex-change surgery. The therapy is aimed at clarifying their attitudes toward irreversible surgery and determining that the desire for surgery is firm and resolute. It can also help them adjust to a new sex role afterward.

As a first step in maximizing the chance of success, the individual is urged to live in the chosen sex role for a year or more before surgery. For example, a man seeking to become a woman might undergo electrolysis to remove unwanted body hair and wear makeup and women's clothing. A woman would conceal her breasts and dress as a man. Both sexes are advised to take on the identity they wish to assume in as many ways as possible.

Several months prior to surgery, hormone treatment is begun to change the body's distribution of fat, alter the growth of body hair, and begin physiological changes in sexual and other organs. Eventually the first surgical steps are taken. The process of surgical reassignment is long, often involving several operations. A female-to-male procedure typically includes removal of breast tissue, possibly a hysterectomy, and sometimes the creation of an artificial penis. A male-to-female procedure includes removal of the penis and testicles and the creation of an artificial vagina.

Even after years of preparation, there is no assurance that surgery will provide a satisfactory outcome, and psychotherapy often continues for years afterward.

12

Sleep Disorders

Neil B. Kavey, M.D., and Jamie Whyte, M.D.

Almost everyone recognizes the importance of restful, refreshing sleep. A good night's sleep has an almost magical ability to make big problems appear smaller, create tranquility in a sea of strong emotions, and turn a sense of discouragement into renewed enthusiasm. By contrast, even a single restless night spent tossing and turning can leave one feeling fuzzyheaded and grouchy. After just a few bad nights, a person will yell at the children, snap at friends, and make mistakes at work.

Most people have difficulty sleeping from time to time, usually in response to stresses in their lives. But for many, sleep difficulties last for an extended period of time, perhaps months or even years. Sleep problems might be just one aspect of a broader physical or emotional condition, or they may qualify as

sleep disorders in their own right. Most sleep disorders fall into four broad categories:

- *Insomnias* are disorders related to not getting enough sleep, or the feeling of having slept insufficiently or poorly.
- *Hypersomnias* are disorders tied to needing *too much* sleep, excessive sleepiness, or sleep at inappropriate times.
- *Biological clock problems* are related to the inappropriate timing of sleep and wakefulness, such as an inability to sleep during the night and a lack of full alertness during the day.
- *Parasomnias* are disturbances associated with sleep, such as sleepwalking or nightmares.

UNLOCKING THE SECRETS OF SLEEP

Despite substantial research, sleep has not yet yielded all its secrets. Scientists are still not certain why we sleep or what role sleep plays in our lives—although much is known about the physiology of sleep and about the diagnosis and treatment of sleep problems. And we do know that nobody can live comfortably (or, indeed, for very long) *without* sleep.

Both physically and mentally, people can suffer severely from lack of sleep. After a day or several days without any sleep whatsoever, many people become irritable, forgetful, and lose the ability to concentrate.

How Much Is "Normal"?

The amount of sleep needed varies enormously among individuals, but about 7 or 8 hours is average. Some people, known as *long sleepers,* actually require 10 or 11 hours of sleep a night. In general, the length of sleep is less important than is its quality. Nine hours of restless sleep can lead to irritability for the same person who feels content with 6 hours of sound sleep.

Sleep Cycles

Whatever its length, normal sleep can be described as a set of cycles that begin when a person prepares for bed and turns out the lights. For about 5 to 10 minutes (on average), a person lies in bed, letting the mind drift from subject to subject. Heart rate, blood pressure, and body temperature gradually drop, and brain waves subtly change.

Without being aware of it, a person enters the first of five sleep phases, each characterized by a slightly different level of consciousness, body physiology, and brain wave patterns. *Stage 1* is light sleep, while *Stage 4* is the deepest, from which arousal can be extremely difficult despite the loudest alarm clock. *Stage 2* and *Stage 3* are distinguished by differences in brain waves, as measured by electroencephalogram (EEG) readings.

Over a period of roughly 90 minutes or so, each person cycles through Stages 1 to 4 and then back up to Stage 2, after which the REM (rapid-eye movement) sleep phase begins. Dreams occur during REM sleep, as the eyes dart back and forth behind closed but fluttering eyelids. After REM, Stage 2 begins again and the sleep cycle repeats itself. Normally the cycle recurs four or five times during a full night's sleep.

All the stages are important to a good night's sleep, but researchers believe that Stages 2 to 4 are those during which the body replenishes itself for the next day. The REM stage, some think, is the time when recent events are integrated into the mind.

This roughly 90-minute cycle continues throughout life, although the time spent in the various stages varies with age. Children, for example, spend more time in deeper stages of sleep than do adults, which explains why often they can be so difficult to rouse. The elderly spend more hours in lighter sleep stages, which is one reason why they tend to awaken in the night. (For more about the sleep experiences and problems of the elderly, see chapter 23.)

The normal sequence of sleep cycles throughout the night is disturbed in many sleep disorders. Studies in sleep laboratories (see the box on page 173) often can reveal which specific stages of sleep are affected.

Diagnosing Problems

Because myriad physical and emotional factors can contribute to disruptions in the sleep cycle, and because some sleep disorders are illnesses in their own right, a doctor experienced in sleep problems must first determine the precise nature of the problem.

The diagnostic process normally includes a thorough physical examination. Often treatment of an underlying physical condition goes a long way toward eliminating the sleep problem. A change in the type or dosage of pain-relief medicine, for instance, might resolve insomnia brought on by serious pain. Mental and emotional history and evaluation are important, as is a detailed history of drug use. (See the box on page 176.)

Sometimes the bed partner (or parent, if a child is having sleep difficulties) might be asked to furnish details about physical problems that occur while a person sleeps, such as breathing difficulties or unusual movements. Once properly diagnosed by qualified professionals, most sleep disorders can be overcome with proper treatment.

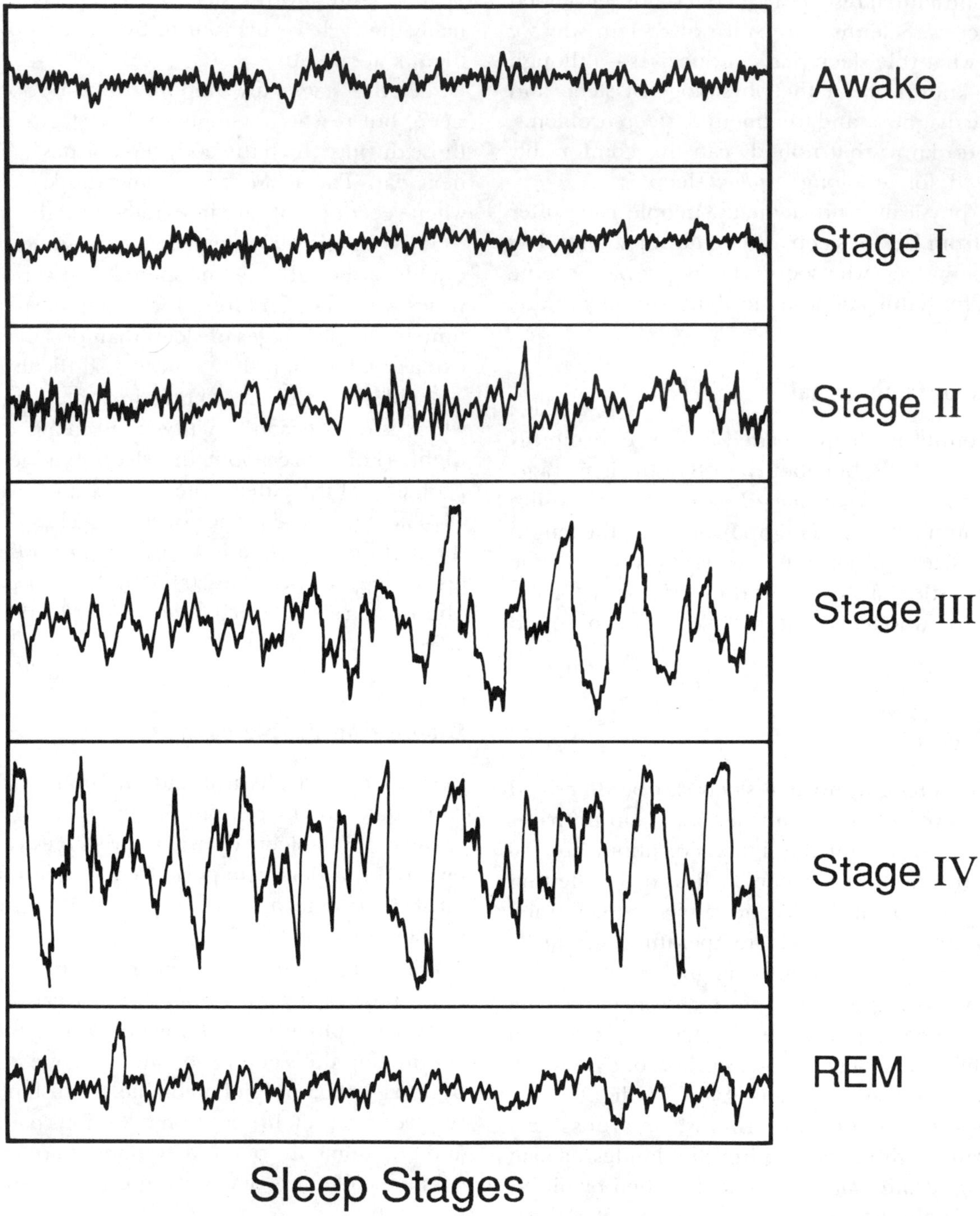

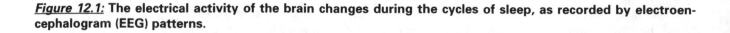

Awake

Stage I

Stage II

Stage III

Stage IV

REM

Sleep Stages

Figure 12.1: **The electrical activity of the brain changes during the cycles of sleep, as recorded by electroencephalogram (EEG) patterns.**

INSOMNIAS

Insomnia is the inability to fall asleep or to stay asleep long enough. It is one of the most common medical complaints in the United States, and one of the most frequently medicated. An estimated 25 million Americans are afflicted with recurrent insomnia, and they spend more than $100 million annually on prescription drugs to help them sleep. Countless millions of dollars more are spent on over-the-counter drugs widely advertised to help promote sleep.

Insufficient or poor sleep can be caused by a range of disturbances in addition to the sleep disorders themselves. Stress-related emotional and behavioral factors head the list. Medical, neurological, and psychiatric disorders and medication use and abuse are common causes as well.

Stress-related Transient and Persistent Insomnia

When stress is the cause of sleep problems and sleep returns to normal within about three weeks (after the stressful event has passed or its memory has faded), specialists call the condition *transient psychophysiological insomnia.*

Stressful life events, whether negative (such as a lost job) or positive (such as a forthcoming wedding), can occupy a person's mind well into the small hours of the night, holding back sleep for hours and/or causing restlessness and frequent awakenings throughout the night. A feeling of listlessness during the day often accompanies the insomnia.

Insomnia that continues for three weeks or more is called *persistent psychophysiological insomnia.* Often it grows out of a short-term condition, in part because the persistent thoughts that initially led to sleeplessness have become a nagging preoccupation—as, for example, when a mid-level executive, worried about a corporate takeover, obsessively begins to ponder the uneasy situation at work as soon as he tries to sleep. People often develop poor sleep habits as they try to deal with a short-term insomnia, and these poor habits enhance the problem. Some people eventually try too hard to fall asleep, unaware that by concentrating on their insomnia they become tense and anxious and encourage themselves to stay awake—as in the case of a young attorney who, after a few weeks of not being able to fall asleep easily, now lies awake worrying about whether she'll be able to sleep. After insomnia becomes chronic, sufferers may no longer even recall when or why it began.

Insomnia Treatments

Both transient and persistent forms of stress-related insomnia can be treated with behavioral therapy that emphasizes good sleep habits. Short-term use of medications may facilitate forming new habits and improve daytime functioning.

Behavior treatments of insomnia appear simple, but many people find that breaking old habits can be difficult. In addition to teaching new sleep habits (see the box on page 174), another method specialists sometimes recommend for persistent insomnia is called *sleep restriction therapy.* The person with insomnia who perhaps stays in bed for a full eight hours but sleeps only four or five is encouraged to adhere rigidly to a schedule that limits time spent in bed, perhaps to five hours nightly to start. Once that five hours is spent totally in sleep, the time is increased gradually in quarter-hour increments. Eventually a full night's sleep is achieved.

In some cases of persistent insomnia, relaxation techniques can be helpful. A well-structured schedule of muscle relaxation prior to bedtime can reduce anxiety and often leads to a sound night's sleep. See chapter 24 for specific relaxation techniques.

A NIGHT IN THE SLEEP LAB

A test known as a polysomnographic study may be necessary to diagnose your sleep disorder precisely and to help a physician suggest the best available remedies. You sleep for one or two nights in a comfortable laboratory room set up as a bedroom. Sensing devices are attached to your body to record brain waves, respiration, and heart rate. The entire session is videotaped for later review.

This study frequently is the only way to identify sleep disturbances that you don't clearly recall when you wake up or that you can't know about because you're asleep, such as thrashing legs or pauses in breathing. The test can also link your sleep disorder to changes in your brain waves or to changes in your stages of sleep.

The short-term use of sleeping pills—also known as *sedative-hypnotics*—can be highly beneficial for some people. The most effective and therefore the most commonly prescribed drugs used today to induce sleep are the *benzodiazepines*. But all sedative-hypnotics must be used carefully and conservatively. Most of these drugs can impair reflexes, and caution must be exercised by anyone who operates machinery or drives a vehicle. Many drugs are dependency-producing, and all interact dangerously with alcohol. (For more on benzodiazepines and other sedative-hypnotics, see chapter 5.)

Drugs are usually most beneficial for short-term insomnia caused by a specific event. A serious problem at work, for instance, may result in transient insomnia for a few nights. Taking medication to assure enough sleep to get through the crisis might be both effective and appropriate. Similarly, sleeping pills can be helpful during an episode of insomnia caused by serious pain—for example, the flare-up of an arthritic knee. Often medication will keep a transient insomnia from becoming persistent.

Persistent insomnia, however, requires more than simply taking pills. Over time medications lose their effectiveness and their side effects become problematic. Long-term use can interfere with normal sleep cycles, causing insomnia that is similar to the condition that the drugs were prescribed to treat. A word of warning: If sleep medication becomes ineffective, do *not* increase or exceed the dosage recommended by the prescribing physician; doing so can lead to dependency and possible overdose.

Another problem with sleeping pills is *rebound insomnia*. Prescription and over-the-counter drugs alike may help bring about sleep, but when they are discontinued, insomnia can be even more severe than it was previously.

Pseudoinsomnia and Other "Noninsomnias"

Some people are convinced they have insomnia even though, by every available measurement, they sleep soundly. They may not realize that their daytime drowsiness and lethargy result from overwork, boredom, or some equally understandable cause rather than from poor sleep. Their problem is considered a disorder of the *perception* of sleep rather than of sleep itself. A firm diagnosis can be made only in a sleep laboratory. The clinician may review details of the sleep study with the patient, including the video por-

---

LEARNING NEW SLEEP HABITS

You can try the basic behavioral treatment approach on your own. Here are the essentials:

- First, go to bed only when you feel drowsy. Many people think that just because it's 10 P.M. or midnight, it's bedtime. But if you go to bed before you're actually sleepy, you'll probably end up lying awake too long and eventually add to the very cycle of insomnia you're tying to break.
- If sleep hasn't come within 20 minutes, get up and do something that is quiet and relaxing— reading a good but not too stimulating book is probably the best choice. Go back to bed about 30 minutes later and try sleeping again.
- Until the insomnia is resolved, set your alarm for the same time every morning, *including* weekends.
- Don't take naps. Relax for a while if you come home tired after work, but that two-hour snooze in the easy chair in front of the television can lead to insomnia later.
- Reserve the bedroom for sleep-related activities only. Reading a disturbing business report in bed can result in a spiral of thoughts that keep sleep at bay. The exception is sexual activity; it generally doesn't interfere with sleep but, on the contrary, usually enhances sleepiness.

---

tions of the person while asleep. Or he or she may awaken the person from deep sleep in the laboratory to demonstrate clearly the differences between sleep and wakefulness.

Sometimes people who normally sleep only a few hours nightly believe that they should be sleeping longer, even though they sleep soundly and awaken refreshed. They sometimes say they are bored by staying awake longer than most people, or that their short sleeping cycle creates social problems. For these *short sleepers*, treatment usually consists of reassurance that a short, sound sleep is adequate and suggestions on how to fill the extra time a short sleep leaves available. Clinicians must be careful to distinguish this normal condition from forms of true insomnia in which people sleep a short time but do not feel refreshed the next day. Many elderly people, who require less sleep than younger people, are short sleepers.

Insomnia Related to Other Disorders

As mentioned, insomnia can be a symptom of numerous mental and physical illnesses. The pain and discomfort of a serious medical condition, as well as worries about recovery, can lead to poor sleep and insomnia. In addition, any number of nervous system disorders can alter the brain's chemistry and structure sufficiently to cause sleep disorders. Insomnia caused by medical and neurological problems usually diminishes when the underlying illness is resolved.

Insomnia also can be a symptom of other sleep disorders that cause repeated nighttime awakenings, such as sleep apnea or jet lag, discussed later in this chapter.

Psychiatric Problems

A number of psychiatric illnesses can cause insomnia. Schizophrenia and other major psychotic disorders often include sleeplessness as a feature of the underlying condition. The insomnia may disappear for a time during the course of the illness but usually will abate completely only if the condition is treated successfully. Depression, too, commonly produces insomnia, often featuring early-morning awakening, which disappears once the depression is treated. In addition, insomnia can result from generalized anxiety, anxiety attacks, and phobias.

Restless Legs Syndrome and Periodic Movements in Sleep

An estimated 1 percent of the U.S. population experiences some form of a condition called restless legs syndrome, marked by an irresistible urge to move the legs. This feeling becomes exaggerated in the evening, especially just prior to sleep and during periods awake in the night. Many people say the movements are due to a "creeping" sensation they feel deep in their legs, usually the calves. Some describe the feeling as "worms inside my legs" or "insects crawling around." As the odd sensations begin, they may keep a person from falling asleep. Insomnia and daytime fatigue may result from the nighttime disturbances.

The disorder has no known cause, but some forms run in families and are presumed to have a genetic basis. Some types of restless legs syndrome occur with rheumatoid arthritis, pregnancy, uremia, iron-deficiency anemia, and diabetes, but no clear cause-and-effect relationship is known. There is no evidence that neurological or muscle disorders contribute to the syndrome. Treatment usually involves one of several drugs (such as mild opioids) that stop the restlessness.

Periodic movements in sleep can accompany restless leg syndrome. These involve regular, brief, slow movements of the toes, feet, or lower legs that make it appear as if the extremities are withdrawing from something. Sometimes termed *nocturnal myoclonus*, these movements are often associated with disturbances in the continuity of sleep and thereby can cause insomnia and fatigue. While they can occur hundreds of times in a single night, they may not be apparent to the bed partner. Unlike restless legs, no unusual sensations accompany this syndrome. The disorder tends to begin in the 30s but can start as early as the teen years. The same drug treatments helpful with restless legs syndrome can benefit people with a periodic movement problem.

HYPERSOMNIAS

Excessive need for sleep, day after day and week after week, eventually adversely affects job performance, family relations, and ability to perform tasks that require concentration, such as driving a car. Seemingly endless tiredness also can lead to emotional problems.

Excessive daytime sleepiness can be caused by many different medical, neurological, and psychiatric conditions, among them diabetes, hypothyroidism, and depression. As discussed in the box on page 176, drug use can also be a factor.

However, several conditions involving excess sleepiness are distinct illnesses unto themselves.

Sleep Apnea

Sleep apnea—in which breathing briefly stops—affects an estimated 2.5 million Americans. Sometimes central nervous system and/or physical factors in the airway cause an obstruction of the air passages during sleep, a syndrome called *obstructive sleep apnea*. Breathing becomes blocked up to several hundred

SLEEP PROBLEMS AND DRUG USE

Sleep can be affected seriously by several common so-called recreational drugs, both legal (such as alcohol and caffeine) and illicit, as well as numerous prescription and over-the-counter medications.

Alcohol, a depressant, dramatically alters the normal sleep-wake cycle and changes breathing patterns during sleep. While a few drinks before bedtime might speed the onset of sleep, as the alcohol is metabolized overnight the tranquilizing effect diminishes and the drinker usually awakens one or more times before morning. Alcohol, like many drugs, also alters the stages of sleep throughout the night; chronic alcoholics tend to suffer from persistent insomnia.

A further complication of alcohol use is that it causes excessive relaxation of the upper airway. In doing so, it worsens both snoring and sleep apnea. (See page 175.)

Caffeine, a stimulant, makes falling and staying asleep more difficult for most people and often is used successfully as a stimulant for people who feel sleepy. Even those who insist coffee doesn't keep them up at night probably are sleeping more lightly than they otherwise would.

Marijuana sometimes causes sleepiness among users, particularly if they are smoking it alone rather than in the company of others. Morning grogginess is common. Withdrawal from chronic marijuana use can cause transient insomnia.

Cocaine is a stimulant so powerful that some users will stay awake for several days and nights using the drug, then "crash" into a sleep binge that might last 24 to 48 hours. Cocaine, like alcohol, interferes with the normal changes in sleep stages, if the user can get to sleep at all. When sleep does occur, it sometimes fails to provide a sense of restoration or renewal.

Prescription medications can have a range of effects on sleep. Those with stimulant properties— such as amphetamines, methylphenidate (Ritalin), and some antidepressants—can produce insomnia. Medications with a depressant effect—including most drugs used as sedatives and in the treatment of anxiety, many antipsychotics, and numerous compounds prescribed for medical conditions—can produce daytime sleepiness and/or lead to poor nighttime sleep.

Antihistamines, most frequently prescribed or purchased over-the-counter to treat allergies, cause daytime drowsiness. This side effect can be used to advantage at night for the person who can't sleep. In fact, antihistamines can be a reasonably safe sleep aid and often are suggested by doctors. A few new antiallergy formulations seem to cause little or no sleepiness, however—a boon to the allergic person who wants to remain alert.

---

times a night. Even though they wake up briefly, gasping for air, people with this condition generally remain unaware of it.

Daytime sleepiness is a very common symptom. Victims of sleep-induced apnea can be so tired from the frequent awakenings that they fall asleep while driving, during dinner, or in the midst of a conversation. Impaired concentration, morning headaches, depression, and even personality changes can result.

Snoring is another common symptom. It and sleepiness may be the only two symptoms of which sleep apnea sufferers are aware. Snoring in sleep apnea is somewhat different from more benign snoring. (See the box on page 177.) In apnea, when the blockage of airflow occurs, the loud vibratory snoring sounds stop suddenly and are replaced by relatively quiet, or gagginglike, noises. The pause ends with a loud snort or snore; then the person takes several good breaths, with loud snoring, before the next pause begins.

Sleep apnea can cause serious harm to the cardiovascular system. The struggle to breathe (and resulting low levels of oxygen in the blood) can strain the heart and lungs and contribute to high blood pressure. Irregular heartbeats and several other heart irregularities are associated with persistent sleep apnea.

Causes

Most people with obstructive sleep apnea are overweight, and in some the obstruction may stem from an overabundance of tissue in the throat that periodically blocks the flow of air during sleep. In people of normal weight, airway blockage can be caused by large tonsils or adenoids, tumors, or unusually small jaws or small airways. Muscles anywhere along the airway, including in the back of the nasal passage and back part of the throat, may relax excessively in sleep and contribute to air blockage. The use of alcohol and other depressant drugs can alter the respiratory system enough to spur obstructive sleep apnea in people already prone to the disorder.

Treatment

Many people gain relief from sleep apnea simply by changing their sleeping positions. Usually sleeping on the back results in many more nightly episodes of sleep apnea than sleeping on the side. (See the box below.) For overweight victims of sleep apnea, a treatment plan might first focus on weight loss. Surgery or a mechanical device that forces air through the nose during sleep and keeps the airway from collapsing may be necessary. Mouthpieces, used for snoring (see the box below) are a new treatment that is gaining in acceptance.

Once the apnea is resolved, people generally feel vastly better than they have in years.

SNORING

As many as half of all adult Americans sometimes snore during sleep. Significantly more men than women snore, and snoring becomes more common in both men and women as they grow older. Snoring is caused by tissue in the upper airway relaxing in sleep and partially blocking the airway. As air rushes past, this tissue vibrates and snoring results. In adults, there is a strong association between snoring and obesity. In children, snoring is usually caused by enlarged tonsils or adenoids; if these organs are blocking the airway enough to cause strained breathing, they may have to be removed.

While snoring is often the butt of jokes, it can indicate the presence of a dangerous medical condition. Not only is it often an integral part of sleep apnea, but it may by itself be associated with a range of heart and circulatory ailments.

Loud snoring often leads to serious social problems. Spouses may move to separate bedrooms to avoid the noise or face restless nights and deprivation of sleep themselves. Marital discord is not infrequent. Some loud snorers refuse to sleep away from home, even in hotel rooms, for fear of disturbing others at night; they therefore may restrict business travel or recreational activities.

What to Do About It

Weight loss can help reduce the excess tissue and relieve snoring in many people. Alcohol relaxes muscles and encourages snoring, so drinking less before bed can help. Avoid smoking, which irritates the nose and throat and sometimes fosters snoring.

Sleeping on your side rather than your back is usually helpful. Researchers have devised a simple, inexpensive, and effective way to encourage sleeping on the side and prevent turning over in the night. Fill a sock with whiffle balls or light, bulky packing material, then pin or sew it firmly to the back of the pajamas. Now try sleeping on your back!

Various pillows are widely advertised to help reduce snoring, although their effectiveness is untested in laboratory settings. Mouthpieces are being developed and offered commercially, but before choosing one, be sure appropriate testing has been conducted. In some cases, as when snoring is very disruptive of one's life, surgery might be recommended.

Narcolepsy

Narcolepsy is an uncommon but serious sleep disturbance with four characteristic symptoms—although an individual may not experience all of them. (There are an estimated half-million sufferers in the United States.)

Uncontrollable sleepiness and sleep attacks. A sudden urge to sleep is the hallmark of this disorder. The so-called attacks are almost irresistible and often occur at inappropriate times, for instance while driving or eating. The need for sleep may begin as general daytime sleepiness, sometimes relieved by frequent naps.

Cataplexy. This is a sudden, brief paralysis, often brought on by laughter, excitement, fear, sexual arousal, or some other sudden strong emotion. In mild cases, it might result in lost control over just a few muscles, perhaps the neck, hands, or knees. In extreme cases, virtually all muscles become paralyzed, leading to the person falling to the ground. Sleep frequently follows the fall; if it doesn't, the person is able to get up after about half a minute or so.

Hypnagogic and hypnopompic hallucinations. These are dreamlike experiences that occur just before (hypnagogic) the onset of sleep or just as sleep ends (hypnopompic). The hallucinations can be vivid and frightening, although they are frequently no more unsettling than normal dreams.

Sleep paralysis. This is a total body paralysis that sometimes occurs just before sleep or just after awakening. Episodes usually last for 30 to 60 seconds (sometimes less). While it can be frightening, the condition is seldom dangerous.

Another frequent symptom of narcolepsy—and one that is somewhat surprising given the nature of the disorder—is poor nocturnal sleep: It is often light, and marred by frequent movements and arousals.

Narcolepsy usually begins gradually, usually starting in adolescence and almost always before age 30; only rarely does it begin after middle age. It is often a seriously disruptive illness, leading to employment problems and family difficulties. The causes of this disorder are unknown; although it does seem to run in families, a genetic basis for narcolepsy has not been established.

Although there is no cure for narcolepsy, treatment usually includes the use of various stimulant drugs. Severe cataplexy, although unrelated to depression, is often treated with tricyclic antidepressants; another drug, gamma-hydroxybutyrate, is sometimes effective when others fail. By learning to take regularly scheduled naps, most people can live much more comfortably with narcolepsy.

Long Sleeper

A long sleeper is a person who needs more sleep than the majority of people and who frequently feels sleep-deprived after a "mere" eight or nine hours of sleep nightly. Often long sleepers try forcing themselves into a "normal" sleep cycle and end up suffering from excessive tiredness. The treatment of choice is for them to try to adapt their lives to their personal sleep needs.

BIOLOGICAL CLOCK DISORDERS

A number of sleep disorders involve disturbances of the daily (or circadian) sleep-wake cycle of about 24 hours.

Jet Lag

The human body is attuned to a roughly 24-hour rhythm, with the sun rising and setting on a fixed schedule and sleep taking place at a certain time during that cycle. When a person crosses several time zones, his or her body must grow accustomed to the new time zone's schedule of light and darkness. Until that adjustment occurs, sleep is fitful and the person awakens or feels sleepy at odd hours.

If the stay in a new time zone is to be short (a day or two), some specialists recommend that the traveler try to go to sleep and get up according to what time it is back home. For longer journeys, some people begin several days in advance to gradually alter their meals and activities, hoping that by the time they arrive they will experience little disruption. They may even try to trick their bodies into believing the new day-night schedule is already in effect by turning on bright lights at night and pulling down blinds during the day or by matching their meals to the appropriate hours in their destination time zone. Medications can sometimes be helpful for getting to sleep in a new time zone, when the clock says it's bedtime but the body, "set" for the old time zone, feels awake.

Irregular Sleep–Wake Schedule

Some people continually alter their sleeping schedules so dramatically that they constantly feel tired or uncomfortable. A job requiring repeated awakenings—a doctor on call for 48 hours straight, for example—can severely alter the normal sleep-wake cycle. Freelance writers and artists often set their own erratic schedules. Eventually, such irregular cycles may snowball into serious problems of falling asleep, staying asleep, or remaining alert during periods of work or social activity.

People who work rotating shifts—such as nurses, police officers, and transportation workers, to name a few—may have little control over their sleep schedules. Irregular sleep-wake cycles may contribute to increased industrial accidents among people who rotate from shift to shift frequently. Studies show that shift work is not so troublesome when the changes take place after long intervals; when shift changes proceed clockwise (that is, moving from the evening shift to the night shift, to the day shift); and when time off accompanies shift changes.

Effective treatment for an irregular sleep-wake cycle requires that the individual maintain a strict sleep-wake schedule under professional supervision. With the person's full cooperation, the problem is often resolved within days or weeks. For the person who can't fully control his or her work schedule, the sleep specialist will try to devise more innovative approaches, but sometimes the problem can't be resolved without returning to regular work hours.

Delayed Sleep Phase Syndrome

Some people can't (or won't) go to sleep until well past conventional bedtime hours—perhaps 3 or 4 A.M. If their jobs or home environments permit them to sleep correspondingly late, these "night people" may go through life with no problems other than minor scheduling difficulties. But when a circumstance requires that they assume a conventional schedule, they may find it difficult to fall asleep and virtually impossible to get up earlier.

One technique sleep specialists use to reset the body's clock is as follows:

The person is told to choose an appropriate new bedtime—for example, midnight. He or she should sleep, or try to sleep, for five hours only. A few days of this firm, five-hour schedule and the person will be sleepy most of the time. Then he or she should increase the sleep time by 15 minutes—the person should get up at 5:15 A.M. Every few days another 15 minutes should be added, until the sleep cycle has been extended to its normal length, at new hours. The technique requires persistence and motivation and may be easiest to accomplish with professional supervision. People must be persistent in adhering to the new schedule to avoid slipping back into the old pattern.

PARASOMNIAS

A number of sleep disturbances involve activity that we usually associate with being awake—such as walking, talking, and urinating.

Sleepwalking

A significant percentage of all children and a much smaller number of adults sleepwalk occasionally. Also known as *somnambulism,* sleepwalking can be limited to simple activities, such as sitting up in bed, reaching for the telephone to make a call, or turning a lamp on and off. In rare cases, a sleepwalker will act dramatically, perhaps by screaming, shouting, or moving about vigorously. Regardless of the amount of activity, sleepwalkers rarely remember the event.

Sleepwalkers move around with eyes open. They usually are able to avoid bumping into anything, although sometimes they do hurt themselves accidentally. They seldom engage in conversation with others or respond to questions or to noise. Some sleepwalkers have been known to engage in eating binges while asleep.

The precise cause of sleepwalking is unknown, but researchers believe there is a genetic factor; identical twins are six times more likely than other siblings to be sleepwalkers. Among adults, a psychological conflict may underlie sleepwalking. Sleepwalking can also be a symptom of a medical or neurological disorder. Laboratory studies show that most episodes take place during the first third of the sleep cycle, and that all incidents occur during non-REM sleep. Sleepwalkers may have some subtle disorder that prevents them from completely waking up, even in circumstances that would wake others.

Most adult sleepwalkers have experienced at least a few episodes during childhood, although children who sleepwalk frequently grow out of it on their own, with no treatment. Because causes are diverse in adults, a complete mental and physical evaluation is required.

With adults and children alike, it is essential to safeguard the individual by keeping the floor area clear of toys and other obstacles and locking windows at night, to minimize the chance of injury. In children, medication is used only if episodes are so frequent or vigorous that they cause special difficulties for the child or family. When sleepwalking occurs repeatedly in adults, physicians regularly prescribe medication (usually benzodiazepines or anticonvulsants).

REM Behavior Disorder

Normally during REM sleep—the period when dreams occur—most muscles are temporarily paralyzed. In rare cases, however, a person's muscles remain active even while dreaming, and the individual—still sound asleep—tries to act out the dream. Speaking, arm-waving, kicking, sleepwalking, and aggression toward others are common; and bed partners can get hit, kicked, grabbed, and even strangled, all while the person is dreaming.

This condition, caused by a biochemical or physical abnormality in the brain, usually begins late in life, at about 50 to 60 years of age, but occasionally earlier. Diagnosis of this disorder requires a sleep center evaluation. Usually it is treated with tranquilizers, anticonvulsants, or antidepressants.

Nightmares and Night Terrors

A nightmare is a vivid, frightening dream that usually results in the dreamer waking up with full or partial recall of the dream itself. A night terror is an episode of extreme fright during sleep *without* any recollection of a dream. Both nightmares and night terrors strike children much more often than adults.

Nightmares occur exclusively during REM sleep. REM sleep phases grow longer in the latter part of the sleep cycle, and the majority of nightmares occur from the middle of the night onward.

Night terrors, by contrast, take place in non-REM (nondream) sleep. During night terrors people wake up sweating heavily, their hearts pounding, and screaming in fear. They are unaware of their surroundings and unresponsive to attempts to comfort them. They may not calm down for 10 or 15 minutes, although they return to sleep quickly once the episode ends. Generally they don't remember what scared them, but rarely a person will retain a vague image of something terrifying. A few children and adults who experience night terrors will sleepwalk during the episode.

Particularly among adults, prescription drugs such as levodopa, reserpine, beta-blockers, and antidepressants, as well as withdrawal from addictive drugs, all can provoke nightmares. Heavy drinking is strongly associated with night terrors.

In both adults and children, nightmares and night terrors also can be caused by unresolved psychological conflicts or traumatic events. They are a frequent feature of post-traumatic stress disorder (see chapter 7). Emotional traumas that disturb the sleep of children can be overlooked easily by adults—such as the loss of a favorite toy or overhearing a loud argument between parents. Although nightmares and night terrors are considered normal developmental events in children, disappearing by adolescence, frequent episodes at any age warrant professional evaluation. Crisis intervention techniques can be very effective in dealing with the trauma. (See chapter 17.) Benzodiazepines and anticonvulsants are prescribed for some people.

Sleep Drunkenness

Immediately upon awakening, some people become confused, irrational, impulsive, and sometimes belligerent or even violent. Lasting as long as an hour, this sleep drunkenness seems to represent a mental state somewhere between full wakefulness and deep sleep. The cause is unknown, but episodes can be minimized by avoiding alcohol and other depressant drugs. When sleep drunkenness becomes a persistent problem, it is sometimes treated with stimulants, which may be administered by a family member shortly before the normal time of rising, with the victim allowed to sleep several more minutes after taking the medicine. When the stimulant takes effect, the person is roused into a more awakened state.

Bruxism

Bruxism is clenching or grinding of teeth during sleep. It usually occurs during childhood, although many adults grind their teeth in sleep; at least 15 percent of the population is thought to have experienced bruxism at some time in their lives. The behavior is thought to be partly genetic in origin but may also be related to stress, a child's intense nature, or even poor alignment of teeth.

Bruxism that continues for several years can wear down teeth and lead to gum disease, sore jaw, facial pain, and headache. Loud tooth grinding may disturb a bed partner. The only treatment widely regarded as effective is a mouthguard worn at night. Dentists should be consulted for information.

Jactatio Capitis Nocturna

Infants are, by nature, restless. But sometimes, for unknown reasons, they perform a series of repetitive, rhythmic movements including head-banging, body-rocking, and rolling of the head, both when going to sleep and during sleep itself. These movements are known as jactatio capitis nocturna. The condition usually begins before 18 months of age and almost always disappears by itself before adolescence. More boys than girls are affected. The cause is unknown.

Each episode of jactatio (as it is commonly called) lasts for 5 to 15 minutes. Injury to the child is the principal danger. Care should be taken that the sides of cribs cannot cause injury during a period of head-banging and that no rigid toys are left in the bed. As the child grows older, he or she may fear social embarrassment and may avoid sleeping away from home.

Some infants are given tranquilizers to control jactatio, but success is inconsistent. Others are treated, again with varying results, by placing a metronome near the bed, tuned to the frequency of the movements; somehow the metronome's regular rhythm calms some affected children. While the incidence of this disorder is high in mentally retarded children, the conditions are not related. Children who experience jactatio generally grow up normally.

WHO CAN HELP

Help is readily available for people with sleep disorders. Physicians may prescribe drugs for the short-term treatment of common problems such as insomnia and as a rule are aware of traditional treatment methods for such conditions as snoring and bruxism. They can also check for physical causes of sleep disturbances.

Psychiatrists and other mental health professionals are versed in dealing with sleep disorders for which a psychological cause is evident.

The diagnosis and treatment of serious or long-standing sleep problems may require the resources of specialists associated with a sleep center. Many hospitals in major metropolitan areas have such facilities. The address of the nearest center can usually be obtained from the family physician or from the American Sleep Disorders Association 604 Second Street, S.W., Rochester, MN 55902; tel. 507 287–6006. This association can also supply information on all types of sleep disorders.

13

Personality Disorders

John M. Oldham, M.D., and Andrew E. Skodol, M.D.

Many persons share certain stylistic traits, such as being organized, outgoing, flirtatious, or timid. Yet every human being thinks, feels, perceives, and reacts to the outside world in a distinctive and unique way. The pattern in which such characteristics are organized forms a unique constellation of emotions, thoughts, and behaviors known as the personality.

Personality is a kind of "automatic pilot" that allows each person to function, grow, and adapt to life. For some people, however, personality grows rigid and inflexible. Rather than providing ways of coping flexibly with challenge, these individuals' characteristic personality styles nearly guarantee that they will be unhappy, unfulfilled, and/or unable to function effectively in life. Having failed to evolve adaptive personality styles, these men and women instead have developed personality disorders.

Because personality disorder is a distortion of normal personality, to understand how it develops, let us first take a closer look at the nature of personality.

TEMPERAMENT AND CHARACTER

Most mental health practitioners agree that personality has two components: temperament and character. Temperament is each person's inborn biological and genetic disposition. For instance, certain individuals are born with a calm and placid nature; others possess a natural proclivity to be active and energetic. Temperament, then, is the preprogrammed, constitutional aspect of personality. Character, on the other hand, is "learned" over time. It is a developing set of behavioral, intellectual, and emotional patterns, influenced by the environment—that is, parents, family, life events, culture, and the world at large.

Temperament and character must be considered together, for each influences and affects the other and both are, in turn, affected by the environment in which the individual exists. For example, the temperamentally excitable or cranky baby may become relatively calm when reared in a relaxed, tolerant family environment. But that same child reared in a stressful, tense family structure may be increasingly irritable and edgy. Similarly, an unflappable, easygoing child can help calm a nervous, anxious parent.

For years, mental health professionals believed that one's personality was formed in childhood and from then on was fixed and unchanging. Newer data refute that thinking, however. It now appears that the interaction between temperament and character is ongoing and that personality maturation is a developmental process that continues throughout an individual's life—unless personality disorder stunts or distorts the process.

PERSONALITY DISORDER: WHAT IT IS AND HOW IT HAPPENS

A personality disorder exists when a person's persistent and enduring patterns of thinking, behaving, perceiving, and feeling are inflexible and maladaptive. Specifically, these patterns cause *significant* impairment in functioning, either socially or occupationally, or *significant* personal distress.

Distinguishing between personality style and personality disorder is generally a matter of degree. Certain personality styles may share certain characteristics with personality disorders, although the features in the former are usually less extreme. For example, the individual who enjoys spending time alone listening to music or reading, and who prefers his own or a good friend's company to that of a group, may be a "loner." However, the person who has no friends, deliberately loses contact with family, has no interest in or feelings for others, and who lives an entirely isolated life may well have schizoid personality disorder, an extreme and maladaptive variation of the "loner" personality style.

How Personality Disorder Develops

At birth, a person immediately begins the process of adapting to the environment. To survive in their particular environments, children cope in unique ways given their genes, temperament, and developing character. In most cases, healthy children with normal, reasonably well-adjusted parents and a relatively trauma-free family environment develop resilient and strong personality styles that allow them to function capably in the world.

Children born to psychologically disturbed parents and/or raised in a stressful, distorted life environment also do their best to survive. They usually do so by adapting, as best they can, to the unreasonable demands and expectations placed on them. Adaptation to a distorted environment, however, may sometimes produce a disordered personality, ill-equipped for healthy social and occupational functioning later in the world at large.

Because most children raised even in extremely stressful environments develop personalities that are normal, and some individuals with personality disorders come from apparently normal families, experts speculate that some people with personality disorders have a biological vulnerability that makes it harder for them to adapt to particular stresses.

How Personality Disorders Affect Functioning

Personality functioning and personality disorders can be assessed in six key areas. These areas are: self, work, interpersonal relationships, feelings, reality testing (perceptions of reality), and impulse control. Each person has ways of thinking, feeling, and behaving in each area, reflecting his or her own personality style or personality disorder.

Self. Personality disorders can affect the way a person sees, thinks, and feels about him- or herself.

For instance, people with narcissistic personality disorder exaggerate achievements and expect to be noticed as special even though they may have done nothing to merit such attention. In contrast, persons with dependent personality disorder lack self-confidence, let others make decisions for them, and belittle their own abilities or talents. It is not unusual for individuals with this disorder to refer to themselves as "dumb" or "stupid."

Work. Personality disorders can reveal themselves in how a person completes tasks, makes decisions, takes charge, follows orders, plans, reacts to criticism, obeys rules, and works with others.

People with passive-aggressive personality disorder, for example, often procrastinate, putting off tasks and constantly missing deadlines. They interfere with the work of others by failing to do their fair share. The individual with obsessive-compulsive personality disorder, sometimes colloquially dubbed a "workaholic," devotes so much time to work and productivity that leisure-time activities and friendships often become excluded from life.

Interpersonal relationships. Personality disorders can affect the nature of an individual's relationships to other people. They can interfere with friendships and hinder a productive and healthy sex life, love life, and/or family life.

For instance, individuals with schizoid personality disorder often choose solitary activities, neither seeking out nor enjoying close relationships with friends or family. On the other hand, persons with borderline personality disorder forge interpersonal relationships that are unstable and intense. They hate being alone and will try desperately to avoid real or imagined abandonment.

Feelings. This area of functioning involves a person's moods and emotional states, including anger, fear, happiness, sadness, and anxiety level. Personality disorders affecting feelings may influence the way praise or criticism is accepted as well as how self-conscious the person generally feels.

People with obsessive-compulsive personality disorder, for example, tend not to express their feelings. They rarely praise others and are often perceived as stilted or "stiff." In contrast, individuals with histrionic personality disorder express emotions with extreme and often inappropriate exaggeration, and they are prone to sudden and rapidly shifting emotional expressions.

Reality testing. How a person perceives and reacts to the outside world strongly depends on the person's personality. Consequently, personality disorders can and often do distort an individual's perception of the world at large.

For instance, individuals suffering from paranoid personality disorder may feel threatened by innocent remarks or events, and they always expect to be hurt or undermined by others. Individuals with schizotypal personality disorder hold odd beliefs and cling to "magical thinking" that influences behavior. For example, they may be highly superstitious.

Impulse control. The extent to which an individual conforms to society's standards of self-control will be affected by his or her personality. Individuals with certain personality disorders will be overly impulsive even though their culture and/or environment dictate keeping their urges in check.

For example, persons with borderline personality disorder may exhibit a marked tendency toward impulsive overspending, sexual promiscuity, substance abuse, or binge eating. Those with antisocial personality disorder often participate in such unlawful behavior as vandalism, stealing, or harassment. These aggressive individuals also find themselves in difficulty due to wildly impulsive behavior leading to brawls or assaults, including spouse- or child-beating.

TYPES OF PERSONALITY DISORDERS

Over the years, mental health professionals have devised numerous ways of describing and categorizing personality types, using such terms as "extravert" or "introvert" to characterize the predominant feature of a given type. Other "dimensional" systems, some more detailed than others, have been devised to classify maladaptive personality patterns. Using such methods, an individual would be described as high or low in each dimension being measured—for

example, orderliness, emotionality, suspiciousness, impulsivity, sociability, and the like.

The most recent classification of personality disorders utilizes a "categorical" system, identifying a limited number of major types of maladaptive patterns. Developed principally by psychiatrists to aid in diagnosing troubled patients as well as for research purposes, the newer classification system has at present identified 11 distinct personality disorders and has suggested two others for further study. An individual may be diagnosed as having a single personality disorder or a mixture of several disorders in varying degrees.

The following descriptions of these disorders are drawn from the third revised edition of the *Diagnostic and Statistical Manual of Mental Disorders* (DSM-III-R).

Paranoid Personality Disorder

The outstanding characteristic of individuals with paranoid personality disorder is a consistent expectation that others are trying to demean, harm, or threaten them. Often these individuals are pathologically jealous, questioning with no apparent reason the fidelity and trustworthiness of friends, lovers, or spouses. Persons with paranoid personality disorder tend to be hypervigilant, quick to anger, guarded, and unforgiving of perceived insults or slights. These individuals refuse to confide in others because of their persistent fear that any information will be used against them. Difficulty in the workplace is common among people with this disorder.

A classic example of an individual with paranoid personality disorder is Captain Queeg of *The Caine Mutiny*.[1] He believed that his crew was "out to get" him, and he attributed any unfortunate occurrences to a plot of his officers against him. He was unforgiving and vindictive, eventually driving his men, who felt threatened by his irrational behavior, to mutiny.

Schizoid Personality Disorder

Individuals afflicted with a schizoid personality disorder are loners in the extreme sense of the word; they almost always prefer solitary activities over those that include others. These persons neither want nor enjoy close relationships, and they usually have no close friends or confidants.

People with schizoid personality disorder reject family members, and they rarely date or marry. To others, these individuals appear cool and unapproachable; rarely do they claim to experience any intense emotion, such as anger or joy. Clearly, then,

their most severe impairment is in the area of interpersonal relationships.

For example, a 26-year-old man who had no friends and had rarely dated succumbed to extreme family pressure and married a young woman from a family they knew from their church. His 19-year-old bride came from a traditional, religious family background, had lived at home, and had not dated frequently before her marriage. She naively assumed that her cool and aloof fiancé would become comfortable with her large family and enjoy their many social gatherings. After the wedding he refused to participate in any family events or social events of any kind. He preferred his own company even to hers, especially when she made emotional or sexual demands on him. He was most comfortable at work, where he functioned well as a computer programmer—as long as he was left alone to do his work.

After five years of marriage, this man's wife had matured and was able to face the reality that her husband was never going to grow closer to her. She convinced him to consult a pastoral counselor with her. In time the best solution for them both was to annul their marriage. While for her the necessary conclusion of their relationship was emotionally very difficult, for him it was a great relief. His parents never pressured him into marrying again.

Schizotypal Personality Disorder

Individuals with a schizotypal personality disorder may suffer from peculiarities of thinking, odd beliefs, or "magical thinking" such as extreme superstitiousness, unusual perceptual experiences such as seeing ghosts, and eccentric behavior. In addition, they experience extreme social anxiety and consequently dislike situations in which they must associate with strangers.

Such individuals live isolated lives, have few or no close friends or confidants, and are suspicious of situations or individuals around them. Additionally, they may display inappropriate behavior in social situations, because they are motivated by their own strong, often eccentric belief systems and may be oblivious to cultural behavioral norms.

An example is the case of the 32-year-old unmarried, unemployed woman on welfare who insisted that she was clairvoyant and could read other people's minds. She spent many hours alone watching television and often dressed in a haphazard, bizarre manner. She trusted no one, and had few friends and no relatives with whom she was in contact. She had

---

[1]Note: Throughout this chapter we have chosen at times to exemplify personality disorders by referring to characters from fiction and film because their personality disturbances and maladaptive behaviors are recognized so easily. We are indebted to our colleague Steven E. Hyler, M.D., for the film examples, which are taken from his article "DSM-III at the Cinema: Madness in the Movies," published in *Comprehensive Psychiatry* 29(1988):195–206. Needless to say, real individuals with personality disorders are just as troubled as these fictional figures, if not more so.

held a few jobs but had lost each one due to her lack of interest.

Antisocial Personality Disorder

An inability to abide by society's rules is the key impairment for the adult with antisocial personality disorder, colloquially referred to as the "sociopath" or "psychopath."

Persons with antisocial personality disorder are defiant and contemptuous of standards of accepted conduct, and they may find themselves repeatedly in trouble with the law. They are irritable and aggressive and get into frequent physical fights. They may also be guilty of assault, including spouse- or child-beating, yet they feel no guilt or remorse for any of their actions.

Along these lines, individuals with antisocial personality disorder repeatedly fail to honor debts or other financial obligations. They may also be hard to pin down; that is, they frequently travel from place to place for undetermined periods of time and lack any fixed address. Squandering money is another common characteristic. They tend to function poorly in the workplace. They have high and unexplained absenteeism and often abandon their jobs without any realistic alternative plans.

Frequent lying is a trait often found in individuals with antisocial personality disorder. These persons often evince a reckless disregard for their own safety and that of others. If they have children, they may abuse or neglect them. Finally, these individuals rarely sustain a monogamous relationship for more than a year.

One of the most infamous cases of an individual with antisocial personality disorder is Gary Gilmore, the subject of Norman Mailer's best-seller, *The Executioner's Song*. Gilmore gained notoriety when he insisted, through a protracted legal battle, that Utah carry out his execution sentence.

The circumstances leading to Gilmore's demise clearly illustrate this disorder. At age 20, he went to prison for burglary and robbery. Later he spent two years in a city jail for a long string of minor offenses. He indulged in illicit drug use and was sexually promiscuous.

In 1976 he moved in with a woman he had met the previous day, later explaining that it was the first "close" relationship he had ever had. He abused the woman's children and constantly got involved in fights whenever he attended any parties. That same year he robbed a gas station and shot the attendant twice in the head because, he said, "I just felt like I had to do it." Convicted of murder, Gilmore was executed in prison in 1977.

Borderline Personality Disorder

Unstable mood, chaotic interpersonal relationships, and vacillating self-image mark the borderline personality disorder. Individuals with this disorder frequently plunge into deep depression, irritability, or anxiety that can last from a few hours to a few days, and they often become inappropriately and intensely angry. They have difficulty controlling that anger, winding up in recurrent arguments or even physical fights.

Their relationships are erratic and intense; they shift rapidly and unpredictably between intense involvement and icy indifference. Moreover, they commonly behave with self-damaging destructiveness. They desperately try to avoid real or imagined abandonment, and they may threaten or attempt suicide repeatedly in a manipulative way to elicit a response from or wreak revenge upon another.

Control over their impulses is difficult for them. They may be sexually promiscuous and take few or no safeguards against disease or pregnancy. They often lose control of their spending and their eating, they may drive recklessly, and they may be involved in impulsive shoplifting. These individuals often report feeling "empty" or bored, and at times they may inflict injury on themselves deliberately.

People with borderline personality disorder have a marked and persistent identity disturbance evident in at least two of the following areas: self-image, sexual orientation, long-term values. In other words, in the most basic areas they don't know who they are or what they want. As a result, these individuals do not seem to develop a normal, gradually maturing life path characterized by a deepening sense of family commitment, a meaningful set of close friends, and a satisfying career.

The character of Theresa, portrayed by Diane Keaton in the film *Looking for Mr. Goodbar*, is an excellent example of an individual with borderline personality disorder. Theresa repeatedly engaged in risky self-damaging behavior; she flirted with suicide, drank too much, and took too many drugs. She was also sexually promiscuous, getting into impulsive, dangerously destructive relationships with men she picked up in bars. She met a gruesome end at the hands of one of these men, who murdered her.

Histrionic Personality Disorder

The men and women who suffer from histrionic personality disorder tend to be overly emotional, often seeming more angry, happy, sad, or pleased than a situation seems to warrant. Such persons lean toward rapid shifts of emotional expression.

They are happiest when at the center of attention, and they constantly seek approval and praise. Often they are excessively concerned about appearance, and they may be inappropriately seductive or sexual. They are self-centered and demand immediate gratification. They adopt a speaking style that is effusive but lacking in detail. For instance if asked "How was your vacation?" the individual with histrionic personality disorder can offer no more information than "Fabulous!"

A classic literary example of someone with this disorder is Scarlett O'Hara of *Gone With the Wind*. Scarlett demanded to be the center of attention and was overly concerned about her appearance, boasting about her "18-inch waist." She was shallow and self-centered, vain and temperamental. She had tantrums when she did not get her way, and she became excessively frustrated and petulant when her needs were not immediately gratified. As is often the case with people with histrionic personality disorder, things did not work out so well in her relationships: "Frankly, my dear, I don't give a damn."

Narcissistic Personality Disorder

The most pervasive elements of narcissistic personality disorder are grandiosity, lack of empathy, and hypersensitivity to the opinions of others. Such persons exaggerate their achievements and assets, and they expect special recognition whether or not their achievements warrant it. These individuals are preoccupied with fantasies of success, power, beauty, brilliance, or "ideal love." A strong sense of entitlement makes them continually expectant of special and favorable treatment.

Because individuals with this disorder often have a fragile sense of self-esteem, others' opinions of them are extremely important to them: They react to any negative criticism with rage, shame, or humiliation, although they may not always show it. They often actively seek compliments from others.

Their interpersonal relationships often suffer. They are chronically envious of anyone they perceive as more successful than they are. Narcissistic individuals are exploitative, often taking advantage of others to achieve their own ends. In addition, they are rarely empathic and may get angry at a friend who cancels plans, no matter what the reason.

An example is the case of a highly successful surgeon who sought psychiatric consultation when his wife threatened divorce. He had been largely oblivious of his haughty, condescending, and tyrannical style both at work and at home. Eventually he irreparably offended his superiors at work and was asked to leave. Life at home deteriorated; one child was hospitalized for alcoholism and a second for depression. His wife blamed him for the disintegration of the family, yet he felt misunderstood and insufficiently appreciated for having provided a large income and luxurious lifestyle.

Avoidant Personality Disorder

Individuals with an avoidant personality disorder yearn for social acceptance and they are often upset by their inability to relate comfortably to others. They are so concerned with how others will react to them that they are unwilling to become involved in relationships unless they are certain of being liked. As a result, they rarely have any close friends or confidants outside the immediate family. Further, they actively avoid situations that will increase their social discomfort.

People with avoidant personality disorder display a generalized timidity. They tend to be quiet in social situations for fear of saying something that would be thought silly or inappropriate. They are easily hurt by criticism or disapproval, and they fear being embarrassed in public.

Such individuals like to stick to their accustomed routines; thus, they may exaggerate risks involved in doing something outside their usual schedule. For example, they may not attend a party held in a distant and strange neighborhood for fear that they would become hopelessly lost.

An inveterate worrier, a 38-year-old woman with avoidant personality disorder felt constantly overwhelmed by her anxieties. She yearned to be accepted socially, yet would agonize so greatly over what to wear, what to say, and how to act that she ended up staying home. When she attended the social functions her husband's job required, she clung to him and often became tongue-tied in her self-consciousness. Yet she constantly dreamed of having a lively social life and of being loved and accepted by others. It always seemed to her that at some point in the indefinite future, when the children were grown, she would "emerge" and her life would be richer and more interesting. In reality, however, her life was narrow and restricted. She rarely traveled alone outside her own neighborhood unless her husband accompanied her.

Dependent Personality Disorder

The essential characteristic of the dependent personality disorder is a pattern of pervasive dependent and submissive behavior. Incapable of making everyday decisions by themselves, people with dependent personality disorder seek excessive advice and reassurance from others before choosing an option. Often, married persons with this personality disorder leave to their spouses any decisions such as where they will live, what kind of house to buy, or where their children will go to school.

Because they are uncomfortable relying on their own resources, persons with this disorder take great pains to avoid being alone. They are heartbroken when a close relationship ends and have a deep-seated fear of being abandoned.

Persons with dependent personality disorder rarely initiate any actions or projects; instead, they always go along with the plans and ideas of others. They will be the ones to volunteer for the task no one else wants in the hope that other people will like them, or at least not reject them.

Most people will recognize dependent personality disorder in the case of the "mama's boy." At age 47, this man continued to live with his mother. She chose his clothes, his food, and his friends, as always. He never had liked making important decisions and, because his mother had never really liked any of the women he had dated, he had never married. He held the same job for many years, worked hard, and was excessively loyal to his employer. Known for being dependable and unobtrusive, he never took any initiative, and he was usually passed up for promotion.

Then suddenly his mother died. The man became extremely depressed and for many months found it difficult to get up, get dressed, feed himself, and go to work. He developed difficulties with his digestion, and when he was hospitalized for tests he developed a close relationship with a nurse's aide some 15 years his senior who was taking care of him. They married three months later. She took over all the roles in

which his mother had functioned for him, and his life regained its particular kind of balance.

Obsessive–Compulsive Personality Disorder

Individuals with obsessive-compulsive personality disorder develop a clear and pervasive pattern of perfectionism and inflexibility. They are so encumbered with the need to do things perfectly that they may never sit down and actually complete a task.

Such persons are keenly aware of their relative status of dominance or submissiveness, but they themselves resist authority and inflexibly insist that others conform to their methods.

Work and productivity take precedence over pleasure and leisure in the lives of individuals with obsessive-compulsive personality disorder. They rarely take vacations or spend time just relaxing, and they are often known as "workaholics."

Because they are so fearful of making mistakes, decision making is avoided. Indecisiveness about what is worth keeping and what isn't may cause these individuals to be dubbed "pack rats" by those who live with them.

People with this disorder are excessively conscientious, scrupulous, and judgmental of themselves and others. They are materially and emotionally stingy and often perceived as "stiff."

A well-known character whose style clearly illustrates obsessive-compulsive personality disorder is "neat freak" Felix Unger of Neil Simon's *Odd Couple*. His extreme attention to the most minute of life's everyday details and his excessive preoccupation with neatness and order drove his roommate, who was his only close friend, crazy. Other characters in the story perceived the overly meticulous Felix as rigid and stilted, though he himself believed he was merely doing things "the right way." He was scrupulous beyond reproach and highly judgmental of those who did not abide by the same standards of behavior.

Passive–Aggressive Personality Disorder

Individuals who have a passive-aggressive personality disorder passively and indirectly resist the demands placed on them for social and occupational performance. The name of the disorder is predicated on the assumption that such individuals are passively expressing their inner aggression.

The resistance of such individuals is expressed through such behaviors as procrastination, stubbornness, intentional inefficiency, and "forgetfulness." Further, their behavior often prevents them from doing their share of the work. When asked to do something they don't want to do, individuals with passive-aggressive personality disorder become irritable and edgy. They often complain to others about the unreasonableness of the demands being placed on them and become scornful and critical of those making the demands.

The case of a 32-year-old freelance artist who constantly missed his deadlines demonstrates the essential characteristics of this disorder. He lost an important magazine account because, according to the editor, he was consistently late with assignments, refused to follow instructions, and seemed unmotivated. Still and all, the artist was surprised and resentful at the loss of this work because he thought he had been doing a great job. Rather than take responsibility for the situation, the artist complained that the editor was "obsessive" and demanding. Significantly, this was not the first such occurrence to befall the artist; he had a long history of difficulty with authority that included his art teachers and other employers.

Self-defeating Personality Disorder[2]

Individuals with a self-defeating personality disorder engage in repeated self-defeating behavior patterns, sometimes referred to as masochistic behavior. For instance, they enter into relationships that have painful or disappointing consequences. They generally are uninterested in people who treat them well and instead are attracted to rejecting partners. They often refuse all opportunities for their own pleasure and advancement, and they engage in excessive and usually unsolicited self-sacrifice. These individuals may not benefit from positive personal experiences; instead, they respond with depression, guilt, or involvement in something that causes pain in order to offset the achievement. For example, they may unwittingly spoil the pleasure of success by careless "accidents," resulting in bodily injury or destruction of valued possessions. These persons fail to complete tasks crucial to their own personal objectives, but

they may spend time helping others to reach their goals. When others offer to help them, however, persons with self-defeating personality disorder turn them down.

People close to them often lose sympathy for their apparently self-induced unhappiness and excessive self-sacrifice. Others' negative responses may be devastating to individuals with this disorder, however.

The case of the chronically unhappy secretary illustrates the self-defeating personality. The 30-year-old woman often felt pessimistic about life, and she consistently became involved romantically and sexually with alcoholic men who abused her.

At her office, she was diligent and self-sacrificing, consistently offering to fill in for colleagues who wanted to leave work early. When she received an unexpected and large inheritance from a wealthy aunt, she felt guilty about her windfall and, within a reasonably short period of time, managed to give all the money away without ever spending any on herself. Eventually her extreme unhappiness spurred her to seek psychotherapy to alleviate some of her distress.

Sadistic Personality Disorder

The essential characteristic of the sadistic personality disorder is a pattern of cruel and aggressive behavior directed at others. Often individuals use sadistic behavior to achieve dominance over others in interpersonal relationships. Individuals with sadistic personality disorder maintain such dominance through tactics that range from verbal intimidation to physical abuse.

Often such people take pleasure in hurting or demeaning their victims. They frequently restrict the freedom of those close to them—such as the husband who refuses to let his wife leave the house unaccompanied by him, or who makes her sleep on the floor while he sleeps on the bed, or who forbids her from eating. Further, these individuals may well be fascinated with instruments of violence or torture.

The portrayal of Joan Crawford in the 1981 film *Mommie Dearest* illustrates sadistic personality disorder at work. In order to assert her dominance over her young daughter, Christina, the Crawford character screamed at the girl, beat her with a wire coat hanger, and banged the child's head against the floor.

---

[2]This disorder and sadistic personality disorder (which follows) have been proposed as new diagnoses. They are being studied and are considered tentative at this time.

TREATMENT OF PERSONALITY DISORDERS

Personality disorders can be extremely disabling. However, individuals with such disorders usually do not seek treatment until the inability to function effectively in one or more areas of their lives—self, work, interpersonal relationships, feelings, perceptions of reality, and impulse control—causes them or those close to them extreme confusion or personal distress. Even then, it is often those close to them, rather than the individuals themselves, who insist that treatment is necessary. Because personality disorders represent a lifetime pattern of being and behaving, people suffering from them very often do not recognize how the disorders have contributed to their failing relationships, career problems, or general unhappiness in life. They are likely to blame others, fate, or life itself for their problems.

Mental health professionals are not in agreement as to which form of treatment is most beneficial for people with personality disorders. In part this is because such deeply ingrained, inflexible, and maladaptive patterns of behavior can be difficult to change. Nonetheless, treatment can be beneficial for many types of personality disorders, and the type of treatment recommended differs depending on which disorder is present.

The three most commonly used treatments for patients with personality disorders are psychoanalytically oriented psychotherapy, psychopharmacology (medications), and cognitive-behavioral therapy. The goals of all three types of therapy (which are explained in chapter 4) are to reduce the interference in functioning caused by personality disorders and to relieve feelings of discomfort or distress that may accompany them.

Psychoanalytically Oriented Psychotherapy

Psychoanalytically oriented psychotherapy focuses on exploration of the roots of maladaptive personality traits and on confrontation with their manifestations. The therapist first strives to make the patient aware of the negative impact of his or her personality on others and consequently on his or her own accomplishments and sense of satisfaction in life. The next steps involve having the patient accept responsibility for the negative traits, understand their origins, and develop adaptive behaviors. A patient may be treated on an individual basis (generally from two to five sessions per week), as a member of a couple (for example, marital therapy), or in a group setting.

Psychopharmacologic Therapy

In using psychopharmacologic therapy, the clinician takes aim at certain target symptoms or syndromes. These may be manifestations of a particular personality disorder or of other psychiatric disorders in association with the personality disorder. Typical goals for medication include reduction of brief breaks with reality; relief of agitation, anxiety, panic, or depression; or stabilization of impulsiveness and mood swings. The medications prescribed are those used to treat major mental disorders—antipsychotic drugs (usually in very small doses), antidepressants, antianxiety agents, and the mood-stabilizing drug lithium (all in full therapeutic doses), and possibly anticonvulsant medication such as carbamazepine (Tegretol). Research into the possible biologic bases of some of the personality disorders, such as borderline personality disorder, promises to yield better psychopharmacologic treatment of symptoms. For example, borderline personality disorder may be strongly related to a fundamental instability of mood and impulse control. In one study researchers at the National Institute of Mental Health found that the antidepressant drug tranylcypromine (Parnate) could help some individuals with this disorder to regain their mood stability and carbamazepine could help them to reestablish control of their impulsiveness.

Psychopharmacologic treatment of personality disorder generally occurs in conjunction with psychotherapy.

Cognitive–Behavioral Therapy

In cognitive-behavioral therapy, the therapist first determines what mechanism underlies the problems presented by the patient. In cognitive terms, the patient has developed a set of basic assumptions about him- or herself and others that leads to maladaptive behavior; this, in turn, may reinforce the original mistaken assumptions. For example, a person suffering from avoidant personality disorder may assume mistakenly that people who love or like each other are never unkind or critical of one another. Therefore, when slighted or criticized by somebody important, this individual overreacts with shock and dismay. His or her oversensitivity makes others very uncomfortable—which serves to confirm to the person with avoidant personality disorder that "Nobody loves me. I am unlovable."

A cognitive therapist attempts to alter the assumptions by challenging and testing their logic or basis in fact; the behaviorist teaches the patient ways to manage distress (for example, relax in the face of social anxiety) and then goes on to train the patient in better social skills.

14

Schizophrenia

Harold A. Sackeim, Ph.D., and Sukdeb Mukherjee, M.D.

Schizophrenia affects an estimated 1 percent of the population in every country of the world. Victims exhibit a range of symptoms that can be devastating to themselves as well as to their families and friends. They may be troubled with hallucinations and delusions. They may express bizarre thoughts. They may have difficulty dealing with the most minor everyday stresses and insignificant changes in their surroundings, such as the use of a different tablecloth or the sound of a squeaky hinge. They may avoid social contact, ignore personal hygiene, and behave oddly, even menacingly.

Misconceptions about this serious illness abound. For example, many people outside the mental health profession believe that schizophrenia refers to a "split personality," or what psychiatrists call a multi-ple personality disorder. The word "schizophrenia" does stem from the Greek *schizo,* meaning "split." But *phrenia* refers to the diaphragm, once thought to be the location of a person's mind and soul. When the word "schizophrenia" was coined by European psychiatrists, they meant it to describe a shattering, or breakdown, of basic psychological functions.

Schizophrenia may well be the most intractable of all the common mental illnesses. Besides the disease itself, sufferers and their families must struggle with the social stigma that this disease casts on them. Some must also attempt to survive without homes or adequate medical services because of deinstitutionalization policies and a subsequent lack of care for them in many communities. (See later in this chapter and also chapter 31.)

There is still no cure for schizophrenia. Yet the picture is not so grim as it may seem. The steady strides in understanding the causes of schizophrenia, its biology and genetics, and its treatment are strong reasons for hope. Already many men and women have been treated successfully and now lead productive lives.

SYMPTOMS

Schizophrenia is a particular form of *psychosis,* a term encompassing several severe mental disorders that result in the loss of contact with reality along with major personality derangements. The illness can best be described as a collection of particular symptoms that usually fall into four basic categories: formal thought disorder, perception disorder, feeling/emotional disturbance, and behavior disorders.

Formal Thought Disorder

People with schizophrenia describe strange or unrealistic thoughts. In many instances, their speech is hard to follow due to disordered thinking. Phrases seem disconnected, and ideas move from topic to topic with no logical pattern in what is being said. In other cases, individuals with schizophrenia say that they have no ideas at all or that their heads seem "empty." More than any other symptom, evidence of a disordered thinking process is key to a proper diagnosis of schizophrenia.

Many schizophrenia victims feel they possess extraordinary powers such as X-ray vision, superhuman strength, or superior insights. They may believe that their thoughts are being controlled by others or are being broadcast over the public airwaves, or that outside thoughts are being implanted in their heads. When such ideas are persistent, organized, and maintained in spite of evidence to the contrary, they are called *delusions.*

Perception Disorder

Those with schizophrenia regularly report unusual sensory experiences, especially when the illness is in an acute stage. Most often these experiences are in the form of hearing voices, or *auditory hallucinations.* Persons may hear one or two (and sometimes more) voices making comments on their behavior. They may not know the voice, or they may believe it is the voice of God, the devil, or a friend or relative.

When the voice issues orders to behave in a particular way, or take a specific action, the experience is known as a *command hallucination.* Such hallucinations can be extremely dangerous to both the sufferer and others, as when the voice commands the person to "jump off the building" or "destroy your family." Even when hallucinations are not particularly dangerous, they can be terrifying to the victim. A parent might repeatedly "hear" his or her child being attacked or crying out for help; a man or woman might face continuous ridicule in the voice of a deceased spouse.

Feeling/Emotional Disturbance

Events that would normally make a person happy or sad—a wedding or funeral, for instance—often produce no emotional response in people with schizophrenia. Their facial expressions and vocal intonations remain the same regardless of what happens around them. Such responses are called *flatness of affect,* which together with thought disorders are important signs of schizophrenia. Some victims do show emotion but at inappropriate times. They might laugh at bad news, grow angry for no apparent reason, or become saddened by what others consider a happy event.

Emotional disturbances frequently result in social withdrawal. People who suffer from schizophrenia often avoid contact with friends and lose interest in daily life and events.

Behavior Disorders

Peculiar *repetitive movements* sometimes also are seen in schizophrenia. Victims might swing one leg back and forth all day or constantly shake their heads. *Catatonic behavior* is another symptom; a victim might keep the same position for hour after hour, unable to talk or eat.

Schizophrenia victims may also become assaultive, making them dangerous to others; or they may be overly intrusive, constantly prying into the affairs of those around them. Although some people with schizophrenia may act dangerously, the vast majority intend no harm and, if anything, prefer to keep to themselves. The popular perception of danger is in large part unwarranted. In fact, studies have not established that people with schizophrenia are any more violence-prone than people without psychiatric illness.

In addition to the specific symptoms common among victims of the illness, they often share other characteristics and traits. These may help the physician in diagnosing the illness. When compared to other people in general, those with schizophrenia are:

- Less likely to marry or remain married;
- More likely to have school problems;
- Often unable to keep their jobs;
- More prone to suicide attempts.

People with schizophrenia also tend to fall into other groupings that can help in diagnosis.

- The majority range in age from adolescence to the mid-20s at the time the psychosis begins.
- As students, many had trouble keeping up with their studies.
- Many became problem employees, with high absenteeism and low work output.
- Unusual, but not necessarily bizarre, viewpoints and speech were common during childhood, accompanied by a social history of being isolated and disliked.

No single patient is likely to show all the symptoms associated with the illness or fall into all the categories described. One person may experience only auditory hallucinations and exhibit only inappropriate emotions. Another might become reclusive and suffer from delusions.

The symptoms themselves are also variable. With the illness, an individual might seem unable to talk one moment and a minute later engage in an extensive, near-normal conversation; another might be agitated in the morning, tranquil by midday, and agitated again later in the afternoon.

DIAGNOSIS

With some symptoms, particularly thought disorders, there may be no clear-cut distinction between "normal" and "abnormal." Obviously, someone who firmly believes he is Jesus Christ and demands to be revered as the Messiah is not normal. But when someone says "The IRS is after me," or "Everybody at school is out to get me," there may be some factual basis to the assertions. The degree to which thoughts are separated from proven reality must be analyzed carefully by a physician before a diagnosis of schizophrenia is made. At times, this requires an independent determination of whether, for example, the IRS *really* is persecuting the individual—perhaps sending repeated letters demanding past-due taxes—or schoolmates *really* are ganging up on a child. Even if a thought is found to be paranoid, this alone does not warrant the diagnosis of schizophrenia.

A diagnosis depends in large part on a group of symptoms observed by a specialist. If enough of the symptoms are evident, are sufficiently intense, and have occurred for a substantial period of time—and if other illnesses and conditions are ruled out—then

a diagnosis of schizophrenia likely will be made. However, recognizing those symptoms is not the only step in making the diagnosis. A physician must rule out a host of other illnesses and possibilities, such as drug abuse. The physician must get information from a variety of sources, rather than from the patient alone, to determine whether the illness is present.

Is It Schizophrenia or Is It . . .

Drug abuse. Chronic use of cocaine, amphetamines, PCP ("angel dust") or other illicit drugs can result in symptoms that are indistinguishable in most respects from those caused by schizophrenia. Even short-term drug use can produce such symptoms, especially with a drug as potent as "crack," the highly purified form of cocaine. Testing for drug use is an important part of the complete examination of a person who may suffer from schizophrenia.

Physical injury or illness. Brain damage from head injuries can cause schizophrenialike symptoms. So can brain tumors as well as physical or chemical damage to the brain's neurological network. A thorough physical and neurological examination always is necessary prior to a diagnosis of schizophrenia.

Peculiar behavior. What appears to some people as a behavior disorder may actually be benign, eccentric behavior. Aunt Mildred and Cousin Harry do not have schizophrenia just because she "speaks" to her departed husband and he lives like a hermit and laughs at funerals. Real life and fictional literature are full of characters whose mental state is questioned by others. The businessman who sells out, then donates his millions to a religious cult living in Rocky Mountain huts may not earn the respect of his colleagues, but he is not necessarily suffering from mental illness.

Much of human behavior is "odd." It is in the nature of human beings to have different preferences and show a variety of personality characteristics. A physician confronting a possible schizophrenia case must rule out the possibility that the patient is totally sane, despite acting in ways unusual in our culture and at variance with our expectations.

Other psychiatric and emotional disorders. A range of psychiatric conditions can cause some of the same symptoms as schizophrenia, among them cocaine psychosis (see chapter 9), bipolar (manic-depressive) illness (see chapter 8), and acute, temporary psychoses caused by extreme stress (psychotic episodes). In general, the diagnosis of schizophrenia is not made unless major, serious symptoms continue for at least six months. This time period permits the physician to eliminate, for instance, the possibility that a person encountered a severe emotional shock that briefly "tipped him or her over the edge" into a psychotic episode that may disappear spontaneously.

Chronic Schizophrenia

Following the "rule-out" process, during which other possible causes of the symptoms are eliminated from consideration, the physician takes a closer look at the history of the symptoms themselves.

Most often, clear manifestations of schizophrenia emerge in adolescence and commonly progress slowly but relentlessly over subsequent years. This pattern is what most often becomes chronic schizophrenia; on a spectrum of schizophrenia illness, it has the least favorable prognosis. Social withdrawal, delinquency, or scholastic trouble may occur even earlier, perhaps during childhood years. A lack of interest in personal hygiene might develop, along with a noticeable lack of interest in everyday school events or family activities. Yet particularly during the early stages, youngsters may have periods of nearly normal behavior.

Early problematic behaviors may, at the time, have been viewed by parents, relatives, and friends as ordinary, expected difficulties of growing up. And it is important to note here that most youngsters who have problems such as social withdrawal or scholastic trouble never develop schizophrenia. But with the onset of more serious symptoms—truly bizarre patterns of thought or actions, for instance—these behaviors might be reinterpreted as early signals of schizophrenia.

Adult-onset Schizophrenia

In other cases, the illness appears more suddenly later in life and reaches a peak rather quickly. Such adult-onset schizophrenia, without a long history of social withdrawal or other noticeable symptoms, usually develops in the late 20s or early 30s and is often less difficult to treat than schizophrenia beginning in adolescence.

Subtypes

Besides distinctions based on how early in life symptoms developed and how rapidly they progress, the illness is commonly assigned a classification depending on its main characteristics. For example, *paranoid schizophrenia* refers to a type in which the predominant symptoms are delusions of persecution or delusions of grandeur (unfounded beliefs that people are trying to harm the individual or that he or she has extraordinary powers). *Catatonic schizophrenia,* on the other hand, can refer either to individuals whose primary symptoms include the lack of spontaneous movement and extended periods of stupor (*stuporous catatonia*) or to those who are highly excited and show extreme agitation (*excited catatonia*). When the symptoms overlap, the individual is said to have *undifferentiated schizophrenia.*

Grouping the illness by category helps physicians anticipate its course and create a specific treatment program for the individual patient. However, there is no known difference in the causes leading to one type of schizophrenia or another; nor is there any way in the early stages of schizophrenia to predict which type may develop eventually. Furthermore, an individual whose main symptoms lead to a diagnosis of, say, paranoid schizophrenia may at a later date show overriding symptoms of, say, catatonia.

Some researchers also classify patients as Type I and Type II, depending on whether their symptoms are mainly "positive" or "negative." It is hard to consider any symptoms as being positive, and, in fact, the term is not meant to denote anything good about schizophrenia. Instead, the term "positive" refers to symptoms associated with psychotic aspects of thought and perception, such as delusions and hallucinations. By contrast, "negative" refers to the emotional withdrawal shown by some people with the illness and their apparent lack of interest in their surroundings.

These may seem fine points in an already complex illness. But some specialists believe that Type I and Type II symptoms have different causes and thus should be treated differently. Type I (positive) symptoms, according to this theory, are the result of over-activity of the brain chemical dopamine, while Type II (negative) symptoms stem from progressive damage to the brain, as shown by studies of abnormalities in the brain structure. Positive symptoms may be more responsive to drugs traditionally used to treat schizophrenia, according to the theory, while negative symptoms may be more difficult to treat with most of the medications currently available.

THE SEARCH FOR CAUSES—PIECES OF THE PUZZLE

Numerous theories have been proposed to explain why some people develop the illness while others do not. The search for the cause, or causes, of schizophrenia has been marked on the one hand by years of careful research and on the other by shaky speculation and dogmatic insistence on the validity of unfounded assertions.

Social Factors

Some illnesses are more common in some socioeconomic groups than in others. For instance, poverty is associated with an increased risk of heart and circulatory disease as well as such disorders as depression. Schizophrenia also develops more often among people in socially and economically disadvantaged groups. Some experts say the everyday stress of such hardship, together with inadequate medical treatment, can contribute substantially to the chance of developing schizophrenia. Others argue that some people end up as social outcasts, perhaps unable to hold a regular job, because the illness—while not yet diagnosed—has already resulted in, say, inadequate education and limited social opportunities.

Parent–Child Relationships

Decades of scientific studies have consistently failed to support the view that abnormal parent-child relationships cause schizophrenia. Yet many parents continue needlessly to blame themselves when the illness develops in their children. While it is true that

the precise role of childhood experiences in the development of schizophrenia remains largely unknown, they are certainly not the critical factor they were once believed to be. In years past many psychiatrists placed special importance on the notion of the so-called schizophrenogenic mother, whose relationship with her child was characterized by the youngster's overdependence. The mother (sometimes both parents) was responsible, according to this theory, by subjecting her children to repeated contradictory messages ("Go out and play," followed by "How could you go out and play, and leave me all alone?" to invoke guilt) and by using abnormal ways to communicate with the children. While some professionals still adhere to this theory, its importance has now been largely discredited. Yet parents should note that blaming attitudes may persist, especially while the child's bizarre behavior is being evaluated and before the diagnosis of schizophrenia is reached. (See also chapter 19.)

Heredity

It has long been observed that schizophrenia tends to run in families. The likelihood of a close relative (mother, father, sibling, children) of a victim developing the illness is 5 to 10 times greater than the chance faced by those with no such illness in the family. If both parents have schizophrenia, their children are at even greater risk. This family tendency might be explained in part by social factors, but other studies point strongly toward a genetic relationship.

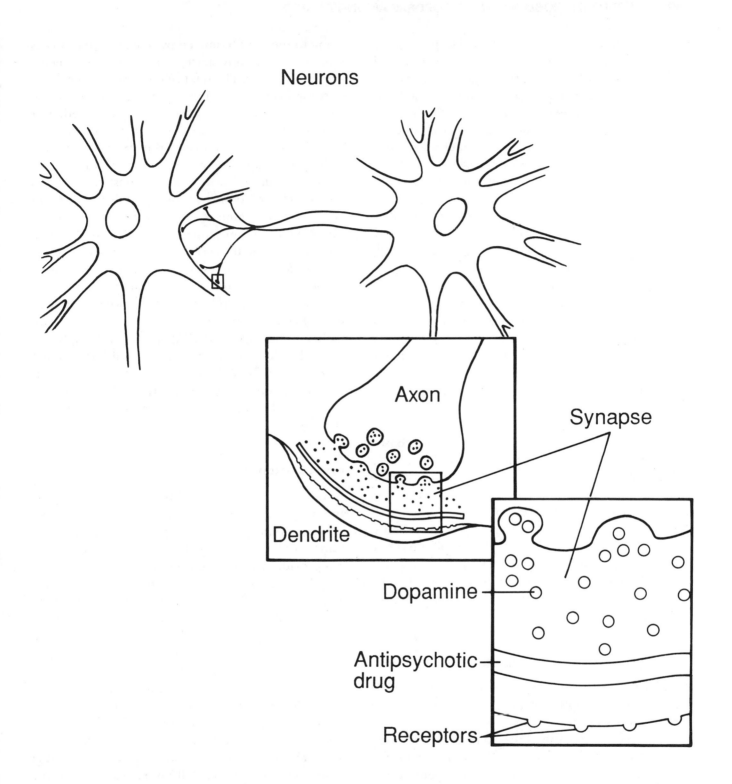

Neurons

Axon

Synapse

Dendrite

Dopamine

Antipsychotic
drug

Receptors

DOPAMINE AND SCHIZOPHRENIA

Figure 14.1: **Some researchers believe that an overabundance of the neurotransmitter dopamine may cause the symptoms of schizophrenia. Here, a neuron (a brain cell) releases high levels of dopamine into the synapse (the space between neurons). Antipsychotic drugs are believed to work by blocking receptors for dopamine in the adjoining cell—hence preventing that cell from absorbing too much dopamine.**

Research on identical twins (who possess the exact same genes) and fraternal twins (who, like all siblings, share only some of their genes) shows that if schizophrenia does develop, the identical twins are more likely to both become ill than are the fraternal twins. Related studies demonstrate that children of parents with schizophrenia face an increased risk—both of schizophrenia and disorders that resemble it—even when they are adopted into other families soon after birth.

Researchers have now determined that in some cases of schizophrenia, parents pass a faulty gene or genes to their offspring. Taken together, however, research findings raise as many questions as answers about the role of heredity. Despite the increased risk associated with genetics, there are many instances where one identical twin develops the illness, while the other does not. It should also be noted that most patients do *not* have immediate relatives with the illness.

What, then, is the real role of heredity? It is possible, of course, that there actually are different types of schizophrenia—with substantially different causes—and that only some can be inherited. Based on current research, it is more likely that one or more biological abnormalities predisposing a person to schizophrenia are passed on genetically but that, for the illness to actually develop, other factors (perhaps social stresses or even a viral disease) must come into play. This would make schizophrenia analogous to, for example, certain forms of heart disease, where a genetic predisposition requires other influences (smoking, poor diet, sedentary lifestyle) for the disease to unfold.

Brain Chemistry: The Dopamine Hypothesis

Researchers have some evidence to suggest that individuals with schizophrenia have specific biochemical abnormalities in their brains.

Within the brain, substances called neurotransmitters are critical to the communication between brain cells. One particular neurotransmitter, dopamine, has been at the center of current research and treatment of schizophrenia. Many researchers believe that in schizophrenia, too much dopamine is present in the brain.

The chemical and electrical activities in the brain are exceptionally complex and, for the most part, still poorly understood. But it is known that when one brain cell is activated, it passes the message along to the next brain cell by releasing neurotransmitters into the tiny space (the synapse) between it and the next cell. The next cell has receptors capable of recognizing the chemical. Generally, only the precise amount of the neurotransmitter needed to deliver the message is present. In many mental disorders, however, the levels of the neurotransmitters within the synapses may be markedly off the mark.

Many drugs used to treat the most severe symptoms of schizophrenia were discovered and used long before the dopamine hypothesis was formulated. It subsequently became apparent that most of the drugs work by blocking the receptors that utilize dopamine. Animal studies suggest that increased dopamine action could explain some common symptoms of schizophrenia, including hallucinations and delusions. Research on the effects of drug abuse on the brain also has suggested a link between schizophrenia and a dopamine imbalance in the brain. Drugs such as cocaine and amphetamines stimulate the transmission of dopamine. Sometimes these drugs also produce a psychosis virtually identical to schizophrenia, although it generally is reversible.

Brain Structure

Some people with schizophrenia show evidence of abnormal brain structure. Studies using sophisticated equipment such as computed tomography (CT scans) or magnetic resonance imaging (MRI), which can provide detailed pictures of the brain, highlight the differences between normal brains and the brains of some of the ailment's victims. Among many of those with the illness, the brain tissue is smaller and the cavities that hold cerebrospinal fluid are larger than in normal brains. These findings suggest that some of the abnormalities seen in schizophrenia may reflect a very early brain injury probably leading to interference with normal development.

Not all schizophrenia patients have gross brain abnormalities. Even though it is not known how the brain abnormalities arise, or precisely what they mean to the individual's illness, research points out the possible relationship between schizophrenia and brain disease. This, in turn, could lead to improved treatment methods.

Brain Metabolism

A minute amount of energy is used every time a single brain cell is "turned on" or "turned off." When millions upon millions of cells are active—which is always the case within the brain—the energy expenditure is enormous. The brain makes up a scant 2 percent of total body tissue, yet it requires fully 20 percent of the oxygen supply available from the blood, along with a substantial amount of the available glucose, a form of sugar, which is needed to fuel the metabolic process.

Using recently developed brain-imaging techniques, it is possible to measure the rates of blood flow, oxygen consumption, and glucose usage in specific regions of the brain. In this way, the amount of "work" being done by various parts of the brain can be determined. By analyzing the brain activity of schizophrenia patients, researchers learned that a particular region, the frontal part of the cortex, was less active than average in some individuals. This part of the brain is believed to be particularly important for abstract thinking, long-range planning, and other activities usually considered distinctly human.

Such test results lead to the belief that some of the psychological abnormalities seen in schizophrenia—such as difficulties in abstract thinking—stem from a specific metabolic problem in the brain.

Psychological Functioning

The environment around us floods us with information we constantly must analyze or block out: The television blares . . . a horn honks in the distance . . . a child smiles . . . a breeze blows through our hair . . . the aroma of dinner fills the kitchen.

To make sense of all the activities around us as well as of our bodily sensations and thoughts, we have to regulate the focus of our attention. We disregard many of the stimuli, act on some, and retain others for later consideration and analysis. At any one moment, then, we may concentrate our attention on some external sound or sight, a body sensation, a vague feeling, or an internal thought. We might concentrate on a single problem at work, perhaps, while ignoring distractions such as a ringing phone and a conversation in the next office. Or we might focus on the feeling of raindrops falling on our arms and ignore the voice of someone offering an umbrella.

When schizophrenia patients talk about their experiences, many say they feel overwhelmed by the stimuli around them. They are distracted easily by things in their environment and are unable to keep their minds on one topic at a time. Instead, they experience a jumble of ideas and sensations and may confuse an internal thought with an external voice. They are distracted so easily that any change in their environment will capture their attention, distracting them from what they were thinking or doing a second before.

Researchers, who long suspected that such attention problems are closely linked to schizophrenia, have now gained evidence to support this view. In various studies, schizophrenia patients typically have serious difficulties performing simple tasks that require sustained periods of concentration. Their responses to simple stimuli are slower than average. When performing tasks under time pressure, they don't benefit, as would normal individuals, from advance warnings of the time limit.

In general, the speed with which those with schizophrenia think appears to be slowed down. They draw less information than average from brief glimpses of pictures or snippets of sound. Their chain of thought is disrupted more easily than average. The various stimuli affect them as if several movies are being shown on the same screen at the same time, with images and sounds overlapping, each one demanding attention and, one on top of the other, hard to interpret.

These difficulties in processing information, together with the sluggish thinking, might explain some of the major thought disorders experienced by people with schizophrenia. The lack of connection between ideas, as reflected in what they say, may be due to an inability to filter out irrelevant associations. A person's social withdrawal might be an attempt to limit the amount of stimulation. This also may be why some people with schizophrenia improve when daily routines, at home and at work, are highly structured and simplified.

Some experts believe that problems in paying attention and maintaining focus on a thought may be genetically determined. They cite research showing that mild forms of attention disturbances, falling far short of psychiatric illness, occur more frequently than average among the close relatives of patients with schizophrenia as well as among youngsters thought to be at high risk for developing the illness.

Perhaps related to the problems with attention is a general decline in intellectual functioning seen in some individuals with schizophrenia. This is noticed more often in those whose illness began suddenly in adolescence or early adulthood. A young person who may have excelled at school or work may suffer a significant intellectual decline within a short period of time. Often, in retrospect, after schizophrenia is diagnosed, it becomes apparent that the individual had a record of increasing difficulty at work or school prior to becoming obviously ill.

TREATMENT

Schizophrenia is a disease that affects each individual differently. Some people may experience only one episode of schizophrenic behavior and then recover completely. Others continue to have symptoms for years, but manage to function well despite their illness. A substantial number of people need supportive help in order to cope, but with it they are still able to live in the community. Some individuals are so impaired by their disease that they will never function normally, however; some require long-term hospitalization, while others can be helped in specialized living arrangements such as group homes.

A few decades ago, many schizophrenia patients who today are living successfully in the community would have required long-term institutionalization. At that time, so little was known about the illness that care often consisted of using whatever means were available to manage poorly understood symptoms and to keep patients from harming themselves or others. Some physicians were willing to try almost virtually any medication or treatment mode, however poorly understood or studied, to help their patients.

That picture has changed dramatically. Knowledgeable professionals and appropriate medications have changed the nature of psychiatric hospitalization and care. Overall, the intensity and duration of symptoms have been reduced substantially, permitting a shift in the locus of care from long-term institutionalization to outpatient care.

When Hospitalization Is Necessary

Generally speaking, hospitalization for patients with schizophrenia is now used only for initial diagnosis and to treat relapses (crisis episodes when symptoms intensify)—for example, when a person becomes assaultive or unable to function because of escalating delusions. Hospitalization lasts only as long as it takes to get symptoms under control.

Choosing a Hospital

In hospitals with psychiatric services, treatment for schizophrenia is fairly standard. The treatment received in a community hospital, for example, is likely to be similar to that offered in a private psychiatric hospital or a Veterans Administration facility. The major exception to this generalization is if a person is interested in trying a new experimental treatment or if the illness is accompanied by unusual medical complications. In these instances, an academic medical center (a teaching hospital connected with a major university) is often the best choice.

More important than *where* treatment is received is *who* will be providing care. The psychiatrist should be experienced in treating schizophrenia and be a professional in whom the family and the patient have a great deal of confidence. In an illness like schizophrenia, continuity of care and rapport with the treating physician are important. It is best to avoid shuttling the patient from one physician to the next. The psychiatrist who will provide outpatient services should have admitting privileges at a facility where the patient is likely to be hospitalized in times of crisis, and he or she should also be willing to supervise inpatient care as well as outpatient care. Because treatment of schizophrenia is often a team approach, with social workers, for example, providing supportive or family care, the psychiatrist's possible network of associated mental health care providers should also be checked.

Drugs for Schizophrenia

Much of the changes in treating schizophrenia came about with the discovery of new medications known as antipsychotics or neuroleptics. There are several "families" of these drugs—such as *phenothiazines, butyrophenones, thioxanthenes, dibenzoxapines,* and *dihydroindolones*—each slightly different from the others in chemical composition, standard dosage, and effect.

Almost all experts agree that the antipsychotic drugs as a group are the first line of treatment for schizophrenia. Many studies have compared the effects of these drugs in treating schizophrenia with the effects of other medications, with psychotherapy, and with the performance of control groups composed of people who received no treatment. Repeatedly, the antipsychotic drugs have proven to be the most effective, both among hospitalized patients and in preventing relapse among those who resume their normal lives while continuing to take the drugs.

One of the most recent advances in treating schizophrenia is the drug clozapine (Clozaril), used in Europe and China for a number of years and now approved by the Food and Drug Administration (FDA) for use in the United States. Clozapine is sometimes effective in cases where other drugs have failed to blunt symptoms, especially the "negative" symptoms (page 196), and it appears to have many fewer side effects than some of the antipsychotic drugs. However, a major drawback to its use is that it can dangerously lower the count of white blood cells (the cells that help fight infection) in a small percentage of people. Thus, everyone using the drug must have a blood count taken weekly. (See chapter 5.) Another drawback is that the cost of the drug and weekly blood counts currently are very expensive. Other new medications that have beneficial effects similar to clozapine but that appear to be safer are now undergoing testing and may be available in the near future.

Specific drugs often are selected for use against certain symptoms of schizophrenia. For example, some phenothiazines with a strong sedative effect frequently are used to treat patients who are agitated.

Various medications are handled by the body in different ways, so one drug may be selected over another because it has less chance of damaging a diseased liver, worsening a heart condition, or affecting a patient's high blood pressure. These drugs have some serious drawbacks: They are extremely powerful medications that alter the brain's chemistry—and therefore the signals the brain sends to the rest of the body—and can lead to a range of side effects. Sometimes side effects can be controlled by changing the drug dosage or switching to a drug with a slightly different chemical makeup; in other cases a second drug must be used to control side effects.

Side effects can include such relatively mild problems as constipation or blurred vision, or more serious effects such as permanent movement disorders, heart rhythm abnormalities, or imbalances in blood chemistry.

Perhaps the most notorious side effect, encountered by as many as one-third of schizophrenia patients being treated with antipsychotic drugs, is a movement disorder called *tardive dyskinesia*, which is often persistent. Considered the most serious long-term side effect of drug therapy, tardive dyskinesia is marked by involuntary, repetitive movements of the mouth, tongue, body, or limbs. These may become irreversible, even when the medications are stopped. In rare cases, the drugs can cause a potentially serious, even lethal, *neuroleptic malignant syndrome* (NMS). NMS causes muscle rigidity and makes the autonomic nervous system unstable. (For a thorough discussion of antipsychotic side effects, see chapter 5.)

Serious side effects also can range from a variety of other involuntary muscle movements and peculiar postures, to the absence of usual movement, particularly of the facial muscles, leading to an immobile, expressionless face. To a large extent, many of the side effects other than tardive dyskinesia can be controlled or reversed with the use of drugs. (For details of drug effects and side effects, see chapter 5.)

For all the benefits that antipsychotic drugs provide, clearly they are far from ideal. Some patients will show marked improvement with drugs, while others might be helped only a little, if at all. A particular antipsychotic compound may bring relief to one person but not to another. The search for new drugs, particularly ones without serious side effects, is underway, and new compounds are being tested continuously. Ideally, drugs soon will be developed to treat successfully the whole range of schizophrenia symptoms.

Psychosocial Approaches

There is new information too about the best ways to treat schizophrenia beyond the use of drugs. Evidence exists that recovering patients do better when stress is kept to a minimum. This has led to increased family involvement in treatment plans, including expanded education and counseling about the nature of the illness. It also has, more than ever, allowed physicians and other professionals to help their patients deal with the stress created both by the everyday environment around them as well as by their illness itself.

The most common cause of relapse is the patient's failure to take medication. Resolving this issue can be difficult and trying to the patience of even the most loving families. However, the more that the patient and the family together can be involved in psychoeducational approaches—regular visits with a mental health professional to learn more about the nature of the illness, the life events and family interaction patterns that are likely to provoke a relapse, medications and their side effects—the more likely it is that relapse can be avoided. (See

THE CASE OF JIM P.: FAMILY TREATMENT WAS KEY

Jim P., who was then 21, was brought by his parents to a psychiatrist's office because, as they told the doctor, their son was "lazy." They were afraid that what they described as his stubbornness and lack of motivation would destroy his chances to attend law school. They reported that he had shut himself in his room and had developed an interest in weird, "hippie" religions.

In conducting a thorough history, the psychiatrist soon discovered that Jim had been hospitalized briefly in college for "hearing things." He had signed himself out of the hospital because of his fear of taking medication. Since then Jim had isolated himself from his friends, spending an increasing amount of time alone in his room, reading books on mysticism and reincarnation. He often laughed and spoke to himself. His grades in school fell from Bs to Cs and Ds until he finally dropped out of college.

Jim had been seeing a psychiatrist for several months after his hospitalization and had been prescribed antipsychotic medication, which he took only sporadically. His mother had attempted to contact his psychiatrist but had been told by him that she was interfering in Jim's treatment. When Jim stopped attending school, his father stopped paying the psychiatrist, because he felt that Jim was being "coddled" and because he and his wife were being excluded from the treatment.

Jim's new psychiatrist decided to involve the family actively in the treatment process. Both Jim and his parents were informed that he was suffering from schizophrenia. The doctor explained clearly how she had arrived at that diagnosis and recommended reading material for Jim's father, who said he was interested in learning more about the disease. The psychiatrist explained that medication was helpful in controlling the symptoms associated with the illness and that taking the medication did not reflect an addiction or weakness of personality, a misconception that had been shared by both Jim and his parents. Side effects were discussed with Jim and his family. As a result, he began taking his medication regularly, which led to a remarkable decrease in his auditory hallucinations and religious preoccupation.

Jim continued to feel ashamed that he could not succeed in college and was saddened by his par-

ents' disappointment. He wanted to take a job doing landscaping work, but his parents discouraged him, telling him that he could be a lawyer if he "just put his mind to it." Jim's father was a lawyer and had always envisioned his son entering his firm. Jim would suffer a worsening of symptoms following these family disagreements. When his parents blamed each other for Jim's mental state, Jim would withdraw to his room and become silent.

In further sessions together, the psychiatrist helped Jim's parents to achieve more realistic expectations for Jim and to understand that his academic difficulties were due to neither laziness nor stubbornness. Over time they began to accept Jim's limitations and stopped talking about law school, as the doctor had urged. Jim began spending less time in his room, and his auditory hallucinations further diminished.

With his parents' encouragement, Jim took a part-time job as an assistant in a small landscaping business. He enjoyed working outdoors and took pride in trimming and planting shrubbery. When Jim became accustomed to his job, the psychiatrist advised Mr. and Mrs. P. to spend a weekend away, leaving their son alone in the house, something which Jim's mother had been reluctant to do since his hospitalization. Arguments between the couple decreased as the therapist helped them understand that neither of them had caused Jim's illness and that they were entitled to time to themselves.

A few months after Jim began his job, the psychiatrist suggested to his parents that they drive to a park where Jim had helped with the landscaping and let him show them around. Jim later told his therapist that one of the happiest moments in his life was when his parents finally accepted his work.

Currently, Jim's parents report an improvement in their marriage. His mother has joined a local support group for parents of the mentally ill, which his father occasionally attends. Jim continues to be stable a year into treatment, only once requiring an adjustment in his antipsychotic medication when auditory hallucinations worsened following the death of an uncle. He was able to continue work nonetheless and has not required any further hospitalization.

chapter 8, page 121, for a discussion on preventing drug noncompliance in bipolar disorder, another mental illness characterized by psychotic episodes.)

Long-term Living Options

Once their most serious symptoms have been brought under control, many patients are able to return home and lead productive lives. Some will need special services, such as community group homes, operated by government or private mental health agencies, religious organizations, for-profit groups, or concerned individuals.

While hard data are not available, it is probable that the majority of people with schizophrenia are cared for at home by members of their families. For those who cannot live at home, either because of personal choice or because their illness places too great a stress on the home environment, there are a number of residential care options to consider—some better than others and, unfortunately, almost all limited in number.

One of the more positive developments in the care of people with schizophrenia is the movement toward halfway programs, which provide medical supervision but allow for independent, outpatient living. For moderately ill individuals, group homes may be among the best long-term options available. Operated by professionals experienced in dealing with schizophrenia, such homes provide day-to-day administration of medications. They are designed to reduce the level of stress confronting the person with schizophrenia, therefore minimizing the frequency of serious episodes of acute illness. Many are geared toward reintroducing their residents into the community.

There are many different models, providing various levels of supervised care. A typical facility might house between 10 and 30 individuals, have several medically trained housekeepers on its staff, and be supervised personally by a psychiatrist or other qualified specialist. Often the facility is located in a large house in a quiet suburban setting.

The best group homes usually fill three important roles: They provide a structured day-to-day environment; they offer some type of rehabilitation, up to and including job training and job placement; and they involve the family as much as possible in treatment, even providing group therapy for family members who want it. Professionals involved in group facilities can help family members understand the patient's illness and also can assist in resolving such basic problems as the financing of treatment.

Other options include *adult homes* or, as they are called in California, *congregate care homes*. These offer no on-site nursing or rehabilitative care, but operate under the supervision of a trained manager who will call on professionals when appropriate. *Board and care homes* are for-profit boarding homes that have no connection to a mental health program and are likely to house individuals with a wide range of conditions in addition to schizophrenia. They vary widely in quality and should be checked out carefully.

A new program offered in some communities provides mental health care in the individual's own setting, whether it is at home with the family, in an SRO (single-room only) hotel, or in a board and care home.

Choosing a Residential Option

Usually it is best to try to match the services in a residential facility to the needs of the person who will live there. Some questions to consider: Is the person a loner or someone who needs contact with others? Will he or she remember to take essential medications, or is a home that sets a medication schedule necessary? Can the activities of daily living (cooking, cleaning, and routine hygiene) be managed, or is a home that provides structured programs, such as weekly trips to the laundry, necessary? Both the patient and family members should visit these homes to see what they offer and whether they are a good match for the patient's level of abilities.

To find out about housing alternatives in a particular community, the state agency (usually the department of health, or social services, or mental health) that licenses residential alternatives for the mentally ill should be contacted and asked for a list of licensed facilities. The mental health professional in charge of the patient's care also can be asked for recommendations. Among the best resources are social workers, who are usually well versed on available community options. If a social worker is not involved in the case, concerned individuals should ask the physician or treating hospital to have one assigned.

Long-term Hospitalization

For some people, family living, group homes, or independent living situations are not viable options; even with medication, they do not have the skills to survive even in supported programs, or their symptoms are so severe that they are disruptive to the lives of others. For these patients, it is often in their best interests to provide the level of care and protective, structured environments offered by 24-hour nursing care facilities.

Unfortunately, the range of options for long-term care is extremely limited. There are excellent private mental health facilities that specialize in the care of patients with schizophrenia, but their numbers are limited and they are usually very expensive. If a family is considering placing a relative in a private facility, it might be best to sit down with a financial advisor first to review the family's resources. In the initial stages of the illness, many families rush to put their loved one into a private facility, hoping that this will speed recovery. But because the length and course of schizophrenia is so variable, it is impossible to predict how long such care will be needed. Often first insurance and then a family's savings and assets are depleted, and the patient winds up in a state hospital facility nonetheless. It is very difficult for families to know when the benefits of private care are worth the financial burden, and there is really no good answer to the problem. But professional counseling may be able to provide some guidelines.

If a family does not have the resources to obtain private care, there is little that can be done except to turn to a public mental health hospital. However, while short-term acute care is usually fairly easy to access, even for the patient without private insurance (Medicaid and Social Security Insurance will usually cover short-term hospitalizations for schizophrenia), in many states long-term admission to public hospitals is limited to those patients who either demonstrate ongoing violent behavior or are clearly incapable of caring for themselves. Many people with schizophrenia, even those with badly deteriorating conditions, do not meet these criteria for admission. For short periods of time, Medicare and Medicaid will pay for hospitalization for patients whose condition is considered acute; however, once their condition has stabilized, they are discharged.

If a person objects to commitment, providing patients with severe schizophrenic symptoms the care that they need can be extremely difficult, sometimes impossible. The evidence of dangerousness must be clear-cut and documentable; verbal threats alone are not considered sufficient for forced commitment. Families should note, however, that it is still important to maintain links to a mental health pro-

WHAT FAMILY AND FRIENDS SHOULD KNOW

- There is no clear evidence that poor parenting causes schizophrenia. Parents should not feel guilty about an illness over which they have no control. Research points to brain structure abnormalities or chemical imbalances (perhaps with some hereditary involvement) as crucial factors in schizophrenia, just as they are in many physical illnesses. Guilt or shame is inappropriate when the illness is, say, diabetes; it is equally out of place with schizophrenia.
- Psychiatric hospitalization, if required, is quite different now from what it was years ago. Diagnostic tests and appropriate medications are available. Many hospitalized patients can return home, and they often resume their normal jobs once their most serious symptoms are resolved.
- Although as youngsters, victims of schizophrenia often experience interpersonal and scholastic problems, the vast majority of children with such problems do *not* develop the illness. Still, parents should be alert to changes in a child's activities and mood, and seek the advice of a mental health professional if the changes are severe.
- Stress and excess stimulation are factors in the sudden worsening of schizophrenia symptoms. Home and work environments should be as free as possible from unnecessarily stressful factors.
- Although the disease is not curable, in many cases the patient with schizophrenia can be helped. A range of drugs can reduce or eliminate many of the symptoms. Other help is also available—including counseling and retraining—and with consistent treatment and realistic expectations, many patients can lead productive lives.
- Ongoing research is making strides toward a better understanding of the illness and improved treatment methods.

HOMELESSNESS AND SCHIZOPHRENIA

Unfortunately, large numbers of people who suffer from schizophrenia do not receive the services they need. The advent of beneficial drugs to stabilize schizophrenia patients allowed psychiatric institutions across the country to release them back into their communities, which in most cases were ill-prepared to provide the care required.

Without the social structure vitally important to people with schizophrenia—including regular, dependable health care, a concerned family, adequate housing, useful employment—many former patients stopped taking their medication, which resulted in a recurrence of their schizophrenia symptoms. Untreated, many thousands have since taken up residence on city streets.

Homelessness constitutes one of the greatest social problems of our time. See chapter 31 for a more complete discussion of mental illness among the homeless.

---

fessional, even though their loved one has refused treatment. The continued involvement of such a practitioner sometimes can help a family convince their loved one that help is necessary, as well as assist the family in accessing treatment, whether on a voluntary or an involuntary basis. (For a discussion on commitment, see chapter 30).

For older patients, nursing homes are sometimes an option, although many are not equipped to treat people with serious mental illness. However, in many cases, the symptoms of schizophrenia abate with age, making this type of facility feasible. If someone has been in a long-term treatment facility for many years, it may be possible to transfer care to a nursing home—although the benefits of doing so, the quality of medical care offered, the financial implications, and the recreational/rehabilitative programs offered by the nursing home should be researched thoroughly first. Supervised housing, discussed earlier, may also be a feasible alternative for the aging person with schizophrenia.

Sources of Help and Information

To date, no national organization specifically targeted to schizophrenia exists. However, NAMI (National Alliance for the Mentally Ill) provides information and support groups for individuals and families affected by mental illness. Contact NAMI at:

NAMI
2101 Wilson Boulevard
Suite 302
Arlington, VA 22201
tel. 703 524–7600

The Schizophrenia Research Branch of the National Institute of Mental Health (NIMH) publishes the *Schizophrenia Bulletin* and helpful information on the illness. To obtain a copy, write to:

Schizophrenia Bulletin
Research Publications and Operations Center
NIMH
Parklawn 10C16
5600 Fishers Lane
Rockville, MD 20857

15

Alzheimer's Disease and Other Organic Causes of Mental Disorders

Davangere P. Devanand, M.D.,
and Richard Mayeux, M.D., M.S.E.

Numerous disorders affecting mood, memory, concentration, intellect, and personality arise from organic, or physical, abnormalities within the brain. As discussed throughout this chapter, there are many organic causes of such psychiatric symptoms as confusion, anxiety, or hallucinations—including, for example, diseases that affect the brain, chemical imbalances associated with illnesses elsewhere in the body, trauma to the head, nutritional deficiencies, drug abuse, or adverse effects of medication.

Increasingly, as the interdependence of the brain and the endocrine and immune systems (among others; see chapter 32) comes into clearer focus, traditional distinctions between what is purely "psychological" and "physical" are eroding. Because all mental and psychological functioning depend on brain function, all psychiatric disorders probably have biological components to some degree (for example, the malfunctioning of neurotransmitter systems that affect multiple mental and organic systems).

In some cases, such as schizophrenia and depression, a number of organic and indeed genetic clues are becoming increasingly apparent, although they have not yet led to definite understandings. Some forms of these disorders and possibly bipolar disorder, among others, may join the organic category in the future. Nonetheless, organic mental disorders remain a distinct class of illnesses in which the physical cause of the psychiatric symptoms is known definitely.

Because organic mental disorders (such as Alzheimer's disease) and other physical contributors to mental symptoms (such as excess blood calcium) can produce the same behavioral and psychological symptoms as the common psychiatric disorders, a physical examination, combined with a full neurologic and psychiatric workup, is necessary to confirm the appropriate diagnosis and institute the correct treatment. Although in some cases psychoactive medication can help treat mental symptoms in both psychiatric and organic disorders, in the latter case, when possible the physical reason for symptoms must be treated to remove their cause.

Organic mental disorders usually require medical intervention. Psychiatric and psychological treatments sometimes can help alleviate some of the symptoms and associated conditions (such as the depression that often accompanies Alzheimer's disease) and help individuals and their families adjust to the diseases and the deficits caused by them—but they are not the primary treatments of the underlying physical conditions.

Brain Functioning and Malfunctioning

The brain performs its myriad functions through a complex system involving electrical, chemical, and physical activity that together regulates everything from heartbeats to menstrual cycles and digestion, and also produces the qualities of personality, emotion, memory, intelligence, and all other factors that make each person a unique human being. To operate efficiently and appropriately, the brain requires a very specific environment. An ample, well-regulated supply of blood, rich in oxygen and other nutrients, is its primary need. If supply is poor, the brain performs its work more slowly, and often erratically, causing overall confusion or incomplete thought processes, or perhaps a more specific inability, such as loss of control over anger.

The brain works best at a precise temperature. Its electrical impulses are disrupted easily by outside signals. Its chemical balance must be so exact that it sets up barriers against many of the molecules readily carried in the blood to other organs. Even small changes in this balance can have significant effects on a person's overall ability to function comfortably or well in society, at least temporarily.

Structurally, the brain is composed mostly of nerve cells (neurons), which are organized into structures and areas that control all its activities. Unlike cells elsewhere in the body, which replace themselves when they are damaged or destroyed, brain cells do not regenerate. A severe cut may destroy numerous skin cells; in time new cells will grow and the wound will heal. A stroke might destroy an entire group of brain cells. If those cells had been involved in holding memories, the memories will be lost; likewise, if the cells had a role in governing mood, some control over mood will disappear. Deficits caused by brain injury or illness can be reversed only when most brain cells in that area remain intact. Thus, conditions such as high fever or nutritional deficiency may cause no permanent injury if the blood supply, oxygen consumption, and chemical balance have been disrupted only temporarily.

Some organic brain disorders, such as Alzheimer's disease, cause widespread death of brain cells and have no known cure. But many others stem from physical illnesses that can be treated and often totally cured, eliminating the mental symptoms completely. The progression of some diseases can be slowed or halted before notable damage occurs.

ALZHEIMER'S DISEASE AND OTHER DEMENTIAS

The term "dementia" refers to any organically caused brain disorder resulting in an overall, or global, loss of intellect or essential mental capacity, usually accompanied by changes in personality, behavior, and other character traits. The most striking changes involve memory and performance in virtually all areas of life. Dementias include some of the most devastating of all mental disorders.

Dementia generally results from a widespread destruction of, or interference with, cells in diverse areas of the brain, with consequent loss of the mental functions previously controlled by those cells.

Dementia can be progressive, as with Alzheimer's, or transient, perhaps as the result of a head injury. Progressive dementias are most common among the elderly, who may be labeled as "naturally" senile. In no case, though, can a dementia be considered a normal part of the aging process. Most people who reach advanced years do *not* develop dementia, and the expectation that "senility" is an inevitable part of the aging process is incorrect.

Physicians generally recognize two broad categories of dementia. *Primary* dementias are those like Alzheimer's in which dementia itself is the major sign of some organic brain disease not directly related to any other organic illness. *Secondary* dementias are those caused by, or closely related to, some other recognizable disease—whether acquired immune deficiency syndrome (AIDS), a chronic subdural hematoma, multiple sclerosis, or one of numerous other identifiable medical conditions. (*Pseudodementia* is another category of dementia that, as the name implies, is not true dementia but rather a set of symptoms that mimic the condition; chapter 23, see page 340.)

All dementias—whether primary or secondary, treatable or untreatable—share a few clinical characteristics in common. Loss of memory and inability to perform routine tasks—such as losing one's way in the neighborhood, difficulties in job performance, language problems—are particularly common. The most recent memories are usually lost sooner than older ones, and new memories, perhaps of something that happened minutes earlier, are difficult to retain. For example, a woman might ask her husband when they're scheduled "to visit the children." "Saturday," he might reply. Just a few minutes later she might ask the identical question. In the early stages of the dementia, however, she probably will have no difficulty identifying photos of the children, or even casual friends, taken 30 years earlier. In addition, behavior changes (such as increased aggressiveness), often mild but sometimes dramatic, almost always accompany dementia.

Alzheimer's Disease

Alzheimer's is the most common of all primary dementias. Estimates of its prevalence vary widely, ranging from 2.5 to more than 4 million victims in the U.S. alone. Some projections indicate that, barring a cure, there will be as many as 14 million victims living in the year 2050. At present, the disease leads to about 100,000 deaths annually.

The disease usually strikes people in their later years, although in rare instances symptoms show up in people in their 30s. Women develop Alzheimer's at a marginally higher rate than men.

The effects of the disease, and some of its immediate causes, were first described in 1907 by Dr. Alois Alzheimer, a German psychiatrist. During an autopsy, he discovered that a large percentage of brain cells of a woman who died with dementia had within them clusters of abnormal protein fibers, called "tangles," and that nearby nerve endings were clotted with dead and dying tissue fragments, called "plaques."

Much detail has since been added to his description. Nonetheless, although tests to detect the presence of the disease are in development, even today the disease cannot be diagnosed with absolute certainty except by microscopic examination of brain tissue, a process possible only after death. Still, studies have shown that in about 80 to 90 percent of all cases where Alzheimer's was strongly suspected, the diagnosis proved accurate at autopsy. The remaining cases demonstrated evidence of other, rarer causes of dementia.

Symptoms and Progression of the Illness

As the box on page 210 indicates, the disease usually involves a gradual, but inevitable, deterioration of virtually every cognitive mental process—memory, attention span, calculating ability, and so on. In its early stages, victims are typically confused, unusually irritable, and mildly forgetful. A small number become withdrawn and apathetic. Later on some are unable to regulate their own emotions, resulting in frequent outbursts of anger and even episodes of violence.

Memory loss progresses steadily, with the most recent memories fading first. Memory loss may begin with victims' inability to recall whom they met for lunch yesterday. Then they may forget where they went on vacation a year ago. Eventually they might no longer remember how many children they have.

In advanced stages of the illness, it becomes evident to others that an enormous body of basic knowledge is gone. Victims forget not only how to straighten the bed, but what a bed is for. They forget to eat, drink, or bathe and must be reminded constantly to do so. Some can't remember names or faces of their own families. Others forget when or where they were born. However, many Alzheimer's victims remember their own names until the disease is well advanced. Finally, many lose the ability to speak or to understand others.

As memory fades, analytical skills also disappear. At first, the mathematician can no longer divide or multiply; a few years later, simple sums are impossible. A dressmaker at first cannot figure out how to cut the fabric to fit the pattern; years later, just reading a ruler is difficult.

After a few years of such deterioration, frequently control is lost over basic body functions. Some people can no longer govern their bowels or bladders and must be diapered. Many cannot move their muscles to walk, or even to lift a spoon, and are unable to connect such movements with simple survival.

The disease continues for anywhere from 5 to 15 years, or more. Most Alzheimer's victims eventually die of infections, including pneumonia and other lung or heart diseases. Their immune systems are overtaxed, and they spend extended periods confined to bed, during which time secondary diseases invade their frail bodies.

Establishing the Diagnosis

At this writing, no medical test is available to accurately determine the presence of Alzheimer's. However, a test to detect a brain protein (ADAP) associated with Alzheimer's is undergoing research and appears promising. Until it or another test becomes available, physicians will continue to rely on a battery of medical, neurological, and psychological tests and careful observation of symptoms conducted over a period of months or years to reach a probable diagnosis.

Suspecting Alzheimer's

The physician examines the person's mental status, with particular interest in changes that took place over the preceding months. Interviews with family members can be very important. Often it is they who notice the earliest signs. Reports such as the following are common.

Three adult siblings visited their elderly mother for the first time in weeks. She had not vacuumed, washed the dishes, or watered the plants, apparently for some time. They had come to celebrate one sibling's birthday and were perplexed to discover that their mother had forgotten it.

Patients may sometimes admit to physicians: "Maybe I have had trouble getting my thoughts together lately." While they may seem slightly depressed by their memory difficulties, they generally feel healthy. Others vehemently deny any problem, and sometimes become angry when clear-cut memory deficits are pointed out. Extensive testing rules out other conditions that could cause the same symptoms. Detailed pictures of the brain itself—through computed tomography (CT) scans or magnetic resonance imaging (MRI)—are usually ordered at this point and may reveal structural brain changes. However, these changes could be caused by other organic conditions as well and are not sufficient to confirm the diagnosis.

If the dementia follows a degenerative course over a period of months, and if all the medical and psychological tests fail to turn up any other clear causes for the dementia, the psychiatrist or neurologist will likely diagnose "probable Alzheimer's."

Medical Treatment

As pointed out earlier, there is no cure for Alzheimer's disease. Numerous medications are under investigation for treating the dementia itself. Many of these experimental drugs seek to replace the neurotransmitter acetylcholine, which is depleted in the brains of Alzheimer's victims. One promising drug currently undergoing tests in the United States, tetrahydroaminoacridine (THA), may diminish the symptoms of Alzheimer's in some cases. During testing done in other countries, THA's major drawback has been its toxic effect on the liver, which can be managed by temporarily stopping the drug or lowering its dose. Another drug being studied is L-acetyl carnitine (Alcar). Both THA and Alcar work by enhancing the brain's cholinergic system, which is activated by acetylcholine and which is deficient in Alzheimer's disease. But because so many other brain functions are also damaged, these drugs may actually provide little more than temporary relief of symptoms.

Medical treatments that physicians now provide make life more bearable for the victim and thus too for those providing care. For example, mild to moderate depression frequently develops among people with dementia at some point in the course of the disease. Often it can be treated successfully with low doses of standard antidepressant drugs. Similarly, symptoms of anxiety sometimes clear up with small to moderate doses of anxiolytic drugs, including the benzodiazepines. Various stimulant drugs, such as methylphenidate (Ritalin), often relieve symptoms such as general fatigue and slow movements, making the management of Alzheimer's easier.

When the illness causes insomnia and other sleep disorders, or leads to frequent periods of aggression, sedatives can be beneficial. If the disease brings about a period of psychosis, as it often does, small doses of antipsychotic drugs can reduce the symptoms. Because Alzheimer's disease destroys many brain cells, patients are particularly susceptible to the side effects of antipsychotics, sedatives, and antidepressants, so small doses are advised.

As the disease progresses, management of victims' basic health needs falls increasingly to others. Because sufferers may not be able to describe their symptoms when they are experiencing pain or common illnesses, caregivers must remain vigilant to their state of health and remind them when it is time to take their medications, drink appropriate liquids, and so on, since they may not be able to follow instructions. They may not fully understand the need to bandage a cut or to leave the bandage in place. Thus, even minor injuries require regular attention by someone else.

Care and Caregivers

Until the illness is well advanced and a professional facility is absolutely necessary, most victims of advanced Alzheimer's receive basic help at home or in the homes of family members or friends, because few government programs or private insurance policies provide benefits for long-term care. Long-term nursing home benefits come primarily from Medicare and Medicaid, which change according to shifting federal policy and also vary considerably from state to state. The emotional drain on family and friends, on top of the considerable economic cost, is enormous. (See "Help for Families," page 214, and "Financial and Legal Considerations," page 219.)

Even for the most devoted family caregivers, dealing with advanced Alzheimer's disease is often a seesaw of emotional turmoil, ranging from one day's devotion to the next day's despair. For example, the demented father takes a short stroll through the neighborhood, doesn't return, and is found hours later at the local police station, where officers describe finding him in a bus entering a garage for the night. The very next day, though, the same man watches a televised baseball game and heartily cheers the team he's followed for decades.

Among the most successful methods of coping with Alzheimer's is a collaborative effort involving the entire family and a neurologist or psychiatrist experienced with the illness. The doctor keeps abreast of the disease's progress in the particular

---

WHAT TO EXPECT WITH ALZHEIMER'S

Alzheimer's disease does not affect any two victims in exactly the same way, or according to the same schedule, but some general stages of the disease have been identified. There is some overlap between the stages, and some people may develop symptoms listed in a later stage much sooner than those listed in earlier stages.

Stage	Typical Symptoms	Stage	Typical Symptoms
1.	None apparent.		needs some help to manage on an ongoing basis.
2. *Forgetfulness*	Sometimes misplaces objects; forgets some names of people.	6. *Middle Dementia*	Forgets name of spouse, recent major events in life, many past events; unaware of surroundings; becomes incontinent; has trouble sleeping; undergoes major personality changes; may become obsessive, anxious, and agitated; sometimes violent or aggressive; loses willpower; cannot concentrate on thoughts.
3. *Early Confusion*	Gets lost when traveling; poor work performance; forgets written material.		
4. *Late Confusion*	Cannot understand current news; forgets major events in personal history; makes financial mistakes; denies any problem exists.		
5. *Early Dementia*	Forgets addresses, phone numbers, or names of close relatives; forgets the day, season, year; has trouble selecting proper clothes;	7. *Late Dementia*	Most verbal abilities and movement (walking) skills disappear; needs help eating, using toilet, bathing.

patient and advises the family on steps to take *before* a problem becomes a catastrophe. For instance, the physician might warn the family in advance that unaccompanied strolls may soon be impossible and advise an in-house exercise regimen.

To conserve energy and prevent "burnout," families are advised to divide among themselves some of the duties of day-to-day care. If one or two people take on the bulk of caregiving, other family members should step in periodically for an evening, a day, or a weekend, so the primary caregivers have a respite from the often grueling task of caring for a person who progressively loses mental and physical function.

Among the physician's most important roles in this kind of unified approach is to inform the family when the Alzheimer's victim requires full-time institutionalization. This subject should be broached well in advance of the actual need, because finding a suitable facility offering qualified care at an affordable price can be a daunting task. Few nursing homes accept patients with advanced dementia, and, among those which do, there is considerable variability regarding the standard of care.

Investigating Causes

The tangles and plaques discovered by Dr. Alzheimer early in the century had clearly led to his patient's

---

DEALING WITH DEMENTIA DAY TO DAY

- Keep a few lights on at night, because some people with dementia experience more confusion and agitation during hours of darkness. During the day, and in a light-filled environment, they receive more visual clues that help them stay aware of the time and place.
- Prevent injuries before they happen. If a person develops trouble walking, keep floors clear of toys, books, loose rugs, and anything else someone might trip over, and move furniture closer to the walls. To prevent falls, install barriers at the top of stairways. Install handrails and grab bars in the bathroom, and purchase a shower chair. Reduce the temperature setting on the water heater to minimize the chance of scalding injuries.
- Help minimize geographical confusion. Tape a BATHROOM sign on the bathroom door, or paint it a distinctive color. Paste red arrows along routes frequently taken, such as from living room to bedroom, from bedroom to bathroom.
- Take control of medications, and learn which drugs you must administer and on what schedule. People with dementia often need a range of drugs for various medical conditions but might not remember when they should take them, or how many should be taken. They can accidentally give themselves overdoses or fail to take a drug essential to their health. Lock drugs away.
- Prepare meals that are very familiar to the person with dementia. He or she may often experience a loss of appetite but may be encouraged to eat if presented with favorite foods.

- Encourage the person to stop driving. Even people in early stages of dementia may forget basic driving rules or respond too slowly to emergencies. Recent evidence indicates that people with Alzheimer's disease who keep driving are several times more likely to be involved in traffic accidents than others in similar age groups.
- Provide exercise. Joining the individual for a daily walk through the neighborhood helps promote sleep at night and keeps muscles in shape.
- Reduce evening liquids. People with dementia commonly wake up at night to use the bathroom, grow confused, and wander around aimlessly, disturbing the sleep of everyone. Having them drink fewer liquids in the evening (but more earlier in the day) helps promote sleep throughout the night. Also eliminate beverages containing caffeine.
- A bracelet engraved with a family member's name, address, and phone number can help locate a person with dementia who has wandered off without identification, and perhaps been found by police or helpful strangers.
- Help select clothing that's easy to put on and take off.
- Try maintaining a regular eating and sleeping schedule. This helps avoid confusion and calms the common fears of change.
- Put off redecorating. Sudden changes in the immediate environment, such as repainting a room, buying new furniture, or installing new lamps, can lead to increased agitation and confusion. If you must make such changes, proceed as slowly as possible.

dementia, he reasoned, but what was behind these irregularities themselves? Since his discovery, researchers have sought in vain to answer that question. Numerous "suspects" have been identified, but none has yet provided more than a hint of the disease's underlying cause.

Among the possibilities being studied are a slow virus, a metallic toxin, genetic flaws, or chemical abnormalities.

A slow virus. A slow-acting virus may set off Alzheimer's and then disappear before symptoms show up, leaving no trace of itself except for the damage in its wake. Or the virus might persist but be too tiny, or too subtle, to be detected by today's instruments.

Metallic toxin. Abnormal deposits of aluminum have been found in the midst of brain-cell tangles, and researchers are studying possible ways the metal could infiltrate the brain and begin killing cells.

Genetic flaws. Victims of Down's syndrome, a disorder linked to a defect on the 21st chromosome, usually develop Alzheimer's if they live to their 40s. Several studies are underway to determine if Alzheimer's is linked to an independent genetic fault on the same chromosome. Furthermore, statistical studies of Alzheimer's in individual families indicate that 30 to 40 percent of cases have some roots in a genetic flaw. However, there is currently no way to determine which family members, if any, will develop the illness.

Chemical abnormalities. The brains of Alzheimer's victims show numerous chemical abnormalities both in and around the affected cells. It is not yet clear, however, if the unusual brain chemistry causes the cells to die, or is instead caused by the already dying cells, or has any direct bearing on the cause or course of Alzheimer's disease. Still, dozens of drugs that may correct the abnormalities and influence the disease are being tested around the world, particularly those that increase the availability within the brain of the neurotransmitter acetylcholine. Studies of some promising drugs have had to be halted when the medications proved too dangerous for human use.

Other Primary Dementias

While Alzheimer's disease comprises well over half of all primary dementias, thousands of people every year fall ill with one of the other primary dementias. They are no less destructive than Alzheimer's, and in some instances their courses are even more tragic.

Multi-infarct Dementia (MID)

Multi-infarct dementia (MID), accounting for about 20 percent of all dementias, is caused by one or more small strokes that destroy or damage brain tissue. MID occurs most commonly after age 65, but it can also strike young or middle-age individuals with high blood pressure. Unlike Alzheimer's disease, more men than women are affected by MID.

As noted earlier, the brain needs a well-regulated supply of oxygen-rich blood in order to function. If supply is interrupted—which is what happens during a stroke—nerve cells in the area deprived of blood die, a process that is called infarction. A single stroke may cause severe damage to some cognitive functions, such as language ability or abstract thinking, but usually will not cause dementia; in fact, many people do recover, at least partially, from a single stroke. In MID, however, successive, multiple infarctions cause increasingly larger areas of cell death and damage. These small strokes or infarctions often occur without the patient experiencing any acute symptoms. When a sufficient area of the brain is damaged, dementia results.

In rare cases, the illness produces such widespread brain damage over a few years that the symptoms and their progression are nearly identical to Alzheimer's. More often, however, multi-infarct dementia results in specific symptoms that point to the cause. For example, if the disease mainly affects the blood supply to the areas of the brain that govern mood, then mood changes will be the dominant symptoms. Victims of multi-infarct dementia usually are keenly aware of their mental deficits and regularly face bouts of anxiety and depression.

Here are some of the clinical symptoms that help physicians differentiate MID from Alzheimer's disease.

- MID comes on abruptly, rather than gradually, as in Alzheimer's (although a number of small strokes may occur before any symptoms of cognitive impairment are evident).

- It progresses in steps, as each successive stroke causes further deterioration.

- The individual still retains his or her unique personality (it is eventually lost in Alzheimer's), although subject to shifting swings of emotional moods—for example, he or she may laugh, cry, or get angry in response to what appears to others to be minor provocations.

- The person with MID usually will have a history of hypertension or of previous strokes.
- Evidence of stroke will show on CT or MRI scans of the brain.

Because both Alzheimer's and MID are common conditions in the elderly, both illnesses can occur in the same individual, making it more difficult to establish an initial difficult diagnosis.

MID cannot be reversed. There is no specific treatment for it, other than the supportive measures for dementia described earlier (page 211). However, it may be possible to stop or considerably slow further damage by treating those factors most responsible for the illness: high blood pressure, smoking, and increased blood cholesterol. An aspirin a day may help prevent further strokes.

Huntington's Chorea Dementia

Huntington's disease is a progressive hereditary disorder with no known cure, although a genetic test is now available to determine whether an individual is a carrier of the gene.

The disease usually becomes evident in the late 30s, and its early symptoms involve involuntary movements of the hands and legs (chorea) and occasionally depression and hallucinations. Dementia symptoms increase over the following months and include gradual loss of muscle control, speech, and cognitive abilities. Death occurs anywhere from a few years to two decades after diagnosis. There is no established treatment, although a few drugs are currently under development.

Pick's Disease Dementia

Pick's disease dementia is almost identical to Alzheimer's in its long-term course and prognosis, but the areas of the brain affected are somewhat different in this disease. It usually causes its own distinctive irregularities in the brain's frontal and temporal cortex.

Early symptoms of Pick's disease, occurring before memory loss becomes prominent, often include mood changes and bizarre behaviors, and often a loss of modesty and sexual inhibitions. Other early symptoms involve inappropriate social behavior, such as laughing in the midst of a funeral service or shouting in a library.

Pick's disease is extremely rare, and little is known about its causes. It does appear to run in families, although no genetic transmission has been established. As with Alzheimer's, an accurate diagnosis is only possible upon autopsy. There is no known treatment.

OTHER ORGANIC BRAIN DISORDERS

Several distinct medical conditions or illnesses sometimes produce dementia. Treatment for these dementias usually consists of addressing the underlying illness or physical problem.

AIDS Dementia

The human immunodeficiency virus (HIV) responsible for acquired immune deficiency syndrome (AIDS) also causes dementia in many victims, as explained in greater detail in chapter 29.

The dementia may start with subtle changes in personality, memory, and behavior, but at first these alterations are usually attributed to the dramatic emotional impact of the disease. In some AIDS patients, however, episodes of depression and psychosis start to occur regularly—often at about the same time that opportunistic infections, such as pneumonia, strike—and considerable memory loss becomes apparent to others. Eventually the victims of AIDS-related dementia themselves acknowledge having serious problems with mental activity and complain of overall lethargy and lack of interest in once-important parts of their lives.

In AIDS victims, dementia symptoms regularly stabilize for months on end, and sometimes for years, before once again continuing a generally downhill course.

While there is no known cure for the disease itself, many symptoms of AIDS dementia (and other psychological problems associated with the illness) often respond to medications. Stimulant drugs such as methylphenidate (Ritalin) and dextroamphetamine improve attention span and overall mental ability for brief periods. Psychotic episodes can be treated with small doses of antipsychotic drugs, and depression responds to small doses of antidepressant drugs.

The use of drugs to treat dementia is complicated by potential interactions with other drugs already being taken to deal with infections or various AIDS-related problems. In general, the smallest effective doses should be prescribed to minimize interactions, and some compounds should be avoided altogether (such as antidepressants with high anticholinergic side effects; see chapter 5).

Other Infectious Diseases

Numerous infectious diseases other than AIDS can cause dementia. Various forms of meningitis, for example, lead to the gradual deterioration of mental ability and, unless treated with antibiotics, are invariably fatal. Viral encephalitis also causes dementia in some patients who do not receive prompt medical treatment.

A rare form of dementia stems from Creutzfeldt-Jakob disease, caused by a slow-acting virus that cannot be seen even with modern microscopes. Symptoms usually appear when patients are in their 50s or 60s; once the disease is diagnosed, severe dementia develops in a few weeks and death usually occurs within a year.

HELP FOR FAMILIES

Caring for a close relative with dementia is always an emotionally draining experience. Sometimes people give up sooner than they would like, place a father or mother in a nursing home, and then face years of guilt feelings over doing so. In other instances they wait too long to find a nursing home, taking many unrealistic burdens upon themselves, and then experience extraordinary stress, sleep disorders, and anxiety, often accompanied by overall emotional instability.

Those caring for dementia victims usually require substantial emotional support. When difficulties dealing with the situation begin to take a toll on everyday life—causing loss of concentration at work, frequent loss of temper, and so on—or when the whole situation seems insurmountable, professional mental health care can be helpful for the caregiver.

Family therapy is particularly useful when overseen by a therapist experienced in the problems of dementia. Support group meetings for the family can be beneficial by confirming that others in similar situations face many of the same problems and by providing practical advice learned from experience. (See the box on page 215.)

Experts suggest that caregivers try to take a distancing approach, by not taking things personally. If someone with dementia angrily shouts at them, for example, it may be helpful to remember that the shouts actually may be a response to fear or to a moment of insight into the loss of mental ability. Coming to terms with the illness is not easy and may take family members several months or years to accept fully.

OTHER MEDICAL ILLNESSES THAT COMMONLY PRODUCE ORGANIC MENTAL SYMPTOMS

In addition to the dementias, over 70 known organic illnesses and conditions can cause mental symptoms of all kinds, although not all produce permanent brain damage. Treatment of the underlying illness is required. Following are some illnesses and conditions that commonly produce mental symptoms. (Medical illnesses also produce emotional *reactions;* these are discussed in chapter 28.)

Brain Tumors and Cancer

Tumors and cancers in the brain press against nerve tissue and sometimes cause its destruction, producing dementia, depression, personality and behavior changes, or hallucinations, depending on their size and location. Detected by CT or MRI scans (see chapter 2), they may be primary, that is, originating in the brain, or secondary, meaning originating elsewhere, such as lung cancer that spreads to the brain.

Nutritional Deficiencies and Toxins

Vitamin B-12 deficiency, which can lead to pernicious anemia; folate deficiency; and chronic drug intoxication (discussed separately on page 217) all can lead to

GETTING HELP AND INFORMATION

The vast majority of people with dementia, whether Alzheimer's or another type, receive most of their essential care from relatives. But some outside assistance is available in most communities across the country, and with perseverance additional help or important information can usually be found.

Organizations for the Aged

Most large cities, and many counties and towns, maintain agencies specifically geared to dealing with the concerns of the elderly. Many can provide information about home care for those with dementia, requirements for admission to area nursing homes, local availability of hospital care, and related concerns. The agencies might be part of the state's social services or mental health offices, or may be locally funded and operated. Phone calls or visits to such agencies listed in the telephone book (usually under "Government Offices") will disclose whether specific services are available.

Associations

The Alzheimer's Association (70 East Lake Street, Suite 600, Chicago, IL 60601; tel. 312 853–3060), the most notable of many dementia research and information groups, has chapters across the country. All provide up-to-date information, and some conduct regular family support meetings. Support groups can be very helpful in understanding and coping with the consequences of the illness.

Adult Day-Care Centers

Adult day-care centers, if they exist in your area, may provide exercise, recreation, or general health advice and support to adults with dementia or other mental difficulties. At the same time, they provide family members with a few hours of freedom from the burden of care. Some are publicly financed, while others are private and charge a fee.

Community Centers

Community centers frequently organize events that can be enjoyed by people in the early to middle stages of dementia, although these centers often cannot deal with those in late stages. Some request that advanced Alzheimer's victims be accompanied during activities.

Home Care Agencies

Whether publicly funded, relying on insurance reimbursements, or requiring immediate payment for services, home care agencies provide trained workers on an hourly, daily, or weekly basis to perform such tasks for dementia victims as preparing meals and cleaning house, as well as giving medications and providing other basic nursing and personal care.

Hospitals

A few large hospitals in major cities, both private and public, have programs specifically designed to help people with dementia. Sometimes they actively seek participants in medical studies to test new drugs or procedures that might help with dementia, and provide those selected with a wide range of support services.

---

disorders characterized by restlessness, irritability, mood changes, intellectual problems, or paranoid thinking. More rarely, emotional symptoms can be traced to lead, mercury, arsenic, or carbon monoxide poisoning. In these cases, other organs—the stomach, kidneys, or blood cells—are affected as well.

Dietary deficiencies—particularly a reduction in thiamine intake—sometimes cause metabolic irregularities within the brain, which in turn can lead to dementia. This most often happens among alcoholics who fail to eat properly. The majority of people recover fully soon after beginning well-balanced diets.

Liver Disease

Liver disease can seriously alter brain chemistry, leading to confusion, agitation, and, in some instances, symptoms of acute psychosis.

Liver problems are fairly common among abusers of alcohol, which itself can cause brain damage. Distinguishing between symptoms caused by chemical changes in the brain due to liver damage and those caused by drinking alcohol is particularly difficult. Treatment also is difficult. Long-term medical treatment of the liver disease usually corrects the accompanying psychiatric problems, if the victim refrains

Table 15.1 SOME MEDICAL CONDITIONS WITH PSYCHIATRIC SYMPTOMS

CONNECTIVE TISSUE DISEASES

Condition	Symptoms
systemic lupus erythematosus	depression, memory impairment, delirium, psychosis

ENDOCRINE/METABOLIC

hyperadrenalism (Cushing's syndrome)	depression, mood swings, anxiety, somatic delusions, psychosis
Addison's disease	depression, apathy, paranoia, psychosis
hyperthyroidism	depression, anxiety, grandiosity, irritability, psychosis
hypothyroidism	impaired thinking, anxiety, irritability, bodily delusions, paranoia, hallucinations, excess sleepiness
hypoglycemia	anxiety, irritability, confusion

INFECTIONS

AIDS-related dementia	depression, irritability, paranoia, psychosis, dementia
tuberculous meningitis	dementia
Creutzfeldt-Jakob disease	rapidly progressive dementia

NEOPLASIAS

pancreatic cancer	depression, apathy

NEUROLOGIC

intracranial tumors	depression, anxiety, personality change
subdural hematoma	irritability, confusion, depression, dementia
postconcussion syndrome	irritability, personality change, depression, dementia
Alzheimer's disease	irritability, personality change, depression, dementia
multiple sclerosis	affective disturbance, memory loss, sensory or motor disorders
myasthenia gravis	anxiety, depression
Parkinson's disease	depression, dependency, dementia, psychosis
Huntington's disease	personality change, irritability, cognitive decline, depression, dementia

NUTRITIONAL

pernicious anemia (vitamin B-12 deficiency)	depression, paranoia, irritability, dementia

Source: Adapted from Susan C. Jenkins, Timothy P. Gibbs, M.D., and Sally R. Szymanski, D.O. *A Pocket Reference for Psychiatrists* (Washington, D.C.: American Psychiatric Press, 1990), 58–66. Used by permission.

from further use of alcohol and minimizes any other risk factors.

Endocrine Disorders

Diseases of the endocrine system commonly produce psychiatric symptoms. Hypothyroidism often leads to depression and apathy; hyperthyroidism can lead to anxiety and panic attacks, as well as eating and sleeping disorders. Affecting the adrenal glands, Addison's disease also produces apathy and depression, while Cushing's syndrome may cause depression or paranoia. Diabetes is quite commonly associated with mood disorders, and hypoglycemia can produce

symptoms ranging from confusion to depression, anxiety, and dementia.

Other Diseases

Multiple sclerosis can cause episodes of unexplained euphoria and periods of mild intellectual impairment, sometimes deteriorating into dementia. Depression is also associated with this disease.

Fevers, even moderate ones, regularly cause delirium. (See page 218.)

Temporal lobe epilepsy can lead to delusions, hallucinations, and schizophrenialike symptoms as well as uncharacteristic episodes of violence and aggres-

Table 15.2   IS THE PROBLEM ORGANIC?

Some clues that suggest an organic mental disorder are the following.

- Psychiatric symptoms arise after age 40.
- The symptoms begin
  —during a major illness.
  —while taking drugs known to cause mental symptoms.
  —suddenly, with no prior psychiatric history or recent severe stressors.
- There is a history of
  —alcohol or drug abuse.
  —physical illness involving major organs.
  —taking multiple medications.
- There is a family history of
  —degenerative or inheritable brain disease.
  —metabolic disease (such as diabetes).

- Mental signs include
  —altered level of consciousness.
  —fluctuating mental status.
  —cognitive impairment.
  —visual, tactile (touch), or olfactory (smell) hallucinations.
- Physical signs include
  —signs of organ malfunction that affect the brain.
  —symptoms such as slowed speech, thinking, or movement, poor muscle coordination, tremors, and the like.
  —neurological symptoms.

Source: R. S. Hoffman and L. M. Koran, "Detecting physical illness in patients with mental disorders." *Psychosomatics* 25(1984): 654–660.

---

sion. It also can cause heightened emotional attachment to people or activities.

Arthritis and abdominal cancers (notably pancreatic cancer) all can cause mood disorders.

Untreated syphilis can cause a wide range of psychiatric disorders, including (in late-stage syphilis) dementia.

Parkinson's disease causes depression and/or dementia in about half of all cases.

Drug and Alcohol Use and Withdrawal

As detailed in chapter 9, alcoholics often experience long periods of amnesia during times of steady drinking. Many who withdraw from heavy alcohol use undergo several hours or days of *delirium tremens,* during which hallucinations and delusions commonly are experienced, along with general signs of confusion and disorientation.

Potent stimulants such as cocaine, especially in fast-acting smokable forms such as "crack," often cause psychosis, paranoia, and other mental disorders both during use and afterward. Milder stimulants such as caffeine and amphetamines can produce anxiety. LSD causes delusions and hallucinations.

In general, most serious psychiatric problems related to drug or alcohol withdrawal begin a day or so after the last drug use and endure as long as a week. But dementia caused by continuous, long-term use of alcohol may never resolve.

Prescription drugs also can produce psychiatric symptoms. For example, some medications pre-

scribed for high blood pressure can reduce the overall flow of blood to the brain, which, particularly in elderly people who already have poor circulation, may lead to such symptoms of dementia as confusion and poor concentration. Reserpine and methyldopa can cause mood disorders, such as unusual sadness or euphoria. Barbiturates and benzodiazepines can produce amnesia. Steroids can cause abrupt mood changes shortly after use, whether by prescription or self-administered. Thyroid drugs sometimes cause psychosis. Birth control pills and hormone drugs can cause mood shifts. Changes in drug dosages are usually effective in the treatment of these conditions.

Trauma

Injury to the head can cause chronic dementia and numerous short- and long-term psychiatric problems. Boxers who repeatedly receive blows to the head over the course of several years often develop dementia indistinguishable from Alzheimer's disease. On autopsy, in fact, their brains may show tangles and plaques similar to those found in Alzheimer's patients.

While even a single major injury to the head can cause dementia, it more often leads to amnesia, temporary confusion, hallucinations, or bursts of aggression. (See chapter 27.) Usually the most serious mental symptoms of physical brain damage appear immediately after the injury, then gradually subside as the wound heals. Some degree of amnesia may remain, though, particularly concerning events shortly before and after the injury occurred.

If the injury causes bleeding under the skull—a subdural hematoma—psychiatric symptoms may develop several days after the injury, as the buildup of blood presses against the brain. Subdural hematomas are medical emergencies that can be fatal without surgery to relieve the pressure. Even a seemingly minor head injury can result in a chronic subdural hematoma, which may cause psychiatric symptoms—including signs of dementia—several weeks or months later. Sometimes a head injury causes persistent changes in personality, behavior, and intellectual ability, and the individual never fully recovers from the damage despite aggressive emergency medical care.

Medical Treatments

In addition to medications, a few medical treatments—including kidney dialysis, radiation therapy, and chemotherapy to treat cancer patients—themselves can lead to symptoms of emotional or psychiatric disturbances and cognitive impairment.

Major operations have sometimes been linked to periods of postsurgical cognitive impairment and depression, which may result from sudden changes of metabolism and blood flow in the brain as well as from the effects of anesthetics and other drugs administered before, during, and after surgery.

DELIRIUM

While dementia is a chronic condition, delirium is usually transient. Delirium is the inability to focus attention on the immediate surroundings, keep thoughts in order, or accurately interpret what the senses perceive. It can result from virtually any of the organic factors described in the previous section. Delirium usually arises suddenly and often abates when the condition causing it is corrected. Visual hallucinations, usually involving the appearance of animals, may precede delirium; this is particularly common during withdrawal from the use of alcohol and illicit drugs.

In hospitals, most often among the elderly, delirium is a common aftermath of surgery, as patients awaken from anesthesia. It may develop in conjunction with a fever caused by infection and subside along with the temperature. During the delirium, the patient might thrash about and tear off bandages or pull out infusion needles.

Sedatives can be used to calm someone with delirium, but extreme care is required, because the drugs might worsen confusion. The only sure way to reverse delirium is by treating the underlying illness or condition causing it.

FINANCIAL AND LEGAL CONSIDERATIONS

Most families caring for someone with Alzheimer's or other dementia do not make adequate long-term financial and legal plans. This is mainly because they feel the difficulties in dealing with today's problems cause enough of an emotional drain; they'll worry about tomorrow's troubles some other day.

Financial Considerations

- Start investigating nearby nursing homes within the first year after diagnosis of probable Alzheimer's is made. Visit them personally, if possible with the individual who has the illness. Study their literature to determine precisely what they offer. Compare prices carefully, paying attention to the cost of "extras." Make a judgment about the friendliness of the staff and their apparent interest in patient care. Ask about waiting lists; if they're more than two years long, consider signing up immediately. Regularly keep in touch with your preferred nursing home choices over the following months and years.
- Find out which agencies in your state handle various aspects of Medicare and Medicaid programs. Study their financial and medical eligibility requirements *immediately*. In some states a complete mental status examination by an approved psychiatrist is required, while in others a diagnosis by a general practitioner is sufficient. Also check whether the person with dementia is entitled to any Veteran's Administration benefits.
- Before providing benefits, federal programs may require that the person with dementia (or the family) first deplete bank accounts and sell personal possessions, thus "spending themselves into poverty." It may be wise to consult an attorney, financial advisor, or social worker to help with financial planning.
- Track down copies of all insurance policies covering the ill person, and determine what benefits are available under specific circumstances. Ask for details from the insurance companies.

Legal Considerations

- Explore how to have someone appointed legal guardian of an individual with dementia, responsible for handling finances and making important legal and medical decisions on behalf of the person. The decision to appoint a legal guardian is best discussed with the victim before paranoia and late-stage dementia set in.
- Whenever possible, encourage open discussion with the person with dementia about attitudes toward emergency medical treatment in case of a life-threatening illness. To avoid future legal problems concerning the competency of a person with dementia, such talks should take place when the individual is still alert and aware enough to comprehend the subject fully. Bring up some hard questions: Should life be prolonged as long as possible? Are feeding tubes and breathing aids desirable? In what circumstances? Consider the benefits and drawbacks in your state of a so-called living will, which clarifies in advance a person's wishes regarding life support methods in the event of a coma or a persistent vegetative state.
- If a will already exists, try to ensure that it still reflects the desires of the person with dementia and the current economic realities. If there is no will, contact a lawyer to help the person write one that is legally valid.

three

• • •

COMMON PROBLEMS AND DISORDERS AMONG CHILDREN AND ADOLESCENTS

16

Introduction to Child and Adolescent Mental Health

David Shaffer, M.D., F.R.C.P., F.R.C. Psych.

It is not always easy for parents to distinguish between normal behavior problems in their children and those difficulties that require special attention. At any stage in the child's development, parents may feel confused and concerned. They may ask: Should I worry if my two-year-old hasn't started talking? Is my six-year-old's bedwetting to be expected? My nine-year-old is as nervous and fearful of leaving home as I was at his age; is this a family trait that he's stuck with or can he get help? Is my teenage daughter's sulking and withdrawing from me a danger signal or just a phase she's going through? Have I done something wrong, or not right enough?

Although it is no simple matter to define what is "normal" mental experience or behavior for adults, it is especially complicated for children, who are changing rapidly. Feelings, thoughts, behaviors, and styles of communicating and coping that are appropriate at one age may no longer be adaptive for the child's developmental level 18 months later. For example, distress when a parent leaves home is ordinary for a toddler but not for a school-age child. Also, a child's developmental level can influence how he or she expresses mental symptoms. Depression in a five-year-old may become most apparent through the child's apathy and frequent headaches and stomachaches; a depressed teenager may complain of boredom and tiredness and prefer to sleep instead of socialize.

Because childhood is a time of change, most of the chapters in this section discuss both what is the normal mental and emotional experience for children at various ages as well as what are signs of common or major problems at particular developmental stages, from preschool through adolescence. Chapter 19, which covers adolescence, focuses particular attention on the normal physical and mental and emotional changes that young people experience in these years and on their often troubling concerns. At all ages, understanding what is normal and individual in their children and spotting the distinguishing characteristics of troubled behavior can help parents communicate with their children and spot problems when they occur, in time to offset the worst consequences of untreated illness.

First, in this introductory chapter, we look at the nature and incidence of mental suffering in childhood, why it occurs, how to recognize it, and what can be done to help children. Fortunately, the child mental health disciplines have amassed a considerable body of knowledge about mental and emotional illness in young people and how it can be treated.

KINDS OF PROBLEMS

Mental disorder and emotional problems afflict at least 12 percent, perhaps as high as 20 percent, of all children at some time before they reach 18. Although virtually all of them can be helped in some way, an estimated 40 percent are never even brought for diagnosis or treatment. Untreated mental disorder takes an enormous toll on children and their families. It can interfere with orderly development of the child and influence the course of his or her entire life. Most disorders that afflict adults can begin during childhood, when diagnosis and treatment could reduce substantially or prevent suffering later. Prompt intervention can provide those with mental retardation (chapter 17) the chance to reach a much greater potential and be productive in life.

Most of the mental problems that afflict children fall into the first three broad groups of problems listed below. Children can and often do suffer symptoms from more than one of these groups.

Developmental Disorders

Children who are greatly delayed in acquiring reading, language, speech, and muscular control are said to have developmental disorders. They may also lag well behind other children their age in their ability to learn or to develop urinary or bowel control. Developmental disorders are not generally considered to be emotional or behavioral problems in and of themselves. However, many children with these disorders have associated emotional or behavioral difficulties.

For example, a third of children who do not learn to read until much later than their peers have behavior problems. Of the developmental disorders, we cover mental retardation and autism in chapter 17 and learning disabilities in chapter 18.

Emotional Disorders

Children who experience a disturbance of feelings or emotions are said to suffer from emotional disorders. They may be depressed or anxious or otherwise acutely or persistently distressed, although they may not experience these problems in ways adults do. In the following chapters we discuss these problems usually as mood and anxiety disorders or symptoms.

Disruptive Behavior Disorders

Children with disruptive behavior difficulties display behavior that upsets others or does not conform to social normals. Children with conduct disorders may steal, fight, lie, upset the classroom, run away, use drugs, and engage in early sexual activity. Hyperactivity (chapter 17) and attention-deficit hyperactivity disorder (chapter 18) fall into this category.

Other Disorders

A number of other disorders also befall children. They are vulnerable to various eating disorders at different developmental stages, such as pica (craving bizarre foods, such as dirt) in early childhood and anorexia nervosa or bulimia in adolescence. Other childhood disorders include sleep problems (including night terrors), speech and articulation

disorders (such as stuttering), elimination disorders (bedwetting, for example), elective mutism (refusal to speak), and gender identity disorders, among others; these are covered in the appropriate chapters in this section.

WHEN DOES A CHILD NEED HELP?

The main gauge of mental health difficulty is whether the child's behavior or emotions cause him or her significant distress or interfere with the child's life or that of the family. The next four chapters provide information on recognizing signs of trouble in children of various ages and in certain situations (such as parents' divorce or abusive environments). In general, however, professionals usually take into account a number of factors when evaluating a child's mental health, including the following. (See also the box on page 226.)

- *Severity, duration, and frequency of the problem.* The difference between troubled and normally troublesome behavior is often one of degree of intensity of the behavior or experience, how long it lasts, and/or how frequently it occurs. For example, all children lose their tempers sometimes, but when a child frequently breaks things and tears clothes while screaming at the top of his or her lungs, these tantrums may indicate a deeper problem. Similarly, although healthy children experience brief periods of feeling down or of

simply being quieter than usual, sadness that lasts for several days or weeks is not normal. Also, most children lie occasionally, often to get out of trouble; when a child lies almost every day, an underlying problem is indicated.

- *Age appropriateness.* Although children develop at their own pace within a given range, certain stages of behavior and learning are appropriate for certain ages. Bedwetting (enuresis), for example, is normal until the child is five or six, after which it may signal a problem in some children and should be evaluated.
- *Number of problems.* When problems accumulate, parents can be more certain that the child is having a mental health difficulty that requires an evaluation. For example, parents may wonder whether their teenager's withdrawal from the family signals a problem or a normal need to assert autonomy. The adolescent is clearly in trouble, however, when the withdrawal is accompanied by retreat from friends and usual activities, neglect of school work, and change in eating and sleeping patterns.

GOING FOR HELP

Whatever the reason, if a child's problems lead to significant distress for him or her, or if they are causing the child to miss out on educational or social opportunities, professional help may be needed. Unfortunately, parents often are reluctant to bring up their concerns with professionals who can help them (such as pediatricians, family physicians, teachers, or school counselors), feeling that they should be able to handle the problems themselves or that the professional will blame them for the child's problems. Professionals understand that by helping parents comprehend the true cause or nature of the behavior or illness, they can often relieve unwarranted

guilt. In most cases, effective treatment closely involves the parents.

Who Can Help

The range and credentials of mental health professionals, and suggestions for evaluating them, are described in chapter 3. When seeking help for a child, it is important to consult only those psychiatrists, clinical psychologists, or clinical social workers who have additional training and experience working with children and adolescents. Although many professionals who are trained to work with

TROUBLED BEHAVIOR

The following patterns of behavior often indicate that a child is having a mental or emotional difficulty. Seek help for the child if the problem persists for more than a few weeks.

- Any sudden, striking change in usual demeanor or behavior, such as loss of interest in usual activities or friendships, change in sleep or eating patterns or school performance.
- Persistent sad mood, low self-worth, and pervasive pessimism or negativity.
- Unexplained lethargy or change in mental alertness.
- Highly changeable moods that appear unrelated to the circumstances in a school-age child.
- Lack of control over behavior, including impulsiveness and aggressiveness out of proportion to the circumstances.
- Inability in a child older than seven or eight to tolerate frustration.

- Highly self-critical and overly controlled behavior, and lack of spontaneity.
- Persistent, extreme shyness and lasting fearfulness of entering into new situations or relationships.
- Withdrawal from or inability to form relationships with friends, siblings, or adults.
- Inability to form relationships with others accompanied by severe delay in language development.
- Persistent difficulty in peer relationships, such as always being picked on by others or picking fights with them.
- Highly distractable behavior at home or at school, with inability to stay focused or attentive, or apparently disorganized behavior that causes problems at school.
- Lack of bladder or bowel control in a child over five or six.
- Sexual behavior that is inappropriate to the child's developmental level (such as public masturbation in a nine-year-old).

children are also qualified to treat adults, the reverse is not usually true; most mental health professionals who treat adults do not have the additional expertise or training necessary to work with children.

Persons seeking referrals to qualified professionals should consult a pediatrician or family physician or the child's school. Other sources of information include the child psychiatry department at the nearest hospital or academic medical center.

As with adults, initial evaluation by a child or adolescent psychiatrist is recommended, because medical assessment of children is especially important when mental health problems are present (see "The Evaluation Process," which follows). Once a diagnosis is made, the psychiatrist will recommend a course of treatment and possibly provide the names of other child mental health professionals in the area who offer that particular kind of treatment. The American Academy of Child and Adolescent Psychiatry (3615 Wisconsin Ave., NW, Washington, D.C. 20016; tel. 202 966–7300) can provide names of qualified child psychiatrists in a specific area and verify the credentials of any who have been recommended.

The Evaluation Process

The evaluation of a child's mental difficulties is necessarily different from that of the adult, as described in chapter 2. For one thing, children are not independent or autonomous; they are reliant on adults and must make do with the school, home, and social environment in which they are born or placed. Usually children do not make the decision to get help; rather, they are referred by the school or sent by their parents, perhaps under protest. It is very common for children initially to deny that they are having the problems that their parents or teachers say they are. Mental health professionals who specialize in the treatment of children are, of course, trained to understand their reactions and symptoms and to communicate with children according to their developmental level. Although a parent's view of the problem may be very different from that of the child (who may insist, perhaps, that the teacher who reported the behavior is lying), the professional must establish a sympathetic alliance with parents and child and is careful not to "take sides." From the start, especially with adolescents, the clinician must also establish that what the child confides in him or her remains confidential.

Professionals perform the evaluation of children in a variety of ways, depending on the age of the child. The assessment process consists of gathering information about the current difficulty from the child and from the parents, possibly also from the school. Some clinicians have parents fill out checklists or use structured (standardized) interviews to gather information from both the parents and the child. In order to understand the child's history, the clinician is usually interested in reviewing the child's entire development, beginning with the mother's pregnancy. (See the box on pages 229–230.) From the parents, in addition to information about problems they are encountering with the child, the professional usually wants to know about child-rearing practices, other children, family life and family stresses, cultural background, and details about their marriage and personal problems, as all these directly affect the child's environment and possibly contribute to the problem.

Equally important is the child's school history (see the box on page 231), because the majority of troubled children exhibit problems in school as well as at home. In addition to asking the child and parents about school performance, the clinician may seek information from the child's teacher.

Drawing, Storytelling, and Playing

During the course of the assessment the evaluating professional will want to spend time with the child alone, without the parents present. To gather information from children, child mental health specialists often use techniques other than direct questioning. For example, some begin their interview by asking the child to draw a picture of anything at all and then to make up a story about it. Through this technique, the clinician will often get the child talking and may detect themes that relate to why the child has been brought for evaluation. Some child specialists ask children to draw a picture of, and tell a story about, a person. These and other techniques may also be used in a more formal testing process (see below).

Also, especially for children who are too young or have significant difficulty putting emotional issues into words, child mental health practitioners use a variety of toys and dolls, as they do in the treatment process itself. (See page 232.) Which of the available toys the child chooses to play with, how he or she plays with them, and what he or she talks about while playing reveal important information about the child's state of mind, troubles, and developmental level.

Additional Psychological Testing

The professional may recommend formal psychological testing to complete or supplement the evaluation process. These tests are generally provided by clinical psychologists who specialize in testing and who later provide a written report to the clinician that may include specific recommendations for the type of remedial help the child may need.

There are two broad types of psychological tests: objective and projective. (For information on some specific types of tests, see chapter 2.)

Objective tests. These types of tests assess a child's specific functioning in numerous areas and determine where he or she stands in relation to same-age children. Through the use of these tests, it is often possible to pinpoint specific deficits that require remediation. Such tests may include measures of intellectual ability (IQ), academic skills, and abilities in specific areas where there seem to be problems (such as ability to pay attention or problems with speech). Numerous tests have been developed for use on children at all levels of development, including infancy. (For example, the Bayley Scales of Infant Development provides an overview of the developmental status of a child from age two months to two and a half years.)

Projective tests. These are used to evaluate personality and areas of psychic conflict for the child. They are not diagnostic or predictive, in that their results do not place anyone in any specific category of illness or provide information about how a child is likely to perform in the future. Rather, from their results the testing psychologist makes various inferences about the nature of the child's thoughts and feelings and confusions at the present time. This information supplements material that the clinician derives from the history and evaluation process but should never be used in lieu of it.

Drawing and storytelling tests are common projective tests, although many researchers and clinicians question their use diagnostically. The child may be asked to tell a story in conjunction with drawing a picture of a person (as mentioned earlier), of a whole family, or of a house, a tree, and a person. From the nature of the drawings and the stories, the tester gathers information about the child's notions about the body, attitudes toward self and family, ideas about gender, aggressive feelings, and so on. Other tests that offer similar types of information include the Rorschach test, in which children are shown inkblot shapes and asked to describe what they are (chapter 2, see page 26); and the thematic apperception test (TAT; chapter 2, page 26) or child's apperception test (CAT), in which the child views cards depicting a variety of scenes or animal cartoons and tells a story about them. These tests, too, are not acceptable evaluation instruments to all child mental health professionals.

Medical Evaluation

It is very common for children who have some kinds of physical illnesses or injuries to exhibit psychiatric symptoms. (See chapter 20.) Evidence suggests that neurological problems often are present in children with behavior and learning difficulties. Malnutrition and lead poisoning can cause learning and behavior problems. Children who cannot hear or see properly also may misbehave or withdraw. Use of mind-altering substances also produces a wide range of mental and physical problems. Therefore, to rule out any physical cause for a child's emotional or behavioral problems, a physical examination is extremely important. Some child psychiatrists perform the examination themselves; others work with the child's pediatrician.

MENTAL HEALTH TREATMENT FOR CHILDREN

Many types of interventions have been designed to treat children with the full range of emotional and mental disorders. All have as a goal the relief of symptoms and promotion of the child's development. All, in various ways, enable children to cope better in their lives. Many forms of psychotherapy used for adults that have been discussed at great length in chapter 4 have been adapted for use in children, as we describe below. Psychiatric drugs (chapter 5) also are used for various mental disorders in children. Although we discuss the common approaches to psychotherapy and to pharmacological treatment separately, in fact drugs and psychotherapy often are used together, and many psychotherapists apply principles of many types of therapy in their treatment, depending on the nature of the child's problems.

How Child Treatment Differs from Adult Treatment

Although the treatment of both children and adults attempt to relieve suffering and enhance the individual's abilities to cope in life, there are necessarily some differences. Not least is the motivation for treatment; most often, adults choose to get help, while children are sent by authority figures whom they are obliged to obey. The goal of the treatment may be to make children more acceptable to parents and teachers. Children may enter treatment feeling angry and/or guilty and bad.

Also substantially different is the role of the therapist. In psychodynamic therapies for adults (chapter 4), the clinician sometimes appears quite passive. In child therapies, the therapist always plays an active role.

Relationship Between Therapist and Parents

Parents are always a part of a child's treatment to some degree, whether it is family therapy in which everyone attends or an individual therapy for the child alone. Especially with younger children, usually the therapist meets with parents and child together at times, or with the parents separately from time to time. The treatment itself ordinarily involves the parents directly, if only to help them become more aware of the child's needs. Indeed, one of the major roles of the mental health professional who works with children is to help explain the child's behavior to the parents and to help children understand their parents' feelings and concerns.

For very young children, parent counseling may be the extent of the treatment. In the treatment of an anxious preschooler, for example, the mental health professional may teach the mother how to become more sensitive to the child and to respond to his or her needs. For conduct problems in older children,

DEVELOPMENTAL AND PAST HISTORY

Depending on the nature of the child's problems, a complete history-taking process can include questions about the mother's pregnancy, the child's birth and infancy, and a detailed overview of the child's entire development, as follows:

Pregnancy and Delivery

Pregnancy

- Past pregnancies, abortions, miscarriages
- Mother's age and health during pregnancy
- Complications of pregnancy
  —medications
  —bleeding
  —accidents
  —excessive weight gain, or weight loss
  —X rays
  —toxemia (high blood pressure, seizures)
  —major illness (diabetes, heart disease)
  —history of measles, venereal disease, urinary infections, vomiting, or Rh negativity
- Addictive habits during pregnancy
  —smoking
  —drug abuse
  —alcohol abuse
- Family attitudes and social stressors
  —Was the pregnancy planned?
  —What sex was preferred?
  —How was the name selected?
  —What was the family going through at that time?

Delivery

- Type of delivery
- Length and type of labor
- Complications
- Anesthesia

Birth and Infancy

Birth

- Apgar scores
- Birth weight
- Complications
  —need for resuscitation, respiratory distress
  —prematurity, blood transfusions
  —jaundice, cyanosis
  —congenital defects or stigmata
  —medications

Infancy

- Undue sleepiness
- Medical problems
- Weak cry, colics
- Did the mother suffer postpartum depression?
- Was the child a twin (identical, fraternal)?
- How long did mother and child remain in the hospital?
- Reaction of siblings

Developmental History

Gross Motor

- When could child keep his or her head up?
- When did he or she crawl, sit, stand with support, stand without support, walk, hop, throw a ball, roller skate, ride a bicycle?
- Was child clumsy or poorly coordinated, or accident-prone?
- Is child overactive or underactive?

Fine Motor

- Pincer grasp, using cup and utensils
- Ability to draw, write, handle small objects, play piano, clap hands, tie shoelaces, use scissors

Language and Communication

- Babbling
- First words
- First phrases
- First sentences, clarity of speech vocabulary, stuttering, lisping
- Delayed speech, echolalia (echoing what is said by others)
- How many languages spoken at home?
- Gestures and postural movements in communication; cadence, rhythm of speech
- Language comprehension and expression when following simple commands
- Confusion or garbled speech and thinking

Personal-Social Behavior

- Feeding
  —breast- or bottle-fed? reaction to weaning?
  —food regurgitation and rumination
  —finicky, over- or undereating, vomiting, pica (eating nonfood substances)
  —food allergies, likes or dislikes

(Continued)

—food habits and dietary intake
—self-feeding
—thumb sucking
—excessive biting or rumination
- Toilet training
—When, how, and by whom was child toilet trained?
—When was child trained day and night for bladder and bowel control?
—constipation, diarrhea, colics, and enemas
—Any bowel movement accidents or bedwetting? When? How often?
- Sexual attitudes
—sexual abuse or excessive visual sexual exposure
—When was child curious about sexual differences? How was this handled?
—Is child well identified with his or her sex? Any history of worrisome cross-dressing, effeminacy, or sexual practices? Response to opposite sex
—family attitudes and reactions to masturbation
—parental attitudes and practices regarding nudity and sex in the household
—sleeping arrangements
—nature and frequency of sex play
—reactions to sexual body changes in puberty; when did they occur?
—sexual or endocrinological anatomical difficulties
- Sleeping
—sleeping habits
—nightmares, sleep talking, sleepwalking, insomnia, early-morning awakening, night terrors
—fear of the dark
—Does child sleep alone? If not, with whom and where in the household?
- Social interactions
—Was child a cuddly infant?
—Style and temperament of relating to peers, siblings, teachers, parents, and other family members?
—How and with whom does child play (content and quality of sharing)? How does he or she get along with others?
—best friend

—interest in group activities versus individual activities
—Aggressive behavior, leadership abilities; is child scapegoated, the clown of the class, shy?
—Responses to separations and baby-sitters?
—Age of playmates; does he or she get along better with younger children or with older children and adults?
—Overly sensitive, overly competitive, cruel with others, bossy, distant, provocative
—Is child gregarious or withdrawn?
—Is child moody, appropriate, constricted, labile, explosive?
- Habits and fears (when, where, how severe)
—head banging, temper tantrums
—rocking
—thumb sucking
—fire setting
—lying
—stealing
—nail biting
—animal cruelty
—tics
—bruxism (teeth grinding)
—hair pulling
—phobias, fears
—substance abuse
—How much television does child watch? What are his or her favorite programs?
—Is child overly concerned about death and dying?
—inappropriate or unusual behavior
- Adaptive behaviors
—ability of child to cope with situations of stress
—malleability, frustration tolerance, ability to delay gratification
—ability to adjust to new situations
—ability to use experience in the solution of new problems
—sports, favorite hobbies, and games
—clubs or groups child belongs to

Source: Adapted from Ian A. Canino, "Taking a History," in *The Clinical Guide to Child Psychiatry*, edited by David Shaffer, Anke A. Ehrhardt, and Laurence L. Greenhill (New York: The Free Press, 1985), pp. 398–400. Reprinted with the permission of The Free Press, a Division of Macmillan, Inc. Copyright © 1985 by David Shaffer, Anke A. Ehrhardt, Laurence L. Greenhill.

SCHOOL HISTORY

Most children with mental or emotional disturbances have problems in performance or behavior in school. Therefore, once a child is old enough to attend school, the evaluating professional needs to gather information from parent, child, and teacher in the following areas.

Parent and Child

- How did the child react to his or her first day of school? Were there any separation problems?
- Is there a history of school phobia or truancy?
- Have there been many school changes?
- Has the child performed consistently, or has he or she gone through ups and down in performance?
- What are his or her grades?
- What classes does he or she enjoy the most? Which does he or she dislike the most, and why?
- Does he or she dislike any particular teacher?
- Is the school or present teacher adequate for the child's particular needs?
- What is the attitude of the parents toward the school, and what is the previous history of the parents' own school experiences?
- Did he or she have to repeat any class? Is he or she in a special class?

Teacher

- Is the child:
  - —quarrelsome
  - —submissive
  - —excitable
  - —a daydreamer
  - —squirmy
  - —a smart aleck
  - —easily hurt
  - —a leader, popular
  - —a follower
  - —scapegoated
  - —immature, sensitive
  - —easily frustrated
  - —uncooperative
  - —organized
  - —overactive
  - —stubborn
  - —fearful
  - —clumsy
  - —moody
- Does the child have learning difficulties? In which areas?
- How does the child get along with other children?
- What are the child's cognitive strengths and weaknesses?
- Does the child work well by him- or herself?
- In what classes is the child doing well and in which is he or she doing poorly? Describe the classes the child participates in.
- Does he or she have many teachers? What are the other teachers like? Does he or she have a favorite teacher or a teacher he or she particularly dislikes?
- Does the child enjoy or avoid gym and sports?
- Is the child involved in extracurricular activities? Which?
- Have there been many changes in the school administration and philosophy?
- Is there a high teacher turnover?
- Is the school safe? What type of neighborhood?
- Is the school public or private? Is it coed or not?

Source: Adapted from Ian A. Canino, "Taking a History," in *The Clinical Guide to Child Psychiatry*, edited by David Shaffer, Anke A. Ehrhardt, and Laurence L. Greenhill (New York: The Free Press, 1985), pp. 405–406. Reprinted with the permission of The Free Press, a Division of Macmillan, Inc. Copyright © 1985 by David Shaffer, Anke A. Ehrhardt, Laurence L. Greenhill.

the professional may work with the parents to design better techniques for discipline and limit-setting. Frequently a therapist works with the parent on ways to change the child's environment, such as by changing schools. Often, when children are responding to problems in the parents' lives, such as depression, divorce, or drug abuse problems, the child mental health professional needs to counsel the adult directly or refer him or her for help.

In family therapy (see page 233), the parents and children (including siblings) are seen together, and their problems in life and styles of interaction are viewed as all interrelated.

Relationship Between Therapist and Child

Despite the parental involvement in child treatment and the child's lack of choice in going for treatment, mental health professionals who treat children work hard to establish a relationship in which the young people can trust and confide in them. They generally do not reveal private material to parents or others without the child's permission. It is especially important that older children recognize that their privacy is assured (unless they are dangerous to themselves or others) and that the therapist is not there to punish them or to make them behave.

The therapist becomes a kind of parent or teacher figure for the child. Although this happens also in the treatment of adults, with children it is much more the actual rather than the imagined role of the therapist in the patient's life.

The Use of Play

In play treatment, therapists rely on symbolic means of communicating with children and finding out what is on their minds rather than using the same kinds of dialogue that are appropriate ways of helping adults. Dolls representing people of various ages, toys, games, and art supplies are among the tools a play therapist uses to assess and treat the child's problems in a variety of treatment settings. For example, a child may use dolls to enact a sexually abusive scene that he or she was unable to verbalize. A child who is having trouble with aggressive or jealous feelings might pick up a lion and mention that it wants to eat its baby sister. When rehearsing a new behavior, a child often "teaches" a puppet how to behave differently, as he or she is presently learning. Children often identify with various dolls or figures, and say such things as "He likes himself a lot more today." With paints or crayons, children can draw imaginary figures about whom they can make up stories that reveal their own fears and conflicts. Storytelling figures prominently in most children's repertoires, and through made-up stories they can let loose their wishes and fantasies that are important in psychodynamic-type therapies.

Therapists who use these techniques believe that drawing and storytelling can both help the child express difficulties and teach him or her new ways to cope. For example, Jimmy T., seven, drew a picture of a tiny boy being attacked by huge dinosaurs. His therapist looked at the picture and said that the little boy in the picture was feeling very small and weak and frightened. He asked Jimmy what the little boy was scared of. Then the therapist suggested that Jimmy draw a picture in which the little boy turned the dinosaur into a puppy and took it home to be his pet. They proceeded to talk about how Jimmy sometimes

feels so frightened, but that there are things he can do to cope with scary situations.

Supportive Psychotherapy

As with adults (chapter 4), supportive therapy helps children to express their feelings, improve their self-esteem, and cope better with what is happening in the present, without urging painful self-awareness or dramatic change. The goal is to restore the child to appropriate functioning. The therapist often offers advice and instruction on finding solutions to specific problems. Frequently the therapist's role also includes educating the child and family about an experience they are going through.

In this broad category of therapies also fall crisis intervention and short-term goal-directed treatments for such situations as coping with parents' divorce, impending surgery, or other traumatic experience.

Psychodynamic Psychotherapy

The many types of long-term (a year or more) or short-term (three to six months) therapies that comprise the psychodynamic psychotherapy are used most commonly for both children and adults. Explained at length in chapter 4, these therapies are derived from psychoanalysis, an intensive psychotherapy that explores the child's unrecognized conflicts that produce troubled behavior. The therapist helps children recognize their feelings, such as anger or fear, of which they may be quite unaware, even though they are acting destructively. ("The dog in the picture is barking at the other dogs so they won't recognize that he's scared of them himself. Perhaps when you get into fights at school, you're really feeling scared yourself.") Through the therapeutic process, children develop the ability to look at themselves and their behavior in ways that are appropriate to their age, to understand that they are responsible for what they do, to recognize what they are feeling, and to translate needs into words rather than to act them out.

Behavior or Cognitive/Behavior Therapy

Behavior therapy works directly to change specific behaviors. Professionals who specialize in behavior therapy do not think it is helpful to explore what might have produced the behavior. Other types of therapy often include some of the techniques of behavior therapy to help deal with a specific behavioral problem.

As explained in chapter 4, behavior therapy offers numerous techniques of changing troubled behaviors and replacing them with more adaptive ones. Techniques of behavior therapy are used to help children with temper tantrums, teens with substance abuse disorders to change their habits, to train children to overcome intense fears and phobias and shyness, to teach them how to control impulsive or angry behavior, to train them to control their bladder, and to help them learn to read despite learning disabilities. Behavior therapy also is used in the treatment of stuttering and asthma.

In the assessment process, the behavior therapist focuses on examples of the problem behavior, especially on the events that seem to precede them and on how the people around the child respond. Behavior therapy is based on the principle that many problem behaviors are inadvertently rewarded, which is why they persist. The behavior therapist works to devise ways to provide rewards for desirable behaviors. For the child who does not complete his or her homework, the therapist may first collect information on all the steps in the process beginning with receiving the assignment to handing it in. Upon discovering that the problem begins when the child fails to write the assignment down, for example, the therapist then might design a system of rewards for the child who successfully learns to record the necessary tasks.

Some of the many techniques of behavior therapy of children include systematic desensitization, time out, cognitive/behavioral techniques, and modeling.

Systematic desensitization. A method of dealing with fears and phobias, this technique is used to expose the child gradually to what he or she fears, in the presence of the therapist, until the fear response is overcome. For example, over a period of weeks a child who is scared of going into dark rooms may be encouraged, first, to step into a pretend closet while holding the therapist's hand, then to go toward a closet in the office but just to stand at the door. Eventually the child will be able to open the door and go in by him- or herself.

Time out. Behavior therapy uses rewards and punishment to reinforce appropriate behavior. An effective punishment is the time-out technique, in which the child who misbehaves is warned that if or when the behavior recurs, he or she will be removed to a specific time-out area. A clock is set for a brief amount of time, and the child stays there until the time is up. It is essential that the child know in advance what will lead to a time out and that the treatment not be given for too many behaviors at the same time.

Cognitive/behavioral techniques. These include methods of thinking and verbalizing the steps in problem solving. For example, an easily distracted child might be trained to catch him- or herself turning away from homework and to say: "I must stop and think here." (See also the next section.)

Modeling. Children often respond well to imitating the way other children overcome the same problems. A shy child may be able to go up and talk to another child once he or she observes another onceshy child doing the same thing.

Other techniques of behavior therapy are detailed in chapter 4.

Cognitive Therapy

Cognitive therapy, developed originally as a short-term treatment for depression (see chapter 4), helps older children especially understand the thinking processes that lead to bad feelings and poor performance. For example, a teenager may conclude that because her boyfriend broke up with her, she will never have another boyfriend. The therapist might point out that this type of thinking ("I'll never . . .") leads to poor feelings about oneself and one's future, and techniques are taught to help the youngster change what he or she is thinking about. Chapter 4, page 54, provides a list of common errors in thinking that are applicable to adolescents as well as to adults.

Family Therapy

Family therapy treats the whole family rather than simply the child who has the symptoms. Family therapy (see chapter 4) holds that the symptomatic individual is part of the whole family system and that the child's problems reflects the family's problems. Although there are many approaches to family treatment, usually the therapy looks at family values, methods of communication, alliances within the family, gender roles, and roles and expectations of members of the different generations. Sometimes the effective treatment for a troubled child combines both family and individual approaches. Family therapy is particularly useful for rebellious and oppositional teenagers and in situations where there are many family disagreements.

Group Therapy

Particularly among adolescents, or for children who share a common illness or disability, going for treatment in a small group can be a very effective way of understanding problems that they share, learning how to overcome them, recognizing how their behavior affects others, and learning how to behave among their peers. As with family therapy, there are many approaches to this kind of treatment. Groups for children who abuse drugs allow the group to support each member's efforts and learn to deal with shared problems (such as how to socialize without drugs). Groups of children with a shared disability (such as diabetes) also can provide support, an opportunity to share pain and disappointment, as well as education in how to manage this lifelong problem.

It is quite common for children to receive both individual and group treatment.

Pharmacological Treatment

As is noted in the chapters that follow, psychiatric medication is used extremely effectively for some childhood and adolescent mental disorders, for example, attention-deficit hyperactivity disorder (ADHD; see chapter 18), depression, certain anxiety disorders, and schizophrenia. These drugs are not prescribed just to relieve minor or transient symptoms; that is, the child who is hyperactive occasionally would not receive medication unless he or she met the diagnostic criteria for ADHD. Likewise, a teenager who felt anxious only when getting ready for a date would not likely be prescribed tranquilizers. However, an adolescent who is anxious in many situations might respond well to such medication. When it is used properly, medication can be an enormous help to an afflicted child.

Medication usually is offered in conjunction with psychotherapy. Although any medical doctor can prescribe medication, it is advisable for parents to seek such treatment from a qualified child psychiatrist, who is trained in the use of psychiatric medications. This expertise is necessary not only to diagnose the child's mental disorder properly but also to choose the type of medication and the appropriate dosage that are best suited to that disorder and that child.

Parents and the child should be sure to talk to the psychiatrist about how the drug works (some drugs, such as antidepressants, take a few weeks to work), what are its benefits, and what are its drawbacks. For example, even though all drugs have side effects, some may be troubling over the long term, as with antipsychotic drugs. (See chapter 5.) Fears about drug therapy should be aired too, because the psychiatrist can usually offset them. Some parents, for example, are reluctant to have their children take psychiatric medications, for fear that the children then will be more likely to get involved with illicit drugs. The psychiatrist will reassure them, however, that there is no increased incidence of drug use among children or adolescents who receive psychiatric medication for a diagnosed mental disorder. Indeed, children whose problems are properly treated may have less reason to self-medicate with street drugs. With the exception of tranquilizers, psychiatric medications are not dependency-producing.

Some children receive medication from a psychiatrist while receiving therapy from a nonmedical mental health professional. In such cases, the psychotherapist also should be informed about the effects and possible ill effects of the drug in order to spot problems. Parents sometimes may wish to inform the school or the school nurse as well.

Use of medication in children and adolescents generally begins at very low dosage, with a gradual buildup to an effective level. For children who are on long-term drug treatment, periodic discontinuation of the medication usually is advised, to determine whether the medication is still needed and to assess side effects. Tapering slowly off the drug usually is recommended as the safest way to stop.

TREATMENT SETTINGS

Children are seen most often in outpatient settings, either at clinics or in a therapist's private office. Hospitalization or other residential treatment or day treatment is sometimes warranted, however. Treatment is provided or is coordinated around schooling and recreational opportunities for the child.

Hospital Treatment

Children require hospitalization under the following circumstances:

- When they are dangerous to themselves or others, such as those who are suicidal, violent toward others, or who have an eating disorder that seriously threatens their life;
- When they are out of control or unmanageable in an outpatient setting, as with disturbed children who persistently run away, who are dangerously hyperactive, or who refuse to eat;
- When their behavior is deteriorating, as with a depressed child who no longer will get out of bed or go to school, or the child with schizophrenia who is having delusions;
- When the diagnosis remains unclear and requires the facilities and 24-hour personnel of the hospital.

Increasingly, hospitalization tends to be short term, from days to weeks, until the child is stabilized, effective treatment is established, or the child can be transferred to a longer-term residential facility. In most cases, psychiatric hospitalization of children and adolescents includes individual care as well as group therapy with other children who are hospitalized.

Residential and Day Treatment

Residential and day treatment settings are useful for children in drug treatment (see chapter 9), for some children with psychotic disorders, and for individuals who are developmentally disabled. Most often, however, residential treatment sites are provided for children who have been removed from their homes for conduct problems and who have not been helped in other settings. Personality and behavior change is the goal, and the environment often simulates that of a family, but one that is functional and sets strict limits on behavior.

CAUSES OF YOUNG PEOPLES' EMOTIONAL PROBLEMS AND DISORDERS

Experts used to seek the roots of children's problems primarily in their environments, especially in their relationships with their parents. Today it is believed that most disorders result from numerous interrelated factors: biological, psychological, and sociopsychological (the results of a child's culture, school, playmates, the media, and so on).

Genetic Predisposition

Inheritance seems to play a strong role in some disorders, including enuresis (bedwetting), schizophrenia, developmental disabilities, and possibly certain mood and anxiety disorders. Genes generally do not confer a certainty that the problem will be inherited. Rather, they produce a susceptibility.

Temperament

Inheritance may also influence behavior through its role in determining temperament. Temperament refers to a child's inborn reaction pattern or style, such as a child's way of responding to new situations. (For example, some children readily explore while others hold back.) Some theorists believe that behavior problems can arise when there is a poor fit between the temperaments of the child and the parents. For example, some parents may be delighted with a child who appears sensitive and cautious, while others feel more comfortable with one who is active and exuberant. Some parents react with anger and rejection to a child whose temperament does not match their own or fit their expectations, or they may not be able to recognize the child's individual needs. Others may feel that the child's temperament difficulties are in some way their fault; this guilt may cause them to be hesitant and inconsistent with the child, which may lead to further problems.

Limited Intelligence and Brain Injury

Severe psychiatric problems are common in children with limited intelligence (such as mentally retarded individuals) and brain injuries (such as those with cerebral palsy and epilepsy or who have suffered falls or infections of the brain, as in encephalitis).

Environmental Factors

The important environmental influences on behavior are family problems, such as marital conflict, and the direct experience of psychologically traumatic events (such as involvement in a destructive fire or other disaster, witnessing the death of a parent, or sexual abuse). Certain aspects of how parents bring up their children are also influential. These include, for example, the extent to which the parents set limits on their child's behavior and their ability to express affection toward their child.

Sometimes it is difficult to tell to what extent parents contribute to a child's behavior and to what extent the child has evoked certain attitudes in the parents. For example, parents of anxious and dependent children are often overprotective, but they may be reacting to rather than causing the behavior.

Mental Disorder in the Parent

The likelihood that a child will have a mental disorder increases dramatically when a parent also suffers from mental illness. While some of this increased risk may result from genetic transmission, parents who are disturbed create a disturbed environment for the child. Illness in the parent often means the mother or father is preoccupied with his or her own problems, or with the partner's problems, or is absent for treatment. Unhappy marriages and disagreements over how to raise the child are extremely common when a parent has mental health problems; these problems can have deleterious consequences for the child's own development and mental health.

As mental health professionals who treat adults become more aware of these risks to children, they are likely to suggest early intervention on behalf of the young people, before their mental health is compromised and their possibilities in life are limited unnecessarily. Parents who battle with mental disorder can help prevent the same suffering in their children by getting help for themselves and for the whole family.

No matter what the cause of a child's mental health problems, numerous forms of intervention and help are available that will make life easier for the child and for the family.

17

Developmental Disabilities and Common Emotional and Behavioral Problems of Preschool Children

Gail A. Wasserman, Ph.D.

The younger the child, the more difficult it can be for parents to detect whether he or she is behaving or developing normally. Is the child's troubling or troublesome behavior a transitory phase or a sign that something is wrong with him or her? Children under five are in the process of acquiring the basic intellectual, emotional, and muscular skills that will allow them to perceive, respond to, and negotiate the world around them. To judge whether their behavior is normal, it needs to be understood both within the context of what is typical of children at each stage of development and what is the nature of each individual child. No child develops along a strict developmental yardstick; each grows and changes in his or her own way.

Early detection of the developmental, emotional, and behavioral problems that afflict young children can help them to continue on their developmental course and prevent future difficulties. In the case of children who are mentally retarded or autistic, early detection can enable parents to minimize the consequences to the child and to access opportunities that can allow him or her to progress beyond initial expectations. Therefore, this chapter is intended to acquaint parents of preschool children with signs that a problem exists, types of treatments offered, and how to cope or come to terms with the child's needs.

The major developmental disabilities (mental retardation and autism) are covered first; although they are usually lifelong problems, they are discussed here primarily in the context of the young child and, of course, the family. The next sections are devoted to the emotional and behavioral problems for which parents often seek pediatric or mental health consultation for their preschool children, including: language and articulation disorders (such as stuttering); intense fears, shyness, and anxieties; aggressive behavior; hyperactivity; eating, sleeping, and toileting disorders; and finally difficulties with sexuality and gender identity. Developmentally disabled children are vulnerable to these problems as well.

Developmental Disabilities

The "Early Developmental Milestones" box on page 239 details the progressive stages through which children are expected to proceed usually well before they are four years old. Although many children demonstrate particular abilities before or after the average age of acquisition, those with developmental disabilities—mental retardation and autism—learn and progress at such a slow pace that they may never acquire the necessary thinking, social, or self-care skills that children must have to begin to adapt to the demands of human life.

MENTAL RETARDATION

An estimated 1 to 3 percent of children do not develop the cognitive (thinking, learning, and problem-solving) capacities that are normal for their age. These children are usually termed "mentally retarded" or "developmentally delayed." These terms generally apply to children who test at 70 or below on standard intelligence tests (a score of 80 to 130 is considered normal intelligence; 100 is average).

The American Association on Mental Deficiency defines mental retardation as "significantly subaverage general intellectual functioning" accompanied by "deficits in adaptive behavior." In other words, mental retardation is characterized by the inability of a child to achieve the independence and perform the social skills expected of his or her chronological age group.

The infant who is mentally retarded is slow in many areas of development, particularly in those related to responsiveness to others and interest in the surrounding environment. Smiling, reacting to sound

EARLY DEVELOPMENTAL MILESTONES

Although every child develops at a different rate, individual progress can be rated according to the following common milestones. These are averages, however, not "deadlines" that necessarily spell difficulties if your child fails to achieve a particular skill by the stated age.

By 4 Months

- Takes an interest in the world and a special interest in the caregiver.
- Responds to sights and sounds as well as to interaction with others.
- Smiles when spoken to or in response to facial expressions; begins to vocalize back by cooing when spoken to.
- Enjoys touch and being cuddled.
- Follows the movement of objects or persons and will turn head in the direction of a pleasant sound.
- Can hold small objects.
- Can lift head and holds head steady when sitting supported on a lap.
- Will sleep for four hours or more at night.

By 8 Months

- Begins to learn how things work and communicates reactions.
- Interacts with caregiver by smiling and responding to her or him. Will begin, for example, to raise arms to be picked up.
- Responds to simple social games such as peek-a-boo or pat-a-cake.
- Will reach out for toys and other objects.
- Shows interest in and cautiousness of new people.
- Focuses on toys or people for longer periods of time.
- Begins to explore the world around him or her with interest and by interacting with it.
- Can pick up small objects.
- Can drink from a cup or glass held by an adult.
- Makes sounds and begins repeating them.
- Can sit unsupported and plays from that position.
- Can creep or crawl.
- Can pull to a standing position in the crib.

By 12 Months

- Begins to initiate complex interactions—hands parents a toy to make it work, rolls a ball, uses gestures to communicate or demand desired objects.
- Uses behavior to establish closeness, such as clinging to a parent's leg.
- Responds to a parent's tone of voice.
- Play becomes more focused and longer.
- Can copy simple gestures—waving bye-bye, shaking the head "yes" or "no."

- Uses hands or eyes to examine a new object or toy. Can throw a ball.
- Looks at simple pictures in a book with help.
- Can feed self small finger food.
- Can walk holding on to furniture.
- Understands simple words and commands.
- Uses sounds for specific objects.

By 18 Months

- Shows intentional planning and exploration in interactions and play.
- Communicates needs and feelings using gestures and words.
- Uses simple two-word sentences and understands simple questions.
- Balances a desire for independence with that of closeness (for example, explores across the room and then comes back for a touch or cuddle).
- Shows assertiveness through behaviors. Can show anger using voice and gesture without having to cry, hit, or bite.
- Uses pretend play or role playing as part of play (cooking with pots, driving toy cars). Plays independently.
- Recognizes pictures of familiar objects. Can do simple shape puzzles. Plays with blocks. Can copy a circle.
- Can balance momentarily on one foot and jump with both feet off the ground. Is able to run.

By 3 to 3½ Years

- Pretend play becomes more complex. Involves themes such as closeness, nurturing, or caretaking as well as assertiveness, exploration, or aggression.
- Knows what is real and what is not.
- Follows rules.
- Realizes how behavior, thoughts, and feelings can be related to consequences.
- Interacts in socially appropriate way with adults and peers.
- Can draw more complex pictures, such as a woman with facial features.
- Can walk up stairs using alternating feet.
- Can kick a large ball or catch it using both hands.
- Sentences become complex with logical connecting words.
- Begins to ask "why?" although is not necessarily interested in the answer.

Source: Adapted with permission from Stanley I. Greenspan, "Emotional and Developmental Patterns in Infancy," in *Handbook of Clinical Assessment of Children and Adolescents*, edited by Clarice J. Kestenbaum and Daniel T. Williams (New York: New York University Press, 1988).

or visual stimulation, and reaching out for comforting or to grasp toys or other objects are abilities that usually are delayed in retarded children.

Many children who are retarded also suffer from numerous physical health problems as well, including congenital heart problems, seizures, and problems with hearing, for example. Many do not live to or beyond middle age, often because they do not receive adequate care. Mental health problems are also very common. (See below.)

How Mental Retardation Is Classified

Mental retardation is not a specific disease that a child has or does not have; it is, rather, a multidimensional condition that encompasses wide variations in behavior and ability. Several classification systems are used to determine a child's level of retardation. Classification is a useful tool that can help in predicting the type and intensity of training and education services that might be most helpful to a child. However, parents, teachers, and physicians should keep in mind that no classification system can foretell with certainty the full developmental potential of any mentally retarded child.

The American Association on Mental Deficiency lists four categories of retardation, ranging in levels from mild to profound. Approximately 85 percent of retarded children fall into the mild range (IQ 50 to 70). While they may require special education, eventually (as late as their teens) they will be able to learn to read and count, and can be helped to achieve some degree of independence later in life. Those in the moderate range (IQ 35 to 49) can manage to take care of themselves and work to some degree if they can live in sheltered or supervised settings. Children with severe retardation (IQ 20 to 34) may be able to learn elementary self-care, but usually have great difficulty with motor and language skills and generally do not benefit from vocational training. The profoundly retarded (IQ below 20) may never be toilet-trained or use language. They require complete care throughout their lives.

Another classification system is based on receptiveness to education: The "educable mentally retarded" (EMR) are those who are judged to be capable of academic achievement on a third- to sixth-grade level, with IQs generally falling in the 50 to 75 range. "Trainable mental retarded" (TMR) children, with IQs of 30 to 50, generally do not develop academic skills beyond a second-grade level.

Diagnosing Mental Retardation

Retardation is sometimes apparent at or even before birth. Prenatal testing can reveal some congenital forms of retardation, including Down's syndrome. (See page 241.) Children with Down's syndrome and some other forms of retardation also have an abnormal physical appearance and other obvious birth defects, which can help establish an early diagnosis.

In most cases, however, because many normal children develop at a slow pace, doctors often take a wait-and-see approach to making a diagnosis of mild retardation. (This waiting period can be agonizing for the parents; see the box on page 245.) Usually, by the second or third year, and almost always before children reach school age, the presence of mental retardation can be determined through the use of psychological and physical tests. Sometimes examination detects other causes for a child's slowed development, including defective hearing, which can delay the acquisition of communication and learning skills. (See page 246.)

It is important to note that the 70-IQ-or-below definition of retardation is somewhat arbitrary. There are children who test below 70 who are capable of leading independent, productive lives. (Indeed, some studies have shown that children from disadvantaged backgrounds or foreign cultures who test below 70 actually have normal IQs once their scores are adjusted to reflect testing biases.) Conversely, there are children who test above 70 but who do not perform at the equivalent level as their same-age peers. Therefore, a child's ability to function, the socioeconomic factors that have shaped his or her life, and the cultural milieu in which a child has been raised must all be considered before a diagnosis is made.

Causes

There are hundreds of known causes of and risk factors for mental retardation, including chromosomal abnormalities (as in Down's syndrome; see the next section), inherited illnesses (such as Tay-Sachs disease), birth injuries, low birth weight and extreme prematurity, hormonal disorders, prenatal infections (such as rubella [German measles] in the first trimester), prenatal nutritional deficiencies, and the mother's use of toxic substances such as cocaine or alcohol. After birth, emotional and physical deprivation of the child, severe malnutrition, brain injury from accidents (falls and near drownings, for example), lead poisoning, and infections (such as meningitis) can all contribute. However, in the majority of cases, the cause of a child's retardation remains unknown.

COPING WITH BEING TOLD THAT YOUR CHILD IS RETARDED

- Remember that your baby, although disabled, is a person with hopes, dreams, rights, and dignity.
- If your friends seem to be avoiding you or seem confused about what to say, understand that most people do not know what to tell you or how to help you. Understand too that some people have little skill in expressing empathy and feeling concern for others.
- Make contact with organizations such as the Association for Retarded Citizens (page 245). Ask to meet other parents of children with retarded children to talk about how they first felt and how they now feel about having a retarded child.
- Accept the full range of your feelings, including guilt, anger, sorrow, and disappointment. These feelings are normal; do not be ashamed of them or of your child.
- Before you can help your child, you may have to come to terms with your loss of the normal child you had hoped to have.
- Although your child has extraordinary needs, do not allow them to shut out the needs of your spouse and other family members. These will be difficult days for everyone.
- Expect good days and bad as you struggle to meet all the problems and feelings that continually face you. Coping with this lifelong situation is difficult and challenging.

Down's Syndrome

The most common form of mental retardation is Down's syndrome, a chromosomal disorder that occurs in about 1 of every 700 births. In many cases, mental development appears to progress normally from birth to about age six months, then stops or regresses. In addition to decreased mental functioning, most children with Down's are born with distinct facial and physical irregularities that can include lack of muscle tone, a small flattened skull, high cheekbones, a protruding tongue, and Asian-shape eyes (which accounts for the former term for this form of

retardation: mongoloidism). In all there are over 100 physical features associated with Down's, although it is very rare for one individual to be affected by all of them.

Causes

Several distinct chromosomal aberrations can cause the disorder. Individuals with *trisomy 21* have 47 chromosomes in every cell instead of the normal complement of 46; they are born with an extra chromosome number 21. This form of Down's is the most common (occurring in about 95 percent of cases) and is not genetically conferred. Some children have an extra chromosome 21, but because of the fusion of other chromosomes, still have the normal 46 chromosomes. Called *translocation,* this form of Down's is inheritable. The parents of a child with this form of Down's should be tested to see if one or the other is a carrier of the gene that causes this condition, and be counseled on the implications for bearing future children. Children whose condition is caused by *mosaicism* (about 1 percent of cases) have a mix of cells—some normal, some with an additional chromosome 21. Children whose syndrome is caused by this genetic arrangement usually have fewer Down's syndrome features and function more closely to normal. No matter what the genetic cause, however, researchers do not know why the chromosomal aberration occurs. Some studies have suggested that it may be caused by pregnancy occurring in later age (although two-thirds of all children with Down's syndrome are born to mothers under 35) or because of maternal exposure to such environmental toxins as X-ray radiation.

Rate of Development

As in other forms of mental retardation, children with Down's syndrome are developmentally delayed compared to other children their age. During the first few months of life, children with this condition are quieter and less responsive than their peers with normal intelligence. Because of low muscle tone, their motor coordination also lags behind. However, most children with Down's begin to respond during the second half of their first year. They smile readily at caregivers, babble, and begin to be able to sit without support, although they may not be able to crawl. During succeeding years development of muscular coordination and competence in language and other skills continue, although the rate of progress still lags behind that of other children. By the second birthday, many children with Down's syndrome are able to say one or two words. Problems with muscle coordination also affect speech: Children with Down's syndrome may have problems coordinating the movements of the tongue, lips, and jaws that are necessary for speech. By age five they are usually able to name many objects and to speak in short sentences, although with many mispronounced words and mistakes in grammar. Parents can help foster the development of language by regularly talking with their child and actively helping him or her practice language skills in social situations. See also the next section and the suggestions in the box below.

LOVE ME!

Providing love and attention is the most basic, essential first step in helping retarded children. Because people with mental and physical disabilities face discrimination and social stigma, it is often difficult for them to like themselves. Being retarded does not spare the majority of retarded people from the painful recognition that they are different and that many people are uncomfortable around them. Knowing that they are loved and wanted has been shown to speed their advancement and build the positive self-image they need to endure the extraordinary difficulties and challenges their lives assuredly will bring.

Treatment

Although mentally retarded children rarely if ever catch up to their normal peers, with active intervention they can be helped to advance to their own potential. The earlier that diagnosis is made, the sooner both family and child can begin a program that stimulates development as well as to cope with the mix of emotions engendered by a diagnosis of mental retardation. (See the box on page 241.)

Most treatment is "habilitative"—that is, it is designed to help the child achieve his or her maximum level of functioning and independence. Increasingly, treatment in the United States is focused on keeping people with mental retardation in the community—either at home with the family or in group homes—and on community-based educa-

tion and training. It is difficult for physicians to predict whether or to what degree a given child will improve. Although a mentally retarded child may achieve a higher IQ score as he or she receives training, the child will not "catch up" in intelligence to a child of the same age with a normal IQ. However, retarded children do learn and progress, and some children do show dramatic improvement.

Many training and educational programs are available to parents who are aggressive about finding them and building their own treatment team. (See the box on page 245.) The types of intervention that a specific child requires depends on professional assessment of his or her needs by an expert in developmental disabilities. Speech and language training, toilet training, and instruction in the basics of dressing and feeding themselves all may be necessary. Parent counseling and education are equally important. Coordination with physicians to treat the child's physical difficulties or disabilities and mental health professionals for possible emotional and behavioral problems also will be necessary.

Help for Emotional and Behavioral Problems

No emotional and behavioral problems are unique to retarded children. However, these children's disabilities make them highly vulnerable to certain difficulties. For example, a number of behavior problems can result from a retarded child's trouble processing information. Because they have short attention spans, retarded children become restless, their behavior is often disruptive, and it can be difficult for them to function in group activities, whether at home or in the classroom.

Also, retarded children commonly have a low tolerance for frustration, often coupled with poor impulse control. It takes them longer to recover from emotional upsets than children with normal cognitive development. A momentary delay in gratification of a desire, a change in routine, a mild reprimand, even a change of food or a rearrangement in furniture can lead to dysfunctional behavior ranging from mild irritability to a violent temper tantrum or self-injurious behavior. Even in normal children, these behaviors are not easy for parents to handle. They are especially difficult to deal with in retarded children because they do not learn behavior control easily. There are ways that parents can help, as shown in the box on page 244. Mental health professionals can intervene with behavior therapy, which focuses on learning new behavior patterns and emotional control and can be particularly effective in retarded children.

Even at a very young age, retarded children often suffer from self-esteem problems. Those with mild developmental disabilities often know that they are "different," either because they are able to compare themselves to a sibling or because of the judgments and comments of those around them—family members, neighborhood children, teachers, and other adult authority figures. As a result, retarded children often suffer from feelings of inadequacy and depression, which in turn can lead to problems such as social withdrawal or aggressive behavior. Mental health professionals can intervene for these difficulties too, sometimes using the play therapy techniques (explained in chapter 16) they use with normally developed children.

Family Problems

Caring for a retarded child can be very rewarding, but it requires great patience and work on the part of the family. Parents commonly feel guilt, pain, and anger that their child is not normal. They also may have trouble bonding with their infant. Other siblings also may feel guilty that they are okay and angry that the retarded child requires so much attention or is different from other children. For these reasons, the family may benefit from counseling as well as the support of other families with retarded children.

Therapy for families of retarded children often has an educational component. Parents learn how to assess the child's developmental level and often receive instruction on how to help the child learn and develop as far as possible.

AUTISM

Also called pervasive developmental disorder, autism is rare (occurring in only 10 to 15 children per 10,000). In addition to lack of development of cognitive and language skills, children with this disorder have significant problems in social interaction. They seem detached, unable to become involved emotionally with those around them. From infancy they may not be responsive to cuddling or to eye contact with their mothers. They prefer to play by themselves and often develop rituals and repetitive behaviors (known as stereotypy), including rocking and head-banging. Their play also tends to be repetitive, and they may spend hours lining up objects or being preoccupied in making patterns with toys. Creative play with dolls or stuffed animals is limited, as is play that requires interaction with others, such as pat-a-cake or peek-a-boo.

About 50 percent of autistic children attain comprehensible speech, although its acquisition is often delayed and the cadence and patterns of speech tend to be abnormal. Most very young autistic children hardly speak; they have great difficulty in sustaining ongoing conversations. When talking, these children may echo what others have said inappropriately or use words in odd ways. Generally the lack of language development, or use of nonsensical, rhyming language, along with the other signs eventually lead to a diagnosis before the age of three.

Some autistic children demonstrate normal behavior initially; then, at about age two or two and a half, symptoms of the disorder develop. In these cases, a differential diagnosis must be made as to whether the symptoms are caused by autism or other conditions, such as elective mutism or schizophrenia (page 249). (Electively mute children differ from autistic children in that they are capable of speaking normally, without disordered language, and are receptive to social contacts with others.)

Although in the past autism popularly was blamed on parental neglect, research suggests that it is a neurological disorder, the cause or causes of which remain unknown. It is rare for families to have a history of autism, although the siblings of autistic children have somewhat higher rates of language disorders, learning disabilities, or mental retardation than is found among the general public. The majority of autistic children demonstrate some degree of mental retardation, but the condition does occur in children of normal intelligence. Unlike Down's syndrome children, autistic children usually have normally developed facial features, although they do not demonstrate the same facial expressiveness as other children.

Having a child with this disorder can be extremely difficult for parents, because the child does not "connect" with them and may exhibit little apparent emotional bond.

HELPING RETARDED CHILDREN CONTROL THEIR PROBLEM BEHAVIORS

Because retarded children progress through the stages of development so much more slowly than other children, they tend to be older and physically bigger than most small children undergoing such difficult development stages as "the terrible twos." Although it is normal and thus tolerable for a two-year-old to throw tantrums, in a retarded child this stage may occur at age four and last for a considerable period. Although it will take considerable patience, exercised over a long term, there are many ways for parents to help their children learn control over their behavior. Here are some suggestions, based on principles of behavior therapy.

- Identify the specific behavior that you want to change, whether it is acquiring a new, good behavior, such as learning potty training, or "unlearning" a bad behavior, such as not running across the street.
- Tackle one problem at a time.
- Assess your child's behavior in terms of his or her developmental age, not chronological age. If you do not know what your child's developmental age is, consult a mental health professional (usually a psychologist) who is trained in working with and assessing children with mental retardation. (See the box on page 245.) Knowing that your child's behavior is appropriate for his or her developmental age may help you to understand why the behavior is occurring.
- Encourage desired behavior by modeling it for the child. Let him or her see how parents and other children do it. If the behavior that you want to encourage occurs, reward the child by praising the behavior. Older children may need some kind of tangible reward—a star on a chart, a toy, an outing, and the like. Smaller awards should be given for behavior that is relatively easy to achieve, bigger awards saved for something that is difficult. Be consistent in giving the award, and make sure that whatever reward you have promised can be given when the desired behavior is performed. You also should gear the reward to the child's developmental stage—a four-year-old who is functioning at the level of a two-year-old may not feel rewarded by a star placed on a chart.
- For bad behaviors, do not scold the child or slap him or her. Children want attention, even such negative attention as scolding. Instead, ignore the behavior, no matter how difficult it is to do so (unless it is dangerous to the child or to others). Once the child sees that he or she is not getting attention from you, the behavior usually stops, eventually.
- Ask yourself if a practical change may make it easier to manage the child's unwanted behavior. Place locks on doors to rooms you don't want him or her to enter, or to kitchen and bathroom cabinets. Hide objects you don't want him or her to play with.
- If a child is engaging in harmful or destructive behavior, use time-out techniques (see page 251), just as you would with a normal child. Ignore any shouting or screaming, and do not take the child out until the screaming has stopped. (Otherwise, the child will learn that time outs stop when he or she screams.) After time out, do not demand apologies. Be friendly and matter-of-fact.
- Frequently, children with Down's syndrome have a habit of sticking out their tongues, due to a combination of a larger-than-average tongue and a smaller-than-average mouth. Using praise and rewards, after the first year you can begin to teach your child to keep his or her tongue in.
- Because of their low muscle tone, children with Down's syndrome are more likely than other children to keep their mouths open and thus to dribble. Using the same praise-and-reward techniques to help them with protruding tongues, you can usually train them to stop this habit too. (If the dribbling persists beyond age four, you may want to discuss with your pediatrician the possibility of an operation to decrease saliva production.)

Source: Adapted with permission from Mark Selikowitz, *Down's Syndrome: The Facts* (New York: Oxford University Press, 1990).

Treatment

There is no known cure for autism. Treatment focuses on attempting to foster normal development, improve communication skills, and reduce abnormal behavior. While the majority of autistic individuals are severely handicapped and unable to care for themselves, an estimated 5 to 17 percent of autistic

GETTING THE HELP YOU NEED

When parents have reason to believe that their child is retarded, getting a diagnosis and referrals to appropriate specialists can be confusing and frustrating. As mentioned earlier, pediatricians often advise a wait-and-see approach, because many normal children are slow in early stages of development, and no one wants to label a child retarded who is not. This waiting period is a time of enormous anxiety for the family. Talk to your doctor about the pros and cons of seeking an early assessment and referral to a specialist.

For a thorough professional evaluation for a child with a suspected or known developmental disability, university medical centers are usually the best resources. Call the department of psychiatry or of pediatrics and ask to see a specialist in childhood developmental disabilities. Treatment usually consists of a team of specialists for particular needs; teaching hospitals usually have such programs or can advise about them in the community.

By law, communities must provide education for developmentally disabled children. Call your local school district and find out what programs are available, if any, for disabled children of preschool age.

Your best resource may well be the Association for Retarded Citizens (ARC), a support and educational organization with chapters in all states. It can provide hard-to-get practical advice on specialists, diagnostic and treatment centers, and training and educational opportunities in your area. Members share information and advice on what to do and where to go for your child, your family, and yourself. For further information, contact ARC, National Headquarters (2501 Avenue J, Arlington, TX 76006; tel. 817 640–0204).

Organizations specifically for Down's syndrome include The National Down's Syndrome Society (141 Fifth Avenue, New York, NY; tel. 800 221–4602) and the National Down's Syndrome Congress (1800 Dempster Street, Park Ridge, IL 60068-1146; tel. 800 232–NDSC). Both can provide information on early intervention and referral to self-help groups.

---

individuals work and function, to some extent, within the community. Most individuals with this disorder, however, need supervision and care throughout life.

To address the problems connected with language, parents of autistic children are sometimes advised to set aside short periods of 30 minutes or so a day exclusively for conversation and play with their child. The focus of these periods is on teaching the child how to communicate, both in words and body language. Progress in developing language will vary widely from child to child. Some children will acquire an extensive vocabulary; others will never learn to speak. Children who do develop language early on and those whose nonverbal skills are well developed may become somewhat self-sufficient later in life.

Because another major feature of autism is the child's isolation, treatment must also focus on developing personal interaction. With a therapist's help, parents should plan activities that engage their child in social interaction, intruding on his or her normally solitary play.

Autistic children can learn, if the teaching environment is structured. The tasks or skills to be learned must be broken down into small manageable steps, and guidance should be provided at each step.

Because autistic children tend to learn by rote, rather than by understanding concepts, learning must be monitored carefully to try to help the child understand what he or she is learning.

Another focus of treatment is to eliminate problem behaviors such as tantrums, aggression, bedwetting, or self-injury. Behavior therapy (see chapter 16) can be effective in helping address these issues. Repetitive, stereotyped behavior is sometimes addressed through a technique called "graded change." Change is brought about by making small changes, one step at a time, in the elements of daily routine or physical environment that appear to provoke stereotyped behavior. Another strategy to reduce stereotyped behavior is to provide stimulating toys and play activities that compete with the stereotyped behavior for the child's attention.

While there are no drugs that treat autism, in some cases medication may help with some of the behavioral manifestations of the disorder. The antipsychotic drugs, for example, sometimes help to reduce agitation and overactivity and facilitate learning. Despite ongoing studies, however, there is little concurrence by researchers on the effectiveness of drug treatment.

Assistance, Support, and Information for the Child and the Family

As with any handicapped child, the families of autistic children face strong stressors. There are pragmatic problems to be dealt with—among them finding professional services and the best care for the child, the financial burden, physical fatigue, and burnout. It is common for parents to experience emotional problems such as depression, anger, and guilt. Caring for an autistic child can strain even the best marital relationships and can impact adversely on siblings as well.

The Autism Society of America (8601 Georgia Avenue, Suite 503, Silver Spring, MD 20910; tel. 301 565–0433) can provide information on help for autistic children and support for families. The organization publishes a membership newsletter and can also refer individuals to local support chapters. The Michigan Society for Autistic Citizens (530 West Ionia Street, Suite C, Lansing, MI 48933; tel. 517 487–9260) operates a mail-order book service.

Common Emotional and Behavioral Problems of Preschool Children

Although the developmental disabilities become apparent in very young children, the major mental disorders such as schizophrenia and depression are highly uncommon. The emotional and behavior problems that commonly afflict children in their earliest years—including children who are developmentally disabled—are discussed throughout the remainder of this chapter.

LANGUAGE AND ARTICULATION DISORDERS

Language is the correct use of words to express meaning. Articulation in this context refers to the physical ability to utter sounds distinctly. While children should be allowed to develop language at their own pace, lack of language development by age two requires investigation.

Language disorders can be obvious—as when speech is totally lacking—or subtle, such as occurs with inappropriate word use or syntax problems. Poor language skills can interfere with learning, because thought and memory are closely interrelated to each other. Language difficulties can cause problems in all spheres of cognitive development, from how a child thinks and perceives the world, to how he or she relates to others. They can also impact on a child's emotions and social adjustment.

Although delayed speech should always be evaluated, parents should be aware that delayed speech does not always signal a problem that needs special treatment. Language problems are fairly common; some young children are simply not verbal. They need to be coaxed and helped to perform rather than pressured or made to feel anxious by worried parents. Many children who do not speak until after age two demonstrate considerable intelligence when they finally do begin to speak.

Hearing Tests

Does the child respond to spoken words or sounds within the environment? Does he or she understand what others say, or accurately distinguish between similar-sounding words? If answers to these questions are no, the language difficulty may be stemming from a hearing problem. A thorough speech and hearing evaluation is the first step in assessing a language difficulty, because the development of speech and language can be hindered by many physical factors, including hearing deficiencies and problems involving facial structure or muscles. Lack of language also may signal mental retardation or autism, discussed earlier in this chapter.

If there is any lag in the development of speech, or if there is any suspicion that hearing may be impaired, the child should be tested by a clinical audiologist. It is important to test as soon as possible, no matter how young the child; the earlier that a hearing problem is detected, the sooner appropriate treatment or remedial training can be initiated. Children whose hearing problem is not detected until the later preschool years often have a harder time learning to speak than do those whose problem was detected earlier.

Pediatricians or hospitals can usually supply referrals. Also, the American Speech, Language, and Hearing Association (ASHA) can provide the names of audiologists and speech and language pathologists who meet their requirements for certification. They can be reached at 800 638–8255. Their address is: ASHA Consumer Division, 10801 Rockville Pike, Rockville, MD 20852.

Stuttering

Most children experience periods of stuttering, or dysfluency, as they learn to speak. But usually, with age, the problem disappears as language proficiency increases. In some children, however, what begins as normal repetition of sounds progresses to frequent repetition of syllables or words and eventually worsens to stuttering. Once children do begin to stutter, they may become anxious, which makes the stuttering worse. In most cases, stuttering disappears spontaneously, although stress can sometimes trigger a recurrence.

Stuttering usually begins between the ages of two and seven and affects about 5 percent of children. Why children start to stutter remains unclear, although both genetic factors and pressure to perform may be involved.

Treatment

Both speech therapy and psychotherapy are used to treat speech problems.

Speech therapy. Approaches that aim to modify behavior by replacing stuttering with fluent speech may help. Some common speech therapy-techniques include:

- *Rhythmic speech.* This technique uses a metronome to train stutterers to speak in a rhythmic pattern. While this therapy appears to be successful, its relapse rate is high, and the resulting speech patterns are unlike normal speech.
- *Slow speech.* This technique teaches children to replace stuttering with speech that is marked by exaggerated vowels and consonants.
- *Easier stuttering.* This technique focuses on helping the child learn new ways of speaking that, while not completely stutter-free, more closely approximate normal speech.

Psychotherapy. Play therapy, in which children are helped to express their emotions (see chapter 16), can be helpful for some children who stutter. Parents can also benefit by therapy that teaches them how to ease whatever pressures in the home may be contributing to the stuttering problem.

FEARS AND ANXIETIES

All children have fears, usually involving certain objects or situations. Indeed, some of these are practical and realistic, protecting the child from harm, such as fear of traffic, great heights, or loud noises.

Certain fears are typical of particular ages and usually do not indicate future problems. Infants can become fearful when exposed to strangers and often have an exaggerated startle response when exposed to loud noises. Very young children may also fear unusual events, unexpected movements, and strange situations and people. The ages of two or three seem to bring with them a fear of animals. Later on, fears of imaginary creatures and of the dark are normal.

Sometimes fears may become so intense that they inhibit a child's daily life, or they may show up or persist at an inappropriate age. When fears cause a child to avoid normal activities or situations, they are called phobias. For a four- or five-year-old to be afraid of monsters in the dark is normal. If, however, the child remains totally unable to sleep because of this fear, or if it persists to later years, he or she is suffering excessively and the family may need outside help to deal with the situation.

Causes

It is not always easy to determine what causes intense fears or phobias in small children. Studies have shown that some children appear to be more vulnerable by nature to anxiety, so individual differences in temperament seem to be important. Inheritance plays a role in temperament, and indeed, severe anxiety often runs in families. Obviously, however, any child brought up in an anxious family has a chance of learning to be anxious and fearful. Research does show that children often adopt their parents' fears, such as fears of dogs, insects, and thunderstorms.

Separation and Stranger Anxiety

Anxiety about separation from the parent is quite common in infants and young children. At about seven months of age the average infant forms a special attachment to the primary caregiver, usually the mother. Once that bond has been established, situations that interrupt it can trigger separation anxiety.

Fear of strangers develops along with separation anxiety. Separation anxiety is particularly apparent in the second year, and begins to decrease after that. It is normal for a two-year-old to cling to a parent when dropped off at preschool, for example, and to be reluctant to interact with others for a brief time. Most children become less concerned about being away from the parent and meeting strangers as they get older and are exposed to more people.

In some cases, however, the child's anxiety does not subside after the parent leaves, and his or her misery makes it impossible for the child to attend nursery school or to be left with a baby-sitter. If this condition persists or recurs, the quality of the child's life can be affected. Children with severe separation anxiety often have trouble sleeping by themselves and may even object to being in a room alone. They may cling desperately to those they feel attached to, and some complain of nonspecific aches and pains when separation is anticipated.

These children fear that each separation from loved ones is the last, because something terrible is going to happen. They thus may be preoccupied with imagined threats to their family from animals, monsters, kidnappers, car accidents, or plane travel (although these fears also can occur in children without separation anxiety). The disorder may develop after the death of a relative or a pet, or after an illness or a change in the child's home environment or neighborhood.

Signs of a Problem

While transient episodes of separation anxiety are normal, excessive or unrelenting anxiety is not. A professional consultation usually is warranted when, for example:

- the child's extreme distress prevents parents from leaving for the day or evening;
- the child cannot leave home without experiencing intense emotional pain;
- the child's fears of separation are manifested through nightmares that interfere with sleep;
- the child develops somatic symptoms (headaches, stomach pains, flulike symptoms) as a reaction to the thought of separation.

Sometimes separation anxiety is also at the root of bad habits such as nail biting, thumb sucking, and temper tantrums.

Treatment

The first step in treatment is to assure the child of the parents' love and approval and to reinforce the child's sense of self-esteem. Sometimes a system of rewards can help ameliorate the symptoms of distress. Changes in the child's daily routine or an important change in life (birth of a sibling, the illness or impending death of a parent, divorce) should be explained carefully, along with an emphasis on the fact that the child is in no way to blame for the change. Behavior modification techniques, in which the child is gradually desensitized to separation, can help in more pronounced cases.

Preventing the Development of Excessive Fear

Because parents' fears rub off on their children, parents may first wish to address their own overreactions and to try not to appear fearful in front of the children.

While children need to be taught to recognize and avoid dangerous situations, it is important not to make them feel overwhelmed by the dangers present in their environment. Providing children with concrete, age-appropriate ways to cope with real dangers will help them feel that they can master the situation. For example, when teaching children to avoid strangers in certain circumstances, instead of dwelling on the frightening aspects of what could happen, advise the children to refuse to enter a stranger's car and to scream if the stranger tries to force them. For the anxious child, or the child who is too young to cope with fearful material, parents can take care to limit exposure to obviously frightening material such as horror movies.

HELPING CHILDREN TO FACE THEIR FEARS

Gradually expose the child to the threatening object or situation while providing encouragement and explaining that nothing bad will happen. For children fearful of dogs, for example, take frequent short trips to a pet store or visit a neighbor's gentle pets to begin to reduce the child's fear.

It often helps to relax the child in the presence of the feared object or situation. For instance, turning out the light and then speaking softly to a child may help reduce his or her fear of the dark. Reward even small increases in willingness to face or endure a fear. Never push too hard or overwhelm a child when he or she is unready.

If all attempts to help the child fail, and if he or she remains in considerable stress, seek professional help.

Shyness and Avoidance of Social Situations

While the two-year-old is still fairly dependent on his or her parents and may be shy with other people, most parents successfully can encourage children of this age to play with others. As they mature and spend more time with other children in playgrounds and at nursery school, young children usually show growing friendliness and interest in each other. Four- or five-year-olds focus on those close to their own age or younger, developing social skills in the process.

As mentioned previously, a child with severe separation anxiety will cling to the mother and not participate in nursery school or other activities with children. But separation anxiety is not the only cause of social withdrawal. Some children are simply shy and slow to warm up by temperament.

Shyness in itself is usually no problem, but it should be distinguished from more serious forms of social avoidance. For example, a preschool child who is bashful at first, when Dad introduces a business acquaintance or upon meeting a nursery school teacher, is reacting appropriately for his or her age. But the child who always refuses to play with other children or to meet new people is probably feeling anxious about entering social situations. Children affected by a rare disorder called elective mutism withdraw by not speaking at all, or by speaking only to family members. (See also page 243.)

Causes
A high level of general anxiety is one reason some children are more shy than others; arrested language development is another. Lack of familiarity with children of a similar age also can lead to withdrawal. An only child raised on a farm who is not used to seeing strangers, for example, may find it particularly stressful to enter nursery school, while a city child used to seeing and playing with other children on the block may have little trouble.

Parental attitudes also can play a part. Some parents make children feel ashamed or even punish them for expressions of dependency that are normal for their age, such as clinging or seeking attention. Rather than risk these consequences, some young children decide to withdraw. The opposite can also be true. A parent may have consistently encouraged dependent, clinging behavior beyond the time when it might be appropriate, discouraging exploration. The child may get the impression that it is risky to venture forth from the mother's lap.

Helping a Shy Child
Most times, shy children will begin to feel more comfortable with other adults and peers if they are introduced to new situations slowly. With plenty of reassurance and encouragement, they can begin to relax in social settings. Some children may remain slow to warm up, however, and their reticence should be respected.

Problems with social interaction most likely will be picked up by nursery school teachers, and parents should discuss their concerns with them to see how the child acts outside of the home. Psychiatric intervention usually is not called for in this age group.

However, serious forms of withdrawal, including elective mutism, usually require professional help, particularly if children are missing many experiences normally enjoyed by others their age.

ANGER AND AGGRESSIVE BEHAVIOR

Healthy assertiveness and the expression of anger cannot always be distinguished from destructive, defiant behavior, nor is it easy to teach a child to express these emotions appropriately. A two-year-old who bangs on the table or a four-year-old who hits a playmate may be showing assertiveness, impulsiveness, or temporary frustration, but not necessarily the desire to hurt someone. Even toddlers can learn that hitting and grabbing are an effective means of getting a desired toy from a playmate. Some children are naturally more energetic and aggressive than others.

If the child is emotionally healthy in other respects and is in a balanced and kind environment, he or she probably will outgrow such behavior. However, children who repeatedly bite, hit, kick, quarrel, destroy property (such as their own toys), abuse animals, or attack others verbally may be exhibiting an abnormal degree of aggressive behavior. Other children will avoid them, and the behavior may thus become self-perpetuating. As early as age five, some children with these kinds of behavior are diagnosed as having oppositional defiant disorder or conduct disorder.

Causes of Aggressiveness

Several factors contribute to intense and persistent aggressive behavior in preschool children, including the parents' attitudes toward such behavior, the influence of aggressive models, and a family history of aggression. Children brought up in aggressive families may inherit the genetic predisposition or simply learn the behavior.

Lack of Firm and Consistent Guidelines
During the preschool years, children begin to adopt standards of behavior to conform with parental expectations. These standards are taught by adults who set limits, reward good behavior, and actively discourage destructive acts. As children grow and develop a conscience, they feel guilty when they transgress these standards. However, until they are much older (usually not before age 11), they judge actions more by consequences than by intent. For this reason, it is futile to expect that four-year-olds will figure out for themselves that hostile behavior is not acceptable. They will assume the action was right unless they are *shown* otherwise.

In fact, overly aggressive children may have been taught that this kind of behavior is effective. Young children are always testing the environment, and especially for those who do not yet have language skills, actions speak louder than words. If they are allowed to get other children's toys by force or to vent their anger by kicking a playmate, they will continue to do so. Even children who are by nature gentle or timid will absorb the same lesson by seeing other children repeatedly getting away with such behavior.

Inconsistent responses toward aggression (punishing it at times and ignoring it at others) is especially damaging. Children have difficulty understanding that something is right in one context and not another. The resulting frustration in itself can lead to more aggressive behavior.

Our culture itself is selective in its condemnation and rewards for aggression. Even in preschoolers, boys are far more aggressive in both action and fantasy than girls. This is due in part to biological differences that affect activity level and aggressiveness. Learning also plays a part, however, and comes from differences in expectation of how boys and girls should behave and what they are permitted to do.

Negative Models
Models for aggression abound in our society, even for the preschooler. In the family, fighting between parents and even physical abuse of spouses or children may be present. Behaviors depicted on television also have enormous impact on children. Studies by researchers L. K. Friedrich and A. H. Stein, among others, have shown that watching violence on television, while it may not in itself create a violent personality in a gentle child, will reinforce a propensity for hostile behavior in a child who already tends to be aggressive.

Child Abuse

The physical and emotional trauma of child abuse disrupts the child's normal development. Children who are physically abused (see chapter 20) tend to exhibit a spectrum of negative behaviors that include lack of impulse control, anger, and hostile behavior. Some abused children are preoccupied with aggressive and violent fantasies. In one study, for example, conducted in a day-care center for young children, researchers found that abused children assaulted their peers twice as often as nonabused children. They were also more likely to be both verbally and physically hostile to the day-care staff and to react to them with distrust.

Stress in the Home

A child who lives in a home in which there are serious problems—acrimonious divorce, financial difficulties, frequent fights, drug or alcohol abuse—is more likely to exhibit aggressive behavior than a child raised in a home without such stressors.

While divorce in and of itself need not cause problems, the typical angry, hostile relationships between parents that usually precede divorce can impact severely on children. (See also chapter 20.) It is typical of children in divorcing families to show bewilderment, depression, confusion, and anger; some young children demonstrate intense anger. And, if a child already has a tendency toward aggressive behavior, divorce often intensifies this tendency.

Preventing and Limiting Aggressiveness

Because hostile behavior often results from the values and attitudes a child witnesses, one way to stop or prevent such behavior is to limit the child's exposure to hostility and violence both in the home and on television. Firm and clear standards should also be set as to what is acceptable behavior and self-expression and what is not. A child who is encouraged to express anger in nonviolent ways such as talking about it, even at a very young age, will be less likely to need to demonstrate it. On the other hand, encouraging a young child to displace his or her anger, such as by hitting a doll, may actually increase aggression, as the child learns that violence in some forms is acceptable.

COPING WITH A CHILD'S ANGRY BEHAVIOR

Coping with angry behavior begins with trying to determine why your child is angry and controlling the circumstances that provoke his or her aggressive behavior.

- Many children model aggressive, bullying behavior on behavior learned from parents. Examine your own behavior at home. Do you and your spouse have explosive arguments in front of your children? If so, you may be teaching that fighting is an acceptable way to get what one wants.
- If your child is learning aggressive behavior from another child, try to limit his or her contact with that child. Arrange for new playmates or enroll the child in group activities where he or she will meet other children. If the child is learning the aggressive activities at a day-care center, discuss the problem with the center's staff. If they cannot resolve the problem, change day-care centers.
- Make sure your child knows that aggressive behavior is unacceptable and that there are more acceptable ways to behave. During periods when your child is not angry, point out good and bad behaviors.
- Teach your child to control anger. Provide an "angry place" where it is acceptable for the child to vent frustrations. Use "time-out" methods—send your child to a quiet room or corner—when behavior gets out of hand. (Some experts recommend that the cooling-off period mirror a child's age: three minutes for a three-year-old, four for a four-year-old, and so forth.) Let your child know that if time out doesn't work, there will be other consequences—a toy will be removed for a certain amount of time, television-watching will be limited, a favorite activity will not be allowed.
- Be firm and consistent. Do not punish aggressive behavior sometimes and ignore it at other times.
- Praise your child for good behavior.

CHILDREN'S ART THERAPY: "THE WATCHFUL HOUSE"

Figure 17.1: **A child in therapy for fearful, withdrawn behavior draws two houses, representing her mother and herself. The "child house" hides behind the "mother house," which looks out at the world with peering suspicious eyes. The closed doors may indicate that the child feels emotionally shut off from her mother.**

When children are overly aggressive, they should not be physically punished; this simply reinforces the idea that such behavior is acceptable. Instead, privileges such as favorite activities or other treats should be removed temporarily. It is important that negative consequences follow quickly upon the child's aggressive behavior so that the child does not associate the punishment with a later, possibly positive, behavior. It is advisable not to follow the punishment by immediately cuddling the child and having a rational chat about what just happened, because this warmth probably will make the child feel rewarded, rather than punished, for his or her actions.

The box on page 251 provides for additional suggestions.

Seeking Help

Severe conduct disorders requiring psychiatric treatment are rare during the preschool years. Aggressive behavior is normal for very young children—they are, after all, still learning how to negotiate their way in life—and most aggressive behaviors disappear as the child grows and develops.

However, if a child continues to exhibit aggressive behavior past the age when his or her peers have outgrown it (usually by the 36th month or so), professional help may be in order. And some behaviors should be evaluated by a pediatric mental health professional no matter how young the child. These include extreme aggression (the child repeatedly hurts other children, intentionally or as a result of losing control of emotions), sets fires, torments animals, or engages in self-mutilating behavior (for example, the child bangs his or her head against the wall or bites or seriously scratches him- or herself).

Some causes of aggression—such as inept parenting, and particularly aggression caused by child abuse or acrimonious divorces—require professional help for the parent as well as the child.

HYPERACTIVITY

Some preschool children are normally very distractible and cannot be expected to stay with any one activity for long periods. Nonetheless, they can remain quiet long enough to focus their attention. Others have such a short attention span and need to keep moving to such an extent that their ability to learn and to relate well to others may be jeopardized. In very young children this hyperactivity is reflected in their inability to stick to any activity, including play, for periods of time appropriate to their age.

Hyperactive children display not only more activity than other children, but activity that is incessant and differs in quality from normal behavior. Hyperactive behavior frequently lacks purpose and is disorganized and haphazard. Enthusiastic children in a hurry may neglect to put away their clothes, but hyperactive children may well run to their dressers on awakening and throw everything out of the drawers. Children who can't be left alone because of their chaotic activity may not have normal control of their impulses.

Parents often remember their child's earliest hyperactive behavior as: "He never walked, he just ran." Hyperactive two-year-olds are not likely to investigate any one object for more than seconds, and they seem to be driven from one object to the next. When they are four, parents may report that they do not listen, are very demanding, cannot play well by themselves or with others, and require constant supervision. At this age they may already have experienced rejection from others for reckless, seemingly destructive behavior.

Attention and hyperactivity problems can be diagnosed in children as young as three. However, children with these problems usually do not come to professional attention until they are in school, where they cannot sit still or pay attention, and the consequences of their behavior magnify.

A more complete discussion of attention and hyperactivity problems, including treatment approaches, outlook for the child, and advice for parents, appears in chapter 18.

PROBLEMS WITH EATING

Parents often worry excessively that their infant is not eating on schedule or that their toddler is more interested in throwing spinach than ingesting it. Young children are often picky about what they eat and usually don't relish new tastes. None of these idiosyncracies is serious, and most abate with maturity. The best gauge for determining if a child is eating properly is general health and growth. Making healthful food available to young children is important; forcing them to eat it is not.

Overeating and Obesity

Young children can overeat, but dieting is seldom if ever recommended for the preschool group. If parents make overeating a big issue, eating problems can develop. For overweight children, parents should make low-calorie foods available and not emphasize weight. Obesity tends to run in families, and while there may be an inherited biological element to this problem, emotional attitudes and learned habits also play a part. Parents who want to avoid self-esteem and body-image problems in their children are advised to adopt a casual attitude about eating, in order to minimize shame and conflict over food. The family needs to find and emphasize sources of shared pleasure other than food and to be sure to communicate affection.

WHEN A CHILD REFUSES TO EAT

Food refusal is both worrisome and aggravating to parents. But there are things you can do to help your child become a better eater. Most appetite problems begin between the ages of 6 to 18 months—the time when a child begins to develop independence. For some children, not eating becomes a way of demonstrating that independence.

- The first and foremost rule is do not force your child to eat. Your child will eat when he or she is hungry enough.
- Do not bribe, persuade, threaten, or punish your child into eating.
- Let your child know that eating is a normal behavior—do not praise him or her for the simple act of eating, and do not let your anxiety show if he or she does not eat.

- If a child is not eating normally, do not feed him or her between meals; let the child realize that he or she will have to wait until the next mealtime to eat.
- Prepare food that looks attractive. Many children are drawn to food that has bright colors.
- Encourage your child to feed him- or herself and to practice self-feeding skills.
- Do not hurry your child into eating faster than he or she wants to—but set limits. Allow a reasonable time to eat, but let the child know that his or her food will be removed once everyone else is done eating.

Source: adapted with permission from Ronald S. Illingworth, M.D., *The Normal Child*, 10th ed. (New York: Churchill Livingstone, 1991).

Pica

Very young children have a habit of putting anything into their mouths, without necessarily swallowing it. But some children, especially those with other psychiatric disorders, persistently eat nonfood substances. Infants with this eating disorder, called pica, typically ingest paint, plaster, string, or hair. Toddlers with pica may eat animal droppings, sand, insects, leaves, or pebbles. They have no aversion to food, however.

Pica usually appears at the age of one or two. Some children with the disorder have cognitive or sensory defects such as retardation or blindness; others may have been left without care for excessively long periods. Consumption of certain materials, especially lead-based paints, may be a considerable health hazard to the young child and must be prevented. Treatment for pica includes psychological training for the child and increased parental interaction and supervision.

PROBLEMS WITH SLEEPING

Infants usually sleep for 45 minutes to 2 hours at a time and total as much as 18 hours of sleep a day. As they develop, they sleep for longer periods at a stretch, and by the time they are three to seven months old they can sleep through the night. For some babies, achieving a regular nighttime schedule is more difficult. While their behavior may be stressful to parents, however, it is not "abnormal."

Nighttime may be stressful for young children, and going to bed is often fraught with complaints and dawdling. Sometimes a change in routine, such as sleeping in an unfamiliar room, having visitors in the house, starting preschool, or being sick can make children more sleepless or reluctant to go to bed. If wakefulness lasts more than a few nights, however, it may be caused by an underlying condition, such as a persistent fear of being left alone in the dark. (See "Fears and Anxieties," earlier in this chapter.)

Walking and Talking in Sleep

Children walk and talk in their sleep far more frequently than adults, for reasons that are not completely understood. A child who sleepwalks will suddenly sit up in bed and then may or may not actually get up and walk around, perhaps appearing distressed. The event may not be recalled the next morning. Some children talk in their sleep, and they may not remember doing so.

These habits usually disappear with time. If a child sleepwalks, it is wise to take precautions to avoid accidents, such as having the child sleep on a lower bunk rather than an upper one. (See also chapter 12.)

Nightmare Disorder and Sleep Terror Disorder

It is not uncommon for young children to experience infrequent but extremely frightening dreams. They usually wake up from these nightmares very alert and able to describe them in detail. Those suffering three or more nightmares a week may have a condition called dream anxiety disorder, or nightmare disorder. This disorder affects less than 5 percent of the total population and usually begins before the age of 10.

Children also may suffer from sleep terror disorder, in which they repeatedly wake up abruptly in the early part of the night and let out a panicky scream. They initially are confused, unresponsive, and disoriented, and cannot recall the dream. These disorders occur most frequently during periods of emotional

---

"MOMMY, CAN I SLEEP WITH YOU AND DADDY?"

Should you allow your youngster to share your bed on a regular basis? Only when he or she awakens scared in the middle of the night? From a mental health perspective, there are no absolute rights or wrongs about it. This is a matter of personal, family, or cultural preference. In some cultures children regularly sleep with their parents, although this is not common practice in the United States.

Remember, however, that the longer the child persists in not sleeping alone, the more difficult the eventual transition may be when he or she is banished to the nursery.

---

stress, but physical fatigue and changes in the sleep environment also may be involved.

Structuring routines and schedules for bedtime and napping may help children suffering from nightmares and sleep terrors. Professional help may be necessary if the child fears the approach of bedtime or if daytime activities become affected by nighttime sleep disturbances. (See also chapter 12.)

TOILETING

Toilet training can begin when a child is physiologically ready to remain dry for significant periods of time and when the child is able to be aware of the relationship between the physical sensations that signal the need to "go" and the result of those sensations.

Children proceed at individual rates. Although failure to be toilet-trained may be associated with a developmental disorder, as described earlier in this chapter, most difficulties that arise do not indicate that the child has "problems." However, the longer the difficulty continues, and the more social disapproval and family pressure young children experience, the more likely they are to develop other problems in reaction.

Wetting

In general, during the second year some children, mostly girls, will begin to stay dry during naptime and occasionally all night. Among two- to three-year-olds, 45 percent of girls but only 35 percent of boys are dry at night. During the third year, dry nights are more frequent, and a full bladder more consistently awakens the child. By age five, the majority of children are reliably dry all night and day, with only infrequent accidents. However, a good proportion (as high as 25 percent) of children who have been dry for as long as six months subsequently begin to wet again, often temporarily, as a reaction to stress.

Among children who continue to wet the bed after age five, most are simply slow to develop nighttime urinary control and will do so eventually. In such cases, a family history of bedwetting is common. Page 270 in chapter 18 provides a full discussion and advice on how to help children who continue to wet their bed.

Consistent rewards for staying dry encourage children in their progress. The process must proceed at the child's own pace, and making him or her feel ashamed for having an accident is not constructive. Many parents, faced with a resistant child or demands on their time caused by the birth of another child, will delay training repeatedly. This may lead to more problems than it avoids.

Bowel Control

Bowel control generally happens at an earlier age than urinary control, in part because this function occurs less frequently and allows the child more time to get to the potty. There is a wide variation in the age at which control over bowel function normally is achieved.

When children do not show significant progress toward bowel control by age three or four, parents often react coercively. Punitive measures may lead to the child's holding back bowel function, however, and chronic constipation and rectal enlargement may result. Once a pattern of constipation and enlargement sets in, the child may no longer feel the usual sensations of pressure that normally precede the production of stools. At the extreme, this may lead to a packed fecal mass, painful constipation, and soiling of underwear from the overflow of fecal material around the blockage. Coupled with the child's growing oppositional behavior, this situation may create a difficult problem for both child and parents.

For the child who repeatedly withholds bowel movements, pediatricians often suggest an enema, followed by supervised use of stool softeners or laxatives. Adding fiber to the child's diet also may be recommended. A psychologist, working in collaboration with the pediatrician, then can help the parents take the focus off the child's failure or opposition and work out a program of regular reward for bowel movements. This training process is slow and gradual; pushing the child will activate resistance.

Children without developmental disorders who cannot be bowel-trained, or who return to soiling, probably have underlying emotional problems or are reacting to family tension. In this situation, soiling is often associated with anxiety (both on the part of the child and the parents) and social withdrawal. Counseling for both the child and parents may be necessary to resolve the problem.

SEXUAL AND CROSS-GENDER BEHAVIOR

People tend to remember their childhoods as periods of nonsexual "innocence," but in fact basic sexual reflexes develop early. The male fetus can and does have penile erections. Similarly, penile erections during sleep begin to occur in infancy. Infant girls experience pleasurable sensations when their genitals are touched.

By age three, most children are asking questions about sexual matters. By age five, most children can correctly distinguish male and female genitals, and they know that babies come from the mother's belly; more detailed understanding about the function of the genitals and reproduction is acquired only very gradually through the subsequent years. It is usually best if parents answer children's questions about sex honestly and matter-of-factly, on the level appropriate to the child's understanding. Not answering questions will encourage the child to seek information elsewhere—often from their similarly uninformed, or misinformed, friends.

Sexual Play

Children are normally curious about their bodies and physical sensations, and they enjoy touching their genitals. This behavior is appropriate; as the child becomes older, parents can teach them about privacy in sexual matters. Reacting with shock and horror when children touch themselves can lead them to think that certain parts of their bodies are "bad."

Sexual curiosity extends as well to bodies of parents, other family members, and other children. Sexual exploration games that involve undressing ("playing doctor" or "playing mother and father") are quite common in children approaching school age. Such exploratory activities may progress into mutual genital fondling, and older children who have had the opportunity to observe sexual activities of adolescents or adults may try to imitate such behavior. Both homosexual and heterosexual play are quite common. Playing doctor also may be a way of coping if the child has had to undergo repeated genital examinations for medical reasons.

There is no need for concern if sexual play occurs sporadically, in which case children may need to learn only about privacy. Parents should intervene if a child tries to force others into sexual play or if there is a large age difference between the children involved. Professional help should be considered only when sexual play becomes highly repetitive and persistent, which may indicate other problems, including sexual abuse. (See chapter 20.)

Cross-gender Behavior

Starting in infancy, a child begins to learn that he is called a boy or she is called a girl; gradually the child develops an identity as one or the other. By the time they are three, most children can correctly answer the question, "Are you a boy or a girl?" The concept of sex differences is developed further over the subsequent years.

Nevertheless, at times most preschoolers do things that in our society generally are thought to be the domain of the other sex. Thus, at times, many girls play with cars and boys play with dolls. Both may dress up in hats, shoes, or even garments of the other sex. They may even say sometimes that they would like to be the other sex. None of this behavior is cause for concern unless it persists. Usually, sporadic cross-gender behavior diminishes with age.

Some children, however, develop a *gender identity disorder*, in which they prefer to be the other sex. The disorder affects boys more than girls. Gender-disordered boys typically are preoccupied with stereotypical girls' activities such as dressing dolls and combing their hair. They like to dress up in girls' outfits and to imitate female television stars. They often avoid other boys and insist that they want to be girls. More rarely, extremely tomboyish girls reject being female or insist that they are really boys and try to dress as much like them as possible.

Persistent cross-gender behavior can occur as early as age two, and the majority of children with gender-identity disorder begin to show signs of it before age five. Boys with a cross-gender condition are especially likely to be progressively isolated and ostracized from their same-sex peer group.

Children with persistent cross-gender behavior require professional help. Pages 168–169 in chapter 11 provide details of treatment as well as a more complete discussion of gender identity disorders.

18

Disorders of School-Age Children

Rachel G. Klein, Ph.D., and
David Shaffer, M.D., F.R.C.P., F.R.C. Psych.

As children reach school age, they need to function outside the home. Types of behavior that may have been tolerated and manageable at home, such as excessive restlessness or aggression, may cause disruption in a classroom and be unacceptable to teachers and even schoolmates. Some problems, such as difficulty in reading or playing with groups of children, may become evident for the first time and significantly hinder a child's development. And certain behaviors that were normal in younger years, such as bedwetting or a fear of imaginary animals, at this stage of development may be a sign of problems that need to be addressed more intensively.

ATTENTION–DEFICIT HYPERACTIVITY DISORDER (ADHD)

Commonly referred to simply as hyperactivity, attention-deficit hyperactivity disorder began to be described in medical journals over 100 years ago. Today it is recognized as one of the most common behavior disorders in children. Hyperactive children move excessively, even in their sleep. What makes them hyperactive, however, is not only that they are overactive, but that they are also not able to control their activity and have a limited attention span. Their behavior sets them apart from other children their age. For reasons that are not yet apparent, the condition seems to occur about 10 times more often in boys than in girls.

Although this disorder can be diagnosed early (see chapter 17), often the scope of the problem does not become apparent until the child enters elementary school. Until then, patient parents and preschool teachers often are able to cope with behavior that becomes intolerable in a structured class setting. Furthermore, the demands for sedentary activities in elementary school make it more difficult for the child to adapt.

Unfortunately, children with this disorder are usually blamed and punished for not controlling themselves. In fact, they would like to cooperate with those around them, if only they could.

Jim B., for instance, is an agile boy of six who appears friendly and cooperative on first meeting. He also seems to be free of any great fear, anxiety, or depression, and he eats and sleeps well. However, Jim has been referred to a counselor by his first-grade teacher, who reports that he requires constant supervision to keep him from disrupting classroom activities. At home, Jim never keeps still for any length of time; he is always running, jumping, rocking, or fiddling with something. He does three or four things at a time without completing any of them, and he disrupts any activity going on around him.

Obviously, Jim's behavior is a problem both at home and at school, but the usual methods of controlling behavior—discipline, rewards, and punishment—do not work with him. He is not willfully "bad," he just cannot turn off his internal motor and control his impulses.

Jim also displays the characteristics of *attention deficit* in his short attention span, difficulty listening, inability to finish things, and easy distractibility. Children with attention problems run into difficulty in

school because they can't stick to tasks. In these children, inattention accompanies impulsiveness; they often talk incessantly or excessively, won't wait in lines, call out in class, and seem to act before thinking.

When Does a Child Have ADHD?

A professional evaluation is always necessary, because not all children who exhibit restless and distractible behaviors suffer from ADHD. Some children who are active and fidgety are normal, although their behavior may be difficult for parents and teachers to handle. Other children with these behaviors suffer from child abuse and neglect (see chapter 20), anxiety, or even boredom. Thyroid disease can sometimes trigger the behaviors, as can certain drugs.

Rating scales and checklists (such as the one in the box on page 260) often can help teachers and other professionals to organize their impressions of a child's behavior as a first step in the evaluation process.

A mental health professional will make an assessment after a review of the child's development from infancy on, including: aberrations in behavior, educational development, psychological makeup, social and familial relationships, medical history, and family history. Often ADHD is associated with developmental disorders, mood disorders, and conduct disorders (page 261).

A clinician will diagnose a child as suffering from ADHD only if the behavior problems have been occurring for over six months and if they have been intense enough to interfere with important aspects of the child's development. The symptoms of the disorder do not disappear from day to day; girls who are giddy at parties or boys who get rowdy in groups are not necessarily hyperactive.

What Causes ADHD?

No one knows for sure what makes some children abnormally active and inattentive. While most experts believe that one or more biological processes in the brain are involved, so far studies have not been conclusive. Hyperactivity seems to run in families, although no one has been able to prove a direct hereditary link.

HYPERACTIVITY SCALE

	Not at All	Just a Little	Pretty Much	Very Much
1. Restless (overactive)	0	1	2	3
2. Excitable, impulsive	0	1	2	3
3. Disturbs other children	0	1	2	3
4. Fails to finish things started (short attention span)	0	1	2	3
5. Fidgeting	0	1	2	3
6. Inattentive, distractible	0	1	2	3

	Not at All	Just a Little	Pretty Much	Very Much
7. Demands must be met immediately	0	1	2	3
8. Cries	0	1	2	3
9. Mood changes quickly	0	1	2	3
10. Temper outbursts (explosive and unpredictable behavior)	0	1	2	3

Professionals often use rating scales such as this to help determine whether a child is hyperactive. A predominance of scores in the 2 and 3 columns indicates the presence of a problem that requires investigation.

Experts used to think that the root of hyperactive behavior was a deficiency in children's thinking processes, which hindered their attention. According to this theory, these children would get up and move on to something else because they were unable to stay focused. This theory did not explain, however, why hyperactive children moved around more than others in their sleep, when presumably they weren't trying to pay attention to anything.

Another theory held that hyperactivity is a conditioned response. According to this idea, children get more attention from parents and others when they "act out," and the extra attention provides a reward that perpetuates the behavior. However, attempts to teach children to change their behavior have largely proved unsuccessful, because these children lack sufficient control over themselves.

A number of experts have attempted to link hyperactivity to diet, including artificial colorings in food, vitamin insufficiency, and excessive sugar. While diets free of artificial colorings (the Feingold diet) and sugar have gained popularity in the United States, none of the diet-related theories is based on scientific evidence, and attempts to document beneficial effects of various diets have largely failed.

Toxic elements in the environment, primarily lead, also have been cited as causes of ADHD, but as yet these claims are not substantiated scientifically. (If a child is found to have high lead levels, however, prompt medical attention is important.)

Future research will probably show that ADHD can result from a variety of factors. Once these are identified conclusively, perhaps the disorder will prove preventable in at least some cases.

Treatment with Medication

So far medication is the most promising treatment for children with ADHD. Three classes of drugs are used: stimulants, tranquilizers, and antidepressants. The most successful and commonly used drugs are stimulants, which have the paradoxical effect in hyperactive children of slowing them down. These drugs include methylphenidate (Ritalin), dextroamphetamine (Dexedrine), and pemoline (Cylert). (See also chapter 5.)

Changes can be striking. Studies have shown that stimulants affect symptoms in up to 80 percent of hyperactive children, reducing aggressiveness, purposeless behavior, and impulsivity, and improving sustained attention and social relationships.

The drawbacks of using medications are the side effects. Studies in the 1960s and 1970s suggested that long-term use of stimulants slowed down the growth rate of children. However, recent studies show that while there may be slower growth in children taking stimulants, when medication is stopped, even for a short time, a growth spurt occurs. Adolescents who took stimulants as children are of normal height.

Short-term side effects of stimulant use can include insomnia, decreased appetite, weight loss, abdominal pain, or headaches. Some children tend to become more emotional, whiny, and irritable. These side effects occur in fewer than 5 percent of children, most frequently in those age five and under. They can usually be controlled by adjusting the dose, and they disappear completely when treatment stops.

Nonpharmacological Treatments

Behavioral and cognitive therapy use reasoning or rewards and punishments in an attempt to teach the child to change the hyperactive behavior. Studies have shown, however, that trying to teach hyperactive children to act differently is not effective in the long run. The children may do well during treatment, but afterward they typically revert to previous levels of impulsiveness and disorganized behavior.

Most children with ADHD do not benefit from extensive psychological treatment, because the disorder is not psychological in origin. However, psychotherapy and other forms of counseling can be helpful if relationships between the child and others, including family members, have become seriously strained, and to help the child cope with the emotional problems that can result from having the disorder. (See below.) Sometimes the goal of psychotherapy is for family members to understand ADHD better and to learn ways to manage its influence on everyone's life.

Outlook for Hyperactive Children

Even though there is no cure for ADHD, over half the children with the condition grow up to lead normal lives. However, there is evidence that about one-third of all hyperactive children, particularly those who exhibit aggressive behavior, will grow up to have problems with antisocial behavior and delinquency.

Some children may require ongoing supportive psychological help and/or medication. Although studies have shown that ADHD children who have difficulties in school are not any more likely than others to develop severe psychiatric disorders, they do tend to be pessimistic and to lack self-confidence.

Many young people who faced great difficulties in school manage to do well as adults in their working lives, and some excel in their professions. Often they compensate for their condition by choosing lifestyles that are not sedentary. Life can be difficult for those adults whose ADHD was never appropriately diagnosed or treated, however, who remain restless, easily distracted, moody, and unable to concentrate. Treatment with medication and psychotherapy can have equally great rewards in adulthood as in childhood.

AGGRESSION AND DEFIANCE

All children at times are difficult to handle. Conduct disorders and oppositional defiant disorders are more severe problems often requiring help for the whole family.

Conduct Disorders

Children with conduct disorders repeatedly disobey authority, pick fights with other children, steal, and lie. Some express little or no remorse about their unruly behavior. Their behavior may affect others directly, such as when children hit people or destroy their property, or it may be more passive, such as with truancy and lying.

In some children, the problem shows up as early as four or five years of age, in the form of extreme anger and aggressiveness. (See chapter 17.) By age eight, the problem may include other antisocial activities: lying, stealing, skipping school, or vandalizing property. Before reaching puberty, these children may be experimenting with drugs, sex, or drinking, or they may be running away from home. All forms of conduct disorder are more common in boys than in girls.

Roy S. is a child with severe conduct disorder. Although he is only seven years old, he has been suspended from school six times in one year. He runs away from the teacher, hits other children, won't take

SUGGESTIONS FOR PARENTS OF HYPERACTIVE CHILDREN

- Praise your child for good behavior, such as sitting quietly or finishing school work.
- Reward the child, and make the accumulation of small rewards into a game or project. For example, if your child collects 50 pennies for good behavior, he or she can trade them in for a special prize or activity.
- Set and enforce consistent limits on the child's behavior.
- Provide a structured environment.
- Make it clear that you love your child, even though you disapprove of some of the things he or she does.
- Help the child find an activity into which to channel all that excessive energy, such as sports.

- Help the child with school work. Organize the work into a series of small tasks to accomplish one at a time, and provide praise and/or rewards for success in each.
- Keep a grip on your own emotions and reactions. Take a brief time out for yourself when you feel yourself losing your control.
- Recognize the warning signs of an impending explosion or tantrum from your child and do not overreact when it happens.
- Share your child's interests and participate in favorite activities, helping him or her to achieve success and to feel accomplished.
- Be open with your child about his or her condition; discuss problems as they arise.

no for an answer, and gets into such rages that his teacher has to restrain him physically. At home he has set fire to his mother's carpet, broken windows of the house next door, and threatened other children with a knife and a toy hatchet.

Possible Causes of Conduct Disorder

Children with conduct disorder usually do poorly in school, sometimes as a result of intellectual handicaps and learning disabilities (pages 263–265). Some experts have suggested that aggressive and antisocial behavior in older children results from their frustrations over early learning difficulties, but recent studies have discredited this theory.

Researchers have linked both genetic tendencies toward aggression and neglectful or abusive treatment from parents to conduct disorders in children. If there is a history of delinquent, antisocial, or criminal behavior in parents, the children, especially the males, run a higher than average risk of having similar problems. Whether the behavior results from genetic predisposition or from early learning, or both, is not clear. As discussed in chapter 17 (page 250), certain parental attitudes and practices (such as poor disciplinary procedures or inadequate monitoring of activities) are known to contribute. Chapter 19 (page 280) details other contributing factors.

Outlook and Treatment

Conduct disorders get better on their own in about 50 percent of cases. In most individual cases, however, it is not possible to predict which children will outgrow their antisocial behavior. Therefore it is advisable to seek help for school-age children with persistent conduct problems.

A professional assessment is important, because aggressive behavior can be symptomatic of, or aggravated by, many childhood disorders, among them mood disorders, attention-deficit hyperactivity disorder, mental retardation, learning disabilities, and substance abuse disorders, among others. Effective treatment depends on the diagnosis.

For the child diagnosed as having a conduct disorder, treatment can be difficult, and one type of treatment alone may not always be successful. Behavioral therapy can be helpful, especially if the child is young. This approach involves rewarding the child for desired behavior with the promise of a treat, extra time for a favorite activity, and so on. As mentioned in chapter 16, when the child is destructive or violent, adults should withdraw attention rather than shout, hit, or scold; this may involve such "time-out" procedures as sending children to their rooms.

Unfortunately, even when behavioral methods of treatment carried out over several months have appeared successful, in many cases the children later relapse into aggressive and antisocial behavior.

Particularly in school or institutional settings, group therapy with the child's peers can sometimes promote new, constructive behavior.

Some children respond to medication to reduce aggressive and impulsive behavior. Anticonvulsants, antidepressants, stimulants, antipsychotics, and lithium are among the pharmacological agents that sometimes are prescribed. (See also chapters 5 and 27.)

Parents and siblings may benefit from help themselves, for many reasons. Parents may find it difficult to carry out the therapist's advice or to deal with the frustrations of living with children with aggressive and violent behavior. Also, many conduct-disordered children come from families in which many members are troubled or in conflict.

Oppositional Defiant Disorder

Oppositional defiant disorder is a less serious pattern of negative, hostile, and defiant behavior than conduct disorder, in that the rights of others are not violated. Defiant children are usually very argumentative with adults, frequently lose their temper, swear, are often angry and resentful, and are easily annoyed by others. These children are often most defiant around adults or peers they know well; thus this pattern of behavior is often at its worst at home.

Experts generally agree that this type of behavior arises most often in homes where parents have not set appropriate limits on such behavior. However, oppositional behavior often occurs in hyperactive children. In these instances, treating the hyperactivity typically improves other behavior problems.

In children whose oppositional behavior is unrelated to hyperactivity, the emphasis in treatment is to work with the child and the family. Parents are trained to set appropriate standards of behavior and to implement negative consequences when these are violated by the child. When possible, it is important that the therapist work with both the parents and the child, because the behavior pattern is influenced by their interaction. Also, all parties need to understand the goals of the treatment and contribute their own views as to how to effect the best outcome.

LEARNING DISABILITIES

Some children may be very bright and yet have specific learning difficulties that make it hard for them to acquire essential types of knowledge, such as reading, language abilities, and arithmetic. There are varying degrees of learning difficulties. Many, if not most, are transitory; with time, and with help from parents and teachers, a child can often overcome a learning problem without any serious longterm consequences.

Some children, however, are *learning disabled.* Their problems are more serious, requiring professional help and intense education efforts to conquer or ameliorate. Some children never overcome a learning disability completely. There is no precise definition of "learning disabled," other than that learning falls significantly below what is expected. The specific disability, and its intensity, will vary from child to child. Overall, learning disabilities affect as many as 15 percent of school-age children. More boys than girls are affected by reading disabilities specifically.

Historically, children who did not learn easily were suspected of simply having bad attitudes or limited intelligence. They received little or no treatment, and they foundered in ordinary school environments. Today children with learning disorders are being identified early, and training is improving their prospects for a normal life.

For some children, the label "learning disabled" is not appropriate. A child may have difficulty in learning but not actually be learning disabled. Difficulty in learning may instead stem from medical problems (such as hearing or vision impairment), behavioral or psychological problems, or disturbances in the home environment. (See page 264.) Parents who suspect that their child has a learning disability should have an assessment performed by an appropriate professional, the sooner the better.

Conversely, some children who need help and should be classified as learning disabled are not. In the United States, a child who is diagnosably learning disabled is legally entitled to education and support services. U.S. Public Law 94-142, passed in 1977, specifies that for every child diagnosed as learning disabled, schools must develop an Individual Education Prescription (IEP)—a formal plan of instruction, based on his or her specific disabilities, bolstered by help from whatever supportive professionals are deemed necessary. Parents may have to fight to have their child classified as eligible for these services.

Learning disabilities can affect a child for life. While most affected children will be able to improve

COPING WITH LEARNING DISABILITIES

- Discuss the learning disability with the child. Be open. Frequently children with learning disabilities have concluded that they are "stupid." Knowing that the problem has a cause can help dispel these feelings of inadequacy.
- Also talk openly to siblings about the problem. Many children feel embarrassed about their learning-disabled sibling or are teased by other children. Helping them to understand that their sister or brother has a problem will help them cope.
- Develop realistic coping strategies. Identify specific goals that need to be addressed. If the child has difficulty remembering, for example, help him or her to make lists that will organize the day.
- Emphasize the child's strengths. Praise the child for accomplishments and help find skills in which the child excels or can express him- or herself. A child who cannot conquer math, for example, may be an excellent artist.
- Help the child develop social skills by inviting other children over to play or by involving the child in recreational activities. Embarrassed or teased by their peers, many children with learning disabilities also suffer from social isolation. Some children need practice in role-playing in social situations.
- Don't expect miracles. There are no cures for learning disabilities, only strategies that compensate for weaknesses. Don't be fooled into putting your efforts into unsubstantiated remedies through diet, vitamins, or elaborate patterning routines.

Source: Adapted with permission from Stephen W. Gabber, Ph.D, Marianne Daniels Gabber, Ph.D., and Robyn Freedman Spizman, *Good Behavior* (New York: St. Martin's Press, 1987), pp. 354–358.

their skills and ultimately do well academically, they may never catch up to their peers completely. The future of a child with learning disabilities depends on a varieties of factors—the severity of the disability, the specific learning problem, and the kind of help the child receives.

Learning disabilities can be difficult for parents as well as the affected child. Frequently parents have trouble adjusting to their child's disability. They blame themselves, the school, or the child for the problem, rather than understanding that a learning disability is a handicap—and like any handicap, measures can be taken to help cope with the problem.

What Causes Learning Disabilities?

As yet, no one is certain what causes learning disabilities, although neurological abnormalities are strongly suspected because many (though not all) learning-disabled children also suffer from neurologically related problems with language or motor skills. Children with neurological conditions such as cerebral palsy and epilepsy or who have suffered head injury trauma often have learning problems as well. Also, children with ADHD, which is believed to have a neurological basis, often suffer from

learning disabilities. (See pages 258–261.) Like ADHD children, learning-disabled children tend to have fewer social skills, short attention spans, and be less organized and more irresponsible than their peers.

However, direct evidence linking learning disabilities to specific neurological abnormalities is lacking. Studies with computed tomography (CT) scans have so far failed to discriminate definitively differences in the brains of children with learning disabilities, although some of the new brain imaging devices such as positron emission tomography (PET; see chapter 32, page 441) one day may help uncover how and where learning disabilities originate. Recent research, still preliminary, suggests that some people with learning disabilities have impairments in the brain's visual and auditory systems and have difficulty processing information correctly. Although dietary factors have been named as causes, thus far no scientific studies have produced reliable evidence. It is also possible that in some cases dietary, visual, and auditory problems exacerbate, but do not cause, learning disabilities.

Reading disabilities particularly appear to run in families and show up much more frequently in identical twins than in fraternal twins, suggesting a genetic factor. Some researchers link the disorder to a particular gene in members of families in which there is a history of reading impairment, but these studies are inconclusive. In other cases, organic damage to the brain before or after birth may contribute; low birthweight and maternal smoking are two factors that have been implicated. Reading disabilities are discussed later in this chapter.

While it is not known if depression can cause learning disabilities, it is clear that it can have a reinforcing role. A child's feelings of failure, frustration, and anxiety over the inability to conquer academic skills can make it all the harder to cope with or overcome the disability. In some children, however, depression may cause symptoms that mimic a learning disability, such as difficulty in concentrating. Also, psychological difficulties or extraordinary stress may prevent some children for learning adequately. (See the box on page 298 in chapter 20.) To establish the correct treatment, expert diagnosis is extremely important.

Reading Disabilities

The most common learning disability, and the one that causes the most problems, involves reading. In order for children to learn to read, they must be able to identify printed words in several ways: by visually recognizing the whole word, by understanding its meaning and context in a sentence, and by breaking a word into its component sound groups (phonics) and "sounding it out." The reading problems that otherwise normal children have are the result of deficiencies in one or more of these functions.

In the past, most reading difficulties were called *dyslexia* and were thought to involve problems in word recognition. Dyslexia came to stand for two related characteristics of this complex disorder: "mirror writing," in which letters in a word are perceived in reverse order (*was* instead of *saw*), and letter reversal (in which a child mistakes a "d" for a "b," for example). For a long time, experts attributed these problems solely to impaired visual sensory development; they believed that children could not *see* the difference between "b" and "d."

Most experts now believe that reading disorders are related to more complex deficiencies. The problem may not be that children hear or see letters in reverse, but that they cannot properly associate the sounds with the symbols.

Children with reading disorders also may suffer from specific memory deficiencies for language.

Children who confuse "pot" for "top," for example, may have difficulty retrieving language-related information from their memory, while they can recall perfectly, say, the earned run averages of favorite baseball players over the past five years. Studies have shown that poor readers who are asked to remember nonsense symbols recall them as well as normal readers. However, when the symbols are actual words, children with reading disorders do poorly.

Overall, children with reading disabilities (also called developmental reading disorder) learn to read much more slowly than their peers, their comprehension is poor, and they have problems spelling. Many also have trouble expressing themselves in writing (including illegible handwriting, poor use of grammar and syntax) and when speaking aloud, and some have coordination problems and seem clumsy. Reading disabilities are common among children with attention and conduct problems. Boys are 3 to 10 times more likely than girls to have reading disabilities.

Diagnosing Reading and Other Learning Disabilities

The diagnosis of a reading disability requires that the child have a reading level that is significantly below his or her general intelligence. The diagnosis requires individualized testing and cannot be based solely on the opinion of parents, teachers, or pediatricians. Most universities and hospital medical centers have child psychology departments that provide the appropriate testing services to evaluate a child for a reading disability. School counselors, pediatricians, and mental health professionals usually can provide referrals.

Emotional problems such as depression or anxiety can interfere with a child's motivation or concentration and make him or her perform poorly. Physical problems such as poor vision or hearing also can interfere with learning. A thorough psychological and physical evaluation is necessary to determine the nature and sources of the child's difficulties.

Once a diagnosis is made, the child usually is referred to a specialist in reading remediation. As mentioned earlier, public schools are required by law to provide special education for children with learning disabilities; remediation programs, as well as their testing capabilities, vary from school to school.

In choosing a private tutor, parents should focus on two factors. First, because the process of reading remediation is laborious and potentially boring to children, parents should make sure that the child likes the tutor. Second, the reading specialist should be trained in teaching phonics and specific decoding (reading) skills. Some specialists undertake to train children to improve their motor skills, such as drawing or copying printed lines of various shapes; the theory behind these techniques is that strengthening these skills—and the brain functions required to master them—eventually will lead to improved reading. However, any approach that does not focus on the reading process should be avoided in favor of teaching the child specific sounds and rules of language.

In some cases, reading disorders have been attributed to psychological problems that impair the child's ability to learn to read. Psychotherapy may be recommended to remove the "block" that is seen as prohibiting the learning process. Although this may be effective in individual cases, there is no evidence that psychotherapy is effective for most children suffering from reading disorders.

One technique that is successful with many children involves teaching them to associate sounds and small units of sounds (such as syllables) with their written symbols, and then to cluster these sounds into words and sentences. The theory behind this phonetic technique is that the failure to learn to read is due to a failure to relate sounds to letters and syllables. Another alternative involves learning the meaning of words within the context of sentences. Most teachers use a variety of techniques, geared to the specific needs of the child.

For a child who is learning disabled, learning to read can be long, hard work. No scientific studies suggest that one technique works better than another. Nor is there any evidence that techniques employing medication, vitamins, or diet control are in any way effective. With one-to-one attention to reading skills, there is often significant improvement, even though these children will probably not become normal readers.

Do Children with Reading and Other Learning Disabilities Get Better?

When parents and teachers recognize and begin treatment for learning disabilities early, children, particularly those with mild difficulties, have a good chance to acquire the necessary skills over time. The outcome of remediation depends on the child's intelligence, the quality of the treatment, and management of the psychological complications of having a learning disability. These complications include the child's frustration at not being able to master the material, dislike of school, anger, unruly behavior, social withdrawal, truancy, and poor self-esteem from feeling "dumb."

To help learning-disabled children to persist in their efforts, it is important for parents to be actively involved in their child's education and to provide support for attempts to learn rather than criticism for failure.

Children with learning disabilities who are highly intelligent learn to compensate for their problem. Some excel in other areas; others practice harder and longer than other children. As a result, their lives are not greatly hindered by the impairment. A number of famous people have overcome learning disabilities to achieve great distinction in life—Alfred Einstein, Thomas Edison, and William Butler Yeats among them.

There is evidence, however, that some people with reading disorders are limited professionally, and many choose careers that do not require the skills they lack. In spite of substantial obstacles, these people do not necessarily suffer future emotional problems, however. Adults with learning disabilities, which were not broadly recognized less than a generation ago, can also benefit from remediation.

For Additional Information

The Learning Disabilities Association of America (4156 Library Road, Pittsburgh, PA 15234; tel. 412 341–1515) can provide further information on learning disabilities.

ANXIETY DISORDERS

For very young children, fearfulness is quite common as they test out the real and imaginary dangers in the world around them. (See chapter 17.) When certain fears and anxieties persist into the school years, however, they may signal more clearly the need for professional attention.

Separation Anxiety Disorder

Experts diagnose a school-age child as having separation anxiety disorder when fears of leaving parents or of being alone interfere with the child's life. The child may not be able to go to bed alone and may often insist on sleeping with his or her parents. Nightmares are common, as is fear of the dark. Physical complaints such as headaches and stomachaches are common. Such children feel the constant need to keep track of their parents or caregivers, sometimes want to call them from school, and sometimes refuse to go to school ("school phobia"). Away from home they may lapse into social withdrawal, become apathetic and sad, and be unable to concentrate on work or play. Occasionally children may become violent toward the person who is forcing separation.

Often children with separation anxiety disorder also suffer from mood disorders (pages 268–269). The most effective treatment usually involves working with both the child and the family to help the youngster overcome unrealistic concerns and to increase a sense of competency and autonomy. Behavior therapy often is helpful in children who have a mild form of this disorder. This approach offers rewards to the child for trying to separate (such as for sleeping alone in his or her own bedroom) and provides a structure for families to participate in the process. For children who continue to be anxious despite therapy, short-term treatment with tranquilizers or antidepressants may be useful. Imipramine (Tofranil), the same drug used to control panic attacks in adults, has been used with some success in children. However, care must be taken in prescribing it, because the drug does have side effects, including symptoms of drowsiness, dry mouth, and, more seriously, possible cardiac complications.

Social Phobia

Two common types of social phobia can show up in late childhood and early adolescence. One is the fear of performing in front of other people; the other is a fear of social situations in general. Both involve a persistent fear of being exposed to the scrutiny of others, or of being humiliated or embarrassed in public.

Children who are afraid to perform in front of others suddenly may be unable to continue talking in the middle of a speech, may choke on food while eating in a group, may be unable to urinate in a public bathroom, or may begin to tremble while writing in front of someone. Children who fear social situations become uneasy around strangers and often avoid going to parties or other social events.

Like adults with social phobia (see chapter 7), children often recognize that these fears are unreasonable but are unable to control their anxiety. The problem is worsened by the perpetual fear of future social situations. In some cases, behavior therapy to help expose them to their fears in a controlled setting may help diminish the anxiety. (However, many children resist such treatment because it can be emotionally stressful.) Therapy that helps a child practice such social skills as how to take part in a game, take turns, and talk to another child can reduce social isolation and help him or her relate better to other children. For children whose social phobia stems from lack of self-esteem, assertiveness training seems to help, as can individual or small-group training in gym or athletic skills.

Overanxious Disorder

Overanxious children worry about everything, suffer from extreme self-consciousness, need excessive reassurance, and are often unable to relax. They may be concerned about every aspect of their lives: their performance at school, their appearance, how they seem in social situations, whether they can live up to what they perceive as their parents' or teachers' expectations of them now or in the future, and even past behavior. While all these worries may crop up in the lives of children at times, overanxious children are preoccupied with them. Their fears may manifest in physical symptoms such as headaches or stomach pains, nausea, or vomiting.

Often overanxious children have anxious parents, from whom they learn to be anxious or inherit their tendency. Sometimes parents of overanxious children may put pressure on them to achieve; these parents may not realize that they are pushing too hard.

Children who exhibit symptoms of overanxious disorder lasting at least six months require evaluation and possibly treatment with supportive psychotherapy and medication, usually mild tranquilizers. Anxious parents may benefit from treatment as well; reduction in parents' anxiety can greatly help the child.

CHILDREN'S ART THERAPY: "FAMILIA"

Figure 18.1: A young boy in therapy for separation anxiety, whose parents are divorced, pictures himself as being the connection between them. His mother holds a club, which the therapist believed represented the child's desire to feel protected and have a strong authority figure in his life.

MOOD DISORDERS IN SCHOOL-AGE CHILDREN

Although mood swings are common in children, prolonged periods of unhappiness (depression) or extreme high mood (mania) are not, and these should receive attention.

Recognizing the Symptoms

It is not easy to determine when young children are depressed, because they have difficulty finding the words to express their emotions accurately. Depressed children often describe their feelings simply as boredom, and indeed their actions connote boredom. Depressed children seem to get no pleasure from activities they used to enjoy, whether it is watching television, playing with favorite toys, or pursuing hobbies. They may avoid playing with friends and prefer to stay at home. They may be irritable, mopey, and withdrawn, and often be tearful for no apparent reason.

Depressed children are often intensely self-critical. They may be preoccupied with thinking about death, although depression prior to adolescence rarely leads to suicide. They seem sluggish and lethargic and often sleep too much. Their appetite may change, and they may start suddenly to eat more or less than usual.

Following a period of depression, some children suddenly will become abnormally enthusiastic about life and display extreme confidence, gregariousness, and energy. If the change in mood lasts for more than a week or two, it may be an unnatural high or mania. The once-lethargic child becomes extremely busy, talkative, and perhaps unable to sleep. Often during the period of extreme buoyancy and energy the child may become irritable and impatient and snap at others without provocation.

Parents and even pediatricians may mistake this manic behavior for hyperactivity. However, hyperactivity is usually present since very early childhood, whereas a dramatic shift in mood contrasts markedly with the child's previous behavior pattern.

Causes of Mood Disorder in School-Age Children

As with mood disorders in adults (chapter 8), the causes of childhood mood disorders seem to lie in a combination of the child's own constitution and life circumstances. Depression is frequently triggered by some type of loss, such as the death of a parent, divorce, serious illness, or a move. There is evidence that some children are more sensitive to loss and may be predisposed biologically to mood disorders. While the mood disorders tend to run in families, children with depressed parents are not necessarily destined to suffer from a mood disorder themselves.

Treating Childhood Mood Disorders

Because of the limited number of long-term studies of children with mood disorders, it is not yet certain which forms of treatment work best, or what the outlook is for such children. If the child's mood seems to be a reaction to a problem in his or her environment, therapy can probably help the child cope or come to terms with those concerns. Sometimes children of school age will respond with anger or sadness if ill-ness or other stressors deprive them of parental approval or their usual activities. Family sessions can mobilize the family to address difficulties that affect the child, and individual psychotherapy may help the child to feel accepted and appreciated.

Patty O., for example, had been a fairly happy child who did well in school and enjoyed playing with her friends and engaging in outdoor activities. When she was 10 years old the family moved to another city, and her mother's drinking, which had been largely in control before, suddenly became dramatically worse. Patty's parents began to fight, and they were too absorbed in their own problems to attend to Patty or her two younger sisters. Patty became withdrawn, staying home indoors after school and making no attempts to find new friends. Her grades fell, and she began to want to stay home from school.

At the suggestion of a teacher, Patty began to see a school guidance counselor, who was able to draw the girl out about her home situation. Exposing her sorrow, anger, and feelings of guilt over "causing" her parents' problems helped lift Patty's depression. The counselor suggested family therapy, which eventually led her mother to seek treatment for her alcoholism. When the fights at home lessened and her mother had more time for her again, Patty's last symptoms of depression cleared up.

Some clinicians prescribe antidepressant medication or lithium to children in conjunction with family and individual psychotherapy, to help reduce the symptoms of mood disorder. (Chapter 19 provides more information on mood disorders in adolescence; depression and bipolar illness, also called manic-depression, are the subject of chapter 8.)

CHILDHOOD SCHIZOPHRENIA

Schizophrenia, which usually begins in adolescence or early adulthood, is rare in childhood. Children with extreme emotional withdrawal and other symptoms, such as an inability to control their repetitive movements, used to be diagnosed as schizophrenic as early as age two. These symptoms are now seen as characterizing pervasive developmental disorder, also known as autism. (See chapter 17.)

Most children who develop schizophrenia before adolescence are male. Symptoms of childhood schizophrenia may begin to appear as early as age five, but this is very unusual and in most cases the child is ten or over. While the symptoms are the same for children as for adults—including disturbance in thinking, delusions, hallucinations, and a marked inability to function—they can be very difficult to assess in young children. Delusions (such as a belief that one's body is inhabited by insects) and hallucinations (hearing voices, for example) may be confused with childhood fantasies. Genuine hallucinations in young children are more likely to be triggered by organic conditions such as high fever.

Additional symptoms that psychiatrists look for in very young children are trouble doing simple tasks, problems with attention, difficulty relating to others, and excessive anxiety over any change. Older children and adolescents also may exhibit loss of the capacity to experience pleasure, excessive dependency, and a profoundly disturbed sense of self.

Causes of Schizophrenia

As discussed at length in chapter 14, researchers have discovered evidence that factors such as genetic predisposition and brain damage play a major role in schizophrenia. Few experts now believe, as they once did, that the illness is caused by poor parenting. However, parenting styles can exacerbate or ameliorate the experience of the child with schizophrenia. These children need sheltered, calm environments, in which a minimum of demands are placed on them. Studies have shown that children with schizophrenia do better in homes where there is not a lot of shouting and conflict.

Treatment and Outcome

Early intervention can make an appreciable difference in the course of schizophrenia and allow some sufferers to lead relatively normal lives. As with adults, treatment should be tailored individually, but it nearly always involves medication, often coupled with supportive psychotherapy, education planning, and parental counseling.

The discussion of schizophrenia continues in the next chapter, on adolescence.

BEDWETTING

In school-age children, wetting and soiling problems (discussed in chapter 17, pages 255–256) can be problematic for both children and parents.

Bedwetting, called *nocturnal enuresis,* is the inability to hold urine while sleeping. An infant wetting the diaper is, of course, behaving normally. But as children grow older, they learn to control their bladders and use a toilet. While there is considerable individual variation among children, most physicians agree that girls who are five years old and boys who are six should be able to control their urine during sleep.

Enuresis is embarrassing and uncomfortable, and just because it is common, it should not be regarded as normal. About 15 percent of five-year-old girls and 7 percent of six-year-old boys have continued episodes of bedwetting. Like sleepwalking and night terrors, it will usually resolve itself by adolescence, with or without treatment. Only about 1 percent of adults regularly experience nocturnal enuresis. However, since it is not possible to predict which child will get better on his or her own, and because the condition is often treatable, if bedwetting persists beyond age seven, help should be sought.

There is some genetic component in primary enuresis. Seventy-five percent of affected children have at least one parent or a sibling who was a bedwetter, and identical twins are twice as likely to be bedwetters as other siblings. Families of bedwetters do, in fact, have a higher than usual incidence of sleepwalking and night terrors.

In girls and less often in boys, bedwetting is often associated with urinary tract infections, and although it is not appropriate to put a child through an uncomfortable urological evaluation, it is wise to have the child's urine tested for infection.

Even though children almost always outgrow their bedwetting, treatment is usually indicated because of the psychological and social consequences. Parents should be aware that the bedwetting child cannot help him- or herself. Punishing or blaming the child, especially when bedwetting is related to psychological conflicts, only adds to the stress the child is already undergoing. The child also should be assured that there is nothing "wrong" with him or her.

Parents can best help their children's progress toward ending bedwetting by praising them for one or more dry nights. Often a physician's guidance can bring about successful management and avoid trauma.

A bedwetting "alarm" is another, often very effective, treatment option. The child wears a device at night that triggers an alarm when it detects moisture. About two-thirds of youngsters using the device soon learn to wake up and visit the bathroom when their muscles begin the process of passing urine. Parents

DOES YOUR CHILD NEED PROFESSIONAL HELP?

As stated in chapter 16, it is not always easy for parents to determine if their child needs professional help. The following are some rules of thumb to help parents of school-age children make this decision. You might want to consult a professional if:

- The child has difficulties in several important situations such as school, camp, extracurricular activities, and home.
- These difficulties are not transient, but persist over time.
- The child finds it difficult to do something that is important to him or her, and it is something that children of that age do readily, such as visit friends, sleep over at a friend's house, get ready in the morning within a reasonable period of time, join a club, do errands, fall asleep at night, or get homework done.
- The child's functioning changes. For example, grades go down, friendships are no longer maintained, interests are not pursued, or self-care or grooming is neglected.
- Emotional responses change. The child worries excessively about school or other concerns; becomes oversensitive to criticism, irritable, nasty, or irresponsible; or stops obeying rules such as curfews.
- The child shows signs of disturbances of thought and attention.

need to be aware that successful treatment nearly always takes more than a month; they should not abandon treatment early just because it does not seem to be working. However, if the alarm has not produced any positive effects after a month, a specialist should be consulted.

In some instances, medications can be prescribed to help the bladder muscles, or to reduce the amount of urine produced during the night. This treatment is simpler than the alarm and therefore reasonable to attempt first. If bedwetting returns when one or two months of treatment ends, the child should then be treated with the alarm. Medication may also be useful in some special circumstances, such as enabling a child to spend a weekend away or to go to camp.

19

Normal Development and Major Problems of Adolescence

Clarice J. Kestenbaum, M.D., and Paul D. Trautman, M.D.

The term "adolescence" commonly refers to the time between puberty and age 19, although many experts now consider this period as extending into the early 20s. This stage of life begins with the physiological changes of puberty that mark the end of childhood. It comes to a close when the individual assumes adult roles, such as work that permits financial independence and the formation of an intimate love relationship.

Psychoanalyst Erik Erikson has described adolescence as a necessary "crisis of development." According to him, the teenage years serve most importantly as a time for identity formation. Peer group affiliation, separation from the family, planning for the future, and the growth of love and intimacy are other

necessary tasks. Erikson also mentions the adolescent's search for fidelity, the ability to be true to something or someone, as described so well by Robert Lindner in *Rebel Without a Cause*. To Erikson, in no other stage of the life cycle are the promise of finding one's self and the threat of losing one's self so closely allied.

Adolescent Turmoil: Is It Necessary?

"Adolescent turmoil" has been defined as an emotional condition that represents significant psychological disruption and leads to mood swings, confused thinking, and rebellion. Many theorists have hypothesized that this turmoil is both typical of and necessary to normal adolescent development. For example, child psychoanalyst Anna Freud (Sigmund Freud's daughter) believed that adolescents who do not experience adolescent turmoil have difficulty separating from their parents and establishing a sense of their own identity.

More recently, however, researchers such as Daniel Offer have reexamined the concept of adolescent turmoil. Studying thousands of high school students, Offer and his colleagues found that most normal adolescents enjoyed their lives, felt relaxed under usual circumstances, and exhibited a positive sense of self-worth. Most did not have major conflicts with their families. On the whole, the adolescents in this survey saw themselves as without significant problems.

However, a large minority of young people did not feel secure about their coping abilities. Twenty percent of adolescents studied demonstrated moderate to serious emotional difficulties, felt empty emotionally, and frequently were depressed, anxious, and confused. While many adolescents who experience such psychological difficulties *are* merely passing through a developmental phase and will emerge as healthy young adults (although counseling or therapy might make that emergence easier), for a small group of troubled teenagers, "adolescent turmoil" may indicate the beginning of serious difficulties such as schizophrenia, depression, and bipolar (manic-depressive) disorder.

Overall, statistics suggest that about 3.4 million of the approximately 17 million adolescents in the United States have significant psychological problems and need mental health services. The major problems (as well as some of the more common difficult behaviors) of adolescence are the focus of the latter half of this chapter. To understand the context out of which these difficulties arise, we look first at the important developments that need to take place at this stage of life. (Note that chapters 21 and 22 discuss many of the adolescent developmental experiences as they relate specifically to females or males.)

THE JOURNEY THROUGH ADOLESCENCE

The Early Phase

During early adolescence (generally ages 12 to 14), a young person's character, or personality, is still in the process of being formed. Tasks that need to be accomplished at this stage include:

- *Loosening of parental ties.* Beginning in early adolescence, children increasingly seek new role models in teachers, counselors, friends, and culture heroes. They identify with these people and use them as examples for themselves as they try to be independent individuals.
- *Resolving earlier traumas.* Adolescents need to come to terms with certain traumatic childhood events. Traumas can range in extremes from recognition that parents have human frailties to death of a parent. (See chapter 20.)
- *Establishing continuity.* Young teenagers begin to understand a larger framework of past, present, and future. They begin to develop a sense of continuity with respect to their previous feelings, remembered experiences, and their own family history. One cannot have a future without having a past, and this becomes apparent to children at this stage of life.

- *Solidifying sexual identity.* In early adolescence people become more certain of their gender identity (that is, who they are as a male or female), which is an aspect of self-awareness that begins in infancy. Young adolescents also begin to experiment with choosing a partner. The goal of the mature individual is to establish an intimate relationship with a partner of (most commonly) the opposite sex.

Effect of Physiological and Sexual Maturation

Hormonal and structural changes (breasts, genitals, musculature, and so on) take place mostly between the ages of 11 and 15. They can lead to confusing and sometimes tormenting conflicts, especially among children who mature at different rates from their classmates. A girl who develops breasts and pubic hair at 11 may be pleased to look like her older sister but confused about being unlike other girls her age. She may feel she is no longer allowed to be a little girl, to enjoy childish games, and to be cared for by her family as a child. She may also sense that she will have to sacrifice aspects of herself and "give herself airs," as she has seen older girls do. Some authorities believe that in extreme cases, she may starve herself and become anorexic in order to keep a child's body. (See page 276.)

Menstruation. The onset of menstruation (menarche) has a deep significance for a girl. As a symbol of sexual maturity, it makes her think about her potential roles as sexual person, wife, and mother. The first menstrual period can be a traumatic event if it has not been explained accurately and helpfully ahead of time.

A young girl's attitude toward menstruation (and toward sex and her role as a woman) will be greatly influenced by her mother's beliefs. Older sisters, schoolmates, female friends, and teachers have less of an influence. The girl will be sensitive not only to what the mother conveys in words about being a woman but, more important, to what she conveys by her gestures, by her relationships with her husband and other men, and by what she chooses *not* to say to her daughter about her entrance into womanhood. If the mother ignores the event or continually refers to it as something unpleasant or a nuisance, the daughter will likely experience menstruation in that light. This attitude possibly can even affect the amount of monthly physical discomfort and cramps that the girl will experience.

Similarly, if a mother gives the impression that women are incompetent and inferior to men, she may convey negative feelings to her daughter not only about menstruation but about all that is uniquely female as well.

Nocturnal emissions. Occasional ejaculation of seminal fluid during sleep is noted in about 9 boys out of 10 after the beginning of puberty and is ordinarily accompanied by erotic dreams. Many boys will talk freely among themselves about such experiences; they will have learned about the universality and meaning of these "wet dreams" from older boys at camp or older brothers or classmates. Some, however, appear to have no idea of what is happening to them and imagine there is something seriously the matter.

Masturbation. For both boys and girls, masturbation is a way of experimenting with, controlling, and integrating new urges. Before intimacy with another person can be achieved at a later stage of development, the young adolescent must first learn how his or her own body functions and to recognize and accept the experiences of sexual tension and response.

Nevertheless, in spite of today's more permissive or sympathetic parental attitudes toward it, adolescents continue to generate many false and frightening ideas concerning masturbation. Guilt feelings, especially in relation to masturbation fantasies, can act as powerful deterrents to an otherwise natural urge. Guilt and shame can also lower self-esteem. Although teenagers probably won't confide in parents about these issues, parents may wish to reassure them nonetheless that masturbation and self-exploration are normal and healthy.

Sexual urges. Throughout adolescence, and most strikingly in its earliest phase, the difference in level of maturity between same-aged boys and girls is profound. Girls are usually two or three years ahead of boys in this respect. Sex for the 14-year-old boy is still mostly a proving ground for genital competence or a way of combating worries about homosexuality. The girl is farther ahead in separating herself from her parents and is beginning to know what it is to seek a new person who will supply love, warmth, nurturance, and devotion.

In relationships with the other sex, early adolescents are still motivated largely by curiosity about their own bodies. New and disruptive sexual urges can cause anxiety as boys find themselves with erections at a high school dance or girls experience disconcerting, although pleasurable, clitoral sensations.

To satisfy their curiosity, or to alleviate anxiety, boys compare their bodies, especially genital size, and often engage in mutual masturbatory acts. Girls discuss the details of their menses and may compare breast size. Peer relationships are still apt to be with the same sex; there usually will be one or two "best" friends and a "gang" or "crowd" with which the young adolescent identifies. Heterosexual exploration at this early stage does not really establish intimate ties but allows the young adolescent to explore and understand new bodily sensations.

The behavior of parents may intensify the sexual conflicts of the young adolescent. A father who used to kiss and fondle his little girl without embarrassment may suddenly discover a nubile young woman capable of arousing him. Both become ill at ease, awkward, and tend to give up this kind of playful activity. Similarly, a mother who may have been comfortable in front of her children when she was only partially clothed may now realize that she arouses sexual feelings in her young adolescent son, who reacts to her presence with both excitement and discomfort.

Middle Adolescence

Although attempting to be free, adolescents at this stage (ages 14 to 17 or 18) still are dependent on their parents and deeply attached. They swing toward and away from parents, forming sudden, intense, and transient attachments to new figures with whom they seek to identify, such as teachers, coaches, rock stars, or sports heroes. Adolescents often see themselves through the eyes of their peers, and any deviation in appearance, dress code, or behavior can cause a loss of self-esteem.

It is important that parents understand behaviors such as changes in friendships, hairstyles, or career goals. As long as adolescents show no signs of major psychological problems or change in their ability to function, changeable behavior is ordinarily no cause for concern. (See the box on page 277.) A teenager may dye his hair purple and shave half his head, but if he joins the family regularly for dinner, seems cheerful, and is keeping up with his school work, the family should try to tolerate the haircut.

At the same time, parents should not abrogate their authority. Teenagers usually will follow consistent guidelines set up to ensure their safety and the comfort and harmony of the household (such as knowing where the teenagers are going and with whom, and that they drive safely), even though they may protest. (See also "What Parents Want to Know" on pages 284–289.)

Sexual Behavior

A study conducted in the late 1980s found that by their 17th birthday, 37 percent of the girls and 54 percent of the boys had had sexual intercourse. Teenagers with gratifying home environments as well as high academic achievements (activities that require a substantial commitment of time) were somewhat less likely to have had sexual intercourse.

Most teenagers in the survey had confidence about their gender identity and heterosexual partner choice. Some adolescents, however, were confused about their identity, including sexual orientation, and engaged in a certain amount of bisexual exploration. A small percentage of teenagers believed themselves to be homosexual from early childhood. It is not abnormal for teenagers to feel some confusion about their sexual orientation. If teenagers experiment with same-sex behavior, it should not automatically be assumed that they are homosexual. The teenage years are a time of trying things out and experimenting; sex and coming to terms with one's sexual identity are among the experiences that mark the passage into adulthood.

If problems with identity or confusion about sexual orientation cause problems with an adolescent's ability to function in academic or social activities, a consultation with a mental health professional should be sought. With sexual orientation problems, the professional consulted must be someone who is sensitive to the issues surrounding same-sex experimentation and who has experience in counseling teenagers about their choice of sexual partners.

Intellectual Development and Judgment

The mid-adolescent period also is a time when intellectual development undergoes considerable change. According to Swiss psychologist Jean Piaget, cognitive development at this stage is characterized by the ability to think in abstractions and reason from hypotheses. Teenagers' awareness increases and they develop a capacity for insight and an ability to make carefully considered judgments. Intelligence and good judgment do not always proceed together, however. At the same time adolescents are developing the ability to solve complicated mathematical problems and discuss historical trends, they can exhibit extremely poor judgment when their emotions take over. For example, a brilliant chemistry student may insist on taking the family car to visit a girlfriend 50 miles away, despite storm warnings and hazardous road conditions. He may believe, in some magical fashion, that nothing can happen to him. In the same way, a girl may believe that she will not become pregnant from unprotected sexual activity.

Parents may have difficulty reasoning with their otherwise intelligent teenagers, who often argue with great intensity and seem unaware of the probable consequences of their actions. As noted, however, the parents' active role is important in forging the bridge to reality and an awareness of the feelings of others.

Reconstructing the Past to Go Forward

Now that they are able to think in abstractions, adolescents begin to develop a more coherent sense of their past and to consider the future. Some adolescents become interested in their roots in the belief that in order to have a meaningful future, one must have a meaningful past. If a child has lost a parent through death or divorce, he or she may now conduct a personal research project on the lost parent's life. An adopted child may try to find the biological parents.

Children who have lost a parent early may not experience full mourning until adolescence. They may then begin to idealize the lost parent. Some adolescents experience a kind of mourning just for "the way things were" in early childhood, within the safe environment of the familiar home and comforting parents. They know they must soon leave home for college or work and that they will form new relationships. While eager to explore the world, they are at the same time reluctant and frightened by the prospect.

Acquiring Personal Values

During the mid-adolescent phase, teenagers are coming to terms with the value systems they have learned from their parents. At this stage, they usually accept the religion, scruples, and moral values of their families, but they are beginning to make their own modifications. Each teenager's conscience now begins to form an integral part of his or her own identity; it is no longer a set of values held merely because of fear of parental disapproval. Teenagers occasionally may need to experiment with peers (perhaps with beer or marijuana) in order to come to their own conclusions about the dangers of such behavior. This does not mean, however, that parents should take a laissez-faire attitude toward such actions. Parents must always make their own views known. (See also "What Parents Want to Know," pages 284–289.)

Late Adolescence

The late adolescent period can range from the late teens through the early 20s. It is a time when the separation process is completed. The young person begins to consolidate realistic work goals and, most important, to establish intimate bonds outside the nuclear family. While the mid-adolescent could mimic sexual intimacy long before he or she was ready (sharing the details of sexual escapades with peers as a way of enhancing self-esteem), the more mature adolescent may be ready for true intimacy.

The first love relationship is very special and will be remembered throughout life. Frequently the adolescent is deeply infatuated with the beloved and may not care to share details of the relationship with anyone. Young people in love often feel that their own passionate feelings are unique and will tend to idolize their lovers. Feelings of empathy and caring now join with sexual passion. The love may deepen as a truly intimate bond develops, or the teenager may find someone else to love.

MAJOR PROBLEMS OF ADOLESCENCE

As noted earlier, as many as one of every five young people manifest specific psychological symptoms as they attempt to negotiate the developmental hurdles of adolescence. Their troubles may be moderate and transient, or they may represent the first appearance of serious disorders. Major psychiatric disturbances that can begin in adolescence include identity disorder, eating disorders, depression, bipolar (manic-depressive) disorder, and schizophrenia.

Problems such as those noted in the box on page 277 are signs that a teenager should be brought to professional attention for a thorough evaluation.

Identity Disorder

Because establishing a unique identity is the hallmark of adolescent development, problems in this area are not uncommon. An adolescent may suffer distress regarding his or her choice of career, long-term goals, family and peer loyalties, and love relationships, finding it almost impossible to select from the myriad groups, careers, lifestyles, and values with which to identify. If the distress is persistent, talking to a professional may help the adolescent sort out the dilemma.

It is normal for a young adolescent to "try on" a variety of roles, perhaps even adopting the dress and mannerisms of a hero, plastering the room with posters of the idol, or listening constantly to a rock star's music. In extreme cases, a disturbed teenager may assume the character of a popular rock star or an older peer and attempt to live out fantasies of being the idol. If the adolescent shows no other signs of disturbance and continues to relate to the parents as before, the phase will probably pass. If, however, the teenager heads off to become a "groupie," joins an extreme cult, or is frequently away from home without explanation, there may be a problem for which professional consultation and individual or group therapy may be warranted.

Eating Disorders

Failure to accept one's body changes is another way that identity disturbance reveals itself. Some girls, fearful of maturation, become convinced at the first sign of breast development or menstruation that they are fat. (In fact, women's dissatisfaction with their bodies is quite common, often fostered by the

GUIDELINES FOR PARENTS

Adolescence is no time to abrogate authority. The adolescent, no longer a child, not yet an adult, at times can be extremely mature and at other times can exhibit a profound lack of judgment. Give the adolescent an opportunity to experiment with independence, such as summers away from home for work, travel, or camp, but always be ready to offer structure, guidelines, and rules. The adolescent who makes some errors of judgment while still in the bosom of the family (getting drunk in his or her room with friends, failing a few exams because of unpreparedness) will most likely do better the first year away from home than the adolescent who is permitted to make no mistakes before leaving home.

It's Okay

The following list shows behaviors that are part of normal development and that need not cause concern.

- *Messy room*
  No matter how much teenagers complain about it, insist that they clean their room once a week. As long as they confine their mess to the bedroom, just shut the door and ignore the chaos.
- *Need for privacy*
  Teenagers need to be alone, behind closed doors much of the time, perhaps listening to music or endlessly talking to friends on the telephone. This is typical behavior and often an important way of achieving separation from the family. Do, however, discuss rules regarding homework, not tying up the telephone lines, and so on.
- *Idealization of role models*
  Transient crushes on "heroes" are an attempt to form a new identity. Your teenager may remove you from the pedestal in the process.

- *Peculiar dress or hairstyles in concordance with peer group*
  Adolescent rebellion can take many forms. This one is mild, transient, and you should probably ignore it as much as possible.
- *Mild mood swings*
  Sudden shifts in mood concerning the future, social roles, and dating are not uncommon. If school work and other activities are up to par, you need not worry.

Causes for Concern

The following list delineates more serious problems in teenagers. Seek a psychiatric consultation if you note:

- A marked loss of interest in usual activities
- Persistent insomnia
- Loss of interest in friends
- Sudden and extreme drop in grades
- Truancy
- Refusal to accept reasonable rules (curfew, household chores, and so on)
- Persistent drug or alcohol use
- Delinquent acts (theft, firesetting, and the like)
- Expressed hatred and contempt toward formerly loved family members
- Sexual promiscuity
- Physical attacks on parents
- Expressed thoughts of suicide
- Joining a cult

All of these behaviors require a consultation in order to determine the cause and appropriate therapeutic intervention. At times a few individual or family sessions may be all that is necessary. Early intervention is important to "nip in the bud" problems in the making and help the adolescent get back on the normal developmental track.

---

media's presentation of idealized bodies that are not necessarily healthy ones.) Unable to eat normally and still attain the ultra-thin look, adolescent girls may develop a pattern of chronic dieting, and sometimes of bingeing and fasting, known as bulimia. It is not uncommon for teenagers who are overweight, or who think that they are, regularly to engage in self-induced vomiting and to use laxatives and diuretics, which can be a serious health threat.

A small number of adolescents, mostly girls,

develop anorexia nervosa. These teenagers often have no concept of how their bodies really look and see themselves as grossly fat, even though they are normal or even emaciated. Because these teenagers may starve themselves and seriously threaten their lives, they should have a professional evaluation if they become significantly underweight. There is some evidence that a predisposition to anorexia nervosa and possibly also to bulimia occurs in girls with a family history of depression. (See also chapters 10 and 21.)

Depression in Adolescence

Mood swings are common in adolescence. Usually these are transient, related to such events as the breakup of a relationship, disappointment in an attempted achievement, or disciplinary measures by a parent. Adolescents may also, as noted earlier, go through a period of sadness as they mourn the loss of childhood. These mood dips usually do not seriously jeopardize their school work or lead to cutting off ties with family or friends. A caring and interested adult, who is not too intrusive, or a best friend or sibling can be a solace during this time.

Although it is uncommon (occurring in less than 5 percent of teenagers), adolescents do experience serious depression in much the same way that adults do. (See chapter 8.) Girls are affected somewhat more than boys. Children and adolescents who have close family members who suffer from depression are at increased risk of suffering depression themselves. About one-third of adolescents with a depressive disorder have parents with the same problem.

Treatment for Depression

Two psychotherapeutic approaches have been found to be successful in treating adolescent depression. Psychodynamic psychotherapy in its many forms (see chapters 4 and 16) explores the adolescent's unconscious wishes, fears, past experiences, and current relationship problems. Cognitive therapy helps the adolescent recognize the kinds of negative thoughts he or she may have that can foster depression. These thoughts include negative beliefs about self, the world, and the future. The thought that "my friends don't want to see me" can cause the adolescent to avoid social situations and thus reinforce the belief, leading to increased isolation, feelings of loneliness, rejection, and overwhelming depression. By helping the youngster recognize these attitudes and change them, the therapist can foster a more positive attitude and help alleviate the problem. More recently, interpersonal therapy, which seeks to modify the depressed person's troubled relationships with family and friends, has been adapted for adolescents.

As an important adjunct to psychotherapy, medication such as antidepressants and lithium have been found to be effective. (See chapter 5.)

There is no way to generalize about how long treatment for depression in adolescence should last or how frequently a teenager should see a therapist.

SIGNS OF DEPRESSION

Depression in adolescence can be a significant impairment. Parents should be concerned if, over a period of time, an adolescent:

- Does not feel able to go to school or to do homework
- Does not wish to see friends or pursue former interests
- Is constantly tearful or irritable
- Engages in dangerous or destructive behavior such as reckless driving or bouts of drinking

Other telltale signs include:

- Change in appetite and weight
- Disturbed sleeping patterns
- Complaints of fatigue
- A seeming agitation or lethargy
- Sudden inattention to appearance
- A sense of worthlessness or self-reproach
- Loss of concentration and an inability to make simple decisions
- A preoccupation with death: *Talk of suicide or suicide attempts require immediate attention.* (See below.)

It depends entirely on the nature and severity of the problem as well as the individual child's response to treatment. In severe cases, parents may wonder whether or not their depressed youngster should be hospitalized for treatment. This decision must be made in consultation with a professional who is experienced in treating adolescents. Usually there is no need to hospitalize a youngster for depression unless there is a risk of suicide (see below) or of the child hurting him- or herself or others. Some teenagers have addiction problems coexisting with depression; in these cases, if outpatient detoxification does not work, inpatient hospitalization might be considered to keep the adolescent away from the drugs or alcohol.

Suicide

Prolonged depression can lead to suicide or suicide attempts in adolescents. Suicide is the third leading cause of death among teenagers. In the United States, an estimated 2,000 youngsters between the ages of 10 and 19 kill themselves every year. Reports of suicide "clusters," in which one suicide appears to trigger several others within a group such as a school or community, have also increased. (See chapter 26.)

The causes of suicide in adolescents, as in adults, are complex and varied; biological, psychological, and environmental factors all play a role. Not all adolescents who talk of or attempt suicide are depressed. Many have serious behavior problems at home or school, and act out aggressively (arguing, fighting, stealing, and so on) toward others as well as themselves. Suicide attempters often have severe conflicts in relationships with their parents.

Teenagers seem prone to see suicide as a solution to life's problems, which they tend to see as overwhelming. While an adult has the experience to know that one setback in life does not mean that all hope is lost, some teenagers may see disappointments as major failures and temporary difficulties as insurmountable crises. An adolescent may see a poor grade as a sign of an irreversible trend and an indication that he or she will never be successful in life. Self-esteem and a sense of identity can be fragile at this age, vulnerable to any major blow.

Adolescents may be particularly susceptible to triggering events such as heartbreaks, school disappointments, or news that people they have known have killed themselves or that a rock star or other hero with whom they strongly identify has done so. The most common trigger, however, is an argument with a parent.

What Should Parents and Friends Do?

If parents are concerned about their teenager, or if he or she is showing any signs of depression as described earlier, parents should keep a close eye out for other warning signs. (See the box that follows.) In particular, if a teenager talks about death or suicide, it is important to listen. If the teenager seems markedly preoccupied with suicide, he or she should be evaluated immediately by a professional. Chapter 26 provides further suggestions.

Treatment for Suicidal Behavior

Many mental health professionals stress that an adolescent who is at risk for suicide needs to know that there is an objective and caring person whom he or she can reach and talk to at any time, day or night.

Because suicide often is prompted by other underlying problems, these problems are usually the focus of treatment. Conditions that are associated

---

WARNING SIGNS OF IMPENDING SUICIDE

The following questions can help parents or others determine if an adolescent is at risk for suicide. While "yes" answers do not mean the child is definitely at risk, they do indicate that an evaluation is important.

- Have there been problems with school or the family?
- Has there been a breakup with a boyfriend or girlfriend?
- Does the adolescent have a history of psychiatric problems such as psychosis, depression, or physical or sexual abuse?
- Has there been a previous attempt?
- Has anyone in the family or a friend attempted suicide?
- Does the adolescent have a history of drug or alcohol abuse?
- Has the adolescent lost interest in school, friends, or former activities?
- Does the adolescent seem depressed?
- Does the adolescent talk of death, dying, or suicide, or make vague threats such as: "You'll be sorry. I won't be around any more"?

Aggravating factors that can contribute to the risk of teenage suicide include severe depression, problems with drugs or alcohol, the presence of a gun in the house, or another family member who has committed suicide.

---

most often with teenage suicides are: previous suicide attempts, major depressive disorder, aggression and conduct disorder, physical illness, drug and alcohol abuse on the part of the adolescent or parents, parental psychiatric illness, marital conflict of parents, and parent-child conflict.

Treatment very often focuses on depression, not only because depression greatly increases the risk of suicide (25 to 30 percent of suicide attempters are depressed) but because this problem often can be treated successfully.

The Case of Dan A.

Dan A. was a 13-year-old seventh-grader when he was sent to the school psychologist after his teacher saw him hanging precariously out a window. He seemed depressed, and the school psychologist referred him to a child psychiatrist. Dan insisted that he was only trying to reach a pencil that a classmate had thrown onto the window ledge, but he admitted that for several months he had felt depressed, tense, irritable, and tired, and had increasing difficulty falling asleep. His grades had fallen recently. "I can't concentrate on anything," he said.

Dan's mother told the psychiatrist that Dan had become distant and uncommunicative at home, although he seemed to be getting along very well with two friends. She believed they were experimenting with alcohol and marijuana. In discussing vacation plans, he had remarked to her, "I'd like to go somewhere very far away. The world isn't big enough."

Dan's family history pointed to trouble. His parents were divorced, his father was an alcoholic, and his maternal grandmother had been treated for depression years before. In light of all these circumstances, Dan's condition was considered quite severe, so he received both a tricyclic antidepressant and psychotherapy. He improved with treatment, becoming more communicative with his mother, doing better at school, and acting more cheerful.

Bipolar (Manic–Depressive) Disorder

Bipolar disorder in adolescence does not vary significantly from that in adults. (See chapter 8.) Characterized by periods of depression alternating with manic periods of excitement, extreme energy, and frenzied behavior, it is particularly difficult to diagnose in adolescents. Bipolar disorder is often confused with schizophrenia, depression, or simply normal mood changes.

Ellen C., a 19-year-old young woman, was hospitalized with an acute psychotic episode after being brought to the emergency room in a state of confusion. Several close family members suffered from emotional disorders, including suicidal depression, anorexia nervosa, and compulsive gambling.

Although prone to periods of depression as a youngster, Ellen had seemed normal to her parents. When she went to college, however, the stress of final examinations in her freshman year led to a period of frenzied activity. Her mind was racing, she began unrealistic projects that could not be finished, she was sexually promiscuous, and she began stealing things throughout her dormitory. Ellen soon was diagnosed as having bipolar disorder. The evaluating psychiatrist recommended a course of lithium treatment combined with continuing psychotherapy. Her prognosis is good.

As in schizophrenia (see page 281), it is important to catch the illness early, particularly before a severe break with reality occurs. In many cases, with the appropriate treatment, the young person may look forward to a normal life. Chapter 8 provides treatment particulars.

Adolescent Conduct Disorders

As mentioned in chapters 17 and 18, socially disapproved behaviors, or conduct disorders, become increasingly serious problems as a child grows older. The behavior associated with these conduct disorders may be socialized (such as gang activities) or unsocialized (the lone firesetter), aggressive (assaultive behavior) or nonaggressive (lying, truancy). Conduct disorders range from less serious problems, such as truancy and school failure, sexual promiscuity, use of alcohol or illicit drugs, and curfew violations, to fighting, running away, incorrigibility, theft, and more violent activities.

Conduct disorder is not just teenage rebellion taken to an extreme; it is a severe problem with a grim outlook. Many adolescents with conduct problems become adults with serious problems. They are more likely than those without such a history to be jailed for criminal behavior, to be hospitalized for severe psychiatric problems, and to have problems in their relationships and with their careers.

Outlook and Associated Factors

Almost all antisocial adults have childhood and adolescent histories of conduct disorder, and approximately 50 percent of conduct-disordered children become antisocial adults. Research in the 1970s showed that children with delinquent behavior were more likely to come from impoverished, large families where the parents had a history of criminality, abuse, and alcoholism. Children with low IQ were particularly susceptible. Many children with conduct disorders suffer from parental abuse, both physical and sexual. Children who come from such homes not only learn that violence is an appropriate model of behavior; they often have to contend with inner feelings of rage that they then displace on their peers and teachers.

A number of other factors have come to be associated with conduct disorders. These include epilepsy, schizophrenia, and serious depressive disorder. Research also points to the relation between conduct disorder and attention-deficit hyperactivity disorder (ADHD; see chapter 18, pages 259–261);

and the overlap of symptoms such as impulsivity, poor judgment, and learning disability (chapter 18, pages 263–266).

Assessment and Treatment

Conduct disorders become a more severe problem in adolescence than in younger years. Teenagers have greater freedom and independence as well as physical strength, and these factors increase the risk that aggressive or destructive behavior will harm others seriously or lead to criminal acts. Any adolescent with serious behavior problems needs a careful evaluation.

Teenagers with conduct disorder usually exhibit a wide range of emotional problems and vulnerabilities in addition to their behavior problems. For this reason, it is important to seek help from a mental health professional who is experienced in diagnosing and treating conduct disorders and who can distinguish whether the problem stems from an underlying mental disorder such as depression or schizophrenia (which may be responsive to drug therapy), or whether the behavior truly merits a diagnosis of conduct disorder. The evaluation usually involves an in-depth exploration of the problem behavior, the events surrounding it, and the social factors in the child's life that may be reinforcing the behavior, such as alcohol abuse (either by the teenager or a parent) or a pattern of violence or neglect in the home. Usually a careful medical history will be taken, to rule out any treatable organic causes (such as a brain tumor or other neurologic injury that may trigger violence; see chapter 27) that may be contributing to the problem.

Parents almost always are involved in the evaluation of the problem, and it is not unusual for the mental health professional also to want to talk to other, nonrelated individuals, such as teachers or peers, to try to learn the full extent of the problem. Parents and teenagers with conduct disorders often have very different perspectives on the extent and seriousness of the problem; the teenager may deny that the problem exists, while the parents are often ignorant of the full extent of their child's behavior.

Some mental health professionals believe that conduct disorders follow a progression of increasingly serious antisocial behaviors. Beginning with truancy and lying, the behavior progresses to drinking and sexual activity, and later escalates to drug use and theft. There is some evidence that the best predictor of adolescent aggression is aggressive behavior at younger ages (although it should be noted that the majority of young children with troublesome behav-

ior do not later develop conduct disorders). Chapter 18, page 261, provides more information on conduct disorders in younger children.

Conduct disorders in adolescence are usually difficult to treat. No one treatment approach has been shown to be more effective than others, possibly because so many factors can contribute to the behavior. What is known is that treatment must address a broad scope of problems, including the reasons underlying the behavior, family interactions, and the social milieu in which the child lives. Because of the seriousness of the problem, treatment is generally long term and ongoing rather than brief.

One type of treatment effective in some cases focuses on teaching parents how to manage better and interact more effectively with their child. Called management training, it theorizes that parents unknowingly contribute to their child's disturbed behavior either by ineffective supervision or by meting out discipline that is too rigid and harsh. Behavior therapy directed toward the teenager is also sometimes effective. This therapy usually focuses on teaching the skills that will help him or her to identify problems that contribute to violence or other problem behaviors and that will then help the teenager cope with feelings of anger, rage, and pain. Some psychiatrists prescribe medication, particularly antipsychotics, although not all experts advocate their use. For some teenagers, treatment at a group home or residential facility is an effective option.

Because of the difficult and often recalcitrant nature of such problems, many therapists are hesitant to treat conduct-disordered teenagers. Parents should look for a professional who has a known interest and success rate with similar cases.

Schizophrenia

As noted in chapter 14, schizophrenia is a serious and generally chronic mental disorder characterized by disturbances of thought and mood and, often, delusions (bizarre beliefs, such as of being possessed by extraterrestrials) and hallucinations (a false sensory experience, such as of hearing voices). This condition rarely begins before puberty and is now distinguished from pervasive developmental disorder (autism), a condition that used to be referred to as childhood schizophrenia (chapter 17).

Schizophrenia can be difficult to diagnose in adolescence, when irrational behavior and "magical thinking" (as with the intelligent high school student who believes he or she is invulnerable to car accidents) are common. In addition, in the acute phase of the illness differentiating schizophrenia from the wild mood swings of bipolar disorder, which may also involve hallucinations and delusions, can be difficult. Drug intoxication or head injury also can cause similar symptoms.

Manifestations of Schizophrenia

Often adolescents with schizophrenia will have a sudden break with reality, demonstrating obvious hallucinations and delusions. Such an acute episode often can be managed within several weeks with appropriate therapy and antipsychotic medication and/or with hospitalization. Afterward the young person may be able to resume a somewhat normal life. In other cases, however, after an acute episode the adolescent may suffer chronically from the illness and have limited ability to function in society.

Not everyone first experiences the illness in such an acute form. In some cases, schizophrenia begins with milder symptoms, such as lack of clarity in thought and periods of irrational behavior that come and go, or an inability to maintain close relationships. As the illness progresses, the behavior becomes more irrational, the withdrawal from reality more complete, and the ability to function diminishes or disappears. Most individuals with schizophrenia never experience total loss of contact with reality, however.

Prevalence and Early Signs

Schizophrenia is most likely to strike between the ages of 15 and 22, and while males and females are equally affected, males are likely to show symptoms earlier. Studies have shown that many people who later develop schizophrenia exhibit certain disordered patterns of behavior in childhood. One study showed that preschizophrenic boys are often unsocialized, aggressive, and loners. Conversely, preschizophrenic girls are often introverted, oversensitive, and shy. Both lack close friends. Several long-term studies of children at genetic risk for schizophrenia reveal that some destined to develop the disease have mild neurological deficits and demonstrate problems in attention, communication, and social interaction long before psychotic symptoms appear.

Treatment of Schizophrenia in Adolescence

Although schizophrenia is rarely cured, most forms will respond to treatment, especially if discovered early. In some cases, a teenager with schizophrenia can grow up to enjoy meaningful work and satisfying relationships. The most crucial therapeutic task is to prevent a psychotic break with reality. Thus, parents who suspect their child has early symptoms should seek psychiatric help. If there is no acute crisis, the young person can be monitored regularly so that later problems can be averted.

Importantly, the professional can advise parents on how to provide the most protective environment in order to prevent a fragile personality from experiencing a breakdown. For example, the therapist might suggest that parents "tone down" their emotional outbursts at one another when they argue, or that they not overwhelm the young person with ambitious plans for the future that may not be appropriate.

The Case of Janet D.

When she was six, Janet D. had been brought to treatment because of hallucinations in which she "saw" eyes on the wall and because she frequently ate flowers. After brief but intense psychiatric treatment (consisting of psychotherapy twice a week, tutoring help, play therapy that focused on making friends, and counseling for her parents) she returned to school, where she did well and developed friendships throughout grade school.

Janet entered intensive treatment again at the age of 13, when she suffered delusions relating to menstruation. (She thought she was bleeding to death and would not be convinced otherwise.) The delusion reflected her fears surrounding sexual issues and her need for help in developing the new, more adult-like social functions that are required of adolescence. After another course of individual and group therapy that focused on age-appropriate social functioning, Janet entered a well-respected college that provided individualized attention, where she did well academically. At 30, she met and married a small-town lawyer, who was able to provide a supportive environment. She works from home and plans to have a family. Although she was diagnosed as having schizophrenia, she never experienced a complete breakdown.

In Janet's case, the important factors for success were early intervention and a warm, protective environment. Although Janet did not require drugs, treatment for schizophrenia (for both children and adults) frequently combines medication and other forms of therapy, often including family therapy. Hospitalization may be necessary, especially in the event of a psychotic break. Follow-up treatment or monitoring is extremely important.

Table 19.1 COMMON DRUGS: SYMPTOMS OF ABUSE

Type of Drug	Drug Name	Street Names	Methods of Use	Symptoms of Use	Hazards of Use
Marijuana Hashish		Pot, Grass, Reefer, Weed, Colombian, Hash, Hash Oil, Sinsemilla, Joint Chiba, Herb, Spliff	Most often smoked, can also be swallowed in solid form	Sweet, burned odor Neglect of appearance Loss of interest, motivation Possible weight change	Impaired memory perception Interference with psychological maturation Possible damage to lungs, heart, and reproduction and immune systems Psychological dependence
Cocaine		Coke, Snow, Toot, White Lady, Blow, Rock, Crack	Most often smoked or inhaled; also injected or swallowed in powder, pill, or rock form	Restlessness, anxiety Intense, short-term high followed by depression	Intense psychological dependence Sleeplessness; anxiety Depression Nasal passage damage Lung damage Death from overdose
Stimulants Drugs that stimulate the central nervous system	Amphetamines* Dextroamphetamine Methamphetamine *Includes lookalike drugs that contain caffeine, phenylpropanolamine (PBA), and ephedrine	Speed, Uppers, Pep Pills Bennies Dexies Moth, Crystal Black Beauties	Swallowed in pill or capsule form, or injected into veins	Excess activity, Irritability, nervousness Mood swings Needle marks	Loss of appetite Hallucinations; paranoia Convulsions; coma Brain damage Death from overdose
	Nicotine	Coffin Nail Butt, Smoke	Found in cigarettes, cigars, pipe and chewing tobacco	Smell of tobacco High carbon monoxide lelels Stained teeth Yellow fingers	Cancers of tho lung, throat, mouth, esophagus Heart disease; emphysema
Depressants Drugs that slow down the central nervous system	Barbiturates Pentobarbital Secobarbital Amobarbital	Barbs, Downers Yellow Jackets Red Devils Blue Devils	Swallowed in pill form or injected into veins	Drowsiness Confusion Impaired judgment Slurred speech Needle marks Constricted pupils	Infection Addiction with severe withdrawal symptoms Loss of appetite Death from overdose
	Quaalude Sopor	Ludes Soapers	Swallowed in pill form	Impaired judgment and performance Drowsiness Slurred Speech	Death from overdose Injury or death from car accident; severe interaction with alcohol
Narcotics Natural or synthetic drugs that contain or resemble opium	Dilaudid, Percodan Demerol, Methadone		Swallowed in pill or liquid form, injected	Drowsiness Lethargy	Addiction with severe withdrawal symptoms including seizures Loss of appetite Death from overdose Nausea and vomiting
	Codeine	School Boy	Swallowed in pill or liquid form, injected		
	Morphine Heroin	Smack Horse	Injected into veins, smoked	Needle Marks	
Hallucinogens Drugs that alter perceptions of reality	PCP (Phencyclidine)	Angel Dust, Killer Hog, Supergrass, PeaCee Pill	Most often smoked; can also be inhaled, (snorted), injected, or swallowed in tablets	Slurred speech; blurred vision, incoordination Confusion, agitation Aggression	Anxiety; depression Impaired memory, perception Death from accidents Death from overdose
	LSD	Acid, Cubes, Purple Haze	Usually swallowed	Dilated pupils Illusions; hallucinations Mood swings	Breaks from reality Emotional breakdown Flashbacks
	Mescaline Psilocybin	Mesc. Cactus Magic Mushrooms	Usually swallowed in their natural form		
Alcohol		Booze, Hooch, Juice, Brew	Swallowed in liquid form	Impaired muscle coordination, judgment Somnolence	Heart and liver damage Death from overdose and accidents Addiction
Inhalants Substances abused by sniffing	Gasoline Airplane Glue Paint Thinner Dry Cleaner Fluid		Inhaled or sniffed, often with use of paper or plastic bag or rag	Poor motor coordination Impaired vision, memory and thought	High risk of sudden death Drastic weight loss Brain, liver, and bone marrow damage
	Nitrous Oxide	Laughing Gas, Whippets	Inhaled or sniffed by mask or balloons	Abusive, violent behavior Lightheadedness Slowed thought Headache	Death by anoxia Neuropathy, muscle weakness Anemia, death by anoxia
	Amyl Nitrite Butyl Nitrite	Poppers, Snappers, Rush, Locker Room	Inhaled or sniffed from gauze or ampules		

Note: Taking drugs of any type during pregnancy can be hazardous to the fetus.

Adapted from "Children and Drugs": distributed by Blue Cross and Blue Shield Plans of Vermont and New Hampshire.

HELP FOR TROUBLED ADOLESCENTS

Getting a troubled young person to seek help may not always be easy. Parents of teenagers should be firm and insist that their child see a professional for at least an initial consultation. If the adolescent does not want to continue, or if the professional does not feel the situation warrants ongoing treatment, at least the adolescent will have someone to contact if there is a future need. If parents are unable to convince the adolescent to seek help, they should call the professional they have selected and ask for advice.

Young and mid-adolescent patients often cooperate better with a therapist of the same sex. Because not all therapists relate well to adolescents, it is best to make sure that the therapist is known to work well with this age group.

Many authorities believe that it is important to work with the parent and child together at least occasionally, because the underlying problem may involve family conflict or problems of other family members. In addition, the family needs to be aware of the treatment process and supportive of the therapy. If the teenager feels uncomfortable with this format, a second professional who counsels the parents may represent a helpful bridge between the family and the teenager's treatment. Family therapy, which focuses on the interactions among family members and often provides concrete suggestions for change, can be especially helpful. (See chapter 4 and chapter 16.)

Confidentiality is always an important issue. Therapists should make it clear to adolescents that their privacy will be respected—except when their behavior is harmful to themselves or others (for example, using dangerous drugs, carrying weapons, having suicidal impulses).

WHAT PARENTS WANT TO KNOW

Parents understandably often are concerned about their teenagers' apparently rebellious or troubled behavior and confused about when, how, and how much to intervene. The following questions are representative of ones that parents commonly ask child mental health specialists, with our responses and recommendations. See also the box on page 277.

Oversleeping

- *My teenager refuses to get out of bed in the mornings, and often not until noon. Is this normal for a child to spend so much time in bed?*
Sleeping long hours or refusing to get out of bed could be a symptom of several problems—depression, an avoidance problem, or drug use. However, it could also be a normal reflection of the teenager's pattern of activities. Does the staying in bed occur only after he or she has stayed up late? Some adolescents are obsessive about homework; a pattern of staying up/sleeping late in these teenagers may be a reflection of their anxiety about performance.

    If your child's sleep habits change abruptly, persist, and/or are accompanied by other symptoms, such as a drop in academic functioning, emotional difficulties could be the cause.

Motivation

- *How can I keep my teenager motivated? She never seems to want to do anything besides sit in her room and listen to music.*
The first step is to be honest with yourself: Are you concerned about your child's motivation and what *she* wants, or are you actually worrying about what *you* are hoping she will achieve? Another facet of this question is whether the daughter only appears unmotivated to you, or whether she really is adrift without goals.

    Your teenager may very well be experiencing an identity crisis—something very normal for a teenager. Not letting you know what she is thinking, feeling, or experiencing may simply be a way of saying "I'm worried about my future too, and I can't cope with your questions." This may be particularly true if the behavior develops around a particularly stressful time—when it is necessary to take college entrance exams, for example. If she is coping with these responsibilities but just not talking to you about them, there is no cause for alarm.

    However, if your teenager's apparent lack of motivation also is affecting her ability to function at school, then you should be concerned.

(Continued)

Ask the school guidance counselor, a teacher, or another trusted adult to talk and/or work with her. If these measures don't seem to help, professional therapy may be useful. Sometimes depression may be at the root of the problem.

Perfectionism

- *My son studies very hard—too hard, I think. He worries about grades, although he has an A– average. When he B+ on an exam last week, he was distraught. I'm proud of my child's abilities, but isn't this going too far?*

The desire to do well and get the best possible grades is normal for many children. The issue is the degree of upset and how fast the child bounces back from it. If a teenager gets a B+ and can't sleep, eat, or threatens suicide, this is a problem that needs professional counseling. To have his self-esteem pricked by such a minor disappointment indicates he has an underlying emotional disorder, and professional counseling is warranted.

Anger and Overreacting

- *My teenager's angry behavior is disrupting the rest of my family's life. If I knew it would pass, I could cope. How can I know?*

Anger that is transitory in response to discipline or family rules about curfews, chores, or family obligations is not abnormal. It may signal rebellion or an attempt to separate from the family—behavior that is normal, though often difficult to cope with.

If the angry behavior persists for long periods or interrupts family life, however, it is very important that parents investigate the extent of the child's angry behavior. Does he or she also display angry behavior at school or with peers? To find out, call the child's principal, guidance counselor, or parents of his or her friends. Anger that spills over into other areas of a teenager's life requires an evaluation by a skilled adolescent mental health specialist to identify the reasons behind the behavior and advise if therapy would be warranted.

In any case, parents should not take *any* abuse, verbal or physical, from a teenager. You need to let him or her know that no matter how angry he or she may be, abusive behavior is never acceptable.

Remember, teenagers need to feel respected and listened to, but they also need the control of

parental judgment. For parents, adolescence is a trying time; they want their children to become assertive and independent but not do things that are destructive—so parents have to set limits and be there. Even if your teenagers are angry that you won't let them stay out late or use the family car, at the same time they will be glad (although this may not be evident) that you care about them and will not let them hurt themselves. Although it may be difficult, you need to ride out the anger and let it pass.

- *My son seems to blow everything out of proportion. Everything—from taking a test to taking out the garbage—seems stressful. To me, it seems like a lot of overreaction. What's going on here? How do I help him put things in perspective?*

Your son is sending messages that something is bothering him. It may be that he is hurt over not being popular, for example, or that he is worried about what the future will bring. The probability is that nothing much is terribly wrong—your son may just need to talk out his concerns and be reassured. He may simply not know how to initiate a heart-to-heart talk about his problems. Someone—yourself, an older sibling, a trusted uncle, or other adult—should try to talk to him about the problem.

However, if your child is completely sullen and withdrawn, resisting any effort to communicate with him, you may have to do some detective work to find out what is bothering him. A family session with a mental health professional can often help to get the teenager to identify and talk about what the trouble is.

- *The last time we tried to talk, my son put his fist through the wall and broke his hand. Does he need professional counseling? How much control should I exert?*

This time your son hurt himself, but the next time his anger could hurt another person. This type of violent reaction needs a professional evaluation immediately, within two to three days of the incident. A teenager who would do this has an enormous amount of inner rage and needs help.

Divorce and Remarriage

- *My wife and I have been having difficulties in our marriage. Our teenager keeps taking his mother's side and is very angry at me. What can I do to keep his love?*

Have an honest heart-to-heart talk with him. It is important for the teenager to realize that what-

(Continued)

ever happens in your marriage, both of you still and always will love him, and that you will continue to have a strong relationship with him independent of the one he has with his mother. He also should be reassured that he is not the cause of the problems and that every marriage has strains and stresses for a variety of reasons.

Be aware that it is normal for a child to feel anger when his parents are having problems, especially if the child blames one parent (usually the father) for breaking up the family. It is important for you and your wife to work on not putting each other in a position of blame. Work out your separation *without* involving the children in the dispute. Clearly, often this is easier said than done—and many parents cannot do it. But it is important to try to have talk to your children about the breakup in as open and honest a way as possible without involving them in the issues surrounding it.

- *I've recently remarried, and my teenage daughter says things to me that are really cruel. How do I react to this?*
Your teenager is having difficulty accepting your new spouse. It is important that you and she spend time together to talk about her feelings and to reassure her that, despite your new relationship, your loving feelings for her have not changed.

If your daughter continues to exhibit angry behavior, you might consider consulting a therapist (perhaps a family therapist) who is skilled in working with "new" or "reconstituted" families. It is important that issues, concerns, and resentments be aired openly.

- *It seems to me that my teenage daughter is acting seductively toward my new husband. What do I do? Is this normal?*
When she is younger, it is normal for a girl to feel attracted to her own father and in competition with her mother for his attention. However, by the time she is an adolescent, societal mores have taught her that such an attraction is taboo. A stepfather, however, can represent a nonincestuous father substitute. Your daughter's seductive behavior may therefore be an acting out of emotions she felt during her childhood, now transferred to a "safe" person because he is not related. (It is also common for a teenage boy to act seductively toward a new stepmother, especially when she is not much older than he is.)

It is important that both you and your new spouse be aware of your daughter's behavior and that he not encourage it or flirt back. Again, family therapy sessions to talk out the problem openly may defuse the situation.

Refusal to Talk

- *My son seems troubled about something, but I can't get him to talk to me. What can I do?*
This type of behavior is most probably a case of moodiness or an attempt by your teenager to separate, be independent, and have his own privacy. And, indeed, this is a time when he *should* have privacy. Is there anyone else he rather would talk to, such as an older brother, a trusted relative, a minister or rabbi, or a teacher—someone who would say, "Your mother told me that she was a little worried, and perhaps we could discuss whatever is bothering you and work it out."

To determine whether your child's behavior is symptomatic of an emotional problem, always look at the level of functioning in other areas of his or her life. If your son's grades are good and the family rules are being followed, there is probably no cause for alarm. However, if your child is not sleeping well, gets into trouble at school, or has suddenly stopped spending time with friends, then it could be a sign of depression or other emotional problem.

- *I found out that my son, who is 18, has been getting counseling from a psychologist at his college, but neither my son nor the psychologist will tell me any details. As I'm paying all college expenses, don't you think I'm entitled to know what's going on?*
No—unless your child is in danger of committing suicide or is seeking counseling for other dangerous behavior. Other than in these situations, the mental health professional is bound by the laws of confidentiality. (See chapter 30, page 421.) However, you do have the right to call the school and inquire about the credentials of the therapist. If you are concerned about the quality of care your son is receiving, arrange for him to see a professional whom you trust, and have him or her talk to the school therapist about your child's treatment.

Discipline

- *What do I do when my child breaks the rules? She insists that every other kid in school is allowed to do what she does, so she does it anyway.*

(Continued)

Discipline your teenager for every rule broken. Make sure that your child knows the rules in advance. (A family conference is an excellent setting for this agenda.)

To determine whether your rules are reasonable, attend PTA groups, parent nights, or other discussion groups. Or you may want to organize a meeting of teenagers and their parents to discuss what other families are doing and what their rules are.

Lying

- *My daughter hides things from me. I can't get a straight answer about anything. I think she often lies about where she's going and with whom. I'm afraid about what she might be doing. What do I do?*

Lying is very serious if it becomes part of a pattern. If your daughter has a history of lying and her current lies are a continuation of this behavior, you must confront her. A child's lies become more serious as the child enters adolescence, because he or she now has more freedom and greater possibilities for harming him- or herself. In this case, you must be open with your teenager, and let her know that you will not trust her until she has proven that she can be trusted. You need to find out what is at the root of this pattern. Has she gotten into bad company? Has there been a change in her habits at school? Has she dropped old friends? Once you discover a pattern of lying, it is important that you check the veracity of what your child is telling you and make sure that she follows your rules. Don't only ask about whom she is going out with and where she is going. *Verify* that what she is telling you is the truth. One way to do this is to develop relationships with the parents of your child's friends; call them and ask if they can confirm what your teenager has told you. Give your child a curfew and make sure she comes in on time. Make sure that she knows beforehand that if she lies, she will be disciplined. Spell out in advance the price to be paid, whether it is being grounded, losing car privileges, or some such.

If your teenager does not have such a pattern of lying but you have nonetheless discovered a lie, talk to him or her openly and nonjudgmentally about the situation. Let the teenager know why you are upset, and find out where the need to lie came from. The issue here is developing a relationship of trust with your teenager. Are you able to trust your daughter, can she trust you?

Clothing

- *My daughter dresses like a prostitute, in my opinion. She says I'm old-fashioned, but I think she's giving boys a message that she is cheap and easy. How can I convince her to have more respect for herself?*

Talk to your daughter and let her know that you will not allow her to dress provocatively. She may think you're old-fashioned and object—but if her dress or makeup goes against family morals and rules, simply lay down the laws. Styles of dress may change from generation to generation, but styles of provocation don't change. However, if the way she is dressing is not actually provocative and sexual, but rather part of the current teenage "uniform," try not to worry about it too much. The fad will pass.

Sexuality

- *I found out that my 15-year-old son is sleeping with his girlfriend. I told him that I don't approve of this behavior. Should I forbid him to see her?*

This is a tricky issue to handle, because it involves not only your son's behavior but also that of the girl and her parents. In addition to your feelings about your son's sexual activities, you must also be concerned both with the possible consequences of his actions (pregnancy, sexually transmitted disease). Every family has a different standard and different rules; there is no right answer as to whether or not the behavior should be condoned—although 15 is young. Someone, however, has to counsel both your son and the girl to make sure that they understand fully what they are doing and the possible consequences of their actions. Often teenagers don't understand the emotional impact their sexual behavior has on them, or how to take precautions to protect themselves. Once your teenager becomes sexually active, you are probably not going to be able to stop him or her from acting sexually. But you need to make sure that he or she is behaving responsibly (using condoms) and realizes that partners bear a responsibility to one another.

- *I walked in on my 14-year-old son lying on the bed naked with his best friend. I was and am very upset about this, but I don't know what to say about it to my son, and he hasn't talked to me about it. Does this behavior mean he's gay?*

Most teenagers will have some sexual exploration with a friend of the same sex by early or

(Continued)

mid-adolescence. Same-sex behavior does not mean that your son is gay, although he may be. It's more likely that he is experimenting, trying to find out how his body works. However, it is important that someone (and preferably a male)—your doctor, an older brother, a trusted friend of the family—talk frankly to your son about his sexual feelings and sexual concerns. The discussion should be completely nonjudgmental and nonpunitive. Do not ignore the incident as if nothing had happened, even if it embarrasses you to talk about it.

Body Image

- *My daughter keeps talking about how much she hates the way she looks. I think she looks fine, but she won't listen.*

Most teenagers hate the way they look. They hate their hair, their pimples, their braces, or they want to look like some teenage idol, such as Madonna. If your daughter's concern about her looks becomes inordinate or has begun to interfere with her behavior (she refuses to go out or to wear a bathing suit, for example) a consultation with a mental health professional, preferably a woman, would be in order.

- *My daughter, who is 14, insists she needs plastic surgery to change her face. I don't know what to make of this; I like her face the way it is.*

Whether or not your daughter has an obvious facial defect, arrange for a consultation with a reputable plastic surgeon who has worked with teenagers to get an expert's opinion about what really would be involved in the surgery and why or why not to do it. If your daughter's nose or other facial feature is indeed disproportionate, and if you could afford such a procedure, the expert will advise you of the right age at which such surgery should be performed. (At age 14, he or she will probably advise that your teenager's features are not yet fully formed and that surgery should be held off until a later date.)

If your daughter has no facial defect, but the perceived flaw is something that exists only in her eye, a good plastic surgeon will let her know that surgery is not going to solve her problem and will advise against the procedure.

Shyness

- *My son doesn't seem to be popular with the other kids. He's shy and self-conscious and seems lonely. I've suggested he get involved in after-school activities, but he refuses, saying they're dumb. What can I do?*

A teenager who is shy, who seems insecure, who refuses to go out or to mix with other children may have a social phobia, an issue that is important to address before it interferes with his life. The behavior warrants a consultation with a mental health professional to find out why he is avoidant and whether treatment is necessary. Often group therapy with teenagers of the same age proves helpful.

Eating Disorder

- *I found laxatives in my daughter's purse. She's always talking about being too fat. Does she have an eating disorder?*

Your daughter's use of laxatives is serious; she can do serious physical harm to herself by using them. However, she doesn't necessarily have an actual eating disorder. Instead, she may be preoccupied with thinness and with dieting, common concerns in our culture, and have started using laxatives because other girls are doing it. I would arrange for an immediate consultation with her doctor, who can talk to her about the risks of using laxatives to control weight. If she continues to use laxatives, or shows symptoms of bulimia or anorexia (see chapter 10), you should schedule an appointment with an expert in eating disorders.

Drug and Alcohol Use

- *I think my son is experimenting with drugs. I asked him pointblank and he said he's not, but I don't believe him. How do I know if he's doing them? What are the signs? What do I do? How do I stop him? I feel so lost.*

Signals of drug use can include tiredness, irritability, secretive behavior, cutting off relationships with former friends and joining a different group, and stealing money. If there is any question of drug use, arrange for a consultation with someone who specializes in treating teenagers who use drugs. He or she can evaluate whether there really is an impairment and whether treatment is needed and, if so, what type. Ask your school or your family doctor for a referral to an appropriate practitioner. Be aware that in this situation, because the child's behavior affects the entire family, everyone may need to participate in treatment to some extent. Alcoholism and drug use is an extreme concern to parents

(Continued)

these days, as you know. It is covered in great detail in chapter 9, which we suggest you read.

- *My son has been hanging with a crowd of boys that is known to drink. We had a big talk about it, and he admitted he's been drinking. He says he doesn't care what I think, everybody drinks and he's not going to stop. What do I do?*

Find out if your child is using alcohol once in a while or regularly. It is extremely important to confront this issue, because drinking can become a serious problem. Like adults, adolescents deny that they have a drinking problem. As with drugs, the professionals best suited to evaluate the extent of the problem are those with experience in treating teenagers with substance abuse problems.

- *I know you can't prevent kids from trying alcohol or other drugs. I did when I was their age. When is drinking or using drugs a problem and when is it not?*

Underage drinking and use of illicit drugs at any age is against the law—and for this reason, they are always a problem. Parents have to keep strict control and not condone drinking or drug use. However, you are right in thinking that it is pretty certain that a teenager will have a few beers. Your reaction should be geared to the nature of the problem: Does your child admit to drinking, or does he or she lie about it? Is it just a few drinks on a special occasion, or is it a weekly, possibly daily, occurrence? Your child may be using alcohol as a way to self-medicate depression or to block out worries and fears about the future. If so, he or she needs help.

Absence of Rebellion

- *My teenager seems too "nice." My friends are always complaining about how awful their kids are—but mine is always so helpful and accommodating. I'm afraid she isn't going through a proper rebellion.*

It's a myth that teenagers have to be rebellious to be normal. Two-thirds of all teenagers sail through adolescence without any trace of rebelliousness and only some subjective feelings of anxiety about future or slight depression. Consider yourself lucky to have a child like this.

20

Stresses and Traumas of Childhood

*Hector R. Bird, M.D., Arthur H. Green, M.D.,
Elliot M. Kranzler, M.D., Boris Rubinstein, M.D., M.P.H.,
and Gail A. Wasserman, Ph.D.*

For most children, vulnerability to mental disorder stems from a combination of factors, including genetic predisposition, temperament, and the environment in which they are raised. Certain life experiences, however, are powerful enough to affect the emotional equilibrium of any child. Such stresses and traumas range from the common, such as birth of a sibling, to the uncommon and horrific, including child abuse and neglect. Parental divorce can have lifelong effects on children, as can the death of a parent. Chronic illness during childhood can severely strain the psychological well-being of the whole family.

While adults also are affected by such stresses, children usually are more vulnerable because they are totally dependent on their caregivers and because they often lack the ability to understand what is happening to them and what the results will be. Because children depend on their parents to interpret and guide them through such traumas, it is important for parents to understand how these stresses can affect both the child and the whole family and what they can do to help.

BIRTH OF A SIBLING

The birth of a brother or sister is a major, frequently unsettling, life event for a child. Although most children cope with birth of a sibling without professional help, it can be one of the most difficult adjustment tasks a child faces. The newborn is a demanding new rival who stirs up competitive, jealous feelings, depletes parents' physical and emotional resources, and takes time away from that which previously had been spent with the older child.

Often young children have limited abilities, both intellectually and emotionally, to cope with the feelings engendered by this situation. For them, accepting the newcomer as an independent individual and family member is at the least an extraordinarily trying task; sometimes their feelings of anger, rage, and isolation are emotionally damaging. How children deal with this experience—or do not deal with it—can be the beginning of problems experienced later in life.

Emotional Response of Siblings

Some children become confrontational, disobedient, and aggressive after a sibling is born. Several studies indicate that these and other behavioral disturbances occur more in children who are under five years of age, perhaps because such young children are more dependent on parental caregiving (and thus resent its diminution more strongly) and have limited control over how they express their feelings.

Jealous young siblings demand attention when parents are attending to the newborn and may become clingy and tearful. Others may withdraw, becoming overly quiet. Sleeping problems, including an inability to fall asleep or repeated wakefulness during the night, are common.

After the birth of a sibling, some children may exhibit regressive behavior, acting younger than their age and resuming behaviors such as bedwetting or baby talk that they have already outgrown. Parents should neither encourage regressive behavior nor become overly concerned with it. As the child adapts to the new sibling, regressive behavior ordinarily stops and age-appropriate behavior resumes.

On the positive side, many children display more independent behavior after a sibling's birth. Most commonly, they demonstrate a new insistence on feeding or dressing themselves, a desire to go to the toilet alone, and an increasing tolerance for self-directed play, especially if parents encourage and support these activities.

When to Seek Help

If regressive behavior continues for months or if it steadily worsens, professional help should be sought. If a child repeatedly attempts to injure a younger sibling, or succeeds in seriously injuring him or her, help should be sought immediately. Parents may find it helpful to seek professional counseling for advice on how best to ease the situation even if a child's behavior is not dangerous or aggressive but is simply hard to manage.

CHRONIC OR ACUTE ILLNESS DURING CHILDHOOD

A chronic handicap—that is, an illness that lasts and tends to impair normal activity, such as severe allergies, eczema, asthma, epilepsy, and cerebral palsy—can pose a threat to a child's long-term emotional health. In fact, children with chronic illness have higher rates of psychiatric disorder than the general population.

The age of the child is less critical in determining the risk to psychological health than are the duration and severity of the illness. If, for example, a child experiences two or three mild attacks of asthma a year, necessitating taking medication but not missing school, the psychological impact will be limited. If, however, a child has severe asthma, must take medicine frequently, misses a good deal of school, and is hospitalized several times a year, he or she is at much greater risk for mental and emotional problems.

Helping Sick Children Cope

Parents should be straightforward and honest and explain as clearly as possible what the illness is. Many

BIRTH OF A SIBLING: HELPING CHILDREN COPE

Preparing the Child for the Arrival

Helping children cope with a new sibling begins before the birth. Adequate preparation may help smooth the transition from only child to older child, or from family baby to older sibling. The purpose is to demystify childbirth and to reassure the older child of his or her valued role in the family. As the birth draws near, parents should:

- Discuss the upcoming birth in terms that are appropriate to the developmental age of the child. Children's books dealing with childbirth and the arrival of a new baby are particularly helpful.
- Allow the child to feel the baby kicking inside the mother and explain that the baby will appear when it is ready.
- Make sure that the child understands where the mother will go to give birth and who will take care him or her while the mother is away. As in any separation, care should be taken to minimize any disruptions in normal routines.
- Involve the child in such prebirth tasks as choosing a name for the newborn and preparing the nursery.
- Take the child to visit the mother just after the birth, allowing him or her to share in the excitement and happiness of the event.

When the New Baby Arrives

The challenge facing parents is to help assuage the older sibling's sense of loss, anger, and rivalry. Consider the following tactics.

- Reassure older siblings that they are loved and still hold a special place in the family by giving them extra attention when you can.
- Encourage the older child to help interpret the baby's needs and wants.
- Make feeding times companionable by feeding the baby on a sofa or chair big enough to include the older child, providing this does not interfere with the feeding itself.
- Encourage children of all ages, including adolescents as well as "adult children," to discuss their feelings about the newborn openly. Permit expressions of anger and resentment as well as more positive emotions.
- Do not permit any physical aggression toward the infant. Children may displace their anger at their parents by wanting to hurt the infant, such as by pinching an arm or leg. Even perfectly normal children have been known to inflict serious injuries on their younger siblings. It must be made clear that no aggression toward the newcomer will be tolerated.
- Accept regressive behavior as a normal way of coping and be reassured that the children will regain their age-appropriate behavior in time.
- Both the newborn and the older siblings need special attention. Set aside time to spend with your older children every day. Read or play a game, or take him or her on outings for walks or to the store. Arrange for the child to spend time in play groups and interesting activities outside the home.

If a child continues to be upset and to show signs of distress long after the new member has been assimilated into the family, consulting a professional may be in order.

---

parents are afraid of upsetting their children by telling them they have a serious illness. However, children usually know when something is being hidden from them, and this secretiveness adds to their fear and confusion. Often they know much more than the parents realize, but they don't say anything for fear of upsetting the parents or simply because they sense the subject is taboo.

One boy with Hodgkin's disease, a life-threatening cancer of the lymph nodes, was told for many years that he simply had anemia and that this was why he had to be hospitalized regularly. By the time he was 12 years old, he knew that his condition was serious. After looking up a number of illnesses in the family encyclopedia, he discovered what his problem was. He was relieved to know the real nature of his disease, rather than tormenting himself in isolated speculation, especially after he told his parents that he knew the truth and was able to discuss his condition freely with them.

Of course, not all children want to know that they are seriously ill. Parents should follow the child's lead. If he or she shows no curiosity and avoids any mention of the illness, parents should wait until the child indicates readiness. Parents need to prepare ahead of time how they will respond to questions when the child begins to ask them, however.

The desire for such information may be expressed in roundabout ways—in irritability, unruly behavior, or refusal to take necessary medication, for example—especially if children feel that grown-ups are withholding information. A child's play and drawings may demonstrate many fears and wishes to the alert parent.

In addition to receiving clear and accurate information, it is helpful for children to feel that they have some say in what is happening to them and how they are treated while they are sick. The decisions can be relatively minor, as to when or where to have a shot. Older children may want to be involved in making important decisions.

Any child who is ill for a significant period of time and cut off from friends and normal activities may begin to doubt his or her abilities and even self-worth. To help maintain a child's self-esteem, parents should stress the abilities a child does have. Sharing activities that the child enjoys and is good at, such as reading or playing games, and finding chores that the child can help with, can foster a sense of mastery and well-being.

Children, like adults, sometimes need professional help to cope with their emotional response to illness. They may feel depressed, fearful of death, anxious about the future, and anger at being ill. As with almost all childhood traumas, supportive therapy can be very helpful, particularly if it employs play therapy as a means of allowing the child to express him- or herself.

Parental Reactions

Parents' mental and emotional health strongly influences the emotional state of the chronically ill child. Parents are a child's main source of emotional support and comfort, which a disturbed or suffering parent cannot adequately provide.

A University of Rochester study took two groups of children with chronic handicaps and placed one under the care of a lay counselor, a mother who had successfully raised handicapped children. The other group received routine pediatric care. The study found that those children under the counselor's care had fewer emotional disturbances, suggesting that the emotional support of a caring adult helped diminish stress on the children and prevented the appearance of new problems.

It is not difficult to understand why parents of chronically ill children may develop emotional problems that, in turn, can have a negative impact on their children. Child rearing is a stressful, demanding job under normal conditions. The physical and emotional demands of a chronically ill child add greatly to the stress.

One of the most difficult aspects of coming to terms with having a chronically ill child is that it is not a one-time occurrence but a lifetime process. Initially, parents' reaction to their child's illness is strikingly similar to the grief response: shock and denial, followed by guilt and anger (often directed at medical staff). Eventually most parents adapt and move ahead with their lives.

Parents who adapt most successfully do not let concern over long-term outcome of the illness detract from current considerations and their enjoyment of the child. Rather than worry excessively about a child's future college potential, for example, they may find it more helpful to stay focused on the next reading test, or simply to make sure the child takes that day's medicine or has fun playing.

Nevertheless, even parents with the best attitudes feel renewed grief at significant points in their child's life, especially in times of transition. When the child was supposed to have started first grade, participated in a religious rite of passage, or gone off to camp with other kids, for example, parents may feel moody, depressed, or irritable. They may even quarrel with each other or snap at other family members.

Because these reactions are so common, doctors encourage parents of chronically ill children to seek support through self-help groups or religious and community programs. Pediatricians are familiar with such groups and can help direct concerned parents to an appropriate program. Chapter 28 provides information on the National Self-Help Clearinghouse and other sources of information. Additionally, many parents of chronically ill children seek the assistance of a mental health specialist to understand and better cope with their feelings.

Impact on Siblings

The siblings of chronically ill children often suffer from depression. They are faced with a confusing mix of emotions, including resentment that the ill child is getting more of their parents' attention and anger at both the sick child and the parents. In addition, siblings may suffer from guilt for having these feelings and simply for being healthy themselves.

It is important that parents assure the well children that they are equally loved and cared for, even if their problems are not as dramatic. Parents should be on the lookout for signs of depression in the well child and pay attention to any irritability, lethargy, disruption in sleeping patterns, or change in eating habits. Parents need to encourage the well child to talk about feelings related to the sibling's illness, and to help him or her join support groups or seek professional help if symptoms persist or worsen.

Hospitalization and Surgery

Separation from parents during hospitalization and/or surgery can be very stressful. Typically, children experience what experts call separation reaction, which involves crying, fearfulness, anger, and moodiness. Next they may go through a period of despair and withdrawal from those around them, before finally settling down and adjusting to their new environment.

Separation reaction is more common and severe in children under the age of 5. Children between the ages of 8 and 12 probably will have a milder reaction, especially if they are not chronically ill and do not have to undergo repeated hospitalizations. Generally, children who experience recurrent hospitalizations, especially if they begin before the child is 5, have more severe and long-term reactions.

Hospitals today tend to be sensitive to the emotional needs of sick children. Liberal visitation policies allow parents to spend as much time visiting children as possible, often including sleeping in the hospital. Other factors that help children adjust to their hospitalization include prehospital visits in which they are shown where they will stay and told what will happen to them, shorter hospital stays, and more playrooms.

Play therapy and helping children imagine beforehand what will happen also can reduce anxiety and trauma significantly. Parents may want to read children stories about other children who were hospitalized, and to tell them about their own operations and how they came out just fine.

MARITAL SEPARATION AND DIVORCE

Marital dissolution numbers among life's most severe stressors for all involved. Since the decade of the 1970s, nearly one-third of American children under the age of 18 have experienced the divorce of their parents.

The Emotional Impact of Divorce on Children

The enormous stress of divorce has a profound emotional impact on children. While reactions vary with each child, some typical ones are:

- *Anxiety.* Most children experience anxiety, especially when the period preceding the separation is marked by turmoil, hostility, anger, and violence between parents.
- *Self-blame.* Children often become the immediate focus of power struggles, which leads them to think that they are causing the problems between the parents. Fights erupting between parents over such trivial issues as whether their

children should be allowed to stay overnight with friends lead children to believe that they caused their parents' breakup.

- *Unlovability/poor self-esteem.* Children perceive a parent's move out of the house as abandonment. Though parents offer explanations, children tend to believe the real reason was their own unlovability. After the divorce, lack of attention from the noncustodial parent reinforces feelings of rejection and further erodes the child's self-esteem.
- *Depression.* Children often experience feelings of bereavement during divorce. Unlike other bereavements, such as when a parent dies, losses caused by divorce can recur frequently. For example, each time a father cancels a much-anticipated weekend together because of a business trip, the child experiences a new loss. Like adults, children often react to such losses by becoming depressed. Also like adults, children react adversely to rapid, disorganized change. During divorce, the upheaval children often

experience in the routine of their lives can bring on anger and depression.

- *Heightened sensitivity to interpersonal slights and rejection.* Because children perceive divorce as a personal rejection, they may try to protect themselves from future hurt by becoming overly sensitive to any slights or perceived rejections.
- *Feeling different from peers.* Despite the increase in divorce rates, children from broken homes remain in the minority. They often perceive themselves to be different from, and less worthy than, their peers. Feelings of guilt over the divorce and shame about fights or other hostile actions that have taken place at home may further this sense of being an outsider. Children's loyalty to their families frequently prevents them from telling anyone about what is happening at home and thereby increases their isolation.

Behavioral Changes During Separation and Divorce

Children's emotional reactions to divorce often reveal themselves through changes in behavior, especially in the immediate aftermath of separation and divorce. "Acting out," or expressing distress through behaviors that have not been typical of the child, is common, particularly in children under 12.

At school, such behavior problems as excessive clowning or angry outbursts may emerge. Children's anxiety and preoccupation with family problems may lead to inattention in the classroom as well as inappropriate attention-seeking behavior that interferes with school work. Academic performance, therefore, may suffer.

Often, reactions to divorce vary with the sex of the child. Girls tend to be more overtly depressed, becoming whiny, clingy, and sulky. Boys, on the other hand, tend to act out their depression through more outwardly aggressive, bullying, hostile behavior.

The Impact of Age

Children's emotional reactions to divorce often relate to their developmental age. Under the age of two, a child lacks the ability to understand what marriage is and what divorce means. As long as the child continues to have contact with both parents, any reactions, such as contrariness and moodiness, are bound to be short-lived. Slightly older children may become fearful and anxious; they may worry about how the change will affect their daily lives.

Divorce may be tougher on the 5- or 6-year-old, who is struggling to work out the interpersonal conflicts natural to that stage in life, often referred to as the Oedipal stage. It is a period when, characteristically, the child develops strong feelings for the opposite-sex parent and feels a rivalry with the same-sex parent. If a young girl's father leaves at this point in her development, she can experience a profound feeling of rejection. If the father moves away from his son, the boy commonly feels he has won the competition for his mother but feels guilt for having "driven" his father away.

At ages 9 or 10, children are forming a strong identification with the same-sex parent. Because the father is usually the parent who leaves, boys suffer the loss particularly. But both boys and girls of this age may suffer grief, anxiety, loneliness, and anger at parents for divorcing.

Although teenagers may be more able intellectually to cope with divorce, they too are vulnerable to emotional reactions. Like the younger child, the adolescent may react with intense feelings of anger and sorrow as well as anxiety about the future. Divorce at this time of a child's life can threaten the adolescent's emerging sense of independence and self-identity. It can also provoke serious and abrupt shifts in the parent-child relationship, with the teenager, perhaps for the first time, feeling a palpable sense of separation from his or her parents. Over the long term, divorce during a child's teenage years can influence how that child views relationships with the opposite sex and, ultimately, his or her own future marriage.

Impact of Personality

A child's personality can have a significant impact on the way he or she reacts to divorce. Divorce often disrupts the familiar patterns of a child's world; frequently it means moving to a new home, going to a new school, or being left for long periods with babysitters, perhaps for the first time. Faced with such disruption, children who are self-critical and who need structure tend to suffer more anxiety, depression, and hostility than children who are less critical of themselves and who are more comfortable in less structured situations.

Sadder
manstr

CHILDREN'S ART THERAPY: "THE SADDER MONSTER"

Figure 20.1: **In this picture, drawn by a young girl in therapy for post-traumatic stress syndrome, the monster sits on the child's head, indicating that she feels burdened by worry. At the start of the therapy session, the child related that she had many "bad things" to talk about; the "X" through the monster was drawn at the end of the session.**

Children who tend to minimize or deny the impact of events may not appear particularly upset or stressed over the divorce. However, because they are not dealing with their feelings and resolving psychological conflicts, these children are at risk of future emotional difficulty.

Impact of Family Finances

In many divorce scenarios, the father, who has been the main financial support of the family, moves out. In these cases, mothers often need to begin to work outside the home. For the children, this new situation represents a loss of the remaining parent as well. Because of new demands on the mother's time, she may be unavailable when they feel they need her. So-called latch-key kids, who have to let themselves into the home after school and wait alone until their mothers get home from work, may feel a greater sense of abandonment, which may manifest itself in depression or misbehavior. Involving the child in after-school programs or arranging for a baby-sitter can help counteract this perceived loss of parental caring and support.

Long-term Effects

Research by psychologist Judith Wallerstein and others has revealed that divorce is not just a short-term crisis, but a long-term trauma that often affects the emotional and psychological well-being of individuals well into adulthood. Wallerstein found that a decade after the divorce, a majority of children expressed feelings of sadness, neediness, and vulnerability, and they voiced a high level of anxiety about relationships, marriage, and personal commitments. As adolescents, they seemed concerned about being betrayed, hurt, and/or abandoned in interpersonal relationships.

For many children who seemed to cope well at the time, the psychological impact of divorce remains dormant until young adulthood. Faced with commitment, love, and sex in an adult context, they become overwhelmed by fears and anxieties.

A Key Factor: How Parents React to Their Own Divorce

The way parents themselves handle their divorce greatly influences the child's emotional health over the short and long term. Research has shown that children whose parents have made separate but stable homes, and who do not indulge in rancor, have many fewer emotional problems than children from unbroken homes where quarreling and hostility continue.

Wallerstein suggests that the emotional stress of divorce on adults is often so great that it may diminish their ability to parent effectively. That is, divorced parents may spend less time with their children, provide less discipline, and be less sensitive to their children's needs.

In fact, parents sometimes can become so upset and depressed by the divorce that they lean on their children for emotional and psychological support. This may result in the child's becoming overburdened by adult responsibilities.

It is essential, then, that parents try to cope with their own emotional reactions to divorce by anticipating and understanding them as much as possible. Among the most common of these reactions are a sense of failure; anger at the ex-spouse; guilt about abandoning familial responsibilities on the part of the parent who moves out; and an overwhelming sense of loss, often the result of idealizing the ex-spouse.

HELPING CHILDREN COPE WITH SEPARATION AND DIVORCE

In order to help children cope effectively with divorce, parents should try to accomplish the following.

- Help children realize that the separation is final. Many children cling to the fantasy that some day their parents will reconcile and that the family unit will reemerge intact. Children must face reality if they are to deal with divorce, and parents must make the finality understood using age-appropriate language.
- It is especially important to young children that parents explain in a concrete and reassuring way what the children's daily life will be like. Children need to be told where they will sleep, where their toys will be, and how often they will see each parent. They need to be reassured that their parents will always be their parents and will always love them.
- Eliminate or minimize conflict. Children clearly are more upset when, as is often the case, parents fight continually. Children suffer most when they are drawn into the conflict.
- Help the child accept the loss of the noncustodial parent if visits stop or become infrequent. The caring presence of an adult of the same sex as the missing parent, such as a stepparent, aunt, or uncle, can be helpful.
- Allow children to express their anger and help them to forgive their parents. Although parents may not find it easy, try to accept this anger as a normal emotional reaction. Also explain that the divorce is no one's fault; children must understand this to have a healthy relationship with both parents.

Getting Help

Because divorce puts a strain on the emotional equilibrium of most children, and because many have no objective adult to turn to, many professionals believe that all children of divorcing parents should receive at least an evaluation from a mental health professional, if only to establish a link to someone if the need arises later.

A good therapist can help in many ways: by giving the child the opportunity to express and then accept the loss; by helping the child understand that the breakup was no one's fault, especially not the child's;

and by helping the child realize that he or she need not get caught up in the parents' conflicts. At the same time, the therapist can help parents understand their behavior and how it affects the child, and perhaps suggest alternate ways of handling the situation.

Because the problem concerns the disruption of the family as a whole, both parents should be involved in the child's counseling, either through joint family sessions or—if both parents cannot be involved together—in individual sessions with the child and therapist.

Some schools and community centers offer groups for children of divorced parents. Young children are encouraged to express their feelings, often through play and the use of dolls and puppets. Children see that their situation is neither unique nor cause for shame or guilt.

THE CASE OF LISA M.

Lisa M., age 6, was referred for a psychiatric consultation by her teacher because she became apathetic and withdrawn after her parents separated. Attempts to draw her into play activities with other children were unsuccessful. During recess she would sit by herself, refusing to talk to other children. During class, rather than listen to the teacher or follow the lesson, she would stare out the window. Although she did not appear to have a learning disability, she was having difficulty in learning to read. Teased by one of her schoolmates during art class, she responded by attacking him with a scissor, puncturing his skin.

During the evaluation interview with the psychiatrist, Lisa talked about being ugly and hated by everyone. The therapist, who specialized in treating children, kept a number of toys, dolls, and puppets in her office. She asked Lisa to pick out ones that reminded her of her mommy and daddy and herself. During her therapy sessions Lisa created a story in which the dolls lived in a magic kingdom. The kingdom was inhabited by a beautiful queen (her mother), a handsome prince (her father), and a little girl (Lisa). The prince was a special friend to the little girl. He played with her a lot, more than with the queen. The queen was very angry. One day a bad man came and threw the prince into the moat, where alligators attacked him. The prince rode off on a big fish. He still came to visit the little girl, but not very often, and he was very sad.

In subsequent play sessions, Lisa played out scenarios with similar themes of loss and separation.

During separate sessions with Lisa's parents, the psychiatrist found out that the divorce was initiated as the result of an affair by Lisa's mother. Her new boyfriend would visit during the day, while Lisa's father was at work. Lisa had been told that these visits were a special secret that could not be told to Daddy. When Lisa revealed the "secret," her parents had a furious fight, which ended with her father walking out of the house. Their subsequent meetings were punctuated by loud, violent arguments. Lisa felt responsible. Her behavior was the result of feelings of guilt, fear that her mother blamed her, and anger over the loss of what had been a close relationship with her father.

During subsequent play sessions, Lisa and the therapist explored Lisa's feelings. The sessions focused on alleviating Lisa's guilt and enhancing her feelings of self-worth. As she came to see that she was not responsible for her father's leaving and that her mother loved her very much, her performance in school improved. She began to make friends. While she still occasionally felt anger, she did not take those feelings out in inappropriately angry acts at other children.

Lisa's therapy, which continued for close to a year, was supplemented by counseling for her parents, who began to learn to control and limit their arguments in front of the girl. She also was directed to a tutor to help her catch up in her reading skills.

DEATH OF A PARENT OR OTHER LOVED ONE

The death of a loved one can be a severe trauma that changes the pattern of family life and calls forth powerful emotions for both children and adults. But whereas an adult's grief is often tempered by an intellectual comprehension of death, a young child may be confused or tormented by a lack of understanding as to what death means.

Death, particularly death of a parent, can leave children extremely vulnerable. Children need and depend on adults for basic caregiving and require the emotional support and coaching of adults to bring them through the bereavement process.

Children are affected critically by what happens following the death and by the quality of their relationship with a surviving parent; indeed, the help or care that a child experiences before and after a loss may affect him or her even more than the loss itself. If the surviving parent is too deeply involved in his or her own mourning to attend to the child's needs, or if the stability and quality of the home life deteriorates, then that child has lost considerably more than just one parent.

As with divorce, children's reactions to death will depend on many other factors, such as the child's age, sex, and maturity; the nature of the relationship to the deceased and to the surviving mother or father; the economic status of the family; and preexisting personal strengths or weaknesses of the child. The loss of a parent in childhood does not necessarily cause problems in later life. Emotionally resilient children who have a strongly supportive parent, a stable environment, good family relationships, and/or a well-developed sense of self probably will cope successfully with parental death.

How Children React to Death

Although children react to a death with the same emotions as adults, including anxiety, grief, and anger, they may express their feelings in different ways and at different times than adults. Indeed, children react differently at different ages.

The following is an outline of reactions that predominate at different developmental stages.

Infancy and Early Childhood

While experts disagree on whether infants actually can mourn, they do agree that young children respond to physical absence. Signs of infant distress include increased crying, withdrawal, and sad facial expression. At this age, however, children are capable of multiple attachments, and the effect that loss will have depends on the quality of care the young child experiences after the parent's death.

By the age of two, the death of an important person in the child's life (such as a parent, grandparent, or sibling) will have a strong impact, even though the child may not clearly realize what death is or be able to put feelings into words. Young children vary in their response to death, depending on their degree of understanding and emotional capacity. They can feel deserted and sense that the security of their world is being destroyed. Some seem unaffected, shutting out their feelings, while others show intense distress. The child may express these emotions through behavioral changes, becoming more demanding or subject to tantrums.

Anxiety—particularly separation anxiety (see chapter 17, page 248)—is a frequent emotional response to death. Sometimes young children cling to surviving parents and caregivers, following them around the room or house and refusing to let them out of their sight, or holding tight to favorite toys or "security blankets." They repeatedly ask for the dead parent, searching for the parent in places they associate with his or her presence. Nighttime fears are common.

Often, if the surviving parent catches a cold or shows any physical frailty, the child will be afraid that this parent too will die. Some children regress to younger behavior, such as returning to poor toilet habits, demanding a bottle, or refusing to eat independently.

Young children tend to express emotions in bursts rather than having consistent, sustained reactions. Often these emotional spikes come in the middle of play or at some other unexpected moment. Sometimes children will express irrational anger, both at the deceased and at the surviving parent. Boys in particular may act aggressively. At other times children may express intense sadness.

Children between the ages of three and six are still trying to figure out what death is all about. Often the reaction to death is a reflection of the child's level of awareness. For instance, young children may view an action or thought as having caused the death, as in the case of a seven-year-old boy who believed that because he sneaked out of school one day, his father had a heart attack and died. This self-centered, guilty explanation may have great power because the child does not have all the information needed to understand the actual cause of death.

Middle and Late Childhood

Older children comprehend what loss means and that it will affect their future. Their growing independence and sense of self is fragile, however, and the death of a parent can rekindle feelings of childishness and helplessness. Some children may react by repressing or holding back feelings, believing it is more "grown up" to do so. They may act as if nothing has happened, continuing to laugh and play in what appears on the surface to be a normal fashion. It may seem to adults that the child does not care. In reality,

WHAT CHILDREN NEED TO UNDERSTAND ABOUT DEATH

1. *Irreversibility.* The dead parent will not come back. Often television shows or cartoons feature apparently "dead" heroes who bounce back to life, making it hard for a child to understand that the body will not come back to life.
2. *Universality.* Death happens to everybody at some stage in life. Children should be assured, however, that they themselves are in no imminent danger of dying.
3. *Causality.* Certain things, such as an illness or an accident, can cause death. Other things, such as a bad thought, cannot.
4. *Awareness of physical reality.* Death is a cessation of bodily function. Often a young child's understanding of death is complicated by the attempts of others, especially parents, to protect him or her from this knowledge or to soften it. Sometimes these "magical" accounts are comforting. Josh, four years old when his father died, was comforted by his cousin's description of heaven. But more often these pictures are confusing, provoking fantasies and making it harder for the child to come to terms with the physical reality of death.

the child is affected very strongly, but needs support and encouragement to express feelings.

Though older children use language more effectively, they may remain silent on the topic of death, in part because they are embarrassed at being "different" because of the loss. At birthday parties and school performances they notice that their friends have both parents present, which can evoke pain because their friends have something they do not. They may also fear being rejected by friends who do not understand, which is often the case.

Adjustment difficulties and stresses often appear in the classroom. Interest in both academics and play can be affected, and school performance often drops. When this behavior continues months after the death, adults may fail to recognize it as a response to the bereavement, and the child may not receive the help he or she needs to resolve the loss. Teachers and surviving parents should let the child know that they understand, and that it is possible and desirable to resume studying and playing even though the pain continues.

Talking to Children about Death and Helping Them Cope

A large part of how a child reacts has to do with what adults are feeling and what they convey. If parents or other surviving adults do not talk about the loss, or if they change the subject when the death is brought up, the child gets the message that this is a topic to be avoided. Sometimes, adults' discomfort in dealing with their own emotions results in a failure to communicate with the child.

Discussion will be easier and more productive if the child has been introduced to concepts of death before a serious illness or death in the family forces the topic. When they are in crisis, parents may be too distraught to discuss the event helpfully or to think through the effect that their words will have.

Even very young children can achieve an understanding of death. The death of a pet, while upsetting to the child, can be used to initiate concepts of death as a physically permanent, irreversible state. Metaphors or analogies can be helpful if drawn from some familiar aspect of life, such as the withering of a flower. However, metaphors can be an adult's way of avoiding being direct and truthful with the child, and parents should make sure the child understands the connection between the story and what is real.

Conveying the News and Working through the Emotions

Soon after a parent, grandparent, or sibling becomes terminally ill or dies, the child should be given clear and realistic information. Children get very frightened when they feel something terrible has happened and they do not know what it is. The news should come from an adult who is close to the child, who is willing to express his or her own reaction, but who is also able to attend to the child's response. The adult should give the child the sense that everyone is very upset, but everyone will work together to deal with this event, including the child.

During the weeks and months following the death, children need frequent opportunities and encouragement to discuss their feelings openly. Talking about the deceased, their memories and their longing for the dead person, is an important part of the grieving process. It helps children to confirm that it is all right to have such feelings, and it helps them to integrate their feelings about the person and the loss into a framework that they can accept and live with. It is also important for the child to know how the surviving parent feels, and that parent and child share a common bond of grief.

Funerals

Whether or not a child should attend the funeral depends on the individual family situation. It may be helpful for a child to feel included in this formal expression of grief as a way of confirming the reality of death and reassuring the child that he or she is an important part of the family. The surviving parent should explain to the child that a funeral is a way of saying good-bye, and allow the child to make the decision of whether or not to go. A child should not be forced to attend a funeral, but certainly should be included if he or she expresses the desire to go.

It may help for the child to participate in the planning of the funeral or to take part in the service itself, perhaps by making a prepared statement or by putting favorite and important mementoes in the casket.

The child must be prepared for the funeral ahead of time. Someone should explain what to expect, including such concrete details as what the room and the casket will look like, and that many people will be there to say good-bye. If the ceremony includes a viewing of the body, this should be described ahead of time simply and factually.

Parents should not expect a child to be on perfect behavior or to follow "established" funeral conventions. With the child at all times should be an adult who can focus beyond his or her own grief. This "buddy" should be aware of what the child is feeling and able to give emotional support. The adult also should be able to answer questions and take the child out of the funeral parlor or chapel when necessary.

When Parents Need Help

Although emotionally most children can survive the loss of a parent or other loved one, a series of ongoing losses can erode a child's ability to cope. If the surviving parent is emotionally overwrought and does not provide sufficient parenting, if before the death the child did not feel emotionally self-confident or secure, or if economic circumstances are unstable, the child who might otherwise have been able to cope well with death may be overwhelmed emotionally.

HELPING CHILDREN DEAL WITH DEATH AND LOSS

- Remember that a child will not grieve in the same way as an adult. Although their feelings may be the same, children will express grief in different ways and at different times.
- Be responsive to the child's signals. When a child needs to cry, respond and comfort the child in a way that acknowledges the way he or she is feeling.
- Recognize that the child will have many questions, and be available to answer them. Do not give the child false reassurances; instead, provide realistic support.
- Let the child know it is okay to grieve and to express feelings. But do not pressure the child to talk if he or she is unready. Follow the child's lead.
- Help the child develop ways to express feelings. A "memory book" can be helpful. Such a book might include pictures of the child and the deceased at different times together as well as poems, thoughts, and memories of shared experiences.
- Arrange for the child to meet and play with other children who have experienced a similar loss, so that the child does not feel so alone in what he or she is going through.

Surviving parents needs to be sensitive both to the needs of their children and to their own grief and limitations. Helping their children through a major loss at the same time that they are called on to assume total parenting responsibilities can be extremely taxing emotionally. If the surviving parent is having a hard time coping with the loss, or is finding it difficult to talk to the child about feelings, he or she should get help. Some people find crisis intervention therapy (see chapter 25) with a professional experienced in bereavement issues particularly helpful.

When Children Need Help

For some children, the death of a parent or sibling can actually be a spur to development. Identification with the deceased's values, goals, or interests can serve as a springboard to defining the young person's life work. Children may also develop new avenues of sensitivity and an awareness of what other people feel. Jayne T., who lost her father at the age of 13, became a child psychologist because of her wish to help other children work through difficult experiences.

But many children do experience problems, and sometimes a professional consultation to evaluate if therapy is needed can be useful.

Signs that the child is troubled include:

- The child persistently refuses to accept the reality of the loss.
- Appetite and sleep disturbance persist.
- The child avoids friends or school functions.
- The child has continuing difficulties in school.
- The severity of the child's reaction goes beyond what the parent can deal with.

In addition to overt, external behavioral problems, parents should watch for quieter signs of emotional pain. The child who responds by internalizing feelings and withdrawing from the world, and who thus receives no attention, may be most likely to have long-term problems.

The first place to look for help, whether it is with caregiving or with emotional responsibilities, is to the people closest to the family—such as supportive relatives, friends, and clergy. If the support network is not sufficient, parents should seek professional help. Short-term individual or group therapy can help to sort out the emotional issues that surface in response to the bereavement and give the parent support and reassurance on how best to help the child. Physicians who were involved in the care of the deceased may be able to recommend a mental health expert skilled in crisis therapy. If practical issues need to be dealt with—day-care arrangements, financial aid, and so forth—a psychiatric social worker may be particularly helpful. Pastoral counselors (see chapter 3), who provide both grief and spiritual counseling, also can be a good source of help.

CHILD ABUSE

The trauma of child abuse has complex mental health consequences for both the child who is the object of abuse and for the family within which the abuse takes place. An estimated 1 to 2 million children are maltreated each year, most of them within their own homes.

Neglect

The most common form of child abuse is neglect—the failure of a parent to provide adequate physical care or supervision for a child. Neglect is generally an act of omission, such as persistently leaving a young child unattended; not providing meals, proper clothing, or adequate shelter; or failing to ensure that a child attends school or receives medical care.

While this form of abuse is the most common, it is the least acknowledged and the least reported to authorities. Thus, often, children who suffer from neglect do not receive help. Neglect is usually a chronic family problem that, when unchecked, can have as significant an impact on a child's development as physical or sexual abuse, discussed at greater length below. Many neglected children, for example, grow up with low self-esteem and poor social skills. They may need professional counseling to help them understand the impact that neglect has had on their lives and to cope with their feelings of anger and abandonment. Neglect, for example, has been associated with such maladaptive behaviors as truancy, aggression toward other children, and poor school performance.

As with physical abuse, helping a child who suffers from neglect is difficult, because it entails convincing an adult who may be unwilling or unable (he or she may simply lack parenting skills) to provide the care needed. If you believe that a child is being neglected to the point of physical endangerment—for example, he or she is in danger of illness from malnutrition or lack of medical care, or of being harmed because of lack of supervision (as can happen when young children are left unsupervised or locked alone in cars)—you *must* call the appropriate child welfare agencies and inform them of the situation. While you may be able to help the child on a one-to-one basis by providing clothes, a good meal, and being there to talk to, only an official agency can assess how serious the situation is and intervene if necessary.

Because neglect often accompanies socioeconomic disadvantage, help in the form of social service/financial assistance is often required. In fact, without this kind of support, therapy for neglect and abuse is often futile. Some communities have adapted a system of case management for dysfunctional families, in which a trained professional provides intense help in finding such resources as mental health counseling for both children and parents.

Physical Abuse

Physical abuse of children is a form of domestic violence. The abuser is most likely to be a parent. Health professionals have documented injuries to abused children that range from skin abrasions, lacerations, and black eyes to broken bones, skull fractures, and internal organ damage, sometimes leading to the child's death.

Risk

Although abuse can happen within any family, rich or poor, physically abused or neglected children are more likely to live in impoverished, single-parent households. Studies have documented a direct relationship between family violence and such factors as poverty, early motherhood, alcohol or drug abuse, and education level. Marital discord figures strongly in child abuse.

The parent most likely to abuse a child is one who was neglected or abused during his or her own childhood. Many of these victims never learned good parenting skills and are not well equipped to cope with or to rear their children. Frequently they harbor unrealistic expectations of how a child should behave. Abusive parents usually have poor problem-solving skills, live isolated lives, and have inadequate emotional support networks. Often the only way they know how to respond to stress is with anger and rage.

Children who are the most at risk to be physically abused are those who are taxing for such parents to care for, such as young children who are difficult to control, are overly active, or who demand a great deal of attention. In some families, one child is singled out as a "scapegoat" for punishment. Understandably, the child's behavior worsens in the face of abuse, to which the parent reacts with increasing violence, perpetuating a cycle of abuse.

Impact on the Child

Physically abused children exhibit a host of difficulties, often compounded by family instability and socioeconomic problems.

Many abused children demonstrate intellectual impairment and experience academic problems in school. A common problem is difficulty with language, but teachers may ascribe the problem to immaturity or learning disabilities rather than to abuse. Often physically abused children are depressed, sometimes to the point of engaging in behavior that is self-destructive, even suicidal.

Conduct problems are typical. A child who is overly aggressive, frequently gets into fights, or, in extreme cases, commits acts of violence may be mimicking what has been done to him or her by an adult.

Boys who are abused are more likely to act out in ways that are aggressive; girls tend to play the part of victims. These behavior patterns can become fixed throughout life if untreated. Boys, for instance, often become delinquents, eventually winding up in the criminal justice system. Abused girls are likely to choose spouses or lovers who abuse them. Some abuse their own children, perpetuating the pattern of child abuse into the next generation.

Help for Physically Abused Children and Their Families

Children may need to be removed from abusive families for their own safety. When possible, psychotherapy for physical abuse should be aimed at both the child and the adult; some experts recommend a combination of family therapy and individual counseling for the child. A child who remains at home can't be protected unless parents accept help for themselves.

Professional counseling can help a parent explore the reasons why he or she responds to stress with anger and violence. It can help parents to develop better parenting and coping skills; learn how to praise and show affection for their children; and use forms of discipline other than physical force. Often learning stress relaxation techniques can help parents defuse their violent reactions.

Without help, abused children are in jeopardy of developing long-term adjustment disorders. The therapist needs to determine the extent of the psychological damage to the child and help the child recover. Particularly important is enabling physically abused children who are themselves destructive to see how their experience of violence leads them to be "bad" themselves.

A typical counseling session with a child might explore the child's fears and anxieties about being hit or examine perceptions about life that have been distorted by violence, such as that it's okay to hit someone if you are angry. Abused children need help understanding their parents' anger and what triggers it, how to control their own impulses, and how to talk to parents or others about their feelings. Some therapists teach children "safety skills"—how to act and whom to tell when a parent turns violent.

Sexual Abuse

Although sexual abuse occurs less frequently than neglect or physical abuse, it is a problem that is receiving increasing attention, and reports of its incidence are on the rise. Unlike physical abuse, which occurs primarily in the privacy of the home, sexual abuse of children occurs both within and outside the home, although abusers most frequently are family members and adults connected to the family rather than strangers. Sexual abuse can occur in any family, rich or poor.

Both boys and girls are at risk for sexual abuse. The more frequent and the more severe the abuse is, the more a child suffers emotionally. Longstanding abuse accompanied by violence and physical threats, for instance, or abuse that is characterized by penetration of the child is more damaging than gentle fondling of short duration.

Incest/Intrafamily Abuse

Many of the risk factors for sexual abuse within the home are the same as for physical abuse, especially the presence of multiple stress factors and social isolation. In addition, the abusing parent, whether it is the father or the mother, is frequently alone with the child and thus has the opportunity for sexual contact. An unrelated male (a stepfather, a boyfriend) living with the family is a major risk factor for sexual abuse, because societal taboos against incest do not apply to them.

In many families where incest occurs, a great difference in power exists between the two parents. Typically, the family is headed by a domineering father who uses force to intimidate and manipulate both his wife and his children. Often alcohol or drug abuse is part of the problem, perhaps because it loosens normal inhibitions about incest. The mother usually is passive, frightened, and dependent; often she is not emotionally equipped to protect her children from her husband. More rarely, the mother is dominant and the father passive and meek; the father sexually abuses a child to feel sexually strong. In both cases, the relationship between parents is characterized by a lack of communication and intimacy.

CHILDREN'S ART THERAPY: A SELF-PORTRAIT

Figure 20.2: **A self-portrait by a six-year old girl who had been sexually abused by a teenage cousin. The outstretched arms signal feelings of vulnerability; the closed eyes, a desire to shut out the world. Initially, the child described the bar in front of her legs as a "magic stick" that protected her. In therapy, she later confided that the "stick" belonged to her cousin, who would use it to touch her in "secret" places.**

In many cases, rather than accepting the reality that his or her spouse or lover is having sexual contact with the child, the nonabusing parent takes sides against the child. Thus, many children experience anger, disbelief, and denial, even blame from the person to whom they go for help.

SIGNS OF SEXUAL ABUSE

The most striking indicator of sexual abuse is if the child begins to have an abnormal curiosity about sexual matters or is hypersexual—he or she displays a precocious knowledge of sex; behaves seductively toward other children or adults; engages in excessive masturbation; or frequently touches people inappropriately.

Some other possible indicators of sexual abuse are:

- Your child might cry a lot or look depressed, be fearful, and exhibit regressive or infantile behavior.
- Your child might not want to go near the person who is abusing him or her, refusing or objecting, for instance, to be left with a baby-sitter, developing a phobia about going to school or visiting a separated parent.
- Your child has medical problems in the genital or anal areas—pain, swelling, or tears in the skin; bleeding, discharge, or an unusual odor.

Impact on the Child

Some of the common responses to sexual abuse are depression, mistrust, suicidal feelings, and poor school performance. Sexually abused children may exhibit a spectrum of sexual behavior that is inappropriate for their age. (See the box above.) For example, they may be prematurely sexual in their behavior, or they may go to extreme lengths to avoid any sexual contact beginning in adolescence.

In many cases, abused children have a close attachment to the person who is molesting them. Thus, they experience painfully conflicting feelings. Feelings of guilt are common for many reasons. They may feel that the abuse was their fault for having consented to it. They may have found some of the activity pleasurable even though they know they were doing something considered wrong. If, as a result of the abuse, a father is removed from the home or a teacher is fired, they may suffer guilt for having broken up the family or disrupted the school.

Sexual abuse impairs a child's self-esteem. The older the child, the more impact the stigma of sexual abuse has on feelings of self-worth. A very young child might not be affected emotionally by sexual abuse at the time it occurs but later may develop a retroactive awareness that what was done to them was "bad." Boys who are abused often feel humiliated. Frequently they have concerns about homosexuality, because they are usually molested by a male, although there is no evidence that sexual abuse affects a child's sexual preference as an adult. Boys are more likely than girls to reenact the abuse when they grow up, becoming sexually aggressive or abusive themselves. A considerable number of sexual offenders have been found to have been sexually abused during childhood.

Girls are likely to respond to sexual abuse by becoming sexual victims later in life. As adults, abused girls seem to be more prone to enter into relationships in which they are not treated well, sometimes becoming battered wives. In fact, many sexually abused women choose a mate who is a sexual abuser; frequently, sexually abused children have mothers with a history of sexual abuse in their childhood. It appears that their sexual traumatization predisposes these women to seek out people who will be abusive. Or, perhaps because the abuse has left them feeling sexually insufficient, they are attracted to men who have difficulties in being sexual with adult women.

Help for Sexually Abused Children and Their Families

Sometimes crisis intervention (discussed in chapter 25) or short-term supportive therapy is sufficient to help a child come to terms with the feelings he or she has about the abuse. Sometimes, however, a child may need long-term therapy to prevent problems that would impair his or her ability to function later in life.

Therapy for sexual abuse has to deal with children's anger and feelings of betrayal by someone whom they trusted, often including the nonoffending parent or others who allowed the abuse to occur. Restoring sexually abused children's feelings of self-acceptance and self-control and teaching them that they have the right to say no are important therapeutic goals.

Many children have problems trusting any adult after they have been sexually abused. Sometimes they will avoid any kind of social or dating situation and have problems with sexual functioning later in life. They have to be helped to know what is normal sexuality and what appropriate sex roles are.

In severe cases, and particularly in cases where children have been threatened with retaliation if they tell anyone about the abuse, children suffer from post-traumatic stress disorder (see chapter 24, page 362), characterized by nightmares or flashbacks. They literally are terrified, their thoughts flooded with bad memories and images.

TALKING TO YOUR CHILD ABOUT SEXUAL ABUSE

If your child is acting frightened, or if you suspect sexual abuse may have occurred, offer your child the opportunity to freely discuss whatever is bothering him or her. Be comforting, supportive, and matter-of-fact in your approach.

Often children are reluctant to talk about sexual abuse because the perpetrator has threatened them in some fashion. A father, for instance, might tell a child, "I'll have to go to jail. You'll have to go to a foster home." Some children deny that they have been sexually molested because of guilt or of a desire to protect the family and its "secret." Because a child will not talk about sexual abuse does not mean that it has not happened.

Questions such as "Has anything happened to make you feel bad? Did anyone touch you in your private parts? Did they give you a bad touch? Did anyone frighten you in this way?" can sometimes help a child to discuss the subject. If your child is exhibiting precocious sexual activity, you should ask where he or she learned the behavior, with questions such as "Did you see any adults do that? Has anyone done this to you?" Do not, however, ask questions that would make a child feel to blame, such as "Why did you let him?"

Don't force your child to talk if he or she refuses.

Avoid trying to lead the child or to impose your ideas of what might have happened on to him or her.

If you suspect that your child has been sexually abused, have him or her examined by a pediatrician who is a specialist in examining children for sexual abuse *and* evaluated by a child psychiatrist, psychologist, or other mental health professional who has experience with abused children. He or she will be better able to determine the kind of emotional stress that your child is experiencing and to develop a therapeutic intervention.

Seeking professional counseling is also important because sometimes children *do* make false accusations of sexual abuse. A child's initial statement cannot always be taken at face value. Occasionally a child either is coached by one parent to wrongly accuse the other or will say what he or she believes a parent wants to hear. Most often, however, if a child says that he or she engaged in sexual activity with an adult, very likely abuse has occurred. A child has more reasons to deny that any molestation has occurred than to fabricate its occurrence.

The Clearinghouse on Child Abuse and Neglect Information (P.O. Box 1182, Washington, D.C. 20013; tel. 202 245–2856) can provide referrals, hotline numbers, information, and advice.

Sexual abuse often precipitates a family crisis. Therapy for the offending parent aims at helping him or her accept rather than deny that abuse has occurred, understand why it happened, and learn ways to refrain from future abuse. Whether the abuse was committed by a stranger, relative, family friend, baby-sitter, or someone else outside the family, parents often have to come to terms with feelings of rage at the perpetrator and of self-blame. Therapy also can help parents to help their child through the crisis.

Prevention

Until recently, the only advice given to most children to protect them against sexual abuse was to "beware of strangers." The fact that most cases of sexual abuse happen with someone the child knows was not fully appreciated. Now many schools offer sex education and prevention programs. Children are taught not to allow themselves to be touched in private places and to distinguish between a good touch and a bad touch. Most important, they are encouraged to tell if *anyone*—even people they know or people in their family—has invaded their privacy. The goal of these programs is to make children aware of sexual abuse and what it is, so that a child may be able to avoid the situation.

four

• • •

SPECIAL ISSUES AND PROBLEMS

21

Women's Issues at a Time of Social Change

Ethel Spector Person, M.D.

All human beings, regardless of their sex, face the same basic life tasks and challenges. Each of us must establish an independent identity, develop relationships, find a means of support, seek pleasure and creative outlets, find meaning in our lives, and face and come to terms with loss and death.

Each individual approaches and copes with these shared human challenges and dilemmas differently, yet some of the differences in approach depend on gender. Each sex appears to have its own set of mental health vulnerabilities. At each stage of life, individuals experience different pressures and expectations from themselves, their families, and society depending on gender; consequently, men and women to some degree experience different psychological and role conflicts.

The past few decades have been a time of social change, perhaps more so for women. While new doors are opening, many women nonetheless find themselves in the throes of confusing, conflicting feelings, values, and experiences. Because other chapters in this book deal with those diagnosable mental disorders that afflict both genders, in this chapter the focus primarily is on issues that are more specific to women. In particular it emphasizes psychological conflicts that are affected markedly by women's roles. These include for some women at some times: role conflicts, obsessive preoccupation with relationships, fear of loss of love, victimization within relationships, work inhibitions, sexual difficulties, inhibitions in expressing anger, and feelings of powerlessness with consequent depression. In addition, problems specific to the female sexual and reproductive cycles (such as premenstrual syndrome and postpartum depression) are discussed. Finally, mention is made of some of the psychiatric disorders that appear to be more common among women. Women, like men, make myriad adaptations to the challenges of their lives, many of them extremely successful and fulfilling; the focus here is on some of the more common maladaptations.

THE WEAKER SEX?

In the past, health professionals and theorists held that the female sex was the emotionally and physically weaker of the two sexes. A female, as an 1827 report explained it, "is far more sensitive and susceptible than the male and extremely liable to those distressing affections which for want of some better term have been determined nervous. . . ." The common explanation for this female vulnerability to emotional distress was her anatomy and reproductive biology, which, according to theorists of past times, made her genetically susceptible to mental afflictions and "weak" personality traits.

At the turn of the century Sigmund Freud, brilliant though he was, was no more free from the biases about women than were his contemporaries. The founder of psychoanalysis believed that masculine personality traits were the norm. Women, he suggested, "retreated" into their feminine personality traits when they discovered at a very early age that they could not be the men that they "naturally" wanted to be. His explanation for female psychology was based on his theory of "penis envy." Freud hypothesized that as soon as a little girl discovered that she had no penis and could never hope to have one, she felt shocked, deprived, inferior, and angry. To resolve this conflict, she normally would begin to retreat into a submissive, passive, masochistic, and childish personality. She then would begin to form dependent attachments to men and in so doing find herself a sort of substitute for her own missing penis.

Freud believed that this personality pattern was normal, inevitable, unchangeable, quintessentially feminine, appropriate, and desirable for all women. (He made exceptions for his female disciples, whose "unresolved masculinity complexes"—so he believed—allowed them to excel in the field.)

Only much later would psychoanalysts and other theorists realize that Freud's theories about female psychology were mired in nineteenth-century cultural attitudes toward women. In Victorian patriarchal culture, women had little or no power or socioeconomic independence, and their welfare and security in life depended entirely on their marriageability and their ability to accept and submit to the authority of their husbands. The woman who was psychologically dependent on men, who did not assert herself, and who was reluctant to voice her own interests if they conflicted with the needs or demands of her husband was making an adaptation to the realities of her life that men found very attractive. With few approved avenues for self-assertion outside the nursery and the kitchen, little authority over the course of their lives, and cultural admonitions to curtail their sexuality, however, many women may well have experienced inward psychological distress—leading, perhaps, to the "nervous afflictions" that apparently were so common among women in that day.

Today the social roles, power relationships, and economic realities remain much the same for many women, especially for those who are poor and who lack education. Yet many women live in a radically changed world, a world in which they are much freer to express themselves and to determine their own direction in life. Women are abundant in the workplace now, in part because one income no longer suffices for most families, but also because new attitudes have surfaced. Many women now are attempting to find meaning for themselves in a wider sphere than the home alone. Opportunities for career success are open to many more women. Still, by no means have women achieved equality in pay or promotion, and, as is discussed shortly, women today generally are still expected to bear full child care responsibilities in addition to going out of the home to work.

Modern studies show that women continue to report more symptoms of mental and physical suffering and to seek help more than men. Whether this means women actually have more problems or that they are perhaps more willing to acknowledge them and seek help is an open question. It is certainly true, however, that many women remain emotionally dependent on and submissive to men for their self-esteem and many have problems with passivity as well as effective expression of anger, among other difficulties. But the explanations for these female vulnerabilities and difficulties are conceptualized quite differently from the way they were in Freud's time.

Mental health professionals no longer believe that women are inherently the weaker sex or more vulnerable to mental health disorders because of their anatomy, hormonal functioning, or penis envy. Instead, we look at the way development, psychology, culture, socioeconomic factors, and biology act together to create conflict or to strain coping capacities or, alternately, to lend strength and resilience to female adaptive capacities. Even those distresses or illnesses that are related to a woman's reproductive cycle—such as premenstrual and postpartum depression—appear to be influenced significantly by social and psychological factors.

FEMALE PSYCHOLOGY AND FEMININE ROLES

For every person, the sense of self as female or as male becomes the scaffolding around which personality develops and behavior takes shape. Little girls and little boys go their separate psychological ways, studies now show, even before they are old enough to recognize that they have different sexual organs. Male and female brains develop somewhat differently after a certain point in fetal life, apparently leading to some differences in behavior, including greater male aggressiveness for example. Nonetheless, most of what society considers masculine or feminine patterns are not inborn. For example, occasionally children are born with malformed or ambiguous sexual organs, and it is not clear which sex they are. These children have an underlying genetic sex, which can be determined by finding out whether they have male or female chromosomes. Studies show that as these children grow up, they develop the traits and identities of the sex in which they are raised, even when their genetic sex is the opposite.

More important than her genes or hormones to the little girl's developing identity as a female is her situation in the family and in society. The process of developing a feminine way of being begins in her earliest relationships within her family. Her parents and the larger culture directly and indirectly teach her about what kinds of emotions, behavior, and reactions are considered ideal for girls, and what kinds of activities and rewards in life are available to her as a female. Meanwhile, the little girl begins to identify herself as female and to imitate her mother. Over time, her sense of femininity is shaped also by her relationships with her father and with her siblings.

As she gets older, a girl learns more from the culture at large, including her peer group, about what constitutes normal, appropriate, approved, and rewarded behavior and roles for girls and women. By the time she is out of adolescence, the young woman has formed an ideal of femininity that she will try to live up to and against which she will measure herself. However, in a time such as ours of changing mores, by the time a girl has reached adulthood, the culture may be changing its values. This is the conflict for some women today: Outwardly they may espouse a "new" femininity, but inwardly they may be influenced as much or more by the feminine ideal with which they grew up.

Women and Relationships

From earliest age, boys and girls are groomed (by parents and cultural dictates) to seek their identities differently. Traditionally, women have learned to value relationships, love, and intimacy as the validation for their femininity, and men to seek autonomy, work, and achievement as the primary proving ground for their masculinity. While men too seek love and family, and women increasingly endeavor to make contributions in the workplace, each gender tends to have its own central psychological mission. A man may not feel comfortable in his relationships until he has established his niche in the working world. A woman who has not found love, marriage, and motherhood despite real accomplishments in the workplace may feel she has fallen short of her ideal of femininity.

The ability and desire to love, to nurture, to share, and to provide emotionally for others lead to lifelong skills and coping strengths for many women, who are able to establish strong and lasting friendships that are so important to maintaining mental and even physical health. For example, studies show that women generally adapt far better than men following the death of a spouse. The widows, unlike their male counterparts, tend to have stronger friendships and ties to others that help sustain them emotionally during their loss. Pursuit and nurturance of love can be self-confirming, self-transcending—a life-enriching experience like none other.

But for some women, the overriding importance placed on success in their roles as wife/lover and mother may make them psychologically vulnerable to certain social factors—among them the relative shortage of men.

How an individual woman responds emotionally to the stresses that all women share in our society depends on her own personality and current psychological functioning and how she weathered conflicts in her early life. Nonetheless, many of the real stresses facing women as a group increase the likelihood of various reactions and adaptations, as we shall shortly see.

Reality Factors: The Shortage of Men, the Double Standard of Aging, and Women Alone

Although relationships with men remain central to the self-concept of many women today, for at least two reasons women do not have equal access to such relationships throughout their life cycle. For one, there are not enough men to go around. Wars, earlier mortality for men, and homosexuality have com-

bined to make men a relatively scarce commodity for women, especially as they age. For another, in our culture men tend to find women less and less desirable as they age. Writer Susan Sontag has called this phenomenon "the double standard of aging"—the inescapable fact that older men are considered attractive and desirable and can more easily find new relationships and produce new families, while women are not viewed similarly and do not have the same opportunity to find new partners.

Thus, women risk aloneness in their lives more than men. The "new" woman who has devoted her 20s and most of her 30s to her career may find that when she is ready to mate and start a family, she may have difficulty finding a partner. The woman who divorces after a marriage of some 20 years may find that she no longer is desired by most men. These women, single or newly single, must endure the prevailing attitude (often from within themselves as well) that being single represents a failure of their femininity. They are deprived of sexual experiences as well.

Women alone face other concrete privations. They often are neglected socially by their paired-off friends and acquaintances, left uninvited to parties and social gatherings. In fending for themselves economically, they almost never have the same earning power as men and may face increasing economic insecurity and material deprivation as they age. In addition, the reality of violence against women may mean that they are not as free to go about in public as they would be in the company of a man.

THE RANGE OF REACTIONS AND ADAPTATIONS TO SHARED STRESSES

Consciously or subconsciously, most women are aware that they must compete for a limited supply of men, that their attractiveness to men is related to their age and appearance, and that if they lose their man, they may not be able to replace him. As a result, women more than men may find their thoughts preoccupied with finding and sustaining love. All too often women accept the greater work of maintaining their relationships. Some women may work hard to sustain relationships not only because they love or value their mates but because they have too much to lose without them. They sometimes tend to fear the loss of love, are possibly more vulnerable to depression, and commonly have difficulty expressing anger in their relationships.

The fear of loss of love and of aloneness may lead some more troubled women to anticipate rejection and abandonment even when there is no current threat. Some may surrender too readily their independent identities and ambitions, seeing their relationships as the only source of meaning in their lives. They may be reluctant to assert themselves or develop themselves as equals in their relationships. Some may concentrate their energy solely on looking young and attractive, rather than experiencing their mature, independent identities.

By making these kinds of accommodations in order to establish and preserve their relationships, these women face many risks. Most commonly, they risk a loss of self-esteem as they make themselves subservient. Then too, their loss of independent identity may make them flat and uninteresting to the mates they wish so desperately to keep. For another, total surrender of their own opportunities leaves them at risk of not being able to survive psychologically or financially should their mates decide to leave. And surrender of the self to an all-powerful person may increase substantially the risk that some women and their children will be the victims of violence and abuse.

Even the woman who can adapt more successfully to her situation and find new meanings for herself may nonetheless judge herself wanting as a woman. Success as wife/lover is so integral to many women's self-esteem that those who remain single or find themselves newly alone respond emotionally to this dilemma by blaming themselves. They may feel not only unloved but bad and unlovable.

The woman who accepted the new cultural norm (that feminine women are successful in the workplace) and concentrated on her career accomplishment may find, as she approaches midlife, that she may begin to measure herself against the traditional norm that she internalized as a girl (that feminine women are those who marry and have children). She may find herself worrying that, despite her proven competence, unless she is married she will not survive.

Being alone is very stressful for most people, especially for those for whom relationships are the principal source of meaning in life. Fortunately, as mentioned, women's ability to form and maintain intimate friendships throughout their life cycle allows most single, divorced, and widowed women to maintain important social ties. With the definition of femininity broadening, the women who remain single today and who are able to make productive, meaningful, mature adaptations will serve as a new kind of role model for the next generation of women.

In such ways as these, ongoing social realities play an important role in challenging each individual woman's self-esteem and coping capacities.

Motherhood

Along with marriage or pair bonding, motherhood for many women today represents the pinnacle of femininity. But mothers today have a hard time indeed fulfilling their dreams of the ideal of motherhood. Some of the problems for which women consult their doctors and therapists—such as exhaustion, guilt, anxiety, depression—can be traced to or triggered by conflicts and demands inherent in the role of today's mothers, especially working mothers.

Mothers of this generation are faced with an unprecedented aloneness in their role. Not only are there more single mothers than in previous times, but women lack the extended family networks that in the past provided emotional support and help with child care. In extreme cases, this lack of social supports combined with weak inner controls could lead the overstressed, emotionally unstable mother to take out her isolation and rage on her children.

Mothers who are less troubled emotionally find themselves nonetheless overwhelmed by guilt and anxiety. Unlike past generations, society today holds mothers completely responsible for the way their children behave and develop. Mothers take this psychological pressure to heart and believe that their children's successes as well as their difficulties or even imperfections reflect their own ability or inability to perform in that all-important role. As more and more women enter the workplace, most of them because they must, society blames them for the stresses of their absence on their children and on their families and for the inadequacy of child care arrangements.

Increasing numbers of men are taking on more child care responsibilities. They are learning to be nurturing and are becoming supportive of their wives in their proliferation of roles. Still, even when fathers participate more actively in parenting, mothers in our society generally remain the "psychological parent"—the one whose thoughts are more occupied with the child and who takes responsibility for remembering the child's schedule, for planning transportation and child care arrangements, and for leaving work if the child becomes ill or if arrangements fall through.

Working Mothers and Their Conflicts

Most women today can expect to work, most because they must, some because they seek self-fulfillment and self-actualization, and many for both reasons. This return to the workplace for mothers with young children represents a break in tradition from times past, when the mother's place was in the home, and it has created many realistic difficulties, role conflicts, and seemingly insurmountable hurdles for today's working mothers. The major unsolved problem for contemporary women is how to integrate work with family life.

Although new values suggest that good mothers also can want to work and to expand their identities outside the home, many women find that they are influenced also by the old values and feel caught between two worlds. Most women who work do not reduce their commitment to being a wife and a mother; rather, they add another full-time role. A woman's internal belief system may require that she be "perfect" in all her roles, and the reality of her inability to measure up to her own ideals and to others' expectations may be hard to bear.

While virtually all mothers want to do the right thing for their children, they now may be confused as to what is right for the children and right for themselves. For example, the decade from the mid-20s to the mid-30s is critical for child rearing as well as for establishing career strategies. Both roles require a deep commitment, and both pose competing concerns and demands on a woman's time and activities, not to mention her thoughts.

Guilt and role strain. Working mothers suffer from two major ailments: guilt and role strain. Women who must work, while they may feel guilty that they do not spend sufficient time with their chil-

dren and may worry that their child care arrangements are inadequate, find some comfort in that they are working to provide the best for their children. Women who choose to work in order to develop their own potential and to prevent the boredom or even depression that may result if they feel forced to stay home may feel guilty that they are "abandoning" their children. Professional women feel guilty also that they are not devoting themselves as thoroughly to their careers as they ought to in order to move forward. These women may have to struggle with their anger at children who present extra, time-consuming demands. Whatever the reasons why they work, few working mothers do not feel a constant undercurrent of guilt about the effects of their working on their children. The guilt is usually most intense for mothers of infants and preschool children.

Role strain is the somewhat euphemistic term for the chronic fatigue, anxiety, sense of always being behind, and near panic that working mothers so commonly feel from trying to manage their separate and often conflicting roles. Working mothers of small children who need them in the night may suffer as well from sleep deprivation, which may leave them less alert, less productive, and some-

---

MOTHERS' NEEDS VERSUS CHILDREN'S NEEDS: SEEKING SOLUTIONS

By far the greatest anxiety for most working mothers with young children is finding adequate child care arrangements. As more mothers return to work while their children are still infants, mental health professionals are paying growing attention to the mother-infant bond. A subject of passionate debate is whether the mother's work-imposed absence puts this important bond at risk. Suggestions that harm will come to infants or very young children who are put in the hands of others so that their mothers can work is a source of torment to most mothers, who are trapped in the crosscurrents of social and economic change.

Does being cared for by others in and of itself harm a child? While there are arguments on both sides, many mental health professionals believe that the critical variable is the quality of the relationship between the child and the mother. A full-time mother who is depressed or disturbed may not be

able to respond appropriately to the child, whereas a mother who is emotionally available to her child a few hours a day may form a good bond. Some studies show that most children do well in high-quality day-care arrangements but that inferior care may cause harm. There is some evidence as well that a child who is cared for by conscientious and nurturing adults at day-care centers may be as well off as a child who is cared for at home by his or her mother.

Because women in all sectors of society are working and must put their children in the hands of others while they are away, establishing quality day-care centers, training programs, and licensing criteria are some of the most critical issues facing our society. The absence of such a system is probably the single greatest stress factor affecting the mental and emotional health of millions of working mothers.

what irritable on the job. Even those rare few who can seem to manage both work and mothering without suffering stress still face periodic exhaustion, lack of private time, and neglect of exercise and appearance.

Common coping strategies. Most working mothers keep their guilt and role strain within tolerable limits, although some may need professional help to deal with the stress and self-criticism. Most try hard to focus on the quality of the time they spend with their children rather than its amount. Many try to compensate with special activities and material benefits. They cope with role strain most often by lowering their career ambitions or slowing down, at least until the children no longer need them as much, and by teaching their children early to be self-reliant and independent.

Women at Work

Whether or not they have children, women are encountering still another range of problems and conflicts with which they must struggle in the workplace. With few exceptions women do not advance as far or earn as much as men. Sexist barriers (sometimes known as the "glass ceiling") prevent them from achieving equal status. Yet many women who are openly ambitious and aggressive are discriminated against, or ridiculed, by male colleagues and management for being too "masculine." In addition to these external handicaps, which though pervasive may not be recognized for what they are, many women bring some common internal conflicts into the workplace that often frustrate their apparent ambitions.

Many of the problems that women encounter at work—including lack of concrete goals, reluctance to compete, fear of success, fear of failure, a feeling of being stuck—can be attributed to the personality traits they developed fulfilling traditional feminine expectations. They learned to be ingratiating, nurturant, supportive, and responsive to men. When they come to the workplace, unlike their male counterparts, they may never have been encouraged to set career goals or to acquire and handle power, or have learned how to parlay their achievements into greater successes.

Women often gravitate to positions in which they are helpful, competent auxiliaries to others. When the bosses get promoted, these women's fortunes may improve, or they may be left behind. They may feel stuck in their careers or angry at being left behind, without realizing how reluctant they are to compete and to take charge themselves. Women are so used to identifying their fortunes with those of other people that they commonly limit their horizons by remaining overly loyal. They may not recognize when the time has come to take off on their own career trajectories, or they may find it hard to deal with the anxiety they experience when it's time to make a change.

Lack of self-esteem plagues many women in the workplace. Although they may yearn to do something "important" with their lives, inside they often believe that as women they cannot achieve anything truly significant. Some women may be so afraid of failing that they dare not tolerate the risks of trial and error through which a person develops skills and confidence. These individuals quickly grow bored and restless with their work. Some who take greater risks may nonetheless devalue their eventual successes, attributing them to luck or to another person's assistance. Even highly accomplished women very often feel as if they did not deserve their successes—and that some day soon someone will expose them for the "fraud" that they think they are.

Perhaps the most pernicious problem for ambitious, successful women, because it strikes at the core of their feminine identity, is the fear of being seen as different from what desirable women are supposed to be. A crucial conflict in professional women today is between achievement and the fear of loss of love. They worry that men will be put off by their competence, which sometimes may be true. They worry that their interest in their careers may present conflicts in their marriages, which also may be true. They are afraid if they "go for it" in their professional lives, they will have to sacrifice having a loving relationship with a man. These women are trapped in a terrible conflict. They dare not go forward for fear of losing love, yet they cannot go backward either. They are stuck.

Most women do not realize that these conflicts may underlie their anxieties, disappointments, loss of meaning, lack of ambition, frustrations, or boredom in their working lives. It is important for working women to recognize the internal obstacles that they bring to the situation. Then they will be freer to spot and deal with the external limitations that society continues to impose on women in the workplace.

Women's Moods

Supposedly, women are moodier than men. As seen in chapter 8, it has been reported that women suffer from depression at rates that are at least twice as high as among men. One suspects, however, that many men have unrecognized mood disturbances that they medicate with alcohol and drugs. Nonetheless, even if depression is not the "women's problem" that the statistics suggest it to be, it is a problem for many women. The depressive disorders are detailed in chapter 8; presented here are some of the social and sex-role factors that may contribute to women's vulnerabilities to depression and to the related difficulty many women have in expressing anger. Depression related to women's reproductive cycles is addressed later in this chapter.

Depression

Two British researchers not long ago reviewed a number of studies and determined that in those studies in which women showed a higher rate of depression, they differed from the male subjects in several important ways. The men, who were found to be less depressed, had better jobs, higher pay, and overall higher socioeconomic status. An ongoing study by psychologist Rosalind Cartwright at Rush-Presbyterian St. Luke's Medical Center in Chicago has looked at separated and divorced individuals and has found no overall difference in the incidence of depression in the male and female subjects—*except* among women who conform to traditional sex roles. In this study, women with traditional values and roles have been found to be twice as likely to become depressed as their traditional male counterparts.

Women as a group, especially those who conform to traditional sex roles, often feel they are less in control of their lives than are men; in some women, this stress may contribute to their fragile self-esteem. In both sexes, life events, patterns, and stresses serve as powerful triggers for all forms of depression. As we have discussed throughout this chapter, women experience different social and cultural stresses than do men. It may well be that their roles as women, rather than their biology or their genes, play a determining part in women's apparent statistical susceptibility to depressive suffering. At the same time, it ought to be noted that men get depressed too and that depression is not a "given" for all women; despite these stresses, many women remain free of it.

Anger

Women have a tendency to inhibit the expression of anger or to suppress it entirely. The inability to express anger commonly lowers a person's self-esteem and leads to depression. Women are socialized to express anger indirectly if at all and to avoid direct confrontation. In the traditional feminine mold, they are taught to be "sugar and spice and everything nice." Women are supposed to please and make things better, to promote harmony; they are not supposed to rock the boat or try to change things.

Despite improvements in women's expectations, it is very difficult to break away from the stereotyped beliefs about how women (and men) are supposed to behave. Many psychotherapists believe that women today continue to fear that their anger would endanger their marriages and love lives, and their fears may, indeed, be realistic. Feeling angry signals that something needs to be changed, and in some cases trying to alter patterns within a relationship may endanger its foundations.

The reluctance to take this risk and to say "No!" when, for example, demands become too great can have serious consequences. It can lead some women to direct their rage against themselves and to feel that they deserve the abuses they may experience. They may submit silently and thus invite exploitation, devaluation, or even violence from others. Some women may project their self-hatred onto their children, whom they may believe are but reflections of their worthless selves. The inhibition of the expression of anger can lead to indirect equivalents, such as attacking the other person and then becoming defensive, taunting, complaining, and blaming, that ultimately may be ineffectual and destructive. Although these forms of anger are generally counterproductive, they may be the only ways some women who feel helpless and powerless may dare to express their negative feelings. They do not lead to correcting the balance of power, however, or to changing an intolerable situation, at home or in the workplace.

Women are better off taking the risk of trying to understand that they are angry and why, determining what needs to change, and trying to negotiate those changes. Some women are able to do this on their own, while others may benefit from social support, assertiveness training, or psychotherapy.

COMMON PROBLEMS OF SEXUALITY AND REPRODUCTION

The differences in male and female sexual and reproductive biology dictate that each sex will have its own set of sexual and reproductive dilemmas. Yet, as we shall see, these dilemmas are not mandated by biology alone.

Female Sexual Response

As with all aspects of their feminine identity, women grow up with ideas about sex that shape their responses and behavior. Nowadays, however, attitudes are changing, in part as a result of research by William H. Masters and Virginia E. Johnson into human sexual response and in part as a result of the women's movement.

In the past, women were believed to be by nature less interested in the physical side of sex. Supposedly, women did not normally wish to masturbate or become familiar with their own sexual responses. During the sex act, the man's sexual urge prevailed; women ideally were passive and submissive to their husbands' desires. The maximum sexual response for the mature woman, it was believed, was a "vaginal orgasm"; this was presumed to occur naturally during the act of intercourse, which ended when the man reached orgasm. The woman who did not have this experience, as few did, were considered "frigid."

Today we know that orgasm for women almost always depends on adequate stimulation of the clitoris, which is outside the vagina. Because this stimulation does not necessarily occur during sexual intercourse, many women do not experience during intercourse the maximum sexual pleasure of which their bodies are capable. The new values about women and sex permit women today to initiate and enjoy sex, be more adventurous, know their bodies and the pathways of pleasure, ask to be pleased rather than simply to concentrate on pleasing, and engage in many sexual practices in addition to intercourse in the missionary position. This information has yet to reach all women, however. Many apparently nonresponsive women (and their partners) suffer only from ignorance about the kinds of stimulation that would enable them to experience greater pleasure.

Yet even many informed women continue to behave in the old patterns and thus inhibit their full sexual response. Out of deference to their partners, or fear of them, or from the fear of appearing unfeminine, they hesitate to say what they would like. They do not ask to be stimulated, they assume that sex must end when the man has an orgasm, and they fake orgasms to please their partners; in other words, they are too preoccupied with pleasing men sexually to experience pleasure themselves. Sexual response is an important vehicle for increased self-esteem for women. Although they may think that they have a sexual disorder because they do not have orgasms or may have little interest in sex, their response usually improves dramatically when they work on self-assertion in their sexual relationships. Chapter 11 provides information on the sexual disorders and their treatment.

Premenstrual Syndrome (PMS)

Great numbers of women experience physical and emotional discomfort during the week before and the first few days of their menstrual cycle. Usually these changes are mild. Perhaps as many as 5 to 10 percent of women, however, suffer intense and incapacitating distress. Some women have mostly physical discomfort, including bloating, headaches, and muscle aches and pains. More apt to come to the attention of psychiatrists and other mental health practitioners are those who suffer from the severe mood swings, irritability, and anger associated with premenstrual syndrome. Most women who come for treatment report that their premenstrual suffering worsens with age.

The American Psychiatric Association has defined a category of psychiatric illness for further research and study called the late luteal phase dysphoric disorder for this small group of women with extreme symptoms. Symptoms of this disorder include marked mood changes, anger and irritability, anxiety, depression, loss of interest in ordinary activities, exhaustion and loss of energy, difficulty concentrating, appetite changes (including food cravings), changes in sleep patterns, and any of a number of physical changes (breast tenderness, headaches, aches and pains, bloating, weight gain). These symptoms may interfere with work, social activities, and relationships. They occur only during the week before and a few days after the onset of menstruation, and the diagnosis can be confirmed only by keeping a daily diary of symptoms during at least two cycles. They do not result from a premenstrual exacerbation of other psychiatric illnesses or disorders, such as major depression or personality disorders.

Researchers have discovered that when these rigorous diagnostic standards are imposed, very few women have true PMS. Rather, their daily diaries often show that they experience symptoms throughout the month and thus suffer instead from an underlying mood instability or other chronic problem that worsens premenstrually. Statistically, women's suicides, suicide attempts, and admissions to psychiatric hospital increase premenstrually; possibly, women who are predisposed to other mental and emotional disorders become particularly vulnerable at this time of the month, which does not necessarily mean that they have PMS. Research studies have also shown that many of the symptoms that women report premenstrually could be caused as well by other illnesses or medications that they may be taking.

At issue within the mental health community and among feminists, however, is whether women with severe premenstrual symptoms should be "labeled" with a psychiatric diagnosis. Despite proposed diagnostic criteria and much continuing study into the symptoms, causes, and treatment of premenstrual syndrome, no one yet fully understands it. Although the suffering for many women is emotional, PMS may be an organic dysfunction. Because it occurs at specific times during the woman's reproductive cycle, presumably the premenstrual shifts in hormones are responsible. The neuroendocrinology of the menstrual cycle is extremely complex and far from completely understood. Some researchers believe that PMS results from an as-yet unidentified neuroendocrine or metabolic defect that needs to be corrected. Others believe that this set of symptoms represents an oversensitivity in some women to the normal shifts in the menstrual cycle.

As with many if not most of women's mental and emotional issues, however, the cultural and social stresses on women may also contribute to this vulnerability. Negative cultural beliefs about the menstrual cycle—that women are moody, emotional, uncomfortable, unpredictable, and unreliable at this time—may even influence how a woman experiences her emotional and bodily states during the premenstrual period.

Postpartum Depression

Seventy to 80 percent of new mothers experience mild "maternity blues" that begin on or about the third day following delivery. Symptoms include tear-

---

TREATMENTS AND SELF-TREATMENTS FOR PMS

Psychiatrists and other practitioners offer a wide range of drug and medical treatments for premenstrual syndrome. These include psychoactive and other drugs (including benzodiazepines, described in chapter 5, and drugs that affect serotonin systems), hormones (including progesterone and birth control pills), diet, and vitamins. While some treatments may be effective for some women, studies have not yet demonstrated an overall effectiveness for any of them, and many, including hormones, can have serious side effects. Keep these facts in mind when you read or hear of claims for sure-fire treatments in popular books, newspaper, and magazine articles.

Certain health strategies recommended by self-help publications—such as eliminating caffeine, alcohol, chocolate, salt, and fats from your diet and enjoying regular exercise—may help and cannot hurt. Without medical advice, avoid taking high levels of vitamins, which may be toxic, especially vitamin B-6, which can cause nerve damage when used at the levels that are often recommended for self-treatment.

So far, whether psychotherapy can help alleviate PMS symptoms has not been systematically studied. Support from an informed, sympathetic mental health professional may be very important to some women. Studies continue to search for effective ways to relieve this form of women-only misery and to identify which women will respond to which treatments. Many academic medical centers, located in large metropolitan areas, have PMS research groups, often within the department of psychiatry. For the woman with intractable PMS, those would be a good place to turn.

fulness, sleeplessness, tension, anxiety, frequent mood changes, and anger. They come and go for a day to a week, then disappear. Some 10 to 20 percent of new mothers, however, move into a full clinical depression, lasting two to eight weeks but sometimes as long as a year. In addition to the usual symptoms of major depression (see chapter 8), women suffering from postpartum depression feel that they are unable to care for their infants. Very rarely—in about 1 or 2 out of 1,000 previously normal women—the depressive symptoms precede an acute psychosis. Most of the psychoses appear within two weeks of childbirth and disappear within two months, although they too can continue longer.

As with premenstrual syndrome, very little is known definitively about psychiatric illnesses that develop following childbirth and whether or not they differ from depressions and psychoses that occur at other times. In addition to the dramatic hormonal shifts that take place following childbirth, stressful life events, marital problems, fear of mothering, overly high expectations of motherhood, and lack of social supports may influence whether a women progresses from the blues to a clinical depression. According to some theories, women who become depressed postpartum may be struggling with internal conflicts regarding the nurturing they received from their own mothers. Depressive symptoms during the pregnancy may predict the appearance of these symptoms following childbirth, and previous psychiatric problems may also be a risk factor. A history of PMS is also a risk.

Even though all these conditions tend to resolve within days, weeks, or months, it is important that the more serious types of postpartum conditions be treated immediately, for the sake of both mother and child. (See chapter 8 for types of treatment for major depression and acute psychoses.) Women experiencing postpartum psychosis occasionally kill their infants, and women who become depressed may kill themselves. While these consequences are rare, the mother's depression can disrupt the important bond with the infant, and without intervention this may affect the future development of the child and the mother-child relationship. Because the more serious postpartum problems occur after mother and baby have returned home, the suffering mother may not receive counseling or referral to a psychiatrist. Obstetricians sometimes are inclined to reassure new mothers that their feelings are normal and fail to take their distress seriously. *Certainly, feelings about wanting to harm oneself or the child are not normal and indicate a strong need for immediate help.*

POSTPARTUM DEPRESSION: WHAT TO DO

New mothers and their families should never take for granted drastic mood or behavior changes following childbirth. Always consult a psychiatrist or other mental health professional when depressive symptoms continue or worsen, when the new mother feels or expresses a wish to harm herself or a fear that she will harm the child, or when she becomes suspicious or begins to act in an unusual, bizarre manner. If bad moods, stress, and conflicts plague the pregnancy, try to head off the probable later depression by getting help before the baby is born. Be assertive; if a doctor does not take the symptoms seriously, get a second opinion.

Treatment of moderate to severe postpartum depression includes antidepressants, lithium, electroconvulsive therapy (ECT), or antipsychotics, depending on the nature of the symptoms and diagnosis. (As these are the same treatments used for mood disorders not related to childbirth, see chapter 8 for details.) Because these drugs may pass through breast milk to the child, check with your physician about the advisability of breast-feeding at this time.

Psychotherapy for the woman and her family can be very helpful to enhance coping skills, educate them on caring for a newborn, and provide support.

Menopause

"Involutional melancholia" was a term once used to refer to a severe form of depression among middle-age women that was believed to result from the biological rigors of menopause. Research has shown that involutional melancholia does not exist and that menopause is *not* a time during which most women can expect to experience severe depression or to become incapacitated. Indeed, for many women menopause may be a time of increased happiness and creativity.

Nonetheless, menopause is an important time of transition for all women, and it may be accompanied by many physical and emotional discomforts. In addition to hot flashes, vaginal drying, and perhaps heavy bleeding, some women may be bothered by a worsening of symptoms commonly associated with the premenstrual phase, including tearfulness, irritability, impatience, and mood changes. Not all these and other emotional difficulties experienced at menopause are necessarily triggered by hormonal changes, however. For example, women who become depressed at menopause may be reacting to their children leaving home at this time—the "empty nest syndrome"—and the loss of the role to which they may have devoted most or all of their attention. Some who have postponed childbearing may be mourning the children they never had. Still other women may be reacting to their feelings that they are now "over the hill" or "too old" for sexuality; this is indeed a myth, for women remain sexual throughout their lifetimes.

Psychotherapy may help some women sort out the conflicts engendered by this transition in their lives. When seeking help for the physical symptoms associated with menopause, the fact that it is a normal time of life for all women should be kept in mind. An important decision, to be made with a gynecologist, is whether or not to take replacement hormones, which can protect against osteoporosis and heart disease (which become risks following menopause) and stabilize mood, but which can increase the risk of breast cancer in some women.

As with premenstrual symptoms, self-help health strategies that many women find useful include regular exercise and limiting their intake of alcohol, salt, fats, and caffeine.

Lesbians and Their Special Mental Health Needs

The loosening of cultural taboos has enabled women, lesbians included, to express their sexuality more openly. Lesbians face many of the same internal conflicts and problems with anger, depression, child rearing, work, relationships, and sexual response as heterosexual women. Because their choices differ so markedly from traditional ideas about what a woman is supposed to feel and do, however, lesbians often face far more resistance and hostility in much of society than do other women. Individual lesbians, who may lack the support and community of others like themselves, may feel very isolated. Some may feel there is something wrong with them for being different. All face great stresses as they encounter prejudices, oppression, and lack of legal rights, and as they try to create role models for productive, meaningful lives.

These pressures as well as the shared human ones that affect everyone may lead a lesbian to seek psychotherapy. Since 1973, the American Psychiatric Association has not considered homosexuality an illness. Nonetheless, some therapists may continue to see lesbianism as a form of sexual deviancy that should be cured. Lesbians should be sure that they feel comfortable with a therapist and that the therapist does not attempt to impose his or her own values. Lesbian organizations and support groups can provide much practical help and emotional sharing.

THE PSYCHIATRIC DISORDERS AMONG WOMEN

Although all the psychiatric disorders afflict both sexes, some seem to favor one sex over the other. For example, the paraphilias (see chapter 11) appear much less frequently among women than among men. Disorders that appear to favor women include kleptomania, depression (which we have discussed in relation to women earlier in this chapter; see also chapter 8), and the eating disorders. The eating disorders are covered in detail in chapter 10; suffice it to say here that women may be especially vulnerable to anorexia nervosa and bulimia because of the strong social pressures on them to fulfill our culture's ideal of feminine beauty. Development of these disorders may also be related to tensions in the mother-daughter relationship. In a symbolic sense, these disorders may represent a woman's desperate, distorted attempt to express her "perfect" femininity or to rebel against it (in extreme anorexia menstrual periods often disappear and the woman becomes so thin she no longer looks feminine at all); sometimes they represent a maladaptive attempt to control their lives. While some women may have a biological propensity to develop an eating disorder, an underlying mother-daughter rivalry may be a psychologically predisposing factor.

PROBLEM SOLVING

All women's mental health issues share both social and individual psychological components. For the woman who is under severe stress and has emotional difficulties, effective problem solving requires that she try to sort out how her real-life situation and cultural values contribute to her problems and the degree to which her own personality and inner psychology are causing her painful reactions to these real-life pressures or interfering with her ability to cope.

For example, all women who balance motherhood and work experience a great deal of stress. Some women, however, may experience severe anxiety and/or depression in their dual role because they demand perfection of themselves in all their undertakings. In other words, they experience a common, shared social problem for women as their own personal failure and they punish themselves for it. Looking for better day-care arrangements or sharing the home responsibilities with their spouses may help lift the burden off most women, while others may benefit also from working with a mental health professional to help lift the self-punitive burden from their own psyches.

Similarly, the woman who worries that her husband will leave her may be reacting appropriately to her husband's real loss of interest in her and to the knowledge that if their long marriage ends, her fortunes in love and life may well suffer. Should the marriage end, she might join a group for women alone and gain support from others in her position. Another woman who worries about her husband's loyalty may be overly sensitive to potential rejection because she lost an important person in childhood or from other losses of emotional closeness early in her life. Or she may perceive a threat to her relationship where none exists because she is afraid of her own inner, unconscious anger. This woman's anxiety about her husband, her excessive submissiveness, and her constant questioning of him may end up driving her husband away. This woman should seek advice from a mental health professional.

In a third example, a woman may remain with a mate who abuses her psychologically or physically because she is poor, has no family or resources, and is realistically terrified of the man's violent response to her attempts to free herself. Another may submit to

HELP FOR WOMEN

All the treatment alternatives and modalities discussed in chapter 4 are appropriate for the various emotional and mental problems that women experience. In addition, support and self-help groups in which women share their problems with one another (for example, mastectomy groups, groups for widows, groups for single mothers), workshops and training sessions on assertiveness and anger, and self-help books addressing women's problems offer various benefits to many women. However, the most important first step is a consultation with a psychologically minded general practitioner or internist or with a psychiatrist or other qualified mental health professional in order to assess the magnitude of the problem and get a recommendation for an appropriate intervention.

Finding a Therapist

Women increasingly seek therapy with female mental health professionals. Do not feel you must confine your choice to female therapists, feminist therapists, or female therapists who limit their practices to women. If you have strong feelings about therapist gender or ideology (as is the case with some women who may feel more comfortable consulting a feminist therapist; see chapter 4 for more information), however, respect your own preference. It is most important to look for a therapist who is not sexist and who does not believe that his or her values should take precedence over your own.

Now is a transitional time in the lives of women. It would be an error for any therapist to assume that a woman should or should not work, should or should not marry, should or should not have a child. A good therapist is one who is objective and can help each individual understand the nature of her values, goals, and conflicts and enable her to be freer to make the decisions of her life.

an abusive or excessively domineering mate out of her own sense of inner unworthiness. The first woman may benefit from social outreach organizations within her community that can shelter and protect her and help her find economic support. The second woman may not be able to benefit from even the most effective organizations without first working with a therapist or counselor to strengthen her sense of herself.

Finally, as women who are highly accomplished in their careers but who have never married or had children reach middle age, they may find themselves battling depression that threatens to undermine their ability to work. These women may feel that their failure to pair up spells a loss of femininity—that in their own eyes and the eyes of society, they are not "whole" or normal, not "real" woman. One woman may be able to bolster her self-worth and regain her balance by recognizing that she is experiencing a conflict between her own internalized traditional notion of feminine identity and her newer notions of female competency and self-direction. This woman has to forge her own path; she lacks a role model to look to for guidance on what to expect of her maturity. Another woman may realize that she has been trying to substitute professional achievement for intimate relationships. She may be ready to face her inner fear of intimacy in order to deal with her depression—and in order to help her form a meaningful relationship.

22

Developmental Issues for Men Throughout Life

Frederick M. Lane, M.D.

Mental health issues are human issues, shared by men and women alike. This is true despite indications from recent physiological research that male and female brains are somewhat different and despite the fact that the sexes face somewhat different developmental challenges. However, throughout the life cycle there are some factors that are especially salient for men; these "male issues" are the focus of this chapter.

Throughout these next pages we look at the concerns and mental health issues that either may characterize each phase of a man's life or may make their first appearance at that time. We begin with adolescence. Keep in mind that these phases only approximate the eras in the life cycle and that a great deal of overlap can occur.

ADOLESCENCE—AGES 12 TO 20

Adolescence is a transitional stage in which many of the psychological potentials seen in childhood

become fixed patterns for adult life. Much of a man's knowledge of who he is within himself and in rela-

323

tion to other people is defined at this time. His search for a place in the world intensifies. Important elements of his sexual life emerge. It is truly an era of change, and, like a landscape that is frequently rocked by earthquakes of varying intensities, it is an unsettled and unsettling place to be. Adolescence is marred by crises large and small and brightened by joys of discovery within oneself and in the world.

Identity Issues

Identity may be defined as a fixed and stable sense of who one is, what qualities one possesses, how one behaves with others, and where one fits into one's society. According to the *Glossary of Psychoanalytic Terms and Concepts,* it is "the experience of the self as a unique and coherent entity which is continuous and remains the same despite inner psychic and outside environmental changes." This fixed emotional and perceptual pattern is a subjective one and is clarified gradually during adolescence. Serious emotional and mental illness may be precipitated by an "identity crisis" in those adolescents whose sense of self, perhaps because of constitutional factors or family dynamics, among other reasons, is chaotic and diffuse.

In some cases, it may be hard to predict how a young man will turn out after adolescence. Some studies, such as those by Harvard psychiatrist George Vaillant, show that many adolescents whose behavior is marked by extremes—for example, rebellion, antisocial acts, or substance abuse—emerge from this stormy period with a firm and well-functioning sense of self, stability, and self-confidence. But other men do not survive a disturbed teenage experience so well. Addiction, criminality, and illnesses marked by psychosis are some of the possible complications of adolescent turmoil.

Social Role and Identity

This aspect of the adolescent boy's sense of self has to do with how he perceives himself in relation to his peers and to society at large. For the boy searching out who he is, peer relationships are of extreme developmental importance. Male bonding at this stage of life is intense, and friendships formed in adolescence have a good chance of surviving throughout adult life. These powerful attachments are the beginnings of a search for intimacy that will peak in the next decade.

Generally, adolescent male bonding is sexually neutral—that is, there are no readily experienced sexual feelings in the love between male friends. Occasionally sexual exploration does occur, but more as a response to the fascination of sexual awakening in puberty than to any real erotic desire for one another. However, the sexual exploration may engender intense worry and concern in a boy—or in his family if they discover it.

Because the acceptance and respect of peers is needed urgently in adolescence, as part of solidifying one's sense of identity, peer pressures and demands for conformity are felt intensely. Slavish conformity is a sign of age-appropriate anxiety regarding one's worth and acceptability. Conformity may have destructive aspects, however, such as the use of drugs and alcohol, criminality, or promiscuous and irresponsible sexual activity. Those adolescents with a stable sense of self and a good sense of self-worth and self-esteem will be able to resist such pressures. Unfortunately, at this time in life, self-confidence and self-esteem may be so shaky for many adolescents that they succumb to peer pressure of a dangerous nature. (Chapter 19 provides help with problems during this stage of life.)

Self-esteem Regulation

The adolescent boy's feeling of self-worth in part has been determined by earlier experiences, including his ability to learn and master childhood tasks. His self-esteem also has been influenced greatly by earlier attitudes and relationships—how his parents valued or failed to value him, and how his relationships with siblings and other important figures such as extended family, teachers, and friends evolved. But by adolescence, this sense of self-worth has not yet become set as a lifelong inner feeling about himself. Thus, the acceptance of peers—both male and, increasingly, female—now becomes extremely important in influencing a boy's ultimate respect for himself. His ability to attract girls and win recognition from them, even his success in gaining sexual experience, all add to self-esteem and self-confidence. Successes and failures in the school setting also are important factors in setting the level of self-worth.

Various handicaps or failures can have a devastating effect on an adolescent boy's confidence and self-esteem. These may not always be obvious. Among the problems are learning disabilities, some quite subtle, such as difficulty with spatial perception and imagery. Children with this problem have trouble visualizing how things are put together and may have a left-right confusion. They fail miserably in shop-work, cannot fix their bikes or hang a picture evenly on a wall. Dyslexia is another subtle learning disorder in which the ability to read and write is impaired. This may cause severe academic problems in an otherwise highly intelligent boy. (Chapter 18 provides more information on childhood learning disorders.)

The impact of minimal neurological deficits may also devastate an adolescent's self-esteem. As the result of MBD (otherwise known as minimal brain disorder), an adolescent may be clumsy, or walk and move awkwardly. He may be unable to dance well—a severe drawback at parties and proms—or perform creditably in sports. Because athletic ability is generally a ticket to peer popularity among adolescents, problems here may have significant ramifications.

A less usual situation that sometimes accompanies other learning disabilities is an inability to read appropriate social cues, a kind of "social dyslexia." This gives rise to a particular social awkwardness, a tendency to say the wrong thing at the wrong time, and an inability to form friendships. It causes peer rejection, social isolation, and severe problems with self-esteem. Psychological counseling aimed toward teaching social skills that ordinarily come intuitively is often beneficial.

An adolescent boy with disabilities such as these may have a constant sense of inadequacy and shame, even self-hatred. These feelings may be greatly relieved when the handicap is discovered and diagnosed, and is presented to him as such—that is, as a problem, but one that can be overcome. Good diagnosis paves the way for corrective measures.

"Ego Ideal" and Moral Function

When adolescence begins, the so-called ego ideal (what kind of person one aspires to be) and the conscience (that which determines good from bad and governs one's actions accordingly) are not fully formed.

Some aspects of the adolescent male's ego ideal are adopted from general peer-group attitudes, shaped in part by the public media (movies, television, magazines, and so on). Qualities of physical courage, aggressiveness, and competitiveness are typical male teenage ideals, although they do not always lead to behavior that is in a boy's best interests. Other ideals are drawn from the boy's socioeconomic background and from important figures in his life who may serve as role models—his father, an older brother, a teacher, or a father surrogate. In this way, ideals of ambition, intellectual achievement, kindness, caring, and responsibility may be transmitted. The adolescent boy's notions of how he should behave are still fluid and may be influenced by charismatic figures and culture heros as well as by general peer attitudes.

One of the major tasks of adolescence is to separate psychologically from the parents—to move from being a dependent child to being an independent young man. Separating from the family frequently takes the form of rebelling against family values. A well-behaved and conforming child then becomes an antagonistic teenager, barely if at all under parental control. He may adopt a moral value system seemingly devoid of conscience or ethical restraint. Antisocial behavior, if severe and recurrent, may warrant intervention in the form of psychological therapy and at times even imprisonment. Often enough, however, this behavior reflects only a passing, albeit disturbing, phase and is followed by a "quieting down" in impulsive action and a resumption of responsible, productive, and more morally constrained behavior. (For more on conduct disorders, see chapter 19.)

Adolescent Sexuality

Adolescence—the psychological emergence of the adult—coincides with puberty, which is the emergence of sexual maturity. It is a time of bodily change, which includes an increase in musculature, growth of body and facial hair, and deepening of the voice. The adolescent boy often feels his penis size is inadequate. Basically, however, unlike the dramatic physical changes that mark the onset of maturation for adolescent girls (the development of breasts, the onset of menstruation), no drastic changes occur in a boy's already established body image with adolescence. Some experts speculate that it is for this reason that adolescent males are less prone to such disorders as anorexia nervosa. (See chapter 10 and chapter 23.)

Masturbation and Wet Dreams

As male hormones pour torrentially into the pubertal boy's bloodstream, erections become more frequent and the penis becomes more sensitive to the pleasurable sensations accompanying them. Masturbation becomes the almost universal "secret" sexual act of the adolescent male. Although often discussed freely among peers, masturbation is hidden from family members. It is often during arousal fantasies in adolescence that a boy learns whether he will choose males or females or both as sexual partners in the future.

Despite its near universality, male masturbation is frequently attended by conflicts and guilty feelings. Sometimes the guilt has a moral or religious content or basis, but more often it is accompanied by fears of a hypochondriacal nature. Abetted by folklore, the adolescent boy may fear he will go insane or blind, develop severe acne, or injure his body or his sexuality by masturbating. In fact, no bodily or psychological harm comes from adolescent sexual self-stimulation. The guilt, which may be severe, probably stems from the boy's discomfort with the fantasies that accompany masturbation.

Masturbation is the most common sexual activity of adolescent males and should be considered perfectly normal and acceptable behavior. There are usually no lasting emotional problems with masturbating, unless it becomes preferred to any sexual activity with a partner. In fact, men who never masturbate may be suffering from serious conflicts and inhibitions in regard to sexual action and expression. On the other hand, masturbation that becomes compulsive and driven should be investigated clinically. In this case, masturbation is being used as a way of releasing tensions other than sexual ones. (Unfortunately, because adolescents conceal this behavior, it is difficult for parents to know if professional counseling should be sought.)

Another experience shared by all male adolescents is the so-called wet dream. This is usually a dream with overt erotic content, culminating in orgasm and ejaculation. With many adolescent males it is an unwelcome event, even though the dream content may be pleasurable, because there is concern that ejaculation stains will be discovered.

The best course of action that parents can take regarding masturbation and wet dreams is to discuss these issues openly with their adolescent.

Gender Identity and Gender Role

A boy's core gender identity—his sense of himself as male—is formed very early in life (between ages two and five). Very occasionally, a boy will develop the feeling that he is really a girl equipped with the wrong genitalia. This rare psychological situation is known as transsexuality. It is different from homosexuality in that male transsexuals feel that they are really female, sometimes to the point of seeking corrective surgery, whereas male homosexuals know as part of their sense of identity that they are indeed male.

How masculine or feminine a boy seems, whether in interests, mannerisms, dress, or the like, determines what is called his gender role. Feminine movements, behaviors, and speech may be seen very early in boys, and are thought to result from a combination of environmental and constitutional influences. Many parents worry that effeminate behavior in boys could be an early sign of homosexuality. However, while there is some speculation that effeminate behavior in childhood—either in boys' play with dolls, friendships mainly with girls, or avoidance of the rough-and-tumble play characteristic of boys—is associated with later homosexuality, occasional effeminate behavior is normal and does not indicate the beginning of a core gender identity problem. Only when a young boy consistently chooses effeminate roles in play may there be a cause for concern.

In any event, male homosexuality is the "final common pathway" of a number of biological and psychological forces and is discussed in detail below. Suffice it to say here that the core gender identity ("I know I am a man and I feel like a man"), the gender role (more or less masculine in traits and behavior), and the choice of sexual partner (heterosexual, bisexual, or homosexual) all emerge fairly clearly during adolescence.

Common Anxieties about Sex and Sexuality

Many men who discover in adolescence that they long sexually for other men go through a great deal of worry; many experience profound guilt and shame. Nevertheless, many after some fear and confusion accept their homosexual longings and go on to have stable, satisfying adult sexual lives with homosexual partners. For an adolescent in particular, though, there is constant peer pressure toward "normality," and a homosexual orientation often causes a sense of isolation and difference from other boys.

The teenager who is squarely heterosexual is also beset by sexual concerns. These have to do with his rivalry with other males and with his emerging attitudes toward females, attitudes that have their origins in his childhood experience with his mother and sisters. Of great concern to the adolescent male is his success in the sexual area. Sexual abilities begin to become an area of concern, one that may persist for a lifetime. Sexual function, manifested by strong erections, and the ability to give pleasure to a woman are issues that often become embroiled in such symptomatic sexual difficulties as sexual impotence and performance anxiety. (See chapter 11.) In these years too, for some men a lifelong fear and distrust of women may well emerge. Often these disturbed feelings stem from maternal conflicts experienced during childhood.

In the arena of sexual competition, there may be new concern with body image, not only with penile size, but with general musculature and stature. This may become a focus of anxiety or of compulsive activity, such as excessive body-building. Connected with sexual rivalry, of course, are competitive strivings for success in athletics, school, and career. These concerns may become even more pressing in later decades.

YOUNG ADULTHOOD—AGES 21 TO 30

In the years between 21 and 30, the emotional turmoil and identity confusion of adolescence tend to abate. One's sense of oneself as a man comes into clearer focus.

Courtship and Sexual Experience

A young man in his 20s constantly is faced with choices about his relationships. He can seek a stable and potentially permanent romantic tie with a woman, or he can pursue a course of experimentation with many women, gathering sexual experience in uncommitted relationships that are mainly pleasure-oriented. A common pattern earlier in the so-called sexual revolution was for a young man to test his sexual appeal and prowess by "scoring" with as many women as possible, using the notion of sexual conquest to enhance his feelings of masculinity. Today, with the danger of acquired immune deficiency syndrome (AIDS), this sort of promiscuity has diminished.

A young man searching for a partner in life often bases his concept of a future mate on idealized images of his mother. These images reside unconsciously in the mind but direct the choice of a mate. Sometimes, however, negative images of mother have become generalized toward all women.

A frequent courtship pattern today is for a young man and his girlfriend to begin living together as a way of exploring the problems and challenges of intimacy. Parents may oppose these courtship experiments, but current mores in a large segment of society do not brand cohabitation as scandalous or immoral. Often in such experiments, the courtship comes apart, especially if one or the other young person experiences conflicts aroused by the demand for intimacy.

A man's response to the prospect of marriage is frequently a dread of commitment. This fear does not necessarily involve deep-seated conflicts regarding intimacy or distrust of women. It usually relates to more superficial layers of anxiety: fear of responsibility, fear of becoming a parent or head of a family, fear of the marital relationship deteriorating and of being "stuck" with a partner when affection has died. But intimacy is difficult for many young men; the sharing of emotions with another person often clashes with the masculine ideal of self-containment—the so-called shroud of silence. For some, the difficulties of adapting to the wishes, attitudes, and desires of another adult may be insurmountable.

Homosexuality

By the time a man reaches his 20s, he generally has confronted the nature of his sexual desires clearly enough to decide whether he is heterosexual, homosexual, or bisexual. Sex researcher Alfred Kinsey in the 1950s delineated a spectrum of sexual orientation that is useful in considering this issue. He rated men (on a scale from 0 to 6) from exclusively heterosexual; to predominantly heterosexual and only incidentally homosexual; to predominantly heterosexual, only more than incidentally homosexual; to equally heterosexual and homosexual; to predominantly homosexual, but more than incidentally heterosexual; to predominantly homosexual, but incidentally heterosexual; to exclusively homosexual.

Although no one knows what causes homosexuality, constitutional and developmental factors are implicated. Research has indicated, for example, that certain hormonal influences on a developing fetus may predispose to brain development of a feminine character. This "feminine brain" will probably, but not always, fix the choice of sexual partner as another man rather than a woman.

Constitutional factors may lead directly to homosexuality or possibly combine with factors in the dynamics of the family to produce a reversal in the usual choice of sexual partner. One situation is a mother who cannot let go of her early symbiotic bonding with her son enough to allow masculinization of the boy's attitudes. Such a mother often shields a boy from his father, who may himself be remote and passive in response to his wife's possessiveness of the boy.

Fathers who are distant and unconcerned, extremely aggressive, or brutal may also prevent their sons from making appropriate masculine identifications with them. A rivalrous father may lead his son to perceive competition with other men in terms of homosexual domination and submission. The boy may then take his own wish to submit to a powerful man (like his father) as a wish to submit homosexually.

Homosexual lifestyle patterns vary a good deal. An active homosexual subculture exists, with its own mores, attitudes, political interests, and activities. A young homosexual man may participate in this subculture exclusively or partially, or may avoid it altogether, depending on his interests and particularly on his acceptance or rejection of his own homosexuality. Those men who cannot accept the notion that they are homosexual often live in torment, participating in homosexual sex but with severe conflict and guilt. Adding to the difficulty of being homosexual in a heterosexual society that largely condemns homosexuality is the dread of fatal infection from the AIDS virus (prevalent in the gay community), transmitted in blood and semen.

Other problems have to do with the nature of homosexual relationships. A major issue is the question of casual relationships, essentially faceless and anonymous, versus a committed, loving, stable relationship. "Cruising," the search for casual sexual partners by homosexual men, bears a great similarity to heterosexual men's search for casual sex. But cruising seems to have a heightened pleasurable excitement connected with it, and for some homosexual men amounts to a compulsion—an impulse that seems irresistible and is connected to attempts to deal with anxiety and stress. In addition to the danger of sexually transmitted illness, casual sex sometimes exposes a homosexual man to violence at the hands of sexual partners.

Establishing a permanent homosexual partnership evokes not only all the problems concerning commitment faced by heterosexual men in lasting relationships, but also frequent reluctance from within the community to find such a relationship socially acceptable. In addition, it often entails revealing one's homosexuality to family, friends, and colleagues. "Coming out of the closet" is a difficult issue for many homosexual men to resolve. Family relationships may not survive such revelations; careers may suffer.

With all these stresses, support from homosexual groups may be very helpful for a man to maintain his sense of self-esteem and worth.

PSYCHOTHERAPEUTIC APPROACHES TO HOMOSEXUALITY: TWO SCHOOLS OF THOUGHT

The question of whether homosexuality requires treatment is highly controversial, even though the American Psychiatric Association and the American Psychological Association do not consider it a disorder. Early childhood therapy with some effeminate boys, who seem to identify strongly with their mothers rather than with their fathers, sometimes has succeeded in reversing this feminization. But it is impossible at present to determine how much of the sexual orientation of any homosexual man is biological and how much is psychological and thus theoretically more malleable.

A number of homosexual men sense in themselves a heterosexual potential and seek therapy in order to achieve a heterosexual adjustment. Two schools of thought exist among psychotherapists on this issue. One maintains that to attempt to change the choice of sexual partner in a homosexual man will produce severe conflicts involving self-esteem and will risk arousing self-hatred and depression. The other holds that the attractions of homosexuality can be reduced, and the fears and inhibitions regarding sex with women can be overcome in a certain number of individuals. Psychiatrists of this school believe that the attempt is worthwhile with those men who are strongly motivated to change. Such a corrective attempt should not be recommended routinely. The risk of encouraging heterosexuality is that a man may become able to court and marry a woman only to have a life devoid of true passion and sexual gratification for himself and his wife.

Career Issues

Young adulthood usually sees the beginning of the process of career consolidation. This becomes a dominant preoccupation in a man's life and affects his self-esteem and social interactions—including marriage and family—for the future.

Work and career bring many emotional issues to the surface. One concerns a man's attitude toward success and failure. Family and society at large frequently demand that a young man be successful. A dread of failure, with its accompanying humiliation, may have a severe inhibiting effect on a young man's assertiveness and ambition. His unwillingness to put himself forth assertively, to take a chance in life, may become a severe obstacle to career advancement.

Another paradoxical problem is "success phobia," an unconscious fear that success will provoke retaliation from rivals. Success phobia leads directly to self-defeating behavior at work. It may derive from the conflicts engendered by a son's competition with his father. If a man exceeds his father's place in life, a sense of guilt may undermine the victory. For some individuals, a raise or other recognition of success may even promote depression. On the other hand, sons of successful and distinguished fathers may lose hope of ever achieving what their fathers did. These are the self-defeating "losers" who become the despair of their successful fathers.

Another issue that arises in the context of a job or career is one's relationships to authority figures. Ambivalent attitudes toward parental authority often are transferred to relationships in the workplace. Patterns shaped by earlier attitudes include compliance, defiance, fear of authority figures, ingratiation, procrastination, competitiveness, and passivity in the face of the boss or supervisor. Old sibling relationships and rivalries are often evoked in the career situation and may foster envy, rivalry, and the deliberate undermining of colleagues—or, alternatively, mutual support. Where psychological issues pose problems, psychotherapy may be particularly helpful. (Chapter 4 discusses the many types of psychotherapy.)

The Armed Forces

For the past seven decades, at unfortunately frequent intervals, this country has inducted its young men into the armed services. In World Wars I and II, the Korean War, the Vietnam War, and the Persian Gulf War, young men have been subjected to the dangers and extraordinary stresses of war. Many have had their lives permanently changed by the experience.

Even in peacetime young men and women in the armed forces are subject to the particular stresses of military life. In a certain number of men, the intimate living conditions of military life arouse extreme anxiety. Problems may range from an inability to urinate and defecate in front of others to fears of homosexual temptation or assault. Intense reactions to authority in basic military training may precipitate violent rebellious behavior, absence without leave, or assault on superiors. Usually an individual with responses of this kind is discharged as being psychologically unable to conform to military life.

The stresses of military life may be enough to precipitate a major psychiatric illness, such as depression or schizophrenia, in those who are predisposed to these illnesses. A major threat to the emotional health of combat veterans—especially those with few or no close friendships with one another—is posttraumatic stress disorder, discussed at length in chapter 24. The intense fraternal feelings that men who serve together often develop for one another, however, can provide strong support both to self-esteem and to the integrity of the personality under severe conditions. This kind of male bonding more than any other single factor has been found protective against post-traumatic stress disorder.

MIDDLE ADULTHOOD—AGES 31 TO 40

Marriage and Sexuality

Some men in mid-adulthood are frozen in their courtship phase by fears of intimacy and commitment. Some may be on their way to becoming "confirmed bachelors," shunning marriage in favor of brief heterosexual relationships or wholehearted devotion to work. Others, though, are able to deepen their relationships with women beyond the romantic-erotic initial phase and experience a true transformation in themselves. Most such transformations lead to a willingness and desire for commitment and marriage

Marriage ushers in new roles for the man. Societal expectations are that he become the breadwinner (though not always the sole breadwinner) for the family, the protector, and the "rock" of the family. He is pledged to sexual fidelity. As sex becomes routine in the marriage, it may lose its initial excitement for him. However, couples today are better informed about sexuality than in the past and perhaps pay more attention to keeping the excitement alive.

The issue of sexual temptation and partners outside the marriage is always present to some degree in a psychologically healthy man. An occasional casual sexual contact outside the marriage does not necessarily imply a profound problem in the marital relationship. If such contacts are sought frequently, however, serious dysfunction in the marriage is more likely and help should be sought. A longstanding extramarital affair destroys closeness and intimacy within a marriage. A secret life with an extramarital lover distances the husband and threatens the integrity of the marriage and the family. Not all such affairs are provoked by bad marriages, but almost all cause a gulf of secrecy in a marriage and eventually may bring about its disruption and, possibly, divorce. Problems in the marriage relationship often are accompanied by intense feelings of mutual resentment, hurt, a good deal of guilt, and a sense of failure.

In addition to sexual infidelity, divorce is often the result of a midlife crisis, which often occurs when a man approaches 40. (See page 332.) Along with a shift in career, a man between 31 and 40 may see divorce as a way of resolving the conflict and engaging life anew. Men who marry at this stage of life may divorce soon after, seeing the new relationship as a mistake. Sometimes the crises in these short-lived marriages are the result of maladaptive patterns of relations learned in childhood and never outgrown—particularly for men with parents whose own married life provided a poor example for a strong, loving union of two people. For example, men who grew up in households where there was no give and take between partners, no demonstrations of affection, or constant arguing simply may not know how to build a strong marriage.

Psychological consequences of divorce include rage, guilt, and feelings of failure. If the breakup was initiated by a wife's infidelity or lack of desire to continue the relationship, it may detract from a man's sense of self-esteem and affect how he functions in other areas of his life. Divorce is a common precipitant for depression.

Marriage counseling sometimes can help to resolve the issues and strengthen the relationship; or it can help clarify the issues, making the decision to divorce a more rational, less emotional one.

Marriage is a complex and demanding enterprise. It requires a certain adaptive ability and thrives on mutuality, flexibility, and perseverance. Both the sharing aspect and the erotic aspect of marriage need to be nurtured and protected by the couple. Remaining aware of the many stresses placed upon the partnership and dealing constructively with these stresses do much to ensure marital health and longevity.

Fatherhood

Most men who become fathers do so in their 30s. In recent decades the role of father has changed, and men's expectations of fatherhood have altered considerably. Today's young fathers expect to participate in the nurturing aspects of child care to a far greater degree than did their own fathers. Because childhood experience of one's own mother and father serves as a template for one's later role as a parent, the newer style of fathering is unfamiliar and may not come easily. Yet there is little doubt that men as well as women have a nurturant capacity. Men can call upon a gentleness and tender caring that can be very advantageous for the infant's growth. Carrying out this nurturant role may be a maturing experience for the man, even though it clashes at times with his ego ideal of what is manly.

With a little effort and support, many men are able to establish a greater closeness to their children than their fathers did. An absent or remote father can hinder the psychological development of both sons and daughters. The young boy needs a masculine role model for identification. Recent studies demonstrate that the father's presence and involvement with his son teach his child "maleness." There are dozens of activities traditionally viewed as masculine in which a father can model a male role for his son. Even the father's presence in teaching the little boy how to urinate standing up is an important masculinizing lesson.

The experience a father can give to his daughter of a nonseductive affectionate bond will go a long way toward shaping her attitudes toward herself and men in her adult life. A father who asks no more of his daughter than cuteness or daintiness contributes little to the growing girl's ambition and potential for accomplishment in life. Women whose fathers expect achievement from them often become significant achievers.

A man's attitude toward his children, though, often is shaped by his own father's attitudes toward him and his siblings. This can be good and bad. Tragic situations of child abuse may be repeated down the generations when the abused children become abusing parents themselves. Psychotherapeutic or other forms of treatment can help break this cycle. Group support, which is furnished by various programs for the treatment of the abusive parent, is also helpful. In any case, professional intervention is essential both for the abuser and the victim.

Being a father calls upon all that is psychologically most sound in a man, but unfortunately the way a man acts as a father may be distorted by preexisting conflicts. For example, a man might feel ambivalent about his relationship with his own father, with new conflicts between them arising after the birth of the child. Or he may suddenly find himself becoming a severe disciplinarian, mimicking the parenting style under which he was raised. Feelings of rivalry for his wife's attention may be severe for some fathers, with this undercurrent of jealousy often causing great strife in the marriage.

Often the problems that emerge when a man becomes a father will lead him to seek psychological help. Therapy at this point might well be an investment in his child's mental health in years to come.

Work and Career

The 30s and the 40s are the major years of career consolidation, as has been shown in a long-term study of university graduates done by psychiatrist George Vaillant. Striving for competitive success and establishing their career is a central focus for men in this era of life. It is a time of conflict between the demands of family life and the demands of work. Where work has become a man's "extramarital lover" or has become his major commitment in life, a marriage may well flounder.

"Workaholism"—the so-called addiction to work—may be a haven of escape from a bad marriage. It may reflect severe security anxieties, whether of financial worries or issues of pride and self-esteem. It may reflect greed and the need to acquire more and more wealth, power, prestige, and influence. This pattern, whatever its roots, may threaten not only the family but also the man's health.

Some men experience considerable tension between their lives at work and their lives at home. A man who is aggressive and competent in the outside world, for example, may be a passive and dependent helpmate, who waits for his wife to anticipate and take care of his every need. Conversely, a man who is meek and subservient at work may be a domestic tyrant.

Self-esteem in mid-adulthood may depend heavily on career and work achievement, which is often measured in financial terms. So much self-approval may rest on the career that severe depressions may be precipitated by business setbacks and failures. Conflicts over success may lead to self-defeating behavior; a man may ironically "snatch defeat from the jaws of victory" and bring about failure through unconscious but deliberate self-sabotage. Issues involving passivity may also determine success or failure, excellence or mediocrity. A significant number of men envy the passive role society frequently assigns women and wish they were exempt from society's expectations of success. Despite Sigmund Freud's equation of masculinity with activity and femininity with passivity, many men struggle with passivity, which may contribute to career problems.

Because of competitiveness and unfortunate mutual distrust, many men become isolated from one another in their 30s and 40s. They may have associates at work, but the close friendships of adolescence and young adulthood often are things of the past. This isolation promotes a tendency to depression and places a heavier than usual burden on the marriage for support. Men would do well to attend to their friendships, for male bonding and mutual support furnish an important protection to a man's mental health.

MIDLIFE—AGES 40 TO 60

Midlife is the time of life in which most men decide whether or not they have achieved their aims. Whatever a man's inner disappointments, his abilities are generally at their height. Though he may not possess all the vitality and physiological strength of youth, he usually still is vigorous, his mental capacities well seasoned due to maturity.

Marriage, Family, and Sexuality

The marriage that has survived the hazards of earlier years reaches a new stage, with attendant assets and liabilities. College tuitions place a severe financial strain on most middle-class couples, but once this stage is over they may find that for the first time in their lives they are financially fit. The children, maturing and leaving home for college or their own careers, leave behind them an "empty nest," and the woman who has remained a homemaker can think about returning to work. For her, a renewed career provides an important opportunity to explore new directions and use long-dormant abilities. For her husband, it means a reorientation in the rhythm and content of his marital life.

With the children leaving, the couple, which has for so long been a part of a multiperson family, is thrown back upon itself. Often lost marital intimacy must be reestablished. If the sexual union is strong and mutually pleasurable, and if the couple continues to have interests and aspirations in common, the marriage goes on with new growth and maturation. But this is often a time of marital tension and instability. With their children's absence, couples may find, seemingly suddenly, that they have grown so far apart that they have little in common. Sometimes the rift is so strong that there is no possibility for reconciliation. In this stage in life a man may perceive divorce as an opportunity to explore new avenues or to find a partner who now fulfills him in ways that his former wife could not. A man may also feel that he is at age where he has "one last chance" before old age to have an extramarital affair. For men who married very young, affairs at this stage may represent a desire to recapture youth or experience a part of life they feel has been missed—although they do not necessarily accomplish these goals and indeed may cause a total disruption in the marriage.

Although sexual appetite is less intense in midlife than in early adulthood, men of this age still possess significant sexual desire. Should sexual dysfunction occur, in the form of impotence or sharply reduced desire, psychological causes are most likely. While sexual problems usually yield nicely to psychiatric intervention, nonetheless, physical causes for the dysfunction should be ruled out. (See chapter 11 for a complete discussion and suggestions for help.)

Finally, an important role reversal begins to occur at this stage of life, in which the man becomes the parent of his aging parents, adding a new dependent responsibility.

The Aging Homosexual Man

Among homosexual men, youth is worshipped to an even greater degree than it is in the general culture. Whereas graying hair and deepening facial lines may make a middle-age heterosexual man seem more attractive and distinguished, many homosexual men fear that these signs of aging will make them less desirable.

For an aging homosexual man, the need for a stable relationship with another man often becomes urgent. Sensitivity to rejection by younger men may become intense, and the threat of aloneness increases. Often the love of a younger man is sought, and the aging homosexual man assumes a fatherly role. It is not clear whether or not homosexual men are more prone to severe midlife crises or to depression in midlife than are heterosexual men. Homosexual men do, however, live in generally more stressful conditions than do their heterosexual counterparts.

The Midlife Crisis

The so-called midlife crisis is a period of unstabilizing emotional conflict that appears to be a normal event in the life cycle, occurring in an estimated 80 percent of men in their 40s. It is a time when neglected parts of the self begin to press for expression.

Sometimes the midlife crisis is precipitated by a sudden illness, such as a heart attack, but more often than not it begins spontaneously. A number of life-cycle developments may be contributory. The man's role as father is diminished as the children leave home. His wife may have established a new career identity or broadened her interests in directions that no longer require his support. Career pinnacles may have been reached, or the man may find his career options painfully limited. With aging, there is some sense of a diminution in physical vitality and in sexual arousal. The death of parents and of friends his own age may make a man suddenly aware of his own aging and mortality.

In some men this developmental crisis occurs undramatically, and, with minor rearrangements in their lives, the transition may be negotiated quietly. But for others it may amount to a major upheaval and be accompanied by serious emotional turmoil, even emotional illness. Whatever the severity, it is often the time in life when an introspective psychotherapy would prove helpful.

The signs and symptoms of the midlife crisis are various. There may be increasing dissatisfaction with the marriage or the children. Often a man who has been faithful up to now will pursue extramarital sex, out of fear of diminishing sexual capacity. He may choose a much younger woman, with the illusion that this is rejuvenating. With the recognition of his mortality and diminishing options in life, a painful self-examination occurs: "What have I done in life? Does all my effort mean anything? Is this all there is and will be to life? I've not fulfilled my promise—I've let myself down." Fatigue and boredom—"burnout"—may set in in a man's daily work. There may be a loss of interest and effort at the job, a growing fear of losing out to young men on the way up, and a general fear of a lack of energy and vitality to apply to work. This fear may be dealt with by increased compulsiveness and "workaholism." There may be an increase in rigid traits such as procrastination, stubbornness, or being oppositional. As a man ages, he becomes "more like himself"—that is, habitual character traits become more dominant, fixed, and repetitive—and these traits may be accentuated in times of crisis.

Generally, men resolve the midlife crisis in one of two ways, both of which involve change. The "autoplastic" solution is to bring about change within oneself, through reflection or counseling or therapy. Although it is the less disruptive solution, it is sought less often and may not always be sufficient. The other mode of solution is "alloplastic"—that is, making changes in one's circumstances. These changes, if made impulsively and desperately, may later cause regret. Fine jobs and careers may be damaged, depression or substance abuse may sur-face, and good marriages may founder. On the other hand, change may lead to marked improvement in a man's mental health and quality of life. A bad marriage, clung to "for the sake of the children," may be severed. A job that has become unsatisfying and pointless may be changed for an occupation that provides more personal gratification. Avocational pursuits and new physical endeavors may bring much-needed psychological and physiological well-being. A move to a new locale may improve the quality of life. Such a "midcourse correction" may indeed amount to healthy maturation and growth. (See chapter 25.)

Career Considerations

Aside from disruptions that may be caused by the midlife crisis, middle age is usually the time of a man's greatest power and prestige in his work. A man's creative powers are at their height, and he becomes a master of his trade. It is also the era that psychologist Erik Erikson, in *Identity, Youth and Crisis,* calls "generativity," a concern for "establishing and guiding" the upcoming generation. The teaching and instructing of younger colleagues becomes a source of gratification rather than of threat.

George Vaillant found that the period of career consolidation is followed by a shift in a man's interests to areas beyond the career. Free of the obsessive dedication to "getting ahead," the midlife man experiences a broadening of horizons and a newfound ease in his work.

LATER ADULTHOOD—AGES 60 TO 70

With medical advances, life expectancy continues to lengthen. It is now clear that the capacity for further psychological growth and maturation, and for further accrual of knowledge and wisdom, continues as well. Later adulthood may be years of some physical decline, but with reasonable luck, a man can expect continued vigor and growth.

Marriage and Sexuality

Aging increases a couple's mutual dependency, and such abrasions of age as diminishing memory will, it is hoped, be viewed by both with good humor. Loss of physical vigor and growing bodily incapacities and discomforts require the couple to accept and adapt to each other's limitations. When acceptance is difficult and depression and despair occur, antidepressant medication and psychotherapy can be effective.

Illness and disability test the solidity and endurance of the marital bond. Having weathered the stresses of midlife, most long-enduring marriages are able to survive these trials. Some end in divorce, but often these are marriages that have been hollow and without intimacy for years or even decades.

Sexual desires are still pressing, but with less frequency and intensity than earlier in life. Potency is still present, except in some cases of illness, and sexuality continues to provide one of the great satisfactions of life. The aging man should inform his partner about his need for greater physical stimulation to aid his arousal—for this is a time in life when mutual frank dealing with sexual matters is of great importance. Even for couples of advanced years, sex therapy may prove very helpful.

To protect his self-esteem, it helps if the aging man's loss of the usual supports for his pride (such as his work) is balanced by increased support from his marriage, his family, and his peers. Communities oriented toward the older adult—so-called adult communities or retirement communities—may provide programs for expanding the interests of the aging man and restoring support for self-esteem.

His family's attitude toward him, especially the way his children treat him, powerfully influences a man's pride and effectiveness at this age. Overprotection merely will hasten regression in an aging person and encourage a kind of childlike, debilitating dependency. Independence, with realistic expectations of an older man's abilities, enhances pride.

Grandfatherhood

Grandfatherhood comes as a repeat of the life cycle and often has a rejuvenating effect on a man. It calls again upon his capacity to nurture and gives him a renewed opportunity to see the world through a child's eyes, to relive the sense of wonder and discovery in growing up. And, as every grandparent acknowledges, it provides these pleasures without the responsibilities and anxieties of parenthood.

Career Considerations

The issue of retirement arises in this stage of a man's life. For some men, the prospect of losing the work on which a great deal of their self-esteem has been based is extremely threatening. They dread the notion of retirement and see it as the beginning of time spent waiting for death. Others go through the painful experience of being informed by colleagues that they are not functioning adequately. In such cases, severe clinical depression may result, and vigorous psychiatric intervention may be indicated. Even when problems and worries are less severe, psychotherapy can be extremely helpful at this age. (See chapter 23.) For other men, however, retirement opens the way for exploring new depths within themselves. It may open up the opportunity for a new career—either paid or, more likely, voluntary—with new challenges and new demands. Self-esteem increases with the mastery of new endeavors, and retirement is welcomed. Whatever a man does about retirement, it is essential that he make as full use of his capacities as possible.

THE ELDER YEARS—AGES 70 AND ABOVE

Erikson has characterized the elder years as the years of wisdom, but they are looked upon with dread by our youth-worshipping society. Many men of 70 maintain a vigorous and active life, however, and, if good fortune spares them significant illness, they may be able to look forward to many more years of creative and meaningful life.

Marriage and Sexuality

Few things in life are more touching than the care and mutual support that a devoted married couple give each other during the elder years. While every attempt should be made to remedy physical and mental disabilities, some simply must be accepted, both in oneself and in one's spouse. Incapacity should be met realistically. The painful situation often arises in which one member of the couple needs more care than can be provided by the other or by a supportive family, and a nursing home facility must be found. Loss of friends and the decimation of the social network is common at this time of life; the elderly man should avail himself of the company of his surviving peers wherever and whenever he can. A man's dependence on his children should be kept to a minimum, even if he is part of their household. He needs a continuing sense of independence and responsibility to support his sense of dignity and integrity. Sexual pleasure and desire never totally die, and the usual cultural attitude that elderly people should no longer have sexual interest is a mistake.

Bereavement is perhaps the gravest stress on body and mind at any stage of the life cycle. The loss of a spouse becomes a greater possibility in the later years. It has long been noted that the year following the loss of his wife is a hazardous time for a man's health. Even such bodily functions as immunity seem to be affected. The danger of severe and suicidal depression is present, particularly in isolated elderly widowers. Family support and encouragement to reestablish peer relationships are helpful, and again, psychologic or psychiatric intervention may be particularly important.

Career Considerations

By now, a man's career is winding down or has come to a close. In the best of circumstances the man will be able to continue to work in some capacity, either in his former field or in a new direction. People who age the most gracefully are those who continue to work in some capacity all their lives.

Living Every Day

Most emotionally healthy elderly people face the inevitability of death with tranquility. Their attitude is one of philosophical acceptance rather than of welcome. Death is welcomed only in depression or in situations of hopeless illness and incapacity. Suicide is a possible result of depression or psychosis at any age and is more likely in despairing elderly people. At this age, any expression of a desire to kill him- or herself, especially in someone who is severely depressed, should be taken seriously. Consultation with a specialist in geriatric psychiatry can help the elderly person learn how better to face the challenges of age.

A man's older age need not be marked by gloom. Most of us hold on to life as precious every day. Most men can look forward to more full and satisfying days than the biblical allotment of threescore and ten.

23

Aging and Mental Health

Barry J. Gurland, M.D., and John Barsa, M.D.

Living to old age is becoming a normal part of the American lifestyle. At present, 11 percent of the population—almost 30 million people—are age 65 or older. These numbers are expected to double by the middle of the 21st century, swelled by "baby boomers" entering their later years and by rising life expectancy rates. With this change in demographics, increasing attention has been focused on mental health issues related to aging.

Some experts on aging categorize the later years as the young old (ages 65 to 74), the old old (75 to 84), and the very old (85 years of age or older), which is the most rapidly growing age group in the United States. Chronological age, however, sometimes bears little relationship to the process of psychological and physiological aging. Each individual ages at a different rate.

THE AGING MIND: WHAT'S NORMAL, WHAT'S NOT

There are many myths about the aging process and its effects on mental health. The later years, for example, are sometimes described as a season of despair marked by physical disability, diminished mental capacity, and overwhelming loss. Yet, although the elderly as a group are confronted by a great many stressful situations, most seniors adapt successfully to the transitions in their lives. Those over 65 by and large find these years satisfying and cope well with adverse life circumstances. The incidence of major mental illness in this group is statistically small.

When mental illness does occur among older individuals, however, it can be devastating, especially when their mental suffering is seen mistakenly as a "normal" part of growing old and thus may go untreated. Therefore, one of the major challenges facing those who treat older individuals is to identify what is normal aging and what is not—to distinguish the normal developmental changes that take place from those that are the result of pathological disease processes that can be treated, reversed, or slowed.

Cognitive Functioning and the Aging Process

A persistent myth is that old age is characterized by impaired intellectual functioning and serious memory loss. While such conditions occur more frequently with age, for the most part those older persons who remain active intellectually and physically reveal no cognitive decline that they cannot learn to deal with through their own personal resources or with memory improvement techniques. The later years in life can be a period of significant accomplishment and new learning, a fact recognized by the many colleges that now offer special courses and tuition packages for senior citizens.

Of course, changes in mental processes do occur with age. As people age, they tend to respond less quickly to stimuli and novel situations compared to when they were younger, and do not do as well in performance tests that have a timed format. Mild memory changes and some forgetfulness, especially concerning recent events, do occur, as do loss of acuity in eyesight and hearing. Older people who seem to respond inappropriately because they do not see or hear well often are mistakenly believed to be "senile."

Moderate to severe forgetfulness, however, is *not* normal. Neither are confusion and severe cognitive impairment, such as that seen in Alzheimer's disease, discussed at length in chapter 15. Impaired memory or intellectual functioning also can result from mental or physical conditions that can be treated successfully and the impairment reversed. Thus, marked changes in mental functioning should not be considered "just the way it is when you get old."

No mental disorders are unique to old age, although some, such as dementia (chapter 15), occur more commonly in this period of life. Also, disorders that are common among all adults, including depression and anxiety, often present different diagnostic and treatment challenges for physicians when treating older individuals, in part because older persons commonly suffer from multiple physical illnesses and take many medications. (See the next section.)

Grieving and sadness are normal responses to the losses experienced in old age, and some degree of anxiety is to be expected in response to life stresses. Major depression and anxiety disorders, however, are not normal. Rather, they indicate the need for treatment (as they would at any other age!) so that a return to normal can be possible.

The Importance of Seeking Help

The individual disorders, as well as the stresses common to older age, are discussed separately throughout the remainder of this chapter. People with mental and emotional distress and disorder can be helped at all stages of life.

Geriatric psychiatry, sometimes called geropsychiatry or psychogeriatrics, is concerned with the range of mental health and adjustment problems that have distinctive age-associated characteristics. The recognition that mental disorder in old age is not the norm has encouraged physicians diligently to diagnose and treat those individuals who show mental and emotional impairment. It is becoming increasingly common for medical physicians to consult with psychiatrists when caring for an older individual.

Psychiatric intervention, either with psychotherapy, medication, or a combination of both, can be very effective in life's later years, but many who could be helped by such therapy do not seek it out. Often this is due to a lack of knowledge about existing mental health resources in the community. In addition, some seniors resist psychiatric care because of long-held, negative stereotypes. For example, many older individuals were raised to believe that one does not share feelings or talk about problems outside of the family. Others are ashamed to admit that they have a mental disorder. Some seniors believe that at their advanced age, either nothing can be done to improve their mental well-being, or that their remaining years are so limited that therapy would be futile. Family members as well may not recognize that mental health treatment for the elderly is available, sometimes at low cost, and helpful.

In fact, studies have demonstrated that mental health care can make dramatic differences in the lives of older individuals (and thus also of their families), helping them to cope with mental and emotional disorders as well as with stressful life events, and to return to a productive and happy life.

THE INTERPLAY OF PHYSICAL AND MENTAL ILLNESS

Differential diagnosis (the consideration of many variables in determining the exact cause of a symptom) is crucial in this age group. Mental and physical illnesses in older people are often closely related. Distinguishing between them can be difficult, especially because many older people have multiple physical disorders or concurrent mental and physical problems.

Psychiatric Symptoms Associated with Organic Mental Disorders and Other Physical Illnesses

As discussed throughout this chapter (as well as in chapters 2, 8, 15, and throughout the other individual disorder chapters), dozens of medical illnesses as well as medications, drugs, and alcohol can cause psychiatric symptoms. Symptoms that often are taken to indicate a psychiatric problem include weight loss, depression, apathy, confusion, agitation, and paranoia. But many of these same symptoms instead may be a reaction to vision or hearing loss or caused by a tumor or Alzheimer's disease. Alzheimer's disease, Pick's disease, and other dementias that affect the elderly increasingly as they age are characterized by confusion, mood changes, aggressiveness, and memory and personality changes—symptoms that can be mistaken for psychiatric problems or passed off as "normal" senility.

When an older person suddenly becomes confused, the most common cause has been found to be a change in medications. Other common, reversible causes of confusion include alcohol abuse, infections such as pneumonia, vitamin deficiencies, trauma, and diseases or conditions that disturb the body's metabolic balance, such as anemia, dehydration, diabetes, and hyper- or hypothyroidism.

Parkinson's disease, stroke, and cardiac illness are three illnesses that more often strike in the later years of life and that often produce psychiatric symptoms.

Parkinson's disease. The incidence of depression in this neurologic syndrome, which usually develops in late life, is extremely high. While the exact cause of Parkinson's disease is unknown, some researchers speculate that it is caused by the depletion of dopamine, a neurotransmitter in the brain, and that this depletion also triggers depression.

Stroke. It is common for victims of stroke to be depressed and confused, often as a result of where in the brain the stroke occurs. People whose infarctions occur in the right brain hemisphere are more irritable, have less ability to concentrate, and show a greater loss of interest than those whose stroke affected the left side. Left-sided stroke victims tend to have symptoms that are closely associated with depression, such as crying, despair, and helplessness.

Cardiac disease. Cardiac disease can strike at any age, but many older people have heart conditions as a result of degenerative disease or lifelong dietary or smoking habits. Sleep disturbance and sexual dysfunction can be intensified by drugs taken to control the disease, such as digitalis, which can have side effects that mimic psychiatric symptoms.

See also chapter 28, page 398, for a discussion of emotional reactions to stroke, heart conditions, and other physical conditions, and chapter 15, page 212, for information on multi-infarct dementia, in which a series of small strokes causes dementia.

Helpful sources of information for these conditions include:

General. The National Health Information Clearinghouse, tel. 800 336–4797. In Arkansas, Hawaii, Virginia, and Washington, D.C.: tel. 703 522–2590.

For stroke. Courage Stroke Network, Courage Center, 3915 Golden Valley Road, Golden Valley, MN 55422; tel. 800 553–6321. Publishes a membership newsletter and can refer callers to local stroke clubs.

For cardiac disease. The American Heart Association, 7320 Greenville Avenue, Dallas, TX 75231; tel. 214 373–6300.

For Parkinson's disease. National Parkinson's Disease Foundation, tel. 800 327–4545; in Florida, tel. 800 433–7022 or 305 547–6666 in Miami.

Emotional Reactions to Chronic Physical Illness

Many elderly individuals—some estimates range as high as 86 percent—have chronic medical conditions that require long-term treatment or for which there is no permanent cure. The stresses resulting from chronic illness are numerous. Lack of mobility can increase isolation; debilitating physical changes can affect feelings of self-worth and self-esteem; concerns about losing independence and the cost of medical care are frequent worries. Although many people adjust well psychologically and physically to their illnesses, it is not surprising to find that depression and anxiety are frequent companions to chronic illness.

After heart disease is diagnosed, for example, some people develop so-called cardiac neurosis, a syndrome characterized by fears that interfere with their ability to function normally. Individuals with a heart condition do, of course, have reason to be concerned for their health, but some people experience such great fear that they become emotionally crippled. Previously productive, these individuals now restrict their lives to such an extent that they are no longer able to work, perform the chores of daily living, or enjoy recreational activities. (This syndrome can occur at any age, of course, but it is more common among older individuals.)

Depression can block rehabilitation and contribute to the debilitating effects of chronic disease. Unfortunately, physicians treating the physical symptoms of chronic illness frequently fail to diagnose depression or anxiety when the patient does not disclose his or her psychological symptoms. People who are depressed very often feel that their conditions are hopeless and that there is no point in taking medication or participating in rehabilitation activities.

Physical Symptoms Associated with Psychiatric Disorders

Many older people feel more comfortable discussing physical problems than mental or emotional ones. Because of this hesitancy to discuss feelings directly, symptoms of psychological distress are frequently either misinterpreted as physical disease or overlooked. Common physical complaints that can indicate mood disorder include aches and pains, a bad taste in the mouth, bowel or bladder discomfort, fatigue, and changes in sleep patterns, appetite, or weight. Many older people may find it hard to accept that a mood or anxiety disorder can affect the body in this way and resist the idea of psychological assistance.

Of course, there may well be an organic basis for these physical complaints—but sometimes these ailments are unconsciously magnified by a person who is emotionally distressed. Disappointments from another area of life can be channeled into the physical symptom and expressed as part of the illness, as in the case of a 75-year-old depressed woman who complained frequently of angina pains. Yet electrocardiograms and laboratory tests showed no evidence of coronary disease. A psychiatric consultation revealed that she felt abandoned by her children, who had moved to the suburbs and rarely visited. The complaints forced her children to be more attentive. Somatic (bodily) complaints are sometimes an older person's only acceptable avenue for expressing feelings and of asking for attention from others.

If, after a thorough evaluation, a physician can find no organic illness to account for physical symptoms or if the symptoms are not relieved by conventional treatments, he or she may recommend a psychiatric consultation.

MAJOR MENTAL ILLNESSES IN THE ELDERLY

As among all adults, anxiety disorders, depression, and schizophrenia take their toll on the elderly. Each is discussed at length elsewhere in this book. (See chapters 7, 8, and 14.) In this chapter we look at how each affects elderly people and how each can be treated.

Depression

Depression is the most common psychiatric problem of the elderly. Nonetheless, it is *not* normal for someone who is elderly to be severely depressed. Older individuals who find that depressed feelings or symptoms interfere with their ability to function normally or enjoy life should seek help—this condition is treatable and frequently reversible.

Common Causes of Depression in the Elderly

As with younger people, depression can result from a number of factors. It can represent a continuing problem, present from earlier years, to which the person may have been predisposed genetically. It can be related to age-associated changes in neurological, endocrine, or other body systems. It can be a reaction to overwhelming life stresses or a biological "side effect" of organic illness or of many medications. The risk of depression in old age is greater in those who have previously experienced it or who have a family history of depression or alcoholism.

Symptoms

Briefly reviewed, the signs of clinical depression include persistent feelings of sadness or a belief that life is not worth living, an inability to enjoy previously pleasurable activities, and a change in ordinary mood. Physical symptoms include changes in sleep, appetite, and weight.

In many elderly people, a hallmark of depression is *hypochondriasis,* an excessive preoccupation with health concerns or exaggerated misinterpretation of minor physical symptoms. (Because such complaints can be irritating to some physicians, they unfortunately may overlook the correct diagnosis in the absence of other obvious symptoms of depression. Often depressed people in this age group talk of feeling useless. They may be uneasy and anxious or fearful. Sometimes severe depression in older individuals is marked by pervasive guilt, often focused on an episode that happened years earlier. One 83-year-old man, for example, had had a brief affair during a troubled period in his marriage. When his wife died from cervical cancer 40 years later, he blamed himself for her death, convincing himself that this betrayal of his wife played a part in her illness.

Delusions are a symptom of depression more common to older individuals than younger ones. They can be very disturbing to the family or neighbors, especially when they take the form of a paranoid belief that someone is harassing or punishing the individual. Delusions are often accompanied by feelings of fear, anxiety, or anger.

Many delusions are related to memory loss or physical problems. A woman with memory problems may find it easier to think that someone is stealing from her rather than acknowledge that she cannot remember where she left her Social Security check. Or a man who is losing his hearing may complain that people are talking about him "behind his back" rather than admit to needing a hearing aid. (Delusions can also signal that the person has a condition called late-onset schizophrenia, discussed on page 343)

Pseudodementia

Sometimes depression can cause symptoms that mimic dementia. These can include apathy, confusion, memory and cognitive problems, incontinence, or loss of self-care skills. Differentiating between depressive pseudodementia (which can be treated and reversed) and true dementia such as that in Alzheimer's disease (which is irreversible and can only be controlled) is a major diagnostic challenge. (See chapter 15 for a more detailed discussion of organic dementias.)

The Risk of Suicide

The elderly have the highest rates of suicide of any age group. Although they constitute 11 percent of the population, those over 65 account for 25 percent of all successfully completed suicides. Suicide is often preceded by a clinical depression or other psychiatric disorder; in the elderly the risk of suicide is increased by bereavement, isolation, and physical illness. Behaviors that are potentially harmful to the self (such as noncompliance with medical regimes, failing to report warning symptoms of illness, neglecting

(See chapter 4, pages 53–55.)

IS IT DEPRESSION OR DEMENTIA?

If an older person is disoriented or is having memory problems, the following symptoms suggest that depression, not dementia, is the cause.

- The symptoms come on suddenly and progress rapidly rather than slowly. (Note, however, that rapid onset can also be a signal of stroke.)
- The person has a previous history of depression, or there is a family history of the disorder.
- The person exhibited symptoms of depression before the changes in intellect and memory occurred.
- The individual is concerned about his or her behavior and memory changes rather than being oblivious to them, or he or she exaggerates the extent of the problem.
- When tested for memory, the individual does not try hard to do well.

diet, fighting, or falling) sometimes may be analogous to suicide attempts. These behaviors are seen quite often among the elderly in nursing homes and call for an investigation of a possible underlying depression.

Treatment

As with younger people, treatment of depression among the elderly includes medication, psychotherapy, and/or electroconvulsive therapy (ECT). One form of short-term psychotherapy, called cognitive therapy, is particularly effective for older individuals. (See chapter 4, pages 53–55.) In some cases these treatments are modified to meet the special needs of older individuals. (See "Mental Health Treatment in Late Life," pages 348–351.)

Drug treatment. Generally, psychiatrists prescribe the same type of antidepressants for older individuals as they do for younger ones. However, older people are more sensitive to drugs and their bodies metabolize them at a slower rate than in younger individuals. Because of this, dosage levels of medication are often lower. They also must be managed more carefully to avoid side effects as well as to minimize potentially harmful interactions with medications being taken for other conditions.

Prior to starting treatment with medications, psychiatrists conduct or refer the patient for a careful

physical examination and take a patient history to assess whether the antidepressant drug will negatively affect an existing physical condition. The exam also includes a discussion of what other medications are being used—particularly important because many seniors are on numerous medications, and taking one drug may provoke a bad response to another. As mentioned earlier, sometimes a medication an individual is taking for a physical condition is actually the cause of the depressed feelings he or she is experiencing. Frequently, the examination includes an electrocardiogram (EKG) to check on heart function. This test is used to ensure that the individual does not have a cardiac condition that would be made worse by the medication.

While the person is on antidepressant medication, the doctor will monitor side effects, taking blood pressures and drawing blood samples to learn the level of medications in the bloodstream.

Not everyone responds to antidepressant medication in the same way: Some people easily tolerate taking these drugs, while others experience discomfort and sometimes serious side effects. Elderly individuals taking these medications need to be aware of what these side effects are and to work closely with their doctors to monitor them. For instance, some of the common minor side effects of antidepressants that can be especially troublesome in older individuals include constipation, a dry mouth, blurred vision, drowsiness, tremors or trembling, or unsteadiness. More serious side effects are postural hypotension, a drop in blood pressure that causes a feeling of lightheadedness or can cause a fall on rising from a sitting or lying position; confusion and clouding of consciousness; difficulty in urinating; alterations in heart rhythm; and aggravation of glaucoma. If side effects do occur, doctors can reduce dosages to build up a tolerance for the drug slowly or switch to another type. Monoamine oxidase inhibitors (MAOIs), for example, are effective in treating some elderly patients, even though they have more potent and dangerous side effects than the traditional tricyclic drugs. (For more on drugs and drug types, see chapter 5.)

Electroconvulsive therapy (ECT). This form of treatment has particularly good results on severe depression in elderly people. It achieves results more quickly than medication, it has far fewer side effects, it does not compromise physical health as drugs might in the presence of serious medical conditions, and it has no long-term effects on memory. Thus, electroconvulsive therapy (ECT), popularly known as "shock therapy," may often be recommended in lieu of drugs, especially when the depression is serious or the individual is suicidal, or when he or she is in poor physical health or taking other drugs that may interact adversely with antidepressants. Or it may be recommended if the depression does not respond to drugs or if side effects force drug treatment to be discontinued. As discussed in chapter 5, with modern techniques, ECT is safe, quick, and painless.

Anxiety Disorders

Many reasonable fears trouble the elderly: Crime, financial difficulties, illness, and disability are among them. Yet the prevalence of anxiety disorders is low among this population. Relatively few older persons become overwhelmed by fears or suffer symptoms of excessive anxiety.

Among those who do, however, the phobias—especially agoraphobia (a condition in which people have a marked fear of leaving home and being in public places, described more fully in chapter 7, pages 104–105)—are most common. Consequences can be serious if the anxiety disorder is not recognized and treated. For example, anxiety can substantially slow rehabilitation and recovery from a physical setback, such as a stroke or a fracture. With age, the chances are increased that an individual who has an anxiety disorder also will have concurrent physical illness, making it more difficult for a physician to diagnose the problem. Also, phobias can cause an individual to limit his or her activities and interests, substantially reducing the quality of life. In those who become housebound because of agoraphobia, isolation and separation from sources of social support can increase the risk for physical or more serious mental illness. All too frequently, older people or their family members accept the fears and resulting limitations of anxiety disorders as an inevitable part of aging rather than as a disorder that can be treated and even overcome.

Symptoms

An individual suffering from an anxiety disorder is assailed by unreasonable and persistent fear or worry, or sometimes simply by a vague, unpleasant, but persistent dread that something is going wrong. Anxiety may accompany depression but frequently occurs independently as a primary condition. The anxiety may be directed at a specific situation (phobias); occur in intense, brief episodes (panic attacks); or be free floating (generalized, pervasive anxiety). Usually the person with abnormal anxiety will recognize that his or her fears are not realistic, but the anxiety persists nonetheless. (For a full discussion of anxiety disorders, see chapter 7.)

Anxiety disorders cause a wide range of physical symptoms, many of which are frightening: trembling, palpitation, sweating, sighing and gasping, difficulty swallowing, dizziness, diarrhea, and disturbed sleep to name some. In the elderly these problems are particularly troublesome, not only because physical symptoms heighten fears of illness and death, but also because they often result in misdiagnoses. It is not uncommon for an older individual who is suffering from anxiety to be diagnosed as having a cardiac or gastric problem and to be inappropriately treated for it, often with medications that further compromise health and well-being.

Treatment

Therapy for anxiety disorders in seniors is similar to that for younger persons. Treatment focuses first and foremost on providing both a reassuring structure in daily routines and supportive encouragement from family and friends. Relaxation techniques (see chapter 24, page 360) and strategies to reduce stress in the individual's physical surroundings are helpful. Use of over-the-counter and prescribed medications containing caffeine, certain bronchodilators, and coffee or tea should be reduced. Regular daytime exercise and regular bedtime rituals will help promote sleep (see also page 344); regular use of sleeping medications may worsen anxiety symptoms.

Short-term drug therapy can be helpful in controlling anxiety, especially when used in conjunction with behavioral or psychological therapies (as described in chapter 4). Benzodiazepines, which have fewer side effects than many other psychotropic drugs, are the most commonly prescribed. As with all medications prescribed for older individuals, these drugs are prescribed initially in low doses. Dosage gradually is raised if not effective. Benzodiazepine use should be monitored carefully by a physician. If taken in doses that are too high, the toxic effects of benzodiazepines can cause confusion, ataxia (an inability to coordinate muscle movements), and even stupor or coma. Benzodiazepines can also cause "sundowning." In this condition, individuals whose behavior is normal during the day become agitated and confused at night, often exhibiting bizarre behavior and delusions. In the morning, normal again, they have no memory of their nighttime behavior.

Chronic Schizophrenia

Schizophrenia is a chronic illness that generally develops in late adolescence and early adulthood. The hallucinations and delusions that are characteristic "positive" symptoms usually abate as a person ages. Some people will recover completely. However, the tendency to become withdrawn and apathetic ("negative" symptoms) persists and may become more pronounced.

Treatment is similar to that of younger individuals, although many older people with chronic schizophrenia no longer require medication or are able to control their symptoms with lower doses. It is important to monitor medications prescribed for schizophrenia and keep them to a minimum because many older individuals have an increased sensitivity to side effects, such as tardive dyskinesia. Many older individuals with schizophrenia are able to live outside of institutions, as long as they remain physically well. They do not have an appreciably increased risk of dementia. (See chapter 14 for a complete discussion of schizophrenia and chapter 5 for more information on tardive dyskinesia and other drug effects.)

Paranoia (Late–Onset Schizophrenia or Paraphrenia)

While true schizophrenia usually develops before the age of 45, some individuals develop delusions or hallucinations that mimic schizophrenia later in life. These can also be caused by organic disease or by other mental disorders, such as depression. One of the major symptoms of late-onset schizophrenia is paranoia. (Hallucinations coupled with paranoia with a chronic but not worsening course are sometimes considered to be a separate syndrome called paraphrenia.)

Those suffering from paranoia imagine or fear being harmed, sexually assaulted, watched, or poisoned. Family members are subjected to unprovoked verbal attacks and abuse; neighbors may find themselves the target of unfounded complaints; police and local authorities may receive so many calls for help that they no longer pay attention to them.

The condition is often preceded by months or years of increasing suspiciousness, anxiety, complaints about health, grudges, bitterness, and resentments. As the paranoia develops in severity, behavior becomes increasingly erratic.

Even so, people suffering from this condition have otherwise normal emotional expression and intellectual functioning; they continue to act in a style consistent with their previous personality, except for their erratic behavior or delusional beliefs. They may suffer from concurrent depression, however.

Contributing factors. Some people who develop paranoia have a long history of suspiciousness. Others in older age may react to stressful situations with paranoid delusions that do not go away when the stress recedes. For others, however, developing deafness and social isolation may be the most significant contributing factors. For unknown reasons, more women than men are likely to suffer from this disorder.

Treatment. The symptoms persist unless treated. Treatment with antipsychotic medication and supportive psychotherapy is very effective if the individual cooperates and takes medications as prescribed. Cooperation is not always easy to obtain, however, because sufferers may be as suspicious of treatment as of everything else.

Medication is usually increased slowly until active psychotic symptoms are controlled and then reduced until improvement can be maintained at the lowest possible dose.

The physical and social circumstances that precipitated the paranoid fantasies should be ameliorated whenever possible. Doing so could include improving hearing impairments, increasing social contacts, explaining any new situation that might make the individual anxious, and encouraging the individual to be actively involved in making decisions.

COMMON PROBLEMS AND STRESSES OF THE LATER YEARS

Certain stresses are common to each developmental stage of life. Those most frequently associated with old age involve loss or change: the death of a spouse and contemporaries, poor health and physical frailty, financial difficulties, and loss of independence or of role, to name a few. It is natural for such stress-causing events to provoke an emotional response.

Individuals who feel overwhelmed or depressed by life circumstances should be made aware that mental health counseling can help them cope and adjust to even the most difficult stresses in their lives. Not only are older individuals every bit as able to cope with change and adversity as younger adults, but their sense of realism and their experience often help them to face loss and illness with greater equanimity and courage.

Physical Illness and Age-related Biological Changes

Of all of the stress factors common to the elderly, physical ones are the most common and the most powerful. Aging can change the body in a number of ways. A general slowing of the body's processes is normal. Vision and hearing become less acute; the metabolism slows; the senses dull, especially those controlling taste and smell; muscles shrink or lose tone, making exercise or common chores more difficult; less food and less sleep are required to maintain the body.

Although the majority of older people report no disabling physical limitations caused by age, many do suffer from chronic conditions that impose some movement restrictions and cause illness-related stress. Chronic illness changes a person's life, and these changes can affect a person's emotions. Anger and frustration are common reactions to limitations brought on by illness, as are feelings of powerlessness or vulnerability. Even for people who are not ill, the fear of becoming ill can be paralyzing. It can shatter a person's self-image of being someone who is strong and productive. For some, illness brings the worry that this is "the beginning of the end" and fear that an illness or injury will force entrance into a nursing home. Such fears are among the reasons why many older people try to hide symptoms of an illness, sometimes letting a minor problem deteriorate into a major one before they seek help.

The interaction of physical illness and psychological illness are discussed at length earlier in this chapter (pages 338–339) and in chapter 28. Psychotherapy, combined with physiotherapy and occupational therapy, can help ameliorate some of the debilitating effects of chronic illness by helping a person learn new coping skills to solve both physical and physiologic problems.

Sleep Problems

Sleep disturbances are a common problem of older age. Some people develop sleep problems as they grow older because their bodies begin to metabolize foods and drugs differently. A single cup of coffee, for example, might keep an elderly individual awake well into the night due to slowed metabolism of the caffeine. Similarly, many drugs commonly used by older people can lead to either sleepiness or insomnia. Physical ailments also can cause repeated awakenings that prevent a full night's sleep—which in turn can exacerbate the physical problem. Heavy snoring and breathing problems are more common as a person ages. As among younger people, insomnia among the elderly also can result from depression and anxiety.

Overall, people sleep less as they age and their sleep is naturally lighter. The importance of sleep and its impact on older individuals is often underrated. Insufficient sleep can affect daytime alertness as well as a person's ability to function physically during the day. Lack of sleep, for example, can contribute to falls and other accidents, and to confused thinking. Although a mild nighttime sedative can help in some situations, long-term reliance on sleeping pills (of which people over 65 are the largest consumers) rarely solves the problem. Indeed, as discussed in the chapters on drugs (chapter 5) and sleep disorders (chapter 12), sedatives have side effects that can intensify sleep problems. Chapter 12 presents solutions to sleep problems.

Sexual Behavior and Sexual Difficulties

The need for physical intimacy continues throughout life. It is normal to have sexual feelings and desires, even into one's late years. While sexual desire gradually reduces as people age, for the most part sexual behavior in older individuals mirrors the patterns of their younger years: Those who were active when young will be more likely to retain an active sexual life when older, and vice versa. There is no norm for appropriate sexual drive or amount of sexual behavior in the later years—as with younger adults, what is normal is what is comfortable between two individuals.

As explained in chapter 11, age does bring some differences in sexual ability, however. Older men usually take longer to achieve an erection and to ejaculate. The volume of seminal fluid is less. These changes are normal and reflect the general slowing down of the body's physiologic processes. They do not interfere with the ability to have sexual intercourse and do not indicate that a man is losing his potency.

In women, changes in sexual function are due primarily to lowered levels of the hormone estrogen. The vagina becomes drier and less elastic, making sex sometimes uncomfortable or painful. Staying sexually active, including by means of masturbation, can help a woman maintain her ability to lubricate. Water-soluble surgical jelly (*not* petroleum jelly) can provide the necessary lubrication when the vagina remains dry. Women who have severe problems are sometimes treated with estrogen.

Specific organic illnesses frequently cause sexual problems in older individuals. For men, the most common organic cause of sexual problems is diabetes, which causes impotency. Prostate problems also can interfere with sexual desire and performance. In most cases, adequate treatment of these medical conditions restores sexual functioning.

While a heart attack does not in itself alter sexual functioning, fear of sex is a common emotional reaction after a heart attack—both in the person who experienced the attack and in the partner, who may be anxious about provoking another one. Although sexual activity does increase blood pressure and pulse rate, studies do not indicate that the risk of a heart attack increases during the sex act.

Medications, for both physical and mental conditions, can cause problems. Among the drugs that can inhibit ejaculation or cause impotency are antihypertensives, heart medications such as digitalis, antidepressants, and tranquilizers.

Sexual functioning also can be inhibited by a variety of psychiatric conditions. Indeed, depression is such a common cause of sexual problems that sudden impotency is often an early clue to the presence of depression. Frequently older people who are depressed believe that their problems with sex are a function of their age rather than of the depression. When the depression is treated, however, sexual functioning returns.

Inappropriate sexual behavior—such as obscene comments, attempts to solicit sex from strangers, and delusions that one is being sexually harassed—can be caused by bipolar illness and by late-onset schizophrenia. Dementia also can lead to inappropriate sexual behavior, particularly among people who have been institutionalized in long-term care facilities. There have been incidents of patients who, in their desire for warmth and human touch, have committed indecent assault or attempted rape, often in the mistaken belief that the person they are approaching is their spouse or that he or she has indicated a desire for sex.

Public acceptance of sexuality in later life is gradually increasing. Most older people want—and are able to lead—an active, satisfying sex life. When and if problems occur, they should not be viewed as inevitable. Usually there is a cause (disease, disability, drug reactions, emotional upset) that requires medical or mental health care.

Isolation and Loneliness

Older people need warm, human relationships and to feel wanted and cared about. One study indicated that those who had at least one close friend to confide in experienced greater life satisfaction and had fewer physical problems than those who lived isolated lives. More than any other age group, however, the elderly are likely to be isolated from people and social activities and to feel lonely. The importance of social networks to well-being is often overlooked.

Not all older individuals who live isolated lives complain of loneliness, however. Some people in fact prefer to live independently; they adapt well to isolation, and their feelings of psychological well-being are not affected by living alone. But isolation can set in motion a downward spiral in which social and self-care skills are lost.

Social isolation has been identified as a major factor contributing to psychiatric disorders, including depression and paranoia. It has been found to increase vulnerability to physical disease and has been implicated in alcoholism and the risk of suicide. Isolation can also render a person more sensitive to the effects of other stresses—intensifying, for example, the impact of the death of a spouse, of chronic illness, or poverty—that may trigger a mental health problem.

Family and friends who are concerned about the effects that living alone may have on an older individual should explore the resources available in their local community. Some cities have organized programs, such as a Friendly Visitor Program, or senior citizen clubs that provide social and exercise programs designed specifically for those over 65. Religious and service organizations such as the YMCAs and YMHAs are also good sources of social activities. Social activities that include physical exercise can be particularly beneficial, because exercise can help promote feelings of well-being. It also provides more energy, helps people to sleep better and feel less tense, improves their appearance and self-confidence, and can keep them socially active.

If an older person consistently complains of feeling lonely, a psychological consultation may be in order. Psychotherapy does not replace the need for social warmth and contact, but it can help a person learn to restructure his or her life and to develop new relationships. Group therapy, in particular, can help people cope with their feelings of loneliness while at the same time providing a vehicle for social contact. (See page 349.)

Death, Grief, and Bereavement

The later years in life are often a time punctuated by multiple bereavements: the loss of one's spouse, of siblings and longtime friends, sometimes of an adult child. Most older individuals do not have excessive fears or concerns about their own death, however. An overly anxious preoccupation with death is sometimes a symptom of depression and should be discussed with a mental health professional.

Bereavement is the process of coming to terms with the death of a loved one. Young or old, people usually experience distinct stages of mourning (as explained in chapter 28), although older individuals sometimes take more time to progress through each stage. The process can take six months to two years.

The immediate reaction to the death of someone close is often emotional numbness, a feeling of disbelief that the person actually could have died. Emotions can fluctuate, from feeling little to feeling overwrought and extremely anxious. Problems with sleeping or with appetite commonly occur.

In the usual progression of grief, the initial feelings of anxiety and disbelief abate after the first few weeks, as the intellectual realization of loss sets in. Then symptoms of depression are common, such as episodes of crying, feeling constantly fatigued, or losing interest in activities or in interacting with others. A person may experience conflicting feelings, such as a desire to be reunited with the loved one mixed with anger for his or her having left. Sometimes people feel anger toward those who were involved in the care of the deceased, such as doctors or nurses, blaming them for not saving the loved one. Some people blame themselves, feeling that they could have done more to prevent the death.

Letting the feelings be expressed is important to the process of grieving. This can involve talking to other family members, to friends, to clergy. When grief is intense, unremitting, or preoccupying, talking to a mental health professional counselor can help. (See chapter 25.) Other signs of difficulty include grief that lasts an excessively long time; continuing depression; persistent feelings of guilt; weight loss; self-deprecation; overidentification with the deceased (sometimes to the point of experiencing the illness symptoms he or she experienced before death); and self-destructive impulses (such as giving away important possessions or making hasty financial decisions), even to the point of suicide. In these cases, it is imperative that help be sought, because unreconciled grief can compromise mental and physical health. Men in particular have a higher incidence of increased physical illness and death in the period following the death of their wives—perhaps because many men have fewer support networks than women.

In recent years many groups have formed to help people share their feelings and cope with their emotions following the death of a spouse. The clergy, senior citizen centers, and local mental health offices can provide information on resources that are available. If problems persist, professional counseling can help a person to put his or her feelings into perspective and promote healing.

Loss of Role: Retirement and Other Lifestyle Changes

Transitions in life's roles are a part of older age. Some can be positive and fulfilling, such as becoming a grandparent. Often, however, losing once-important activities can compromise a person's identity and feelings of self-esteem.

Retirement is one of the major transitions of later life. For many people, work provides a sense of purpose and direction in life. It can be hard for a person to accept and adjust to the loss of both the external structure that organized the days and to the companionship of friends in the work environment.

Interestingly, studies show that retirement from work is *not* a common cause of depression. This is not to say that retirement never causes depression, but that the incidence of people who consult psychiatrists for this specific reason is low. Signs of depression after retirement may signal a true clinical illness rather than a short-term adjustment problem.

Retirement also can add stress to marital relationships as couples suddenly find themselves being involved with each other on a full-time basis, sometimes in a brand-new community lacking their usual social supports. Couples who have lived very divergent lives may find that they have little in common. Arguments may become common as unresolved conflicts, sometimes of many years' duration, become exacerbated.

Loss of role can also affect relationships with children. Some older individuals have problems giving up the role of parental authority and complain of feeling abandoned and rejected by their children. Exchange of roles also can be a source of conflict. Both children and parents often are uncomfortable or resentful when an adult child must suddenly provide care for a disabled or impoverished parent, especially if the child becomes overprotective and tries to make all the decisions for a parent.

Psychotherapy can help people learn to adapt and negotiate new roles. Marriage and family counseling, often seen as the province of younger adults, also can help resolve role conflicts in later life. Self-help groups and retirement-preparation counseling can also help. (See "Mental Health Treatment in Late Life," pages 348–350.)

Dependency/Institutionalization

One of the greatest fears of older people is that physical illness or financial or other social circumstances will force a loss of independence. Relocating to a long-term care facility or to a child's home can have adverse effects on how a person perceives him- or herself, which in turn can affect mental and physical health. Common reactions to forced dependency can include depression, anxiety, and anger. Behavior changes are common, especially withdrawal from outside activities. Studies have shown higher mortality and illness rates following involuntary relocation to a nursing home.

One of the major factors affecting how well a person adjusts to this major life change is his or her perception of control. The more control a person has in making decisions, the higher his or her life satisfaction and the greater the corresponding ability to cope with stress. Some people can be so frustrated by nursing home regimes and the loss of their independence that they experience feelings of hopelessness. They may respond with behavior that psychiatrists call "infantilization"—a learned helplessness that is reinforced when well-meaning relatives or inpatient staff insist on doing things for older people that they could do for themselves.

One of the ways to make the move easier is to give the person some choices, such as over when the move will occur or which facility will become home. When a facility is being considered, administrators should be asked to specify what kind of schedules are followed, what type of recreational programs exist, and whether a person can choose to participate or not. (See also the box below.)

If an older person is relocated to a long-term care facility because of mental health problems, psychi-

---

WHEN CHOOSING A NURSING HOME, YOU SHOULD:

- Check to see that the home has a current license from the state and that the administrator's license is current as well. Ask if the home has been cited for any violations; then double-check the answer with the state licensing board.
- Ask about access to medical and nursing services, and about types of arrangements for handling medical emergencies. If medical or psychological care is needed, ask what the specific care plan will be.
- Ask what types of rehabilitation and social programs are offered and if any type of group counseling is available.
- Evaluate the food service and the facilities. The better nursing homes are designed with the needs of older people in mind. Features such as handrails, low elevator buttons for those in wheelchairs, and furniture that is comfortable and easy to get in and out of can help residents be more independent and mobile, helping to ward off depression and withdrawal.
- Talk to other residents and their families. Drop in once or twice unannounced, perhaps in the evening, to get an idea of staffing levels and resident activities.
- Privacy can be an important issue. Ask if single rooms are available, and at what cost. If the facility only offers semiprivate accommodations, find out if individuals can select their roommates.

SLEEP PROBLEMS AND LONG-TERM CARE FACILITIES

Many older people who live in nursing homes or other care facilities complain of having difficulties with sleep. Numerous factors in a nursing home can contribute to the problem: the unfamiliarity of the surroundings; new, uncomfortable bedding; noise from staff and other residents; lack of physical activity; taking too many daytime naps or going to bed too early in order to escape boredom; medications taken at the wrong time of day.

Another common complaint is that these institutions force unwanted sleep schedules on individuals. In many nursing homes, staffing at night is minimal, which can lead to problems of supervising and safeguarding people if they get up and wander. To ease the transition from home:

- Talk to the staff about schedules and bedtime routines before you or your relative enters the nursing home. If these do not coincide with cur-

rent sleep patterns, find out what alternatives can be worked out.

- Investigate the kind of activities the facility arranges for its residents. Try to choose a facility that provides daytime stimulation, such as physical activities, arts and crafts recreation, or educational programs.
- Bring a pillow from home. Find out if the institution will provide foam padding for beds that are too hard or boards for those that are too soft.
- Keep a soft light on at night and perhaps a tape of soothing music or of familiar sounds from home—sometimes people get up at night because they want reassurance.
- Make sure that medications are taken on a schedule that will take advantage of their side effects: those with sedative effects should be taken at night; those that are stimulating in the morning.

atric consultation and treatment must be part of the treatment he or she receives. A facility that provides therapeutic care directed toward maintaining or increasing levels of competency, not merely custodial care, should be chosen.

The issue of whether to move an elderly person to a nursing home can be emotionally charged. Family members may feel overwhelmed by providing care for a parent who is physically disabled or cognitively impaired. Their feelings of guilt may delay the move,

sometimes to the detriment of both the older adult and family relationships. Sometimes there are strong conflicts between siblings over the issue of who will care for a parent or if the move should be made at all, and over who will pay for the care.

Psychotherapy can help families to recognize that their feelings and conflicts are normal reactions and help them to work through their feelings. It also can aid them to make decisions concerning institutional care versus care at home.

MENTAL HEALTH TREATMENT IN LATE LIFE

Throughout this chapter, the importance of psychiatric care for older adults has been emphasized. Here we discuss some of the specific issues of treatment related to age as well as appropriate use of these treatments to achieve maximum benefit.

Drugs

People over 65 are the largest consumers of drugs generally in this country—almost all of them legally prescribed by physicians. They are also the population most likely to suffer from serious side effects or

misuse of drugs, for two reasons. First, many older people suffer from coexisting medical conditions and take multiple medications. Sometimes a psychiatric drug interacts negatively with these medications.

Second, the body metabolizes drugs differently with age. The gastrointestinal tract absorbs drugs more slowly; age-related changes in the liver and kidneys (the organs responsible for metabolizing and excreting drugs) affect how the blood circulates drugs and increase the length of time that they remain active in the body.

In addition, older individuals can be more at risk of drug side effects that would be less consequential to younger people. A common side effect of tricyclic antidepressants, for example, is orthostatic hypotension, a drop in blood pressure that causes a feeling of light-headedness on rising from a sitting or lying position. For older people, this side effect increases the risk of falling and incurring fractures or other injuries.

Although psychoactive drugs must be used with discretion, many older individuals with mental health disorders respond favorably to them, as discussed earlier in this chapter. The general rule that physicians use in treating older patients with psychoactive medications is to start with low levels and to increase the dose slowly. When prescribed appropriately and monitored carefully, drug therapies for the elderly are much more effective and are accompanied by fewer side effects than was true even a decade ago.

Psychotherapy

Older individuals respond just as well as their younger counterparts to all forms of psychotherapy. Psychotherapy may be recommended for a wide range of psychiatric disorders, including depression and anxiety, and for difficulties in coping. The type of psychotherapy used will be tailored to the individual's condition and capabilities and to the treatment goal (that is, what the therapist and individual hope to accomplish). Frequently, medication may be part of the treatment regimen.

Overall, psychotherapy (described fully in chapter 4) can help an older person learn new problem-solving and interpersonal skills. It can address feelings of self-worth and correct assumptions about what being "old" means. Psychotherapy can enhance a person's sense of competence and independence, as he or she realizes that change is possible at any age. Some common age-related problems addressed in psychotherapy sessions include how to cope with and adjust to stressful life circumstances; how to compensate for losses, such as memory decline; resolving conflicts with others; and mourning what has passed and facing the future with hope.

Cognitive Therapy

Cognitive therapy has been found to be particularly well suited for older individuals suffering from depression. Cognitive therapy is an approach that is short term and problem-oriented. Therapeutic goals—usually addressed at examining and correcting faulty thinking patterns—are broken down into manageable steps. As part of the therapy, individuals are taught problem-solving, coping, and interpersonal skills.

Family Therapy

When an older individual is experiencing emotional difficulties or problems in coping with stress, the entire family is often affected as well. Family therapy can be particularly helpful in cases where there are conflicts between older people and their adult children or where the behavior of an elderly person causes conflict among the children. It also can ease the situation when an individual suffers from dementia, when cognitive deterioration and behavior changes can try even the most tolerant of families.

Group Therapy

In group therapy, a group of individuals with common age-related concerns explore their problems and feelings under the guidance of a therapy leader. Some groups have specific focuses, such as the stresses involved in taking care of someone who is chronically ill or coping with the death of a spouse. One of the reasons that these groups work so well is that seniors feel comfortable in the presence of their peers.

A group therapy technique that has gained popularity in recent years is *reminiscence*, or *life review*, therapy. This technique uses exploration of the past to resolve emotional problems. Individuals are encouraged to compile scrapbooks and photo albums, listen to popular music of the past, visit those places connected with their pasts, and write accounts of their life histories. The psychotherapist uses tools to facilitate an understanding of how prior life events can affect the present, to help reestablish a person's sense of self-esteem, and to assist an individual in coming to terms with the present.

Group therapy can be particularly helpful in institutions, where it can help elderly individuals with cognitive problems. *Reality orientation* therapy, for example, is a technique designed to help someone who is confused use more of his or her mental abilities. It uses props and pictures to stimulate the senses, and asks individuals to respond to basic questions about such things as the day, time, and their current location.

Cooperating in Treatment

Treatment of mental and emotional problems is complex and requires a high degree of coordination and cooperation among doctors, patients, and their families. Often what appears to be a failure of treatment or a bad reaction to medication is in reality a lapse of this teamwork.

"Patient noncompliance" is the term used when individuals do not follow a doctor's orders (such as to take a medication at a particular hour or for a specific period of time) or stop treatment altogether. Noncompliance is a significant cause of treatment failure with the elderly.

With drug therapy, noncompliance can occur when a person experiences uncomfortable or frightening side effects that the doctor did not adequately explain. Or it can occur because the person does not tell the doctor about the problem and thus he or she cannot adjust the medication. Physicians and family members also should be aware that anxiety or physical problems, such as with hearing or vision, can contribute to an older individual's noncompliance. Sometimes the problem is that the individual does not understand the importance of taking the drug as prescribed, or fails to remember the instructions on how to take it. The cost of medication also can be an obstacle to compliance, as can problems in obtaining the medication if the individual does not have easy access to a pharmacy.

With psychotherapy, noncompliance can mean that a person refuses to continue to see a doctor or to attend therapy sessions. There can be a number of reasons for this—perhaps the psychotherapist's office is too far from where the patient lives or transportation is difficult. Here too cost of treatment also can be a major deterrent. Sometimes an older person has mental barriers against psychological counseling and allows fear or biases against psychotherapy to interfere with treatment. Individuals who have been forced by their children to visit a mental health specialist against their will may particularly resist treatment.

Here are some suggestions that might help convince an older person to seek help.

- Ask the person's primary physician not only to recommend treatment but actually to make the appointment.
- Call a family meeting in which everyone shares their concern with the older individual.
- Enlist the aid of the senior's close friends who realize that he or she needs help, or who have received such help themselves.
- Offer to make an occasion out of it—a visit to the therapist, then lunch at a nice restaurant or a drive in the country.
- Call the mental health professional and make an appointment for yourself. Discuss the senior's problems and ask how to help.

Once senior citizens are convinced to see a therapist, mental health professionals who are experienced in working with older people often can put them at ease.

The following suggestions may help older individuals and their families communicate better with the treatment team and can help ensure that adequate information is provided.

- Make sure that in the first visit, adequate time is spent with the doctor. Psychiatrists who routinely treat older patients know that first visits often take longer than with their younger patients: there is more to discuss and explain, and information sometimes needs to be repeated or conveyed in simpler terms.
- During the visit relay all symptoms and how they developed; ask the doctor questions to clarify what may be wrong; discuss with him or her what further investigations may be required or what treatment options are available. Take notes on what the doctor says; have a family member help. Ask the doctor to write it down for you.
- If the doctor prescribes medications, ask what side effects there might be and which of these effects should be tolerated and which reported immediately to the doctor. Ask if there are any foods or medications that must not be taken at the same time as that medication.
- When a particular treatment is recommended, ask your doctor what symptoms it will improve and how long it will take to have an effect (it may be several weeks).

Remember, cooperation does not mean that the older patient should follow the doctor's orders passively and blindly. Rather, there should be a full exchange of information between patient and doctor, and decisions on treatment should be considered together and implemented in a way agreed upon by both.

GETTING HELP

The practitioner's experience with the elderly is essential. He or she needs to have a feel for what makes seniors comfortable as well as be versed in more technical aspects, such as age-related reactions to drugs and physical problems that mimic psychological symptoms. Someone who has empathy for the problems of older individuals and who will spend extra time with a patient when necessary should be selected. Some therapists work with a nurse practitioner or a social worker who is readily available to answer questions. Someone who can explain clearly what the goals of therapy are and what the patient can hope to achieve should be chosen. In the end, however, it is the patient's rapport with the mental health professional that provides the essential ingredient for a truly therapeutic relationship.

Family doctors, local hospitals, or the nearest university medical center can provide a referral to a geriatric psychiatrist, as can one of the following sources.

Helpful Addresses and Phone Numbers

American Association of Geriatric Psychiatry
P.O. Box 376A
Greenbelt, MD 20768
tel. 301 220–0952

American Psychiatric Association
Council on Aging
1400 K Street, NW—4th Floor
Washington, D.C. 20005
tel. 202 682–6143

National Institute on Aging
Information Office
Federal Building 6C12
Bethesda, MD 20892
tel. 301 496–1752

National Association of Area Agencies
on Aging
600 Maryland Avenue, SW, Suite 208
Washington, D.C. 20024
tel. 202 484–7520

The American Association of Retired Persons
(AARP)
1909 K Street, NW
Washington, D.C. 20049
tel. 202 872–4700

24

Stress and Stress Management

Kenneth A. Frank, Ph.D., and Donald S. Kornfeld, M.D.

Stress has always been part of the human experience. Each period of history has had its own particular sources of stress, its predators and plagues, wars, cataclysms, famines. In the late twentieth century, many of the characteristic stressors we face are at least partly of our own making: crowding, noise, urbanization, socioeconomic mobility, new family structures, loss of traditions, and loss of the social supports that traditionally could be called upon in times of hardship and suffering. Change is rapid and constant in our world, and for many change is the most potent stressor of all.

A substantial body of research indicates that stress is a factor in a variety of diseases, including coronary heart disease, hypertension, immune-system disorders such as rheumatoid arthritis and ulcerative colitis, migraine headaches, and some cancers. Preliminary research in the infant science of psychoneuroimmunology shows that the biochemistry of immunity is influenced by psychological and social factors—among them, stress. Stress also contributes to a spectrum of health-risk behaviors: overeating, smoking, and abusing alcohol and other drugs. By definition it plays an essential role in the development of post-traumatic stress disorder, and it is thought to contribute strongly to the development of depression and anxiety, two of the most prevalent psychiatric disturbances.

WHAT IS STRESS?

In colloquial usage, the expression "under stress" or "stressed out" refers to a state of nervous tension brought about by the experience of something unpleasant or taxing. But to many researchers—

including Hans Selye, the "father" of stress research—stress is a biological state that occurs as an individual attempts to adapt to every challenge and change in daily life. By this definition in its broadest sense, stress could be defined as the rate of wear and tear on the body caused by daily living—everything from a game of tennis, to a malfunctioning car, to the death of a loved one. Thus, not all stress is negative or pernicious. Selye identified two different types, *eustress* and *distress*. Eustress is positive and is associated with joy, intense concentration, and high self-esteem. An actor on opening night experiences stress of this kind. Distress, on the other hand, is negative stress—uncomfortable, disruptive, and associated with poor self-esteem.

According to another definition, stress involves the psychological and physical responses to a situation that is perceived by individuals as challenging or exceeding their resources and endangering their well-being. In this view, adapted from that of the researchers Richard Lazarus and Susan Folkman, the stressor may be an actual event (being fired from a job) or an internal, imagined one (worrying about an anticipated firing).

The level of stress is a significant factor in the degree to which it is experienced as negative. At manageable levels, stress challenges an individual's motivation, efficiency, and creativity, but at high levels it becomes disabling.

MIND–BODY REACTION TO STRESS

Fight or Flight

The stress reaction is usually identified with the "fight-or-flight" response described by Walter Cannon in 1929, in which the body becomes mobilized to deal with a threat by either staying and fighting or beating a hasty retreat. In the face of fear, pain, anger, or rage, the body reacts automatically and almost instantaneously. The pituitary gland releases adrenocorticotrophic hormone (ACTH), prompting the adrenal glands to pour corticosteroids and epinephrine, the so-called stress hormones, into the bloodstream. In the resulting "rush of adrenaline," these hormones activate the autonomic nervous system. As a result, the heart speeds up and blood pressure rises, the breathing rate accelerates, the muscles tense, blood-clotting mechanisms are activated, glucose pours from the liver to provide fuel, perspiration increases, the pupils of the eyes dilate, and all the senses become keener. The body is thus in a state of readiness, prepared to deal with the threat. This state will persist for about half an hour. However, when the threat posed by the stressor is particularly intense or persistent, the body may not be able to respond effectively.

For earlier people, living in a world full of real physical danger, the fight-or-flight response was vital for survival; it worked adaptively in providing our early ancestors with extra energy to fight harder or run faster for survival. It remains a suitable and desirable response to some threatening situations today—you spot a rattlesnake in the desert and you beat a fast retreat. But the same automatic physiological activation also is elicited by relatively minor psychological stressors, such as interpersonal conflict or social change—even, as one study showed, by the challenge of doing mental arithmetic under time pressure. In such situations, neither fight nor flight is appropriate or socially acceptable. Your boss criticizes you; you can't very well attack or storm out of the office.

The General Adaptation Syndrome

The fight-or-flight response corresponds to the first phase of what Selye identified as the "general adaptation syndrome" ("general" because the hormones involved have an arousal effect on the whole body; "adaptation" because stress stimulates the body's defense systems and so increases the chances for survival; "syndrome" because the various manifestations of stress occur together).

Selye found that the body makes no distinction among the sources of stress: What counts is the demand for adaptation. Physical stressors, such as extreme cold or starvation, and social stressors, such as the death of a spouse, produce the same three-part syndrome. First comes the alarm phase, in which the body is activated to cope with the stressor, discharging adrenal hormones in response to the "nocuous agent." This is followed by the resistance or acquired adaptation phase as the body attempts to resist the stressor and adapt to the derangement it has caused. Energy stores are replenished and the adrenal cortex accumulates new reserves of corticosteroid-secreting hormones.

If the stressor is stubborn or persistent enough to outlast the body's resistance, however, the acquired adaptation is eventually lost and the body enters the exhaustion phase. A second alarm response occurs and corticosteroids are discharged again. The depletion of the adaptive reserves and the wear and tear generated by repeated alarm and resistance are precursors of illness. In Selye's words, "No living organism can exist continuously in a state of alarm."

Stress and Illness

Repeated activation of the autonomic nervous system during the stress response causes wear and tear on the body and may bring about or worsen a disease state. For example, cortisol, one of the stress hormones, raises the level of cholesterol and other lipids in the blood. This, in turn, can cause arterial blockage and coronary heart disease. Both epinephrine and cortisol have been found to depress the immune system, lowering the body's resistance to disease. This finding supports the popular observation that stressful events and illness are closely related—for example, that widows often become seriously ill in the months following their husband's deaths. Elevated levels of cortisol have also been found in many people suffering from major depressions.

Signs and Symptoms of Chronic Stress

It is relatively easy to recognize the signs of alarm-phase stress—pounding heart, tense muscles, increased perspiration, racing thoughts, and so on. Chronic stress (stress in the exhaustion phase) has manifestations that are more subtle. In those people who are unable to deal with stress adaptively (see below for more information), chronic stress buildup may be evidenced in physical symptoms, behavioral problems, emotional difficulties, or in all of these. The emotional and behavioral problems tend to develop gradually and may be missed easily. Often they manifest themselves only as exaggerations of a person's usual characteristics.

Physical symptoms include a broad spectrum of problems. Among them are eating disorders, bowel and stomach disturbances, heart palpitations, tingling in the hands and feet, headache, neck and back pain, light-headedness, elevated blood pressure, and a weakened resistance to disease. Behavioral symptoms—overeating, substance abuse, proneness to accidents, and impaired performance on the job or at school—may signal stress buildup. Family conflict, interpersonal problems, and social withdrawal are also common. Emotional symptoms include feelings of anxiety, irritability, or anger; depression; insomnia; difficulty in concentrating; fatigue; and negative thinking.

Stress follows a self-perpetuating cycle, making easy identification of causes and results difficult. Excessive stress can produce physical and psychological weakness that, in turn, can increase an individual's vulnerability to further stress. Resistance sometimes lowers and overload comes more quickly. Moreover, because behavior is often impaired by stress, leading to poor interactions and lack of confidence, an overstressed individual tends to encounter more than the usual number of stressful situations.

The experience of stress can also result in a psychiatric stress disorder including adjustment disorder and post-traumatic stress disorder, discussed on pages 362–363.

SOURCES OF STRESS

Just as people vary in their reaction to physical stressors—one person is comfortable in a snowstorm without hat or gloves; another shivers despite layers of clothing—so they do to psychological and emotional ones. One person sees the loss of a job as a defeat and a severe blow to self-esteem; another takes it as an opportunity to explore new and perhaps more exciting possibilities. In other words, one person's eustress may be another's distress. However, the events and situations that are, in general, most likely to lead to the development of stress are those characterized by uncontrollability, unpredictability, or uncertainty. It is important to note that each of these properties in a stressor is a product of the individual's perception of what is happening, his or her coping resources, and the demands of the situation. Note too that these properties apply both to everyday stress and to severe states, including the psychiatric stress disorders described later in this chapter.

Uncontrollability. A sense of lacking control does much to determine the perceived stressfulness of a situation. Numerous studies in both animals and humans have substantiated this key factor. For example, a study in Sweden found that commuters who boarded a train late in the trip and had to stand or push their way through to a seat had significantly higher levels of certain stress hormones than those who boarded earlier. These early-comers could exert some control over their environment by choosing their seats and settling their belongings.

In another study, people were given tasks requiring concentration while disturbances went on in the background. Those who were told that they could stop the disturbances whenever they wished were able to perform much better than those who had no such sense of control, even though the former group did not actually use the option.

Unpredictability. The unpredictability with which a stressor occurs—such as the occurrence of earthquakes in areas prone to them—is another factor. In one study, two groups of rats were subjected to electric shocks. One group heard a beeping sound exactly 10 seconds before each shock, while for the other group the beep came at random intervals. Both groups of rats developed ulcers, but the rate was six times higher in the group for which the timing of the stressor was unpredictable.

Uncertainty. Knowing that a stressful event is about to happen, but not knowing exactly what will occur, is a common source of stress. Examples abound: tests and examinations, surgery, a family gathering. In anticipating a stressful event, an individual has the opportunity to prepare, which may make the event easier to handle. However, if the anticipation of a stressor is itself stressful, the benefits of being able to prepare may be undermined.

Rating Stress

Because people have different perceptions of what is stressful and cope with stress in different ways, it is difficult to measure stress levels of life events or to say with certainty what their effect on any particular individual will be. Nevertheless, a number of self-rating scales have been developed to help pinpoint which life events are most stressful to most people. One of the most useful is the Social Readjustment Scale, developed by Drs. Thomas Holmes and Richard Rahe of the University of Washington. (See table 24.1.)

Working with thousands of patients of diverse backgrounds, the researchers ranked 43 specific life events according to their generally perceived stressfulness and assigned a numerical value to each. The death of a spouse—even a former spouse—was almost unanimously seen as the most stressful event in life and was rated 100. Marriage had the midway position of 50. The researchers followed their patients for several years, comparing life-event scores with medical histories. The results suggested that an accumulation of 300 or more stress points in a year translated into an 80 percent risk that a major physical or emotional illness would occur within two years; with a score between 150 and 300, the odds were about 50/50.

Loss and change are threads that run through the list and characterize the most stressful events. But even events that recur every year (Christmas) or are generally thought of as relaxing (vacation) carry a significant number of stress points.

Using this scale, people can take the measure of the stresses in their lives and so be aware of their risk of stress-related problems. More important, the scale is a tool that can be used to manage life changes, avoiding excessive change wherever possible. While some stressful events cannot be anticipated, the timing of others is under an individual's control; sometimes these events can be spaced so that major stressors do not come too close together in time. For example, a newlywed who has just moved to a new town and started a new job might be well advised to postpone other major changes.

Stress and the Workplace

Corporations are spending increasing sums to combat the negative effects of stress on workplace morale, attendance, accidents (85 percent of industrial accidents are said to be stress-induced), and employee health and productivity. According to the National Institute of Occupational Health and Safety, stress costs the American economy $10 to $20 billion a year.

No work is without stressors, but some jobs seem to produce particular stress and to have clear risks to health. Air-traffic controllers, for example, who must make split-second decisions that affect the lives of hundreds of people, have an extremely high turnover rate and an incidence of gastric ulcers that is well above average. People who must adapt their sleep patterns to the changing hours of a rotating shift suffer stress as a result of the disruption of their circadian (daily) rhythms. Women who must balance the demands of a job with those of child care are

Table 24.1   THE SOCIAL READJUSTMENT RATING SCALE

Life Event	Mean Value
1. Death of a spouse	100
2. Divorce	73
3. Marital separation	65
4. Jail term	63
5. Death of close family member	63
6. Personal injury or illness	53
7. Marriage	50
8. Fired at work	47
9. Marital reconciliation	45
10. Retirement	45
11. Change in health of family member	44
12. Pregnancy	40
13. Sex difficulties	39
14. Gain of new family member	39
15. Business readjustment	39
16. Change in financial state	38
17. Death of close friend	37
18. Change to different line of work	36
19. Change in number of arguments with spouse	35
20. Mortgage or loan for a major purpose (home, etc.)	31
21. Foreclosure of mortgage or loan	30
22. Change in responsibilities at work	29
23. Son or daughter leaving home	29
24. Trouble with in-laws	29
25. Outstanding personal achievement	28
26. Spouse begins or stops work	26
27. Begin or end school	26
28. Change in living conditions	25
29. Revision of personal habits	24
30. Trouble with boss	23
31. Change in work hours or conditions	20
32. Change in residence	20
33. Change in schools	20
34. Change in recreation	19
35. Change in church activities	19
36. Change in social activities	18
37. Mortgage or loan for a lesser purpose (car, TV, etc.)	17
38. Change in sleeping habits	17
39. Change in number of family get-togethers	16
40. Change in eating habits	15
41. Vacation	13
42. Christmas	12
43. Minor violations of the law	11

Adapted from T. H. Holmes and R. H. Rahe, "The Social Readjustment Scale," *Journal of Psychosomatic Research* 2 (1967): 213–218. © 1967 Pergamon Press, Inc. Reprinted with permission.

twice as likely to suffer from coronary heart disease as housewives with the same number of children.

What makes a job stressful? A research team headed by Dr. Robert Karasek questioned people working in a variety of fields about two aspects of their jobs: (1) the amount of psychological demand in their work—how hard or fast they had to work, the time pressure involved, how hectic they felt their jobs were; and (2) the amount of decision control they had—did they have any control over working conditions, did their jobs offer variety or an opportunity to use their skills and learn new things? Then Karasek and his team tallied the rates of cardiovascular disease in different occupations. Thus far, the research has revealed a consistent and significant finding: Jobs with high psychological demand and low decision control are associated with high rates of heart disease.

While this research cannot be taken as definitive evidence that certain occupations result in a high risk of heart disease, it does indicate an apparent link between job-related stress and heart disease. The research defines a high-stress job as one that is repetitive and machine-paced. The work is monotonous and yet demands close attention. The workers have little or no control over their working situation. Some of the many jobs that fit this description are assembly-line work, freight-handling, and garment assembly.

Low-stress jobs, according to Karasek's findings, are those with low psychological demand or those with high levels of control. For chief executive officers and top professionals, high demand is offset by high levels of decision control. Popular wisdom to the contrary, such high-level jobs have relatively low levels of cardiovascular risk. In fact, a study of male employees at a major corporation found that the rate of coronary disease was lower with each step up the corporate ladder.

Other important factors in determining the levels of job-related stress are the management style and personality of the supervisor. One study of personnel management showed that the single factor that correlated with evidence of stress in employees (specifically, high blood cholesterol levels) was a supervisor who gave more attention to trivial details than to larger goals of efficiency and productivity. The attitudes of co-workers is also a factor in job-related stress. Camaraderie and social support can do much to buffer the effects of a stressful work environment.

COPING WITH STRESS

Coping mechanisms come into play as an individual seeks to adapt to a stressful event—to master, tolerate, minimize, or reduce stress. It is the way we respond to stress, not so much the stressors themselves, that determines whether the impact will be large or small—even whether the individual experiences eustress or distress.

Poor coping may fail to address the stressor and may even worsen it, as with a student who dreads an examination and puts off studying to the last moment. Or a person may attempt to distract him- or herself from the immediate distress, perhaps with drug or alcohol use or by overeating, and the stressor simply may be ignored. Sometimes the methods used to cope with a stressful situation become symptoms of psychopathology themselves. For example, a man whose feelings of masculine inadequacy make social situations stressful might "cope" by avoiding such situations entirely.

Good coping, on the other hand, enables an individual to meet the demands of a stressful situation effectively and at the same time promotes psychological and physical well-being. (The box on page 359 presents an example.)

Personality Factors

Some people simply are more effective than others in dealing with the vicissitudes of life. Research by Dr. W. Doyle Gentry has shown that an individual's coping resources can buffer the effects of stress, as reflected in the development of illness.

Some personality traits found to be associated with protection against illness under stress are an active (versus passive) coping orientation, a positive (versus negative) attitude, a sense of personal control over one's life, personal commitment, and adaptive flexibility—that is, the ability to try various approaches in seeking a satisfactory one.

Coping Principles

People who cope successfully with stress tend to adopt the following strategies. It is important to note that skilled professional help (described in more detail below) can help in implementing these strategies and maximizing their chances for success.

Cope actively. Whenever possible, stressors should be dealt with by taking direct action. Individuals must also learn to recognize what is beyond their control, however.

Manage time. Pacing oneself, refusing to take on too much, and learning to say "wait" or "no" are valuable ways of reducing stress.

Regulate the stress. Stressful information can be handled better in manageable amounts and at manageable intervals. For example, a distant goal can be redefined as a number of short-term objectives. A stressful situation often can be broken down into units, to be dealt with separately. Or, if there are several concurrent stressful events, possibly they can be faced one at a time.

Identify priorities. Long- and short-term priorities can be distinguished from one another and a realistic, flexible plan of action set up. From time to time, and as dispassionately as possible, the plan should be reevaluated.

Make contact. In times of stress, human contacts are helpful in sorting out priorities and making choices.

Refuse to admit defeat, and rely on others. Studies of people who have survived situations of extreme stress or danger show that two further coping strategies were of particular importance to them: a refusal to admit defeat and a reliance on the support of others. Both strategies have been found, for example, in those who survived the Nazi death camps. A notable feature of the support system in this group was the exchanging of gifts—insignificant except for the message of caring that they conveyed.

Although little is known about the underlying processes by which social support affects health, that it plays an important role in protecting people from the effects of stress has been well demonstrated. It may act as a buffer against the destructive effect of adverse events, or it may have an intrinsic positive effect. Another possibility is that lack of support itself may be a stressor.

TYPE A BEHAVIOR AND STRESS

The term "Type A behavior" was coined by two California heart specialists, Drs. Meyer Friedman and Ray Rosenman, to describe a behavior pattern shared by many of their heart-attack patients. Type A behavior, they wrote, is "an action-emotion complex that can be observed in any person who is aggressively involved in a chronic, incessant struggle to achieve more and more in less and less time, and if required to do so, against the opposing efforts of other things and other persons." Type A people are always in a hurry, often doing or thinking two or more things simultaneously, and creating deadlines where none exist. They tend to be aggressive and hostile, frequently challenging and competing with others. They are prone to speaking explosively, dominate conversations, and impatiently finish other people's sentences. Type Bs, in contrast, are more relaxed, less competitive, less driven by "hurry sickness" and the desire to achieve, and, very importantly, less susceptible to heart attacks. Friedman and Rosenman suggested that Type A behavior is associated with high levels of the so-called stress hormones cortisol, epinephrine, and norepinephrine. They noted also that Type As tend to have an excessive amount of insulin in their bloodstream and take much longer to rid themselves of dietary cholesterol after a meal than do Type Bs. These Type A physiological changes could produce narrowed blood vessels and increase the deposits of plaque on the vessel walls, leading to heart attack.

Recent research has attempted to identify the most damaging component or components in the Type A behavior pattern. Rather than the stress-related time urgency characteristic of Type A behavior, it appears that it is free-floating hostility—described by Friedman as "a permanently indwelling anger that shows itself with ever greater frequency in response to increasingly trivial happenings"—that is the major contributing factor in heart disease. This finding notwithstanding, it is clear that Type A behavior is closely associated with a stressful lifestyle.

Changing Type A Behavior

According to Friedman and Rosenman, the goal is not to change the personality of a Type A person but, rather, to eliminate the destructive components of the behavior. Attempts to modify Type A behavior are best tried in a group setting, with the guidance of a trained professional. However, such a group may not be available, or may be accessible only to those who have already suffered a heart attack. Under such circumstances, someone who recognizes a propensity to Type A behavior in him- or herself might usefully note these guidelines:

- Evaluate your strengths and weaknesses. Ask yourself whether your real interests are being satisfied and your abilities realized.
- Establish realistic long-term goals for your working and private lives and review these goals frequently.
- Regularly give time to pursuits unrelated to your vocation. Learn to recognize the value of rituals and tradition. Learn to enjoy time alone.
- Manage your time so that you are not competing against the clock. Revise your daily activities so that there is more than enough time for things that are important; eliminate activities that do not make a contribution to your well-being.
- Set priorities. Learn to delegate responsibility and to say "no."
- Avoid the people and situations that provoke your hostility. If avoiding them is not possible, call on your humor and good sense.
- Forget the "standards of excellence" that are in fact excuses for anger at those who will inevitably fail to live up to them.
- Learn to recognize and accept calmly those anger-provoking situations that you cannot control.
- Smile at other people and laugh at yourself.

Adapted with permission from Meyer Friedman and Ray Rosenman, *Type A Behavior and Your Heart* (New York: Alfred A. Knopf, 1974).

Social support allows someone to know that he or she is cared for, is esteemed and valued, and is a member of a network of communication and mutual obligation. The sources of such support may be family members, friends and neighbors, a person's supervisor or co-workers, health professionals, or a self-help group. Accumulating evidence suggests that, when people are undergoing severe distress, those who have had similar experiences are in a unique position to provide effective support.

Stress Management Programs

Many self-help books have been published on the topic of stress reduction. Typically, they recommend exercise, dietary modification, hobbies, or confiding in friends as well as more sweeping lifestyle changes as ways of combating stress. While these publications may be helpful to people who need to manage light stress loads, most people who suffer severe chronic stress do not achieve much success with self-help approaches.

There are many reasons for this. For one, chronic stress can develop slowly and insidiously so that the original stressors are no longer clearly recognizable; thus, people often lack insight into the real causes of their stress reactions. Further, an individual's motivation to lead the kind of life that has resulted in stress may be so deep-rooted or complex that it can override even the most conscientious efforts to reform. Another reason that self-help approaches may fail is that economic, vocational, or family pressures may counteract the individual's efforts to lighten the stress burden.

Responding to the widespread personal, physical, social, and economic costs associated with stress, clinicians have developed a number of direct, short-term techniques for dealing with the problem. Some are designed to provide relief from subjective distress, while others teach improved ways of dealing with stressors. Although they have been shown to be effective over the short term, as yet their long-term effectiveness has not been demonstrated with certainty.

Combinations of these techniques are often taught in comprehensive stress management programs. Because such programs are usually administered in a series of group sessions lasting over a period of weeks, they are usually quite affordable. More and more hospitals are offering stress management programs through their psychiatry or psychology departments. At the Columbia-Presbyterian Medical Center, for example, this program is offered within the Behavioral Medicine Program, which is designed specifically to teach the use of psychological techniques for promoting health and managing medical problems. Independent professionals working in private practice also are increasingly skilled in teaching stress management techniques.

Stress management programs typically begin with an assessment of an individual's stress problems and his or her coping deficiencies and potentials. Because stress management is not intended to help with more serious psychological disturbances, individuals with such problems will be screened out for

SUCCESSFUL LIFE-CHANGE MANAGEMENT: A CASE HISTORY

Mrs. G., an accountant, was in her late 50s. Her family doctor, who was seeing her for her low back pain, observed symptoms of depression and referred her to a psychotherapist.

In the course of the first few sessions, it became clear to the therapist that Mrs. G. was suffering from chronic stress buildup, manifesting itself as depression. The stressors in her life were numerous and interrelated. During the previous year, both her father and her husband had died, the latter after a long illness. She had been left with a pile of debts, a large house that was difficult to maintain and expensive to run, and a host of legal and practical responsibilities that were new to her, as previously her husband had handled them. As a widow, Mrs. G. also faced the task of redefining her relationships with those friends who had remained in touch (many had drifted away during Mr. G.'s illness) and with family members, whom she found cold and unsupportive. There was the further question of whether she should continue to work or take early retirement. And, as if she needed any further stressor in her life, her family doctor insisted that she lose at least 30 pounds, because her excess weight was exacerbating her back problem.

With the therapist's guidance, Mrs. G. began to manage the changes that had come into her life. First, she sold the house and moved into a nearby apartment building. The sale and the move introduced additional stress, but there were many immediate compensations: Mrs. G. no longer had the burden of looking after the house; in her new surroundings, she was not reminded of her husband at every turn; her financial situation improved. She also soon found that there were many people of her own age in the building. She began to make new friends, took up bridge again after a gap of years, and started to walk regularly for exercise and weight reduction. Needing something to love and care for, she adopted a cat.

During these months of change, Mrs. G.'s depression began to lift. She was able to resolve with equanimity the career problem that she had "put on the back burner." She decided to continue working because, as she said with a laugh, "If I retire, there will be too much time for moping—as opposed to coping!"

referral to more appropriate, specific therapies. (See "Psychotherapy for Stress and for the Psychiatric Stress Disorders," beginning on page 362.) Then, depending on the results of the assessment, a number of different coping techniques (some of which are described next) may be taught.

Relaxation Techniques

Mental or deep-muscle relaxation can help to moderate feelings of tension and tame the physical reactions characteristic of the stress response. Learning to relax at will may well be the first step in prevention of stress disorders.

Dr. Herbert Benson of Harvard University has described an innate "relaxation response" that can be elicited to counteract the increased activity of the autonomic nervous system that occurs with stress. The relaxation response is characterized by decreased heartbeat and respiration rate, lowered metabolic rate, and lowered blood pressure. The technique Benson recommends to elicit this response is simple, straightforward, and easily learned, although it is not recommended without supervision for all individuals. (See the box on this page.)

Research by Benson and his colleagues suggests that in order to achieve long-term benefits, such as reduced blood pressure and enhanced immune response, relaxation must be practiced on a regular basis over a period of time. However, once learned, the technique may also be called upon as needed to induce "quick relaxation" to help cope with stressful situations.

Another relaxation technique often taught in stress management programs is "progressive relaxation," developed by Dr. Edmund Jacobson in the 1930s. Jacobson had observed that anxiety states and similar conditions were often accompanied by contraction of the skeletal muscles and that his patients were unaware of this muscle tension. The Jacobson technique involves actively tensing and then relaxing different muscle groups in order to increase awareness of both tension and relaxation. With this training, stress can be recognized early and countered with a relaxed state.

Controlled Breathing

Rapid breathing is part of the stress reaction and becomes a vicious circle. "Overbreathing" causes the

---

RELAX!

- Sit in a comfortable position in a quiet environment, and with the eyes closed.
- Consciously relax all the muscles, beginning with the feet and ending with the forehead.
- Breathe naturally and easily through the nose, silently repeating the word "one" (or some other word, or a brief phrase or prayer) with each exhalation.
- Concentrate on the rhythm of the breathing and the regular silent repetition. If distracting thoughts or images intrude, adopt a passive attitude: Let them pass and return to the repetition.
- Continue for 10 to 20 minutes.

---

body automatically to activate regulatory mechanisms that can cause stresslike symptoms, including light-headedness, dizziness, and tingling and coldness of the extremities. Surprisingly, the symptoms of overbreathing, including shortness of breath, may be experienced as oxygen deficiency, causing the individual to breathe even more rapidly and thereby worsen the condition, sometimes to the point of panic. To deal with this stress-related sequence of symptoms, individuals can be taught to pace their respiratory rate. Diaphragmatic breathing ("belly-" as opposed to "chest-" breathing) further enhances the effects of controlled breathing.

Biofeedback Training

Effective biofeedback training combines general deep-relaxation techniques with specific biological feedback by way of electronic monitoring equipment. Biological phenomena such as pulse rate and muscle tension are measured and the information simultaneously displayed, either visually or audibly. Guided by the electronic feedback, the trainee learns, through a process of trial and error, to control physical responses to stress that normally are involuntary. With this training, and in a relatively short time, many people learn to lower their heart rate and blood pressure, prevent migraine headache, and ameliorate irritable bowel syndrome—to name some of the physical problems associated with the stress response that are amenable to the biofeedback approach.

Cognitive Restructuring

Cognitive restructuring assumes that stress commonly results from certain patterns of thinking, especially negative thinking, and teaches individuals to think more realistically about stressors. For instance, to reduce feelings of time urgency, an individual might be taught to "think twice" about the boss's request to get a job done "as soon as possible." The employee can learn to question whether such instructions mean "when you can get to it" rather than the pressure-filled "right away!"

Induced Imagery Techniques

Positive fantasies can have a profound effect on emotions and behavior. Clinically, induced imagery techniques have long been used in hypnosis and behavior therapy. Many people, for example, have been helped to reduce public speaking anxiety and to perform more effectively through fantasy rehearsals and imagining successful outcomes. Imagery techniques, especially in conjunction with relaxation, can help individuals develop stress-reducing feelings of mastery over the perceptions of threat and danger that so often accompany the stress reaction.

Exercise

Exercise provides a way to discharge tension, resulting in heightened feelings of well-being. Moreover, scientists have found that regular aerobic exercise can reduce the levels of stress-related hormones in the body. In addition, physical fitness may reduce the cardiovascular component—the rise in blood pressure and heart rate—of an individual's stress reaction.

Diet

When stress is prolonged, and especially when physical action is not an appropriate response to the stressor, the body quickly can become drained of its reserves. Body protein, drawn chiefly from the muscles, will be used to provide energy. Calcium will be lost from the bones, and, as the result of sodium retention, blood levels of potassium will fall. A balanced diet combined with exercise to help maintain bone and muscle is therefore a basic prescription in stress management.

Other nutrients that may be depleted are the water-soluble vitamins—vitamin C and the B vitamins—and approximately two dozen minerals. The appetite usually is suppressed during severe stress, as part of the body's adaptive response. Moreover, the food that is eaten may not be digested and absorbed properly, as a result of the redirection of blood to the muscles. If caloric intake is less than 1,200 to 1,500 calories, a balanced vitamin-mineral supplement is sometimes recommended.

While some people undergoing stress find it difficult to eat adequately, others eat too much. The explanation for "stress-eating" may lie partly in the fact that high-carbohydrate foods—often the first choice of people under stress—bring about a rise in the level of the brain chemical serotonin, which has a soothing effect on the body. Those who tend to respond to stress by overeating can be guided to find some other way of dealing with the discomfort—exercise, for example, or the pursuit of a hobby.

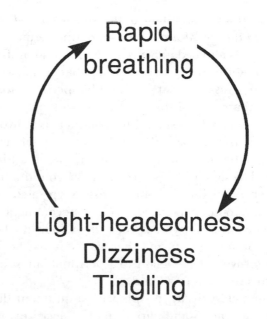

BREATHING AND STRESS REACTION

**Figure 24.1:** **Rapid breathing is part of the stress reaction; it can cause light-headedness, dizziness, and tingling in the hands and feet. The response is often to breathe even more rapidly, causing the symptoms to worsen.**

PSYCHOTHERAPY FOR STRESS AND FOR THE PSYCHIATRIC STRESS DISORDERS

Short-term group stress management programs are designed for the "average" member and do not always address adequately the needs of all members. Moreover, a group coping skills approach is not always suitable for stress-related problems, including two psychiatric syndromes: adjustment disorder and post-traumatic stress disorder. In these as well as other psychiatric disorders, the psychological symptoms may be severe, even disabling; a pervasive dysfunctional self-defeating motivational pattern may be apparent; the problem may be chronic and deeply entrenched; or the problem may be supported by factors beyond an individual's control. Such stress-related problems are treated more appropriately with longer-term intensive psychotherapy, appropriate medication, or a combination of both.

Adjustment Disorders

The third revised edition of the *Diagnostic and Statistical Manual of Mental Disorders* defines adjustment disorder as a maladaptive reaction to an identifiable psychological stressor, or stressors, that occurs within three months of the stressor and has persisted for no longer than six months.

There may be a single stressor, such as a divorce, or many stressors, as is the case in ongoing family difficulty. The stressor may recur, as in a business marked by seasonal crises, or it may be continuous, as with chronic illness. Some stressors are associated with developmental stages, such as becoming a parent. The syndrome can affect a single individual or a group or community; in other words, it may be seen in an individual's reaction to a personal illness or in a town's reaction to a flood.

Characteristically, people with adjustment disorder experience some impairment of social or occupational functioning, or symptoms that exceed the normal and expectable reaction to a stressful event. For example, although it is common for people who are undergoing divorce to feel angry, sad, and somewhat confused about their present and future, a person who had extensive difficulty concentrating at work would be suffering from an adjustment disorder. The disturbance generally improves when the individual has achieved a new level of adaptation.

Treatment for adjustment disorders can include a wide range of psychotherapeutic interventions depending on the symptoms (such as anxiety, depression, or antisocial behavior) and whether the individual has underlying chronic difficulties (such as a mood disorder or a physical illness) that may be related to the current problem.

Post–Traumatic Stress Disorder

While some stressors are predictably part of most people's lives—for example, bereavement or chronic illness—others lie outside the range of these common experiences. These include hurricanes, floods, and other natural disasters; airplane accidents and car crashes where there is considerable injury; rape and assault; and armed combat, torture, and existence in a death camp. Such traumatic events would produce distress in almost everyone of any age. In some, they give rise to a syndrome known as post-traumatic stress disorder (PTSD).

The symptoms of PTSD usually begin shortly after the stressful event. A major symptom is the reexperiencing of the event in painful memories, dreams, or nightmares. Another major symptom is what has been called "psychic numbing" or "emotional anesthesia." Sufferers exhibit a pervasive feeling of being detached from other people, from the outside world, and from activities that used to be enjoyable. They also have a greatly diminished ability to experience emotion, especially tenderness and the feelings associated with intimacy and sex. Other symptoms reflect an overaroused autonomic nervous system. Sufferers have difficulty falling asleep or staying asleep; they are keyed up and their startle response is heightened.

Anxiety and depression are common in those with PTSD. Irritability is a further problem. Guilt about surviving when others did not, and about the behavior that was necessary for survival, may be constant and painful. Some of those with this disorder turn to alcohol or drugs for escape; others may become self-defeating or suicidal.

People with PTSD often experience a worsening of their symptoms when they find themselves in situations that resemble the original trauma or that may be taken as symbols of it—for example, a spell of hot, humid weather for a Vietnam veteran or a dark street for a woman who has been raped. In avoiding, or attempting to avoid, such situations, an individual's ability to function socially and at work may be impaired severely.

If such functional impairment occurs, or if the symptoms are severe and prolonged, some form of psychotherapeutic treatment is indicated. With psychodynamic psychotherapy, the individual has the opportunity to discuss the event, relive it, and achieve a better understanding of why it has triggered so severe a psychological and physiological reaction. Cognitive-behavioral techniques may be used to reduce anxiety and depression, aid with insomnia, and treat any phobic symptoms that may have developed. As with other stress problems, tranquilizers such as benzodiazepines (including Xanax, for example) may be useful in decreasing symptoms, but they must be used under medical supervision in order to avoid dependency. In those with depression, antidepressant medication also may prove useful.

How the Psychotherapies Combat Stress

The psychotherapeutic approaches are discussed at length in chapter 4. A brief look at how the common approaches help relieve stress and stress-induced reactions follows.

Psychodynamic (Psychoanalytic) Therapy

Psychodynamic psychotherapists take the view that psychological problems, including problems in coping with stress, typically result from personality vulnerabilities dating back to childhood. Such vulnerabilities may be caused by adverse childhood events, negative parenting experiences, or a poor "fit" between parent and child. They exist relatively silently within the personality until a particular stressor activates them, causing symptoms of distress.

An example is the individual who responds to the loss of a loved one with protracted and pervasive anxiety, depression, or social withdrawal. From a psychodynamic point of view, such a person might be responding with the reactivated anguish of childhood loss, or with anxiety engendered by a relationship with an overprotective parent or by some inadequately resolved separation early in life. Gaining insight into the problem, coupled with a positive relationship with the therapist, should enable such a person to resolve or at least modify these vulnerabilities and thus cope more effectively.

Cognitive–Behavioral Therapy

In a relatively short-term therapy, cognitive-behavioral therapists attempt to promote positive coping skills in order to replace counterproductive ones. Generally this approach, in contrast with psychodynamic therapy, emphasizes the present almost exclusively. Cognitive-behavioral therapists hold that faulty beliefs or ways of thinking contribute to the maintenance of maladaptive behavior patterns and that these behavior patterns in turn play a role in creating or perpetuating the damaging effects of stressors.

In cognitive-behavioral therapy, people learn to identify and modify their dysfunctional ways of thinking about or behaving toward stressors, so that they may alter their emotional responses. Therapists rely on self-monitoring techniques such as diary-keeping to identify ways of thinking that are counterproductive. New behaviors often are rehearsed or role-played in therapy sessions and then attempted "by prescription" in order to develop improved coping strategies.

Medication

Medications are available to ease the suffering of an individual in acute distress. If appropriately used, they can serve a useful function. Such medications must be used under medical supervision and only on a short-term basis because some produce lethargy and many have an addictive potential. For individuals under chronic stress, however, the various nonpharmacological techniques described are the better approaches. There is, after all, no "cure" for the stressful situations that face all individuals throughout life. People can, however, work to eliminate the patterns within themselves that worsen or complicate the impact of stress. People also can learn, with or without help, to manage the common life events that produce stress and to deal with the impact of the inevitable blows.

25

Emotional Crises

Robert E. Feinstein, M.D.

Normally most people feel a sense of balance between themselves and the environment. They feel reasonably calm, alert, and able to function in their daily routines. Then something happens—a job loss, a relationship breakup, an illness in the family—or the stresses of life pile up, and suddenly the normal order of life is shattered. In a state of emotional crisis, anyone will feel panicked, helpless, overwhelmed, and unable to carry out even basic activities such as working, shopping, or socializing—temporarily.

This crisis state is a reaction to specific stresses in an individual's life. It is a *normal* response to troubling events, not a sign of mental illness. Indeed, almost everyone experiences a crisis at some time in life,

whether it is precipitated by a typical life experience such as leaving home for the first time, by a trauma such as the death of a child, or by an extraordinary national tragedy such as the space shuttle explosion. Everyone is vulnerable to emotional crisis, although the events that trigger it vary from individual to individual. Disasters such as an airplane crash, flood, mass murder, or war are traumatic enough to precipitate a crisis in almost anyone. (See the box on page 368.)

Most people recover spontaneously from a crisis within a short period of time, often feeling that they have grown from the experience. Others may need professional help in order to get their lives back in balance.

WHAT IS A CRISIS? HOW IS IT TRIGGERED?

Mental health practitioners since Freud have recognized that severe trauma produces characteristic psychological reactions. In the 1940s, for example,

psychiatrist Eric Lindemann studied individuals who lost family members in Boston's Coconut Grove fire, which claimed 500 lives. Lindemann discovered that

g such a disaster, normal people experience
ional crisis of pain, confusion, anxiety, and
ry difficulty in daily functioning that rarely
er than six weeks. He also observed that the
f the reaction is *not* related primarily to pre-
hiatric illness but rather to the specific cir-
es that trigger the crisis.

1960s psychiatrist Gerald Caplan, synthe-
vork of his predecessors, defined a crisis as
onal psychological upheaval, precipitated
r or hazard, which produces such emo-
oil that a person temporarily is unable to
, or function normally. Caplan demonstrated that most crises resolve in about six weeks,
with four possible outcomes: People come through
their trauma with an improved ability to meet future
challenges; they return to their previous level of
functioning; they are able to function as well as
before but will be susceptible to further crises; or
they stabilize at a lower level of functioning.

Whether individuals navigate the emotional
storm on their own or with professional help, the
evolution and outcome of the crisis will depend on
the following five factors: the severity of the trauma
or precipitant; the personalized meaning of the
event; the strength of the support network of family
and friends; individual coping styles and adaptability;
and, in some cases, preexisting personality patterns
or mental disorders.

Precipitants and Stressors

Sometimes the cause of a crisis is obvious, such as a
fire, a rape, a kidnapping, or another shocking experience. More often emotional crises are precipitated
by a combination of stressful circumstances. These
so-called stressors, or precipitants, can be real-life
events or disturbing ideas or feelings but are typically
a combination of both.

The onset of a crisis is usually immediate—either
the same day or within several days of the precipitating events—and, less commonly, within six weeks.
Events from long ago can be a factor in a new crisis if
they are linked to a past emotional trauma that never
fully healed.

Stressful Life Events
The well-known Social Readjustment Rating Scale by
Holmes and Rahe (presented in chapter 24, page
356) lists 43 typical negative and positive life events
likely to cause significant upheaval in normal people.

They range in severity from death of a spouse (1) and
divorce (2), through trouble with in-laws (24) and
outstanding personal achievement (25), to Christmas (42) and minor violations of the law (43). Of
course, a relatively low-stress event such as a vacation
or an argument with a co-worker isn't likely to trigger
a crisis in and of itself. But if a number of stresses
occur together, or if the event has special meaning
for the person (as is discussed later), a crisis can
develop.

Developmental Conflicts
In the 1960s psychoanalyst Erik Erikson observed
that people routinely experience a crisis when they
try to resolve the normal developmental issues that
arise as they progress through life. For example, a
child swings between trust versus mistrust; an adolescent struggles toward a clear identity; an adult
grapples with procreativity and creativity versus self-
absorption and stagnation. Erikson postulated eight
critical phases, but other theorists expanded his idea
of developmental crises to include key turning
points such as marriage, childbirth, the departure of
the last child from home (the "empty nest syndrome"), the "midlife" crisis, and retirement.

People can juggle the emotional conflicts of each
stage for years without experiencing outward disruption. However, issues that are not worked through at
the appropriate stage of development tend to resur-
face as the themes of crises later in life. For example,
a 55-year-old man who had lived with his widowed
mother until her death found himself in crisis over
becoming independent and taking charge of his
own life for the first time—a crisis most people experience in late adolescence. Similarly, a middle-age
man experienced a midlife crisis when he began an
extramarital affair that threatened to destroy both
his family and his career. The affair triggered the crisis, but the underlying emotional issue was his regret
over opportunities he felt he had missed in his
youth.

Psychological "Events"
Sometimes the events precipitating a crisis are
obscure because they are largely internal experiences, such as a disturbing thought or dream or an
overwhelming impulse to hurt oneself or someone
else. Usually it is such thoughts together with outward events that trigger a crisis. Jane C., a 25-year-old
pregnant woman, seemingly out of nowhere began
having obsessive thoughts of harming her mother.

The idea first occurred to her two days before her husband was due to leave on an overnight business trip. Terrified by these thoughts, unlike any she remembered ever having before, Mrs. C. asked her husband to cancel his trip and take her to the doctor. The external stressors (her pregnancy and her husband's imminent departure) plus the terrifying internal impulse to hurt her mother combined to create an acute crisis.

The Personalized Meaning of the Stressor

Events affect individuals differently, depending how a person interprets or adds meaning to them, as Mrs. C.'s case shows. Even a mild stressor can produce a crisis if it has some special significance to the individual. Most people would not consider a spouse's overnight business trip to be a very distressing event, but to Mrs. C., who was expecting her third child, the impending separation was catastrophic. As she told the psychiatrist to whom her doctor referred her, she had an "inexplicable" feeling that the husband was being unfaithful, despite the fact that he denied ever having an affair and was angry at her for even thinking it.

Therapy revealed the personal significance of these events. Mrs. C.'s father had abandoned his family "inexplicably" when her mother, like Mrs. C. now, was 25 years old and pregnant for the third time—with Mrs. C. Her father never returned, and Mrs. C. never knew why. Not surprisingly, she felt unwanted and unloved as a child, and now she felt ambivalent about the birth of her own third child. Mrs. C. associated her husband's trip in the middle of her third pregnancy with her worst fears—that her husband, like her father, would abandon her and that she would wind up feeling useless and bitter, as her mother did. This triggered old resentments toward her mother and raised suspicions about her husband's fidelity.

This sequence of current events—the pregnancy, the husband leaving, the murderous and jealous feelings—was filtered through Mrs. C.'s past experience and personalized with meaning, leading to her distorted interpretation and precipitating a crisis.

Sometimes people become deeply upset by world events that seem not to affect them directly, such as the death of Martin Luther King, Jr., or John Lennon, the Chernobyl nuclear disaster, or the *Challenger* space shuttle disaster. Again, such incidents precipitate severe personal crises because of their special meaning to an individual. For example, they may symbolize the demise of hopes and ideals or reawaken feelings associated with past unresolved traumas.

The Support Network

Virtually everyone lives within a social network, large or small, of family, friends, neighbors, lovers, coworkers, shopkeepers—the people with whom one interacts daily. That network generally encompasses an array of resources for living, such as work, housing, food, medical care, recreation, and so on.

The disruption of this support network through illness, divorce, personal catastrophe, or simply moving away can precipitate a crisis. Indeed, a minor disturbance in a small or loosely formed support system can produce acute problems. Thus, a housebound elderly woman, who has no family or friends and no telephone, can experience a major crisis when her home health aide misses an appointed visit.

On the other hand, a strong social support system can make a great difference in the development and outcome of a crisis, and to some extent provides protection against stressful life events. Thus, a woman who has close ties to her family and community can survive a divorce without excessive turmoil because of support from her social network. A man who suddenly loses his job copes without crisis because he has a working spouse and money in the bank.

In Mrs. C.'s case, her husband was very understanding (he canceled his trip and even attended her initial therapy sessions), and she had close women friends in whom she could confide. Their availability and support minimized the severity of her crisis and contributed to her successful recovery. However, had her husband left on his trip with no concern, or had he actually abandoned her, Mrs. C. might have suffered a more severe trauma.

Coping Style and Problem-solving Skills

Another important influence on the severity and outcome of a crisis is the effectiveness and flexibility of coping styles, defenses, and adaptations to reality—people's individual ways of reacting to and dealing with stress and conflict. Some people cope by tackling challenges head on, while others deny there is a problem or refuse to think about it, at least right away. Additional styles include imitating others' successful strategies and relying on a support network for help. While each of these ways of coping may work in some situations, one habitual mode of reacting usually will not be successful all the time. Indeed, people who have rigid coping styles may be predisposed to crises, particularly under stressful circumstances.

For example, John S., a young advertising executive, always responded to difficulty on his new job by asking his boss what to do. This coping style worked well for him until his boss took a sudden sick leave. With his boss gone and no other support network, Mr. S. felt unable to gather data for an important client report. He subsequently lost the account and began to fear for his job. His feelings of helplessness and failure began to pervade his life, causing him to become sexually impotent and paralyzing him at work. Unable to perform even routine tasks, Mr. S. was in a state of crisis. He sought help and resolved his difficulty. (See page 370.)

On the other hand, people who have flexible, effective coping styles and well-developed problem-solving skills may be less susceptible to emotional crises when they are under pressure. Had Mr. S. been better able to establish a support network or to find resources on his own, he could have avoided the upheaval precipitated by his boss's illness.

Adaptation

Gerald Caplan stressed the importance of one's ability to adapt to reality in preventing or resolving a crisis. The process of adaptation is not very different from developing flexible coping styles and new skills. However, it is an ability that is most necessary when dealing with more permanent and pervasive life changes, such as those associated with long-term developmental issues. For example, a working woman who has her first child must learn over time to be comfortable as a mother; to adjust to "family life," including a different relationship to her spouse, and perhaps to parents and in-laws; and to juggle the conflicts between home and career. An adaptable person—one who can anticipate and plan for potential problems and modify goals to suit new life circumstances—is more likely to handle the constant demands of parenthood or other significant life change without crisis.

Personality and Psychiatric Factors

A preexisting personality style or psychiatric condition can play a role in crisis development. Consider the case of David B., an executive in a major chemical corporation, who suffered from obsessive-compulsive personality disorder. (See chapter 13.) Always on time, extremely organized and competent, Mr. B. did so well that he was promoted to head of his department—despite the fact that he was also stubborn, rigid in his thinking, and generally unaware of and unable to express his feelings. His new position demanded heavy client contact and the development of new business, tasks that called for a sociable, flexible person who could make others feel at ease, who could deal successfully with many different types of people, and who could make convincing, dynamic presentations. Mr. B.'s lack of these qualities and inability to change caused him to do poorly. His failure upset him so much that he became totally unable to work, and he found himself in crisis.

Chronic psychiatric problems were also a factor in the case of Aaron D., a mentally retarded boy who became extremely violent after his radio was stolen. For most people, the theft of a radio would be a minor stressor, yet to Aaron, it was akin to the loss of his favorite and only companion. The low intelligence and lack of verbal skills directly associated with his disability predisposed him to develop a crisis of violence.

TREATMENT IN A CRISIS

Crisis intervention or crisis therapy is a brief form of treatment that is particularly effective in psychiatric emergencies or disasters, or when a person is trapped in painful life circumstances, such as loss of a spouse and of a means of support. It is used when treatment must be immediate and flexible and offer pragmatic solutions, and when the cost of treatment is a major consideration. For those with psychological conflicts, personality problems, or other long-standing conditions, crisis treatment is at best only an adjunct to other forms of therapy.

During World War I, British military surgeon Thomas Salmon discovered the fundamentals of crisis treatment in his study of why French soldiers suffered fewer psychological casualties of war than did British soldiers. He found four factors that seemed to

SURVIVING DISASTER: THE CASE OF THE K. FAMILY

During a return flight from a family vacation, the K. family—husband, wife, and six-year-old son—heard the flight attendant announce that their plane was in trouble and that passengers should prepare for a crash landing. "Nonsense—nothing can happen to my family," thought Mr. K. Suddenly bewildered, he unbuckled his seat belt and began to get up. Mrs. K. remained calm and efficient. She buckled her son's seat belt and then her own. She reached for her husband and pulled him back into his seat. She instructed her son and husband to brace themselves for the crash by bending over and holding their knees. Mr. K. followed his wife's instructions while in a daze. He later said, "I was shocked, stunned, unable to get my mind in gear. I was watching my wife. I simply didn't know what to do or think." Totally involved in her actions, Mrs. K. showed no fear or confusion.

The plane crashed and caught fire. Mrs. K. was killed. In the hour that followed the crash, Mr. K. was in shock as he held his whimpering son. Neither was badly hurt.

In the week that followed, although he was able to plan the funeral and to bury his wife, Mr. K. pushed the events of the crash from his mind (using the psychological defense of denial). He went to live with his parents, who were helping him care for his son.

Over the next month, Mr. K.'s disbelief and denial gradually gave way to grief. He became filled with self-recriminations—if only he had been more level-headed, his wife would have survived, he believed. He also found himself inexplicably angry at his son, although he realized his feelings made no sense. Mr. K. sought medical attention for many troublesome aches and pains, but no physical cause was ever found. He became preoccupied with images of the disaster, envisioning his wife being consumed by fire.

Six weeks after the disaster he returned to work. He could perform his job but he felt numb. After work, he felt alternating periods of numbness, grief, and self-recrimination. Gradually over many weeks, he began to recover his composure, although he was plagued by nightmares about the disaster. He real-

ized that he had "sort of forgotten" about his son's suffering, so preoccupied had he been with his own loss. He began to be more attentive to the boy.

Over the next year, Mr. K. returned to his previous level of functioning. He continued to relive aspects of the disaster and of his wife's death, especially on their anniversary and during the Christmas holidays.

How someone will react during a disaster is not really predictable based on psychological makeup. It is well known, for example, that a person with schizophrenia may act clearly and lucidly during a disaster, whereas previously stable individuals may unravel completely during these extreme events. Seventy-five percent of those who survive disasters report experiences similar to those of Mr. K.: the confusion, bewilderment, and paralysis of action. The other 25 percent respond like Mrs. K.: cool, action-oriented, without signs of fear. Everyone experiencing a disaster will suffer severe emotional turmoil and brief impaired functioning. Individuals who respond adaptively during a disaster generally will recover more easily.

Psychological recovery also will depend on survivors' capacity to grieve, the presence or absence of physical injury or disability from the disaster, the coping style people use to process the events, and the nature of the support system after the disaster. Mr. K. used denial initially, which, at the beginning, was helpful in dealing with the acute shock. However, as time progressed, his denial became less adaptively helpful to him and his son. Later he was able to grieve and to talk about the events, his nightmares and self-recriminations. He worked through the experience and was able to resume his normal functioning at work and with his son and to begin to rebuild his life.

Disasters such as earthquakes and floods that destroy the fabric of entire communities and drastically alter inhabitants' lifestyles tend to have the most long-lasting effects on survivors. Recovery from those mass disasters can be very difficult and require much time. Victims may be vulnerable to post-traumatic stress disorder (see chapter 24) in the future.

account for the French advantage: French soldiers were told that they could expect to recover from their psychological trauma; they received immediate psychological help; treatment was close to the front; and they were returned to battle as quickly as possible. These principles became the cornerstones of modern crisis intervention, which aims to provide immediate treatment to crisis victims while they continue to live at home and which stresses the likelihood of recovery and a speedy return to normal life.

Today crisis intervention treatment generally lasts two to six weeks. Sessions usually are held two to three times in the first week, with one or two follow-up sessions each week thereafter—approximately five to 10 sessions in all. The first session may last several hours, with follow-up meetings lasting 45 minutes to two hours.

TYPES OF PROBLEMS TREATED BY CRISIS INTERVENTION

- Acute grief
- Suicidal behaviors or thoughts
- Acute medical problems (particularly organic problems such as dementia, which are confused with emotional disorders)
- Intrapsychic crises (acute problems originating in psychological conflicts, involving disturbances of mood, perception, or thinking, or physical problems with no organic basis)
- Violence (including homicide, assault, spouse abuse, child abuse, rape, incest, and the like)
- Family crises (especially deaths, divorce, separations, drug addiction)
- Family developmental crises (such as the "empty nest syndrome," midlife crisis, or a crisis of retirement)
- Individual developmental crises (adolescence, marriage, birth of first child, menopause, and so on)

- Interpersonal crises (acute problems with friends, lovers, and others)
- Therapeutic crises (a patient already in treatment who is not getting along with the therapist)
- Economic or financial crises (acute problems involving income loss or problems of housing, shelter, or food)
- Occupational crises (acute loss of work or school difficulties)
- Religious crises (acute crisis of faith or other problems in the religious community)
- Public crises (an acute personal crisis related to a world event, such as an environmental disaster, death of a leader or other famous person, economic depressions, and so on)

Identifying Psychiatric and Medical Emergencies

The first priority in any crisis treatment is identifying and treating psychiatric emergencies. These are immediate and life-threatening situations involving suicidal behaviors, potential violence, or the possibility of an unrelated organic problem, such as stroke, that require an immediate medical evaluation. Some medical conditions, including seizures, brain tumors, Alzheimer's disease, metabolic problems, and drug addiction, have symptoms that at first glance may be mistaken for psychiatric illness. Therefore, the crisis evaluation usually begins with a medical history including appropriate tests.

Dealing with Distress and Denial

Individuals who are in a crisis state may be in obvious psychological distress and pain. They may be crying, trembling, sitting quietly in a detached state, or completely mute. Some may be suicidal or violent. They may appear confused and bewildered, severely anxious, depressed, or occasionally even psychotic. Most likely they cannot function in their daily routine or interact normally with others.

When the emotional response seems highly volatile, the emotional level needs to be lowered before the person in crisis can explore the precipitants and their meaning. At the other end of the spectrum, some people may "seal over" the crisis, or deny that it exists, so that they don't have to experience the painful feelings. They may register the pain unconsciously perhaps as anxiety or depression, but it is not identified logically in their minds with a particular cause. In such cases, intense emotions may need to be brought to the surface before the crisis can be resolved.

Determining the Precipitants: Why Now?

In general, there is no sharp distinction between diagnosis and treatment in crisis intervention: Analysis of the problem often yields solutions as well. Thus, the clinician usually begins treatment by exploring the precipitants of the crisis: Why is it happening now? The primary focus is on the events of the last few days to six weeks in the patient's life. Past history that is not specifically related to the crisis is not explored. The therapist gathers information from the individual in crisis and, when possible, interviews family, friends, caregivers, and others in the patient's support network, such as a landlord, priest, lawyer, or teacher.

Indeed, a major part of the initial evaluation is to "map" the extent of the patient's social supports. Particularly when the crisis has no obvious precipitant, a detailed history about the nature of the support system usually reveals the cause. Rarely, except with disasters, does a single problem in a support network bring on a crisis. Typically multiple problems in social interactions and/or in the network conspire to bring on a crisis. For example, Joseph P. found himself in crisis when his wife became ill, he was laid off his job, *and* his parents retired and moved away. Sylvia R. went into crisis when her husband left her *and* she was evicted from her apartment.

People who have "sealed over" the crisis, or denied that it exists, often are surprised to discover during treatment that there had been a significant stressful event either the same day or several days before the onset of their crisis. One such case involved a teenage girl who had taken an overdose of pills after breaking up with her boyfriend and arguing with her mother. The mother went to the psychiatrist's office with the girl two days after the suicide attempt. The girl said that she had not tried to kill herself. It was "no big deal," she insisted, she had simply taken pills for a headache. In an attempt to bring the girl in touch with the feelings she had experienced two days before, the therapist asked her to recall the events of that day. When she showed little emotion, the psychiatrist asked the mother how she would have felt had her daughter died. The daughter began to sob when the mother started describing her anguish. Once the girl had opened herself up to her real emotions, it became possible to identify the problems and begin to work through the crisis.

After identifying the precipitating problems, the clinician and patient decide together which to handle immediately.

The Steps to Recovery

The focus of the remaining days or weeks of treatment is on helping the person locate strengths and return to his or her previous level of functioning.

Sometimes medication is prescribed. With the patient, the therapist may design and implement a plan of action to resolve the problems.

Learning to Cope or Adapt

If inadequate or inflexible coping styles are part of the problem, the therapist will help the patient develop a new approach to problem solving. This process may include learning necessary skills or designing detailed strategies to tackle practical problems such as obtaining food, shelter, employment, public assistance, medical care, or legal advice—or even making new friends.

A young woman who became suicidal while staying alone in her apartment during the Christmas holidays made out a plan in conjunction with her therapist to reduce her isolation. She agreed she would volunteer her services at an orphanage and invite colleagues to have lunch with her.

John S., the advertising executive mentioned on page 367 who couldn't function at work when his boss suddenly became ill, learned a whole new style of coping. Previously he had relied exclusively on his boss to answer questions or handle difficulties; now, in treatment, Mr. S. learned to find his own solutions to problems by developing a resource network. With his newfound skills, he became more confident and more self-reliant.

A person who is experiencing a developmental crisis may need to make long-range plans in addition to coping with the immediate issues. Retirees, for instance, may have to find new ways of coping with financial matters now that they're on fixed incomes, which may require learning new financial skills. They may have handled personal problems in the past by burying themselves in their work; now they will need to find more effective ways of coping.

Getting Support

Improving communication within a social support system is a mainstay of crisis treatment. Suicide attempts and domestic violence can be treated successfully in the context of crisis family therapy, which helps to increase each member's awareness of the problems within the family. A job crisis may be averted by helping the patient learn how to communicate better with the boss. In crises involving external events such as an eviction or severe financial hardship, the practitioner may direct the patient toward other sources of information or help, such as attorneys or social welfare organizations.

Often exploration of the support network reveals that individuals have many more resources available to them than they realized. For example, an adolescent girl in crisis after a severe argument with her mother was helped to realize that her grandmother could intervene and help her with her mother.

Exploring Feelings

Crises that have been precipitated in part by overwhelming thoughts or feelings may require more in-depth exploration of emotions, psychological conflicts, or maladaptive behaviors. People suffering acute grief may need help in fully expressing their feelings as they go through the stages of mourning. Those enduring a marital separation may need help in understanding the confusing and often contradictory desires to stay and to leave. Rape victims may need help in coping with the reality of physical and psychological damage—particularly feelings of fear, guilt, shame, and anger typically aroused by such a trauma.

Crisis treatment of maladaptive behaviors such as violence, abuse, or neglect often is geared toward preventing further damage. The clinician may help a person who is prone to violence to get in touch with the feelings that precipitate the behavior and then learn to substitute more adaptive behaviors, such as walking away, delaying impulsive action, verbally expressing the anger, or taking medication.

During the termination phase of crisis therapy, plans will be made for follow-up treatment if required. Some patients may enter long-term psychotherapy or return to have their medication monitored. Others may wait awhile and enter long-term or short-term treatment later. Further treatment is recommended in about half the cases because crisis therapy commonly identifies other, sometimes chronic problems that require other forms of treatment.

If the crisis treatment goes well, a patient will have improved skills and functioning. For some people, the crisis will have made them stronger and promoted growth. Ms. G. is one such example. Currently a 40-year-old attorney with one child, Ms. G. was married at age 17 to a man 10 years her senior. She was just out of high school and became pregnant almost immediately. Her husband was a successful professional who was a workaholic. Ms. G. idealized her husband as a father figure. He treated her like a little girl, often criticizing her harshly. He demanded that she entertain all his prospective clients, yet he preferred to discuss his business concerns and other important aspects of his life only with his friends. He

spent little time with their child. Sex was always on her husband's terms, and Ms. G. always felt obligated to do as he said. She couldn't wait till each sexual encounter was over.

She lived like this until she was 30, when she began to realize she was dissatisfied with her life. She tried to discuss her feelings with her husband, but Mr. G., as always, blamed her. Nonetheless, Ms. G. decided she wanted to go to college. Mr. G. became furious and subsequently had an affair.

Ms. G. went into a crisis. Her marriage was in shambles, and she felt trapped with no means of support. She became depressed and suicidal before finally entering a crisis treatment. During the brief therapy, she recognized her passivity and her tendency to want her husband to direct her life. She decided upon a divorce. She enlisted her parents for temporary financial aid, hired a divorce attorney, and subsequently went to college and then to law school. Recently she remarried. In her new marriage, to an attorney, she has a more balanced relationship. Ms. G. finds that now she is able to combat her occasional tendency to become passive. The couple enjoy their sex life and are contemplating having a child of their own.

While not everyone benefits so dramatically from crisis intervention, most people at least will be able to return to their level of functioning prior to the crisis. However, some may be so traumatized by the crisis that they can be stabilized only at a new level of lower functioning. Those people who emerge from a crisis with only a partial or incomplete resolution probably will be more susceptible to future crises precipitated by less stressful events.

Kinds of Crisis Therapy

While all crisis treatments adhere to the basic principles and techniques just discussed, many different applications are provided by people with a wide variety of skills and credentials. Most crisis treatments fall under three broad categories: individual, family-oriented, or group. One practitioner may be skilled in all three types.

Individual therapy. Individual crisis treatment often is appropriate when there are personal psychological issues that need exploration or require privacy or confidentiality, or when there is no support network.

Family therapy. Many practitioners feel that family crisis therapy is the treatment of choice when dealing with suicidal or violent behaviors, or when complex medical issues are involved. Family therapy must be coordinated with individual evaluation and care. It is the most effective treatment for problems within families or when much help is required from the support network. Practitioners should be trained in both crisis and family treatment.

Group treatment. The number of groups for various kinds of stress is growing. Group treatments are based on the idea that people who undergo similar severe traumas will be able to understand and help others with similar problems. Such groups may be organized by professionals or by former patients and usually revolve around specific events or issues, such as suicide, incest, divorce, drug addiction, and the like. Members share experiences, feelings, coping styles, and skills for dealing with specific situations.

Disaster self-help groups. People who have lost loved ones through disasters have begun to form self-help support groups to assist others in similar situations. One such group, Compassionate Friends, has more than 600 chapters nationwide.

Some groups have emerged after specific disasters. Relatives of the 156 passengers who died in a crash on a plane flying from Detroit to Phoenix in 1987 formed an organization called "Flight 255—The Spirit Lives On." Members of this group go to the scene of other flight disasters to offer solace and practical information to others involved in such a tragedy.

Where to Get Help

Information and referrals generally are available through psychiatric facilities, social agencies, hospital or emergency rooms, suicide and rape hotlines, or private doctors. Specialized local social service agencies may provide direct assistance or referrals, particularly in cases of domestic violence, child abuse, incest, homelessness, or other family crises. Rape crisis centers and shelters for battered women are also established in many cities. The local chapter of Alcoholics Anonymous or Narcotics Anonymous is a good resource for information regarding substance abuse crises. Police and fire departments, the Red Cross, and local hospitals are the best referral sources for disaster relief and management services.

A SELF-HELP STRATEGY FOR CRISIS RESOLUTION

The following self-help strategy, adapted from crisis treatment principles, can be useful when trying to come to terms with a major life change or any crisis that is not life-threatening. *Self-help strategies are not recommended if a crisis involves suicide, violence of any sort, substance abuse, or medical conditions that contribute to or cause the crisis situation.* Keep in mind that people who are embroiled in crises frequently do not recognize these emergency situations, because during the crisis state they simply are not able to identify emotions and problems accurately, nor are they able to think clearly enough to find solutions.

1. *Recognize the early warning signs of a crisis.* These are any dramatic or sudden changes in feelings, thoughts, perceptions, mood, or behavior over the previous six weeks that are accompanied by an emotional storm involving severe anxiety, panic, and feeling overwhelmed, and/or an inability to cope with your daily life.
2. *Talk to a trusted person.* It is very difficult to resolve a crisis by yourself because your own psychological conflicts are frequently outside your conscious awareness. Talking with a trusted friend or loved one who is *not* directly involved in the crisis may help you see things that you are not able to see by yourself.
3. *Discuss painful feelings and emotions.* Concentrate on the emotions that you are feeling right now. If you are feeling suicidal or violent, immediately seek professional help.
4. *Try to identify the specific precipitant to the crisis.* The acute stressor is most typically something that happened or was felt the day the emotional crisis ensued or several days previously. It is unlikely that a precipitant is something that happened more than six weeks ago. The Social Readjustment Rating Scale (chapter 24, page 356) may be useful to help identify common stressors.
5. *Identify the specific area of your life most affected by crisis.* Review your relationships, family life, work or school issues, economic or financial situation, religious life, developmental phase, and housing, food, and clothing needs. Try to locate the *one* specific

(Continued)

problem area that is most upsetting. Do not attempt to move on to a second or related problem until the first is completely and successfully resolved. If your crisis involves multiple problems, make a list and set priorities. If the crisis involves interrelated areas that need to be handled simultaneously, consider seeking professional help. If you think that your own psychological conflicts contribute to your crisis, definitely seek help.

6. *Gather as much information from as many sources as you can.* Once you identify the one problem to begin to work on, gather all the information you can about the problem. During a crisis, information gives you the power to know where to intervene to correct the problem. Learn as much as you can about the *system* within which your crisis has developed—the school system, the corporate bureaucracy, the criminal justice system, the municipal housing authority, and so on. If it is a school or work crisis, for example, knowing how those systems operate and the resources that they offer might suggest solutions. If it is a problem of obtaining resources, knowing about various government bureaucracies and how they work also will be helpful. When the crisis involves your own psychology, you are more likely to need the help of a confidante or professional to discover new information about yourself. If the crisis involves an interpersonal relationship, a detailed review of its history might suggest solutions to the current crisis.

Gather information by calling others, contacting agencies, reading, or learning as much as you can about how others who are involved in the crisis feel and think.

7. *Decide who must be involved to help resolve the crisis.* In addition to others who are directly involved in your crisis, whom can you call on to help find a solution? For example, a problem with a spouse means that at some point he or she must be involved in the resolution. Who else might be helpful—children, parents, a close friend, a member of the clergy? If it is a problem related to work, can you involve a co-worker, the boss, the employee assistance program, or the union? Actively enlist help in resolving the crisis.

8. *Make a specific plan based on new information or newly discovered feelings.* For the most pressing problem you have identified, plan the sequence of step-by-step actions you need to take, including conversations you need to have, in order to resolve the problem. Plan a timetable for each action or conversation. Set limited concrete goals. For example, confront a husband about an affair, not about what's gone wrong during the entire marriage. Or address a salary dispute at work, not broad problems within the work environment.

9. *Implement the plan.* It's one thing to know what you have to do, and another thing to do it. Take one step at a time.

10. *Assess the results.* Was the plan successful? Did the problem resolve? Do you feel better? If your answer is yes, now you can consider handling a second problem. If the plan only was partially successful, you can reevaluate and begin again. If you got nowhere or remain overwhelmed, seek professional help.

11. *Seek professional help.* Consider this any time you feel that proceeding on your own is too difficult.

26
Suicide

Thomas Kranjac, M.D.

Suicide has long been recognized as a major public health problem. According to government statistics, about 55,000 people in the United States—nearly 13 out of every 100,000—deliberately kill themselves each year. This rate has remained stable over recent decades. Most experts believe the actual rate is substantially higher, perhaps closer to 75,000, because many suicide deaths are incorrectly listed as accidents (particularly single-car accidents) or homicides.

Why do people commit suicide? What brings someone to act with such awful finality? What message, if any, was meant? How do we make sense of it? What can be done to prevent it? Many of these questions have begun to yield to scientific scrutiny. Suicide is considered to be preventable in most cases, *if* those at risk receive the medical and psychological help they need.

THE SUICIDE SPECTRUM

"I Wish I Were Dead": Suicidal Fantasies

Thoughts of suicide and death are not in and of themselves signs of mental illness. Most people at one time or another will ponder suicide as an abstract concept. In the midst of a particularly stressful event, it is not unusual to hear phrases such as "I wish I were dead," or "I can't live like this." Most often statements such as these serve as psychological safety valves for venting strong emotions—much like swearing, shouting, or crying. Expressing these feelings can be helpful if it spurs the person to decide to tackle a specific problem and seek a workable solution.

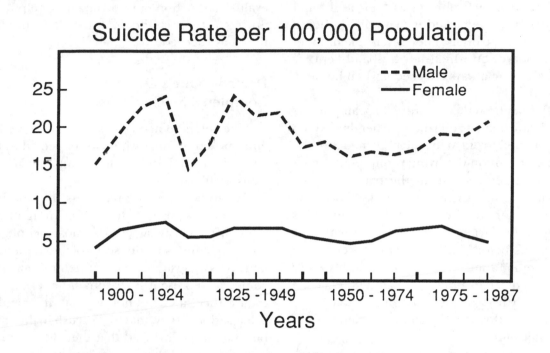

Suicide Rate per 100,000 Population

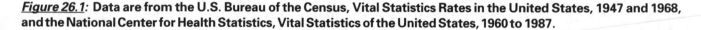

SUICIDE RATES IN THE UNITED STATES FOR MEN AND WOMEN, 1900-1987

Figure 26.1: Data are from the U.S. Bureau of the Census, Vital Statistics Rates in the United States, 1947 and 1968, and the National Center for Health Statistics, Vital Statistics of the United States, 1960 to 1987.

Casual, short-term contemplations of suicide commonly are overcome by the passage of time: The immediate crisis is resolved, or an anticipated problem turns out to be less serious than supposed. Often just talking things over with a friend may allow even a serious situation to be seen from a different perspective and allow the troubled person to plan for the future again.

A Cry for Help: Suicide Gestures

Suicide attempts, or "gestures," are estimated to take place at least 10 times more frequently than completed suicides. Studies show that most people who attempt suicide exhibit psychological characteristics substantially different from those who succeed. Many who attempt suicide fail because the method they select stands little real chance of success or because the attempt takes place where help is readily at hand. Often the person making the failed attempt has mixed feelings about seeking death; part of the motivation may be to get help.

Gaining attention is a conscious primary goal for many people who make suicide gestures. For example, a teenager who "slashes" his or her wrists with a dull pair of scissors, producing minor wounds, and who then joins a family gathering in tears, may be seeking more time with parents, protesting a family move to a new home, or hoping the incident will keep together parents who are planning a divorce.

Nonetheless, despite the underlying motivation, people who attempt suicide may "accidentally" succeed. The tragic story of a young married woman is an example of an apparent suicide gesture that went awry. Her husband was a hard-working law student who regularly stayed at school studying until late into the night. As a teenager, her emotional problems had led her to abuse tranquilizers frequently, which sometimes resulted in overdoses from which she had always fully recovered.

The woman had long been plagued with feelings of intense jealousy. One evening the couple attended a party together, and she became infuriated when her husband seemed to pay undue attention to an attractive woman. After several drinks she stormed home. She wrote an angry note to her husband, replete with such phrases as "end it all" and "it's over with us." She tacked it to a bulletin board just inside the front door. They often joked about the bulletin board, on which her husband kept his weekly schedule; he always checked it when he came home.

Then she swallowed a handful of tranquilizers (which had not been prescribed to her but which she had obtained from a friend), turned off the lights, and lay down on the living-room sofa. At midnight, when he returned from the party, her husband was angry and drunk. He walked past the bulletin board without checking it. He assumed his wife had gone to a friend's house, as she had after similar blowups before, and he went to sleep. The next morning he found both the note and his wife's body. The medical examiner concluded that the woman probably had died after her husband went to bed. Had he seen the note, he almost certainly could have saved her life.

This woman probably did not know that tranquilizers and alcohol together are much more potent than either substance alone. She took about the same dose of sleeping pills from which she had recovered easily as a teenager, but those earlier episodes had not included alcohol. It seemed as if she had expected her husband to rescue her. Nonetheless, her apparent gesture proved fatal.

While those who attempt suicide and those who complete it comprise different groups, there is significant overlap between the two. More often than not, suicide attempts are impulsive acts that take place with little planning; they often can be viewed as psychological cries for help. Nevertheless, it is estimated that about 8 percent of those who attempt suicide will repeat the attempt within 10 years, often planning it more deliberately and succeeding. Thus, every suicide gesture or attempt, no matter how minor it may appear, deserves serious evaluation. Action must be taken to help the person during the crisis and to forestall future attempts that may succeed.

Death by One's Own Hand: Completed Suicide

Suicide refers to acting *consciously* and *deliberately* to end one's own life, with death expected as the *direct result* of the act. Rarely do individuals make such decisions hastily or easily.

While nearly everyone wants to experience life for as long as possible, to find meaning in it, and to enjoy life's satisfying events, most people who are contemplating suicide seriously experience problems or feelings that so overwhelm them that death comes to represent a reasonable alternative. While their difficulties need not be what others might consider serious, they may feel crushed by impossible burdens and convinced that their lives can never be satisfying, hopeful, or free of pain.

For these people, a decision to commit suicide usually comes slowly. At first, they may have fleeting notions of death in general. Soon they focus on the concept of their own death, perhaps as one of many potential answers to a particular problem. Finally they may concentrate on suicide as the *sole* available option, believing there is nothing else they possibly can do that would offer a way out of their difficulties. Even then they may still consider other possibilities, but will reject each option in turn as untenable, unworkable, or unlikely to achieve the desired result. Eventually they find themselves trapped between just two options: seemingly unbearable life on the one hand and the possibility of relief through death on the other. The person who resorts to suicide is, in effect, blind to all other possibilities.

THE DECISION TO ACT NOW

Not everyone who is in severe physical or emotional distress commits suicide. Studies of people who attempt or commit suicide reveal that three factors converge when a person takes action to end his or her life: recent occurrences that act as a precipitant, the individual's particular motives, and the availability of a means of self-destruction.

The Precipitant

A precipitant is any extremely upsetting event that, when added to other stresses, provokes the suicide. The most common of these are disruptions of close relationships, such as a heated argument with a loved one, a divorce, or the death of a spouse, child, or parent. The threat of jail, loss of a job, or failure to accomplish an important task are also common precipitants.

The precipitating event usually occurs within six weeks of the suicide. (See chapter 25.) When various stressful events take place repeatedly over a period of several months or a year, the single event triggering strong suicidal thoughts or suicidal action may not seem any different from the other events. In fact, to an outsider they might appear less significant. But for the person who resorts to suicide, this most recent event is just too much to bear.

An executive with a major multinational company committed suicide when another corporation announced its intent to purchase his firm. He already had faced two takeover attempts. Both times he had worked hard to help his firm remain independent, constantly aware that his own job—and his family's security—was on the line. After the third takeover bid, he told his wife: "I don't think I can go through this again."

He knew that this particular corporate battle would be easier to fight than the first two. But he foresaw an endless string of similar takeover attempts in the future. He was convinced that eventually his firm would lose and he would be fired. On the other hand, generous pension benefits would fall to his family in the event of his death. Two weeks after the announcement of the takeover bid, he locked himself in his garage, started the car's engine, and was asphyxiated. In his detailed suicide note, he reiterated what he had told his wife earlier. "You'll be well taken care of," he wrote, "and I won't have to suffer again through all the worry."

For this man, the stresses of the previous events had accumulated, and, even though the most recent problem appeared less serious, it was sufficient to push him to the brink of despair and suicide.

The Motive

The majority of people who survive suicide attempts describe a range of complex, often conflicting motives. Some perceive suicide as a solution to a particular problem—as a way to escape financial difficulty, for example. A long-running dispute might lead to suicide, as it did for a man who died of a self-inflicted gunshot wound after the most recent in a series of heated arguments with his son.

Others think their suicide will keep a bad situation from growing worse. That was the case with a young actress who had played a series of notable roles in quick succession, but who in the months before her death had been offered only minor parts in films unlikely to succeed.

For some individuals, the motivation may be a wish to punish someone important in their lives—a spouse, a parent, or a teacher—or to gain their attention at last. When a close friend or relative dies, a particularly vulnerable individual may attempt suicide in order to rejoin the person in death.

Some people who survived suicide attempts say afterward that they believed they somehow would be aware, even after their death, of a response from their family and friends. In their fantasies they perceive suicide as an escape from an unbearable pain yet also a state of continued consciousness. They fail to recognize the finality of death.

The Means

The determined individual can find a means to end life; a lethal suicide method is available to almost everyone—firearms, drugs, tall buildings, sharp objects, highway traffic, and so on. Studies have found that a direct relationship does exist, however, between the *easy* availability of lethal agents and the suicide rate. In Great Britain, inhaling home cooking gas used to be a common suicide method. That nation's suicide rate dropped markedly when the gas was made nontoxic. Similarly, in Australia many suicides once involved prescription drugs; the suicide rate decreased when the availability of these drugs was reduced substantially.

In the United States, guns are the most common lethal suicide method among men, followed closely by hanging, strangulation, or suffocation. Prior to 1970 women more often used poisons, including overdoses of prescription medication. In the last two decades, the use of firearms among women has increased drastically. Many mental health experts believe that a nationwide ban on guns would reduce the suicide rate among both sexes. It is unknown, however, whether making firearms unavailable would result in some other suicide method becoming dominant.

THE KEY QUESTION: WHY?

How can life become so bleak? Numerous mental, emotional, and physical conditions promote the kind of hopelessness associated with the decision to commit suicide.

Depression

Suicide most commonly occurs in the presence of psychiatric disorders that cause intense emotional suffering or weaken the normal constraints against self-destruction.

Among all mental disorders, depression is associated most closely with suicide. Vast numbers of people suffering from major depression, from the depressive phase of bipolar illness, or from anxiety disorders will have strong thoughts of suicide or actually will attempt to kill themselves. As many as 70 percent of suicide victims in the United States are known to have suffered from depression just before their deaths.

Those who have never confronted serious depression in themselves or in someone close may find it difficult to understand the depths of despair that someone suffering from this illness experiences. From the viewpoint of a severely depressed person, there is no joy left in work, family, sex, leisure, or any of the other activities that once brought happiness. Instead of offering the possibility of challenge and improvement, the future appears foreboding and hopeless. When a person is severely depressed, he or she cannot see that a change for the better ever could be possible. Without successful treatment, the anguish may become the person's primary focus.

Depression also can bring on a number of physical problems—fatigue, difficulty sleeping, loss of appetite, weight loss, loss of sexual interest or pleasure—which add discomfort and pain to the uninterrupted emotional turmoil. In addition, a number of people with depression may experience delusions that they are afflicted with a serious and perhaps terminal physical illness.

The depressed person wishes for an end to the misery but cannot believe the depression will ever vanish. In such an emotional environment, thoughts of escape through death easily may take hold and recur with increasing frequency as the untreated depression continues.

Well over half of those people with moderate to severe depression consider suicide as one option for ending their pain. For most of them, fortunately, the suicidal thoughts are fleeting and their depressions lift spontaneously or with treatment. But suicide accounts for about 15 percent of deaths among this group, with most taking place soon after the depression begins or during a relapse while recovery is underway.

Other Psychiatric Disorders

Roughly 10 percent of all those who commit suicide were suffering from a psychiatric illness other than a mood disorder at the time of their deaths. The high-risk disorders (excluding drug abuse disorders, which we discuss separately) include schizophrenia, organic brain syndromes, and personality disorders. These and other psychiatric disorders often feature depression among their symptoms. Suicide may result directly from the specific ailment's depressive aspect or from other features of the illness. Symptoms such as hallucinations, delusions, and confusion, for example, can make suicide seem like a logical and even desirable action to take. With schizophrenia (chapter 14) a person may hear "voices" urging suicide.

Some personality disorders are marked by a powerful inclination toward impulsive actions. Most notable among them is borderline personality disorder; in severe cases, sufferers commonly act self-destructively, often attempting to take their lives. Histrionic personality disorder can sometimes lead to suicide when individuals fail to gain the high levels of attention they demand and plunge into despair. Personality disorders may also lead to poor coping patterns in response to severe stress, which may make suicide more likely.

Alcoholism

As many as one out of every four people committing suicide is an alcoholic, and an even larger percentage of suicides have high blood-alcohol levels at the time of their deaths. Overall, alcoholics face a suicide risk 10 times the national average, according to government statistics.

Alcohol is also a key ingredient in countless auto accidents, brawls, and other illegal or antisocial behavior, and experts believe that at least some of the resulting deaths may have coincided with strong suicidal feelings. Furthermore, alcohol by itself—and in combination with other drugs—is a chemical capable of bringing about death from overdose.

While heavy drinking is sometimes a by-product of depression—the depressed person might try to overcome or mask the depressive illness through drinking—there is substantial evidence that excessive drinking can lead to suicide even in the absence of depression. Alcoholism frequently causes severe marital, employment, and legal difficulties, any of which can engender a sense of self-loathing and guilt. The alcoholic's inability to stop drinking and gain control of events and conform to social standards compounds the psychological pressure.

The physical ailments associated with alcoholism can be chronic and painful, including liver disease, eating and digestive problems, and neurological disorders. All these difficulties can play an important role in an alcoholic's decision to commit suicide.

At the same time, the chemical action of alcohol within the brain leads to a reduction of inhibitions. In one heavy drinker, the loss of social restraints might lead only to embarrassing behavior in public, while in another drinker, an equally widespread loss of inhibitions might overcome strong social restraints against suicide.

Drug Use

In vulnerable individuals, the use of illicit drugs can encourage suicidal thoughts, which sometimes may be turned to actions. The suicide rate among narcotics abusers is four times higher than that among the general public.

Users of heroin and other narcotics face many of the same work and family problems as do alcoholics, and they confront legal complications even more frequently, due to the illegal nature of the drugs. As with alcohol, narcotics usage also can cause many physical illnesses, ranging from infections and blood disorders to permanent brain damage.

Heavy cocaine use can cause psychosis, a profound derangement in the ability to think rationally. Cocaine users who suffer a paranoid psychosis, which may include vivid hallucinations and delusions, have been known to kill themselves to avoid what they irrationally believed to be, for instance, an effort by others to attack and torture them. Cocaine is an exceptionally powerful stimulant, and when its use (or the chronic use of any strong stimulant) is dis-

continued, the individual may experience several days of depression, which can result in suicidal thinking and actual attempts at suicide. Users of another illicit drug commonly known as "angel dust" or PCP (phencyclidine piperidine) sometimes experience bizarre hallucinations that can lead to a desire to commit suicide. (See chapter 9.)

Numerous prescription drugs also have the power to alter mood and cause depressionlike symptoms. These include steroids, some medications used to treat high blood pressure, and various other drugs. The depression that can result from these drugs is no less real to the victim than depression stemming from any other cause, and it can lead to the same feeling of hopelessness. Fortunately, drug-induced depression usually ends soon after the drugs are withdrawn or another therapeutic drug is substituted.

Severe Medical Illness

Contrary to widespread belief, the nationwide suicide rate is not dramatically increased among people with serious medical illnesses such as heart disease or cancer, even when their ailments are diagnosed as terminal or are associated with extreme pain. Instead, statistics show that their suicide risk is only slightly above normal.

In those cases of suicide where medical disease did play a role, the illnesses most often involved were cancer, digestive disorders, and epilepsy. Suicides among the medically ill most often take place soon after a diagnosis is made.

A Genetic Predisposition?

Much research has focused on those who commit suicide who were not depressed, did not abuse alcohol or other drugs, exhibited no obvious signs of emotional or mental disorders, and were not physically ill. Yet it is still uncertain whether anyone is genetically predisposed to suicide, although research has been undertaken to determine if there are important chemical differences between the brains of suicide victims and those who died naturally. The known genetic factors in depression and alcoholism may be closely associated with suicide.

Some research indicates that the brains of suicide victims—as well as those of people who engaged in certain types of violent behavior—had unusually low levels of serotonin, a neurotransmitter associated with depression, impulsive behavior, and aggression.

It is not yet known whether low serotonin levels are one reason why some people commit suicide or whether depression or suicidal thoughts result in the low serotonin levels. Studies are underway to discover whether a low level of this important brain chemical is a "biological marker" for suicide, which could lead to better identification of potential suicide victims in time to take preventive treatment measures.

SUICIDE RISK FACTORS: THE STATISTICS

Each instance of suicide is different from every other in detail, but most suicide victims have in common one or more underlying risk factors that substantially increase the chance that a suicide attempt may occur. These risk factors are compiled from statistical evidence and point to the likelihood of suicide within a specific group. However, there are no sure ways to pinpoint which individuals within a high-risk category are likely to make an attempt. In addition, suicides occur among people who do not fall within these high-risk categories.

- *Race*
  Caucasians commit suicide at a rate vastly higher than any racial group in the United States except native Americans.
- *Gender*
  Men *commit* suicide at a rate seven times that of women, while women *attempt* suicide four times more often than men. Faced with a serious medical condition, however, women have a greater rate of completed suicides than men.
- *Mental Disorders*
  The suicide rate among people with symptoms of depression is about 80 times higher than among the general population. Organic brain syndromes, schizophrenia, mood disorders other than depression, severe personality disorders, and severe panic/anxiety disorders also are frequently associated with suicide.
- *Marital Status*
  Most people who resort to suicide are single, widowed, or divorced, and living alone at the time of death.
- *Alcohol/Substance Abuse*
  A substantial percentage of those who commit suicide are alcoholics or abuse some other drug. Close to 20 percent of suicides are intoxicated at the time of death. About 15 percent of alcoholics die of suicide.

- *Age*
  Suicides are most common among people over 40. The highest suicide rate by age group is found in those over 65. The suicide rate has increased in the last 20 years among white males between the ages of 15 and 35. In the single decade between 1970 and 1980, the suicide rate among young men under 24 increased by a full 50 percent and has been rising even higher since.
- *Stressors*
  Suicide rates increase dramatically when a major crisis takes place in an individual's life, such as the loss of a job, the death of a spouse, or a personally humiliating experience.
- *Previous Suicidal Behavior*
  The risk of successful suicide is markedly greater for people who have previously attempted it, had strong suicidal thoughts, or actually contemplated a method of committing suicide. Such suicidal behavior is often, but not always, known to others. Large numbers of those who commit suicide have a history of previous attempts.
- *Exposure to Suicide*
  People who have lost a family member or close friend through suicide are at greater-than-average risk themselves. Vulnerable individuals exposed to publicity about suicides of celebrity role models are also at risk.
- *Discharge from a Psychiatric Hospital*
  The risk of suicide among psychiatric patients is greatest during hospitalization and, for women, in the first six months after discharge from the hospital. For men, the risk remains high for up to a year after discharge.
- *Adolescent Depression and Crisis*
  Adolescents who exhibit some signs of depression and who simultaneously suffer what they view as a major defeat or personal crisis (in school, during a romance, in a sport) are at a higher-than-normal suicide risk.

SUICIDE CLUSTERS

While most suicides are incidents involving one person who acts to end his or her life for personal reasons, sometimes suicides occur in "clusters"—either a single mass suicide at the same place and time or a series of suicides in the same region over a period of days or weeks. The reasons for suicide clusters are varied, and understanding their origins can help in recognizing someone potentially at risk.

Mass Suicides

Suicide clusters are not new events. Early Greek and Roman literature records episodes of mass suicides as early as 600 B.C. In Jewish history the deaths of several hundred defenders of Masada in A.D. 73 are well remembered. In the centuries since, suicide clusters have occurred throughout the world.

In the 1960s many Buddhist monks in Vietnam killed themselves by fire during dramatic demonstrations against their government. Some American war protesters adopted the same suicide method in Detroit, New York City, and Washington, D.C. Similarly, 16 French youngsters burned themselves to death in 1970 protesting their country's actions in Biafra. In the next decade Americans, most from California, drank from a vat of poison and killed themselves in a jungle settlement in Jonestown, Guyana, when ordered to do so by their fanatic religious leader, James Jones.

Mass suicides such as the ones at Jonestown involve religious or political fervor guided to a fever pitch by a messianic leader. These leaders frequently suffer from personality disorders or other mental illnesses that may be obvious to all but their adherents.

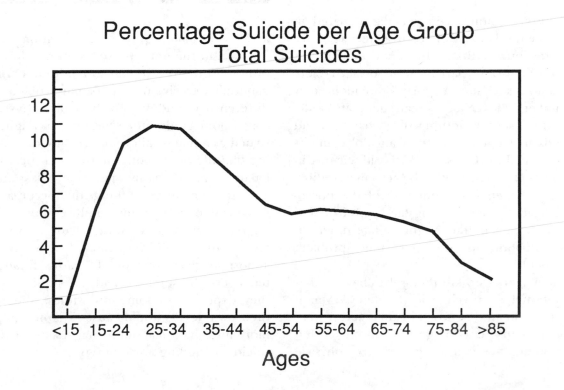

PERCENTAGE OF SUICIDES BY 5-YEAR AGE GROUPS FOR CENSUS YEARS 1970 AND 1987

Figure 26.2: **Data are from the National Center for Health Statistics, Vital Statistics of the United States.**

In some cases the followers (often people who have trouble adjusting to the daily demands of society in general) repeatedly are provided with misinformation about the group, its function, and the true activities of its leaders. With the addition of physical control over the disciples' activities—when and what to eat, when to sleep, when to marry, what labor to perform—the leader completes a process popularly known as brainwashing and achieves total control over the followers, who will believe and obey the leader even when logic and personal experience offer more reasonable alternatives.

While occasionally suicide clusters may reflect ideology or altruism, most suicides occurring in a cluster are, in fact, committed by people who fall into the groups identified as high risk. In most cases these individuals have contemplated suicide previously and gain "courage" to carry out the act through knowledge that others are not flinching at making such a decision. An alcoholic, for example, who previously attempted suicide, and who carries a genuine intent to die, might adopt a widely publicized cause or method.

Adolescent Suicides

Suicide clusters among teenagers have soared in number since the 1970s. By and large, teenagers are more impressionable than adults, and imitation of others is an important part of their social development. A famous rock star or sports figure idolized by large numbers of teenagers can generate widespread enthusiasm for clothing styles, haircuts, and even trends in language. If such an idol commits suicide—as did Phil Ochs in 1976, Sid Vicious in 1979, and Ian Curtis in 1980—the act gains credibility among the teenagers. Imitation of the not-so-famous also takes place. A youngster deeply troubled by a romantic attachment might imitate others in a similar situation who "solved" their problem through suicide.

Most teenagers who kill themselves have underlying emotional or psychiatric problems, even if these have not been diagnosed or their severity has not been recognized. Teenagers are in an accelerated and sometimes confusing period of physical and emotional growth and transition. They are involved in the normal process of developing their own identities on the way to adulthood. Teenagers generally perceive their personal problems in ways different from adults. To the typical 15-year-old, a single poor grade on a school exam might be construed as a major failure in life; an adult, recognizing that life offers both failures and successes, may balance more easily personal disappointment against the many good things that occur, and therefore be able to put a single failure in perspective.

Teenagers who attempt suicide also view their own deaths in different ways. They often have an almost magical concept of death's finality. Many teenagers who survive suicide attempts say later that they expected to somehow witness the reactions their own deaths would cause. Chapter 19 provides more information about teenagers, depression, and suicide, including warning signs.

IF YOU ARE HAVING THOUGHTS OF SUICIDE

- Let others know how badly you're feeling. Allow your friends, family doctor, teacher, pastoral counselor, or a mental health professional to help you.
- Call your local suicide hotline (listed in most telephone directories) or your local community mental health center or hospital emergency service and ask for help. Your telephone operator can assist you in finding these phone numbers as well.
- If you feel that you may act on your suicidal thoughts, let others know how you feel and ask them to stay with you until you get help. Or if you are unable to contact someone else, go directly to the nearest facility that has emergency services and ask for help.

Treatment that can help is available in virtually all parts of the United States. Professionals and volunteers experienced in helping people when they feel suicidal are available 24 hours a day.

HELP FOR THE SUICIDAL PERSON

Several treatment options are available whenever a person who might attempt suicide is identified. For the most part, treatment is aimed at the current precipitating stressors in the person's life as well as the

WHAT TO DO WHEN SOMEONE YOU KNOW IS SUICIDAL

Many people who attempt suicide—and a large number who complete it—give some advance indication that suicide is on their minds. Not even trained professionals can be totally certain which suicide threats are likely to result in actual attempts. Thus, *every* expression of suicidal intent must be taken seriously.

When you are faced with a person who hints through words or actions that he or she is considering suicide, take the following steps.

Ask/Discuss

When someone you know expresses a suicidal idea, immediately engage the person in further discussion about it. Suppose, for example, your teenage daughter breaks up with her boyfriend, arrives home in tears, and rushes to her room shouting: "It's just not worth living anymore." Do not ignore this kind of veiled suicide threat. Ask about it. Without a discussion, you have no way of knowing the depth of turmoil experienced by the youngster, or how seriously you need to respond to it. What may seem trivial to you can take on overwhelming importance to a teenager. Approach the youngster directly and express your concern, perhaps by saying "It must be a terrible feeling to break up with your boyfriend," or "I want to try to understand what you're going through, but you have to help me by talking about it."

Similarly, suppose your spouse learns of a serious business setback, sits staring at the wall, and says, "That company is my whole life; without it, I might as well be dead." Ask *directly* about those feelings and show sympathy and concern. "It really means the world to you, doesn't it?" is one possible opening to encourage a discussion.

Consider

After talking to the person, however briefly, ask *yourself* some questions and *answer them honestly.* Is the suicidal expression a completely isolated incident (indicating a low risk)? Or have there been hints that you've overlooked before—perhaps the use of peculiar phrases ("If I wasn't here," or "If I suddenly died," or "There's just no way out of this situation")? Have there been recent actions that, in retrospect, seem somewhat baffling—the sudden desire to write a will (after putting it off for years), a surprising dedication to "getting these documents in order" or giving away personal possessions?

These questions are especially important when the person falls within one of the major suicide risk groups. Is he or she being treated for depression or, in the absence of a diagnosis and treatment plan, showing any signs of depression or a continuing "low" mood? Is there evidence of excessive drinking or drug use? Is there a significant disruption in work, school, or a personal relationship? Has there been a significant change in sleeping or eating patterns? Has the person withdrawn from family and friends, or shown less interest in activities he or she usually finds pleasurable? Does the person express feelings of hopelessness? Did anything happen earlier that you passed off at the time as an accident but, looking back, might have been viewed as a suicide attempt?

Act

If it is clear that the person is considering suicide seriously, *do not leave him or her alone* before obtaining help.

The telephone is one of the greatest suicide-prevention tools available. If you have any question about the chance of suicide or wish to know how to proceed if you decide that suicide is a possibility, *immediately* call a mental health professional. If there is a suicide hotline in your area (usually listed under "Suicide" in the telephone book), you can quickly reach someone trained to give appropriate advice and assistance on how and where to get help. Your state, city, or county mental health department can put you in touch with someone experienced in dealing with these situations.

If the person you're concerned about is already under treatment by a psychiatrist, other mental health worker, or any physician, do not hesitate to inform the practitioner of your suspicions or worries regarding suicide. By the same token, urge the person you think is suicidal to contact a professional or to call a hotline him- or herself. Once again, do not leave this person alone until you are sure that he or she is receiving help.

AFTER SUICIDE: EFFECTS ON FAMILY AND FRIENDS

Following a suicide, the grief and mourning among loved ones can be compounded by anger and self-blame. Some will ask: "How could he or she have done this terrible thing to me?" Others might say: "I drove him or her to it; it's all my fault."

These feelings and reactions are common, even though they are based on faulty assumptions. As has been mentioned earlier in the chapter, the vast majority of people who commit suicide suffered from depression, alcoholism, or some other illness in the months or years before their deaths. They were not responsible—nor are the survivors—for the high level of hopelessness that drove them to take their own lives, any more than someone is responsible for failing kidneys or a heart defect.

One of the best ways to recover from the emotional aftermath of a suicide is through discussions with others who faced, or are still facing, the same situation. Many hospitals and mental health agencies across the country host discussion groups comprised of men and women who have lost someone to suicide. Knowing you are not alone, sharing feelings, and coming to a better understanding of suicide permit the normal process of grieving to proceed. In addition, many people find that individual counseling is very helpful in this process.

Often families face complex and costly legal difficulties. Police agencies may scrutinize a suspected suicide more closely than a death that was clearly accidental, and the presence of investigators burdens those already feeling overwhelmed by the death. In addition, insurance policies that would have covered a natural death may not pay if the death was considered a suicide, adding a financial blow.

An attorney can be helpful in sorting out some of the legal or financial problems. The self-help groups just mentioned can also provide invaluable information about dealing with this aspect of the aftermath of suicide. During the grieving and recovery process, it is advisable to delay making major life decisions—such as selling the house or giving away possessions—until the immediate shock of loss has abated somewhat and future plans and decisions can be formulated better.

significant underlying emotional or physical problem that led to thoughts of suicide, the expression of a wish for death, some degree of suicide planning, or an actual suicide attempt.

The most important part of treatment planning is an accurate assessment of the seriousness of the suicide intent. Is suicide only a passing consideration? Is the thought of suicide a constant preoccupation? Has a precise plan for suicide been considered? Is the means of suicide—for example, a gun—readily available?

When the risk is judged to be serious—the person has expressed an intent to die and has a plan in mind—a psychiatrist most often will recommend immediate hospitalization where protection against suicide is assured. Once the suicidal patient is safe, treatment of the underlying disorder can proceed.

In addition to individual psychotherapy and/or family counseling, treatment might involve the use of antidepressant drugs or electroconvulsive therapy (ECT) for severe depression, lithium carbonate for bipolar affective disorders, or antipsychotics for schizophrenia. Treatment for alcoholism and drug abuse sometimes includes the use of medications during the initial detoxification process.

Learning to See Alternatives

Psychotherapy almost always is beneficial in helping someone who feels suicidal. Initial treatment usually is accompanied by supportive psychotherapy, which often provides an immense relief to the patient, who may for the first time come to realize that someone understands his or her situation. More probing, intensive psychotherapy, if appropriate, begins only after the most serious symptoms have resolved.

Suicide has been called a permanent solution to a temporary problem. People who are feeling suicidal cannot see that there are ways to solve their difficulties and to go on living. With help, a person can begin to recognize alternatives and to recover control of his or her life.

27

Violence and Aggression

Jonathan M. Silver, M.D., and Stuart Yudofsky, M.D.

Violent and aggressive behavior is a major social health problem. In the United States, close to 25,000 homicides are committed yearly; aggravated assaults total more than a million cases. Over 10 percent of wives are physically abused by their husbands, sustaining more injuries than result from all rapes, muggings, and automobile accidents combined. Every year over 1.6 million children are reported to be victims of abuse and neglect, and it is certain that the problem is underreported. Child abuse results not only in direct emotional and physical trauma to the child, but also in the increased risk that these children will grow up to be abusing, violent adults.

In addition to the violent acts that become part of official statistics, aggressiveness spans a wide spectrum of behavior that can have disabling consequences for the individual and for others. Consider these examples of irritability and outbursts of anger:

- A 30-year-old engineer drives home from work after having two drinks at a local bar. He is cut off accidentally by another driver, and, in a sudden angry reaction, he tailgates, accelerates to pass, then suddenly swerves in front of the "offender," forcing him off the road.
- A 75-year-old demented woman has been cared for at home by her daughter and son-in-law. But they are no longer able to tolerate her increasingly irritable and agitated behavior, and they regretfully place her in nursing home.
- A 20-year-old man with paranoid schizophrenia decides to seek revenge on those who he mistakenly believes want to hurt him. He threatens a family member with a kitchen knife.
- A 15-year-old girl has been using cocaine several times a day for the past month. She has become irritable and paranoid and is brought to the emergency room by the police. She is kicking and screaming obscenities.

Individuals become violent for complex and various reasons. Social, environmental, cultural, eco-

385

nomic, developmental, psychiatric, and neurological factors can all contribute. Circumstances contribute even when a violence-producing substance is involved. For example, some people who frequently lose control after drinking alcohol in a bar—such as the 30-year-old engineer—will remain calm when alcohol is administered in a carefully controlled laboratory situation.

Not all those who commit violence are suffering from a psychiatric disorder. Nor are the vast majority of people with psychiatric disorders violent. Among those psychiatric patients who do exhibit aggressive behaviors, few become involved in violent crimes. However, many psychiatric conditions—including alcohol and drug intoxication—predispose those who suffer from them to develop irritability, outbursts of rage, or antisocial behavior. The spectrum of their aggressiveness ranges from agitation to verbal abusiveness, aggression against objects, aggression against self, and aggression against others.

THE SPECTRUM OF AGGRESSIVE BEHAVIOR

Verbal Aggression

- Makes loud noises, shouts angrily.
- Yells mild personal insults ("You're stupid!")
- Curses viciously, uses foul language in anger, makes moderate threats to others or self.
- Makes clear threats of violence toward others ("I'm going to kill you") or self or requests help to control self.

Physical Aggression Against Objects

- Slams doors, scatters clothing, makes a mess.
- Throws objects down, kicks furniture without breaking it, marks the wall.
- Breaks objects, smashes windows.
- Sets fires, throws objects dangerously.

Physical Aggression Against Self

- Picks or scratches skin, hits self on arms or body, pinches self, pulls hair (with no injury or minor injury only).

- Bangs head, hits fist into objects, throws self onto floor or into objects (hurts self without serious injury).
- Inflicts small cuts or bruises, minor burns.
- Mutilates self, makes deep cuts and bites that bleed. Acts in such a way as to cause internal injury, fracture, loss of consciousness, loss of teeth.

Physical Aggression Against Others

- Makes threatening gestures, swings at people, grabs at clothes.
- Strikes, kicks, pushes, pulls hair (without injury).
- Attacks others causing mild to moderate physical injury (bruises, sprains, welts).
- Attacks others causing severe physical injury or death (broken bones, deep lacerations, internal injury).

Adapted from Jonathan M. Silver, M.D., and Stuart Yudofsky, M.D., "Documentation of Aggression in the Assessment of the Violent Patient." *Psychiatric Annals* 17:6 (June 1987), p. 30.

AGGRESSION AND THE BRAIN

As previously noted, violence has many causes, and tracing aggression to its roots often is difficult. In some cases, however, it is clear that problems in the anatomy or chemistry of the brain are immediately responsible.

Uncontrolled rage and violent behavior often result from damage to specific areas of the brain. Individuals who suffer from the frontal lobe syndrome, for example, in which there is damage to the frontal lobes and deep structures of their brains, are unable to control angry feelings, among other unfortunate consequences. Deeper in the brain, the limbic area, site of many of our emotions, also controls aggressive behavior. In laboratory settings, stimulation of this area with electrodes often provokes episodes of rage in animals and in humans.

Studies have also examined the role of brain neurotransmitters in violent and aggressive behavior. The brain's increased use of the neurotransmitters norepinephrine and dopamine has been

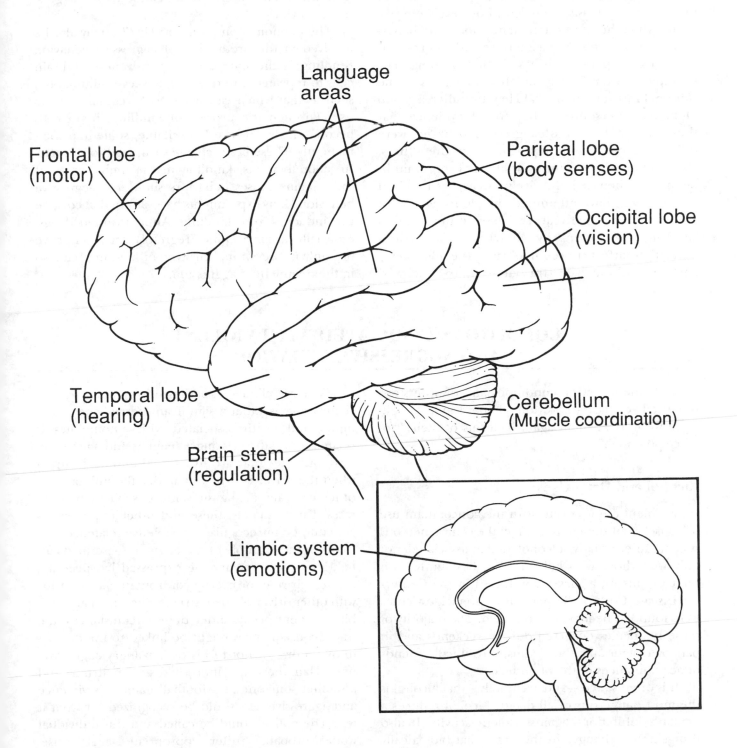

Language areas

Frontal lobe (motor)

Parietal lobe (body senses)

Occipital lobe (vision)

Temporal lobe (hearing)

Cerebellum (Muscle coordination)

Brain stem (regulation)

Limbic system (emotions)

THE BRAIN AND VIOLENT BEHAVIOR

Figure 27.1: View of the brain's surface, showing location of major lobes. Individuals who have damage to the frontal lobe of the brain (which controls motor behavior) sometimes demonstrate violent behavior. Inset: A cross-section of the brain showing its limbic (emotional) area. Laboratory studies have shown that stimulating this area can provoke episodes of rage.

found to be associated with rising agitation and an increase in aggressive behavior. Low levels of serotonin, which helps regulate many mood and behavioral functions, also are associated with aggression.

Clinical experience bears out these findings. For example, Walter Brown and his colleagues at the National Institute of Mental Health studied a group of military personnel. They found evidence that those with a history of aggressive behavior were utilizing more norepinephrine than the others. Other studies have found low levels of serotonin in people who behave impulsively and aggressively and in those who have attempted suicide using violent means, such as with firearms. These findings tend to confirm observations by clinicians that medications that affect norepinephrine (beta-blockers) and serotonin activity (trazodone, fluoxetine, and lithium) often are effective treatments for aggressive behavior.

The phenomenon known as *kindling* may also be involved in the production of aggressive behavior. Kindling is the increased responsiveness of brain cells to repeated, intermittent, low-level stimulation, such as that which can occur with regular cocaine use. Through the process of kindling, brain cells become, in effect, overly excitable, sometimes permanently. These brain changes can lead to seizures. In laboratory rats, kindling in the limbic areas of their brains causes behaviors similar to aggressive behavior. Many experiments have shown that cocaine can induce seizure kindling. Anticonvulsant drugs, especially carbamazepine (Tegretol), can be effective not only in preventing this type of kindling but also in the treatment of aggression.

CONDITIONS ASSOCIATED WITH VIOLENT AND AGGRESSIVE BEHAVIOR

Many of the following conditions and disorders are discussed at length in previous chapters in this book. Here we look at them again in terms of their "violence potential."

Alcohol and Drug Use

Most violent crimes occur with the concomitant use or abuse of substances that affect the central nervous system. Interestingly, alcohol use is associated not only with those who kill but also, frequently, with their victims. In a survey conducted by the Centers for Disease Control, 30 percent of homicide victims were found to be legally intoxicated. The majority of these homicides occurred during weekends and in bars or restaurants; the victims were usually friends or acquaintances of the offenders.

It is often stated—and accurately—that alcohol is the most dangerous of all drugs. Alcohol reduces a person's inhibitions against violent activity. It also brings about changes in the brain that biologically lower the threshold of violent behavior. In other words, it takes less to provoke a person who has had a few drinks than it does to set off a person who has had no drinks at all. Factors that increase the propensity of alcohol to cause violence include brain injury, a history of antisocial behavior, and psychosis. When these factors are combined with an automobile, the potential for disaster is high.

Extensive clinical experience in treating trauma victims suggests that a significant percentage of the injury and death associated with automobiles is related to the driver's angry feelings and aggressiveness. Such feelings are intensified and acted upon when the driver is drunk or under the influence of other centrally acting substances, such as barbiturates. Unfortunately, these and other tragic events generally go unrecognized as violence-related.

As in the example of the engineer described earlier, angry feelings may be expressed by speeding, reckless driving, or overtly confrontational behavior with other drivers or pedestrians. Should an automobile accident occur under these circumstances, the tragic consequences might be linked to the driver's intoxication but not to his or her angry aggressiveness. Had the same individual gotten drunk and assaulted someone at a football game, his violence and aggressiveness would be recognized for what it was. The police would be called and this individual would probably suffer appropriate legal consequences. The angry drunken driver, however, might only lose his license for a while.

The association between violent behavior and cocaine use is of increasing importance because of the epidemic use of cocaine, especially "crack." In a survey of people who telephoned the 800 COCAINE help-line, over 80 percent admitted to irritability. Psychiatrist William Honer and colleagues at Presbyterian Hospital in New York studied the records of emergency-room patients who were intoxicated on cocaine and found violence to be common. Thirty-six percent of users of crack had threatened others, 29 percent had attempted suicide, 19 percent were agitated, and 11 percent were irritable.

With cocaine intoxication, there is a release of inhibitions, resulting in behavioral changes. Fighting, impulsiveness, and agitation are common. Some people, when high on cocaine, show manic symptoms, such as exaggerated feelings of well-being or powerfulness plus poor judgment. When their grandiose actions are thwarted, they may become physically abusive. In others, paranoid delusions may appear, increasing the propensity for violence. For example, a man who has been taking large amounts of cocaine for a long time may become violent because he believes that his neighbor is about to do him harm.

Outbursts of rage also may occur during intoxication with inhalants, marijuana, PCP ("angel dust"), and opiates. Withdrawal from drugs results not only in irritability but also often in paranoid thinking, which increases the risk of openly violent behavior. Intoxication and withdrawal also may cause a delirium, in which the individual is less able to maintain attention to the environment and/or starts to ramble and becomes incoherent and disorganized in thinking. In this state, the individual may become very agitated, especially if restrained.

Irritability, frustration, and anger frequently accompany even nicotine withdrawal. Anyone who has lived or worked with someone who has stopped smoking recently knows how jumpy and quick to anger such a person can be. Society's increasing restriction and disapproval of cigarette smoking make it certain that these symptoms of withdrawal will be seen more often in the future.

Organic Mental Disease

The association between brain disease and aggressiveness was first made by the Dutch physician Hermann Booerhaave in the eighteenth century. He noted that patients with rabies—which scientists now know affects the limbic "emotional" areas of the brain—developed uncontrollable outbursts of rage and violent behavior. Researchers now know too that many types of brain dysfunction predispose a person to becoming aggressive. Tumors of certain areas of the brain and viral infections of the central nervous system, for example, can result in agitation and, in rare instances, even homicidal aggression.

Episodic Dyscontrol Syndrome

Episodic dyscontrol syndrome is the term commonly used for outbursts of rage associated with neurological impairments. It is also known as *organic aggressive syndrome,* to emphasize the strong connection between brain disease and aggression. People with this disorder commonly react with sudden explosive outbursts. They have nothing to gain over the long run from these reactions, which are unpremeditated, and afterward they are extremely concerned and regretful about their behavior. Frank Elliott, emeritus professor of neurology at Pennsylvania Hospital, reviewed the histories of 286 patients with recurrent attacks of uncontrollable rage. He found that in almost all of them there was evidence of developmental or acquired brain defects, and that many had a history of brain injury. Significant neurological impairment has been documented in seriously delinquent children, in adolescents arrested for murder, and in many prisoners with violent behavior. For example, psychiatrist Dorothy Otnow Lewis and her colleagues conducted comprehensive examinations of 15 death-row inmates. All of them had histories of severe head injury, five had major neurological impairments, and seven had other, less serious neurological problems such as blackouts or nonspecific "soft" signs of neurological dysfunction.

Brain Injury

Each year there are approximately 1 million new cases of brain injury caused by strokes, tumors, and traumatic brain injury. If the frontal lobes of the brain are damaged, the result will be *frontal lobe syndrome.* Violent behavior and poor control of rage is one aspect of this complex disorder. Victims react to minor provocations with aggressive outbursts that are usually unplanned, unsustained, and largely ineffectual.

For some 70 percent of people with traumatic brain injury, irritability and aggressiveness develop either very shortly after the brain injury or months later during rehabilitation. These symptoms significantly interfere with the patient's and family's ability to cope. For example, a 20-year-old man who suffered a severe head injury during high school had been an exceptional athlete and student. After the injury he had marked intellectual difficulties, problems with coordination, and frequent explosions of rage—to the extent that his family was frightened to stay with him. Despite several attempts at rehabilitation, he continued to be irritable and explosive. He described these rages as "like when you are at the beach and hit with a wave." After treatment with beta-blocking drugs, he was able to detect surges of anger as they were beginning and to control his outbursts.

Dementia

Men and women who suffer from dementia, including that characteristic of Alzheimer's disease, are especially prone to agitation and irritability. Violent and aggressive behavior is the most common and serious concern of almost all families of patients with dementia. Studies have found that over one-fourth of all nursing home residents are agitated or aggressive. This proportion is similar to that among patients with documented Alzheimer's disease.

Mental Retardation

Aggressive behavior more than anything else is what prompts families to bring people with mental retardation to emergency rooms or to give them over to the care of hospitals and other institutions. Aggressive behavior, irritability, and self-injury are common, chronic problems among many individuals who are severely mentally retarded.

Epilepsy

Scientists disagree as to whether or not there is an association between temporal lobe epilepsy and violent behavior. A study at the National Institute of Mental Health that examined the scientific literature on the topic concluded that the significant factor predisposing to violence is not the epilepsy itself but whether there is damage in the limbic area of the brain. However, other studies indicate that patients with temporal lobe epilepsy frequently report intensified feelings of anger or irritability and that anger in the period between seizures is a common and serious problem. Relatively few violent episodes occur during the seizures themselves. After an act of violence, the individual may recall the aggressive behavior with much regret.

It should be emphasized that most persons suffering from epilepsy, or even temporal lobe epilepsy, do not become violent.

Psychotic Disorders

While it is true that most people with schizophrenia are not violent, studies show that the risk of violence among those with schizophrenia is greater than in people of the same age and sex who do not have the disease. Aggressive or violent behavior is the immediate cause of emergency hospital admission for many people with schizophrenia. Not surprisingly, a family member is the most common victim of this violence.

Of all mental disorders, the schizophrenic disorders (particularly paranoid schizophrenia) and other disorders associated with paranoia carry the highest risk for severe violent behavior, such as murder. Significant symptoms are delusions that the mind or body is being controlled, grandiose delusions, and delusions having to do with persecution or jealousy, particularly if these are accompanied by auditory hallucinations with a similar content.

While these psychotic and persecutory symptoms are associated most commonly with the schizophrenic disorders, they may also occur in other psychiatric illnesses, such as delusional disorder, bipolar disorder, and major depressive disorder.

The risk of violence is very great when someone with paranoid schizophrenia believes he or she has been harmed or is now in danger and broods about revenge. It becomes greater yet if thoughts of revenge become focused plans, or if the individual has hallucinations of being ordered by some outside power to act against another person. In such circumstances, the person should be hospitalized, either voluntarily or involuntarily.

Mood Disorders

Irritability may be a prominent symptom of a mood disorder. Indeed, in children and adolescents, irritability rather than sadness may be the primary manifestation of a minor or major depression, even of bereavement. With bipolar disorder, the manic phase may be characterized by irritability, intrusiveness, and aggression as well as by the typical symptoms of grandiosity, rapid speech, decreased need for sleep, and increased energy. At times, irritability rather than mood swing is the most noticeable problem in bipolar disorder. For example, a 53-year-old executive was known for his sudden outbursts of temper. He terrified his associates at work and his wife and children at home. Only after a psychiatrist carefully questioned him was it discovered that his periods of irritability coincided with a decreased need for sleep and increased energy, and that these episodes alternated with periods of lowered self-esteem, fatigue, and sadness—all symptoms of bipolar disorder, which he never knew he had.

Anxiety Disorders

People suffering from severe generalized anxiety may seem "high strung" and noticeably irritable. In post-traumatic stress disorder, when the sufferer has committed acts of violence in the past—as in war—the fear of losing control and acting violently again can be severe and pervasive. And in fact, episodes of rage and violent behavior are not uncommon in combat veterans with this disorder.

Personality Disorders

Some individuals have a lifelong history of antisocial behavior. In childhood or adolescence, antisocial behavior commonly takes such forms as physical violence, cruelty to animals, use of weapons, and fire-setting. This is termed *conduct disorder*. Children who receive this diagnosis sometimes have a history of neurologic difficulties, such as traumatic brain injury, that may contribute to their behavior. In *oppositional defiant disorder*, the behavior is less extreme and does not seriously violate the rights of others. These children often lose their temper, argue with adults, and defy adults' rules.

An estimated 3 percent of adult men have *antisocial personality disorder*. (The disorder is uncommon among women; see chapter 13.) These individuals are likely to be involved in fights and assaults and reckless behavior. As opposed to brain-injured people who experience violent episodes, they feel no remorse over their behavior. Conduct disorder always precedes the development of antisocial personality disorder (although most children with conduct disorder do not develop the adult personality disorder); like their childhood counterparts, adults sometimes have a history of neurologic illness (encephalitis, brain injury, seizures, or developmental difficulties) that may be related to the personality disorder. In addition, developmental factors such as having been abused as a child may make it more likely that these antisocial behaviors will develop.

Although not all people who have been treated violently as children become violent adults, most individuals who act violently have been treated violently as children. Physical and sexual abuse in childhood leads to feelings of helplessness and to angry feelings that, later in life, increase the risk of violent behavior. Another circumstance that increases the risk of violence is witnessing violence within the family. An environment in which violence is common will lead to violent behavior in future generations. Antisocial personality disorder is a common diagnosis among prison inmates.

Individuals who suffer from *borderline personality disorder* have intense moods that often change rapidly. They may be irritable, may have frequent outbursts of rage, and often act with violent impulsiveness, frequently directed against themselves.

Metabolic Conditions Associated with Aggression

Hypoglycemia—low blood sugar—is sometimes associated with irritability and violent behavior. When Finnish investigators induced hypoglycemia in violent prison inmates, violent behavior was the result. However, the rarity of this disorder makes it unlikely that it is a significant factor in many episodes of violent behavior.

Another metabolic condition associated with irritability is premenstrual syndrome (also known as late luteal phase dysphoric disorder). This disorder is not nearly as common as is believed, but for those women who have it, moodiness or short temper during the week preceding a menstrual period may be severe enough to make normal functioning very difficult. These feelings of irritability resolve after the first few days of the menstrual cycle. (See chapter 21.)

INTERVENTIONS AND TREATMENT

The first step in the intervention process is to ensure one's own safety.

Warning Signs and What to Do about Them

Although it is difficult to predict whether or when any individual will become violent, there are several characteristic warning signs that an individual is about to lose control. The first indication is in motor behavior—pacing, making fists, biting movements, and physical agitation. Abusive language and loud, rapid speech indicate difficulty in controlling emotions. Fear or anger may show in the person's eyes. Cuts around the knuckles or bruises on the face may suggest recent fighting. Signs of drug or alcohol use—slurred speech, unsteady gait, dilated pupils—are clear warnings that violence is a definite possibility. When any of these warning signals are noted and it is suspected that an agitated person may be about to lose control, the physical safety of those who might be harmed must be the first priority. Reducing the tension may ease the situation (see the box below), but it may not work. People confronted with an individual who may become violent should first plan an escape route, to be used if necessary.

HELPING A POTENTIALLY VIOLENT PERSON TO STAY IN CONTROL

If you are confronted by someone who threatens to become violent:

- Talk in a quiet tone of voice, and try to give the person the sense that he or she is in control of him- or herself and the situation.
- Give the person an "out"—a nonviolent way of backing out of the situation without losing self-esteem. If possible, provide a choice of "outs."
- Give the person room—crowding a fearful, paranoid, or agitated person may increase the likelihood of violence.
- Keep everything as quiet and calm as possible. Sometimes decreased stimulation from the environment helps to alleviate a crisis.

Intervention for Hospitalized Individuals

In the hospital setting, acutely violent patients may need seclusion (a locked, padded room) or restraint (a straitjacket or camisole) to prevent them from injuring themselves or others. Specific hospital and mental health law guidelines carefully regulate the use of these treatments, including the frequency with which someone checks on the patient and the duration of the seclusion or restraint. Seclusion and restraint should never be used as punishment, but rather as appropriate emergency measures to ensure the safety of the patient and others. Several staff members and security officers always should be present when a patient is told that seclusion is necessary to help him or her remain in control. Sometimes a show of strength is all that is necessary for the patient to regain control.

Getting Help

When someone becomes acutely violent and agitated, the police should be called. In most instances they can determine whether the person will be managed more appropriately in the emergency room or in a cell at the police station.

Shelters for battered women can provide a temporary haven for both women and their children. Local hospitals or law enforcement agencies can help locate these shelters and other organizations that offer assistance.

Chronic aggressiveness or irritability in a family member warrants medical help. A thorough medical, neurologic, and psychiatric examination will provide a diagnosis. In very many instances—but unfortunately not in all—appropriate treatment can do much to alleviate the problem.

Treatment for Violence and Aggression

Because violence and aggressive behavior are generally symptomatic of the range of conditions covered in this chapter, treatment depends on first identifying the underlying disorder. Once an accurate diagnosis is made and the disorder itself is treated, the behavior may cease. Patients whose irritability results from a manic episode may well respond to antimanic drugs, such as lithium carbonate. Some impulsive, self-injuring patients who are diagnosed as having borderline personality disorder may respond to the antidepressants tranylcypromine (Parnate) and fluoxetine (Prozac) or the anticonvulsant carbamazepine (Tegretol). Those patients who are aggressive in response to persecutory delusions need antipsychotic medication. When a patient is severely out of control, drugs with sedating properties may be needed to deal quickly with the aggressive or impulsive outburst.

There is no approved "antiaggression" drug. Several drugs currently are being investigated for the treatment of chronically violent patients, however. Drugs that may be especially effective in the treatment of the rage and violent behavior that results from organic brain injury include the beta-blocking drugs, such as propranolol (Inderal) and nadolol (Corgard) and the anticonvulsant drug carbamazepine (Tegretol).

Medication is not the only approach to the treatment of people who become violent. Depending on the individual and his or her underlying condition, behavioral forms of therapy may teach some individuals to better control their impulses. Long-term psychotherapy for underlying personality disorders, particularly borderline conditions, in time may help a sufferer develop increased self-control. Group therapy and self-help groups for child- or wife-abusers, for example, also can provide an effective approach for those who are strongly motivated to deal with their problems.

For great numbers of people who become aggressive, drug abuse intervention and subsequent abstinence can be the most important form of treatment of all. The fact is that without drugs or alcohol, many of these people would not become violent or be provoked to act aggressively toward themselves or anyone else.

Helpful Numbers

Violent Behavior
The National Institute of Mental Health
The Center for Antisocial and Violent Behavior
5600 Fishers Lane
Room 6C-15
Rockville, MD 20857
tel. 301 443–3728

Child Abuse
Child Help USA
tel. 800 422–4453

National Clearinghouse on Child Abuse
 and Neglect Information
P.O. Box 1182
Washington, D.C. 20015
tel. 301 251–5157

Domestic Violence
Project Share
P.O. Box 2309
Rockville, MD 20852
tel. 301 231–9539 or 9540

Rape
The National Center for the Prevention and Control
 of Rape
5600 Fishers Lane
Room 6C-12
Rockville, MD 20857
tel. 301 443–1910

Alcohol Abuse
National Clearinghouse for Alcohol Information
 (NCALI)
P.O. Box 2345
Rockville, MD 20852
tel. 301 468–2600

Victims Resource
National Victims Resource Center
Office of Victims of Crime
Department of Justice
Room 1352
633 Indiana Avenue, NW
Washington, D.C. 20351
tel. 202 724–5947

28

Coping with Medical Illness and Dying

Philip R. Muskin, M.D., and Eve Caligor, M.D.

The loss of health almost always provokes apprehension, anxiety, and even broad psychological problems for the sick person as well as for family and friends. Serious illness may cause emotional problems severe enough to hinder care, treatment, and recovery. And sometimes the psychological reactions to being ill are as harmful to long-term health as the illness itself. In these cases, the emotional consequences must be treated just as aggressively as the medical condition. The types of emotional challenges a person faces when ill often depend, first, on whether he or she is acutely, chronically, or terminally ill.

ACUTE, CHRONIC, OR TERMINAL?

Acute Illness

Becoming acutely ill means an abrupt change in health or physical status, as occurs with heart attack, kidney stones, or an automobile accident. Normal activities, including going to work and having a social life, are swiftly replaced by pain, confusion, an unfamiliar hospital routine, and possibly the fear of long-lasting disabilities or even death.

A serious acute condition can cause higher levels of anxiety than a more slowly progressing disease. At first, people often respond to such illnesses just as they would to hurricanes, fires, or other major disasters. (See chapter 25.) They are stunned, cannot believe what has happened, often feel numb, and may refuse for hours or days to contemplate the illness consciously. Expressions of understanding and support from family and friends can be extremely helpful at such times.

When the person who is acutely ill expects to recover fully, the slightest improvements tend to act as positive reinforcements and lead to significant reductions in anxiety levels, in turn bringing about yet more progress. It pays to point out even modest advances, especially when the individual becomes depressed or discouraged. When progress is evident, people with acute illness usually grow increasingly self-reliant and also develop more confidence in their doctors, which can help to speed recovery.

Not everyone can expect to recover from an acute illness, however. Some acute illnesses develop into, or are the first signs of, chronic conditions that persist for months, years, or even for life.

Chronic Illness

In the category of chronic illness fall those that cause long-lasting adverse effects. They may respond to treatment, but they usually cannot be cured. Some chronic conditions, including arteriosclerosis, arthritis, asthma, and multiple sclerosis, may not improve even with treatment. Instead they may stay the same or worsen gradually over the course of months or years. The individual must knowingly face a progressive decline in health and frequently also confront concerns about long-term financial support, loss of self-esteem, and the possibility of a reduced life span.

The slow course of many chronic illnesses, however, often enables a person to develop a way of dealing with concerns and setbacks as they happen. Many people cope well with whatever limitations their illness brings. Still, the stresses of chronic illness, such as ever-increasing pain, or new difficulties with previously simple tasks, may lead to giving up hope prematurely. Because the illness itself cannot be conquered completely, some people may cope inappropriately by becoming angry at their doctors, spouses, children, or colleagues at work. Some people suddenly may lose confidence in their treating physicians or begin shopping for a "miracle cure." Family members can sometimes help by learning more about the illness and guiding the sick person's efforts in directions likely to be constructive. (See "Sources of Help and Information," pages 405–406.)

Periodic depression occurs quite commonly in chronic illness, particularly when an individual notes a lack of improvement, is increasingly forced to rely on others, and feels a sense of helplessness. Depression occurring along with a medical illness or in other situations can be treated with a variety of therapies, including counseling, psychotherapy, medication, electroshock treatment, or some combination of these.

Terminal Illness

Terminal illnesses are diseases that lead inevitably to death, either in the immediate or the more distant future. Treatment may prolong life or make symptoms more bearable, but only temporarily.

Terminally ill people have experiences similar to those who are chronically sick, but they also must confront the added stress of a shortened life span. Ways of coping vary widely. For example, some people respond by withdrawing completely from medical care, reasoning that if they cannot be cured, they have little reason to undergo treatment; others accept every treatment available.

In their remaining months or weeks, many people with terminal conditions focus their attention on putting their affairs in order to reduce problems for their heirs. Some devote the balance of their lives to helping others with similar ailments. A discussion of the psychological effects of impending death can be found later in this chapter.

COMMON STRESSES OF MEDICAL ILLNESS

Powerful stresses confront people facing serious illness or injury, whether acute, chronic, or terminal. Although each individual deals with these stresses differently, depending on his or her personality style (discussed on page 399), the following discussion focuses on the most common stresses that sick people experience.

Until they become ill, most people feel relatively indestructible. A person's self-image can be deeply shaken by illness as well as by the dependence on doctors, nurses, and medical technology that illness often brings. Almost always, sick or injured people are concerned about the loss of independence and self-sufficiency, and they may worry about being permanently incapacitated or disfigured.

An illness can provoke feelings of guilt and shame, or a perception of the illness and hospitalization as punishment for some wrongdoing. For example, a person suffering from a lung disease may feel guilty about having smoked. Similarly, someone with coronary heart disease might feel to blame for having ignored a cholesterol-reducing diet.

Prior experiences of illness and hospitalization—both the patient's own experiences as well as those he or she has heard about or witnessed in others—will influence reactions to a current illness. Positive experiences in the past tend to reduce the stress of a current illness, whereas negative ones tend to increase the person's stress.

The extent and gravity of the stresses depend not only on the illness itself, but also on numerous independent factors. A person's economic situation can play an enormous role, especially if treatment for the illness is expensive and insurance insufficient, or if a return to work is not possible.

A person's age and developmental stage will influence the types of stresses he or she faces when ill. Children, for example, whose understanding of death is often not very clear, might focus their attention on the pain caused by cancer therapy and may not be able to grasp the possibility that the illness could be fatal without treatment. (See chapter 20.) A woman of child-bearing age may focus her concerns on the influence her illness might have on her reproductive capacity. A man in his 40s who is the primary wage earner for his family often faces concerns about financial problems as well as the loss of his usual role within the family.

The Stress of Hospitalization and Medical Treatment

Illness demands that substantial trust be placed in the hands of strangers: doctors, nurses, and other health-care professionals. This dependence on others can be a frightening experience for many people. Often it requires an unaccustomed act of faith, especially when there is no relationship with a medical professional predating the illness, or when information and knowledge to help assess the medical competence of those providing care are not available.

Hospitals threaten a person's sense of being in control. Suddenly others are making the important decisions and demanding passive compliance. The sick person, perhaps for the first time in decades, has to sleep, wake up, eat, and use the bathroom according to someone else's schedule.

A hospital stay requires separation from family, friends, job, pets, and home. Most people, especially children and the elderly, are quite frightened by being away from their customary surroundings and routines, which they rely on to function effectively and to feel like "whole" people.

In order to diagnose and treat a medical illness, it is often necessary repeatedly to examine and probe a person's body, to sample bodily fluids regularly, and to use a range of high-tech medical appliances. If the reasons for the poking and prodding are not clearly explained, the examinations and treatments can increase the stress of the illness substantially. (See also page 397.)

Loss of Love and Approval

Finally, illness and injury commonly evoke a fear of losing love and approval of family, friends, and society. A woman may feel less attractive and lovable after a mastectomy, despite her husband's reassurances. The high achiever, forced to slow down by a heart attack, might believe that working less will diminish peer respect. The threat of rejection can be especially frightening to the person with acquired immune deficiency syndrome (AIDS), cancer, or disfiguring illness, because these conditions often provoke a horror in others, as discussed at greater length on page 399.

Some conditions cause the loss of previously mastered bodily and mental functions, such as physical strength, motor functions, bladder control, or the ability to regulate emotions. Such losses cause anxiety even when there is assurance that they are only temporary. When the losses are permanent, they can cause major injuries to self-esteem as well as concern about the loss of love and respect.

PAIN

The stress stemming from pain and from the potential for pain can aggravate any of the stress factors discussed earlier. Sudden, unanticipated pain, whether or not the cause is known or suspected, often causes anxiety and fear. Chronic pain usually results in depression at some point in its course, typically after several months or years when treatment has not provided substantial relief.

Emotional and psychological factors influence the perception of pain. For example, a person's understanding of the illness, feelings about treatment, and even emotional attitudes toward the doctors and nurses caring for him or her can play an important role.

Even for the person whose pain from a physical illness varies with emotional factors, medication and pain-reducing therapies are very important. Sometimes people in pain are concerned about taking narcotic medication because they fear becoming addicted. Addiction is rarely a consequence of narcotics taken to reduce acute pain, and narcotics should be used as needed in this setting. In the long-term treatment of chronic pain, the use of narcotics is sometimes appropriate, although antidepressants, hypnosis, or nonnarcotic drugs might also be considered.

Before surgery or medical procedures, patients should be told about the degree of pain or discomfort likely to follow; advance information can reduce the intensity of the pain and the amount of medication a person needs for it. If not informed, patients should ask. They also should ask about whether they can have a say in when pain relief is provided, rather than having to follow a rigid schedule, such as every four hours. Sometimes, knowing that relief will come whenever the pain occurs can lessen feelings of helplessness and anxiety, which in turn can actually reduce the intensity of the pain.

REACTIONS TO TESTS, TREATMENTS, AND PROCEDURES

Tests to detect the presence or course of an illness and treatments to cure or arrest it can be as emotionally stressful as the illness. Much of the stress can be reduced or prevented by physicians who explain in advance appropriate treatment options, their benefits and their drawbacks, so that the patient understands and is in favor of a particular treatment approach. An individual who is not unduly surprised by the pain after surgery, the discomfort of a barium test, or the overall slow progress of treatment will experience significantly less stress than someone who doesn't know in advance what to expect.

Drugs

Most medications have some unwanted side effects. These can be minor or major, and usually differ in intensity from person to person. Someone who is aware before taking the drugs of the most likely side effects and instructed to report them to the doctor may have fewer emotional reactions if and when side effects occur. For example, for men a common side effect of numerous high blood pressure medications is some sexual dysfunction. (See chapter 11.) Although individuals made aware of this possibility still may be affected emotionally if a problem occurs, they will find ways to cope with the situation more quickly without necessarily stopping the medication.

Therapies

Numerous medical therapies can be stressful and lead to responses that should be addressed with clear coping strategies. For example, even before radiation or chemotherapy treatment for cancer begins, anxieties may arise over impending hair loss. One way of coping might be to accept consciously temporary hair loss as a trade-off for being cured, or at least for slowing the advance of the illness. Another might be to wear a hat or scarf when leaving home. People specifically cautioned in advance that they might lose their hair sometimes shop for an attractive wig long before it is needed, thus staving off the surprise and stress that sudden hair loss can cause. Coping styles and strategies are discussed at greater length beginning on page 400.

Kidney dialysis regularly leads to mood and attention disorders, induced in part by temporary chemical alterations in the brain but also by an unwanted dependency on other people and on technology. Dialysis patients who are shown in detail how the machines work and who learn more about the way kidneys function tend to have significantly fewer emotional problems. Self-help groups for dialysis patients can also offer much-needed support.

Prostheses and Implants

The need for a prosthesis (an artificial body part or aid), such as a hearing aid, a pacemaker, an artificial leg or hip joint, sometimes creates a strong emotional response, usually stemming from a general fear of declining health or an unaccustomed need to rely on the products of technology. Many people cope by eventually thinking of the device as part of their own body, but others never may come to accept it. People with pacemaker or heart valve implants frequently cope by convincing themselves that the artificial part prevents the possibility of further heart disease.

Transplantation

Emotional reactions associated with organ and bone marrow transplantation often start with the stress of waiting, sometimes for years, for a suitably matched donor. After receiving a donor organ, recipients may be either uncharacteristically ebullient over a renewed lease on life or unusually morose and contemplative, feeling guilty about the donor's death. Most people, however, adjust quickly and easily to obtaining a donor organ.

Surgery

Although many patients hope that surgery will provide a "sure" cure for a specific ailment, there is almost always some degree of uncertainty and apprehension about the procedure, the anesthesia, and their aftermath. Such concerns usually can be resolved by informative talks with the anesthesiologist and surgeon about the operation and its post-surgical and recuperative stages. Clinical studies have shown that people fully informed in advance about all aspects of surgery, including the potential risks, need significantly less pain medication during recovery.

After surgery, emotional concerns commonly revolve around pain and recovery, including the chance of returning to everyday life fully functional. Minor changes in appearance or loss of body integrity, such as reduced muscle tone or scars, are usually less traumatic if their likelihood was known prior to surgery.

When surgery leaves disfiguring scars, when the loss of an organ or limb requires dramatic changes in lifestyle, or when the procedure was performed only as a temporary stopgap, serious psychological problems often result and usually must be addressed by trained mental health professionals.

STROKES, HEART CONDITIONS, AND CANCER

In addition to the common stresses experienced by most people undergoing any sudden or serious illness, particular diseases or conditions present predictable emotional hurdles or psychiatric consequences. For example, psychiatrists who study and treat the psychiatric complications of medical illness (who are known as consultation/liaison psychiatrists) have identified certain reaction patterns resulting from three of the most common potential killers:

stroke, heart disease, and cancer. (For the mental health consequences of AIDS, see chapter 29.)

Stroke

About half of all people suffering a stroke experience depression, usually minor but occasionally quite severe. The depression can be accompanied by pronounced apathy. Some people develop a mental state characterized by apathy alternating with inappropriate cheerfulness.

Such mood disturbances sometimes stem in part from the stroke's destruction of brain cells. (See chapter 15.) They are also attributable to the enormous stresses brought about by the continuing disabilities, such as partial paralysis or speech problems, new dependency on others, or the need for long-term physical therapy to regain lost functions, which strokes commonly cause.

Symptoms of depression sometimes appear as long as two years after the stroke, perhaps following a series of disappointments in the recovery process or due to lingering physical problems within the brain. More commonly, however, they show up within the first few months. When depression does occur, it requires the same level of psychiatric care as depression experienced by someone without a stroke. Antidepressant medications, along with active rehabilitation and psychotherapy, are often helpful.

Heart Attack and Heart Disease

Heart attacks also lead regularly to depression, often beginning as early as the third day of the illness. Therefore, once the acute phase of the medical condition has passed, the management of depression becomes an important task for the physician. A thorough explanation of the heart attack's probable causes and consequences, information about future preventive measures, and suggestions about ways to adjust can be helpful in combating this depression.

Many people fear resuming sexual activity. Physicians can provide clear guidelines that will help in the return to a normal, active life.

Cancer

Cancer remains the second most common cause of death in the United States. A cancer diagnosis usually causes deep concerns about the possibilities of a cure, the progression of the illness, the chance of death, and the discomforts and side effects of treatment. It frequently elicits strong emotional responses including fear, a sense of hopelessness, feelings of isolation, and a loss of self-esteem.

A sense of shame is also common, because many people continue to stigmatize cancer victims and those who suffer from AIDS. (See chapter 29.) Cancer victims may be rejected even by family and friends. They often face unjust discrimination, sometimes in finding or keeping a job, and often when discussing coverage with their insurance companies. As a result, many people with cancer hesitate to talk about the illness. Yet most victims would find comfort in discussing a cancer diagnosis with family members and close friends; they need understanding, sympathetic, and nonjudgmental listeners. The isolation adds to the stress of the disease and the emotional toll it takes.

The stigma and shame are best fought with education about the disease, aimed both at the sufferer and the public. Self-help groups for cancer victims can provide crucial support.

COMING TO TERMS WITH THE ILLNESS

Each person copes with illness in his or her highly personal way. Becoming familiar with one's own style of dealing with frightening events can enable a person to use constructive coping mechanisms.

Personality Styles

An individual's personality largely determines what the illness means to each person and influences the way he or she attempts to deal with its stresses. Someone who habitually laughs off problems likely will attempt to deal with medical illness in a similar manner. By contrast, a person who constantly worries is likely to brood over every aspect of medical care. People who have

troubled personality patterns (personality disorders; see chapter 13) generally reveal a similarly troubled pattern of coming to terms with the illness.

Defense Mechanisms

Psychological defense mechanisms are ways through which individuals find relief from conflict and anxiety. Usually defense mechanisms—ways people automatically, unconsciously respond to threats such as illness—are outside the person's awareness. Many personality and coping styles rely on specific defense mechanisms, which serve to make the illness seem more understandable or more acceptable and the dangers less serious. (See also the box on page 48 for additional information on defenses.) The following rank among the most common defense mechanisms:

- *Repression.* Involuntarily forgetting an unpleasant or threatening experience. A person may repress the pain of medical tests, for example, by either wiping it out of memory or remembering only a blur of activity.
- *Suppression.* Deliberately putting the disturbing matter out of mind. A person who suppresses the unpleasant reality of medical illness instead may focus full attention on family activities or work, finding comfort for hours or days by choosing not to even think about the illness.
- *Denial.* Not acknowledging the existence of an unpleasant reality. People diagnosed with cancer, for example, may not think of themselves as having a malignancy but rather a "growth" or a "condition."
- *Displacement.* Transferring emotional reactions from one thing or person to another. For example, a sick person may feel extreme anger at the disease, but aim that anger at a friend, relative, or doctor.
- *Intellectualization.* Replacing feelings with facts and reason. A person intellectualizes his or her illness by becoming an expert on it and/or the treatment. This defense can give people a powerful, comforting sense of control. It may permit them to undergo many difficulties and tribulations because they "know" what is going on.

Coping Styles

Defense mechanisms and personality styles together create a person's individual style of coping with the stress of medical illness. Most people have more than one way of coping, and strategies frequently change during the course of an illness. For instance, someone who denied the existence of a tumor for the first week or so after diagnosis and refused treatment might suddenly demand to be seen and treated "before it's too late." An individual who initially seemed uninterested in the details of an illness might begin asking specific questions that show an unexpectedly high degree of understanding about the disease. Such changes are part of the process of coming to terms with the illness.

Coping Constructively
Beneficial coping strategies can aid recovery. These strategies are evident when an ill person seeks more information about the disease or injury, shares major worries with others, and takes decisive actions based on a reasonable understanding of the situation. Other coping styles are less constructive, as when a person displaces anger onto medical personnel and family members, becomes morose and excessively self-pitying, withdraws into isolation, or indicates that the illness or injury was inevitable or "fated." A few coping strategies become so extreme or psychologically and physically destructive that professional psychiatric care is needed.

Often the same coping method can be used constructively or destructively. Seeking direction from an authority and going along with expert medical opinion can be a beneficial coping strategy. A person's ability to become a "good" patient, implicitly trusting caregivers and obeying a hospital's myriad rules, is usually helpful to all and may speed recovery. But when it leads to total submission—a disowning of personal responsibility—or apathy about the medical care, it may signal the use of a destructive coping strategy.

The Two Sides of Denial
Constructive denial is often vital in keeping a sick person functioning. A 56-year-old woman was diagnosed with cancer. Her response was "Okay, I have a disease, but it can't possibly kill *me* with all the therapy available today. Sure, the treatment might make me sick, but I'll just get on with it." After a few weeks of chemotherapy and radiation, she was focusing her attention exclusively on the scheduling of, and recovery from, her treatment. She had begun to insist that the disease itself, which she never named, was "the least of my problems." This woman chose to deny the significance of the cancer, because it was too disturbing for her to face, but she nevertheless accepted the need for continuing care.

Had this woman disbelieved the cancer diagnosis, as many people do, and sought additional opinions until the time for early, effective treatment was long overdue, her denial would constitute a destructive coping strategy.

Denial, the feeling that "this just can't be happening to me," is quite common after a heart attack or other acute cardiac emergency. Some heart attack victims have actually tried to walk out of emergency rooms shortly after being brought in by ambulance.

Yet constructive denial may increase the chance of survival in the hours immediately following a heart attack or other health crisis. A person who believes that no real emergency exists remains calmer and provides more accurate information to treating physicians than does someone who is frightened and agitated. This decreased anxiety provided by con-structive denial mechanisms may actually improve the prognosis following a heart attack.

HOW TO COPE WITH MEDICAL ILLNESS

- For most people, it is best to be as active and as well informed as possible.
- Ask questions of your doctors. If you find this difficult to do, have a spouse or other relative or friend join you when you are meeting with your doctor.
- If you still have unanswered questions, there are other places to turn for information. Some-times a second opinion from another physician can be helpful. Often local medical libraries or patient advocacy groups (such as the MS Soci-ety or the National Epilepsy Foundation) can be useful resources.
- Information ahead of time is important at each step in the evaluation and treatment of your illness. For example, before having diagnostic tests, starting a medication, or going into the hospital, you should know what to expect. Ask your doctor what the rationale is for taking this step, what it will feel like, what the expectable side effects and potential risks are. Knowing ahead of time can diminish pain, anxiety, and even the rate of certain side effects and complications.
- Make sure you have a doctor you have confi-dence in and you feel you can work with long term. While endless "doctor shopping" is not helpful, it is a good idea early on in the course of an illness to find a doctor who is right for you. Often friends and relatives can be good sources of information, as can the patient advo-cacy groups mentioned above.
- Designate one doctor as your primary doctor. Often a person ends up with several specialists involved in his or her care. This can lead to crossed communications and confusion as to who is in charge. It is helpful to have a single physician (for example, your internist or general practitioner) be responsible for coordinating your care and helping you to get answers and make decisions.
- Having an illness is one of life's most stressful experiences. Expect that you will have power-ful emotional reactions, some of which may seem irrational and out of character. It is normal to feel frightened, anxious, angry, or depressed at various points in an illness. (The same applies to your loved ones.) Most of these reac-tions are transient. They are normal parts of the response to illness, and over time they often become part of the coping process.
- Pay attention to your feelings, do not be frightened or embarrassed by them, and ask for help. If you find yourself worrying, ask for answers and reassurance. Medical questions can be directed to medical staff, financial and insurance-related concerns to social workers. Emotional problems and fears can be shared with these professionals as well as with your loved ones.
- Contact with a counselor can be helpful in the coping process. Often even one or two visits with a professional can make an enormous dif-ference. He or she can help to address effec-tively your feelings and concerns and those of your family as well. There are many people to turn to, including pastoral counselors, social workers, psychotherapists, and psychiatrists. You can always ask your doctor for a referral. When it comes to coping with chronic or poten-tially life-threatening illness, patient support and self-help groups can be very helpful. Many organizations provide support to spouses and family members as well.

THE SUPPORT NETWORK

Recent research has demonstrated that a strong support network of professional health-care pro-viders, family, and friends can significantly affect the emotional well-being of people who become ill. For family and friends to be of help, they must become involved as early as the time of a diagnosis. They need to know as much as the person affected by the illness, because they too will experience many of the responses typically associated with med-ical crises, such as the initial shock and disbelief, fear, concern over finances, and worry about the future.

Armed with the medical facts, family and friends have more of a chance to develop positive emotional responses to the situation and to become truly supportive of the sick person and of one another. With accurate information, they are more prepared to listen to the fears and concerns of the ill person and can better face the risks involved in treatment.

Unfortunately, the majority of seriously ill people in hospitals receive few visits from family members or friends. Healthy people also use constructive or destructive coping strategies for dealing with others' illnesses. Presumably, by not visiting, they do not have to contemplate such issues as their own vulnerability to illness and suffering. Another way of denying their own anxiety is to blame the sick person for "causing" his or her own illness through supposedly irresponsible or careless behavior. While such defensive tactics may serve to protect the healthy person from his or her uncomfortable feelings in the face of someone else's illness, they also lead to the withdrawal of support precisely when it is most needed.

HELPING OTHERS TO COPE WITH ILLNESS

Family and friends can contribute to or help moderate the stress of illness at all stages. Facing illness is easier when one is surrounded by people willing to listen to problems, worries, and complaints. In addition to providing sympathy, others may be able to offer constructive advice. (See "The Support Network," page 401.)

- Be available. Regular phone calls and visits from relatives and friends, even if very brief, are extremely important for the person trying to cope with illness. This can be especially true during hospitalizations. Even if little is said during your visit or call, your ongoing attention, concern, and commitment can play a critical role in fending off the feelings of isolation and hopelessness that often accompany illness.
- Don't be afraid to talk about the illness. Ask how things are going. If the person who is ill doesn't want to talk about it, he or she will let you know. But more often than not, it is a relief for ill people to be able to share their complaints, hopes, and fears with the people they care about.
- As you listen, don't feel you need to solve problems or make fears or sadness go away. That you are able to listen sympathetically and express your concern is what's most important.
- Don't be surprised to hear about angry feelings directed at others and even at yourself. This is a normal response to illness and shouldn't be taken personally. Allow the ill person to express these feelings in the same way you allow them to express their hopes and fears.
- Just as it's natural for ill people to feel angry, it is also natural for them to use denial. People absorb information at their own pace. Don't feel that you need to correct them; neither do you need to encourage widely unrealistic expectations. Maintaining hope is extremely important. One way you can help with this in a realistic way is to continue to talk about the future in reasonable terms—for example, making reference to your next visit or to plans for an upcoming holiday.
- Offer to help with the things that are worrying the person who is ill or that are unduly burdening the family members and caregivers. This might include going over finances, helping to deal with medical bills or insurance companies, offering a hand with household chores, babysitting, or transportation to and from the doctor.

Knowing the Truth about Illness

Doctors who make themselves available to patients and family members to answer all questions that arise generally provide the most effective medical support. It is reasonable for the ill person and the family to expect that the physicians will share as much information as possible through simple, nontechnical explanations and will describe all procedures and tests clearly.

Questions regularly arise over whether someone with a major medical illness should be told the truth about the diagnosis and probable course of the illness. Research suggests that most people recover more thoroughly, or cope better with a chronic condition, when they face a known illness rather than some unspecified "problem." These studies have encouraged many doctors to present a diagnosis directly and unambiguously and to explain the prognosis in a comprehensive yet compassionate manner.

Such openness permits an honest and thorough discussion of a sick person's questions and fears, and thus lowers the possibility that emotional problems will develop later. Doctors are learning to negotiate treatment plans with their patients, instead of just issuing orders that stand little chance of actually being obeyed. Patients, meanwhile, are becoming increasingly active and informed partners in their own treatment.

Nevertheless, physicians must gear their use of medical information to the individual and must deliver it in a supportive manner. People accept information at their own pace, and physicians must allow them time to assimilate it.

Hiding the truth, however, is seldom beneficial and, indeed, is poor medical practice. Unless an ill person says he or she does not want to know the truth, withholding medical facts creates an unhealthy atmosphere of secretiveness and dishonesty. Such "conspiracies of silence" are nevertheless common. They frequently lead to social and emotional isolation of the ill person as well as the family, and deprive everyone of needed emotional support. Furthermore, these falsehoods may rob the sick person of the chance to come to terms with the illness, accomplish tasks he or she had always wanted to do, and concentrate on living even while facing a possibly shortened life span.

The Stress on Families of Changing Roles

Families are highly complex units in which each individual's role developed slowly over the course of many years. During a family member's illness, the spouse and children may have to suddenly adopt new lifestyles to accommodate the convalescent, learn new skills, enforce an exercise regimen, maintain strict prescription drug schedules, or face any number of other changes, including taking over responsibility for major decisions and perhaps assuming new financial responsibilities or becoming the breadwinner.

Most family members, including the ill individuals themselves, find it difficult to adjust to role changes or to accept major new tasks. These difficulties sometimes can be eased by full and complete discussions within the family. Sometimes a physician, hospital social worker, or other health professional can provide advice on how to resolve particular problems created by role reversals or other stresses resulting from the illness. Attending group meetings with family members who have faced similar situations is almost always beneficial, and many groups exist in hospitals and other locations. (See "Sources of Help and Information," pages 405–407, and chapter 25.)

Coping with Placing the Sick Person in a Nursing Home

For a variety of reasons, families may not be able to care for an ill person at home. Reaching this decision often creates emotional problems for the family as well as for the sick person. Family members often feel a deep sense of guilt about taking such a step. The ill individual, meanwhile, may be fearful over entering a new environment, and often feels rejected and abandoned by the family. These emotions often lead to outbursts of anger. Whatever the immediate and long-range responses, family relationships undergo major changes that produce new stresses and require new coping strategies. (See also "Family Therapy" in chapter 4, pages 58–61; "Dependency/Institutionalization" in chapter 23, pages 347–348; crisis intervention in chapter 25, pages 367–373; and "Sources of Help and Information," later in this chapter.

Whenever possible, the person who will be moving to the nursing home should participate actively in the selection. Various nursing homes must be visited and evaluated, and the available levels of care carefully compared. Numerous questions need to be asked. Which nursing home best meets the nursing needs of the ill person? What other important services are available? Is the nursing home properly licensed by state or local agencies? Is it close enough to allow frequent visits? Does the staff discourage visiting or enforce strict visiting schedules? How much does it cost, and will insurance cover the charges? Is the nursing home safe, well staffed, and well maintained? Is the food adequate, nutritious, and nicely prepared? Is privacy respected? What activities are available? For information on finding a nursing home, see page 406.

DEATH AND DYING

Few subjects are more stressful to discuss than death and dying. Cultural background helps to determine one's attitudes toward death. In a religious society, in which people view the process of dying as a natural transition from one state of being to another, the thought of death often causes less fear. Western culture, on the other hand, has long viewed death as a forbidden subject. It has been customary to cope with death by pretending that it wasn't approaching, despite all evidence to the contrary. This denial isolated the dying person from society, friends, and even close family members. In recent years attitudes have begun to change somewhat, and death and dying now are discussed more candidly.

Dr. Elisabeth Kübler-Ross, psychiatrist and author of *On Death and Dying* (1974), was among the first to study the emotional responses and needs of the terminally ill. She found them usually willing and eager to know about and discuss their circumstances. Moreover, she noticed that most people sensed they were dying without being told. According to her research and to several more recent studies, openness enables the dying person, the family, and the medical community to share some of the emotional burdens of terminal illness and to show compassion for one another. Frankness also permits the terminally ill individual to deal with such issues as reconciliation, resolving conflicts, and pursuing treatment options that provide some amount of continuing hope.

Furthermore, openness gives dying people more chances to determine their own destinies. They even may prove able to manage much of their own care in their final days. Some people decide to avoid aggressive medical treatment, particularly involving machines capable of artificially maintaining life, while continuing to accept everyday care. Some terminally ill people and their families choose hospice care for their final weeks or days. (See "Hospices," page 406.)

The Right to Refuse Treatment

Saving lives is the goal of medical care. The dying person who wishes to refuse life-sustaining measures (such as mechanical ventilation or artificial feeding) and to specify "no code" or "DNR" (hospital terminology for no cardiopulmonary resuscitation if the heart stops beating) must express the intent clearly to family members and medical caregivers. The

wishes must be made known as early in the illness or hospitalization as possible, or even beforehand, when the individual's mental competence to make such decisions is unquestionable.

A living will (instructions to family and doctors about what should be done, or not done, in the event of a medical emergency), prepared in advance, may be of great help in guiding family members and physicians who may have to make critical decisions. See page 406 for further information.

Grieving and Mourning

Every major loss elicits grief and necessitates adjustments through a process of mourning. The sudden disappearance of good health or the need to make dramatic changes in customary routines will cause varying degrees of grief for the person who is ill. For close relatives and friends left behind after a death, mourning is a complex and often long-term matter, frequently leading to bouts of intense sadness and feelings of loneliness, guilt, and abandonment. These emotions may persist in some form even years later. (See also chapters 20 and 23 for more about mourning and bereavement.)

Those who are facing imminent death also grieve the loss of their own life. Research by Kübler-Ross and others has identified five emotional stages of grieving commonly experienced by the terminally ill. (See the box on page 405.) These stages may occur consecutively, or they may overlap or diminish, before returning with greater intensity than before. Some people who enter the first stage refuse to believe that they are dying and therefore do not experience the remaining stages.

For a terminally ill person, acceptance of death may be extraordinarily difficult to attain. Coming to terms with the life already lived—acknowledging, for instance, that some goals were accomplished, while others will never be achieved—enhances the possibility of accepting one's inevitable mortality and focusing on the life that still remains.

Acceptance of impending death goes hand in hand with a loss of interest in, and withdrawal from, outside attachments, including close family ties. It is important for family members and dear friends not to confuse the normal process of separating from life with rejection.

THE FIVE STAGES OF FACING DEATH

- *Stage One*
  Denial, shock, and disbelief. Feeling of numbness. The inability to accept what has happened and insistence that no change has taken place.
- *Stage Two*
  Anger that the situation could occur, possibly directed at others.
- *Stage Three*
  Beginning to accept the reality of the situation, but trying to "bargain" for a bit more time to live, whether through expressions of religious belief or increased compliance with medical instructions.

- *Stage Four*
  Depression, characterized by feelings of hopelessness and despair about what has already been lost and what else will be lost.
- *Stage Five*
  Acceptance of the loss, and quiet discussions of death with closest friends and relatives. An emotional reprieve from negative emotions. Feelings of peaceful resignation about one's own fate. Lack of interest in, and withdrawal from, the everyday affairs of life, such as political affairs, social events, news stories, and so on.

SOURCES OF HELP AND INFORMATION

Individual professionals and agencies can be very helpful to people with serious illness as well as their families. Many hospitals and clinics employ mental health professionals trained to assist in coping with the many stresses of illness and dying. There are also numerous independent, patient-run organizations. They deal with specific illnesses and offer programs ranging from informal social gatherings to group therapy sessions. Participation can lower significantly the sense of isolation many ill people and their families feel. The groups often become major sources of support. The National Self-Help Clearinghouse (33 West 42nd Street, New York, NY 10036) can provide information on such self-help and support groups nationwide.

In addition to suggestions from the treating physician, up-to-date information about illnesses and treatments can make decision-making quicker and easier. Some hospitals have libraries for patients and their families. Independent medical libraries for the consumer also exist in some cities. For example, The Planetree Health Resource Center (2040 Webster Street, San Francisco, CA 94115; tel. 415 923–3680) offers health research services to area residents and will send information to people outside the area, for a small fee.

Psychotherapy and other mental health treatment modes can be of great benefit when illness brings on strong feelings of hopelessness, anxiety, fear, anger, and depression. The primary-care physician is a good resource for finding the appropriate counselor or therapy program. Within hospitals, it is increasingly common for medical patients to receive psychiatric assistance for emotional difficulties in coping with their illness.

Home Care

When there is no family to provide needed care at home, or when the family needs additional help, a variety of services offer in-home and out-of-home assistance. More and more people are returning home from the hospital more quickly than ever, or are avoiding hospitalization completely by using such services as visiting nurses, home health aides, homemakers, home therapists, night-sitters, Dial-a-Ride, Meals-on-Wheels, day care and family respite organizations, and public centers geared to the needs of senior citizens.

Doctors and hospital social workers as well as state, county and city agencies can help find appropriate local support services. The Family Service Association of America (11700 West Lake Park Drive, Milwaukee, WI 53224; tel. 414 359–1040) can provide the address and telephone number of the nearest local service.

THE LIVING WILL

A living will, also known as an advanced directive, helps you plan the direction of your medical care should you become physically or mentally incapacitated. It helps to ensure that your preferences concerning medical treatment are known. You can also use a living will to designate an individual you trust to make decisions on your behalf.

A number of organizations provide information or sample living wills. The American Association of Retired Persons is one such organization (write to AARP Fulfillment, 1909 K Street NW, Washington, D.C. 20049). Another is Choice in Dying, 200 Varick Street, New York, NY 10014, which can provide sample wills as well as literature on such associated issues as patients' rights and pain management.

If you are using a living will sample kit, make sure that it is specific to the state in which you live, since different states have different laws. The National Council on Death and Dying (250 West 57th Street, New York, NY 10107) can provide living will forms for every state.

Living wills generally include the following:

- Designation of a health-care representative (a person to whom you grant the legal right to make decisions on your behalf).
- Alternative health-care representatives, should the original person designated be unable, unwilling, or unavailable to make decisions on your behalf.
- A statement specifying that all measures be taken to sustain life; or alternatively,
- A statement requesting that no heroic or unwanted measures be initiated to prolong life.
- Your specific wishes concerning CPR (cardiopulmonary resuscitation), artificially provided fluids and nutrition (such as by use of a feeding tube or intravenous line), and other life-sustaining measures such as mechanical ventilation.
- A statement of your understanding of such terms as "terminal," "permanently unconscious," and "incurable or irreversible illness."
- Descriptions of circumstances that would lead you to forgo medical treatment, or special concerns that you have about treatments. (These kinds of descriptions can help provide guidance to those who may become responsible for your care.)
- A statement of whether you agree that death should be defined on the basis of whole-brain death (the irreversible cessation of all functions of the entire brain) or on the traditional criteria by which death is judged to occur (when breathing and heartbeat stop).
- Your wishes concerning organ donations.
- The signatures, addresses, and telephone numbers of at least two individuals who have witnessed your signing of the living will.

A copy of the living will should be given to your physician and to the person(s) designated to be your health-care representative(s). You may also wish to give a copy of it to your attorney.

If you decide to make a living will, you should:

- Discuss it with others, especially those who will be involved in carrying out its terms.
- Make sure that your physician and designated health-care representative(s) understand your wishes.
- Make sure that your designated health-care representative(s) understands his or her responsibilities.

Additional information on home health care is available from the Visiting Nurse Association of America (800 426–2547) and the American Association of Retired Persons (202 872–4700). Information about the licensing of home health care agencies is available from the Joint Commission on Accreditation of Healthcare Organizations (312 572–2818).

Nursing Homes

Compiling a complete list of nursing homes can start with the telephone book. Other helpful sources include the doctor, a hospital social worker, the local medical society, the state chapters of the American Health Care Association, or the American Association of Homes for the Aging. (See also chapters 15 and 23.)

Hospices

Hospices are alternatives to hospitals for terminal care. The National Hospice Organization (NHO) defines a hospice as "a medically directed, nurse-coordinated program providing a continuum of home and inpatient care for the terminally ill and their family." More than a place in which to die, hospice represents a concept of care for the dying. The emphasis is on providing terminally ill patients with comfort care, in a warm and understanding atmosphere, surrounded by family and friends who frequently participate in the care. Such a setting enables everyone involved to experience the dying process in a more humane and compassionate way.

NHO will provide names and addresses of hospices throughout the United States to anyone calling its toll-free help-line: 800 243–8728. It may also be contacted at 1901 North Moore Street, Suite 901, Arlington, VA 22209.

29

Coping with AIDS

Judith Godwin Rabkin, Ph.D., M.P.H.,
and Robert M. Kertzner, M.D.

AIDS—acquired immune deficiency syndrome—is a multidimensional health threat unprecedented in our times. Caused by the *human immunodeficiency virus (HIV)*, it is an infectious, apparently fatal disorder for which there is now no cure or vaccine. Most of those who develop the disease die in their prime.

Many of the emotional issues confronting men and women with AIDS are common to other chronic debilitating or terminal illnesses. (See chapter 28.) But people with AIDS must also contend with a barrage of societal reactions—rejection, social and emotional isolation, and often homophobia—that are fueled by a terror of contracting the deadly disease combined with ignorance of the illness and its processes.

In this chapter we discuss what experts now know about the psychological and psychiatric aspects of AIDS and ways for individuals, their friends, and their families to cope and to find appropriate help. Because accurate information about the disease and its transmission is indispensable to better coping—

not only for individuals who have the disease but also for their families, friends, and indeed for society in general—we also present "The Facts About AIDS," beginning on page 414.

An inescapable fact, especially in major cities, is the sheer number of people who harbor the infection. In 1981, 350 cases were reported. By mid-1992, there were 218,000. The Centers for Disease Control projects 390,000 to 489,000 cases in the United States alone by the end of 1993. While the overall rate of growth is slowing, especially among gay men, it is increasing among minorities and teenagers. The number of people affected both directly and indirectly will increase in the foreseeable future.

For each person with AIDS, an estimated 10 or more carry the virus but do not yet have AIDS. Many thousands more are or believe themselves to be at risk for infection. The partners, families, and friends of people with AIDS are affected dramatically and suffer considerable emotional distress.

Because the emotional aspects of HIV illness are partly rooted in medical realities, how infected individuals and their loved ones adapt to HIV undoubtedly will be influenced by changing treatments, possible vaccines, and greater scientific wisdom. As an example, recent evidence from clinical trials suggests that several HIV-related infections can now be treated successfully. Yet, while scientific understanding and treatment of HIV illness are advancing rapidly, social accommodation to this illness is moving more slowly. A widely perceived "them" versus "us" mentality often overshadows the psychological, emotional, and personal predicament of those infected. Nonetheless, many individuals who are either infected with or closely touched by AIDS are able to move beyond personal aversion and fears and get on with the business of living fully. For everyone, coping with AIDS means reconciling one's emotions to a new fact of life, here to stay for the foreseeable future.

MENTAL AND EMOTIONAL ASPECTS OF HIV INFECTION

Infection with HIV has profound psychological effects. Infected individuals face a shortened life expectancy and fears of prolonged dependency, possible dementia, and, ultimately, death. More immediately, HIV-seropositive people must educate themselves about their condition and learn to cope with the health-care system. Individuals planning to have children must consider the approximately 30 percent chance of maternal-fetal HIV transmission. In addition to these issues, people who are HIV seropositive contend with personal rejection, stigmatization, and discrimination.

Yet many people cope remarkably well, responding throughout the course of their illness with resilience. Many maintain a remarkably high level of positive feelings—perhaps because the disease progresses slowly, over a period of months or even years, leaving room for the hope that a cure will be developed.

Depression and Anxiety

Early reports of high rates of depression and anxiety syndromes among people with HIV infection have not been confirmed by recent studies. While feelings of anxiety and distress are characteristic reactions to the news of infection and are part of dealing with any severe disease, rates of clinical depressive or anxiety disorders are no higher among gay men with HIV illness than in the general population.

Many people with HIV infection or AIDS who find themselves overwhelmed by persistent depression or anxiety have been troubled similarly at other times in their lives. They may react to discovering that they have the virus or to other crisis points during the course of the illness by becoming anxious or depressed once again. Whether the difficulties are new or represent an exacerbation of a preexisting condition, treatment for anxiety and depression can be very helpful for people with HIV illness.

Jerry T., for example, was a 43-year-old designer referred to a psychiatrist because of severe depression. While he had known for a while that he was HIV seropositive, Mr. T. was beginning to have physical symptoms, and several of his close friends had recently died from AIDS. He felt that all was hopeless, that his life as a productive and useful human being was over. Therapy gave him the opportunity to talk in stark terms about his fears of dying and being alone and to share some of his most private thoughts and feelings. After several months of therapy and antidepressant medication, he came to realize that he still could act to make changes and to find pleasure in life; he even decided to take a vacation.

Symptoms of depression and anxiety may be caused or exacerbated by underlying medical problems, or perhaps by drugs used to treat HIV conditions, such as interferon. Therefore, in evaluating emotional distress in someone with AIDS, a direct organic or medical cause must always be considered, and psychological support must always be coordinated with medical follow-up.

For more information on mental health care for people with AIDS, see page 412.

Suicide

Some people with AIDS do contemplate suicide, although these thoughts usually are fleeting and not accompanied by an intention to act. When a person contemplates progressive deterioration and the likelihood of severe pain, incontinence, or dementia (the things people most fear), it can be reassuring to think, "Then I will kill myself." But that is not suicidal thinking in the usual clinical sense; rather, it is a way of maintaining control in a potentially untenable situation. As people get sicker, they modify their definition of "untenable," and even when these feared outcomes occur, suicide or requests for assisted death are uncommon. In the rare instances when suicide attempts do occur, they may be associated with the presence of organic brain syndromes such as dementia (see below). Active thoughts of suicide may reflect an underlying depression and should be evaluated professionally and treated.

AIDS Dementia Complex

The one neuropsychiatric condition specific to HIV infection is AIDS dementia complex. In about 10 percent of those infected, the first manifestations of HIV infection are mild changes in cognition (memory, abstract thinking, and concentration), which do not necessarily interfere with activities of daily living, at least initially. These early clinical symptoms resemble depression and are sometimes difficult to distinguish. Eventually, late in the course of illness, one-half to two-thirds of people with AIDS are likely to develop at least some cognitive symptoms, usually accompanied by other AIDS-related conditions.

AIDS dementia complex may cause impaired balance or coordination and weakness in the legs. Individuals may progressively withdraw, losing interest in life and becoming apathetic. Intellectual changes include mental slowness, confusion, the loss of ability to read and sometimes even to converse. Some people become agitated and disoriented, or have delusions and visual hallucinations. The late stages of AIDS dementia complex can include inability to speak, incontinence, and paralysis.

Preliminary evidence suggests that zidovudine (Retrovir; often referred to as AZT; see page 418) and psychostimulant medications such as methylphenidate (Ritalin) may improve HIV–associated cognitive symptoms. If these symptoms become severe, several practical measures can be helpful. Prompts—such as a pocket-size notebook for recording appointments and information of importance—can help organize day-to-day schedules. Pill boxes compartmentalized by dose and digital wristwatches with alarms can help keep track of medication schedules.

Men and women with advanced dementia often need home health care or treatment at a day-care facility. It helps to surround them with familiar objects, which provide orientation. Lights should be left on at night; a calendar and a clock should be kept nearby, which they can see easily. Clear and explicit language should be used, and requests, directions, or explanations should be simple to understand. Chapter 15 provides more advice on dealing with dementia.

ADJUSTING TO THE ILLNESS AND COPING WITH THE STRESSORS

It is difficult to generalize about how any individual will react to HIV infection and AIDS. The psychological course varies as widely as the medical course and often reflects it. Also, each person brings the force of his or her existing personality to bear on coping. The person who habitually responds angrily to upsetting events, for instance, is likely to respond to each new crisis with renewed anger. Finally, and frequently overlooked, is the fact that economic and social circumstances can mediate the stresses. A young, poor, minority, single woman with an infant child living in the inner city, for example, has a completely different set of stressors than a 40-year-old successful lawyer. Both must come to terms with premature illness and physical decline. The single mother, however, also will have to deal with stresses that are more practical and immediate, such as arranging for child care, finding a clinic to treat her, getting transporta-

tion to a clinic, and arranging for Medicaid coverage. With adequate insurance and disability coverage, good medical care, and the support of friends and family, the lawyer has more time to dwell on the premature end of his or her hopes and dreams in life.

AIDS is a disease with many crisis points. These typically include testing positive for HIV antibodies, deciding to start an antiviral medication, developing medication side effects or new symptoms, and becoming sick with an illness associated with HIV infection, such as Pneumocystis carinii pneumonia. However, individuals vary greatly in their emotional reaction to HIV infection, responding positively as well as negatively. Some individuals, for example, say that HIV infection has given them a greater sense of purpose or meaning in life. Some individuals progress through sequences of denial, anger, sadness, and acceptance in contemplating death (see chapter 28, page 405, for a discussion of the stages of emotional reaction to dying), but others follow a less linear path, experiencing emotional upheaval and anguish throughout the course of the disease.

Dealing with Test Results

Testing for the presence of HIV antibodies (see page 417) is often the first major emotional task to face. Many of those in high-risk groups live with the ever-present fear of infection. A positive result is often not a great surprise. Some people even report they find it easier to cope with finding out they have the virus than with living with the fear that they might have it.

Following a positive test result, many report feelings of emotional turbulence. One young man said he felt as if "time were rushing toward me." For most people, the acute distress diminishes over the course of a few weeks. They find that life goes on, that nothing—at least immediately—has really changed, and that they have time to think about major decisions. Those who remain extremely anxious or depressed are generally people who have a predisposition to anxiety or depression, as mentioned earlier.

Learning that one does *not* have the disease can have profoundly positive effects on one's life. A 47-year-old chronically anxious journalist in a high-risk group began to experience intermittent fever and chills and to lose weight. He was terrified to take the HIV antibody test. After months discussing with his psychiatrist what being tested would mean and how the results would affect his life, he finally made an appointment. To his surprise, that test and another one six months later proved to be negative. His physical symptoms subsided and did not return. Although he subsequently felt a sense of guilt that he did not have the virus when so many people close to him did, he became far less anxious than he had been for almost a decade.

In order to prepare for test results, pretest counseling is strongly recommended and is mandatory in some states, including New York. Unfortunately, there are no uniform guidelines on what the counseling should include.

Contending with People's Reactions

In addition to confronting one's own fears, telling others is not easy, for their reactions can be painful, even cruel. Many people are confused and frightened by the effects of the disease; some respond by shun-

---

COMMON COPING STYLES

There are several ways that people cope with testing positive for HIV, among them:

- *Altruism.* Some people who are infected find that working on behalf of others with AIDS eases their own stress. Many get involved in AIDS activities or donate their professional services to people with AIDS, offering help with financial consulting or providing legal assistance, for example.
- *Increased spirituality.* Some find solace in seeking spiritual support, whether in formal religion or in nontraditional sources.
- *Hypervigilance about health.* Most people pay much more attention to their health, hoping to stave off infections by changing their habits. This may include smoking cessation, cutting down on drinking or recreational drugs, exercising, and eating properly.
- *Denial.* Others ignore their HIV-positive status while asymptomatic, or continue to live as if there has been no change in their lives. As long as they engage in no behaviors that put themselves and others at risk, and they do not avoid important medical decisions that may prevent illness progression, this psychological defense can sometimes work quite well, allowing the individual to maintain emotional control.

---

ning or stigmatizing those who have been infected. Some people with AIDS have been abandoned by their parents; some have been fired or asked not to go to work. In the early days of the epidemic, some health aides refused to enter the hospital rooms of AIDS patients, leaving food trays outside the door and debilitated patients unfed. Hospital information programs to teach workers about the disease and its transmission have now corrected this situation in most places—yet even today some doctors are reluctant to provide care for people with AIDS.

In large cities where there is by now more familiarity with the disease and its transmission, people with AIDS may face less ostracism. Yet for many gay people, telling their families both that they are gay and that they have AIDS can be especially wrenching—and risky if the parents have strong feelings against homosexuals. Homophobia also affects many people with AIDS who are not gay, who must deal with presumptions that they are homosexual and acquired the disease in a "bad" way.

Other Common Stresses and Concerns

How to pay for medical care, what to do about insurance, where to find nursing care when one can no longer take care of oneself, how to handle the needs of dependent children while ill oneself, how to sustain existing relationships, how to cope with the deaths of so many of one's friends or family members, where to turn for public financial assistance—all are pressing questions for people who also must deal with the stresses of being seriously ill.

Legal problems fall into several categories: issues regarding confidentiality of HIV status; discrimination in the areas of insurance, employment, housing, or medical care; potential disputes over wills, power of attorney designation, hospital visitation privileges, and funeral arrangements; and difficulties in receiving benefits from government programs such as Medicaid and Social Security. In recent years, federal legislation aimed to protect the disabled has been extended to include those with AIDS and HIV infection.

The Stresses on Families, Partners, and Friends

People who are tied emotionally to those with AIDS are the so-called second wave of the epidemic. Caregivers often underestimate the impact of illness on their lives and, in so doing, neglect their own needs for support. In addition, because of the widespread fear of and ignorance about the disease, besides the real frustration of dealing with a very sick person who may at times be confused or uncooperative, caregivers must deal with their own sometimes contradictory responses.

Parents may vow to care for their dying son or daughter but be terrified of touching him or her for fear they will catch the disease and die. (See page 414 for a further discussion on how the virus is transmitted.) Feelings of profound sadness and grief may vie with shame and worry that others will find out.

The disclosure of homosexuality or intravenous drug use may be as or in some cases more upsetting than learning of HIV infection. In such cases, family members may have to contend with a confusing mixture of shock, anger, guilt, and despair. Longstanding emotional and geographic estrangement may make any reconciliation more difficult and, indeed, impossible, especially if time is short.

Following the death, caregivers may feel suddenly shut off from hospitals, physicians, and others who helped care for the individual. They may feel isolated suddenly, particularly if little social support has been available, as is often the case when the illness has been shrouded in secrecy. Contradictory feelings may still be unresolved and prove more distressing during the period of bereavement.

GETTING HELP

Fortunately, there are increasing numbers of places to turn for medical, social, financial, and legal advice and assistance. Most larger cities have a network of counseling, support, and information services for people with HIV illness and their loved ones.

Community Organizations

Community-based organizations in urban areas are perhaps the greatest source of assistance. They may offer counseling, peer support, and psychotherapy groups; legal and social services; recreational and occupational therapies; and current information about medical treatment, among other services. An individual can often turn to a community health organization for help in preparing a will, obtaining disability payments, finding a personal physician, or getting some help at home, such as a "buddy" who can assist with miscellaneous chores. Information (including addresses and phone numbers) about community based health organizations can be obtained from the National AIDS Network (2033 M Street, NW, Washington, D.C.; tel. 202 293–AIDS).

Of inestimable value for many people with AIDS are peer groups in which members share feelings, experiences, and information and provide emotional support. Groups for caregivers are similarly helpful.

Mental Health Care

Professional mental health care is available for those who need or prefer additional support or who need help assessing and managing problems with anxiety, depression, concentration, or memory.

Once coordinated with medical care for AIDS, supportive psychotherapy for those who continue to experience significant distress can be enormously helpful. Provided he or she is knowledgeable about AIDS, the therapist can offer reassurance and correct misconceptions about HIV infection and can clarify further treatment options. It is common for people who are HIV positive to feel that they did something wrong or that the disease is their fault. Psychotherapy can often help to defuse this self-incrimination and, in so doing, reduce feelings of social and emotional isolation. Perhaps most important, it can help individuals regain a sense of control over their lives.

Support for Loved Ones

Some communities now offer support services for families, lovers, spouses, and others closely affected by those with AIDS. For example, some organizations offer support groups for caregivers with AIDS, spouses of people with AIDS, concerned family members, and the recently bereaved. National hotlines and organizations have been created in recent years to decrease the isolation and stigma felt by many caregivers, particularly families and partners with little social or community support. The National AIDS Network (see page 412) can provide further information.

HOW TO HELP PEOPLE WITH AIDS

When someone you know becomes ill, especially with a serious illness such as AIDS, you may feel helpless or inadequate. Here are some suggestions that may help you to help someone who is ill.

- Don't avoid him or her. Be there—it instills hope. Be the friend or loved one you've always been, especially now when it is most important.
- Touch. A simple squeeze of the hand or a hug can let a person know that you still care. (Don't be afraid . . . you cannot contract AIDS by simply touching.)
- Call before you plan to visit. The person may not feel up to a visitor that day. Don't be afraid to call back and visit on another occasion. The person needs you, and may be lonely and afraid.
- Help caregivers, lovers, and roommates. Though not ill, they may also be suffering. Caregivers may also need a small break from the illness from time to time. Offer to stay with the person who is sick in order to give the loved ones a break. Invite them out. Offer to accompany them places. They may need someone to talk with as well.
- Don't be reluctant to ask about the illness. The person may need to talk about his or her condition. Find out by asking: "Do you feel like talking about it?"
- Don't feel that you both always have to talk. It's okay to sit together silently reading, listening to music, watching television, holding hands. Much can be expressed without words.
- Help the person feel good about his or her looks, if possible. Say he or she looks good, but only if it is realistic to do so. If the person's appearance has changed, don't ignore it. Acknowledge the fact. But be gentle, and remember: never lie.
- Include the person in decision making. He or she has been robbed of so many things and has lost control over many aspects of life. Don't deny him or her a chance to make decisions, no matter how simple or silly they may seem to you.
- Be prepared for a person with AIDS to get angry with you for no obvious reason, although you've been there and done everything you could. Permit the person this, and don't take it personally. Feel flattered that he or she is close enough to you to risk sharing anger or frustration.
- Offer to do household chores, perhaps taking out the laundry, washing dishes, watering plants, feeding and walking pets. This may be appreciated more than you realize. However, don't do what the person can do him- or herself. Ask before doing anything.
- Don't lecture or be angry if the person seems to be handling the illness in a way that you think is inappropriate.
- Do not confuse acceptance of the illness with defeat. This acceptance may free the person and provide a sense of his or her own power.
- Don't allow the person or the caregivers to become isolated. Let them know about the support groups and other concrete, practical services offered without charge by various organizations.
- Talk about the future . . . tomorrow, next week, next year. Hope is important.

Source: Adapted from "When a Friend Has AIDS . . . ," a publication of the GMHC (The Gay Men's Health Crisis), The AIDS Service and Education Foundation, New York City.

THE FACTS ABOUT AIDS

AIDS is the subject of a huge worldwide research effort. Since the first cases of AIDS were reported in 1981, we have learned much about what AIDS is, how it is transmitted, who is at risk, how to prevent it, and how to treat it. While no cure or vaccine has been found, great strides have been made in treat-ing many of the opportunistic infections that actually cause AIDS-related deaths. The following review is accurate at press time. For the most up-to-date information, consult local public or community health agencies.

The Human Immunodeficiency Virus (HIV) and the Diagnosis of AIDS

AIDS is caused by the *human immunodeficiency virus,* or HIV, which weakens the immune system and renders the person vulnerable to many different infections. The organisms that cause these infections are common and carried by almost everyone, but they flourish once HIV weakens the body's natural ability to fight them off. The resulting infections are called *opportunistic.* People with AIDS die from these opportunistic infections or other consequences rather than from the AIDS virus itself.

Testing positive (or seropositive) for the presence of HIV (see page 417) is not the same as being diagnosed as having AIDS; diagnosis of AIDS is actually a late stage of infection with HIV. A person is diagnosed as having AIDS when he or she has developed one or more of the AIDS "indicator" diseases, such as pneumocystis carinii pneumonia or Kaposi's sarcoma, a type of cancer common with AIDS. However, in 1992 the definition of AIDS was expanded to include very low levels of CD4 (T4) lymphocytes (a type of white blood cell) even in the absence of any clinical illness.

One common source of confusion is the difference between the time it takes to develop HIV antibodies (and hence to "test positive") and the time it takes from initial infection to the diagnosis of AIDS. Whereas most individuals develop antibodies within six months of exposure to HIV, the length of time to developing AIDS is much longer; on average, 10 years.

Illness Course

While there is great variation in illness course, the first several years are often characterized by relatively good health accompanied by a progressive but often symptomless decline in the immune system. Then a series of infections and symptoms successively appear and an opportunistic infection eventually leads to a diagnosis of AIDS, on average after about 10 years. (In infants, the course of the illness is much faster.)

Symptoms of HIV infection include persistent swollen lymph nodes (referred to as *generalized lymphadenopathy*) and chronic fever; unexplained weight loss, diarrhea, and/or fatigue not due to other causes; as well as night sweats and chronic cough. Some people with HIV infection develop conditions such as oral thrush (a mouth infection), persistent herpes simplex (cold sores), or herpes zoster (shingles).

Physicians used to describe these symptoms as *AIDS-related complex* or *ARC,* a term never precisely defined. But because some people develop AIDS without ever having ARC—and because ARC diseases can be as serious and life threatening as AIDS diseases—the term has limited value and is no longer widely used in the medical or scientific communities. The National Academy of Sciences has recommended that HIV infection itself be considered a disease encompassing a series of illness stages and conditions.

Knowledge about what happens after a person has been infected with HIV is advancing and has permitted significant gains in clinical treatment. Early medical interventions and medications that offer some preventive capacity have increased survival time after the diagnosis of AIDS and may delay progression of the illness at earlier stages of HIV infection. Experimental treatments are becoming progressively "smarter" as science homes in on the intricate secrets of cell biology and basic immunology. Eventually, with the advent of new treatments and longer survival, AIDS may come to be regarded as a chronic debilitating disease (albeit like no other in recent memory) rather than a swift death sentence.

Who Gets AIDS and How?

All studies to date agree that HIV is passed from one person to another *only* in infected bodily fluids, primarily semen, vaginal secretions, or blood. The possibility of HIV transmission through saliva has been raised by very rare reports of infection transmitted during oral sex. The disease does not strike randomly. Most of those who are at risk for AIDS are men and women who are exposed to the possibility of infection by these described routes. Many of these risks can be avoided.

(Continued)

Sexual Behavior

HIV infection can be passed via vaginal or anal intercourse through the partners' semen or vaginal secretions. Whether between homosexuals, bisexuals, or heterosexuals, all sexual activities involving these body fluids—except those that take place within relationships that have been monogamous since 1979—potentially are risky. Some sexual practices (such as anal intercourse, especially for the receptive partner) are considered especially high risk. Having multiple sexual partners increases the risk, especially if partners are only casual acquaintances or strangers. Oral sex conceivably may transmit HIV, particularly if ejaculate is swallowed, although this risk is less than that for anal or vaginal intercourse.

Even though in the United States most people with AIDS are male and sexual transmission of AIDS among adults is generally male to male or male to female, in Africa, where the disease is rampant, women are equally affected and transmit it to their male partners. Among adults in the United States in 1991, the ratio of infected heterosexual males and females was 7 to 1. Among adolescents, however, the ratio was 7 to 4, indicating a comparatively high rate among female adolescents compared to adults. HIV infection, in other words, is not limited to men or to gay men.

In the United States, gay men continue to constitute the largest segment of AIDS cases cumulatively and annually in terms of newly reported cases.

Although their proportion is declining overall, each year there continue to be more new cases among gay men than there were the year before.

AIDS was first identified among gay men, and in the very beginning it actually was called "gay-related immune deficiency" or "GRID." This gays-only notion was disproved quickly, but the major spread of HIV infection did occur first in urban gay communities, notably San Francisco, New York, and Los Angeles. The "gay liberation movement," which grew within the context of profound social change among all young people in the late 1960s, encouraged an openly gay lifestyle, including sex with multiple, casual partners. Consequently, HIV infection spread rapidly in this particular segment of the population.

Once the disease and its risk factors were identified, aggressive education programs within the gay community led to dramatic behavioral and social change, which curbed the increase of the disease. Between 1982 and 1987 in San Francisco, for example, the rate of new infection dropped from 20 percent to less than 1 percent. Nevertheless, the damage was done early, and it is estimated that as many as 50 percent of the members of some urban gay communities have HIV infection.

For men and women, the risk of acquiring AIDS through sexual activity can be reduced substantially by *always* using condoms and by following "safer sex" procedures. (See below.)

PRACTICING "SAFER SEX"

The principles behind "safe sex" are simple. Because the AIDS virus is passed from one person to another only through bodily secretions such as blood, semen, or vaginal fluids, practicing "safer sex" means using barriers that prevent these fluids from entering your body or your partner's body.

- Use condoms. If a lubricant is desired, use a water-based lubricant, such as KY Jelly. Don't use Crisco, baby oil, hand lotions, or any product containing oil or petroleum, such as Vaseline. They can make the condom break.
- Because condoms can come off and break, withdrawal before ejaculation is recommended.
- Spermicides containing nonoxynol-9 used with a condom may give better protection, especially if the condom breaks. Some women have allergic reactions to it, so try it first on a patch of skin. If it is irritating, try another brand.

- The best protection is to choose sexual activities that do not allow semen, blood (including menstrual blood), or vaginal fluids to enter your body or to touch your skin where there is an open cut, scratch, or sore.
- If using objects to enhance sex, such as vibrators, use your own, clean shared ones with bleach or alcohol, or use condoms and change them after use.

Talking about sex and insisting on precautions can be difficult or awkward, but it also can be a very rewarding shared experience. With AIDS, it is also a matter of life and death.

Source: Adapted from "Women Need to Know About AIDS" prepared by the Gay Men's Health Crisis, Inc.

(Continued)

Needle Sharing

Sharing unsterilized hypodermic needles presents an extraordinary risk. In the United States needle sharing occurs almost entirely in the context of illicit drug use, particularly heroin and cocaine. By mid-1992 intravenous drug abusers accounted for some 23 percent of the total of AIDS cases reported, and their numbers are growing. On the East Coast, about 50 to 60 percent of methadone maintenance clinic clients (former heroin users) are believed to have HIV infection, and among street addicts the estimates rise to 70 to 80 percent. Because most needle-sharing drug abusers are male and heterosexual, at present they constitute the major route of infection to women and their fetuses.

The risk of passing the infection via needles can be reduced by cleaning the needle and "works" with bleach before every use.

Blood Transfusions

Because AIDS is transmitted in blood, nearly 3 percent of reported AIDS cases are associated with transfusions of contaminated blood during medical procedures, almost all received before 1985. *A national screening program of donated blood, introduced in 1985, has substantially eliminated this infection source in the United States—except for the small but identifiable risk from recently infected donors who have not yet developed detectable antibodies.* Some people facing elective surgery decide to have their own blood drawn in advance and used in their surgery to avoid this risk.

New cases among people suffering from hemophilia—a disorder often requiring treatment with a blood derivative taken from multiple donors—are minimal because of the screening procedures. Unfortunately, an estimated 80 percent of those with hemophilia severe enough to require transfusion became infected before 1985. Today they account for 1 percent of AIDS cases.

Pregnancy and Childbirth

Some 30 percent of babies born to infected mothers develop AIDS. It is not clear whether infants acquire the virus only through the placenta or whether it is also passed on during childbirth. Scientists have found the HIV virus in fetal tissue as early as 13 weeks' gestation. Children are currently the smallest but the most rapidly growing group to become vulnerable to HIV infection. Most HIV-infected children are Black or Hispanic, reflecting the disproportionate distribution of HIV in Black and Hispanic mothers who themselves are infected by sexual contact with HIV-positive men or by intravenous drug use. Care for these children is particularly difficult, because many of their mothers are impoverished single parents and ill themselves. Often AIDS babies are abandoned and remain indefinitely in hospitals, for lack of alternative placements.

AIDS TRANSMISSION: WHAT *NOT* TO WORRY ABOUT

HIV is a weak and fragile virus. Compared to other viruses, it is easy to kill before it enters the body (with heat, bleach, alcohol, and similar substances) and hard to acquire. It is rare for a person to become infected after a single exposure, just as it is rare to become pregnant after a single encounter. No household members of AIDS patients have been known to become infected unless they themselves engaged in high-risk behavior. The very few health-care workers not in high-risk categories themselves who have acquired the disease have been exposed to patients' blood products accidentally, such as by pricking their skin with used hypodermic needles.

To date, there has been no documented case in which HIV has been spread through tears, saliva in nonsexual contact, urine, or sweat, even though virus in small quantities has been isolated from these fluids. While scientists are not prepared to state unequivocally that such transmission never will or never can occur, the risks are vanishingly small if they in fact exist. Accordingly, there is nothing to worry about from coughs and sneezes, public toilet seats, gym equipment, a shared eating utensil, or food handlers. Nor can social contact lead to HIV infection. This includes ordinary classroom contact, workplace contact, and friendly encounters of any nonsexual kind.

(Continued)

A few years ago sensational newspaper articles suggested that mosquitoes and other insects can transmit HIV. This is untrue: The pattern of distribution of HIV infection does not correspond to that of insect-transmitted diseases such as malaria. Except for transfusion recipients, children between ages five and 15 have almost no cases of HIV infection, nor do the elderly, even though both groups are exposed to mosquitoes. Careful laboratory studies also have ruled this out as a mode of transmission.

The only things to worry about are exchange of blood products by sharing needles, transfusions, accidents in handling infected material that can puncture the skin, and specific sexual activities. In contrast to former years when routes of HIV infection were not known, today HIV infection is avoidable. Take precautions where they count.

HIV TRANSMISSION BY DOCTORS AND DENTISTS

In 1991 considerable public anxiety was generated by the report that a Florida dentist had infected five of his patients before he died of an AIDS-related condition. To date these are the only documented cases of patient infection by any health-care worker, and even in this instance no one has been able to provide a convincing explanation of how the dentist infected his patients. In the past 10 years there has not been a single instance of transmission from physician, nurse, or hospital worker to a patient.

In response to congressional initiatives, the American Medical Association asked dozens of medical groups and specialty societies to identify invasive procedures that could pose a risk to patients if performed by an HIV-infected physician. Over 40 of these groups refused to comply on the grounds that such a policy is counterproductive, recommending instead the enforcement of universal precautions to prevent transmission of any infectious agent.

In August 1991 at a press conference, former Surgeon General C. Everett Koop, M.D., joined representatives from the American Medical Association, Centers for Disease Control, and the Society for Hospital Epidemiology of America in efforts to allay the widespread and misguided fears about risk of HIV transmission by health-care workers. He stated that the chances of a physician's passing HIV to a patient "are essentially nil unless they are having a sexual relationship or are sharing needles."

Testing for the Presence of HIV Antibodies

HIV tests, which detect antibodies to the viruses in the blood, have been used for clinical diagnosis of HIV infection, to screen blood and blood products, for epidemiological studies of the distribution of HIV in the general population, and to test individuals concerned about exposure to HIV. The currently used HIV test actually has two stages. A blood sample is first analyzed using a test called *ELISA (enzyme linked immunosorbent assay)*. If it is positive, meaning that HIV antibodies are found, the test usually is repeated. After a second positive result, the *Western blot* test is performed to confirm the ELISA. If all three procedures are positive, the person is said to be HIV positive (or seropositive). It is *not* a test for AIDS and it does not necessarily mean that the person has AIDS or will develop AIDS in the near future.

It is important to know that HIV antibodies do not develop immediately, usually taking six to 12 weeks (sometimes longer) to appear in measurable quantities. Even though the individual does not test positive during this period, he or she is infected and can pass the virus on to another person. Because of this "silent" period between infection and antibody detection, a single negative test is *not* proof of absence of HIV infection. To be certain, the HIV test needs to be repeated, generally six months after the first negative test. If the person does not engage in any high-risk activity between tests and the second is also negative, absence of infection is confirmed. Of course, absence of the disease in the present does not mean that the person will not contract it in the future, especially if he or she engages in high-risk activities.

Although voluntary (and even mandatory) testing has been advocated for a long time by many federal and state officials, gay community leaders initially discouraged it, convinced that the risks (of losing jobs, housing, insurance, and the like) were significant while the benefits were not. In August of 1989, with the announcement of scientific evidence

(Continued)

showing that AZT (or zidovudine; see below) postponed illness in HIV-positive people even without current symptoms, attitudes have changed dramatically. At that time, the Gay Men's Health Crisis in New York, the world's largest community-based organization, called a news conference to announce a policy reversal and undertook an advertising campaign to encourage voluntary HIV testing.

Treatments

In 1987 the first drug to work directly against HIV was marketed in the United States, altering the outlook for AIDS survival. Known as zidovudine, azidothymidine (AZT), or by its brand name, Retrovir, the drug reduces HIV activity and may protect against new opportunistic infections.

Zidovudine is not a cure and its effects do not last indefinitely: It works only while the patient is taking it. It also can cause severe side effects, forcing many patients to discontinue use or reduce dosage. While zidovudine is not the final treatment answer, this drug has brought hope to thousands and extended life to many. It is now recommended for use by HIV-infected patients who do not yet have AIDS or even any HIV symptoms but whose immune systems show impairment.

In 1991 the Food and Drug Administration (FDA) approved a second antiviral medication to treat HIV infection, dideoxyinosine, or ddl. This medication

The advantages of the individual knowing he or she is infected are increasing. For the couple considering having a child, knowledge of maternal infection may influence decision making. Testing thus can be crucial for those women whose sexual partners are intravenous drug users or bisexual men. For anyone who is HIV positive, early treatment may well prolong life. Those who fear discrimination should consider taking the test anonymously.

was approved for patients who developed severe side effects on zidovudine or who no longer respond to that drug. A third antiviral, dideoxycytidine (ddC) is under evaluation at press time and may be particularly useful if taken in combination with zidovudine. As mentioned earlier, other drugs have been identified that successfully treat AIDS-related diseases (that is, opportunistic infections).

Because the FDA does not approve drugs that have not undergone extensive clinical trials, often taking years, and because approved drugs such as zidovudine can be extremely expensive, underground networks and "buyers' clubs" bring unapproved drugs illegally into the country at the lowest possible cost. While these drugs are of uncertain worth medically and in fact may carry risks, some people with HIV infection take them in the hopes of finding something that can help them live longer.

FOR FURTHER INFORMATION

Information on clinical trials and AIDS research is available by calling the National Institutes for Health, Centers for Disease Control (800 TRIALS–A). In addition to advice on the latest research, it will send a complimentary copy of the "AIDS/HIV Experimental Treatment Directory," a subscription newsletter published by The American Foundation for AIDS Research. Another source of information and publications on AIDS treatment, research, and sources of help is the National AIDS Clearinghouse (P.O. 6003, Rockville, MD 20850; tel. 800 458–5231).

30

Legal and Ethical Issues

Francine Cournos, M.D., and John Petrila, J.D., LL.M.

To ensure the delivery of the best possible care and protect the rights of patients, the actions and responsibilities of mental health practitioners are governed by a number of basic guidelines. Some are legal, such as restrictions imposed by governmental licensing agencies or laws that regulate involuntary commitment. Some are ethical, such as guidelines set by professional organizations that describe what is appropriate conduct and what is not. Ethical principles do not generally carry the force of law, although their violation may lead to censure by professional organizations to which a practitioner belongs. However, ethical principles are considered so basic to good care that a conscientious practitioner will adhere strictly to them. And while laws may vary from state to state, in many instances legal and ethical codes overlap.

In this chapter many of the references to the legal and ethical duties of the "psychiatrist" or "doctor" also apply to any person involved in providing mental health care—psychiatrists, psychologists, nurses, counselors, social workers, and even medical office staff.

THE PATIENT–THERAPIST AGREEMENT

The patient-therapist relationship is much like a contract. The practitioner agrees to provide services within his or her area of competence and according to generally accepted professional standards. (See "Standard of Care" page 421.) The patient, in turn, agrees to treatment and to compensate the therapist for services rendered.

The patient-therapist relationship begins when both agree to it. However, in emergency situations, the law allows the relationship to begin in the absence of an overt agreement if the patient is incapable of agreeing to treatment. (See pages 422–423 for a discussion of informed consent and competency.) The patient's consent to treatment may involve or extend to more than one therapist or professional, as is often the case, for example, when a patient is treated in a hospital or group practice.

Ending the Relationship

Either the patient or the therapist can end the relationship. The patient can end it in any way he or she pleases—by not attending any more appointments, by changing therapists, or by telling the therapist that he or she no longer wants treatment.

A therapist might recommend that treatment terminate for a number of reasons. He or she may not have the necessary skills to treat a specific problem, for example, or may believe that further therapy would prove unproductive. The therapist, however, may not stop treatment abruptly and is required to refer the

patient to another source of care if treatment is still needed. The absence of such a referral may constitute what the law terms "patient abandonment."

PAYMENTS

Before treatment begins, you and your therapist should discuss fees as well as how and when payment should be made. In many instances insurance covers only part of the fee, and patients must pay the balance or the full fee prior to being reimbursed by their insurance company. If you do not pay, the therapist can terminate the treatment after helping you find other care, if you still need treatment.

In most situations, no laws prohibit a therapist from charging for missed appointments or for meetings that are short because a patient is late, but the therapist should be explicit about these policies before treatment begins.

LICENSES AND "SCOPE OF PRACTICE"

For his or her own safety, before beginning treatment, an individual should be sure to determine whether the mental health professional is licensed. Every state has licensing laws, with the requirements typically including educational criteria and qualifying examinations. A licensed professional cannot exceed the authority permitted by his or her license. Most states, for example, grant only to physicians the right to prescribe medications; psychologists or social workers may not do so. It is often very difficult to assess the qualifications of individuals who call themselves psychotherapists but who are not licensed professionals.

Scope of practice also means that a therapist is expected to practice only within the limits of his or her individual competence. For example, a therapist who is not trained to treat children should not attempt to do so; rather, he or she should refer the patient to a more qualified practitioner. If a therapist attempts to do something for which he or she is unqualified and the patient is harmed, the therapist may be held accountable. Similarly, a therapist cannot delegate to a nonmedical person any matter requiring the exercise of professional medical judgment.

An individual entering treatment should feel free to ask questions about areas of specialty, licensing, professional experience, and any other matter relevant to the therapist's qualifications. (See chapter 3 for a discussion of the types of mental health professionals and their qualifying credentials.)

JOINT OR COMBINED TREATMENT

Combined treatment is when a patient sees more than one professional for psychiatric care, as when a patient sees a psychiatrist for medication and another mental health professional for psychotherapy. In this situation, a patient should have ongoing, face-to-face contact with both professionals. As a general rule, any

questions a patient has about treatment should be directed to the professional who is best trained to evaluate the question. For example, questions about medications or physical health should be directed to the psychiatrist, who has the appropriate medical training to answer them.

STANDARD OF CARE

All mental health professionals are obligated to practice in accordance with the standards of their profession. Failure to do so could constitute negligence or malpractice as well as pose an unacceptable risk to patients. This obligation does not mean, of course, that the outcome of treatment can be guaranteed; rather, it means mental health practitioners have a duty to act *reasonably* in reaching a diagnosis, providing medications (if they are licensed to do so), and performing treatment. Nor does it mean that there is only one correct treatment. There are numerous approaches to understanding and explaining human behavior and mental disability and an equally diverse range of treatment approaches.

Standards of care evolve and change over time, refined by research and scientific advances that help to develop new treatments. A number of sources shape the standard of care at any given time, and practitioners are expected to be familiar with them.

Professional organizations (such as the American Psychiatric Association or the American Psychological Association) establish standards and help members keep up-to-date in their field. Professional manuals offer guidelines and current information on mental health diagnosis or treatment. Scholarly journals report on the latest treatment advances.

Health-care facilities themselves can establish standards of care through internal policies and review boards. Government regulation also can establish the standard of care, such as by mandating the minimum number of staff needed to provide good care in a hospital.

Professionals are responsible for keeping up-to-date with developments in their fields and with the policies of accrediting bodies, regulatory agencies, and employers.

CONFIDENTIALITY

Therapists must keep confidential all communications about treatment, any records of it, and even the very fact that treatment is taking place. A therapeutic relationship is based on trust, and that trust is difficult to maintain if information about a patient's mental state and innermost feelings is widely available.

If the therapist asks for permission to disclose information, a patient should find out precisely why the information must be passed on, what details will be disclosed, and to whom. Before giving permission to disclose information, the advantages and possible disadvantages of releasing information should be considered. For instance, if a patient asks that a diagnosis or treatment summary not be released to an insurance company, the company may refuse to cover the treatment expenses. The patient's decision rules, however.

It is also important to understand that there are limitations to confidentiality. For example, a therapist must report suspected child abuse and, if he or she is treating a parent, subsequently may be ordered into court to testify about that treatment. In many states the therapist is obligated legally to reveal to appropriate authorities dangerous behavior or threats that a patient has made. Listed in the box on page 422 are a number of important legal exceptions to the general requirement for medical confidentiality.

Professionals ethically are allowed to consult their peers on behalf of patients. However, when a case is discussed among professionals without a patient's specific approval, the therapist must avoid any description that might identify the patient. It is a breach of the patient's right to confidentiality for the doctor, his or her employees, or anyone else in the health-care establishment to discuss the patient for any purpose other than his or her benefit.

Sometimes permission to disclose medical information is implied. For example, a clerical worker employed by the doctor to maintain records and organize files might have some knowledge of the information in those records, and the patient automatically approves of that knowledge merely by accepting the doctor's standard office practices. Similarly, by providing a blood sample for testing, the patient grants permission to those conducting the test to know the results and communicate them to the doctor.

INFORMED CONSENT

Patients are entitled to know their diagnosis; the available treatments and the risks and benefits of each; and the potential outcome if no treatment is pursued. This information should be conveyed in a way that is easily understood, not in complicated technical language. It also should include details of the treatment itself—how it is performed, how long it takes, when results can be expected, and the overall likelihood of success. In some instances, costs may be relevant to the issue of informed consent. For example, if two drugs are equally effective, but one is considerably more expensive than the other but has fewer side effects, the physician might very well include this as part of the discussion. (However, the mental health professional does not have a legal obligation to project costs for treatment.)

When a patient sufficiently understands these issues, his or her decision to accept a particular treatment is called informed consent. The law assumes that most people are competent to give informed consent. Often it is given verbally. However, for admission to a hospital or for certain medical procedures such as electroconvulsive therapy (ECT), a patient or family member generally must provide written consent.

Studies suggest that many patients do not understand sufficiently the treatment they are offered. Therefore, before treatment begins, it is important that patients talk to their therapists about any questions that they have regarding treatment. If a patient does not sufficiently understand the doctor's explanation, he or she should not hesitate to ask for additional information or another review of what the treatment involves.

Competency

In a psychiatric emergency a psychiatrist may begin treatment without informed consent if it is clear that the individual is unable to make a competent decision. This situation might arise, for instance, when it is necessary to intervene in a suicide attempt, or when

---

CONFIDENTIALITY—COMMON EXCEPTIONS TO THE RULE

A psychiatrist or other mental health care professional must keep confidential all information about the patient's diagnosis, treatment, or prognosis, except in certain circumstances:

- When a court orders disclosure, such as in a civil commitment proceeding, or some other legal action in which the mental state of one of the parties is relevant.
- In a custody dispute, where the best interests of the child are considered to be at stake (if, for example, the parent's ability to care for the child is in question because of a mental health problem), the judge might require the treating psychiatrist to testify. The judge will hear arguments from both sides regarding the testimony's relevance before ordering it admitted into evidence.
- In cases of suspected child abuse (many professionals have both a legal and ethical obligation to report this possibility).
- When an insurance company or government agency is paying for or regulating the mental health services being provided.

- When a minor child requires parental consent for therapy (although today's trend is to limit as much as possible the scope of information provided to parents and to give children much the same confidentiality enjoyed by adults).
- When the therapist has reason to believe a patient is suicidal or may endanger another person. (However, rules encouraging therapists to warn potential victims vary from state to state and are not uniform in all professional associations.)
- When an individual is evaluated by a therapist at the request of a third party—such as when a court orders an independent psychiatric examination, in which case the therapist works for the third party, not the patient; no therapeutic relationship is established and information uncovered in the examination will be made available to the third party.
- If a patient decides to initiate a legal action against a therapist because of questions about treatment received.

a violent patient poses a clear danger to others. But even in cases such as these, treatment must be limited to the immediate, life-threatening emergency. Once the emergency ends, consent must be given before treatment continues.

Under most circumstances the law upholds the right of the competent person to refuse treatment, even though it would be beneficial. However, if a patient lacks the capacity to make informed treatment decisions, a psychiatrist can initiate procedures to obtain permission to treat from a surrogate (a third party). These procedures are intended to safeguard the rights of patients while at the same time ensure that a patient who is incapable of making a treatment decision still can receive needed care.

The laws regarding surrogates vary widely from state to state. In the case of an adult who lacks capacity, a family member, a legal guardian, or a court may make the decisions depending on the nature of the treatment and the relevant law. Children are generally considered unable to give informed consent, and the parents must act for them. However, in some circumstances adolescents are permitted to make their own treatment decisions. The doctor is obligated to make certain that a surrogate is at least as well informed as a fully competent patient would be.

Consent and Treatment Side Effects

As in any branch of medicine, some psychiatric treatments contain a degree of risk. Common or severe side effects of a treatment or diagnostic test should be described in advance. Informed consent requires that these risks be explained to the patient in an understandable manner. Many doctors do not review every possible side effect, because many are quite uncommon.

Some drugs require special measures to ensure a patient's safety while using them. In these instances, informed consent means that a patient understands what these measures are and why they are necessary. For example, lithium and clozapine (Clozaril) both require frequent blood tests to reduce risks and ensure the best therapeutic results. Monoamine oxidase inhibitors require a special diet to avoid significant medical complications. (See chapter 5 for a full discussion of drugs and their side effects.)

Consent to Research

Occasionally a doctor suggests that a patient participate in a research investigation or an experimental treatment. Two types of situations are involved. The first involves a therapeutic approach that is not common practice. Generally a doctor recommends experimental treatment if other approaches have not worked, or if he or she believes that the treatment under investigation will be more beneficial than the patient's current treatment. For example, a psychiatrist might prescribe a medicine that has not yet been firmly established for use in a particular psychiatric illness, if some studies suggest it could be helpful. In this case, informed consent requires that the patient be told what the treatment is, the fact that its efficacy has not yet been firmly established, and what complications are possible.

The second involves an organized study that seeks to gain new knowledge of a disorder or its treatment. Although participants often benefit, the primary purpose of such a study is not to treat individual patients but to attempt to answer important scientific questions. Those who are asked to volunteer for the study have the condition that is under investigation. Participants sign consent forms that contain full descriptions of the purpose of the research, its risks and benefits, alternative treatments, protection of confidentiality, compensation for injury, and the name of a researcher who can answer any questions about the study. In addition, the consent forms must make it clear that a patient can withdraw from the study at any time and that such a withdrawal will not jeopardize his or her care. A patient should never feel pressured or obligated to join in a research study if he or she does not wish to do so.

PATIENT RECORDS

In general, an individual has the right to review his or her medical records, although that right varies from state to state and does not necessarily include receiving a full copy of the actual record. Sometimes a psychiatrist will agree to go over the chart with the patient and explain entries. More often the practitioner will consider the request within the context of treatment (Is the patient worried that the therapist is hiding something important? Does the patient want more control over treatment?) and encourage the patient to discuss fully the reasons for making the request. In some states a written request from the patient to review his or her own records is sufficient; in others, a court order is necessary.

Generally, psychiatrists are willing to release the records to another professional who has assumed responsibility for the patient's treatment, following a written request by the patient to release records. If there is material that the mental health professional considers sensitive and is reluctant to release, usually he or she will call the new treating professional to discuss the issues involved.

In a situation where the records are requested in anticipation of a malpractice suit, the mental health professional may well be reluctant to release records and, in fact, probably will be advised by his or her attorney not to do so. Currently, no states have laws mandating an absolute duty on the part of a mental health professional to turn over records. In this situation, a patient may well have to hire an attorney and subpoena the records.

VOLUNTARY AND INVOLUNTARY HOSPITALIZATION

Voluntary admission to a psychiatric hospital is in some ways similar to checking into a standard medical unit. Often, however, the rights of a voluntary patient in a psychiatric hospital are somewhat more limited than those of a patient with a purely medical condition. The doors of psychiatric facilities are often kept locked, for instance, and patients must receive a pass in order to leave. In some cases a hospital can detain a voluntary patient for a limited period of time even after the patient asks to be discharged, if the attending psychiatrist believes continuing treatment is necessary and plans to ask for involuntary commitment.

Most therapeutic relationships are entered into voluntarily. Sometimes, however, people do not seek treatment, even when it appears needed to protect them or others from harm. Their behavior may prompt others to seek a civil commitment on their behalf. Civil commitment means that someone with authority decides that a person must be hospitalized against his or her will.

A request for involuntary hospitalization usually is made by a family member, a friend, a psychiatrist, or a representative of a government agency. (In most states statutes define who may serve as an applicant for commitment.) The decision to commit can be made only after an evaluation of the person's mental status reveals that the standards of commitment have been met. In general, hospitalization is permitted for a limited period of time, after which the facility either must release the patient or must seek court permission for an extension.

Both physicians and judges have a role in the commitment process. In most states a preliminary decision is made by a psychiatrist or physician and then reviewed by a judge, who decides whether involuntary commitment for a longer period of time is warranted. However, the specific time frames concerning commitment and the specific duties of judges and physicians vary from state to state.

Criteria for Commitment

There are two primary criteria for commitment. First, a person must be found to have a mental disorder. Second, as a result of the illness, he or she must present a clear danger to self or another person. While legal definitions of "dangerousness" vary from state to state, the general concept is the same. A person who attempts suicide is considered a danger to self; in most states someone who threatens suicide falls into the same category. In many states someone unable to provide for basic needs—food, shelter, medical care—as a result of a mental disorder is also considered a danger to self. Direct threats or actions against others are evidence that a person is dangerous to someone else. In every state a link between a mental disorder and "dangerousness" must be shown prior to commitment.

In a psychiatric emergency, individuals may be detained briefly in a hospital as long as they appear to present an immediate danger to themselves or others. In such situations the patient must be released when the immediate danger has passed, unless he or she agrees to continued hospitalization or the psychiatrist seeks a civil commitment.

Involuntary commitment also can result from the disposition of criminal charges. Before a trial, a judge can order a suspect to undergo psychiatric observation and/or treatment. Following conviction, psychiatric hospitalization can be part of sentencing. Criminal defendants who are found "not guilty by reason of insanity" also can be confined to psychiatric hospitals, even though they have been acquitted.

Patients' Rights

After commitment, individuals still retain basic civil rights. For example, they can still manage their monetary affairs and they have the right to vote. Nor does involuntary hospitalization exempt patients from paying taxes and meeting other civic obligations.

In most states involuntarily hospitalized patients can refuse to take medications—unless there is an immediate danger to self or others or the patient is found to lack the capacity to make treatment decisions. This right is consistent with the general principles of laws governing health care, which assume that adults have the right to make decisions about the course of their own medical treatment.

FOR FURTHER INFORMATION ABOUT INVOLUNTARY COMMITMENT

To find out what the specific laws regarding involuntary commitment are in your state, call the state department of mental health (sometimes a component of the department of health) and ask for the legal or other appropriate division.

Neither involuntary nor voluntary psychiatric patients can be restrained physically or placed in seclusion unless clear and immediate risk of harm to self or others exists and no other reasonable alternative is available. Restraint or confinement must be limited to the period of danger and cannot be used as punishment. Most states have specific laws that regulate restraint and seclusion and also require clear, unambiguous documentation to support such action.

PROFESSIONAL MISCONDUCT

Although the overwhelming majority of therapists adhere to ethical guidelines, unfortunately not all do. Therapist misconduct can be particularly damaging because the nature of the relationship between a patient and therapist leaves patients vulnerable to any inappropriate conduct on the part of a therapist. This misconduct may be financial, as in the case of a therapist engaging in business deals with the patient or using confidential information for personal profit; or it may involve social or sexual contact. It is essential that a patient's treatment needs come first. The introduction of any other purpose into the treatment relationship undermines its outcome.

The patient's vulnerability results in part from a phenomenon called transference. Transference is the tendency to experience people in the present in ways similar to important individuals in childhood, such as parents. It is especially powerful in the very intimate relationship that occurs in psychotherapy. Often transference provokes intense, but unrealistic, feelings for the therapist, including anger, idealized love, or sexual attraction. An ethical therapist will not respond to the patient's transference feelings in any way other than as an important source of information that assists him or her in understanding and helping the patient. (See chapter 4, page 50, for an additional discussion of transference.)

Sexual contact is never a valid method of treatment, even if the patient has sexual problems. Sexual contact is unethical (and in some states illegal) even if the patient consents to it and even if a patient initiates it. A practitioner who engages in sexual activity with a patient directly violates ethical standards set by numerous professional organizations. Even the Hippocratic Oath, which established basic ethical guidelines over 2,000 years ago, prohibits a doctor from "all seduction and especially from the pleasures of love of women and men." Nor will an ethical therapist engage in a sexual relationship even after treatment ends; transference feelings for a therapist are lifelong, and a patient continues to be at risk for emotional harm.

PROBLEMS WITH TREATMENT—WHAT TO DO

If you are concerned about the efficacy of your treatment or if you suspect that someone involved in your mental health care has violated legal or ethical guidelines, you can follow several courses, depending on whether your goal is to resolve a problem in treatment or to change its direction, to obtain monetary compensation for damages caused by substandard care, or to censure the mental health professional.

Resolving a Problem

Sometimes patients in treatment consider bringing lawsuits because they are unhappy with their progress or with some other specific aspect of care. Bringing a lawsuit is not the best way to resolve such a conflict, however.

If your goal is to resolve a problem in treatment, often it is best to begin by speaking directly to the therapist about the problem. Sometimes the complaint may be only a misunderstanding between the two of you. Talking it over can often resolve the problem without interrupting treatment.

Keep in mind that misunderstandings between you and your therapist could be symptomatic of the problem for which you have sought help, and thus, they need to be explored. For example, a patient who wants to end treatment without good reason may have a pattern of ending important relationships. A paranoid patient's desire to see medical records may be related to the disorder. Or a patient who repeatedly misses or is late for appointments and is angry at the therapist for charging for this time may have a history of provoking confrontations.

If talking to your therapist does not resolve your complaint, consult another mental health professional for an evaluation of your treatment. He or she may be able to clarify whether the treatment is or is not appropriate, or whether it might be better to switch therapists. Often the simplest way to resolve the problem is simply to change therapists.

Some patients, however, do not have this choice. Patients in state mental hospitals or publicly funded clinics, for example, may not have the financial resources to switch to another therapist or treatment facility. Or a person may live in a rural area where the options for treatment are limited. In this instance, a patient may want to take action that is designed to change some aspect of treatment—medication or its schedule, a hospital's policy on restraining patients or restricting them to a ward, or even uncourteous treatment by staff.

There is always some supervising authority to which you can direct an appeal if the problem has not been resolved by talking it over with the therapist. In a clinic or hospital, this may be the therapist's supervisor, the chairman or director of the department of psychiatry, the hospital's director or chief administrator, or someone assigned by the hospital to handle patient complaints.

If the problem is not resolved within the clinic or hospital, or if you feel that you cannot get satisfaction because the mental health professional and hospital are ignoring or dismissing your complaint, you can take further steps. Many agencies strictly regulate health care; a complaint can be addressed to any one of them, or to several agencies simultaneously. (See "Pursuing Complaints about Care" on page 427.)

Relatives' Concern about Treatment

If you are concerned about a family member's treatment, be aware that there are many limitations on what a therapist ethically can discuss with third parties. Without patient consent, a doctor can release information only in those cases where the third party has a legal right to receive that information or has a legal responsibility for the patient's care. Even with consent, a doctor will provide information only to the extent that he or she judges it to be in the best interest of the patient.

Disciplinary Action

If you believe that stronger action against a therapist for ethical or legal wrongdoing is necessary, you may attempt to have a hospital reconsider a professional's right to practice there or to have a government agency revoke his or her license. In general, the place to start is with whatever agency in your state has jurisdiction over the practitioner's license. This may be the state's department of health or professional education office. Call and ask what their procedures are for filing a complaint.

In cases of sexual or financial exploitation, you also could consider going to your city's district attorney to see if there is sufficient basis for a criminal charge. Particularly in cases where the therapist has induced a patient to engage in sexual relations, an element of sexual assault may be involved. You should be forewarned, however, that these cases often are difficult to prove and, if prosecuted, sometimes may receive a great deal of media attention. You may find yourself having to expose intimate details of your sexual behavior in a public courtroom.

(Continued)

Malpractice Suits

You also can resort to civil suits, known as malpractice suits, in which you demand monetary compensation for damages. (Malpractice suits and disciplinary action can be pursued simultaneously or separately.) In such cases, the person filing the suit must demonstrate four factors: (1) the therapist had an obligation to the patient; (2) the doctor failed to meet that obligation by deviating from an accepted standard of care; (3) the patient suffered damages; and (4) the damages were the direct result of the doctor's failure.

To find out whether a malpractice suit is warranted, consult an attorney who is experienced in malpractice as it pertains to mental health issues. You might also ask another mental health professional to review your situation and advise if your case has merits, although it may be difficult to find someone who is willing to provide this service. An attorney who deals with medical malpractice may know of mental health professionals who specialize in case review.

Often the issue of malpractice is not clear-cut. It can be very difficult for a patient to know what constitutes malpractice and what does not. For instance, if a patient takes a medication and suffers a serious side effect that makes him or her very ill, that is probably not malpractice if the prescribing physician has followed normal precautions and has obtained informed consent. Many drugs do have side effects, and a physician cannot be held accountable for the action of a drug. Nor can a physician be held accountable simply because a specific drug that he or she has prescribed does not work. However, if the physician prescribed the drug at a much higher dose than recommended by its manufacturer, or if he or she failed to monitor the patient adequately, then there *might* be grounds for malpractice. Or if a physician only recommended psychotherapy when the accepted approach to treatment is with medication, then, again, there *might* be malpractice.

Pursuing Complaints about Care

Several agencies, both public and private, are prepared to investigate and respond to complaints about mental health care. They range from state licensing departments, to congressional committees studying proposed legislation involving the medical profession, to agencies that regulate the quality of care.

You can find out where to address your questions by phoning your city or state health department (or a similarly named agency in your area), local legislators, or a professional organization such as the American Psychiatric Association. Many states and even some large cities have an ombudsman office that can assist in directing you to the proper agency.

If you have a complaint concerning hospital care, check whether your hospital has a patients' rights advocate or ombudsman to help handle your complaint or a panel of professionals willing to study your situation.

A local politician may be able to help you reach the appropriate authorities. You also might try complaining to an organization that provides funding to the hospital or clinic. (These are often listed in a hospital's annual report.) Or you may wish to consult an attorney to assist you.

Advocacy groups such as FAMI (Friends and Advocates of Mentally Ill) and NAMI (National Alliance for the Mentally Ill) can also provide help and information as well as emotional support. (See chapter 31, page 435, for a list of advocacy groups.)

It is important to document your complaint as thoroughly as possible. Include in your letter of complaint the specifics of the case, what you believe the problem to be, what was done and what was not done, the date treatment started, its nature, and any conversations you have had with the practitioner or staff member of an institution relevant to your complaint. A complaint that is not thoroughly documented is dismissed more easily as lacking merit.

As you pursue your complaint, keep a record of whom you have talked to and when, as well as notes on your conversations. Follow up your conversations in writing, and keep copies of any letters and any backup correspondence you have sent.

Be aware that winning redress for your problem may not be easy. Licensing boards are sometimes ineffective in sanctioning bad practitioners. Government agencies can move slowly and be frustrating to deal with. Hiring an attorney can be expensive, and there is no guarantee that you will win a suit. But if you feel strongly that your case has merit, be persistent and follow up on every avenue.

31

National Policy and Mental Health

Herbert Pardes, M.D., Frederic I. Kass, M.D., and Francine Cournos, M.D.

Much of the discussion regarding national mental health policy revolves around people's attitude toward mental illness and the government's commitment to pay for mental health treatment and research. It has been difficult for people to conceive of mental illnesses as medical disorders and worthy of the same kind of sympathy and attention. This fact has led to a reluctance to fund treatment and research in this area.

In recent years research linking mental illness to biological disorders, and efforts by people who suffer from mental illness and their family members to overcome prejudice and stigma, have begun to improve the situation. But there is a long way to go. This chapter reviews some of the policy challenges the mental health field now faces.

STIGMA

In spite of how common mental disorder is, there is still great fear of and prejudice against those who suffer from it. Within any given one-month period, about 15 percent of adults and 12 percent of children suffer from a psychiatric disorder. And yet, because mental illness is not widely understood, sufferers may not receive the care they need. Most people have only a vague concept of what mental illness is, and make little distinction between the different types of mental disorders.

Some people believe mentally ill persons are invariably dangerous or violent, even though studies show that as a group, mentally ill people are in fact no more inclined to violence than the general population. Others wrongly believe that mentally ill persons have somehow brought their illnesses upon themselves. Sufferers from mental illness—and their families—often attempt to hide the problem rather than seek treatment. Even those who do accept help may not apply for insurance benefits, fearing that their treatment will become known to their employers or others.

Often mentally ill people are portrayed negatively in popular television shows, movies, or books, and the labels "maniac" and "lunatic" have become a familiar part of our vocabulary. Even mental health professionals often are portrayed negatively—

disturbed themselves, or uncaring and incompetent.

Research has shown that attitudes toward mental illness have a direct correlation to education level and exposure. The well educated tend to have less fear of mental illness and less prejudice against those who suffer from it.

Relatives or friends of those who have had mental disorders tend to be more accepting. These people, banding together with current and former patients, have created citizen advocacy groups that are leading a growing effort to fight the stigma of mental illness. They are educating the public, demanding a greater recognition of the plight of mentally ill people, and making their needs known. Recently, more sensitive portrayals of mentally ill patients have appeared in popular books and on television.

THE PUBLIC MENTAL HEALTH SYSTEM

In a small percentage of cases, mental illness is so disabling that those affected by it cannot take care of themselves, and the cost and effort of caring for them exceeds the resources of their families. This group of patients presents a special challenge to government, which has gone through cycles of neglecting mentally disabled citizens and then creating new institutions or programs to care for them.

In this century, state mental hospitals were once viewed as a solution to the problem of disabled mentally ill Americans. The state hospital system reached its peak in 1955, when about 560,000 patients were housed in these institutions. At that time, one out of every two hospital beds in this country was occupied by a person with mental illness.

Today, the state hospital system is much smaller; however, most people do not fully understand the reasons for its decline. Many factors contributed to the reduction of state hospital beds. Revelations of deplorable conditions spurred demands for reform. Powerful psychotropic drugs, such as chlorpromazine (Thorazine) and lithium, made it possible for the first time to control some of the more bizarre symptoms of psychotic illness. Civil rights legislation, spawned by the climate of social change of the 1960s, limited the circumstances under which mentally ill persons could be committed.

Yet people who have studied the decline of state hospitals have suggested that one of the most important reasons was the creation of new federal programs that paid for care in nursing homes, supervised residences, and outpatient clinics. In the 1960s the federal government created Medicare and Medicaid and expanded the opportunities for people with mental disorders to receive disability payments from the Social Security Administration. In addition, the Community Mental Health Centers Act in 1963 allowed for the establishment of a network of outpatient programs. Many states saw this as an opportunity to save money by reducing the number of state hospital beds and allowing the federal government to pay for the care of mentally ill persons.

Many illnesses that were once treated in state hospitals, such as mental retardation and neurological disorders such as Alzheimer's and Huntington's diseases (two severe forms of dementia), are now managed elsewhere. Although the term "deinstitutionalization" is often used to refer to the reduction of state hospital beds in the 1960s, 1970s, and 1980s, these were replaced by other types of residential care, mostly nursing homes for elderly people and supervised homes for mentally retarded and mentally ill patients. In fact, more people are under institutional care today than before "deinstitutionalization" began.

Nonetheless, the attempt to shift caring for mentally disabled persons from state hospitals to other settings created a tremendous upheaval in the public mental health system, and a number of unanticipated problems arose. In many areas community alternatives to state mental hospitals were virtually nonexistent, yet patients were released nonetheless. The services these patients needed were much greater than anyone had planned for. In addition, state hospitals had provided food, shelter, and psychiatric and medical care in a single location. Many patients found it difficult to meet all these needs on their own. Some resisted treatment; their connection to care became tenuous or too often lost altogether. Finally, a significant minority of mentally ill persons became involved in alcohol and drug use. Only recently has the problem of the dual-diagnosis patient (one who has coexisting mental illness and substance abuse problems) gained recognition in the public mental health system.

In spite of all these problems, phasing out the state hospital system had significant advantages. Most patients accepted services voluntarily and experienced an improved quality of life outside the hospital. For example, in one account of sheltered care in California following deinstitutionalization, 84 percent of those interviewed objected to the idea of returning to a state hospital. Having experienced new opportunities for autonomy and improved functioning, few could imagine returning to the restricted atmosphere of the hospital. Virtually every study that compares patients who remain in the hospital with those who are placed in residential settings demonstrates that patients function better once they leave the hospital.

To solve what are perceived as problems caused by deinstitutionalization (such as homelessness, as discussed later in this chapter), some factions of the public are calling for wholesale *re*institutionalization of mentally ill persons in state hospitals. Yet warehousing patients in these institutions is clearly not the answer. Deinstitutionalization rests on a philosophy of safeguarding individual civil liberties, of granting every individual the right to self-determination and simple human dignity. For ethical and compassionate reasons, this must be the standard of care that prevails.

Today's challenge is to create alternatives that provide the same level of services given by hospitals yet still allow people to function outside of them. Solutions must be found to the constant struggle among the local, state, and federal governments to shift the burden of costs to each other.

A Better Way

A comprehensive system today would provide the following components of care to seriously mentally dis-

abled persons, including those with substance abuse problems:

Medication management. The purpose of medication is to reduce unwanted symptoms and give an individual the best possible chance of recovery and rehabilitation. Often, however, serious side effects can undermine a patient's willingness to take drugs, as can negative attitudes about taking medications or confusion about medication instructions. One study found that some 41 percent of patients do not comply with medication prescribed by their psychiatrists. Resolving this problem rests, in part, on developing a system that emphasizes and enhances the relationship between patient and doctor. Both must become partners in treatment.

Family support and education. Helping the family understand and manage an ill member is crucial. Preserving social supports is one of the most important nonpharmacological interventions for people with serious mental illness. "Psychoeducation"—teaching patients and families about the illness and how to reduce stress—is often helpful, as are group counseling sessions in which families can offer support and advice to each other.

Day programs. Organized, day-long programs that focus on diverse elements of social functioning as well as self-care, occupational skills, and use of leisure time are also important. Surveys have shown that many individuals with mental illness find a lack of productive activity and work to be their greatest source of life dissatisfaction.

Day programs can help by combining treatment with education about day-to-day living skills. Today many program models are in use, including partial hospitalization, day treatment, social skills training, transitional employment, and vocational rehabilitation. Studies have shown that these types of programs work best when they focus on activities and skills rather than on achieving psychological insight.

Emergency services. Because of the frequency of relapse in serious mental illness, around-the-clock emergency services are a necessary part of any treatment program. Hospitals, for example, should include as part of their emergency room staffing psychiatrists and other mental health professionals who evaluate patients in crisis. Drop-in centers are another way to provide help to those who are not yet ready to accept conventional mental health services but who have serious, unmet needs.

Residential programs. Residential programs are one of the most essential elements of a comprehensive care plan. These programs offer a variety of levels of supervision—from around-the-clock to independent living situations—and allow patients to receive care according to their ability to function.

Outreach and case management. Case management links patients with all needed services, including financial benefits, health care, and psychiatric treatments. Outreach is important when patients are unable or in some cases unwilling to access these services on their own.

Long-term hospitalization. Even when comprehensive community care is available, some patients continue to need long-term hospitalization. State hospital beds, or their equivalent, are therefore still necessary.

Mental health care is headed toward this kind of comprehensive system, although many obstacles still exist.

THE HOMELESS MENTALLY ILL

The General Problem of Homelessness

Today, any discussion of the public mental health system leads naturally to a debate about homelessness. But no understanding of this problem is possible without carefully distinguishing between mental illness on the one hand and social and political issues on the other as causes of homelessness.

Homeless people as a group have a high incidence of many different types of problems. These include mental illness, physical illness, substance abuse, and a lack of experience with stable family structures. Homeless people include not only isolated adults but many families, often single mothers with children. Many of these children are preschoolers, spending their formative years without the basic resources needed for optimal development. Extreme poverty, lack of affordable housing, unmet medical needs, and inadequate social supports create severe stress in homeless family members, which is likely to cause or exacerbate existing emotional problems.

Most accounts of homelessness have linked it with deinstitutionalization. However, the phasing out of state hospital beds occurred primarily in the 1960s and 1970s, when it caused no serious problem with homelessness. It became a serious problem in the 1980s, when the federal government reduced entitlement benefits for poor and disabled Americans. At the same time, little money was spent on public housing, and many cities replaced hotels that housed transient people with upgraded housing for the middle class. For the entire population—healthy and ill alike—the cost of housing as a percentage of income increased. All these factors made it difficult for people depending on federal benefits to pay for a place to live.

Homeless Persons Who Are Mentally Ill

Although homelessness is a distressing social problem that cannot be remedied by the mental health system, among homeless persons exists a group of people with chronic mental illness who need special attention from the public mental health system. Debate still rages over how large this group is. Data from the National Institute of Mental Health suggest that about one-third of single homeless people suffer a serious psychiatric problem, and at least one-third of single homeless persons also are incapacitated by drug or alcohol abuse.

Compared to people with chronic mental disorders who have a home, homeless mentally ill persons lack supportive social networks, are more likely to have drug and alcohol abuse problems, and are less likely to be involved in a therapeutic program or to take medicines that would help control their disorders.

These facts do not prove that mental illness causes homelessness. Nonetheless, it falls on the public mental health system to try to change the lives of these people. Psychiatric disorders are made worse by the overwhelming environmental stress of being homeless. Public shelters offer a place to sleep but little more; in some shelters crime and transmissible illness are epidemic, and food is of poor quality.

Many homeless mentally ill people fear and distrust mental health providers and have developed a pattern of avoiding traditional mental health services. People clearly in need of help wander the streets, their conditions deteriorating further. Special efforts must be made to include them in a system of care.

In addition, the traditional mental health system is not well suited for the needs of homeless people. Psychiatric and social services, for example, often are not accessible to those who are homeless. Many community mental health programs are geared toward treating a better-functioning population, not one that is frightened and has extraordinary service needs.

Help for Homeless Mentally Ill People

The first priority in helping homeless mentally ill persons is housing. The current emphasis on shelters and temporary housing in hotels is an incomplete solution. Many mentally ill people will never be able to live completely independently; others need transitional housing that will lead eventually to independence. An array of housing programs is needed, in particular supported housing staffed to provide for psychiatric needs.

New approaches to outpatient treatment must be developed and funded. The most effective way to reach homeless mentally ill people is to approach them on their terms. For example, rather than expecting these people to show up at set appointment times in formal offices, psychiatric outreach workers need to go out to the streets, to assess and counsel people on their own territory. Training programs for mental health professionals must be developed to increase the number of workers entering the field with clinical experience in reaching this population.

Sources of income need to be explored and maximized. Many homeless mentally ill people are entitled to Social Security disability benefits, but do not receive them because of problems with paperwork or because of restrictive residency requirements. The Social Security Administration has an outreach program for homeless mentally ill persons, but it is not widely available and many people are unaware of its existence.

The need of many people for assistance from multiple human service systems, including those providing mental health services, medical treatment, substance abuse counseling, and social welfare benefits, underscores the merits of comprehensive case management. To better ensure that homeless people are able to live in community-based housing and obtain the necessary treatment and support in that setting, case managers need to function as arrangers, expediters, troubleshooters, and liaisons. Effectiveness is increased when follow-up is done by the same case manager for a long time, and when the case manager has the authority to designate and implement a service plan.

SUBSTANCE ABUSE: THE NEED FOR A NATIONAL POLICY

In the United States, an estimated 10.5 million adults show some symptoms of alcoholism or alcohol dependency and an additional 7.2 million abuse alcohol. Addictions to illicit drugs are also common, as well as costly. One estimate puts the cost to society of illicit drug use at over $60 billion a year.

Alcohol or drug abuse impairs a person's ability to function. It also frequently accompanies other forms of both mental and physical disorders—as either an effect or a cause of the accompanying condition. About 25 percent of all hospitalized patients have alcohol-related problems.

In the private sector, cocaine and alcohol abuse are viewed as diseases and treated as such, with many excellent facilities available for those who can pay. In the public sector, society has adopted a punitive approach. Drug addiction in particular has been dealt with as a crime rather than a mental health problem that deserves a rehabilitative treatment approach. Law enforcement efforts have been bolstered while insufficient funds are allocated to research and treatment.

A national education program is needed as well as an approach that recognizes that substance abuse is a treatable mental disorder. Funding for research on substance abuse is also critical. In the future, for example, research may be able to uncover clinical and biochemical markers that will help identify those at genetic risk for substance abuse as well as develop new treatment programs.

INSURANCE COVERAGE FOR PSYCHIATRIC CARE

Most working people and their dependents have private health insurance, often provided by their compa- nies. Usually these insurance plans offer much less coverage for mental health treatment than other kinds of medical care—even though this may not be cost effective, because several studies have shown that costs for physical health care drop substantially for many who receive needed mental health services. In addition, mental health treatment may reduce employee absenteeism and increase productivity. Ironically, cost-containment policies prevent access to treatment at a time when mental disorders can be diagnosed and treated much more effectively than ever before.

Because the cost of health care has been increasing, psychiatric patients who lack adequate coverage for their illnesses find it ever more difficult to pay for needed care. In 1983, 53 percent of employed workers had coverage for inpatient treatment of mental illness equal to coverage for other illnesses; in 1986 this figure had dropped to 37 percent. For outpatient care, by 1986 only 6 percent had coverage equal to that for other illnesses.

Many employers are now shifting to prepaid insurance plans such as health maintenance organizations (HMOs). These plans often control costs by creating barriers to availability, such as requiring prior authorization of treatment or rejecting the use of specialists. Virtually all HMOs offer only tightly controlled benefits for psychiatric treatment.

Aided by their families and advocacy groups, patients with serious mental disorders, such as schizophrenia and bipolar disorder, are now challenging the reluctance of health insurers to cover these illnesses. Pointing out that these disorders are associated with biological abnormalities and comparing them to physical illnesses have been helpful in winning judgments in court. However, mental health professionals, while pleased with the prospect of increasing coverage in these areas, remain concerned about gaining better reimbursement for conditions that are treated by psychotherapy or other interventions not based on a purely biological model of illness.

FUNDING FOR RESEARCH

Even though nearly 40 million people in the United States suffer from psychiatric disorders, funding for psychiatric research has not yet reached a level of support commensurate to other disorders. The primary source of funding has been the Alcohol, Drug Abuse, and Mental Health Administration (ADAMHA), slated for reorganization. This agency oversaw three independent institutes—the National Institute of Mental Health (NIMH), the National Institute on Alcohol Abuse and Alcoholism (NIAAA), and the National Institute on Drug Abuse (NIDA). These institutes decide which investigators in the mental health field will receive federal support and conduct research on their own as well.

Psychiatric research is overwhelmingly dependent on federal funding. Some 88 percent of all psychiatric research is funded by the federal government, in contrast to 58 percent, on average, in other medical fields. With few exceptions the level of state funding for research is low; most state dollars are applied to clinical care only. Because few private foundations and individual philanthropists contribute to psychiatric research, cuts in federal spending are particularly damaging.

Yet psychiatric research proves to be a good investment, helping in the long run to save money in the delivery of services. For example, one researcher has projected that lithium, used to treat bipolar illness, has saved some $15 billion in health-care costs since its introduction. Even though it can take years, even decades, for research to bear fruit, the efforts of dedicated scientists may turn out to be the most critical element in reshaping mental health systems and in bringing hope to patients and their families.

THE MENTAL HEALTH PROFESSIONS AND THE PUBLIC

Psychiatry, psychology, and the mental health professions in general play an important role in many other arenas besides the direct provision of services to persons with mental illness. They help to shape the social response to a broad spectrum of issues that affect the public.

For example, they have a powerful role to play in educating the public about the range of responses to human stress. When disasters or national tragedies strike—the *Challenger* space shuttle explosion in 1986, the San Francisco earthquake in 1989, the 1991 war with Iraq, to name a few—psychiatrists and psychologists are called on by the media and other public forums. They are also called on to counsel the public, through the media, on more common traumas such as rape or other crimes such as child or spouse abuse.

Often mental health professionals are asked to give advice on managing ordinary, day-to-day problems as well, on such issues as how to cope with children, lose weight, or improve communication between married partners. Many medical illnesses are affected by behavior that could be changed, and, again, psychiatrists are drawn into many public discussions about behavior and health. Some of these issues, for example, are maternal drinking that damages the fetus; smoking that can cause heart and lung disease; and the risk of acquired immune deficiency syndrome (AIDS) through sexual and drug use behaviors.

Psychiatry and psychology help to define societal norms and values. Among the public, there is a great desire to know what is "normal" and acceptable behavior and what is not, and many articles about these concerns use mental health professionals as sources. Sexual practices, or difficult emotions such as jealousy or anger, are examples of areas where psychiatry and psychology help define what is normal.

Finally, there are many national issues that involve psychiatry and the courts. Among the mental health questions that have legal implications, for example, are: Should the insanity defense exist at all? If so, under what circumstances? Is alcoholism a disease or a willful act of wrongdoing?

HELP FOR FAMILIES

Mental illness impacts not only on the patient but also on relatives, friends, and children. However well loved, people with severe mental illness can be exceptionally difficult to care for. Many families live in loneliness and despair, cut off from friends and community supports.

Families need information about mental illness and its causes and treatment. They need to know where to get help. Families also need to be able to share their feelings, whether of guilt, confusion, or anger. But few programs exist to meet their special needs.

One type of program that holds hope is respite care, which provides temporary relief from a family's burden. Respite care can take many forms, including day hospital centers, caregivers to visit the home and spell family members for a few crucial hours, or crisis centers that offer overnight lodging when the ill family member is in trouble. Another approach is psychoeducational, teaching family members, often in a group setting, how to better understand and manage mental illness.

Advocacy Groups

One of the most vital developments of the 1980s was the rapid growth of citizens' advocacy groups, comprised of patients, family members, or both. Building on the self-help/mutual support models developed by groups such as Alcoholics Anonymous, these groups provide emotional support but are also emerging as effective and persuasive advocates for better care for mentally ill people. In addition, some groups have raised significant sums for research.

A number of organizations, of varying philosophies, lobby on behalf of those with specific types of mental illness. Generally these citizens' groups are battling not only the public's ignorance and fear about mental illness but also entrenched government indifference. The National Alliance for Research on Schizophrenia and Depression (NARSAD) is one that is focusing with increasing success on raising private money for research.

A list of the major citizen-advocacy groups follows, with the addresses of their national headquarters. Many also have local branch offices. The National Association for the Mentally Ill (NAMI) and the National Mental Health Association (NMHA) have the most offices nationwide.

American Mental Health Fund
Woodburn Medical Park
Suite 335
3299 Woodburn Road
Annandale, VA 22003-1275
tel. 703 573–2200

Mental Illness Foundation
7 Penn Plaza
New York, NY 10001
tel. 212 629–0755

National Alliance for Research on Schizophrenia
  and Depression (NARSAD)
60 Cutter Mill Road
Suite 200
Great Neck, NY 11021
tel. 516 829–0091

National Alliance for the Mentally Ill (NAMI)
2101 Wilson Boulevard, Suite 302
Arlington, VA 22201
tel. 703 524–7600

National Mental Health Association
1021 Prince Street
Alexandria, VA 22314-2971
tel. 703 684–7722

32

Outlook for the Future

Jack M. Gorman, M.D.

The preceding chapters describe significant advances in treating mental illness. Yet many problems continue to elude a clinician's best treatment efforts. Schizophrenia, for example, remains a devastating disease of unknown cause and often unsatisfactory outcome. A variety of dementias, including those arising from Alzheimer's disease, stroke, and aquired immune deficiency syndrome (AIDS), are still virtually untreatable. Efforts to prevent or stop people from abusing alcohol and drugs are far from satisfactory.

For these and other disorders, psychiatric research holds great promise. New insights and technologies have placed the field on the brink of major breakthroughs in understanding mental illness—breakthroughs that derive from fields as diverse as genetics, biochemistry, neurology, and pharmacology, to name a few.

THE BRAIN AND MENTAL HEALTH

The brain, the body's most complex organ, regulates cognitive awareness, emotions, and behavior through an elaborate set of neural systems. In order to better understand mental illness, scientists are studying brain structure and have begun to make compelling strides toward understanding the processes that enable the brain to perform its unique functions. Much remains to be uncovered, however, in determining precisely how abnormalities in the brain are related to abnormalities in thought and behavior.

Neurotransmitters

One area under intense study involves how the brain communicates at the cellular level. Brain cells, called neurons, consist of a cell body and extending arms

436

called dendrites and axons that carry electrical impulses to and from the cell. To communicate with each other, neurons must transmit information across a juncture site, or synapse. This process occurs through the release and uptake of chemical messengers called neurotransmitters, a feature that has led the eminent scientist Stephen Paul to describe the brain as "the organ of the body that turns life's experiences into chemicals."

Although only a few have been identified so far, it is likely that at least 100 different kinds of neurotransmitters exist. Each neurotransmitter is tuned exquisitely to attach, or bind, only to specific receptors in the receiving cell. The binding of a neurotransmitter to a receptor initiates a complex cascade of events within the cell that affects the permeability of its outer membrane, its chemical composition, and electrical potential.

Ultimately, the specifics of which neurotransmitter is released and which receptors are stimulated determine whether a piece of neural information—such as a good mood—will be transmitted, stored in memory, or discarded. If there is a malfunction in the way a neurotransmitter is released or taken into a neuron, then an abnormality in thought, feeling, or behavior may result. Schizophrenia (with its symptoms of incoherent speech, delusional ideas, and abnormal thought processes) is thought to be associated with the excessive release of a neurotransmitter called dopamine, for example. (See chapter 14.)

Neuroscientists now have the knowledge and technology to influence many aspects of neural transmission and to study the strength of nerve cell–receptor binding. Research has revealed that the brain constantly is changing its pattern of neurotransmitter release as well as the number, kind, and sensitivity of its receptors. Already this knowledge has been applied to understanding the mechanisms of action of several psychiatric and neurologic drugs. For example, tricyclic antidepressants appear to work by enhancing the effects of norepinephrine and serotonin, neurotransmitters that are believed to play a major role in depression and other mood disorders.

(For further discussion of drugs, neurotransmitters, and receptors, see page 442.)

Learning and Memory

In the immediate future, much more will be uncovered about the rules governing chemical neurotransmission and receptor physiology in the human brain. For example, scientists are now using this information to explore the cellular basis for learning.

Short-term memory appears to involve a process that is chemically different from long-term memory. When an individual learns something to be remembered only briefly (perhaps the telephone number of a restaurant), research suggests that certain proteins in brain cells are altered slightly. But when something is to be remembered for long periods of time, the brain cell's DNA probably is activated to facilitate more permanent changes in the composition of brain proteins. (See "Molecular Genetics," below.)

Understanding how brain cells learn will have diverse applications. It could someday provide insight into how differences in early childhood experience appear to produce such powerful influences on lifelong personality characteristics, for example. There may be a critical period during development in which various kinds of learning take place that affect ultimate personality.

Such understanding also could help explain how psychotherapy works on the cellular level. Dr. Eric Kandel of Columbia University is studying how animal learning is translated into changes in the function of brain chemicals, using a large sea slug called *Aplysia* that has relatively few and quite large nerve cells. Kandel has been able to teach this primitive animal new tasks, such as avoiding shocks administered by electric prods. He is mapping out how this newly acquired learning is translated into changes in the *Aplysia*'s nerve transmission system. Kandel has attempted to link these experimental findings with scientific speculation to explain how "talk therapies" might produce biological changes in the human brain.

MOLECULAR GENETICS

The discovery of the double helix of deoxyribonucleic acid (DNA) by Francis Crick and James Watson revolutionized genetic research, and today molecular biology has become a dominant field in science.

Genes are lengths of DNA found in the nucleus of human cells in thread-shaped bodies called chromo-

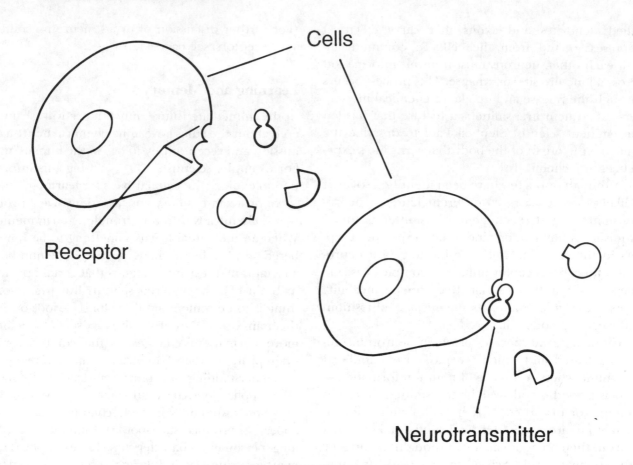

Cells

Receptor

Neurotransmitter

THE BRAIN'S NEUROTRANSMITTERS

Figure 32.1: **To understand how the brain functions, scientists are studying neurotransmitters—chemical messengers that transmit information from one cell to the next. An individual cell has many surface receptors; a neurotransmitter can bind to (and therefore transmit information through) only the specific receptor that fits its chemical shape.**

somes. Normally, a person inherits 23 pairs of chromosomes (one-half of each pair from each parent) including a combination of X and Y chromosomes that determines sex. The specific matchup of chromosomes determines what traits are inherited—for instance, whether a person has blue eyes or brown, is tall or short, and so forth.

Genes also determine how a cell acquires its precise form and function. Cells are made of proteins; genes direct the construction of these proteins and ultimately are responsible for the development of a human being from a single cell into a whole, functioning person. Disorders can occur when there is a defect in a gene or chromosome, causing the genetic programming to go awry. Disorders so far proven to be caused by genetic defects range from the mild, such as color blindness, to life threatening or impairing, such as cystic fibrosis.

For many years scientists have had strong suspicions that at least some psychiatric disorders have a heritable component. Illnesses such as anxiety disorders, depression, and schizophrenia, for example, appear to run in families. This kind of evidence comes from family studies that trace lineage and disease patterns in first-degree relatives. While important in establishing that genetics might be involved, family studies cannot prove a genetic basis to a psychiatric illness. It is perfectly possible that merely growing up in an environment that includes exposure to people with psychiatric illness influences a person's susceptibility to developing that same illness. When this is true, the illness is more properly called familial, not genetic. However, understanding that a illness is familial is still extremely important, because it suggests that changes in the environment of growing children conceivably

THE SEARCH FOR THE MIND–BODY CONNECTION

An association between emotional factors and physical responses has long been recognized but remains poorly understood. Everyone is familiar with stories that go something like these:

- A couple tries for years to achieve pregnancy without success, submitting to multiple medical workups and consulting fertility specialists. After adopting a child, the wife becomes pregnant.
- A man loses his wife to cancer. Even though he seemed in perfect health himself, he becomes ill and dies within a year of his wife's death.
- A hard-driving business executive has a heart attack and is warned to cut down on his work schedule and relax. He tries this for a while but quickly resumes his old habits and suffers another heart attack.
- A person with a fatal illness, perhaps AIDS, is told he has only a few months to live. Rather than giving up hope he makes plans to enjoy the remaining time, see friends, and perhaps finish writing a book. To everyone's surprise, including the doctors, the person survives for two more years.

All of these anecdotes have in common an impression that emotions can affect the course of medical illness, that what happens in the mind has great influence over what happens in the body. But do these familiar stories represent real cause-and-effect relationships?

Only two systems in the human body have the capacity to remember: the nervous system and the immune system. For a long time experts suspected that people under stress or suffering depression develop deficiencies in the immune system, rendering them more susceptible to infections, cancer, and other illnesses. Now research is revealing that the nervous and immune systems are indeed linked. Parts of the brain have direct control over the immune system; conversely, those cells of the immune system called lymphocytes and macrophages produce substances that directly affect the brain.

Research scientists also are now demonstrating that stress affects blood flow through the heart, thus validating the idea that too much stress indeed may put vulnerable hearts at risk for heart attacks. Researchers are uncovering ways in which the brain controls precisely how the heart beats. One source of information on heart-brain interactions is transplant patients, whose new hearts cannot be reconnected to the nerves that link them to the brain. This situation allows scientists to study the effects of stress on a heart that is "denervated," or isolated from the brain.

The brain also serves an important role as the regulator of the organs of the body that produce hormones. Hormonal releasing factors secreted by the brain's "master gland," the hypothalamus, regulate the production of thyroid hormone, cortisol from the adrenal gland, growth hormone, testosterone, estrogen, and others. By the secretion of releasing factors, the brain exerts direct control over many basic aspects of life, such as metabolism, growth, and sex drive. There is mounting evidence that the hypothalamus secretes too many releasing factors in some forms of depression and anxiety disorder. Very likely research will uncover in the not too distant future how abnormalities in hypothalamic function are integral parts of many psychiatric illnesses. Scientists may also find that psychiatric illness affects physical functions such as sleep, appetite, immune response, and sex drive through changes in hypothalamic secretion of releasing factors.

None of these mind-body findings should be of any surprise. The human brain with its billions of nerve cells and connections is the most complex organ in the body. The brain controls every facet of life, including the function of every organ in the body, not only directly through the networks of nerves but indirectly through the hormones and other chemical messengers it sends throughout the body.

could reduce the risk of developing a mental illness later in life.

Twin and Adoption Studies

To decide whether a disease is familial or genetic, scientists use twin and adoption studies. Identical (monozygotic) twins share almost identical genetic information. Fraternal (dizygotic) twins, on the other hand, are no more similar genetically than other brothers and sisters. If a psychiatric illness tends to occur regularly in both members of an identical twinship, but in only one member of a fraternal twinship, there is a very good chance that an inherited gene is responsible for the illness. Such a situation has now been found in a number of psychiatric illnesses, including bipolar illness (manic-depression), schizophrenia, panic disorder, and alcoholism.

Adoption studies produce similar evidence in a different way. In these studies researchers look to see whether people adopted away from their natural parents at birth develop the same mental problems as their natural parents or as their adoptive parents. When adopted children develop the mental disturbances of their biological parents rather than their adoptive parents, evidence indicates that genes, rather than environment, are controlling the development of the illness.

Illness-causing Genes

Now researchers are beginning to locate the abnormal genes actually responsible for disease. Using the techniques of molecular genetics, it is possible to find which chromosome contains a gene for a particular disease and, increasingly, to isolate the responsible gene. To date, however, no major mental illness has been traced to a specific gene. In part, this is due to the difficulty of identifying and isolating a gene, for the nucleus of a single cell in the human body is estimated to contain well over 100,000 genes. Multiply this by the number of cells in a human body, and it is clear that the search for a single gene is daunting. And for diseases such as depression, the search is complicated further by the wide range of symptoms and the many external stressors that can contribute to its cause.

Yet genetic researchers remain hopeful that specific genes for mental illnesses will be identified. In the last decade, chromosomal clues to several psychiatric disorders have been discovered or hinted at, particularly with schizophrenia and bipolar disorder. One study, for example, has shown a linkage between bipolar illness and the X chromosome, although the gene for this disorder has not been located specifically and scientists are still a good way from knowing how an illness such as this is transmitted or caused by genes.

Another area of interest in molecular genetics is how genes control the functioning of neurons. Columbia University's Dr. Martin Chalfie, for example, is studying how genes might cause nerve cell death, using for a model a small, almost invisible worm called *Caenorhabditis elegans* that has a simple nervous system. He has identified two genes responsible for mutations that cause toxic proteins and kill specific nerve cells in these worms. While it has not yet been shown that human beings have comparable genes, Chalfie's work ultimately may help to discover how brain cells die in such neurodegenerative diseases as Alzheimer's and Huntington's.

Finding the gene that causes a disease is an important first step in learning how to prevent or cure an illness. As has already happened with Huntington's disease, among others, it can lead to the development of tests to detect carriers, who can then be counseled about the possibility of transmitting the disease to their children. Or it may one day be possible to develop therapies to treat mental illness, perhaps by replacing or altering abnormal genes.

IMPROVED DIAGNOSIS

Epidemiology

Previously, in the absence of objective evidence such as blood tests and X-ray results, mental health professionals had to rely on mostly subjective impressions to make diagnoses. Now that situation is changing. Epidemiologists—scientists who study disease frequency and distribution—have helped to identify how many people actually suffer from mental symptoms, what kinds of risk factors predispose a person to acquire a mental disorder, and what the natural course of mental illness actually is for most patients. Their work has practical importance in guiding experts in recognizing when illness is most likely to occur and helping them distinguish which symptoms may be early signs of a problem.

Epidemiological work, for example, has taught that bipolar illness usually begins in the early 20s, while depression without mania commonly begins later in life. It also has revealed that anxiety disorders are far more common than previously believed, that schizophrenia rarely begins in elderly people, and that clusters of adolescent suicides may be related to television shows dramatizing teenage suicide.

Laboratory Tests

At present, few psychiatric disorders can be diagnosed definitively by biological tests. This is largely because abnormalities in the brain are rarely reflected by corresponding abnormalities in blood or urine, and it is not possible to take "brain samples" from living patients. However, for some disorders laboratory tests show promise of ultimately becoming useful for clinical diagnosis.

Panic disorder. Researchers are using a "challenge test" model to study panic disorder. Patients with panic disorder (chapter 7) suffer from recurrent anxiety attacks that last about 10 to 30 minutes. They occur sporadically and therefore are difficult to study in a laboratory. In the 1960s, however, researchers discovered that infusing a substance called sodium lactate into a patient with panic disorder almost always provoked a panic attack, while people without panic disorder were unaffected. This finding led to developing even more sophisticated methods of challenging the patient and provoking an attack. It is now hoped that one of these challenge methods will result in a diagnostic test to sort out panic disorder patients from patients suffering from related but nevertheless different conditions.

Depression. Another use of challenge tests is to reveal biological abnormalities that otherwise would remain silent. As explained earlier, many hormones, such as thyroid hormone and growth hormone, are controlled by other hormones called releasing factors that are secreted from the hypothalamus in the brain. When a releasing factor is injected into the bloodstream, it produces a rapid rise in the level of the hormone it controls. But depressed patients and some anxiety disorder patients often have an abnormal response to the injection of releasing hormones. Once again, this biological difference between people with a psychiatric illness and normal people may someday become a standard laboratory procedure for diagnosing specific types of mental illness.

Another test for depression may come from sleep studies. Some depressed people experience a shortening of the amount of time it takes after falling asleep to enter the stage of sleep in which dreams occur (REM sleep). This finding can be confirmed by studying brain waves during sleep. Unfortunately, while it appears that only depressed people exhibit this abnormal pattern, not all of them develop it. Thus, the test cannot be used clinically at present to confirm the diagnosis of depression. Further research may produce refinements of the test that will result in better diagnostic power, however.

Brain Imaging

One of the factors inhibiting both laboratory diagnosis and progress in mental health research is the brain's inaccessibility to study. Nephrologists can take biopsies of the kidney for their research. Hematologists and immunologists easily obtain blood samples. Cardiologists can send catheters directly into the heart and with injected dyes and X-ray pictures accurately map its structures and blood vessels. But those who study the brain rarely can take samples of brain tissue from living people to study. As for understanding brain function by analyzing fluids that pass in and out of the brain, the brain's "blood-brain barrier" presents a difficulty. Like an impregnable protective fortress, the blood-brain barrier keeps most substances from getting into or out of the brain. Thus, blood or urine samples reflect little of what is going on in the brain.

A major breakthrough occurred when neuroscientists discovered ways of making detailed computerized images of the brains of living subjects. (See the photographs on page 24.) The first technique to be developed, now a standard part of clinical medical practice, is called *computerized tomography* or *CT scanning*. This sophisticated X-ray technique yields very precise, detailed X-ray pictures of the brain itself. It already has led to the discovery of some structural brain abnormalities in patients with schizophrenia.

An even newer technique, fast becoming a standard part of medical diagnostic practice, is *magnetic resonance imaging* (MRI). This technique makes even more detailed pictures of the brain than CT without exposing the patient to radiation. It has been used in studies of schizophrenia and panic disorder.

The experimental and related techniques of *regional cerebral blood flow* (rCBF), *single photon emission tomography* (SPECT), and *positron emission tomography* (PET) not only yield pictures of brain structure but also show patterns of blood flow through the brain and, especially in the case of SPECT and PET, reveal the actual activity of different parts of the brain. These techniques provide a dynamic picture of how the human brain works. They all involve giving the subject small amounts of safe radioactive tracer material that can transverse the blood-brain barrier and be taken up by brain cells. Sensors then detect which brain cells actively process the tracer material.

Because of PET, experts can now label brain neurotransmitters and their receptors and determine exactly where in the brain different drugs and chemicals actually work. It is possible to study which parts of the brain are active when someone thinks, talks, cries, or sleeps. Also, scientists can begin to understand which parts of the brain are not working properly in patients suffering from psychiatric disorders. For example, PET studies have shown that individuals with Alzheimer's disease have low levels of metabolic activity in the brain's parietal lobe. While the significance of these findings is not yet clear, one day PET may be used to help determine whether a problem with memory might be due to early Alzheimer's disease or other causes.

The use of imaging techniques helps to compensate for the inability to obtain brain tissue from living subjects for study. Indeed, imaging of the brain (used primarily in research settings) holds enormous promise for the study of mental problems. In schizophrenia, for example, rCBF scanning often indicates a defect in function of a part of the brain called the dorsolateral prefrontal cortex. It also has hinted at blood-flow abnormalities in patients with specific types of dementia. PET scan work also has suggested that an imbalance in blood flow exists between the right and left sides of the brain's parahippocampal gyrus in panic disorder.

BETTER TREATMENTS

Psychopharmacology

The 1960s were a decade of pharmacologic revolution in psychiatry, with the rapid introduction of new and extremely effective agents for the treatment of schizophrenia, depression, mania, and anxiety disorders. Good luck and hard work went into discovering such important medications as lithium, the benzodiazepines, the tricyclic antidepressants, and the antipsychotic drugs. As neuroscience advances, a second "drug revolution" in psychiatry is imminent.

Knowing exactly how a drug works in the brain opens sweeping new avenues of research. As discussed earlier, all nerve cells have structures called receptors. Each receptor has a very specific molecular shape. Only when chemicals with the corresponding molecular shape attach to them, like keys into locks, do receptors transmit that chemical's message. When scientists discovered not many years ago that some brain cells have receptors that respond only to the molecular shape of opiate drugs, they realized that the body must produce its own opiatelike substances. They searched for and found natural substances produced in the body, which they called endorphins and enkephalins. These chemicals have qualities similar to those of opiate drugs, including relief of pain.

In 1977 two research groups independently discovered that the human brain also has a receptor that binds the benzodiazepine class of drugs. (Many of the most widely used tranquilizers and sleeping medications fall into this class of drugs; see chapter 5, pages 65–67.) Once a benzodiazepine drug binds to its receptor, it initiates a stream of biochemical events that produce a quieting of the nervous system. This is the mechanism behind the drug's ability to reduce anxiety and muscle tension.

Similar to their search for the body's own opiates, scientists are now working to find an antianxiety, benzodiazepinelike substance that is manufactured by the body. After all, the body would not have a receptor only for a substance manufactured by a drug company. Finding this substance could provide important information on causes of anxiety disorders. Perhaps people with anxiety disorders do not make enough of the body's natural calming substance or have receptors that do not bind these compounds well enough for them to work properly.

Of more immediate practical importance, while some scientists are searching for the natural substance, others are studying the exact way benzodiazepine drugs bind to their receptors, in the hope of developing new drugs that offer improved antianxiety effect without adverse consequences. While they offer many benefits, artificially manufactured benzodiazepines have some side effects that limit their usefulness, including sedation and dependence. Efforts to improve antianxiety drugs are but one example of the new emphasis on searching for better drug treatments based on an understanding of underlying brain mechanisms. New and better drug treatments continue to be developed for bipolar disorder, depression, and schizophrenia.

Psychotherapy Research

The excitement surrounding the introduction of such sophisticated technologies as molecular genetics and brain imaging to the study of mental disorders may give the misleading impression that psychiatric research now is focused only on biology and chemistry. In fact, research into psychotherapy and psychosocial management of mental illness also is undergoing a revolution.

Until recently, many scientists and mental health professionals were frustrated by the very idea of trying to submit to rigorous study the psychotherapies that clinicians and patients have found extremely helpful.

How could these be tested scientifically? How could anyone know which therapy would be best suited for which patient and which disorder? Now new advances are being made in understanding how people acquire new knowledge, remember it, and change their behavior. For the first time, these aspects of life can be studied under rigorously controlled circumstances.

When medical researchers study a new medication, they usually use what is called a double-blind placebo-controlled trial. This means that half of the patients who have volunteered for a new medication study actually receive the active drug while the other half are given a placebo—an inactive pill. Neither the doctor nor the patient knows if that particular patient is receiving the drug or the placebo—the so-called double blind. This tried and tested research design eliminates the possibility that bias on the part of the doctor or patient will influence the assessment of whether or not a drug works. Under these conditions, if the group that receives the drug does better than those on the placebo, it can be said fairly that the drug is useful for the particular disorder. If those taking the drug do not improve or actually worsen as compared with those taking the placebo, the conclusion is that the drug has proven ineffective.

In studying psychotherapies, however, conducting double-blind placebo-controlled research is more difficult. How could a researcher come up with a placebo psychotherapy treatment and then keep this a secret from the doctor and the patient? Would any patient agree to a five-year "placebo" psychoanalysis as part of a study to see if psychoanalysis works? Could a behavioral therapist give "placebo" behavioral modification treatment and not know that the treatment was really inactive?

As discussed in chapter 6, researchers are beginning to find ways of resolving these issues so that psychotherapy can be studied scientifically. One of the most important examples of this improved research was a recently completed collaborative study of the treatment of depression sponsored by the National Institute of Mental Health and conducted at several leading medical school departments of psychiatry. In this study, outpatients with depression were randomly assigned to one of three treatments: cognitive psychotherapy, interpersonal psychotherapy, and drug therapy with the tricyclic antidepressant imipramine (Tofranil). The results of this research, although complex and somewhat controversial, indicated that for milder forms of depression, the psychotherapeutic treatments were as good as the antidepressant drug. For more serious depression, medication appears the superior therapy. Hence, psychotherapy can hold great promise as a viable alternative to drugs in the treatment of some forms of depression.

In a similar vein, studies are now comparing behavioral and cognitive therapies to antianxiety drugs in the treatment of conditions such as panic disorder, obsessive-compulsive disorder, and social phobia. And even in the area of schizophrenia, excellent scientific research is examining the usefulness of non-drug interventions with patients and their families in preventing relapse and rehospitalization.

Of great interest is a recent study suggesting that psychotherapy actually is able to influence biological processes. Preliminary evidence by Dr. Katherine Shear at Cornell University and Drs. Abby Fyear and Jack Gorman at Columbia University indicates that successful psychotherapy can change the way a patient with panic disorder responds to a challenge test of sodium lactate infusion. While this work is still in its early stages, it raises the possibility that psychotherapy produces biological changes that are not so different from those produced by medications.

COMPASSION AND SCIENCE

Basic science and improved treatment techniques have brightened the future of mental health care considerably. Attitudes toward individuals with mental disorders also seem to be improving. As discussed in chapter 31, private foundations and citizen activist groups are lobbying successfully for more attention for and education about psychiatric illness. Results could mean more hospital beds, more access to treatment with less fear of social ostracism and economic reprisal, and more money for research. While the legal system has long grappled with the problem of protecting people from unnecessary forced institutionalization (see chapters 30 and 31), now it is struggling also with the right of every citizen to obtain fast, safe, and effective treatment for mental disorders. There is a movement to reverse insurance company discrimination against patients with psychiatric illness so that they and families do not have to bear the cost of treatment alone. And greater numbers of medical students are recognizing the potential of psychiatry; the critical shortage of psychiatrists in the United States, especially those treating patients with the most serious mental disorders, may be reversed someday soon.

Today the mental health profession has sharpened its diagnostic skills and introduced powerful scientific methods to the study of the brain and its dysfunctions. Scientific journals are replete with new and exciting findings that will lead the way to improved treatments. Now as never before, those of us who work in the field are convinced that a combination of compassion and science will show us the way to relieving the pain and suffering of mental illness.

Glossary

Tia Powell, M.D.

Note: Following are a list and definitions of many of the terms used throughout this book. Words that are italicized in the text of a definition are defined elsewhere in the glossary.

Acetylcholine A chemical found in a number of body organs and tissues including the brain; it is believed to play a major role in how cells communicate with each other through transmitting nerve impulses.

Acquired immune deficiency syndrome Commonly called AIDS, a disease caused by a virus that destroys the body's immune system. Those who are infected are vulnerable to a variety of infections, cancers, and neurologic problems. A condition called AIDS dementia can occur when brain cells are infected by the virus, with symptoms ranging from mild memory loss to severe cognitive impairment.

Acute illness An illness that is marked by rapid onset and severe symptoms; it is of short duration, as opposed to *chronic illness.*

Addiction The inability to stop using a substance without suffering discomfort. The term is often used to refer specifically to physical dependence on a substance such as alcohol or drugs. Depriving an addict of his or her substance may cause withdrawal symptoms.

Addison's disease A disease caused by a deficiency in hormones secreted by the adrenal glands. Psychiatric symptoms can include apathy, irritability, and depression. Named for the British physician Thomas Addison (1793–1860).

Adjustment disorders Disorders that have as a primary symptom an inability to adapt to stressful life events such as divorce, business setbacks, or family crises. The response to stressful events includes impaired functioning and emotion or behavior that is excessive to the provoking situation. By definition, symptoms of these disorders last less than six months.

Adrenocorticotrophic hormone (ACTH) A hormone released by the pituitary gland in response to fear, pain, anger, or rage. Abnormally high or low levels of ACTH occur in a number of diseases, including *Cushing's syndrome.*

Affect The type and degree of emotion a person displays, such as the sadness that accompanies depression. "Appropriate affect" describes emotions that properly reflect a situation; "inappropriate affect" describes emotions that are an abnormal response, such as laughing when confronted with tragedy. A "blunted affect" signifies a lack of emotional expression and can be a sign of depression.

Affective disorder A disorder characterized by mood disturbances. Examples include *depression* and *bipolar disorder.*

Agoraphobia A marked fear of leaving home and/or being in public places.

AIDS, AIDS dementia See *acquired immune deficiency syndrome.*

Akathisia Compulsive, constant motor restlessness; attempting to be still provokes intense anxiety. It can be a medication side effect.

Alcoholism A chronic and progressive disease characterized by *addiction* or dependence on alcohol.

Alzheimer's disease A chronic, progressive organic mental disorder, involving irreversible loss of memory and deterioration of intellectual functioning. It is the leading cause of dementia in later life. Named for Dr. Alois Alzheimer, who first described the disease in 1907.

Amphetamines A generic name for a group of drugs that are central nervous system stimulants.

Angel dust A slang term for phencyclidine (PCP), an illegal drug that is frequently used as a *hallucinogen*. Even small doses can cause symptoms mimicking *psychosis*.

Anhedonia An inability to experience pleasure.

Anorexia nervosa An *eating disorder* characterized by intense fear of obesity and self-imposed dietary restrictions, often to the point of endangering life. Those suffering from this condition believe themselves to be fat even when their weight is far below normal.

Anorgasmia In females, the inability to achieve orgasm.

Antianxiety drug A drug used to reduce the symptoms of anxiety; commonly called tranquilizers or anxiolytic drugs.

Anticholinergic Relating to an agent that blocks impulses in the *parasympathetic nervous system*. A drug with anticholinergic effects can cause symptoms such as dry mouth and blurred vision; more serious effects include agitation, disorientation, and hallucinations.

Antidepressant drug A drug used to treat depression. Two main classes include *tricyclic antidepressants* and *MAO inhibitors*.

Antipsychotic drug A drug used to treat *psychosis;* drugs in this class are also known as neuroleptic drugs.

Antisocial personality disorder A disorder marked by inability to get along with others or abide by societal rules. Individuals with this disorder are sometimes referred to as psychopaths or sociopaths.

Anxiety A feeling of uneasiness, apprehension, or impending danger—even when no real threat exists. The feeling can be accompanied by physical symptoms, including, for example, increased heart rate, palpitations, difficulty with breathing, and sweating.

Anxiety disorder Any psychiatric disorder that features anxiety as the prime symptom. Common anxiety disorders include *generalized anxiety disorder (GAD), obsessive-compulsive disorder, panic attacks, phobias,* and *post-traumatic stress disorder.*

Anxiolytic drug Another term for an *antianxiety drug.*

Ataxia Inability to coordinate muscle movements.

Attention-deficit hyperactivity disorder (ADHD) Also called attention deficit disorder, or ADD. A disease beginning in childhood and characterized by short attention span, impulsive behavior, poor concentration, and excessive motor behavior.

Atypical Deviating from the normal. In psychiatry, the term frequently is used as an adjective to describe common mental disorders with unusual variations (for example, atypical depression).

Autism A syndrome, first appearing in childhood, characterized by complete self-absorption, inability to relate to others, and removal from reality. Autistic children exhibit a wide range of abnormal behaviors, including difficulty in communicating and rocking movements. Also called pervasive developmental disorder or childhood schizophrenia.

Autonomic nervous system The part of the nervous system that directs involuntary body functions such as breathing, heart rate, and digestion. It is divided into the *sympathetic nervous system* and the *parasympathetic nervous system.*

Avoidant personality disorder A disorder marked by avoidance of situations that provoke social discomfort, often leading to withdrawal from all social contact. Individuals with this disorder sometimes yearn for social acceptance and are overly sensitive to rejection.

AZT Azidothymidine, a drug used to treat AIDS. Also called *zidovudine (ZDV).*

Barbiturate A class of drugs, used primarily to induce anesthesia and to treat pain, that depresses the functioning of the central nervous system.

Bedwetting See *enuresis.*

Behavioral therapy A type of short-term psychotherapeutic treatment that focuses on changing specific behaviors.

Benzodiazepines A class of drugs used mainly for their antianxiety or sleep-inducing properties. Drugs in this class include diazepam (Valium) and alprazolam (Xanax).

Bereavement The feelings of grief and loss felt at the death or loss of a loved one.

Beta-blocking drugs Medications that interfere with the transmission of the neurotransmitters *norepinephrine* and *epinephrine;* many drugs in this class are used to treat high blood pressure. Some also may be effective in the treatment of *performance anxiety.*

Biofeedback Relaxation training that combines deep-relaxation techniques with electronic monitoring equipment to measure such biological phenomena as pulse rate and muscle tension.

Biological clock Informal term denoting the internal regulating system that governs biological functions such as growth, the sleep-wake cycle, and the menstrual cycle. A circadian rhythm is about 24 hours long.

Bipolar disorder   A disorder characterized by periods of *depression* alternating with *manic* periods of excitement, extreme energy, and frenzied behavior. Also known as manic-depression.

Bisexual   A person who is sexually attracted to members of both sexes.

Borderline personality disorder   A disorder characterized by lack of identity, intense unstable relationships, and moods that change rapidly.

Brainwashing   A technique that uses intense psychological pressure to replace a person's existing beliefs with another set of doctrines.

Brief dynamic psychotherapy   A form of *psychotherapy* that lasts a limited time, usually no more than 10 to 15 sessions.

Bruxism   Grinding of the teeth, most often occurring during sleep.

Bulimia   An eating disorder characterized by binge-eating followed by purging by vomiting or using laxatives.

Cataplexy   Sudden loss of muscle control precipitated by strong emotional stimulation. The reaction usually lasts only a few seconds to a minute or two.

Catatonia   A clinical syndrome characterized by *mutism*, rigidity, grimacing, and stupor or marked excitement and aggression.

Catecholamines   *Neurotransmitters,* including *norepinephrine, epinephrine,* and *dopamine,* that help to regulate the nervous and cardiovascular systems. They are believed to play a role in both psychotic and *mood disorders.*

Character   Each person's unique set of behavioral, intellectual, and emotional patterns that are stable over time and are influenced by environment. Often used synonymously with *personality.*

Cholinergic   Relating to nerve cells that release *acetylcholine,* a chemical that affects the *parasympathetic nervous system.* A number of psychiatric drugs have *anticholinergic* effects.

Chronic illness   An illness of long duration, as opposed to *acute illness.*

Circadian rhythm   See *biological clock.*

Client-centered psychotherapy   A form of psychotherapy developed by Carl Rogers; in it, a therapist uses understanding and empathy to help patients clarify their feelings and thoughts.

Clitoris   The female sexual organ that produces sensations of orgasm.

Cocaine   A drug obtained from leaves of the coca plant. It stimulates the central nervous system and is among the most addictive of all known substances. It is illegal to use for nonmedical purposes.

Codependent   A colloquial term that gained popularity in the 1980s. Describes a participant in a mutually reinforcing set of *maladaptive* or addictive behaviors; for example, a spouse who supports *addiction* by excusing, denying, or concealing evidence of the partner's alcoholism.

Cognition   Mental awareness encompassing such functions as perception, reasoning, intuition, judgment, and memory.

Cognitive development   The acquisition of thinking, intelligence, and problem-solving skills.

Cognitive therapy   A short-term psychotherapy that seeks to replace poor or counterproductive coping skills with positive ones. It emphasizes changing behavior or distorted ways of thinking that contribute to problems.

Compulsion   The need or uncontrollable urge to repeat an action again and again, such as washing hands; failure to perform the act causes anxiety.

Conditioning   Changing behavior through learning. Classical, or Pavlovian, conditioning uses a stimulus to provoke a response. It is named for the late Russian physiologist Ivan Pavlov, who found that dogs can be conditioned to salivate when a bell is rung. In operant conditioning, developed by B. F. Skinner, behavior is modified by rewards or punishments.

Conduct disorder   An *antisocial personality disorder* generally diagnosed in children under the age of 15. Children with conduct disorders repeatedly disobey authority, pick fights with other children, steal, and lie.

Confusion   In psychiatry, a mental state characterized by lack of orientation to reality and reduced mental functioning.

Controlled study   Study in which the effect of a drug or therapy is measured against a similar group given a placebo.

Coprophilia   A *paraphilia* characterized by an abnormal interest in feces.

Corticosteroids   Hormones released by the adrenal gland in response to stress. They help to activate the *autonomic nervous system.*

Couple therapy   Counseling that focuses on the dynamics of the relationship between two people. Can be done with one couple or groups of couples. Also called marriage therapy.

Crisis intervention   A time-limited therapy used to intervene during psychiatric crises and help restore coping abilities.

Cross-dressing Dressing in clothing of the opposite sex; for example, when men dress in a skirt or other typical female clothing.

CT scan Also called CAT scan. Short for computerized axial tomography scan, an *imaging device* that can detect various abnormalities in the body. CAT scans of the brain can sometimes reveal abnormalities associated with some mental problems.

Cushing's syndrome A disease of the adrenal glands in which excessive hormones are excreted; psychiatric symptoms can include depression or paranoia.

Cyclothymia An *affective disorder* with mood swings that are similar to, but not of the same severity, as those of *bipolar disorder.*

Day hospital A type of psychiatric hospital care in which patients are admitted during the day but allowed to return home at night. It is a midway alternative to outpatient care or full inpatient hospitalization.

Defense mechanism An automatic, unconscious response to a threat, often triggered by conflict or *anxiety.* There are many different defense mechanisms, such as *repression, suppression,* or *denial.*

Deinstitutionalization The release of institutionalized psychiatric patients into the community. The term is frequently used to describe the reduction in state mental hospital beds that began in the 1960s.

Delirium An acute state of mental confusion, characterized by disorientation and an inability to process information or focus on immediate surroundings.

Delirium tremens Colloquially, the "DTs." An acute physical reaction experienced by alcoholics deprived of alcohol. Symptoms can include *hallucinations* and disoriented behavior as well as fever and cardiac problems.

Delusion, delusional A false belief to which a person clings, despite proof that it is false. Frequently occurring in *schizophrenia,* delusional ideas commonly reflect feelings of grandeur or persecution.

Dementia Loss of intellect, memory, or mental capacity, usually accompanied by changes in personality and behavior. Some causes of dementia, such as a brain tumor, are possibly reversible; others, such as *Alzheimer's disease,* are not. See also *pseudodementia.*

Denial A defense mechanism in which unpleasant realities are kept from conscious awareness.

Dependent personality disorder A disorder marked by lack of self-confidence, decisiveness, and self-denigration.

Depression A mental disorder characterized by low mood. It can include loss of interest in usual activities, changes in appetite and sleep, fatigue, feel-ings of despair, worthlessness, and suicidal thinking. Depression can range from chronic *dysthymia* to severe *major depression.* In common usage, depression also refers to transitory, normal dips in mood.

Detoxification Treatment aimed at removing drugs or alcohol from the body.

Developmental disability Failure to develop age-appropriate intelligence and cognitive ability. Also known as mental retardation.

Differential diagnosis A list of all those diseases—in order of decreasing likelihood—that might be the underlying cause of a particular symptom; many diseases, for instance, are in the differential diagnosis for *delirium.*

Displacement A *defense mechanism* in which emotional reactions are transferred from one thing or person to another, as when a person feels anger at being ill but directs that anger at a relative or doctor instead.

DNA Deoxyribonucleic acid. A complex protein found in the cells of all living things; it is what carries each individual's genetic information.

Dopamine A *catecholamine neurotransmitter* that affects a large number of areas in the brain, including the basal ganglia, pituitary, and anterior cortex. Abnormalities of dopamine regulation may cause *depression* or *psychosis.*

Double-blind placebo trial A research study in which subjects are given either an active treatment or a *placebo;* both the subject and the person administering the study are ignorant (that is, "blind") as to which subjects are receiving active treatment and which placebo, until a code is broken at the end of the trial.

Down's syndrome A congenital form of mental retardation. Children suffering from this syndrome also have an abnormal physical appearance and obvious birth defects.

Drug holiday Stopping the administration of drugs for a limited period; usually in response to side effects or to evaluate the continued need for the drug.

Dyslexia A learning disability related to subtle language deficiencies. Children who are dyslexic often place letters in a word in reverse order or read letters backward. Or they may be unable to associate sounds with symbols.

Dyspareunia Pain felt by women during sexual intercourse.

Dysphoria A mood or feeling of depression or unrest, anxiety, restlessness.

Dysthymia, dysthymic disorder A chronic, less intense, but life-disrupting form of *depression.*

Dystonia Impaired muscle tone. Acute dystonia is characterized by uncontrollable movements and facial expressions.

Eating disorder Any disorder whose primary characteristic is a disturbance in eating behavior, such as *anorexia nervosa, bulimia,* or *pica.*

ECT See *electroconvulsive therapy.*

EEG See *electroencephalogram.*

Electroconvulsive therapy A form of *somatic* therapy using electric currents, primarily to treat *depression.* Also called ECT and colloquially known as shock therapy.

Electroencephalogram Also known as EEG; a recording of the brain's electrical activity.

Empathy The ability to sense the feelings and ideas of another person beyond a mere intellectual understanding.

Endocrine system A group of glands that secrete hormones affecting the functioning of a number of the body's tissues. Glands in the endocrine system include the hypothalamus, the pineal gland, the thyroid, the adrenal glands, the pancreas, and the ovaries and testes.

Enuresis Involuntary discharge of urine; bed-wetting.

Epinephrine A hormone released by the adrenal gland in response to stress, fear, or anxiety. It activates the *autonomic nervous system.*

Episodic dyscontrol syndrome A syndrome characterized by outbursts of rage associated with neurological impairments. (Also called organic aggressive syndrome.)

Euphoria An exaggerated feeling of well-being.

Exhibitionist, exhibitionism A man who exposes his genitalia to women in public places; it is rare for women to be exhibitionists. The act of exhibitionism is considered to be a *paraphilia.*

Extrapyramidal dyskinesia Movement disorders (such as tremors, muscle contractions, and gait disturbances) that involve the extrapyramidal system, which helps to maintain equilibrium and muscle tone. It can be caused by illnesses such as *Parkinson's disease* or be a side effect of *antipsychotic drugs.*

Family therapy Therapy that focuses on treating the entire family system rather than just one individual within it.

Fantasy Images created by the mind, as in day-dreams; they can be consciously directed or reflect unconscious wishes and desires.

Feminist therapy Therapy that takes into account the impact of societal mores and norms on patients.

Fetish, fetishism A *paraphilia* in which sexual gratification is obtained from inanimate objects, such as shoes or underwear, rather than a person.

Flooding Form of *behavioral therapy* that treats phobias by repeated exposure to the thing or event that triggers the phobia.

Free association A psychoanalytic therapeutic technique in which thoughts are freely expressed without censorship.

Free-floating anxiety Pervasive anxiety that is not provoked by any specific event.

Freud, Sigmund (1856–1939). The founder of *psychoanalysis.* Freud developed the fundamental techniques and concepts of psychoanalysis.

Frontal lobe syndrome Mental disorder with marked personality changes, including violent behavior and poor control of rage; associated with organic head injury and/or damage to the frontal lobes of the brain.

Frottage The act of rubbing up against someone, usually in a crowd, to achieve a sexual orgasm; the person who performs this *paraphilia* is called a frotteur.

Gender identity A person's sense of him- or herself as male or female. Gender identity is distinct from sexual identity, as determined by sexual organs.

Gender identity disorder Confusion about sexual role; for example, boys with this disorder are preoccupied with stereotypical girls' activities or prefer to dress in female clothing.

Generalized anxiety disorder (GAD) A disorder characterized by *free-floating anxiety,* ranging from mild nervousness to continuous feelings of dread.

Gene The basic unit of heredity. Physical traits—hair and eye color, height, and so on—are passed on depending on the match-up of genes inherited from each parent. Increasingly, researchers are finding that many mental disorders have a genetic component.

Geriatrics The branch of medicine concerned with diseases of aging.

Geropsychiatry Psychiatric specialty focusing on the treatment of older adults.

Group therapy Therapy session conducted with two or more patients at the same time; the group dynamics become part of the therapeutic process.

Halfway house A facility for psychiatric patients who no longer need full hospitalization but are not yet ready for independent living.

Hallucination   An unreal apparition or false perception that has no grounding in reality. Hallucinations can be tactile, visual, auditory, or olfactory.

Hallucinogen   A class of drugs that cause a sense of an altered, heightened, or "expanded" consciousness, such as LSD.

Health maintenance organization (HMO)   A type of group health plan in which comprehensive health services are offered to subscribers who pay a fixed fee.

Histrionic personality disorder   A disorder in which emotions are expressed with extreme and often inappropriate exaggeration. Individuals with this disorder are prone to sudden and rapidly shifting emotional expressions.

HIV   See *human immunodeficiency virus.*

HMO   See *health maintenance organization.*

Homophobia   Intense fear of homosexuals.

Homosexual   Sexual preference for members of one's own sex.

Hospice   A program of care for the terminally ill.

Hotline   Also called crisis line. A telephone manned by counselors trained to deal with emotional crises.

Human immunodeficiency virus (HIV)   The virus responsible for *acquired immune deficiency syndrome (AIDS).*

Huntington's chorea   A progressive hereditary disorder characterized by abnormal brain chemistry. Symptoms involve involuntary movements of the hands and legs and sometimes depression and hallucinations.

Hyperactivity   Conduct characterized by short attention span and overactivity. See *attention-deficit hyperactivity disorder.*

Hypersomnia   Sleeping for excessive amounts of time.

Hypnagogic hallucination   *Hallucination* that occurs just before falling asleep.

Hypnopompic hallucination   *Hallucination* that occurs before one is fully awake.

Hypochondriasis, hypochondria   An excessive preoccupation with health concerns or exaggerated misinterpretation of minor physical symptoms.

Hypomania   Feelings similar to mania, though not quite as severe; accompanied by excited behavior.

Identity   A person's sense of who he or she is, and the combination of characteristics that form *personality.*

Identity disorder   Any disorder characterized by a sense of loss of self.

Imaging, imaging device   Equipment such as *CT scans, magnetic resonance imaging (MRI)* or *positron emission tomography (PET)* that produce diagnostically helpful pictures of the internal structures, tissues, or metabolic functions of the body.

Implosion   A *behavioral therapy* technique for treating *anxiety* in which the patient is repeatedly exposed to anxiety-provoking experiences.

Impotence   Inability to achieve erection of the penis.

Informed consent   Agreement to accept treatment after being briefed by a physician, psychotherapist, or other professional on the risks and benefits of a suggested treatment; can be granted only by a mentally competent person.

Inpatient treatment   Care given in a hospital setting, with the patient staying overnight.

Insight   In psychoanalytically oriented therapy, an understanding of the unconscious forces that affect a particular behavior.

Insomnia   Difficulty sleeping.

Intellectualization   A *defense mechanism* in which reasoning and analysis replace emotional reactions.

Interpersonal therapy (IPT)   A type of therapy, used primarily to treat depression, that concentrates on current interactions with others.

Intrapsychic conflict   The clash of opposing wishes, thoughts, and desires within one's self.

Light therapy   See *phototherapy.*

Lithium, lithium carbonate   A mood-stabilizing drug, made from naturally occurring lithium salts, that is used primarily to treat *bipolar disorder.*

Lymphadenopathy   Disease of the lymph nodes; it is often one of the first presenting symptoms of AIDS.

Magnetic resonance imaging (MRI)   A type of *imaging* procedure used with increasing frequency to detect brain lesions such as stroke, malignancy, and atrophy; produces detailed scans of soft tissues.

Major depression   A serious and often recurrent mental disorder characterized by depressed mood or loss of interest and pleasure in most activities for at least two weeks without relief. Associated symptoms may include changes in sleep, appetite, weight, energy, self-image, and ability to concentrate, as well as inappropriate guilt and suicidal thoughts.

Maladaptive   Behavior that interferes with an individual's ability to cope or adjust to new life circumstances or stress.

Mania, manic behavior Mood disorder characterized by euphoria, agitation, excessive activity; it is one stage of *bipolar disorder.*

Manic-depression, manic-depressive disorder See *bipolar disorder.*

MAO inhibitor (MAOI) Monoamine oxidase inhibitor. A group of drugs used to treat depression; they work by inhibiting the action of an enzyme, monoamine oxidase, that metabolizes the *catecholamines.*

Masochism, sexual The need to suffer physical or psychological pain in order to attain sexual gratification.

Masturbation Sexual arousal achieved by stimulating one's own genitals.

Menarche The onset of menstruation.

Mental retardation See *developmental disability.*

Mental status examination Evaluation of a patient's mental functioning.

Meta-analysis A form of research analysis combining data from a number of different studies.

Methadone A synthetic *opiate* used to treat heroin *addiction.*

Minimal brain disorder Minor neurological deficits that impact on learning and movement ability.

MMPI Minnesota Multiphasic Personality Inventory. A psychological test.

Modeling Acquiring behavior by following the patterns set by others.

Monoamine oxidase inhibitor See *MAO inhibitor.*

Mood A person's sustained and predominant internal emotional experience; examples include depression and euphoria. Distinct from *affect,* which is the external manifestation of emotion.

Mood disorder A disorder characterized by disturbance in mood, such as *major depression* and *bipolar disorder.*

MRI See *magnetic resonance imaging (MRI).*

Multidisciplinary treatment team Treatment by physicians and/or other professionals from more than one medical field.

Multi-infarct dementia (MID) *Dementia* caused by one or more strokes that destroy or damage brain tissue.

Mutism The absence of speech; its causes can be *organic* or psychologic.

Narcissistic personality disorder A disorder characterized by a pathological need to be admired. Elements of this disorder include an exaggerated sense of self-importance, lack of empathy, and hypersensitivity to the opinions of others.

Narcolepsy Excessive daytime sleepiness, accompanied by nocturnal sleep that often is disrupted by temporary paralysis, multiple arousals, and nightmares.

Narcotic Any drug that depresses the central nervous system, producing pain-relieving effects. Narcotics have the capacity to become addicting.

Necrophilia Intense sexual urges and sexually arousing fantasies involving corpses.

Neuroleptic drug See *antipsychotic drug.*

Neuroleptic malignant syndrome (NMS) A potentially fatal *toxic* reaction to *antipsychotic drugs.* Symptoms include *catatonia,* stupor, fever, rigidity, and problems with blood pressure.

Neurologist, neurology A physician who specializes in diseases of the nervous system. Neurology is the branch of science concerned with diseases of the nervous system.

Neuropsychiatry An emerging medical discipline that combines *neurology* and *psychiatry.* Neuropsychiatrists treat illnesses that have both neurologic and psychiatric symptoms, such as *Parkinson's disease* or *alcoholism.*

Neurosis, neuroses (pl.) Mental disorders characterized by *anxiety* and maladaptively using *defense mechanisms;* neuroses affect behavior, although not to the point of rendering an individual nonfunctional. There is some controversy among mental health professionals regarding the use of the term.

Neurotransmitters Chemicals, produced by nerve cells, that play a role in nervous system communication. Some neurotransmitters, such as *dopamine,* are believed to play a role in regulating moods and emotions.

Night terror A symptom, occurring primarily in children, in which *panic attack*like fear is experienced while dreaming.

Nocturnal enuresis See *enuresis.*

Nocturnal penile tumescence Erections that occur during sleep.

Noncompliance Failure to take medications and/or follow a physician's recommended treatment course.

Norepinephrine A *neurotransmitter* that controls a number of brain functions and is implicated in mood and anxiety disorders as well as aggressive behavior.

Nystagmus Rapid movement of the eyeballs, as occurs with dizziness.

Obsession A thought that occurs again and again, uncontrollably, often leading to a *compulsion.*

Obsessive-compulsive disorder A disorder in which uncontrollable patterns of thought and action develop, becoming major preoccupations. Symptoms may cause extreme distress and interfere with a person's occupational and social functioning.

Occupational therapy The use of work or other purposeful activities to promote therapeutic goals.

Operant conditioning See *conditioning*.

Opiate A drug derived from opium that dulls pain; opiates can also create a sense of pleasure and well-being.

Opportunistic infection An infection that occurs when the immune system is damaged, as in *acquired immune deficiency syndrome* (AIDS).

Oppositional defiant disorder A childhood disorder characterized by defiant behavior. Children with this disorder are usually very argumentative, angry, and resentful.

Organic brain syndrome A mental disorder caused by physical or chemical brain damage. Examples include *delirium, dementia,* and intoxication.

Organic disease Physical illness.

Orgasm Sexual climax.

Orthomolecular treatment Treatment with megadoses of vitamins.

Orthostatic hypotension See *postural hypotension*.

Over-the-counter (OTC) drugs Nonprescription drugs.

Outpatient care Brief care in a hospital or clinic setting that does not require an overnight stay.

Panic Severe anxiety.

Panic attack An acute and frightening episode of *anxiety,* accompanied by feelings of intense fear and physical symptoms such as hyperventilation, chest pains, sweating, or nausea.

Paranoia A mental syndrome characterized by delusions of persecution.

Paranoid personality disorder A disorder characterized by a chronic tendency to see the actions of others as threatening or untrustworthy.

Paraphilia A psychosexual disorder in which sexual arousal is achieved through strange, unusual, or bizarre acts; formerly known as perversion. Paraphilias include *fetishes, frottage, exhibitionism,* and *voyeurism,* among others.

Paraphrenia A mental disorder, occurring in older age, that has as its primary symptom *paranoia*.

Parasympathetic nervous system A part of the *autonomic nervous system* that controls smooth muscle movements, heart rate, and gland secretion.

Parkinson's disease A neurologic disease characterized by tremors, rigidity, and muscular weakness. Psychiatric symptoms can include depression.

Passive-aggressive personality disorder A disorder in which aggressive behavior is manifested in passive ways. Individuals who exhibit this disorder indirectly resist the demands placed upon them; their resistance is expressed through such behaviors as procrastination, stubbornness, and intentional inefficiency.

Pathological Pertaining to disease.

Pavlov, Ivan (1849–1936). Russian physiologist best known for his work on classical conditioning.

Pedophilia A *paraphilia* characterized by a desire for sexual relations with children.

Performance anxiety Anxiety felt about the ability to perform sexually.

Personality The unique constellation of emotions, thoughts, and behaviors that determine who a person is. It is a kind of "automatic pilot" that allows each person to function, grow, and adapt to life.

Personality disorder A distortion of normal personality. A personality disorder exists when a person's persistent and enduring patterns of thinking, behaving, perceiving, and feeling are inflexible and *maladaptive*.

Pervasive developmental disorder See *autism*.

Perversion See *paraphilia*.

PET See *positron emission tomography (PET)*.

Pharmacotherapy Treating diseases with drugs.

Phencyclidine See *angel dust*.

Phobia A persistent, irrational fear accompanied by a compelling desire to avoid the object, activity, or situation that provokes the fear.

Phototherapy The use of light to treat depression; it is used to treat *seasonal affective disorder (SAD)*.

Physiology The study of the living organisms and their biological functions.

Pica An *eating disorder* in which children persistently eat nonfood substances.

Pick's disease A hereditary disease characterized by *dementia;* it is caused by irregularities in the brain's frontal and temporal cortex. Symptoms can include mood changes and bizarre behaviors.

Placebo A preparation that contains no medicine, often referred to colloquially as a "sugar pill." Placebos are used in *controlled studies* to measure the effectiveness of a drug under study.

Play therapy A form of therapy in which children use dolls or other toys to act out problems; therapists use the same vehicle to provide counseling.

Pneumocystis carinii pneumonia A type of pneumonia; it is a common *opportunistic infection* of *acquired immune deficiency syndrome*.

Positron emission tomography (PET) New technology that is able to image the processes of the brain and other soft tissues by measuring metabolic processes that have been observed to be abnormal in several psychiatric disorders, including *Alzheimer's disease, bipolar disorder,* and *schizophrenia*.

Postpartum depression Depression following pregnancy; occurs in some 3 percent of women. Symptoms include feelings of guilt, inadequacy, and inability to cope with the newborn child.

Post-traumatic stress disorder (PTSD) A syndrome that can develop after a severe, traumatic experience. PTSD can affect individuals of all ages. The traumatic event is reexperienced in realistic memories, dreams, or nightmares.

Postural hypotension A sudden and sometimes dangerous drop in blood pressure that causes a feeling of light-headedness on rising from a sitting position; it can be a side effect of some antidepressant medications. Also called orthostatic hypotension.

Premature ejaculation disorder Ejaculation of semen too soon after arousal.

Premenstrual syndrome (PMS) Also called late luteal phase dysphoric disorder. A syndrome characterized by moodiness, short temper, and numerous psychological symptoms during the week preceding a menstrual period.

Projection In psychiatry, a *defense mechanism* in which one's own unacceptable ideas or feelings are construed as motivating the behavior of others.

Projective test A psychological test in which the subject is asked to tell a story or to freely relate feelings or emotions evoked by an illustration or other object. The *Rorschach test* is the best-known projective test.

Prolactin A hormone that helps stimulate the formation of breasts and the production of milk.

Prostate A gland that is part of the male reproductive system.

Prosthesis An artificial replacement for an organ or body part.

Pseudodementia A set of symptoms that mimic *dementia*. The condition often is produced by *depression*, especially among the elderly. The symptoms do not arise from organic brain damage and are reversible.

Psychiatrist A medical doctor who has received specialized training in the treatment of mental disorders.

Psychiatry The branch of medicine concerned with mental disorders.

Psychoanalysis A technique for understanding and treating psychological symptoms. Developed by Sigmund Freud, it probes unconscious conflicts and motivations to explain behavior and effect change.

Psychoanalyst One who uses the techniques of *psychoanalysis*.

Psychodynamic psychotherapy A class of *psychotherapies* derived from *psychoanalysis*. The approach postulates that psychological distress and consistent *maladaptive* behaviors result from *unconscious* conflicts, often dating back to childhood.

Psychogeriatrics The psychiatric specialty that treats older adults. (Also referred to as *geropsychiatry*.)

Psychologist A practitioner in the field of psychology; generally speaking, psychologists hold a Ph.D. degree.

Psychology The science that studies mental processes and their effect on behavior.

Psychomotor agitation Increased physical activity due to mental unrest.

Psychomotor retardation Slowing down of mental and physical activity.

Psychopharmacology The science of treating mental disorders with drugs.

Psychosis A mental state in which contact with reality is severely impaired by such symptoms as *delusions, hallucinations,* and bizarre behaviors. Mental disorders that can produce psychosis include *schizophrenia, mania,* and delusional *depression*. The psychosis can be *acute* and temporary, as in severe reactions to extreme stress (sometimes called a psychotic episode), or *chronic* and lifelong, as in schizophrenia.

Psychosocial Pertaining to both psychological and sociological/cultural factors.

Psychosomatic illness An illness in which the physical symptoms are the result of psychological factors.

Psychotherapy A form of treatment for mental disorders that uses "talk therapy" rather than *somatic* means to achieve symptom relief, behavior changes, and/or self-growth.

Psychotherapist One who practices *psychotherapy*.

Psychotic Pertaining to *psychosis*.

Psychotropic drug Drugs that affect the functioning of the mind.

Rapid eye movement sleep See *REM sleep*.

Reality orientation therapy A therapeutic technique that uses props and questions to stimulate the senses, in order to help orient confused individuals to reality.

Recreational drugs   Drugs that are taken for their pleasurable effect rather than for medicinal or therapeutic purposes.

REM sleep   The stage of sleep in which most dream activity occurs.

Reminiscence therapy   A therapeutic technique frequently employed with older individuals. It uses exploration of the past to help resolve current emotional problems.

Repression   A *defense mechanism* that involves the unconscious forgetting of an unpleasant, stressful, or threatening experience.

Restless legs syndrome   A condition in which there is an intense sensation of internal discomfort in the lower extremities, leading to the movement of the legs in an attempt to alleviate the feeling.

Rorschach test   A type of *projective test* in which the respondent is asked to describe what he or she associates with a series of 10 inkblot pictures. Named for its creator, Hermann Rorschach (1884–1922).

SAD   See *seasonal affective disorder (SAD)*.

Sadism   A *paraphilia* in which pleasure or sexual gratification is obtained by inflicting pain on another.

Sadistic personality disorder   A disorder characterized by a pattern of cruel and aggressive behavior directed at others.

Schizophrenia   A serious, chronic mental disorder characterized by loss of contact with reality and disturbances of thought, mood, and perception. Symptoms often include *delusions* and *hallucinations*.

Schizotypal personality disorder   A disorder characterized by peculiarities of thinking, odd beliefs, and eccentric behavior.

Seasonal affective disorder (SAD)   A mental disorder characterized by *depression* and sometimes *mania* that fluctuates with the various seasons; it appears to be related to changes in seasonal sunlight.

Sedative-hypnotics   Drugs that depress the central nervous system to induce sleep or reduce *anxiety*.

Self-actualization   Fulfilling one's potential.

Self-defeating personality disorder   A disorder marked by a pattern of self-defeating or masochistic behavior patterns.

Self-help group   A group in which people with emotional or behavioral problems band together for emotional support. See also *support group*.

Senile dementia   Mental deterioration occurring in old age.

Sensate focus exercises   A set of exercises that uses tactile and increasingly intimate touch to treat sexual problems.

Serotonin   A *neurotransmitter* that helps to regulate *mood* and behavior. Abnormalities in serotonin levels appear to be associated with such behaviors as aggression, impulsivity, *anxiety*, and eating.

Sex therapy   Treatment for sexual dysfunctions, including *psychotherapy, sensate focus exercises*, or laboratory studies to rule out organic problems.

Sexual dysfunction   Inadequate enjoyment of sex and/or problems that interfere with the enjoyment of sex, such as arousal disorders or pain.

Sexual orientation   An individual's gender preference for a sexual partner; it can be heterosexual (different sex), homosexual (same sex), both sexes (bisexual), or absent (asexual).

Shock therapy   See *electroconvulsive therapy*.

Side effect   Any action of a drug that occurs in addition to desired therapeutic effect.

Single photon emission computer tomography (SPECT)   A new form of *imaging* equipment; it measures cerebral blood flow to map the response of the brain to various stimuli.

Sleep apnea   Condition in which breathing stops during sleep. In obstructive sleep apnea there is an effort to breathe, but the airway is blocked.

Somatic   Pertaining to the body.

Somatic treatment, somatic therapy   Physical treatments, such as drug therapy or *electroconvulsive therapy*.

Somnambulism   Sleep walking.

SPECT   See *single photon emission computer tomography*.

Stigma   A mark of shame, used to discriminate against a person or group, as in the stigma of mental illness.

Stressor   That which causes stress.

Stereotypy, stereotypical behavior   Rote, mechanical repetition of words or physical movements. Frequently seen in individuals with schizophrenia or children with autism.

Sublimation   A *defense mechanism* in which unacceptable drives are channeled into socially acceptable channels.

Substance abuse   Regular, habitual use of any substance (including drugs, alcohol, or tobacco) to the degree that it causes self-detrimental behavior.

Suicide   The intentional taking of one's life.

Sundowning   A condition in which individuals exhibit bizarre behavior and delusions only at night; behavior is normal during the day.

Supportive therapy A form of *psychotherapy* treatment that focuses on relieving symptoms and restoring coping.

Support group A group of people with common goals who band together for mutual self-help.

Support network Family members, friends, and professionals who can be approached or counted on for help during crises.

Suppression A *defense mechanism* in which disturbing thoughts or emotions are deliberately put out of mind.

Sympathetic nervous system The part of the *autonomic nervous system* that controls motor nerves and involuntary muscles.

Syndrome A group of symptoms that together are characteristic of a specific disorder. Examples include *neuroleptic malignant syndrome (NMS)* and *premenstrual syndrome (PMS)*.

Tardive dyskinesia A serious, sometimes irreversible, *side effect* of antipsychotic drug therapy. Symptoms include involuntary movements of the facial muscles, mouth, tongue, body, or limbs.

Telephone scatologia A *paraphilia* in which anonymous, obscene phone calls are made.

Temperament An aspect of *personality;* it is each person's inborn biological and genetic disposition.

Testosterone A male hormone.

Therapeutic alliance The healing relationship developed between a psychotherapist and the person in treatment.

Therapist One who provides therapy.

Toxic Any substance that is poisonous; for example, a drug that has a poisonous effect on the body is described as being toxic.

Tranquilizer A general term for an *antianxiety* or anxiolytic drug.

Transference In psychiatry, the tendency to relate to important people in one's current life with patterns of behaviors and feelings learned in one's early life. For instance, a patient's feelings about a psychiatrist may reflect feelings about the patient's parents.

Transsexual A person who alters physical characteristics (by surgical, chemical, or hormonal means) to assume those of the opposite sex.

Transvestism A *paraphilia* in which an individual assumes the dress and mannerisms of the opposite sex.

Trauma An injury or wound; in psychiatry, it is a disturbing event or experience.

Tricyclic antidepressant (TCA) A class of *antidepressant drug* named for its three-ringed chemical composition. TCAs are believed to affect the *catecholamine neurotransmitters.*

Twelve-Step programs Therapeutic programs that use the 12 recovery guidelines developed by Alcoholics Anonymous.

Type A behavior A term coined by Drs. Meyer Friedman and Ray Rosenman to describe a behavior pattern, dominated by aggressiveness and competitiveness, that appears to be shared by many heart-attack patients.

Unconscious A Freudian concept that holds that behavior is motivated by a complex set of feelings and drives existing beyond conscious awareness.

Voyeurism A *paraphilia* in which sexual gratification is obtained by observing others nude or engaging in the sex act.

Wet dreams Ejaculation of seminal fluid during sleep.

Word salad An incomprehensible mixture of words and phrases.

Zidovudine (ZDV) A medication used to treat *acquired immune deficiency syndrome (AIDS)*. Also known as *AZT.*

Index